OMNIBUS

MAYA ANGELOU

virago

OMNIBUS

I Know Why the Caged Bird Sings

Gather Together in My Name

Singin' and Swingin' and Gettin'
Merry Like Christmas

This omnibus edition first published in Great Britain by
VIRAGO PRESS Limited 1991
20–23 Mandela Street, Camden Town, London NW1 0HQ

I Know Why the Caged Bird Sings
Published by VIRAGO PRESS Limited 1984
First published in USA by Random House 1969
Copyright © 1969 by Maya Angelou
The title *I Know Why the Caged Bird Sings*, is from the Poem
"Sympathy," by Paul Laurence Dunbar.
Acknowledgements is extended to Edward B. Marks Music Corporation
for permission to reprint "Lift Ev'ry Voice and Sing," words by James
Weldon Johnson, music by J. Rosamond Johnson. Copyright Edward B.
Marks Music Corporation.

Gather Together in My Name
Published by VIRAGO PRESS Limited 1985
First published in USA by Random House 1974
Copyright © 1974 Maya Angelou
"If You're a Viper" by Rosetta Howard, Horace Malcolm and Herbert
Moran. © Copyright 1938 MCA Music, a Division of MCA, Inc.
Copyright renewed and assigned MCA Music, a Division of MCA, Inc.
Used by permission.

Singin' and Swingin' and Gettin' Merry Like Christmas
Published by VIRAGO PRESS Limited 1985
First published in USA by Random House 1976
Copyright © 1976 Maya Angelou
Grateful acknowledgement is made to the following for permission to
reprint previously published material:
Chappell & Co., Inc.: For eight lines of lyrics from the Song "Street
Song," by George Gershwin, and three lines of lyrics from "There's a
Boat That's Leavin' Soon for New York," by George Gershwin.
Copyright © 1935 by Gershwin Publishing Corp. Copyright renewed.
All rights reserved. International Copyright Secured.
Harper & Row Publishers, Inc.: For lines from the poem "For a Lady I
Know" from *On These I Stand* by Countee Cullen. Copyright 1925 by
Harper & Row Publishers, Inc.: renewed 1953 by Ida M. Cullen.
Northern Music Company: For four lines of lyrics from the song "Stone
Cold Dead in the Market (He Had It Coming)," words and music by
Wilmoth Houdini. Copyright © 1945, 1946 Northern Music Company.
All rights reserved.

*A CIP catalogue record for this book is available from the British
Library.*

Printed in Great Britain.

Typeset by The Design Team, Ascot, Berks
Printed in Great Britain by Mackays of Chatham PLC
Chatham, Kent

CONTENTS

I
Know Why
the Caged Bird
Sings

ACKNOWLEDGEMENTS

I thank my mother, VIVIAN BAXTER, and my brother, BAILEY
JOHNSON, who encouraged me to remember, Thanks to the
HARLAM WRITERS' GUILD for concern and to JOHN O. KILLENS who
told me I could write. To NANA KOBINA NKETSIA IV who insisted
that I must. Lasting gratitude to GERARD PURCELL who believed
concretely and to TONY D'AMATO who understood. Thanks to
ABBEY LINCOLN ROACH for naming my book.
A final thanks to my editor at Random House, ROBERT LOOMIS,
who gently prodded me back into the lost years.

This book is dedicated to
MY SON, GUY JOHNSON,
AND ALL THE STRONG BLACK BIRDS OF PROMISE
who defy the odds and gods and sing their songs

"What you looking at me for?
I didn't come to stay..."

I hadn't so much forgot as I couldn't bring myself to remember.
Other things were more important,

"What you looking at me for?
I didn't come to stay..."

Whether I could remember the rest of the poem or not was
immaterial. The truth of the statement was like a wadded-up
handkerchief, sopping wet in my fists, and the sooner they accepted
it the quicker I could let my hands open and the air would cool my
palms.

"What you looking at me for . . . ?"

The children's section of the Colored Methodist Episcopal Church
was wiggling and giggling over my well-known forgetfulness.

The dress I wore was lavender taffeta, and each time I breathed it
rustled, and now that I was sucking in air to breathe out shame it
sounded like crepe paper on the back of hearses.

As I'd watched Momma put ruffles on the hem and cute little tucks
around the waist, I knew that once I put it on I'd look like a movie
star. (It was silk and that made up for the awful color.) I was going to
look like one of the sweet little white girls who were everybody's
dream of what was right with the world. Hanging softly over the
black Singer sewing machine, it looked like magic, and when people
saw me wearing it they were going to run up to me and say,
"Marguerite [sometimes it was 'dear Marguerite'], forgive us, please,
we didn't know who you were," and I would answer generously,
"No, you couldn't have known. Of course I forgive you."

Just thinking about it made me go around with angel's dust
sprinkled over my face for days. But Easter's early morning sun had
shown the dress to be a plain ugly cut-down from a white woman's

5

once-was-purple throwaway. It was old-lady-long too, but it didn't hide my skinny legs, which had been greased with Blue Seal Vaseline and powdered with the Arkansas red clay. The age-faded color made my skin look dirty like mud, and everyone in church was looking at my skinny legs.

Wouldn't they be surprised when one day I woke out of my black ugly dream, and my real hair, which was long and blond, would take the place of the kinky mass that Momma wouldn't let me straighten? My light-blue eyes were going to hypnotize them, after all the things they said about "my daddy must of been a Chinaman" (I thought they meant made out of china, like a cup) because my eyes were so small and squinty. Then they would understand why I had never picked up a Southern accent, or spoke the common slang, and why I had to be forced to eat pigs' tails and snouts. Because I was really white and because a cruel fairy stepmother, who was understandably jealous of my beauty, had turned me into a too-big Negro girl, with nappy black hair, broad feet and a space between her teeth that would hold a number-two pencil.

"What you looking..." The minister's wife leaned toward me, her long yellow face full of sorry. She whispered, "I just come to tell you, it's Easter Day." I repeated, jamming the words together, "I just come to tell you it's Easter Day," as low as possible. The giggles hung in the air like melting clouds that were waiting to rain on me. I held up two fingers, close to my chest, which meant that I had to go to the toilet, and tiptoed toward the rear of the church. Dimly, somewhere over my head, I heard ladies saying, "Lord bless the child," and "Praise God." My head was up and my eyes were open, but I didn't see anything. Halfway down the aisle, the church exploded with "Were you there when they crucified my Lord?" and I tripped over a foot stuck out from the children's pew. I stumbled and started to say something, or maybe to scream, but a green persimmon, or it could have been a lemon, caught me between the legs and squeezed. I tasted the sour on my tongue and felt it in the back of my mouth. Then before I reached the door, the sting was burning down my legs and into my Sunday socks. I tried to hold, to squeeze it back, to keep it from speeding, but when I reached the church porch I knew I'd have to let it go, or it would probably run right back up to my head and my poor head would burst like a dropped watermelon, and all the brains and spit and tongue and eyes would roll all over the place. So I ran down into the yard and let it go. I ran, peeing and crying, not toward the toilet out back but to our house. I'd get a whipping for it, to be sure, and the nasty children would have something new to tease me about. I laughed anyway, partially for the sweet release; still, the greater joy came not only from being liberated from the silly

6

church but from the knowledge that I wouldn't die from a busted head.

If growing up is painful for the Southern Black girl, being aware of her displacement is the rust on the razor that threatens the throat.

It is an unnecessary insult.

1

When I was three and Bailey four, we had arrived in the musty little town, wearing tags on our wrists which instructed—"To Whom It May Concern"—that we were Marguerite and Bailey Johnson Jr., from Long Beach, California, en route to Stamps, Arkansas, c/o Mrs. Annie Henderson.

Our parents had decided to put an end to their calamitous marriage, and Father shipped us home to his mother. A porter had been charged with our welfare—he got off the train the next day in Arizona—and our tickets were pinned to my brother's inside coat pocket.

I don't remember much of the trip, but after we reached the segregated southern part of the journey, things must have looked up. Negro passengers, who always traveled with loaded lunch boxes, felt sorry for "the poor little motherless darlings" and plied us with cold fried chicken and potato salad.

Years later I discovered that the United States had been crossed thousands of times by frightened Black children traveling alone to their newly affluent parents in Northern cities, or back to grand-mothers in Southern towns when the urban North reneged on its economic promises.

The town reacted to us as its inhabitants had reacted to all things new before our coming. It regarded us a while without curiosity but with caution, and after we were seen to be harmless (and children) it closed in around us, as a real mother embraces a stranger's child. Warmly, but not too familiarly.

We lived with our grandmother and uncle in the rear of the Store (it was always spoken of with a capital s) , which she had owned some twenty-five years.

Early in the century, Momma (we soon stopped calling her Grandmother) sold lunches to the sawmen in the lumberyard (east

Stamps) and the seedmen at the cotton gin (west Stamps). Her crisp meat pies and cool lemonade, when joined to her miraculous ability to be in two places at the same time, assured her business success. From being a mobile lunch counter, she set up a stand between the two points of fiscal interest and supplied the workers' needs for a few years. Then she had the Store built in the heart of the Negro area. Over the years it became the lay center of activities in town. On Saturdays, barbers sat their customers in the shade on the porch of the Store, and troubadours on their ceaseless crawlings through the South leaned across its benches and sang their sad songs of The Brazos while they played juice harps and cigar-box guitars.

The formal name of the Store was the Wm. Johnson General Merchandise Store. Customers could find food staples, a good variety of colored thread, mash for hogs, corn for chickens, coal oil for lamps, light bulbs for the wealthy, shoestrings, hair dressing, balloons, and flower seeds. Anything not visible had only to be ordered.

Until we became familiar enough to belong to the Store and it to us, we were locked up in a Fun House of Things where the attendant had gone home for life.

Each year I watched the field across from the Store turn caterpillar green, then gradually frosty white. I knew exactly how long it would be before the big wagons would pull into the front yard and load on the cotton pickers at daybreak to carry them to the remains of slavery's plantations.

During the picking season my grandmother would get out of bed at four o'clock (she never used an alarm clock) and creak down to her knees and chant in a sleep-filled voice "Our Father, thank you for letting me see this New Day. Thank you that you didn't allow the bed I lay on last night to be my cooling board, nor my blanket my winding sheet. Guide my feet this day along the straight and narrow, and help me to put a bridle on my tongue. Bless this house, and everybody in it. Thank you, in the name of your Son, Jesus Christ, Amen."

Before she had quite arisen, she called our names and issued orders, and pushed her large feet into homemade slippers and across the bare lye-washed wooden floor to light the coal-oil lamp.

The lamplight in the Store gave a soft make-believe feeling to our world which made me want to whisper and walk about on tiptoe. The odors of onions and oranges and kerosene had been mixing all night and wouldn't be disturbed until the wooded slat was removed from the door and the early morning air forced its way in with the bodies of people who had walked miles to reach the pickup place.

8

"Sister, I'll have two cans of sardines."

"I'm gonna work so fast today I'm gonna make you look like you standing still."

"Lemme have a hunk uh cheese and some sody crackers."

"Just gimme a coupla them fat peanut paddies." That would be from a picker who was taking his lunch. The greasy brown paper sack was stuck behind the bib of his overalls. He'd use the candy as a snack before the noon sun called the workers to rest.

In those tender mornings the Store was full of laughing, joking, boasting and bragging. One man was going to pick two hundred pounds of cotton, and another three hundred. Even the children were promising to bring home fo' bits and six bits.

The champion picker of the day before was the hero of the dawn. If he prophesied that the cotton in today's field was going to be sparse and stick to the bolls like glue, every listener would grunt a hearty agreement.

The sound of the empty cotton sacks dragging over the floor and the murmurs of waking people were sliced by the cash register as we rang up the five-cent sales.

If the morning sounds and smells were touched with the supernatural, the late afternoon had all the features of the normal Arkansas life. In the dying sunlight the people dragged, rather than their empty cotton sacks.

Brought back to the Store, the pickers would step out of the backs of trucks and fold down, dirt-disappointed, to the ground. No matter how much they had picked, it wasn't enough. Their wages wouldn't even get them out of debt to my grandmother, not to mention the staggering bill that waited on them at the white commissary downtown.

The sounds of the new morning had been replaced with grumbles about cheating houses, weighted scales, snakes, skimpy cotton and dusty rows. In later years I was to confront the stereotyped picture of gay song-singing cotton pickers with such inordinate rage that I was told even by fellow Blacks that my paranoia was embarrassing. But I had seen the fingers cut by the mean little cotton bolls. and I had witnessed the backs and shoulders and arms and legs resisting any further demands.

Some of the workers would leave their sacks at the Store to be picked up the following morning, but a few had to take them home for repairs. I winced to picture them sewing the coarse material under a coal-oil lamp with fingers stiffening from the day's work. In too few hours they would have to walk back to Sister Henderson's Store, get vittles and load, again, onto the trucks. Then they would face another day of trying to earn enough for the whole year with the heavy knowledge that they were going to end the season as they started it. Without the money or credit necessary to sustain a family for three months. In cotton-picking time the late afternoons revealed the harshness of Black Southern life, which in the early morning had been softened by nature's blessing of grogginess, forgetfulness and the soft lamplight.

2

When Bailey was six and I a year younger, we used to rattle off the times with the speed I was later to see Chinese children in San Francisco employ on their abacuses. Our summer-gray pot-bellied stove bloomed rosy red during winter, and became a severe disciplinarian threat if we were so foolish as to indulge in making mistakes.

Uncle Willie used to sit, like a giant black Z (he had been crippled as a child), and hear us testify to the Lafayette County Training Schools' abilities. His face pulled down on the left side, as if a pulley had been attached to his lower teeth, and his left hand was only a mite bigger than Bailey's, but on the second mistake or on the third hesitation his big overgrown right hand would catch one of us behind the collar, and in the same moment would thrust the culprit toward the dull red heater, which throbbed like a devil's toothache. We were never burned, although once I might have been when I was so terrified I tried to jump onto the stove to remove the possibility of its remaining a threat. Like most children, I thought if I could face the worst danger voluntarily, and *triumph*, I would forever have power over it. But in my case of sacrificial effort I was thwarted. Uncle Willie held tight to my dress and I only got close enough to smell the clean dry scent of hot iron. We learned the times tables without understanding their grand principle, simply because we had the capacity and no alternative.

The tragedy of lameness seems so unfair to children that they are embarrassed in its presence. And they, most recently off nature's mold, sense that they have only narrowly missed being another of her jokes. In relief at the narrow escape, they vent their emotions in impatience and criticism of the unlucky cripple.

Momma related times without end, and without any show of

emotion, how Uncle Willie had been dropped when he was three years old by a woman who was minding him. She seemed to hold no rancor against the baby-sitter, nor for her just God who allowed the accident. She felt it necessary to explain over and over again to those who knew the story by heart that he wasn't "born that way."

In our society, where two-legged, two-armed strong Black men were able at best to eke out only the necessities of life, Uncle Willie, with his starched shirts, shined shoes and shelves full of food, was the whipping boy and butt of jokes of the underemployed and underpaid. Fate not only disabled him but laid a double-tiered barrier in his path. He was also proud and sensitive. Therefore he couldn't pretend that he wasn't crippled, nor could he deceive himself that people were not repelled by his defect.

Only once in all the years of trying not to watch him, I saw him pretend to himself and others that he wasn't lame.

Coming home from school one day, I saw a dark car in our front yard. I rushed in to find a strange man and woman (Uncle Willie said later they were schoolteachers from Little Rock) drinking Dr. Pepper in the cool of the Store. I sensed a wrongness around me, like an alarm clock that had gone off without being set.

I knew it couldn't be the strangers. Not frequently, but often enough, travelers pulled off the main road to buy tobacco or soft drinks in the only Negro store in Stamps. When I looked at Uncle Willie, I knew what was pulling my mind's coattails. He was standing erect behind the counter, not leaning forward or resting on the small shelf that had been built for him. Erect. His eyes seemed to hold me with a mixture of threats and appeal.

I dutifully greeted the strangers and roamed my eyes around for his walking stick. It was nowhere to be seen. He said, "Uh... this this... this... uh, my niece. She's... uh... just come from school. "Then to the couple—"You know... how, uh, children are... th–th–these days... they play all d–d–day at school and c–c–can't wait to get home and pl–play some more."

The people smiled, very friendly.

He added, "Go on out and pl–play, Sister."

The lady laughed in a soft Arkansas voice and said, "Well, you know, Mr. Johnson, they say, you're only a child once. Have you children of your own?"

Uncle Willie looked at me with an impatience I hadn't seen in his face even when he took thirty minutes to loop the laces over his high-topped shoes. "I... I thought I told you to go... go outside and play."

Before I left I saw him lean back on the shelves of Garret Snuff, Prince Albert and Spark Plug chewing tobacco.

11

"No, ma'am... no ch—children and no wife." He tried a laugh. "I have an old m—m—mother and my brother's t—two children to l—look after."

I didn't mind his using us to make himself look good. In fact, I would have pretended to be his daughter if he wanted me to. Not only did I not feel any loyalty to my own father, I figured that if I had been Uncle Willie's child I would have received much better treatment.

The couple left after a few minutes, and from the back of the house I watched the red car scare chickens, raise dust and disappear toward Magnolia.

Uncle Willie was making his way down the long shadowed aisle between the shelves and the counter—hand over hand, like a man climbing out of a dream. I stayed quiet and watched him lurch from one side, bumping to the other, until he reached the coal-oil tank. He put his hand behind that dark recess and took his cane in the strong fist and shifted his weight on the wooden support. He thought he had pulled it off.

I'll never know why it was important to him that the couple (he said later that he'd never seen them before) would take a picture of a whole Mr. Johnson back to Little Rock.

He must have tired of being crippled, as prisoners of penitentiary bars and the guilty tire of blame. The high-topped shoes and the cane, his uncontrollable muscles and thick tongue, and the looks he suffered of either contempt or pity had simply worn him out, and for one afternoon, one part of an afternoon, he wanted no part of them.

I understood and felt closer to him at that moment than ever before or since.

During these years in Stamps, I met and fell in love with William Shakespeare. He was my first white love. Although I enjoyed and respected Kipling, Poe, Butler, Thackeray and Henley, I saved my young and loyal passion for Paul Lawrence Dunbar, Langston Hughes, James Weldon Johnson and W.E.B. Du Bois' "Litany at Atlanta." But it was Shakespeare who said, "When in disgrace with fortune and men's eyes." It was a state with which I felt myself most familiar. I pacified myself about his whiteness by saying that after all he had been dead so long it couldn't matter to anyone any more.

Bailey and I decided to memorize a scene from *The Merchant of Venice*, but we realized that Momma would question us about the author and that we'd have to tell her that Shakespeare was white, and it wouldn't matter to her whether he was dead or not. So we chose "The Creation" by James Weldon Johnson instead.

3

Weighing the half-pounds of flour, excluding the scoop, and depositing them dust-free into the thin paper sacks held a simple kind of adventure for me. I developed an eye for measuring how full a silver-looking ladle of flour, mash, meal, sugar or corn had to be to push the scale indicator over to eight ounces or one pound. When I was absolutely accurate our appreciative customers used to admire: "Sister Henderson sure got some smart grandchildrens." If I was off in the Store's favor, the eagle-eyed women would say, "Put some more in that sack, child. Don't you try to make your profit offa me."

Then I would quietly but persistently punish myself. For every bad judgment, the fine was no silver-wrapped Kisses, the sweet chocolate drops that I loved more than anything in the world, except Bailey. And maybe canned pineapples. My obsession with pineapple nearly drove me mad. I dreamt of the days when I would be grown and able to buy a whole carton for myself alone.

Although the syrupy golden rings sat in their exotic cans on our shelves year round, we only tasted them during Christmas. Momma used the juice to make almost-black fruit cake. Then she lined heavy soot-encrusted iron skillets with the pineapple rings for rich upside-down cakes. Bailey and I received one slice each, and I carried mine around for hours, shredding off the fruit until nothing was left except the perfume on my fingers. I'd like to think that my desire for pineapples was so sacred that I wouldn't allow myself to steal a can (which was possible) and eat it alone out in the garden, but I'm certain that I must have weighed the possibility of the scent exposing me and didn't have the nerve to attempt it.

Until I was thirteen and left Arkansas for good, the Store was my favorite place to be. Alone and empty in the mornings, it looked like an unopened present from a stranger. Opening the front doors was pulling the ribbon off the unexpected gift. The light would come in softly (we faced north), easing itself over the shelves of mackerel, salmon, tobacco, thread. It fell flat on the big vat of lard and by noontime during the summer the grease had softened to a thick soup. Whenever I walked into the Store in the afternoon, I sensed that it was tired. I alone could hear the slow pulse of its job half done. But just before bedtime, after numerous people had walked in and out, had argued over their bills, or joked about their neighbors, or just dropped in "to give Sister Henderson a 'Hi y'all,'" the promise of magic mornings returned to the Store and spread itself over the family in washed life waves.

Momma opened boxes of crispy crackers and we sat around the meat block at the rear of the Store. I sliced onions, and Bailey opened two or even three cans of sardines and allowed their juice of oil and fishing boats to ooze down and around the sides. That was supper. In the evening, when we were alone like that, Uncle Willie didn't stutter or shake or give any indication that he had an "affliction." It seemed that the peace of a day's ending was an assurance that the covenant God made with children, Negroes and the crippled was still in effect.

Throwing scoops of corn to the chickens and mixing sour dry mash with leftover food and oily dish water for the hogs were among our evening chores. Bailey and I sloshed down twilight trails to the pig pens, and standing on the first fence rungs we poured down the unappealing concoctions to our grateful hogs. They mashed their tender pink snouts down into the slop, and rooted and grunted their satisfaction. We always grunted a reply only half in jest. We were also grateful that we had concluded the dirtiest of chores and had only gotten the evil-smelling swill on our shoes, stockings, feet and hands.

Late one day, as we were attending to the pigs, I heard a horse in the front yard (it really should have been called a driveway, except that there was nothing to drive into it), and ran to find out who had come riding up on a Thursday evening when even Mr. Steward, the quiet, bitter man who owned a riding horse, would be resting by his warm fire until the morning called him out to turn over his field.

The used-to-be sheriff sat rakishly astraddle his horse. His nonchalance was meant to convey his authority and power over even dumb animals. How much more capable he would be with Negroes. It went without saying.

His twang jogged in the brittle air. From the side of the Store, Bailey and I heard him say to Momma, "Annie, tell Willie he better lay low tonight. A crazy nigger messed with a white lady today. Some of the boys'll be coming over here later." Even after the slow drag of years, I remember the sense of fear which filled my mouth with hot, dry air, and made my body light.

The "boys"? Those cement faces and eyes of hate that burned the clothes off you if they happened to see you lounging on the main street downtown on Saturday. Boys? It seemed that youth had never happened to them. Boys? No, rather men who were covered with graves' dust and age without beauty or learning. The ugliness and rottenness of old abominations.

If on Judgment Day I were summoned by St. Peter to give testimony to the used-to-be sheriff's act of kindness, I would be unable to say anything in his behalf. His confidence that my uncle and every other Black man who heard of the Klan's coming ride would scurry under their houses to hide in chicken droppings was too humiliating to hear. Without waiting for Momma's thanks, he rode out of the yard, sure that things were as they should be and that he was a gentle squire, saving those deserving serfs from the laws of the land, which he condoned.

Immediately, while his horse's hoofs were still loudly thudding the ground, Momma blew out the coal-oil lamps. She had a quiet, hard talk with Uncle Willie and called Bailey and me into the Store.

We were told to take the potatoes and onions out of their bins and knock out the dividing walls that kept them apart. Then with a tedious and fearful slowness Uncle Willie gave me his rubber-tipped cane and bent down to get into the now-enlarged empty bin. It took forever before he lay down flat, and then we covered him with potatoes and onions, layer upon layer, like a casserole. Grandmother knelt praying in the darkened Store.

It was fortunate that the "boys" didn't ride into our yard that evening and insist that Momma open the Store. They would have surely found Uncle Willie and just as surely lynched him. He moaned the whole night through as if he had, in fact, been guilty of some heinous crime. The heavy sounds pushed their way up out of the blanket of vegetables and I pictured his mouth pulling down on the right side and his saliva flowing into the eyes of new potatoes and waiting there like dew drops for the warmth of morning.

4

What sets one Southern town apart from another, or from a Northern town or hamlet, or city high-rise? The answer must be the experience shared between the unknowing majority (it) and the knowing minority (you). All of childhood's unanswered questions must finally be passed back to the town and answered there. Heroes and bogey men, values and dislikes, are first encountered and labeled in that early environment. In later years they change faces, places and maybe races, tactics, intensities and goals, but beneath those penetrable masks they wear forever the stocking-capped faces of childhood.

Mr. McElroy, who lived in the big rambling house next to the Store, was very tall and broad, and although the years had eaten away the flesh from his shoulders, they had not, at the time of my knowing him, gotten to his high stomach, or his hands or feet.

He was the only Negro I knew, except for the school principal and the visiting teachers, who wore matching pants and jackets. When I learned that men's clothes were sold like that and called suits, I remember thinking that somebody had been very bright, for it made men look less manly, less threatening and a little more like women.

Mr. McElroy never laughed, and seldom smiled, and to his credit was the fact that he liked to talk to Uncle Willie. He never went to church, which Bailey and I thought also proved he was a very courageous person. How great it would be to grow up like that, to be able to stare religion down, especially living next door to a woman like Momma.

I watched him with the excitement of expecting him to do anything at any time. I never tired of this, or became disappointed or disenchanted with him, although from the perch of age, I see him now as a very simple and uninteresting man who sold patent medicine and tonics to the less sophisticated people in towns (villages) surrounding the metropolis of Stamps.

There seemed to be an understanding between Mr. McElroy and Grandmother. This was obvious to us because he never chased us off his land. In summer's late sunshine I often sat under the chinaberry tree in his yard, surrounded by the bitter aroma of its fruit and lulled by the drone of flies that fed on the berries. He sat in a slotted swing on his porch, rocking in his brown three-piece, his wide Panama nodding in time with the whir of insects.

One greeting a day was all that could be expected from Mr. McElroy. After his "Good morning, child," or "Good afternoon, child," he never said a word, even if I met him again on the road in front of his house or down by the well, or ran into him behind the house escaping in a game of hide-and-seek.

He remained a mystery in my childhood. A man who owned his land and the big many-windowed house with a porch that clung to its sides all around the house. An independent Black man. A near anachronism in Stamps.

Bailey was the greatest person in my world. And the fact that he was my brother, my only brother, and I had no sisters to share him with, was such good fortune that it made me want to live a Christian life just to show God that I was grateful. Where I was big, elbowy and grating, he was small, graceful and smooth. When I was described by our playmates as being shit color, he was lauded for his velvet-black skin. His hair fell down in black curls, and my head was covered with black steel wool. And yet he loved me.

When our elders said unkind things about my features (my family was handsome to a point of pain for me), Bailey would wink at me from across the room, and I knew that it was a matter of time before he would take revenge. He would allow the old ladies to finish wondering how on earth I came about, then he would ask, in a voice like cooling bacon grease, "Oh Mizeriz Coleman, how is your son? I saw him the other day, and he looked sick enough to die."

Aghast, the ladies would ask, "Die? From what? He ain't sick."

And in a voice oilier than the one before, he'd answer with a straight face, "From the Uglies."

I would hold my laugh, bite my tongue, grit my teeth and very seriously erase even the touch of a smile from my face. Later, behind the house by the black-walnut tree, we'd laugh and laugh and howl.

Bailey could count on very few punishments for his consistently outrageous behavior, for he was the pride of the Henderson/Johnson family.

His movements, as he was later to describe those of an acquaintance, were activated with oiled precision. He was also able to find more hours in the day than I thought existed. He finished chores, homework, read more books than I and played the group games on the side of the hill with the best of them. He could even pray out loud in church, and was apt at stealing pickles from the barrel that sat under the fruit counter and Uncle Willie's nose.

Once when the Store was full of lunchtime customers, he dipped the strainer, which we also used to sift weevils from meal and flour, into the barrel and fished for two fat pickles. He caught them and hooked the strainer onto the side of the barrel where they dripped until he was ready for them. When the last school bell rang, he picked the nearly dry pickles out of the strainer, jammed them into his pockets and threw the strainer behind the oranges. We ran out of the Store. It was summer and his pants were short, so the pickle juice made clean streams down his ashy legs, and he jumped with his pockets full of loot and his eyes laughing a "How about that?" He smelled like a vinegar barrel or a sour angel.

After our early chores were done, while Uncle Willie or Momma minded the Store, we were free to play the children's games as long as we stayed within yelling distance. Playing hide-and-seek, his voice was easily identified, singing, "Last night, night before, twenty-four robbers at my door. Who all is hid? Ask me to let them in, hit 'em in the head with a rolling pin. Who all is hid?" In follow the leader, naturally he was the one who created the most daring and interesting things to do. And when he was on the tail of the pop the whip, he would twirl off the end like a top, spinning, falling, laughing, finally stopping just before my heart beat its last, and then he was back in the game, still laughing.

Of all the needs (there are none imaginary) a lonely child has, the one that must be satisfied, if there is going to be hope and a hope of wholeness, is the unshaking need for an unshakable God. My pretty Black brother was my Kingdom Come.

In Stamps the custom was to can everything that could possibly be preserved. During the killing season, after the first frost, all neighbors helped each other to slaughter hogs and even the quiet, big-eyed cows if they had stopped giving milk.

The missionary ladies of the Christian Methodist Episcopal Church helped Momma prepare the pork for sausage. They squeezed their fat arms elbow deep in the ground meat, mixed it with gray nose-opening sage, pepper and salt, and made tasty little samples for all obedient children who brought wood for the slick black stove. The men chopped off the larger pieces of meat and laid them in the smokehouse to begin the curing process. They opened the knuckle of the hams with their deadly-looking knives, took out a certain round harmless bone ("it could make the meat go bad") and rubbed salt, coarse brown salt that looked like fine gravel, into the flesh, and the blood popped to the surface.

Throughout the year, until the next frost, we took our meals from the smokehouse, the little garden that lay cousin-close to the Store and from the shelves of canned foods. There were choices on the shelves that could set a hungry child's mouth to watering. Green beans, snapped always the right length, collards, cabbage, juicy red tomato preserves that came into their own on steaming buttered biscuits, and sausage, beets, berries and every fruit grown in Arkansas.

But at least twice yearly Momma would feel that as children we should have fresh meat included in our diets. We were then given money—pennies, nickels, and dimes entrusted to Bailey—and sent to town to buy liver. Since the whites had refrigerators, their butchers bought the meat from commercial slaughterhouses in Texarkana and sold it to the wealthy even in the peak of summer.

Crossing the Black area of Stamps which in childhood's narrow measure seemed a whole world, we were obliged by custom to stop and speak to every person we met, and Bailey felt constrained to spend a few minutes playing with each friend. There was a joy in going to town with money in our pockets (Bailey's pockets were as good as my own) and time on our hands. But the pleasure fled when we reached the white part of town. After we left Mr. Willie Williams' Do Drap Inn, the last stop before whitefolksville, we had to cross the pond and adventure the railroad tracks. We were explorers walking without weapons into man-eating animals' territory.

In Stamps the segregation was so complete that most Black children didn't really, absolutely know what whites looked like. Other than that they were different, to be dreaded, and in that dread was included the hostility of the powerless against the powerful, the poor against the rich, the worker against the worked for and the ragged against the well dressed.

I remember never believing that whites were really real.

Many women who worked in their kitchens traded at our Store, and when they carried their finished laundry back to town they often set the big baskets down on our front porch to pull a singular piece from the starched collection and show either how graceful was their ironing hand or how rich and opulent was the property of their employers.

I looked at the items that weren't on display. I knew, for instance, that white men wore shorts, as Uncle Willie did, and that they had an opening for taking out their "things" and peeing, and that white women's breasts weren't built into their dresses, as some people said, because I saw their brassieres in the baskets. But I couldn't force myself to think of them as people. People were Mrs. LaGrone, Mrs. Hendricks, Momma, Reverend Sneed, Lillie B, and Louise and Rex. Whitefolks couldn't be people because their feet were too small, their skin too white and see-throughy, and they didn't walk on the balls of their feet the way people did—they walked on their heels like horses.

People were those who lived on my side of town. I didn't like them all, or, in fact, any of them very much, but they were people. These others, the strange pale creatures that lived in their alien unlife, weren't considered folks. They were whitefolks.

5

"Thou shall not be dirty" and "Thou shall not be impudent" were the two commandments of Grandmother Henderson upon which hung our total salvation.

Each night in the bitterest winter we were forced to wash faces, arms, necks, legs and feet before going to bed. She used to add, with a smirk that unprofane people can't control when venturing into profanity, "and wash as far as possible, then wash possible."

We would go to the well and wash in the ice-cold, clear water, grease our legs with the equally cold stiff Vaseline, then tiptoe into the house. We wiped the dust from our toes and settled down for schoolwork, cornbread, clabbered milk, prayers and bed, always in that order. Momma was famous for pulling the quilts off after we had fallen asleep to examine our feet. If they weren't clean enough for her, she took the switch (she kept one behind the bedroom door for emergencies) and woke up the offender with a few aptly placed burning reminders.

The area around the well at night was dark and slick, and boys told about how snakes love water, so that anyone who had to draw water at night and then stand there alone and wash knew that moccasins and rattlers, puff adders and boa constrictors were winding their way to the well and would arrive just as the person washing got soap in her eyes. But Momma convinced us that not only was cleanliness next to Godliness, dirtiness was the inventor of misery.

The impudent child was detested by God and a shame to its parents and could bring destruction to its house and line. All adults had to be addressed as Mister, Missus, Miss, Auntie, Cousin, Unk, Uncle, Buhbah, Sister, Brother and a thousand other appellations indicating familial relationship and the lowliness of the addressor.

Everyone I knew respected these customary laws, except for the powhitetrash children.

Some families of powhitetrash lived on Momma's farm land behind the school. Sometimes a gaggle of them came to the Store, filling the whole room, chasing out the air and even changing the well-known scents. The children crawled over the shelves and into the potato and onion bins, twanging all the time in their sharp voices like

20

cigarbox guitars. They took liberties in my Store that I would never dare. Since Momma told us that the less you say to whitefolks (or even powhitetrash) the better, Bailey and I would stand, solemn, quiet, in the displaced air. But if one of the playful apparitions got close to us, I pinched it. Partly out of angry frustration and partly because I didn't believe in its flesh reality.

They called my uncle by his first name and ordered him around the Store. He, to my crying shame, obeyed them in his limping dip-straight-dip fashion.

My grandmother, too, followed their orders, except that she didn't seem to be servile because she anticipated their needs.

"Here's sugar, Miz Potter, and here's baking powder. You didn't buy soda last month, you'll probably be needing some."

Momma always directed her statements to the adults, but sometimes, Oh painful sometimes, the grimy, snotty-nosed girls would answer her.

"Naw, Annie..."—to Momma? Who owned the land they lived on? Who forgot more than they would ever learn? If there was any justice in the world, God should strike them dumb at once!—"Just give us some extry sody crackers, and some more mackerel."

At least they never looked in her face, or I never caught them doing so. Nobody with a smidgen of training, not even the worst roustabout, would look right in a grown person's face. It meant the person was trying to take the words out before they were formed. The dirty little children didn't do that, but they threw their orders around the Store like lashes from a cat-o'-nine-tails.

When I was around ten years old, those scruffy children caused me the most painful and confusing experience I had ever had with my grandmother.

One summer morning, after I had swept the dirt yard of leaves, spearmint-gum wrappers and Vienna-sausage labels, I raked the yellow-red dirt, and made half-moons carefully, so that the design stood out clearly and masklike. I put the rake behind the Store and came through the back of the house to find Grandmother on the front porch in her big, wide white apron. The apron was so stiff by virtue of the starch that it could have stood alone. Momma was admiring the yard, so I joined her. It truly looked like a flat redhead that had been raked with a big-toothed comb. Momma didn't say anything but I knew she liked it. She looked over toward the school principal's house and to the right at Mr. McElroy's. She was hoping one of those community pillars would see the design before the day's business wiped it out. Then she looked upward to the school. My head had swung with hers, so at just about the same time we saw a troop of the powhitetrash kids marching over the hill and down by the side of the school.

I looked to Momma for direction. She did an excellent job of sagging from her waist down, but from the waist up she seemed to be pulling for the top of the oak tree across the road. Then she began to moan a hymn. Maybe not to moan, but the tune was so slow and the meter so strange that she could have been moaning. She didn't look at me again. When the children reached halfway down the hill, halfway to the Store, she said without turning, "Sister, go on inside."

I wanted to beg her, "Momma, don't wait for them. Come on inside with me. If they come in the Store, you go to the bedroom and let me wait on them. They only frighten me if you're around. Alone I know how to handle them." But of course I couldn't say anything, so I went in and stood behind the screen door.

Before the girls got to the porch I heard their laughter crackling and popping like pine logs in a cooking stove. I suppose my lifelong paranoia was born in those cold, molasses-slow minutes. They came finally to stand on the ground in front of Momma. At first they pretended seriousness. Then one of them wrapped her right arm in the crook of her left, pushed out her mouth and started to hum. I realized that she was aping my grandmother. Another said, "Naw, Helen, you ain't standing like her. This here's it." Then she lifted her chest, folded her arms and mocked that strange carriage that was Annie Henderson. Another laughed, "Naw, you can't do it. Your mouth ain't pooched out enough. It's like this."

I thought about the rifle behind the door, but I knew I'd never be able to hold it straight, and the .410, our sawed-off shotgun, which stayed loaded and was fired every New Year's night, was locked in the trunk and Uncle Willie had the key on his chain. Through the fly-specked screen-door, I could see that the arms of Momma's apron lifted from the vibrations of her humming. But her knees seemed to have locked as if they would never bend again.

She sang on. No louder than before, but no softer either. No slower or faster.

The dirt of the girls' cotton dresses continued on their legs, feet, arms and faces to make them all of a piece. Their greasy uncolored hair hung down, uncombed, with a grim finality. I knelt to see them better, to remember them for all time. The tears that had slipped down my dress left unsurprising dark spots, and made the front yard blurry and even more unreal. The world had taken a deep breath and was having doubts about continuing to revolve.

The girls had tired of mocking Momma and turned to other means of agitation. One crossed her eyes, stuck her thumbs in both sides of her mouth and said, "Look here, Annie." Grandmother hummed on and the apron strings trembled. I wanted to throw a handful of black pepper in their faces, to throw lye on them, to scream that they were

22

dirty, scummy peckerwoods, but I knew I was as clearly imprisoned behind the scene as the actors outside were confined to their roles.

One of the smaller girls did a kind of puppet dance while her fellow clowns laughed at her. But the tall one, who was almost a woman, said something very quietly, which I couldn't hear. They all moved backward from the porch, still watching Momma. For an awful second I thought they were going to throw a rock at Momma, who seemed (except for the apron strings) to have turned into stone herself. But the big girl turned her back, bent down and put her hands flat on the ground—she didn't pick up anything. She simply shifted her weight and did a handstand.

Her dirty bare feet and long legs went straight for the sky. Her dress fell down around her shoulders, and she had on no drawers. The slick pubic hair made a brown triangle where her legs came together. She hung in the vacuum of that lifeless morning for only a few seconds, then wavered and tumbled. The other girls clapped her on the back and slapped their hands.

Momma changed her song to "Bread of Heaven, bread of Heaven, feed me till I want no more."

I found that I was praying too. How long could Momma hold out? What new indignity would they think of to subject her to? Would I be able to stay out of it? What would Momma really like me to do?

Then they were moving out of the yard, on their way to town. They bobbed their heads and shook their slack behinds and turned, one at a time:

" 'Bye, Annie."

" 'Bye, Annie."

" 'Bye, Annie."

Momma never turned her head or unfolded her arms, but she stopped singing and said, " 'Bye, Miz Helen, 'bye, Miz Ruth, 'bye, Miz Eloise."

I burst. A firecracker July-the-Fourth burst. How could Momma call them Miz? The mean nasty things. Why couldn't she have come inside the sweet, cool store when we saw them breasting the hill? What did she prove? And then if they were dirty, mean and impudent, why did Momma have to call them Miz?

She stood another whole song through and then opened the screen door to look down on me crying in rage. She looked until I looked up. Her face was a brown moon that shone on me. She was beautiful. Something had happened out there, which I couldn't completely understand, but I could see that she was happy. Then she bent down and touched me as mothers of the church "lay hands on the sick and afflicted" and I quieted.

"Go wash your face, Sister." And she went behind the candy

counter and hummed, "Glory, glory, hallelujah, when I lay my burden down."

I threw the well water on my face and used the weekday handkerchief to blow my nose. Whatever the contest had been out front, I knew Momma had won.

I took the rake back to the front yard. The smudged footprints were easy to erase. I worked for a long time on my new design and laid the rake behind the wash pot. When I came back in the Store, I took Momma's hand and we both walked outside to look at the pattern.

It was a large heart with lots of hearts growing smaller inside, and piercing from the outside rim to the smallest heart was an arrow. Momma said, "Sister? that's right pretty." Then she turned back to the Store and resumed, "Glory, glory, hallelujah, when I lay my burden down."

6

Reverend Howard Thomas was the presiding elder over a district in Arkansas that included Stamps. Every three months he visited our church, stayed at Momma's over the Saturday night and preached a loud passionate sermon on Sunday. He collected the money that had been taken in over the preceding months, heard reports from all the church groups and shook hands with the adults and kissed all small children. Then he went away. (I used to think that he went west to heaven, but Momma straightened me out. He just went to Texarkana.)

Bailey and I hated him unreservedly. He was ugly, fat, and he laughed like a hog with the colic. We were able to make each other burst with giggling when we did imitations of the thick-skinned preacher. Bailey was especially good at it. He could imitate Reverend Thomas right in front of Uncle Willie and never get caught because he did it soundlessly. He puffed out his cheeks until they looked like wet brown stones, and wobbled his head from side to side. Only he and I knew it, but that was old Reverend Thomas to a tee.

His obesity, while disgusting, was not enough to incur the intense hate that we felt for him. The fact that he never bothered to remember our names was insulting, but neither was that slight, alone, enough to make us depise him. But the crime that tipped the scale and made our "hate not only just but imperative was his actions at the dinner table. He ate the biggest, brownest and best parts of the chicken at every Sunday meal.

The only good thing about his visits was the fact that he always arrived late on Saturday nights, after we had had dinner. I often wondered if he tried to catch us at the table. I believe so, for when he reached the front porch his little eyes would glitter toward the empty dining room and his face would fall with disappointment. Then immediately, a thin curtain would fall over his features and he'd laugh a few barks, "Uh, huh, uh, huh, Sister Henderson, just like a penny with a hole in it, I always turns up."

Right on cue every time, Momma would answer, "That's right, Elder Thomas, thank the blessed Jesus, come right in."

He'd step in the front door and put down his Gladstone (that's what he called it) and look around for Bailey and me. Then he opened his awful arms and groaned, "Suffer little children to come unto me, for such is the Kingdom of Heaven."

Bailey went to him each time with his hand stretched out, ready for a manly handshake, but Reverend Thomas would push away the hand and encircle my brother for a few seconds. "You still a boy, buddy. Remember that. They tell me the Good Book say, 'When I was a child I spake as a child, I thought as a child, but when I became a man, I put away childish things.' " Only then would he open his arms and release Bailey.

I never had the nerve to go up to him. I was quite afraid that if I tried to say, "Hello, Reverend Thomas," I would choke on the sin of mocking him. After all, the Bible did say, "God is not mocked," and the man was God's representative. He used to say to me, "Come on, little sister. Come and get this blessing." But I was so afraid and I also hated him so much that my emotions mixed themselves up and it was enough to start me crying. Momma told him time after time, "Don't pay her no mind, Elder Thomas, you know how tender-hearted she is."

He ate the leftovers from our dinner and he and Uncle Willie discussed the developments of the church programs. They talked about how the present minister was attending to his flock, who got married, who died and how many children had been born since his last visit.

Bailey and I stood like shadows in the rear of the Store near the coal-oil tank, waiting for the juicy parts. But when they were ready to talk about the latest scandal, Momma sent us to her bedroom with warnings to have our Sunday School lesson perfectly memorized or we knew what we could expect.

We had a system that never failed. I would sit in the big rocking chair by the stove and rock occasionally and stamp my feet. I changed voices, now soft and girlish, then a little deeper like Bailey's. Meanwhile, he would creep back into the Store. Many times he came flying back to sit on the bed and to hold the open lesson book just before Momma suddenly filled the doorway.

"You children get your lesson good, now. You know all the other children looks up to you all. "Then, as she turned back into the Store Bailey followed right on her footsteps to crouch in the shadows and listen for the forbidden gossip.

Once, he heard how Mr. Coley Washington had a girl from Lewisville staying in his house. I diidn't think that was so bad, but Bailey explained that Mr. Washington was probably "doing it" to her. He said that although "it" was bad just about everybody in the world did it to somebody, but no one else was supposed to know that. And once, we found out about a man who had been killed by whitefolks and thrown into the pond. Bailey said the man's things had been cut off and put in his pocket and he had been shot in the head, all because the whitefolks said he did "it" to a white woman.

Because of the kinds of news we filched from those hushed conversations, I was convinced that whenever Reverend Thomas came and Momma sent us to the back room they were going to discuss whitefolks and "doing it." Two subjects about which I was very dim.

On Sunday mornings Momma served a breakfast that was geared to hold us quiet from 9:30 A.M. to 3 P.M. She fried thick pink slabs of home-cured ham and poured the grease over sliced red tomatoes. Eggs over easy, fried potatoes and onions, yellow hominy and crisp perch fried so hard we would pop them in our mouths and chew bones, fins and all. Her cathead biscuits were at least three inches in diameter and two inches thick. The trick to eating catheads was to get the butter on them before they got cold—then they were delicious. When, unluckily, they were allowed to get cold, they tended to a gooeyness, not unlike a wad of tired gum.

We were able to reaffirm our findings on the catheads each Sunday that Reverend Thomas spent with us. Naturally enough, he was asked to bless the table. We would all stand; my uncle, leaning his walking stick against the wall, would lean his weight on the table. Then Reverend Thomas would begin. "Blessed Father, we thank you this morning..." and on and on and on. I'd stop listening after a while until Bailey kicked me and then I cracked my lids to see what had promised to be a meal that would make any Sunday proud. But as the Reverend droned on and on and on to a God who I thought must be bored to hear the same things over and over again, I saw that the ham

26

grease had turned white on the tomatoes. The eggs had withdrawn from the edge of the platter to bunch in the center like children left out in the cold. And the catheads had sat down on themselves with the conclusiveness of a fat woman sitting in an easy chair. And still he talked on. When he finally stopped, our appetites were gone, but he feasted on the cold food with a non-talking but still noisy relish.

In the Christian Methodist Episcopal Church the children's section was on the right, cater-cornered from the pew that held those ominous women called the Mothers of the Church. In the young people's section the benches were placed close together, and when a child's legs no longer comfortably fitted in the narrow space, it was an indication to the elders that that person could now move into the intermediate area (center church). Bailey and I were allowed to sit with the other children only when there were informal meetings, church socials or the like. But on the Sundays when Reverend Thomas preached, it was ordained that we occupy the first row, called the mourners' bench. I thought we were placed in front because Momma was proud of us, but Bailey assured me that she just wanted to keep her grandchildren under her thumb and eye.

Reverend Thomas took his text from Deuteronomy. And I was stretched between loathing his voice and wanting to listen to the sermon. Deuteronomy was my favorite book in the Bible. The laws were so absolute, so clearly set down, that I knew if a person truly wanted to avoid hell and brimstone, and being roasted forever in the devil's fire, all she had to do was memorize Deuteronomy and follow its teaching, word for word. I also liked the way the word rolled off the tongue.

Bailey and I sat alone on the front bench, the wooden slats pressing hard on our behinds and the backs of our thighs. I would have wriggled just a bit, but each time I looked over at Momma, she seemed to threaten, "Move and I'll tear you up," so, obedient to the unvoiced command, I sat still. The church ladies were warming up behind me with a few hallelujahs and Praise the Lords and Amens, and the preacher hadn't really moved into the meat of the sermon.

It was going to be a hot service.

On my way into church, I saw Sister Monroe, her openfaced gold crown glinting when she opened her mouth to return a neighborly greeting. She lived in the country and couldn't get to church every Sunday, so she made up for her absences by shouting so hard when she did make it that she shook the whole church. As soon as she took her seat, all the ushers would move to her side of the church because it took three women and sometimes a man or two to hold her.

Once when she hadn't been to church for a few months (she had taken off to have a child), she got the spirit and started shouting, throwing her arms around and jerking her body, so that the ushers went over to hold her down, but she tore herself away from them and ran up to the pulpit. She stood in front of the altar, shaking like a freshly caught trout. She screamed at Reverend Taylor. "Preach it. I say, preach it." Naturally he kept on preaching as if she wasn't standing there telling him what to do. Then she screamed an extremely fierce "I said, preach it" and stepped up on the altar. The Reverend kept on throwing out phrases like home-run balls and Sister Monroe made a quick break and grasped for him. For just a second, everything and everyone in the church except Reverend Taylor and Sister Monroe hung loose like stockings on a washline. Then she caught the minister by the sleeve of his jacket and his coattail, then she rocked him from side to side.

I have to say this for our minister, he never stopped giving us the lesson. The usher board made its way to the Pulpit, going up both aisles with a little more haste than is customarily seen in church. Truth to tell, they fairly ran to the minister's aid. Then two of the deacons, in their shiny Sunday suits, joined the ladies in white on the pulpit, and each time they pried Sister Monroe loose from the preacher he took another deep breath and kept on preaching, and Sister Monroe grabbed him in another place, and more firmly. Reverend Taylor was helping his rescuers as much as possible by jumping around when he got a chance. His voice at one point got so low it sounded like a roll of thunder, then Sister Monroe's "Preach it" cut through the roar, and we all wondered (I did, in any case) if it would ever end. Would they go on forever, or get tired out at last like a game of blindman's bluff that lasted too long, with nobody caring who was "it"?

I'll never know what might have happened, because magically the pandemonium spread. The spirit infused Deacon Jackson and Sister Willson, the chairman of the usher board, at the same time. Deacon Jackson, a tall, thin, quiet man, who was also a part-time Sunday school teacher, gave a scream like a falling tree, leaned back on thin air and punched Reverend Taylor on the arm. It must have hurt as much as it caught the Reverend unawares. There was a moment's break in the rolling sounds and Reverend Taylor jerked around surprised, and hauled off and punched Deacon Jackson. In the same second Sister Willson caught his tie, looped it over her fist a few times, and pressed down on him. There wasn't time to laugh or cry before all three of them were down on the floor behind the altar. Their legs spiked out like kindling wood.

Sister Monroe, who had been the cause of all the excitement, walked off the dais, cool and spent, and raised her flinty voice in the hymn, "I came to Jesus, as I was, worried, wound, and sad, I found in

28

Him a resting place and He has made me glad."

The minister took advantage of already being on the floor and asked in a choky little voice if the church would kneel with him to offer a prayer of thanksgiving. He said we had been visited with a mighty spirit, and let the whole church say Amen.

On the next Sunday, he took his text from the eighteenth chapter of the Gospel according to St. Luke, and talked quietly but seriously about the Pharisees, who prayed in the streets so that the public would be impressed with their religious devotion. I doubt that anyone got the message—certainly not those to whom it was directed. The deacon board, however, did appropriate funds for him to buy a new suit. The other was a total loss.

Our presiding elder had heard the story of Reverend Taylor and Sister Monroe, but I was sure he didn't know her by sight. So my interest in the service's potential and my aversion to Reverend Thomas caused me to turn him off. Turning off or tuning out people was my highly developed art. The custom of letting obedient children be seen but not heard was so agreeable to me that I went one step further: Obedient children should not see or hear if they chose not to do so. I laid a handful of attention on my face and tuned up the sounds in the church.

Sister Monroe's fuse was already lit, and she sizzled somewhere to the right behind me. Elder Thomas jumped into the sermon, determined, I suppose, to give the members what they came for. I saw the ushers from the left side of the church near the big windows begin to move discreetly, like pallbearers, toward Sister Monroe's bench. Bailey jogged my knee. When the incident with Sister Monroe, which we always called simply "the incident," had taken place, we had been too astounded to laugh. But for weeks after, all we needed to send us into violent outbursts of laughter was a whispered "Preach it." Anyway, he pushed my knee, covered his mouth and whispered, "I say, preach it."

I looked toward Momma, across that square of stained boards, over the collection table, hoping that a look from her would root me safely to my sanity. But for the first time in memory Momma was staring behind me at Sister Monroe. I supposed that she was counting on bringing that emotional lady up short with a severe look or two. But Sister Monroe's voice had already reached the danger point. "Preach it!"

There were a few smothered giggles from the children's section, and Bailey nudged me again. "I say, preach it"—in a whisper. Sister Monroe echoed him loudly, "I say, preach it!"

Two deacons wedged themselves around Brother Jackson as a preventive measure and two large determined-looking men walked down the aisle toward Sister Monroe.

While the sounds in the church were increasing, Elder Thomas made the regrettable mistake of increasing his volume too. Then suddenly, like a summer rain, Sister Monroe broke through the cloud of people trying to hem her in, and flooded up to the pulpit. She didn't stop this time but continued immediately to the altar, bound for Elder Thomas, crying "I say, preach it."

Bailey said out loud, "Hot dog" and "Damn" and "She's going to beat his butt."

But Reverend Thomas didn't intend to wait for that eventuality, so as Sister Monroe approached the pulpit from the right he started descending from the left. He was not intimidated by his change of venue. He continued preaching and moving. He finally stopped right in front of the collection table, which put him almost in our laps, and Sister Monroe rounded the altar on his heels, followed by the deacons, ushers, some unofficial members and a few of the bigger children.

Just as the elder opened his mouth, pink tongue waving, and said, "Great God of Mount Nebo," Sister Monroe hit him on the back of his head with her purse. Twice. Before he could bring his lips together, his teeth fell, no, actually his teeth lumped, out of his mouth.

The grinning uppers and lowers lay by my right shoe, looking empty and at the same time appearing to contain all the emptiness in the world. I could have stretched out a foot and kicked them under the bench or behind the collection table.

Sister Monroe was struggling with his coat, and the men had all but picked her up to remove her from the building. Bailey pinched me and said without moving his lips, "I'd like to see him eat dinner now."

I looked at Reverend Thomas desperately. If he appeared just a little sad or embarrassed, I could feel sorry for him and wouldn't be able to laugh. My sympathy for him would keep me from laughing. I dreaded laughing in church. If I lost control, two things were certain to happen. I would surely pee, and just as surely get a whipping. And this time I would probably die because everything was funny—Sister Monroe, and Momma trying to keep her quiet with those threatening looks, and Bailey whispering "Preach it" and Elder Thomas with his lips flapping loose like tired elastic.

But Reverend Thomas shrugged off Sister Monroe's weakening clutch, pulled out an extra-large white handkerchief and spread it over his nasty little teeth. Putting them in his pocket, he gummed, "Naked I came into the world, and naked I shall go out."

Bailey's laugh had worked its way up through his body and was escaping through his nose in short hoarse snorts. I didn't try any longer to hold back the laugh, I just opened my mouth and released sound. I heard the first titter jump up in the air over my head, over

30

the pulpit and out the window. Momma said out loud, "Sister!" but the bench was greasy and I slid off onto the floor. There was more laughter in me trying to get out, I didn't know there was that much in the whole world. It pressed at all my body openings, forcing everything in its path. I cried and hollered, passed gas and urine. I didn't see Bailey descend to the floor, but I rolled over once and he was kicking and screaming too. Each time we looked at each other we howled louder than before, and though he tried to say something, the laughter attacked him and he was only able to get out "I say, preach." And then I rolled over onto Uncle Willie's rubber-tipped cane. My eyes followed the cane up to his good brown hand on the curve and up the long, long white sleeve to his face. The one side pulled down as it usually did when he cried (it also pulled down when he laughed). He stuttered, "I'm gonna whip you this time myself."

I have no memory of how we got out of church and into the parsonage next door, but in that overstuffed parlor, Bailey and I received the whipping of our lives. Uncle Willie ordered us between licks to stop crying. I tried to, but Bailey refused to cooperate. Later he explained that when a person is beating you you should scream as loud as possible; maybe the whipper will become embarrassed or else some sympathetic soul might come to your rescue. Our savior came for neither of these reasons, but because Bailey yelled so loud and disturbed what was left of the service, the minister's wife came out and asked Uncle Willie to quiet us down.

Laughter so easily turns to hysteria for imaginative children. I felt for weeks after that I had been very, very sick, and until I completely recovered my strength I stood on laughter's cliff and any funny thing could hurl me off to my death far below.

Each time Bailey said "Preach it" to me, I hit him as hard as I could and cried.

7

Momma had married three times: Mr. Johnson, my grandfather, who left her around the turn of the century with two small sons to raise; Mr. Henderson, of whom I know nothing at all (Momma never answered questions directly put to her on any subject except religion); then finally Mr. Murphy. I saw him a fleeting once. He came through Stamps on a Saturday night, and Grandmother gave me the chore of making his pallet on the floor. He was a stocky dark man who wore a snap-brim hat like George Raft. The next morning he hung around the Store until we returned from church. That marked the first Sunday I knew Uncle Willie to miss services. Bailey said he stayed home to keep Mr. Murphy from stealing us blind. He left in the middle of the afternoon after one of Momma's extensive Sunday dinners. His hat pushed back off his forehead, he walked down the road whistling. I watched his thick back until he turned the bend by the big white church.

People spoke of Momma as a good-looking woman and some, who remembered her youth, said she used to be right pretty. I saw only her power and strength. She was taller than any woman in my personal world, and her hands were so large they could span my head from ear to ear. Her voice was soft only because she chose to keep it so. In church, when she was called upon to sing, she seemed to pull out plugs from behind her jaws and the huge, almost rough sound would pour over the listeners and throb in the air.

Each Sunday, after she had taken her seat, the minister would announce, "We will now be led in a hymn by Sister Henderson." And each Sunday she looked up with amazement at the preacher and asked silently, "Me?" After a second of assuring herself that she indeed was being called upon, she laid down her handbag and slowly folded her handkerchief. This was placed neatly on top of the purse, then she leaned on the bench in front and pushed herself to a standing position, and then she opened her mouth and the song jumped out as if it had only been waiting for the right time to make an appearance. Week after week and year after year the performance never changed, yet I don't remember anyone's ever remarking on her sincerity or readiness to sing.

Momma intended to teach Bailey and me to use the paths in life that she and her generation and all the Negroes gone before had found, and found to be safe ones. She didn't cotton to the idea that whitefolks could be talked to at all without risking one's life. And certainly they couldn't be spoken to insolently. In fact, even in their absence they could not be spoken of too harshly unless we used the sobriquet "They." If she had been asked and had chosen to answer the question of whether she was cowardly or not, she would have said that she was a realist. Didn't she stand up to "them" year after year? Wasn't she the only Negro woman in Stamps referred to once as Mrs.?

That incident became one of Stamps' little legends. Some years before Bailey and I arrived in town, a man was hunted down for assaulting white womanhood. In trying to escape he ran to the Store. Momma and Uncle Willie hid him behind the chifforobe until night, gave him supplies for an overland journey and sent him on his way. He was, however, apprehended, and in court when he was questioned as to his movements on the day of the crime, he replied that after he heard that he was being sought he took refuge in Mrs. Henderson's Store.

The judge asked that Mrs. Henderson be subpoenaed, and when Momma arrived and said she was Mrs. Henderson, the judge, the bailiff and other whites in the audience laughed. The judge had really made a gaffe calling a Negro woman Mrs., but then he was from Pine Bluff and couldn't have been expected to know that a woman who owned a store in that village would also turn out to be colored. The whites tickled their funny bones with the incident for a long time, and the Negroes thought it proved the worth and majesty of my grandmother.

8

Stamps, Arkansas, was Chitlin' Switch, Georgia; Hang 'Em High, Alabama; Don't Let the Sun Set on You Here, Nigger, Mississippi; or any other name just as descriptive. People in Stamps used to say that the whites in our town were so prejudiced that a Negro couldn't buy vanilla ice cream. Except on July Fourth. Other days he had to be satisfied with chocolate.

A light shade had been pulled down between the Black community and all things white, but one could see through it enough to develop a fear-admiration-contempt for the white "things"—white folks' cars and white glistening houses and their children and their women. But above all, their wealth that allowed them to waste was the most enviable. They had so many clothes they were able to give perfectly good dresses, worn just under the arms, to the sewing class at our school for the larger girls to practice on.

Although there was always generosity in the Negro neighborhood, it was indulged on pain of sacrifice. Whatever was given by Black people to other Blacks was most probably needed as desperately by the donor as by the receiver. A fact which made the giving or receiving a rich exchange.

I couldn't understand whites and where they got the right to spend money so lavishly. Of course, I knew God was white too, but no one could have made me believe he was prejudiced. My grandmother had more money than all the powhitetrash. We owned land and houses, but each day Bailey and I were cautioned, "Waste not, want not."

Momma bought two bolts of cloth each year for winter and summer clothes. She made my school dresses, underslips, bloomers, handkerchiefs, Bailey's shirts, shorts, her aprons, house dresses and waists from the rolls shipped to Stamps by Sears and Roebuck. Uncle Willie was the only person in the family who wore ready-to-wear clothes all the time. Each day, he wore fresh white shirts and flowered suspenders, and his special shoes cost twenty dollars. I thought Uncle Willie sinfully vain, especially when I had to iron seven stiff starched shirts and not leave a cat's face anywhere.

During the summer we went barefoot, except on Sunday, and we learned to resole our shoes when they "gave out," as Mamma used to say. The Depression must have hit the white section of Stamps with cyclonic impact, but it seeped into the Black area slowly, like a thief with misgivings. The country had been in the throes of the Depression for two years before the Negroes in Stamps knew it. I think that everyone thought that the Depression, like everything else, was for the whitefolks, so it had nothing to do with them. Our people had lived off the land and counted on cotton-picking and hoeing and chopping seasons to bring in the cash needed to buy shoes, clothes, books and light farm equipment. It was when the owners of cotton fields dropped the payment of ten cents for a pound of cotton to eight, seven and finally five that the Negro community realized that the Depression, at least, did not discriminate.

Welfare agencies gave food to the poor families, Black and white. Gallons of lard, flour, salt, powdered eggs and powdered milk. People stopped trying to raise hogs because it was too difficult to get slop rich enough to feed them, and no one had the money to buy mash or fish meal.

Momma spent many nights figuring on our tablets, slowly. She was trying to find a way to keep her business going, although her customers had no money. When she came to her conclusions, she said, "Bailey, I want you to make me a nice clear sign. Nice and neat. And Sister, you can color it with your Crayolas. I want it to say:

1   5 LB. CAN OF POWDERED MILK IS WORTH 50¢ IN TRADE
1   5 LB. CAN OF POWDERED EGGS IS WORTH $1.00 IN TRADE
10   #2 CANS OF MACKEREL IS WORTH $1.00 IN TRADE."

And so on. Momma kept her store going. Our customers didn't even have to take their slated provisions home. They'd pick them up from the welfare center downtown and drop them off at the Store. If they didn't want an exchange at the moment they'd put down in one of the big gray ledgers the amount of credit coming to them. We were among the few Negro families not on relief, but Bailey and I were the only children in the town proper that we knew who ate powdered eggs every day and drank the powdered milk.

Our playmates' families exchanged their unwanted food for sugar, coal oil, spices, potted meat, Vienna sausage, peanut butter, soda crackers, toilet soap and even laundry soap. We were always given enough to eat, but we both hated the lumpy milk and mushy eggs, and sometimes we'd stop off at the house of one of the poorer families to get some peanut butter and crackers. Stamps was as slow coming out of the Depression as it had been getting into it. World War II was well along before there was a noticeable change in the economy of that near-forgotten hamlet.

One Christmas we received gifts from our mother and father, who lived separately in a heaven called California, where we were told they could have all the oranges they could eat. And the sun shone all the time. I was sure that wasn't so. I couldn't believe that our mother would laugh and eat oranges in the sunshine without her children. Until that Christmas when we received the gifts I had been confident that they were both dead. I could cry anytime I wanted by picturing my mother (I didn't quite know what she looked like) lying in her coffin. Her hair, which was black, was spread out on a tiny little white pillow and her body was covered with a sheet. The face was brown, like a big O, and since I couldn't fill in the features I printed M O T H E R across the O, and tears would fall down my cheeks like warm milk.

Then came that terrible Christmas with its awful presents when our father, with the vanity I was to find typical, sent his photograph. My gift from Mother was a tea set—a teapot, four cups and saucers and tiny spoons—and a doll with blue eyes and rosy cheeks and yellow hair painted on her head. I didn't know what Bailey received, but after I opened my boxes I went out to the backyard behind the chinaberry tree. The day was cold and the air as clear as water. Frost was still on the bench but I sat down and cried. I looked up and Bailey was coming from the outhouse, wiping his eyes. He had been crying too. I didn't know if he had also told himself they were dead and had been rudely awakened to the truth or whether he was just feeling lonely. The gifts opened the door to questions that neither of us wanted to ask. Why did they send us away? and what did we do so

35

wrong? So Wrong? Why, at three and four, did we have tags put on our arms to be sent by train alone from Long Beach, California, to Stamps, Arkansas, with only the porter to look after us? (Besides, he got off in Arizona.)

Bailey sat down beside me, and that time didn't admonish me not to cry. So I wept and he sniffed a little, but we didn't talk until Momma called us back in the house.

Momma stood in front of the tree that we had decorated with silver ropes and pretty colored balls and said, "You children is the most ungrateful things I ever did see. You think your momma and poppa went to all the trouble to send you these nice play pretties to make you go out in the cold and cry?"

Neither of us said a word. Momma continued, "Sister, I know you tender-hearted, but Bailey Junior, there's no reason for you to set out mewing like a pussy cat, just 'cause you got something from Vivian and Big Bailey." When we still didn't force ourselves to answer, she asked, "You want me to tell Santa Claus to take these things back?" A wretched feeling of being torn engulfed me. I wanted to scream, "Yes. Tell him to take them back." But I didn't move.

Later Bailey and I talked. He said if the things really did come from Mother maybe it meant that she was getting ready to come and get us. Maybe she had just been angry at something we had done, but was forgiving us and would send for us soon. Bailey and I tore the stuffing out of the doll the day after Christmas, but he warned me that I had to keep the tea set in good condition because any day or night she might come riding up.

9

A year later our father came to Stamps without warning. It was awful for Bailey and me to encounter the reality one abrupt morning. We, or at any rate I, had built such elaborate fantasies about him and the illusory mother that seeing him in the flesh shredded my inventions like a hard yank on a paper chain, He arrived in front of the Store in a clean gray car (he must have stopped just outside of town to wipe it in preparation for the "grand entrance"). Bailey, who knew such things, said it was a De Soto. His bigness shocked me. His shoulders were so wide I thought he'd have trouble getting in the door. He was taller than anyone I had seen, and if he wasn't fat, which I knew he wasn't, then he was fat-like. His clothes were too small too. They were tighter and woolier than was customary in Stamps. And he was blindingly handsome. Momma cried, "Bailey, my baby. Great God, Bailey." And Uncle Willie stuttered, "Bu—Buh—Bailey. "My brother said, "Hot dog and damn. It's him. It's our daddy." And my seven-year-old world humpty-dumptied, never to be put back together again.

His voice rang like a metal dipper hitting a bucket and he spoke English. Proper English, like the school principal, and even better. Our father sprinkled *ers* and even *errers* in his sentences as liberally as he gave out his twisted-mouth smiles. His lips pulled not down, like Uncle Willie's, but to the side, and his head lay on one side or the other, but never straight on the end of his neck. He had the air of a man who did not believe what he heard or what he himself was saying. He was the first cynic I had met, "So er this is Daddy's er little man? Boy, anybody tell you errer that you er look like me?" He had Bailey in one arm and me in the other. "And Daddy's baby girl. You've errer been good children, er haven't you? Or er I guess I would have er heard about it er from Santa Claus." I was so proud of him it was hard to wait for the gossip to get around that he was in town. Wouldn't the kids be surprised at how handsome our daddy was? And that he loved us enough to come down to Stamps to visit? Everyone could tell from the way he talked and from the car and clothes that he was rich and maybe had a castle out in California. (I later learned that he had been a doorman at Santa Monica's plush Breakers Hotel). Then the possibility of being compared with him occurred to me, and I didn't want anyone to see him. Maybe he wasn't my real father. Bailey was his son, true enough, but I was an orphan that they picked up to provide Bailey with company.

I was always afraid when I found him watching me, and wished I could grow small like Tiny Tim. Sitting at the table one day, I held the fork in my left hand and pierced a piece of fried chicken. I put the knife through the second tine, as we had been strictly taught, and began to saw against the bone. My father laughed a rich rolling laugh, and I looked up. He imitated me, both elbows going up and down. "Is Daddy's baby going to fly away?" Momma laughed, and Uncle Willie too, and even Bailey snickered a little. Our father was proud of his sense of humor.

For three weeks the Store was filled with people who had gone to school with him or heard about him. The curious and envious milled around and he strutted, throwing *ers* and *errers* all over the place and under the sad eyes of Uncle Willie. Then one day he said he had to get back to California. I was relieved. My world was going to be emptier and dryer, but the agony of having him intrude into every private second would be gone. And the silent threat that had hung in the air since his arrival, the threat of his leaving someday, would be gone. I wouldn't have to wonder whether I loved him or not, or have to answer "Does Daddy's baby want to go to California with Daddy?" Bailey had told him that he wanted to go, but I had kept quiet. Momma was relieved too, although she had had a good time cooking special things for him and showing her California son off to the peasants of Arkansas. But Uncle Willie was suffering under our father's bombastic pressure, and in mother-bird fashion Momma was more concerned with her crippled offspring than the one who could fly away from the nest.

He was going to take us with him! The knowledge buzzed through my days and made me jump unexpectedly like a jack-in-the-box. Each day I found some time to walk to the pond where people went to catch sun perch and striped bass. The hours I chose to go were too early or late for fishermen, so I had the area to myself. I stood on the bank of the green dark water, and my thoughts skidded like the water spiders. Now this way, now that, now the other. Should I go with my father? Should I throw myself into the pond, and not being able to swim, join the body of L.C., the boy who drowned last summer? Should I beg Momma to let me stay with her? I could tell her that I'd take over Bailey's chores and do my own as well. Did I have the nerve to try life without Bailey? I couldn't decide on any move, so I recited a few Bible verses, and went home.

Momma cut down a few give-aways that had been traded to her by white women's maids and sat long nights in the dining room sewing jumpers and skirts for me. She looked pretty sad, but each time I found her watching me she'd say, as if I had already disobeyed, "You be a good girl now. You hear? Don't you make people think I didn't raise you right. You hear?" She would have been more surprised than I had she taken me in her arms and wept at losing me. Her world was bordered on all sides with work, duty, religion and "her place." I don't think she ever knew that a deep-brooding love hung over everything she touched. In later years I asked her if she loved me and she brushed me off with: "God is love. Just worry about whether you're being a good girl, then He will love you."

I sat in the back of the car, with Dad's leather suitcases, and our cardboard boxes. Although the windows were rolled down, the smell of fried chicken and sweet potato pie lay unmoving, and there wasn't enough room to stretch. Whenever he thought about it, Dad asked, "Are you comfortable back there, Daddy's baby?" He never waited to hear my answer, which was "Yes, sir," before he'd resume his conversation with Bailey. He and Bailey told jokes, and Bailey laughed all the time, put out Dad's cigarettes and held one hand on the steering wheel when Dad said, "Come on, boy, help me drive this thing."

After I got tired of passing through the same towns over and over, and seeing the empty-looking houses, small and unfriendly, I closed myself off to everything but the kissing sounds of the tires on the pavement and the steady moan of the motor. I was certainly very vexed with Bailey. There was no doubt that he was trying to butter up Dad; he even started to laugh like him, a Santa Claus, Jr., with his "Ho, ho, ho."

"How are you going to feel seeing your mother? Going to be happy?" he was asking Bailey, but it penetrated the foam I had packed around my senses. Were we going to see Her? I thought we were going to California. I was suddenly terrified. Suppose she laughed at us the way he did? What if she had other children now, whom she kept with her? I said, "I want to go back to Stamps." Dad laughed, "You mean Daddy's baby doesn't want to go to St. Louis to see her mother? She's not going to eat you up, you know."

He turned to Bailey and I looked at the side of his face; he was so unreal to me I felt as if I were watching a doll talk. "Bailey, Junior, ask your sister why she wants to go back to Stamps." He sounded more like a white man than a Negro. Maybe he was the only brown-skinned white man in the world. It would be just my luck that the only one would turn out to be my father. But Bailey was quiet for the first time since we left Stamps. I guess he was thinking too about seeing Mother. How could an eight-year-old contain that much fear? He swallows and holds it behind his tonsils, he tightens his feet and closes the fear between his toes, he contracts his buttock and pushes it up behind the prostate gland.

"Junior, cat's got your tongue? What do you think your mother will say, when I tell her her children didn't want to see her?" The thought that he *would* tell her shook me and Bailey at the same time. He leaned over the back of the seat—"My, it's Mother Dear. You know you want to see Mother Dear. Don't cry." Dad laughed and pitched in his seat and asked himself, I guess, "What will she say to that?"

I stopped crying since there was no chance to get back to Stamps and Momma. Bailey wasn't going to back me up, I could tell, so I decided to shut up and dry up and wait for whatever seeing Mother Dear was going to bring.

St. Louis was a new kind of hot and a new kind of dirty. My memory had no pictures of the crowded-together soot-covered buildings. For all I knew, we were being driven to Hell and our father was the delivering devil.

Only in strict emergencies did Bailey allow me to speak Pig Latin to him in front of adults, but I had to take the chance that afternoon. We had spun around the same corner, I was sure, about fifty times. I asked Bailey, "Ooday ooyay inkthay isthay is our atherfay, or ooday ooyay inkthay atthay eeway are eeingbay idkay appednay?" Bailey said, "My, we're in St. Louis, and we're going to see Mother Dear. Don't worry." Dad chuckled and said, "Oohay oodway antway ootay idkay appnay ooyay? Ooday ooyay inkthay ooyay are indlay ergbay ildrenchay?" I thought that my brother and his friends had created Pig Latin. Hearing my father speak it didn't startle me so much as it angered. It was simply another case of the trickiness of adults where children were concerned. Another case in point of the Grownups' Betrayal.

To describe my mother would be to write about a hurricane in its perfect power. Or the climbing, falling colors of a rainbow. We had been received by her mother and had waited on the edge of our seats in the overfurnished living room (Dad talked easily with our grandmother, as whitefolks talk to Blacks, unembarrassed and unapologetic). We were both fearful of Mother's coming and impatient at her delay. It is remarkable how much truth there is in the two expressions: "struck dumb" and "love at first sight." My mother's beauty literally assailed me. Her red lips (Momma said it was a sin to wear lipstick) split to show even white teeth and her fresh-butter color looked see-through clean. Her smile widened her mouth beyond her cheeks beyond her ears and seemingly through the walls to the street outside. I was struck dumb. I knew immediately why she had sent me away. She was too beautiful to have children. I had never seen a woman as pretty as she who was called "Mother." Bailey on his part fell instantly and forever in love. I saw his eyes shining like hers; he had forgotten the loneliness and the nights when we had cried together because we were "unwanted children." He had never left her warm side or shared the icy wind of solitude with me. She was his Mother Dear and I resigned myself to his condition. They were more alike than she and I, or even he and I. They both had physical beauty and personality, so I figured it figured.

Our father left St. Louis a few days later for California, and I was neither glad nor sorry. He was a stranger, and if he chose to leave us with a stranger, it was all of one piece.

10

Grandmother Baxter was a quadroon or an octoroon, or in any case she was nearly white. She had been raised by a German family in Cairo, Illinois, and had come to St. Louis at the turn of the century to study nursing. While she was working at Homer G. Phillips Hospital she met and married Grandfather Baxter. She was white (having no features that could even loosely be called Negroid) and he was Black. While she spoke with a throaty German accent until her death, he had the choppy spouting speech of the West Indians.

Their marriage was a happy one. Grandfather had a famous saying that caused great pride in his family: "Bah Jesus, I live for my wife, my children and my dog." He took extreme care to prove that statement true by taking the word of his family even in the face of contradictory evidence.

The Negro section of St. Louis in the mid-thirties had all the finesse of a gold-rush town. Prohibition, gambling and their related vocations were so obviously practiced that it was hard for me to believe that they were against the law. Bailey and I, as newcomers, were quickly told by our schoolmates who the men on the street corners were as we passed. I was sure that they had taken their names from Wild West Books (Hard-hitting Jimmy, Two Gun, Sweet Man, Poker Pete), and to prove me right, they hung around in front of saloons like unhorsed cowboys.

We met the numbers runners, gamblers, lottery takers and whiskey salesmen not only in the loud streets but in our orderly living room as well. They were often there when we returned from school, sitting with hats in their hands, as we had done upon our arrival in the big city. They waited silently for Grandmother Baxter.

Her white skin and the pince-nez that she dramatically took from her nose and let hang free on a chain pinned to her dress were factors that brought her a great deal of respect. Moreover, the reputation of her six mean children and the fact that she was a precinct captain compounded her power and gave her the leverage to deal with even the lowest crook without fear. She had pull with the police department, so the men in their flashy suits and fleshy scars sat with churchlike decorum and waited to ask favors from her. If Grandmother raised the heat off their gambling parlors, or said the word that reduced the bail of a friend waiting in jail, they knew what would be expected of them. Come election, they were to bring in the votes from their neighborhood. She most often got them leniency, and they always brought in the vote.

St. Louis also introduced me to thin-sliced ham (I thought it a delicacy), jelly beans and peanuts mixed, lettuce on sandwich bread, Victrolas and family loyalty. In Arkansas, where we cured our own meat, we ate half-inch slabs of ham for breakfast, but in St. Louis we bought the paper-thin slices in a strange-smelling German store and ate them in sandwiches. If Grandmother never lost her German accent, she also never lost her taste for the thick black German *Brot*, which we bought unsliced. In Stamps, lettuce was used only to make a bed for potato salad or slaw, and peanuts were brought in raw from the field and roasted in the bottom of the oven on cold nights. The rich scents used to fill the house and we were always expected to eat too many. But that was a Stamps custom. In St. Louis, peanuts were bought in paper bags and mixed with jelly beans, which meant that we ate the salt and sugar together and I found them a delicious treat. The best thing the big town had to offer.

When we enrolled in Toussaint L'Ouverture Grammar School, we were struck by the ignorance of our schoolmates and the rudeness of our teachers. Only the vastness of the building impressed us; not even the white school in Stamps was as large.

The students, however, were shockingly backward. Bailey and I did arithmetic at a mature level because of our work in the Store, and we read well because in Stamps there wasn't anything else to do. We were moved up a grade because our teachers thought that we country children would make our classmates feel inferior—and we did. Bailey would not refrain from remarking on our classmates' lack of knowledge. At lunchtime in the large gray concrete playground, he would stand in the center of a crowd of big boys and ask, "Who was Napoleon Bonaparte?" "How many feet make a mile?" It was infighting, Bailey style.

Any of the boys might have been able to beat him with their fists, but if they did, they'd just have had to do it again the next day, and Bailey never held a brief for fighting fair. He taught me that once I got into a fight I should "grab for the balls right away." He never answered when I asked, "Suppose I'm fighting a girl?"

We went to school there a full year, but all I remember hearing that I hadn't heard before was, "Making thousands of egg-shaped oughts will improve penmanship."

The teachers were more formal than those we knew in Stamps, and although they didn't whip students with switches, they gave them licks in the palms of their hands with rulers. In Stamps teachers were much friendlier, but that was because they were imported from the Arkansas Negro colleges, and since we had no hotels or rooming houses in town, they had to live with private families. If a lady teacher took company, or didn't receive any mail or cried alone in her room at night, by the weeks' end even the children discussed her morality, her loneliness and her other failings generally. It would have been near impossible to maintain formality under a small town's invasions of privacy.

St. Louis teachers, on the other hand, tended to act very siditty, and talked down to their students from the lofty heights of education and whitefolks' enunciation. They, women as well as men, all sounded like my father with their *ers* and *errers*. They walked with their knees together and talked through tight lips as if they were as afraid to let the sound out as they were to inhale the dirty air that the listener gave off.

We walked to school around walls of bricks and breathed the coal dust for one discouraging winter. We learned to say "Yes" and "No" rather than "Yes, ma'am," and "No, ma'am."

Occasionally Mother, whom we seldom saw in the house, had us meet her at Louie's. It was a long dark tavern at the end of the bridge near our school, and was owned by two Syrian brothers.

We used to come in the back door, and the sawdust, stale beer, steam and boiling meat made me feel as if I'd been eating mothballs. Mother had cut my hair in a bob like hers and straightened it, so my head felt skinned and the back of my neck so bare that I was ashamed to have anyone walk up behind me. Naturally, this kept me turning quickly as if I expected something to happen.

At Louie's we were greeted by Mother's friends as "Bibbie's darling babies" and were given soft drinks and boiled shrimp. While we sat on the stiff wooden booths, Mother would dance alone in front of us to music from the Seeburg. I loved her most at those times. She was like a pretty kite that floated just above my head. If I liked, I could pull it in to me by saying I had to go to the toilet or by starting a fight with Bailey. I never did either, but the power made me tender to her.

The Syrian brothers vied for her attention as she sang the heavy blues that Bailey and I almost understood. They watched her, even when directing their conversation to other customers, and I knew they too were hypnotized by this beautiful lady who talked with her whole body and snapped her fingers louder than anyone in the whole world. We learned the Time Step at Louie's. It is from this basic step that most American Black dances are born. It is a series of taps, jumps and rests, and demands careful listening, feeling and coordination. We were brought before Mother's friends, there in the heavy saloon air, to show our artistry. Bailey learned easily, and has always been the better dancer. But I learned too. I approached the Time Step with the same determination to win that I had approached the time tables with. There was no Uncle Willie or sizzling pot-bellied stove, but there was Mother and her laughing friends, and they amounted to the same thing. We were applauded and given more soft drinks and, more shrimp, but it was to be years later before I found the joy and freedom of dancing well.

Mother's brothers, Uncles Tutti, Tom and Ira, were well-known young men about St. Louis. They all had city jobs, which I now understand to have been no mean feat for Negro men. Their jobs and their family set them apart, but they were best known for their unrelenting meanness. Grandfather had told them, "Bah Jesus, if you ever get in jail for stealing or some such foolishness, I'll let you rot. But if you're arrested for fighting, I'll sell the house, lock, stock, and barrel, to get you out!" With that kind of encouragement, backed by explosive tempers, it was no wonder they became fearsome characters. Our youngest uncle, Billy, was not old enough to join in their didoes. One of their more flamboyant escapades has become a proud family legend.

Pat Patterson, a big man, who was himself protected by the shield of a bad reputation, made the mistake of cursing my mother one night when she was out alone. She reported the incident to her brothers. They ordered one of their hangers-on to search the streets for Patterson, and when he was located, to telephone them.

As they waited throughout the afternoon, the living room filled with smoke and the murmurs of plans. From time to time, Grandfather came in from the kitchen and said, "Don't kill him. Mind you, just don't kill him," then went back to his coffee with Grandmother.

They went to the saloon where Patterson sat drinking at a small table. Uncle Tommy stood by the door, Uncle Tutti stationed himself at the toilet door and Uncle Ira, who was the oldest and maybe everyone's ideal, walked over to Patterson. They were all obviously carrying guns.

Uncle Ira said to my mother, "Here, Bibbi. Here's this nigger Patterson. Come over here and beat his ass."

She crashed the man's head with a policemen's billy enough to leave him just this side of death. There was no police investigation nor social reprobation.

After all, didn't Grandfather champion their wild tempers, and wasn't Grandmother a near-white woman with police pull?

I admit that I was thrilled by their meanness. They beat up whites and Blacks with the same abandon, and liked each other so much that they never needed to learn the art of making outside friends. My mother was the only warm, outgoing personality among her siblings. Grandfather became bedridden during our stay there, and his children spent their free time telling him jokes, gossiping with him and showing their love.

Uncle Tommy, who was gruff and chewed his words like Grandfather, was my favorite. He strung ordinary sentences together and they came out sounding either like the most profane curses or like comical poetry. A natural comedian, he never waited for the laugh that he knew must follow his droll statements. He was never cruel. He was mean.

When we played handball on the side of our house, Uncle Tommy would turn the corner, coming from work. He would pretend at first not to see us, but with the deftness of a cat he would catch the ball and say, "Put your minds where your behinds are, and I'll let you on my team." We children would range around him, but it was only when he reached the steps that he'd wind up his arm and throw the ball over the light post and toward the stars.

He told me often, "Ritie, don't worry 'cause you ain't pretty. Plenty pretty women I seen digging ditches or worse. You smart. I swear to God, I rather you have a good mind than a cute behind."

They bragged often about the binding quality of the Baxter blood. Uncle Tommy said that even the children felt it before they were old enough to be taught. They reminisced over Bailey's teaching me to walk when he was less than three. Displeased at my stumbling motions, he was supposed to have said, "This is *my* sister. *I* have to teach her to walk." They also told me how I got the name "My." After Bailey learned definitely that I was his sister, he refused to call me Marguerite, but rather addressed me each time as "Mya Sister," and in later more articulate years, after the need for brevity had shortened the appellation to "My," it was elaborated into "Maya."

We lived in a big house on Caroline Street with our grandparents for half the year before Mother moved us in with her. Moving from the house where the family was centered meant absolutely nothing to me. It was simply a small pattern in the grand design of our lives. If other children didn't move so much, it just went to show that our lives were fated to be different from everyone else's in the world. The new house was no stranger than the other, except that we were with Mother.

Bailey persisted in calling her Mother Dear until the circumstance of proximity softened the phrase's formality to "Muh Dear," and finally to "M'Deah." I could never put my finger on her realness. She was so pretty and so quick that even when she had just awakened, her eyes full of sleep and hair tousled, I thought she looked just like the Virgin Mary. But what mother and daughter understand each other, or even have the sympathy for each other's lack of understanding?

Mother had prepared a place for us, and we went to it gratefully. We each had a room with a two-sheeted bed, plenty to eat and store-bought clothes to wear. And after all, she didn't have to do it. If we got on her nerves or if we were disobedient, she could always send us back to Stamps. The weight of appreciation and the threat, which was never spoken, of a return to Momma were burdens that clogged my childish wits into impassivity. I was called Old Lady and chided for moving and talking like winter's molasses.

Mother's boyfriend, Mr. Freeman, lived with us, or we lived with him (I never quite knew which). He was a Southerner, too, and big. But a little flabby. His breasts used to embarrass me when he walked around in his undershirt. They lay on his chest like flat titties.

Even if Mother hadn't been such a pretty woman, light-skinned with straight hair, he was lucky to get her, and he knew it. She was educated, from a well-known family, and after all, wasn't she born in St. Louis? Then she was gay. She laughed all the time and made jokes. He was grateful. I think he must have been many years older than she, but if not, he still had the sluggish inferiority of old men married to younger women. He watched her every move and when she left the room, his eyes allowed her reluctantly to go.

11

I had decided that St. Louis was a foreign country. I would never get used to the scurrying sounds of flushing toilets, or the packaged foods, or doorbells or the noise of cars and trains and buses that crashed through the walls or slipped under the doors. In my mind I only stayed in St. Louis for a few weeks. As quickly as I understood that I had not reached my home, I sneaked away to Robin Hood's forest and the caves of Alley Oop where all reality was unreal and even that changed every day. I carried the same shield that I had used in Stamps: "I didn't come to stay."

Mother was competent in providing for us. Even if that meant getting someone else to furnish the provisions. Although she was a nurse, she never worked at her profession while we were with her. Mr. Freeman brought in the necessities and she earned extra money cutting poker games in gambling parlors. The straight eight-to-five world simply didn't have enough glamor for her, and it was twenty years later that I first saw her in a nurse's uniform.

Mr Freeman was a foreman in the Southern Pacific yards and came home late sometimes, after Mother had gone out. He took his dinner off the stove where she had carefully covered it and which she had admonished us not to bother. He ate quietly in the kitchen while Bailey and I read separately and greedily our own Street and Smith pulp magazine. Now that we had spending money, we bought the illustrated paperbacks with their gaudy pictures. When Mother was away, we were put on an honor system. We had to finish our homework, eat dinner and wash the dishes before we could read or listen to *The Lone Ranger*, *Crime Busters* or *The Shadow*.

Mr. Freeman moved gracefully, like a big brown bear, and seldom spoke to us. He simply waited for Mother and put his whole self into the waiting. He never read the paper or patted his foot to radio. He waited. That was all.

If she came home before we went to bed, we saw the man come alive. He would start out of the big chair, like a man coming out of sleep, smiling. I would remember then that a few seconds before, I had heard a car door slam; then Mother's footsteps would signal from the concrete walk. When her key rattled the door, Mr. Freeman would have already asked his habitual question, "Hey, Bibbi, have a good time?"

His query would hang in the air while she sprang over to peck him on the lips. Then she turned to Bailey and me with the lipstick kisses. "Haven't you finished your homework?" If we had and were just reading —"O.K., say your prayers and go to bed." If we hadn't—"Then go to your room and finish... then say your prayers and go to bed."

Mr. Freeman's smile never grew, it stayed at the same intensity. Sometimes Mother would go over and sit on his lap and the grin on his face looked as if it would stay there forever.

From our rooms we could hear the glasses clink and the radio turned up. I think she must have danced for him on the good nights, because he couldn't dance, but before I fell asleep I often heard feet shuffling to dance rhythms.

I felt very sorry for Mr. Freeman. I felt as sorry for him as I had felt for a litter of helpless pigs born in our backyard sty in Arkansas. We fattened the pigs all year long for slaughter on the first good frost, and even as I suffered for the cute little wiggly things, I knew how much I was going to enjoy the fresh sausage and hog's headcheese they could give me only with their deaths.

47

Because of the lurid tales we read and our vivid imaginations and, probably, memories of our brief but hectic lives, Bailey and I were afflicted—he physically and I mentally. He stuttered, and I sweated through horrifying nightmares. He was constantly told to slow down and start again, and on my particularly bad nights my mother would take me in to sleep with her, in the large bed with Mr. Freeman.

Because of a need for stability, children easily become creatures of habit. After the third time in Mother's bed, I thought there was nothing strange about sleeping there.

One morning she got out of bed for an early errand, and I fell asleep again. But I awoke to a pressure, a strange feeling on my left leg. It was too soft to be a hand, and it wasn't the touch of clothes. Whatever it was, I hadn't encountered the sensation in all the years of sleeping with Momma. It didn't move, and I was too startled to. I turned my head a little to the left to see if Mr. Freeman was awake and gone, but his eyes were open and both hands were above the cover. I knew, as if I had always known, it was his "thing" on my leg.

He said, "Just stay right here, Ritie, I ain't gonna hurt you." I wasn't afraid, a little apprehensive, maybe, but not afraid. Of course I knew that lots of people did "it" and that they used their "things" to accomplish the deed, but no one I knew had ever done it to anybody. Mr. Freeman pulled me to him, and put his hand between my legs. He didn't hurt, but Momma had drilled into my head: "Keep your legs closed, and don't let nobody see your pocketbook."

"Now, I didn't hurt you. Don't get scared." He threw back the blankets and his "thing" stood up like a brown ear of corn. He took my hand and said, "Feel it." It was mushy and squirmy like the inside of a freshly killed chicken. Then he dragged me on top of his chest with his left arm, and his right hand was moving so fast and his heart was beating so hard that I was afraid that he would die. Ghost stories revealed how people who died wouldn't let go of whatever they were holding. I wondered if Mr. Freeman died holding me how I would ever get free. Would they have to break his arms to get me loose?

Finally he was quiet, and then came the nice part. He held me so softly that I wished he wouldn't ever let me go. I felt at home. From the way he was holding me I knew he'd never let me go or let anything bad ever happen to me. This was probably my real father and we had found each other at last. But then he rolled over, leaving me in a wet place and stood up.

"I gotta talk to you, Ritie." He pulled off his shorts that had fallen to his ankles, and went into the bathroom.

It was true the bed was wet, but I knew I hadn't had an accident. Maybe Mr. Freeman had one while he was holding me. He came back with a glass of water and told me in a sour voice, "Get up. You peed in the bed." He poured water on the wet spot, and it did look like my mattress on many mornings.

Having lived in Southern strictness, I knew when to keep quiet around adults, but I did want to ask him why he said I peed when I was sure he didn't believe that. If he thought I was naughty, would that mean that he would never hold me again? Or admit that he was my father? I had made him ashamed of me.

"Ritie, you love Bailey?" He sat down on the bed and I came close, hoping. "Yes." He was bending down, pulling on his socks, and his back was so large and friendly I wanted to rest my head on it.

"If you ever tell anybody what we did, I'll have to kill Bailey."

What had we done? We? Obviously he didn't mean my peeing in the bed. I didn't understand and didn't dare ask him. It had something to do with his holding me. But there was no chance to ask Bailey either, because that would be telling what we had done. The thought that he might kill Bailey stunned me. After he left the room I thought about telling Mother that I hadn't peed in the bed, but then if she asked me what happened I'd have to tell her about Mr. Freeman holding me, and that wouldn't do.

It was the same old quandary. I had always lived it. There was an army of adults, whose motives and movements I just couldn't understand and who made no effort to understand mine. There was never any question of my disliking Mr. Freeman, I simply didn't understand him either.

For weeks after, he said nothing to me, except the gruff hellos which were given without ever looking in my direction.

This was the first secret I had ever kept from Bailey and sometimes I thought he should be able to read it on my fane, but he noticed nothing.

I began to feel lonely for Mr. Freeman and the encasement in his big arms. Before, my world had been Bailey, food, Momma, the Store, reading books and Uncle Willie. Now, for the first time, it included physical contact.

I began to wait for Mr. Freeman to come in from the yards, but when he did, he never noticed me, although I put a lot of feeling into "Good evening, Mr. Freeman."

One evening, when I couldn't concentrate on anything, I went over to him and sat quickly on his lap. He had been waiting for Mother again. Bailey was listening to *The Shadow* and didn't miss me. At first Mr. Freeman sat still, not holding me or anything, then I felt a soft lump under my thigh begin to move. It twitched against me and started to harden. Then he pulled me to his chest. He smelled of coal dust and grease and he was so close I buried my face in his shirt and listened to his heart, it was beating just for me. Only I could hear the thud, only I could feel the jumping on my face. He said, "Sit still, stop squirming." But all the time, he pushed me around on his lap, then suddenly he stood up and I slipped down to the floor. He ran to the bathroom.

For months he stopped speaking to me again. I was hurt and for a time felt lonelier than ever. But then I forgot about him, and even the memory of his holding me precious melted into the general darkness just beyond the great blinkers of childhood.

I read more than ever, and wished my soul that I had been born a boy. Horatio Alger was the greatest writer in the world. His heroes were always good, always won, and were always boys. I could have developed the first two virtues, but becoming a boy was sure to be difficult, if not impossible.

The Sunday funnies influenced me, and although I admired the strong heroes who always conquered in the end, I identified with Tiny Tim. In the toilet, where I used to take the papers, it was tortuous to look for and exclude the unnecessary pages so that I could learn how he would finally outwit his latest adversary. I wept with relief every Sunday as he eluded the evil men and bounded back from each seeming defeat as sweet and gentle as ever. The Katzenjammer kids were fun because they made the adults look stupid. But they were a little too smart-alecky for my taste.

When spring came to St. Louis, I took out my first library card, and since Bailey and I seemed to be growing apart, I spent most of my Saturdays at the library (no interruptions) breathing in the world of penniless shoeshine boys who, with goodness and perseverance, became rich, rich men, and gave baskets of goodies to the poor on holidays. The little princesses who were mistaken for maids, and the long-lost children mistaken for waifs, became more real to me than our house, our mother, our school or Mr. Freeman.

During those months we saw our grandparents and the uncles (our only aunt had gone to California to build her fortune), but they usually asked the same question, "Have you been good children?" for which there was only one answer. Even Bailey wouldn't have dared to answer No.

12

On a late spring Saturday, after our chores (nothing like those in Stamps) were done, Bailey and I were going out, he to play baseball and I to the library. Mr. Freeman said to me, after Bailey had gone downstairs, "Ritie, go get some milk for the house."

Mother usually brought milk when she came in, but that morning as Bailey and I straightened the living room her bedroom door had been open, and we knew that she hadn't come home the night before.

He gave me money and I rushed to the store and back to the house. After putting the milk in the icebox, I turned and had just reached the front door when I heard, "Ritie." He was sitting in the big chair by the radio. "Ritie, come here." I didn't think about the holding time until I got close to him. His pants were open and his "thing" was standing out of his britches by itself.

"No, sir, Mt. Freeman." I started to back away. I didn't want to touch that mushy-hard thing again, and I didn't need him to hold me any more. He grabbed my arm and pulled me between his legs. His face was still and looked kind, but he didn't smile or blink his eyes. Nothing. He did nothing, except reach his left hand around to turn on the radio without even looking at it. Over the noise of music and static, he said, "Now, this ain't gonna hurt you much. You liked it before, didn't you?"

I didn't want to admit that I had in fact liked his holding me or that I had liked his smell or the hard heart-beating, so I said nothing. And his face became like the face of one of those mean natives the Phantom was always having to beat up.

His legs were squeezing my waist. "Pull down your drawers." I hesitated for two reasons: he was holding me too tight to move, and I was sure that any minute my mother or Bailey or the Green Hornet would bust in the door and save me.

"We was just playing before." He released me enough to snatch down my bloomers, and then he dragged me closer to him. Turning the radio up loud, too loud, he said, "If you scream, I'm gonna kill you. And if you tell, I'm gonna kill Bailey." I could tell he meant what he said. I couldn't understand why he wanted to kill my brother.

Neither of us had done anything to him. And then.

Then there was the pain. A breaking and entering when even the senses are torn apart. The act of rape on an eight-year-old body is a matter of the needle giving because the camel can't. The child gives, because the body can, and the mind of the violator cannot.

I thought I had died—I woke up in a white-walled world, and it had to be heaven. But Mr. Freeman was there and he was washing me. His hands shook, but he held me upright in the tub and washed my legs. "I didn't mean to hurt you, Ritie. I didn't mean it. But don't you tell... Remember, don't you tell a soul."

I felt cool and very clean and just a little tired. "No, sir, Mr. Freeman, I won't tell." I was somewhere above everything. "It's just that I'm so tired I'll just go and lay down a while, please," I whispered to him. I thought if I spoke out loud, he might become frightened and hurt me again. He dried me and handed me my bloomers. "Put these on and go to the library. Your momma ought to be coming home soon. You just act natural."

Walking down the street, I felt the wet on my pants, and my hips seemed to be coming out of their sockets. I couldn't sit long on the hard seats in the library (they had been constructed for children), so I walked by the empty lot where Bailey was playing ball, but he wasn't there. I stood for a while and watched the big boys tear around the dusty diamond and then headed home.

After two blocks, I knew I'd never make it. Not unless I counted every step and stepped on every crack. I had started to burn between my legs more than the time I'd wasted Sloan's Liniment on myself. My legs throbbed, or rather the insides of my thighs throbbed, with the same force that Mr. Freeman's heart had beaten. Thrum... step... thrum... step... STEP ON THE CRACK... thrum... step. I went up the stairs one at a, one at a, one at a time. No one was in the living room, so I went straight to bed, after hiding my red-and-yellow-stained drawers under the mattress.

When Mother came in she said, "Well, young lady, I believe this is the first time I've seen you go to bed without being told. You must be sick."

I wasn't sick, but the pit of my stomach was on fire— how could I tell her that? Bailey came in later and asked me what the matter was. There was nothing to tell him. When Mother called us to eat and I said I wasn't hungry, she laid her cool hand on my forehead and cheeks. "Maybe it's the measles. They say they're going around the neighborhood." After she took my temperature she said, "You have a little fever. You've probably just caught them."

Mr. Freeman took up the whole doorway, "Then Bailey ought not to be in there with her. Unless you want a house full of sick children."

She answered over her shoulder, "He may as well have them now as later. Get them over with." She brushed by Mr. Freeman as if he were made of cotton. "Come on, Junior. Get some cool towels and wipe your sister's face."

As Bailey left the room, Mr. Freeman advanced to the bed. He leaned over, his whole face a threat that could have smothered me. "If you tell..." And again so softly, I almost didn't hear it—"If you tell." I couldn't summon up the energy to answer him. He had to know that I wasn't going to tell anything. Bailey came in with the towels and Mr. Freeman walked out.

Later Mother made a broth and sat on the edge of the bed to feed me. The liquid went down my throat like bones. My belly and behind were as heavy as cold iron, but it seemed my head had gone away and pure air had replaced it on my shoulders. Bailey read to me from *The Rover Boys* until he got sleepy and went to bed.

That night I kept waking to hear Mother and Mr. Freeman arguing. I couldn't hear what they were saying, but I did hope that she wouldn't make him so mad that he'd hurt her too. I knew he could do it, with his cold face and empty eyes. Their voices came in faster and faster, the high sounds on the heels of the lows. I would have liked to have gone in. Just passed through as if I were going to the toilet. Just show my face and they might stop, but my legs refused to move. I could move the toes and ankles, but the knees had turned to wood.

Maybe I slept, but soon morning was there and Mother was pretty over my bed. "How're you feeling, baby?"

"Fine, Mother." An instinctive answer. "Where's Bailey?"

She said he was still asleep but that she hadn't slept all night. She had been in my room off and on to see about me. I asked her where Mr. Freeman was, and her face chilled with remembered anger. "He's gone. Moved this morning. I'm going to take your temperature after I put on your Cream of Wheat."

Could I tell her now? The terrible pain assured me that I couldn't. What he did to me, and what I allowed, must have been very bad if already God let me hurt so much. If Mr. Freeman was gone, did that mean Bailey was out of danger? And if so, if I told him, would he still love me?

After Mother took my temperature, she said she was going to bed for a while but to wake her if I felt sicker. She told Bailey to watch my face and arms for spots and when they came up he could paint them with calamine lotion.

That Sunday goes and comes in my memory like a bad connection on an overseas telephone call. Once, Bailey was reading *The Katzenjammer Kids* to me, and then without a pause for sleeping, Mother was looking closely at my face, and soup trickled down my chin and some got into my mouth and I choked. Then there was a doctor who took my temperature and held my wrist.

"Bailey!" I supposed I had screamed, for he materialized suddenly, and I asked him to help me and we'd run away to California or France or Chicago. I knew that I was dying and, in fact, I longed for death, but I didn't want to die anywhere near Mr. Freeman. I knew that even now he wouldn't have allowed death to have me unless he wished it to.

Mother said I should be bathed and the linens had to be changed since I had sweat so much. But when they tried to move me I fought, and even Bailey couldn't hold me. Then she picked me up in her arms and the terror abated for a while. Bailey began to change the bed. As he pulled off the soiled sheets he dislodged the panties I had put under the mattress. They fell at Mother's feet.

13

In the hospital, Bailey told me that I had to tell who did that to me, or the man would hurt another little girl. When I explained that I couldn't tell because the man would kill him, Bailey said knowingly, "He can't kill me. I won't let him." And of course I believed him. Bailey didn't lie to me. So I told him.

Bailey cried at the side of my bed until I started to cry too. Almost fifteen years passed before I saw my brother cry again.

Using the old brain he was born with (those were his words later on that day) he gave his information to Grandmother Baxter, and Mr. Freeman was arrested and was spared the awful wrath of my pistol-whipping uncles.

I would have liked to stay in the hospital the rest of my life. Mother brought flowers and candy. Grandmother came with fruit and my uncles clumped around and around my bed, snorting like wild horses. When they were able to sneak Bailey in, he read to me for hours.

The saying that people who have nothing to do become busybodies is not the only truth. Excitement is a drug, and people whose lives are filled with violence are always wondering where the next "fix" is coming from.

The court was filled. Some people even stood behind the churchlike benches in the rear. Overhead fans moved with the detachment of old men. Grandmother Baxter's clients were there in gay and flippant array. The gamblers in pin-striped suits and their makeup-deep women whispered to me out of blood-red mouths that now I knew as much as they did. I was eight, and grown. Even the nurses in the hospital had told me that now I had nothing to fear. "The worst is over for you," they had said. So I put the words in all the smirking mouths.

I sat with my family (Bailey couldn't come) and they rested still on the seats like solid, cold gray tombstones. Thick and forevermore unmoving.

Poor Mr. Freeman twisted in his chair to look empty threats over to me. He didn't know that he couldn't kill Bailey... and Bailey didn't lie... to me.

"What was the defendant wearing?" That was Mr. Freeman's lawyer.

"I don't know."

"You mean to say this man raped you and you don't know what he was wearing? "He snickered as if I had raped Mr. Freeman." Do you know if you were raped?"

A sound pushed in the air of the court (I was sure it was laughter). I was glad that Mother had let me wear the navy-blue winter coat with brass buttons. Although it was too short and the weather was typical St. Louis hot, the coat was a friend that I hugged to me in the strange and unfriendly place.

"Was that the first time the accused touched you?" The question stopped me. Mr. Freeman had surely done something very wrong, but I was convinced that I had helped him to do it. I didn't want to lie, but the lawyer wouldn't let me think, so I used silence as a retreat.

"Did the accused try to touch you before the time he or rather you say he raped you?"

I couldn't say yes and tell them how he had loved me once for a few minutes and how he had held me close before he thought I had peed in the bed. My uncles would kill me and Grandmother Baxter would stop speaking, as she often did when she was angry. And all those people in the court would stone me as they had stoned the harlot in the Bible. And Mother, who thought I was such a good girl, would be so disappointed. But most important, there was Bailey. I had kept a big secret from him.

"Marguerite, answer the question. Did the accused touch you before the occasion on which you claim he raped you?"

Everyone in the court knew that the answer had to be No.

Everyone except Mr. Freeman and me. I looked at his heavy face trying to look as if he would have liked me to say No. I said No.

The lie lumped in my throat and I couldn't get air. How I despised the man for making me lie. Old, mean, nasty thing. Old, black, nasty thing. The tears didn't soothe my heart as they usually did. I screamed, "Ole, mean, dirty thing, you. Dirty old thing." Our lawyer brought me off the stand and to my mother's arms. The fact that I had arrived at my desired destination by lies made it less appealing to me.

Mr. Freeman was given one year and one day, but he never got a chance to do his time. His lawyer (or someone) got him released that very afternoon.

In the living room, where the shades were drawn for coolness, Bailey and I played Monopoly on the floor. I played a bad game because I was thinking how I would be able to tell Bailey how I had lied and, even worse for our relationship, kept a secret from him. Bailey answered the doorbell, because Grandmother was in the kitchen. A tall white policeman asked for Mrs. Baxter. Had they found out about the lie? Maybe the policeman was coming to put me in jail because I had sworn on the Bible that everything I said would be the truth, the whole truth, so help me, God. The man in our living room was taller than the sky and whiter than my image of God. He just didn't have the beard.

"Mrs. Baxter, I thought you ought to know. Freeman's been found dead on the lot behind the slaughterhouse."

Softly, as if she were discussing a church program, she said, "Poor man." She wiped her hands on the dishtowel and just as softly asked, "Do they know who did it?"

The policeman said, "Seems like he was dropped there. Some say he was kicked to death."

Grandmother's color only rose a little. "Tom, thanks for telling me. Poor man. Well, maybe it's better this way. He was a mad dog. Would you like a glass of lemonade? Or some beer?"

Although he looked harmless, I knew he was a dreadful angel counting out my many sins.

"No, thanks, Mrs. Baxter. I'm on duty. Gotta be getting back."

"Well, tell your ma that I'll be over when I take up my beer and remind her to save some kraut for me."

And the recording angel was gone. He was gone, and a man was dead because I lied. Where was the balance in that? One lie surely wouldn't be worth a man's life. Bailey could have explained it all to me, but I didn't dare ask him. Obviously I had forfeited my place in heaven forever, and I was as gutless as the doll I had ripped to pieces ages ago. Even Christ Himself turned His back on Satan. Wouldn't he turn his back on me? I could feel the evilness flowing through my body and waiting, pent up, to rush off my tongue if I tried to open my mouth.I clamped my teeth shut, I'd hold it in. If it escaped, wouldn't it flood the world and all the innocent people?

Grandmother Baxter said, "Ritie and Junior, you didn't hear a thing. I never want to hear this situation nor that evil man's name mentioned in my house again. I mean that." She went back into the kitchen to make apple strudel for my celebration.

Even Bailey was frightened. He sat all to himself, looking at a man's death—a kitten looking at a wolf. Not quite understanding it but frightened all the same.

In those moments I decided that although Bailey loved me he couldn't help. I had sold myself to the Devil and there could be no escape. The only thing I could do was to stop talking to people other than Bailey. Instinctively, or somehow, I knew that because I loved him so much I'd never hurt him, but if I talked to anyone else that person might die too. Just my breath, carrying my words out, might poison people and they'd curl up and die like the black fat slugs that only pretended.

I had to stop talking.

I discovered that to achieve perfect personal silence all I had to do was to attach myself leechlike to sound. I began to listen to everything. I probably hoped that after I had heard all the sounds, really heard them and packed them down, deep in my ears, the world would be quiet around me. I walked into rooms where people were laughing, their voices hitting the walls like stones, and I simply stood still—in the midst of the riot of sound. After a minute or two, silence would rush into the room from its hiding place because I had eaten up all the sounds.

In the first weeks my family accepted my behavior as a post-rape, post-hospital affliction. (Neither the term nor the experience was mentioned in Grandmother's house, where Bailey and I were again staying.) They understood that I could talk to Bailey, but to no one else.

Then came the last visit from the visiting nurse, and the doctor said I was healed. That meant that I should be back on the sidewalks playing handball or enjoying the games I had been given when I was sick. When I refused to be the child they knew and accepted me to be, I was called impudent and my muteness sullenness.

For a while I was punished for being so uppity that I wouldn't speak; and then came the thrashings, given by any relative who felt himself offended.

We were on the train going back to Stamps, and this time it was I who had to console Bailey. He cried his heart out down the aisles of the coach, and pressed his little-boy body against the window pane looking for a last glimpse of his Mother Dear.

I have never known if Momma sent for us, or if the St. Louis family just got fed up with my grim presence. There is nothing more appalling than a constantly morose child.

I cared less about the trip than about the fact that Bailey was unhappy, and had no more thought of our destination than if I had simply been heading for the toilet.

14

The barrenness of Stamps was exactly what I wanted, without will or consciousness. After St. Louis, with its noise and activity, its trucks and buses, and loud family gatherings, I welcomed the obscure lanes and lonely bungalows set back deep in dirt yards.

The resignation of its inhabitants encouraged me to relax. They showed me a contentment based on the belief that nothing more was coming to them, although a great deal more was due. Their decision to be satisfied with life's inequities was a lesson for me. Entering Stamps, I had the feeling that I was stepping over the border lines of the map and would fall, without fear, right off the end of the world. Nothing more could happen, for in Stamps nothing happened.

Into this cocoon I crept.

For an indeterminate time, nothing was demanded of me or of Bailey. We were, after all, Mrs. Henderson's California grandchildren, and had been away on a glamorous trip way up North to the fabulous St. Louis. Our father had come the year before, driving a big, shiny automobile and speaking the King's English with a big city accent, so all we had to do was lie quiet for months and rake in the profits of our adventures.

Farmers and maids, cooks and handymen, carpenters and all the children in town, made regular pilgrimages to the Store. "Just to see the travelers."

They stood around like cutout cardboard figures and asked, "Well, how is it up North?"

"See any of them big buildings?"

"Ever ride in one of them elevators?"

"Was you scared?"

"Whitefolks any different, like they say?"

Bailey took it upon himself to answer every question, and from a corner of his lively imagination wove a tapestry of entertainment for them that I was sure was as foreign to him as it was to me.

He, as usual, spoke precisely. "They have, in the North, buildings so high that for months, in the winter, you can't see the top floors."

"Tell the truth."

"They've got watermelons twice the size of a cow's head and sweeter than syrup." I distinctly remember his intent face and the fascinated faces of his listeners. "And if you can count the watermelon's seeds, before it's cut open, you can win five zillion dollars and a new car."

Momma, knowing Bailey, warned, "Now Ju, be careful you don't slip up on a not true." (Nice people didn't say "lie.")

"Everybody wears new clothes and have inside toilets. If you fall down in one of them, you get flushed away into the Mississippi River. Some people have iceboxes, only the proper name is Cold Spot or Frigidaire. The snow is so deep you can get buried right outside your door and people won't find you for a year. We made ice cream out of the snow." That was the only fact that I could have supported. During the winter, we had collected a bowl of snow and poured Pet milk over it, and sprinkled it with sugar and called it ice cream.

Momma beamed and Uncle Willie was proud when Bailey regaled the customers with our exploits. We were drawing cards for the Store and objects of the town's adoration. Our journey to magical places alone was a spot of color on the town's drab canvas, and our return made us even more the most enviable of people.

High spots in Stamps were usually negative: droughts, floods, lynchings and deaths.

Bailey played on the country folks' need for diversion. Just after our return he had taken to sarcasm, picked it up as one might pick up a stone, and put it snufflike under his lip. The double entendres, the two-pronged sentences, slid over his tongue to dart rapier-like into anything that happened to be in the way. Our customers, though, generally were so straight thinking and speaking that they were never hurt by his attacks. They didn't comprehend them.

"Bailey Junior sound just like Big Bailey. Got a silver tongue. Just like his daddy."

"I hear tell they don't pick cotton up there. How the people live then?"

Bailey said that the cotton up North was so tall, if ordinary people tried to pick it they'd have to get up on ladders, so the cotton farmers had their cotton picked by machines.

For a while I was the only recipient of Bailey's kindness. It was not that he pitied me but that he felt we were in the same boat for different reasons, and that I could understand his frustration just as he could countenance my withdrawal.

I never knew if Uncle Willie had been told about the incident in St. Louis, but sometimes I caught him watching me with a far-off look in his big eyes. Then he would quickly send me on some errand that would take me out of his presence. When that happened I was both relieved and ashamed. I certainly didn't want a cripple's sympathy (that would have been a case of the blind leading the blind), nor did I want Uncle Willie, whom I loved in my fashion, to think of me as being sinful and dirty. If he thought so, at least I didn't want to know it.

Sounds came to me dully, as if people were speaking through their handkerchiefs or with their hands over their mouths. Colors weren't true either, but rather a vague assortment of shaded pastels that indicated not so much color as faded familiarities. People's names escaped me and I began to worry over my sanity. After all, we had been away less than a year, and customers whose accounts I had formerly remembered without consulting the ledger were now complete strangers.

People, except Momma and Uncle Willie, accepted my unwilling-ness to talk as a natural outgrowth of a reluctant return to the South. And an indication that I was pining for the high times we had had in the big city. Then, too, I was well known for being "tender-hearted." Southern Negroes used that term to mean sensitive and tended to look upon a person with that affliction as being a little sick or in delicate health. So I was not so much forgiven as I was understood.

15

For nearly a year, I sopped around the house, the Store, the school and the church, like an old biscuit, dirty and inedible. Then I met, or rather got to know, the lady who threw me my first life line.

Mrs. Bertha Flowers was the aristocrat of Black Stamps. She had the grace of control to appear warm in the coldest weather, and on the Arkansas summer days it seemed she had a private breeze which swirled around, cooling her. She was thin without the taut look of wiry people, and her printed voile dresses and flowered hats were as right for her as denim overalls for a farmer. She was our side's answer to the richest white woman in town.

Her skin was a rich black that would have peeled like a plum if snagged, but then no one would have thought of getting close enough to Mrs. Flowers to ruffle her dress, let alone snag her skin. She didn't encourage familiarity. She wore gloves too.

I don't think I ever saw Mrs. Flowers laugh, but she smiled often. A slow widening of her thin black lips to show even, small white teeth, then the slow effortless closing. When she chose to smile on me, I always wanted to thank her. The action was so graceful and inclusively benign.

She was one of the few gentlewomen I have ever known, and has remained throughout my life the measure of what a human being can be.

Momma had a strange relationship with her. Most often when she passed on the road in front of the Store, she spoke to Momma in that soft yet carrying voice, "Good day, Mrs. Henderson." Momma responded with "How you, Sister Flowers?"

Mrs. Flowers didn't belong to our church, nor was she Momma's familiar. Why on earth did she insist on calling her Sister Flowers? Shame made me want to hide my face. Mrs. Flowers deserved better than to be called Sister. Then, Momma left out the verb. Why not ask, "How *are* you, *Mrs.* Flowers?" With the unbalanced passion of the young, I hated her for showing her ignorance to Mrs. Flowers. It didn't occur to me for many years that they were as alike as sisters, separated only by formal education.

Although I was upset, neither of the women was in the least shaken by what I thought an unceremonious greeting. Mrs. Flowers would continue her easy gait up the hill to her little bungalow, and Momma kept on shelling peas or doing whatever had brought her to the front porch.

Occasionally, though, Mrs. Flowers would drift off the road and down to the Store and Momma would say to me, "Sister, you go on and play." As I left I would hear the beginning of an intimate conversation. Momma persistently using the wrong verb, or none at all.

"Brother and Sister Wilcox is sho'ly the meanest—" "Is," Momma? "Is"? Oh, please, not "is," Momma, for two or more. But they talked, and from the side of the building where I waited for the ground to open up and swallow me, I heard the soft-voiced Mrs. Flowers and the textured voice of my grandmother merging and melting. They were interrupted from time to time by giggles that must have come from Mrs. Flowers (Momma never giggled in her life). Then she was gone.

She appealed to me because she was like people I had never met

61

personally. Like women in English novels who walked the moors (whatever they were) with their loyal dogs racing at a respectful distance. Like the women who sat in front of roaring fireplaces, drinking tea incessantly from silver trays full of scones and crumpets. Women who walked over the "heath" and read morocco-bound books and had two last names divided by a hyphen. It would be safe to say that she made me proud to be Negro, just by being herself.

She acted just as refined as whitefolks in the movies and books and she was more beautiful, for none of them could have come near that warm color without looking gray by comparison.

It was fortunate that I never saw her in the company of powhitefolks. For since they tend to think of their whiteness as an evenizer, I'm certain that I would have had to hear her spoken to commonly as Bertha, and my image of her would have been shattered like the unmendable Humpty-Dumpty.

One summer afternoon, sweet-milk fresh in my memory, she stopped at the Store to buy provisions. Another Negro woman of her health and age would have been expected to carry the paper sacks home in one hand, but Momma said, "Sister Flowers, I'll send Bailey up to your house with these things."

She smiled that slow dragging smile, "Thank you, Mrs. Henderson. I'd prefer Marguerite, though." My name was beautiful when she said it. "I've been meaning to talk to her, anyway." They gave each other age-group looks.

Momma said, "Well, that's all right then. Sister, go and change your dress. You going to Sister Flowers's."

The chifforobe was a maze. What on earth did one put on to go to Mrs. Flowers' house? I knew I shouldn't put on a Sunday dress. It might be sacrilegious. Certainly not a house dress, since I was already wearing a fresh one. I chose a school dress, naturally. It was formal without suggesting that going to Mrs. Flowers' house was equivalent to attending church.

I trusted myself back into the Store.

"Now, don't you look nice," I had chosen the right thing, for once.

"Mrs. Henderson, you make most of the children's clothes, don't you?"

"Yes, ma'am. Sure do. Store-bought clothes ain't hardly worth the thread it take to stitch them."

"I'll say you do a lovely job, though, so neat. That dress looks professional."

Momma was enjoying the seldom-received compliments. Since everyone we knew (except Mrs. Flowers, of course) could sew competently, praise was rarely handed out for the commonly practiced craft.

62

"I try, with the help of the Lord, Sister Flowers, to finish the inside just like I does the outside. Come here, Sister."

I had buttoned up the collar and tied the belt, apron-like, in back. Momma told me to turn around. With one hand she pulled the strings and the belt fell free at both sides of my waist. Then her large hands were at my neck, opening the button loops. I was terrified. What was happening?

"Take it off, Sister." She had her hands on the hem of the dress.

"I don't need to see the inside, Mrs. Henderson, I can tell..." But the dress was over my head and my arms were stuck in the sleeves. Momma said, "That'll do. See here, Sister Flowers, I French-seams around the armholes." Through the cloth film, I saw the shadow approach. "That makes it last longer. Children these days would bust out of sheet-metal clothes. They so rough."

"That is a very good job, Mrs. Henderson. You should be proud. You can put your dress back on, Marguerite."

"No ma'am. Pride is a sin. And acording to the Good Book, it goeth before a fall."

"That's right. So the Bible says. It's a good thing to keep in mind."

I wouldn't look at either of them. Momma hadn't thought that taking off my dress in front of Mrs. Flowers would kill me stone dead. If I had refused, she would have thought I was trying to be "womanish" and might have remembered St. Louis. Mrs. Flowers had known that I would be embarrassed and that was even worse, I picked up the groceries and went out to wait in the hot sunshine. It would be fitting if I got a sunstroke and died before they came outside. Just dropped dead on the slanting porch.

There was a little path beside the rocky road, and Mrs. Flowers walked in front swinging her arms and picking her way over the stones.

She said, without turning her head, to me, "I hear you're doing very good school work, Marguerite, but that it's all written. The teachers report that they have trouble getting you to talk in class." We passed the triangular farm on our left and the path widened to allow us to walk together. I hung back in the separate unasked and unanswerable questions.

"Come and walk along with me, Marguerite." I couldn't have refused even if I wanted to. She pronounced my name so nicely. Or more correctly, she spoke each word with such clarity that I was certain a foreigner who didn't understand English could have understood her.

"Now no one is going to make you talk—possibly no one can. But bear in mind, language is man's way of communicating with his fellow man and it is language alone which separates him from the lower animals." That was a totally new idea to me, and I would need time to think about it.

"Your grandmother says you read a lot. Every chance you get. That's good, but not good enough. Words mean more than what is set down on paper. It takes the human voice to infuse them with the shades of deeper meaning."

I memorized the part about the human voice infusing words. It seemed so valid and poetic.

She said she was going to give me some books and that I not only must read them, I must read them aloud. She suggested that I try to make a sentence sound in as many different ways as possible.

"I'll accept no excuse if you return a book to me that has been badly handled." My imagination boggled at the punishment I would deserve if in fact I did abuse a book of Mrs. Flowers. Death would be too kind and brief.

The odors in the house surprsied me. Somehow I had never connected Mrs. Flowers with food or eating or any other common experience of common people. There must have been an outhouse, too, but my mind never recorded it.

The sweet scent of vanilla had met us as she opened the door.

"I made tea cookies this morning. You see, I had planned to invite you for cookies and lemonade so we could have this little chat. The lemonade is in the icebox."

It followed that Mrs. Flowers would have ice on an ordinary day, when most families in our town bought ice late on Saturdays only a few times during the summer to be used in the wooden ice-cream freezers.

She took the bags from me and disappeared through the kitchen door. I looked around the room that I had never in my wildest fantasies imagined I would see. Browned photographs leered or threatened from the walls and the white, freshly done curtains pushed against themselves and against the wind. I wanted to gobble up the room entire and take it to Bailey, who would help me analyze and enjoy it.

"Have a seat, Marguerite. Over there by the table." She carried a platter covered with a tea towel. Although she warned that she hadn't tried her hand at baking sweets for some time, I was certain that like everything else about her the cookies would be perfect.

They were flat round wafers, slightly browned on the edges and butter-yellow in the center. With the cold lemonade they were sufficient for childhood's lifelong diet. Remembering my manners, I took nice little lady-like bites off the edges. She said she had made them expressly for me and that she had a few in the kitchen that I could take home to my brother. So I jammed one whole cake in my mouth and the rough crumbs scratched the insides of my jaws, and if I hadn't had to swallow, it would have been a dream come true.

As I ate she began the first of what we later called "my lessons in living." She said that I must always be intolerant of ignorance but understanding of illiteracy. That some people, unable to go to school, were more educated and even more intelligent than college professors. She encouraged me to listen carefully to what country people called mother wit. That in those homely sayings was couched the collective wisdom of generations.

When I finished the cookies she brushed off the table and brought a thick, small book from the bookcase. I had read *A Tale of Two Cities* and found it up to my standards as a romantic novel. She opened the first page and I heard poetry for the first time in my life.

"It was the best of times and the worst of times..." Her voice slid in and curved down through and over the words. She was nearly singing. I wanted to look at the pages. Were they the same that I had read? Or were there notes, music, lined on the pages, as in a hymn book? Her sounds began cascading gently. I knew from listening to a thousand preachers that she was nearing the end of her reading, and I hadn't really heard, heard to understand, a single word.

"How do you like that?"

It occurred to me that she expected a response. The sweet vanilla flavor was still on my tongue and her reading was a wonder in my ears. I had to speak.

I said, "Yes, ma'am." It was the least I could do, but it was the most also.

"There's one more thing. Take this book of poems and memorize one for me. Next time you pay me a visit, I want you to recite."

I have tried often to search behind the sophistication of years for the enchantment I so easily found in those gifts. The essence escapes but its aura remains. To be allowed, no, invited, into the private lives of strangers, and to share their joys and fears, was a chance to exchange the Southern bitter wormwood for a cup of mead with Beowulf or a hot cup of tea and milk with Oliver Twist. When I said aloud, "It is a far, far better thing that I do, than I have ever done..." tears of love filled my eyes at my selflessness.

On that first day, I ran down the hill and into the road (few cars ever came along it) and had the good sense to stop running before I reached the Store.

I was liked, and what a difference it made. I was respected not as Mrs. Henderson's grandchild or Bailey's sister but for just being Marguerite Johnson.

Childhood's logic never asks to be proved (all conclusions are absolute). I didn't question why Mrs. Flowers had singled me out for attention, nor did it occur to me that Momma might have asked her to give me a little talking to. All I cared about was that she had made tea cookies for *me* and read to *me* from her favorite book. It was enough to prove that she liked me.

Momma and Bailey were waiting inside the Store. He said, "My, what did she give you?" He had seen the books, but I held the paper sack with his cookies in my arms shielded by the poems.

Momma said, "Sister, I know you acted like a little lady. That do my heart good to see settled people take to you all. I'm trying my best, the Lord knows, but these days..." Her voice trailed off. "Go on in and change your dress."

In the bedroom it was going to be a joy to see Bailey receive his cookies. I said, "By the way, Bailey, Mrs. Flowers sent you some tea cookies—"

Momma shouted, "What did you say, Sister? You, Sister, what did you say?" Hot anger was crackling in her voice.

Bailey said, "She said Mrs. Flowers sent me some—"

"I ain't talking to you, Ju." I heard the heavy feet walk across the floor toward our bedroom. "Sister, you heard me. What's that you said?" She swelled to fill the doorway.

Bailey said, "Momma." His pacifying voice—"Momma, she—"

"You shut up, Ju. I'm talking to your sister."

I didn't know what sacred cow I had bumped, but it was better to find out than to hang like a thread over an open fire. I repeated, "I said, 'Bailey, by the way, Mrs. Flowers sent you—' "

"That's what I thought you said. Go on and take off your dress. I'm going to get a switch."

At first I thought she was playing. Maybe some heavy joke that would end with "You sure she didn't send me something?" but in a minute she was back in the room with a long, ropy, peach-tree switch, the juice smelling bitter at having been torn loose. She said, "Get down on your knees. Bailey, Junior, you come on, too."

The three of us knelt as she began, "Our Father, you know the tribulations of your humble servant. I have with your help raised two grown boys. Many's the day I thought I wouldn't be able to go on, but you gave me the strength to see my way clear. Now, Lord, look down on this heavy heart today. I'm trying to raise my son's children in the way they should go, but, oh, Lord, the Devil try to hinder me on every hand. I never thought I'd live to hear cursing under this roof, what I try to keep dedicated to the glorification of God. And cursing out of the mouths of babes. But you said, in the last days brother would turn against brother, and children against their parents. That there would be a gnashing of teeth and a rendering of flesh. Father, forgive this child, I beg you, on bended knee."

I was crying loudly now. Momma's voice had risen to a shouting pitch, and I knew that whatever wrong I had committed was extremely serious. She had even left the Store untended to take up my case with God. When she finished we were all crying. She pulled me to her with one hand and hit me only a few times with the switch. The shock of my sin and the emotional release of her prayer had exhausted her.

Momma wouldn't talk right then, but later in the evening I found that my violation lay in using the phrase "by the way." Momma explained that "Jesus was the Way, the Truth and the Light," and anyone who says "by the way" is really saying, "by Jesus," or "by God" and the Lord's name would not be taken in vain in her house.

When Bailey tried to interpret the words with: "Whitefolks use 'by the way' to mean while we're on the subject," Momma reminded us that "whitefolks' mouths were most in general loose and their words were an abomination before Christ."

16

Recently a white woman from Texas, who would quickly describe herself as a liberal, asked me about my hometown. When I told her that in Stamps my grandmother had owned the only Negro general merchandise store since the turn of the century, she exclaimed, "Why, you were a debutante." Ridiculous and even ludicrous. But Negro girls in small Southern towns, whether poverty-stricken or just munching along on a few of life's necessities, were given as extensive and irrelevant preparations for adulthood as rich white girls shown in magazines. Admittedly the training was not the same. While white girls learned to waltz and sit gracefully with a tea cup balanced on their knees, we were lagging behind, learning the mid-Victorian values with very little money to indulge them. (Come and see Edna Lomax spending the money she made picking cotton on five balls of ecru tatting thread. Her fingers are bound to snag the work and she'll have to repeat the stitches time and time again. But she knows that when she buys the thread.)

We were required to embroider and I had trunkfuls of colorful dishtowels, pillowcases, runners and handkerchiefs to my credit. I mastered the art of crocheting and tatting, and there was a lifetime's supply of dainty doilies that would never be used in sacheted dresser drawers. It went without saying that all girls could iron and wash, but the finer touches around the home, like setting a table with real silver, baking roasts and cooking vegetables without meat, had to be learned elsewhere. Usually at the source of those habits. During my tenth year, a white woman's kitchen became my finishing school.

Mrs. Viola Cullinan was a plump woman who lived in a three-bedroom house somewhere behind the post office. She was singularly unattractive until she smiled, and then the lines around her eyes and mouth which made her look perpetually dirty disappeared, and her face looked like the mask of an impish elf. She usually rested her smile until late afternoon when her women friends dropped in and Miss Glory, the cook, served them cold drinks on the closed-in porch.

The exactness of her house was inhuman. This glass went here and only here. That cup had its place and it was an act of impudent rebellion to place it anywhere else. At twelve o'clock the table was set. At 12:15 Mrs. Cullinan sat down to dinner (whether her husband had arrived or not). At 12:16 Miss Glory brought out the food.

It took me a week to learn the difference between a salad plate, a bread plate and a dessert plate.

Mrs. Cullinan kept up the tradition of her wealthy parents. She was from Virginia. Miss Glory, who was a descendant of slaves that had worked for the Cullinans, told me her history. She had married beneath her (according to Miss Glory). Her husband's family hadn't had their money very long and what they had "didn't 'mount to much."

As ugly as she was, I thought privately, she was lucky to get a husband above or beneath her station. But Miss Glory wouldn't let me say a thing against her mistress. She was very patient with me, however, over the housework. She explained the dishware, silverware and servants' bells. The large round bowl in which soup was served wasn't a soup bowl, it was a tureen. There were goblets, sherbet glasses, ice-cream glasses, wine glasses, green glass coffee cups with matching saucers, and water glasses. I had a glass to drink from, and it sat with Miss Glory's on a separate shelf from the others. Soup spoons, gravy boat, butter knives, salad forks and carving platter were additions to my vocabulary and in fact almost represented a new language. I was fascinated with the novelty, with the fluttering Mrs. Cullinan and her Alice-in-Wonderland house.

Her husband remains, in my memory, undefined. I lumped him with all the other white men that I had ever seen and tried not to see.

On our way home one evening, Miss Glory told me that Mrs. Cullinan couldn't have children. She said that she was too delicateboned. It was hard to imagine bones at all under those layers of fat. Miss Glory went on to say that the doctor had taken out all her lady organs. I reasoned that a pig's organs included the lungs, heart and liver, so if Mrs. Cullinan was walking around without those essentials, it explained why she drank alcohol out of unmarked bottles. She was keeping herself embalmed.

When I spoke to Bailey about it, he agreed that I was right, but he also informed me that Mr. Cullinan had two daughters by a colored lady and that I knew them very well. He added that the girls were the spitting image of their father. I was unable to remember what he looked like, although I had just left him a few hours before, but I thought of the Coleman girls. They were very light-skinned and certainly didn't look very much like their mother (no one ever mentioned Mr. Coleman).

My pity for Mrs. Cullinan preceded me the next morning like the Cheshire cat's smile. Those girls, who could have been her daughters, were beautiful. They didn't have to straighten their hair. Even when they were caught in the rain, their braids still hung down straight like tamed snakes. Their mouths were pouty little cupid's bows. Mrs. Cullinan didn't know what she missed. Or maybe she did. Poor Mrs. Cullinan.

For weeks after, I arrived early, left late and tried very hard to make up for her barrenness. If she had had her own children, she wouldn't have had to ask me to run a thousand errands from her back door to the back door of her friends. Poor old Mrs. Cullinan.

Then one evening Miss Glory told me to serve the ladies on the porch. After I set the tray down and turned toward the kitchen, one of the women asked, "What's your name, girl?" It was the speckled-faced one. Mrs. Cullinan said, "She doesn't talk much. Her name's Margaret."

"Is she dumb?"

"No. As I understand it, she can talk when she wants to but she's usually quiet as a little mouse. Aren't you, Margaret?"

I smiled at her. Poor thing. No organs and couldn't even pronounce my name correctly.

"She's a sweet little thing, though."

"Well, that may be, but the name's too long. I'd never bother myself. I'd call her Mary if I was you."

I fumed into the kitchen. That horrible woman would never have the chance to call me Mary because if I was starving I'd never work for her. I decided I wouldn't pee on her if her heart was on fire. Giggles drifted in off the porch and into Miss Glory's pots. I wondered what they could be laughing about.

Whitefolks were so strange. Could they be talking about me?

69

Everybody knew that they stuck together better than the Negroes did. It was possible that Mrs. Cullinan had friends in St. Louis who heard about a girl from Stamps being in court and wrote to tell her. Maybe she knew about Mr. Freeman.

My lunch was in my mouth a second time and I went outside and relieved myself on the bed of four-o'clocks. Miss Glory thought I might be coming down with something and told me to go on home, that Momma would give me some herb tea, and she'd explain to her mistress.

I realized how foolish I was being before I reached the pond. Of course Mrs. Cullinan didn't know. Otherwise she wouldn't have given me the two nice dresses that Momma cut down, and she certainly wouldn't have called me a "sweet little thing." My stomach felt fine, and I didn't mention anything to Momma.

That evening I decided to write a poem on being white, fat, old and without children. It was going to be a tragic ballad. I would have to watch her carefully to capture the essence of her loneliness and pain.

The very next day, she called me by the wrong name. Miss Glory and I were washing up the lunch dishes when Mrs. Cullinan came to the doorway. "Mary?"

Miss Glory asked, "Who?"

Mrs. Cullinan, sagging a little, knew and I knew. "I want Mary to go down to Mrs. Randall's and take her some soup. She's not been feeling well for a few days."

Miss Glory's face was a wonder to see. "You mean Margaret, ma'am. Her name's Margaret."

"That's too long. She's Mary from now on. Heat that soup from last night and put it in the china tureen and, Mary, I want you to carry it carefully."

Every person I knew had a hellish horror of being "called out of his name." It was a dangerous practice to call a Negro anything that could be loosely construed as insulting because of the centuries of their having been called niggers, jigs, dinges, blackbirds, crows, boots and spooks.

Miss Glory had a fleeting second of feeling sorry for me. Then as she handed me the hot tureen she said, "Don't mind, don't pay that no mind. Sticks and stones may break your bones, but words... You know, I been working for her for twenty years."

She held the back door open for me. "Twenty years. I wasn't much older than you. My name used to be Hallelujah. That's what Ma named me, but my mistress give me 'Glory,' and it stuck. I likes it better too."

I was in the little path that ran behind the houses when Miss Glory shouted, "It's shorter too."

For a few seconds it was a tossup over whether I would laugh (imagine being named Hallelujah) or cry (imagine letting some white woman rename you for her convenience). My anger saved me from either outburst. I had to quit the job, but the problem was going to be how to do it. Momma wouldn't allow me to quit for just any reason.

"She's a peach. That woman is a real peach." Mrs. Randall's maid was talking as she took the soup from me, and I wondered what her name used to be and what she answered to now.

For a week I looked into Mrs. Cullinan's face as she called me Mary. She ignored my coming late and leaving early. Miss Glory was a little annoyed because I had begun to leave egg yolk on the dishes and wasn't putting much heart in polishing the silver, I hoped that she would complain to our boss, but she didn't.

Then Bailey solved my dilemma. He had me describe the contents of the cupboard and the particular plates she liked best. Her favorite piece was a casserole shaped like a fish and the green glass coffee cups. I kept his instructions in mind, so on the next day when Miss Glory was hanging out clothes and I had again been told to serve the old biddies on the porch, I dropped the empty serving tray. When I heard Mrs. Cullinan scream, "Mary!" I picked up the casserole and two of the green glass cups in readiness. As she rounded the kitchen door I let them fall on the tiled floor.

I could never absolutely describe to Bailey what happened next, because each time I got to the part where she fell on the floor and screwed up her ugly face to cry, we burst out laughing. She actually wobbled around on the floor and picked up shards of the cups and cried, "Oh, Momma. Oh, dear Gawd. It's Momma's china from Virginia. Oh, Momma, I sorry."

Miss Glory came running in from the yard and the women from the porch crowded around. Miss Glory was almost as broken up as her mistress. "You mean to say she broke our Virginia dishes? What we gone do?"

Mrs. Cullinan cried louder, "That clumsy nigger. Clumsy little black nigger."

Old speckled-face leaned down and asked, "Who did it, Viola? Was it Mary? Who did it?"

Everything was happening so fast I can't remember whether her action preceded her words, but I know that Mrs. Cullinan said, "Her name's Margaret, goddamn it, her name's Margaret." And she threw a wedge of the broken plate at me. It could have been the hysteria which put her aim off, but the flying crockery caught Miss Glory right over her ear and she started screaming.

I left the front door wide open so all the neighbors could hear. Mrs. Cullinan was right about one thing. My name wasn't Mary.

17

Weekdays revolved on a sameness wheel. They turned into themselves so steadily and inevitably that each seemed to be the original of yesterday's rough draft. Saturdays, however, always broke the mold and dared to be different.

Farmers trekked into town with their children and wives streaming around them. Their board-stiff khaki pants and shirts revealed the painstaking care of a dutiful daughter or wife. They often stopped at the Store to get change for bills so they could give out jangling coins to their children, who shook with their eagerness to get to town. The young kids openly resented their parents' dawdling in the Store and Uncle Willie would call them in and spread among them bits of sweet peanut patties that had been broken in shipping. They gobbled down the candies and were out again, kicking up the powdery dust in the road and worrying if there was going to be time to get to town after all.

Bailey played mumbledypeg with the older boys around the chinaberry tree, and Momma and Uncle Willie listened to the farmers' latest news of the country. I thought of myself as hanging in the Store, a mote imprisoned on a shaft of sunlight. Pushed and pulled by the slightest shift of air, but never falling free into the tempting darkness.

In the warm months, morning began with a quick wash in unheated well water. The suds were dashed on a plot of ground beside the kitchen door. It was called the bait garden (Bailey raised worms). After prayers, breakfast in summer was usually dry cereal and fresh milk. Then to our chores (which on Saturday included weekday jobs)—scrubbing the floors, raking the yards, polishing our shoes for Sunday (Uncle Willie's had to be shined with a biscuit) and attending to the customers who came breathlessly, also in their Saturday hurry.

Looking through the years, I marvel that Saturday was my favorite day in the week. What pleasures could have been squeezed between the fan folds of unending tasks? Children's talent to endure stems from their ignorance of alternatives.

After our retreat from St. Louis, Momma gave us a weekly

allowance. Since she seldom dealt with money, other than to take it in and to tithe to the church, I supposed that the weekly ten cents was to tell us that even she realized that a change had come over us, and that our new unfamiliarity caused her to treat us with a strangeness.

I usually gave my money to Bailey, who went to the movies nearly every Saturday. He brought back Street and Smith cowboy books for me.

One Saturday Bailey was late coming back from the Rye-al-toh. Momma had begun heating water for the Saturday-night baths, and all the evening chores were done. Uncle Willie sat in the twilight on the front porch mumbling or maybe singing, and smoking a ready-made. It was quite late. Mothers had called in their children from the group games, and fading sounds of "Yah... Yah... you didn't catch me" still hung and floated into the Store.

Uncle Willie said, "Sister, better light the light." On Saturdays we used the electric lights so that last-minute Sunday shoppers could look down the hill and see if the Store was open. Momma hadn't told me to turn then on because she didn't want to believe that night had fallen hard and Bailey was still out in the ungodly dark.

Her apprehension was evident in the hurried movements around the kitchen and in her lonely fearing eyes. The Black woman in the South who raises sons, grandsons and nephews had her heartstrings tied to a hanging noose. Any break from routine may herald for them unbearable news. For this reason, Southern Blacks until the present generation could be counted among America's arch conservatives.

Like most self-pitying people, I had very little pity for my relatives' anxiety. If something indeed had happened to Bailey, Uncle Willie would always have Momma, and Momma had the Store. Then, after all, we weren't their children. But I would be the major loser if Bailey turned up dead. For he was all I claimed, if not all I had.

The bath water was steaming on the cooking stove, but Momma was scrubbing the kitchen table for the umpteenth time.

"Momma," Uncle Willie called and she jumped. "Momma." I waited in the bright lights of the Store, jealous that someone had come along and told these strangers something about my brother and I would be the last to know.

"Momma, why don't you and Sister walk down to meet him?"

To my knowledge Bailey's name hadn't been mentioned for hours, but we all knew whom he meant.

Of course. Why didn't that occur to me? I wanted to be gone. Momma said, "Wait a minute, little lady. Go get your sweater, and bring me my shawl."

It was darker in the road than I'd thought it would be. Momma

73

swung the flashlight's arc over the path and weeds and scary tree trunks. The night suddenly became enemy territory, and I knew that if my brother was lost in this land he was forever lost. He was eleven and very smart, that I granted, but after all he was so small. The Bluebeards and tigers and Rippers could eat him up before he could scream for help.

Momma told me to take the light and she reached for my hand. Her voice came from a high hill above me and in the dark my hand was enclosed in hers. I loved her with a rush. She said nothing—no "Don't worry" or "Don't get tender-hearted." Just the gentle pressure of her rough hand conveyed her own concern and assurance to me.

We passed houses which I knew well by daylight but couldn't recollect in the swarthy gloom.

"Evening, Miz Jenkins." Walking and pulling me along. "Sister Henderson? Anything wrong?" That was from an outline blacker than the night.

"No, ma'am. Not a thing. Bless the Lord." By the time she finished speaking we had left the worried neighbors far behind.

Mr. Willie Williams' Do Drop Inn was bright with furry red lights in the distance and the pond's fishy smell enveloped us. Momma's hand tightened and let go, and I saw the small figure plodding along, tired and old-mannish. Hands in his pockets and head bent, he walked like a man trudging up the hill behind a coffin.

"Bailey." It jumped out as Momma said, "Ju," and I started to run, but her hand caught mine again and became a vise. I pulled, but she yanked me back to her side. "We'll walk, just like we been walking, young lady." There was no chance to warn Bailey that he was dangerously late, that everybody had been worried and that he should create a good lie or, better, a great one.

Momma said, "Bailey, Junior," and he looked up without surprise. "You know it's night and you just now getting home?"

"Yes, ma'am." He was empty. Where was his alibi? "What you been doing?"

"Nothing."

"That's all you got to say?"

"Yes, ma'am."

"All right, young man. We'll see when you get home."

She had turned me loose, so I made a grab for Bailey's hand, but he snatched it away. I said, "Hey, Bail," hoping to remind him that I was his sister and his only friend, but he grumbled something like "Leave me alone."

Momma didn't turn on the flashlight on the way back, nor did she answer the questioning Good evenings that floated around us as we passed the darkened houses.

I was confused and frightened. He was going to get a whipping and maybe he had done something terrible. If he couldn't talk to me it must have been serious. But there was no air of spent revelry about him. He just seemed sad. I didn't know what to think.

Uncle Willie said, "Getting too big for your britches, huh? You can't come home. You want to worry your grandmother to death?" Bailey was so far away he was beyond fear. Uncle Willie had a leather belt in his good hand but Bailey didn't notice or didn't care. "I'm going to whip you this time." Our uncle had only whipped us once before and then only with a peach-tree switch, so maybe now he was going to kill my brother. I screamed and grabbed for the belt, but Momma caught me. "Now, don't get uppity, miss, 'less you want some of the same thing. He got a lesson coming to him. You come on and get your bath."

From the kitchen I heard the belt fall down, dry and raspy on naked skin. Uncle Willie was gasping for breath, but Bailey made no sound. I was too afraid to splash water or even to cry and take a chance of drowning out Bailey's pleas for help, but the pleas never came and the whipping was finally over.

I lay awake an eternity, waiting for a sign, a whimper or a whisper, from the next room that he was still alive. Just before I fell exhausted into sleep, I heard Bailey: "Now I lay me down to sleep, I pray the Lord my soul to keep, if I should die before I wake, I pray the Lord my soul to take."

My last memory of that night was the question, Why is he saying the baby prayer? We had been saying the "Our Father, which art in heaven" for years.

For days the Store was a strange country, and we were all newly arrived immigrants. Bailey didn't talk, smile or apologize. His eyes were so vacant, it seemed his soul had flown away, and at meals I tried to give him the best pieces of meat and the largest portion of dessert, but he turned them down.

Then one evening at the pig pen he said without warning, "I saw Mother Dear."

If he said it, it was bound to be the truth. He wouldn't lie to me. I don't think I asked him where or when.

"In the movies." He laid his head on the wooden railing. "It wasn't really her. It was a woman named Kay Francis. She's a white movie star who looks just like Mother Dear."

There was no difficulty believing that a white movie star looked like our mother and that Bailey had seen her. He told me that the movies were changed each week, but when another picture came to Stamps starring Kay Francis he would tell me and we'd go together. He even promised to sit with me.

He had stayed late on the previous Saturday to see the film over again. I understood, and understood too why he couldn't tell Momma or Uncle Willie. She was our mother and belonged to us. She was never mentioned to anyone because we simply didn't have enough of her to share.

We had to wait nearly two months before Kay Francis returned to Stamps. Bailey's mood had lightened considerably, but he lived in a state of expectation and it made him more nervous than he was usually. When he told me that the movie would be shown, we went into our best behavior and were the exemplary children that Grandmother deserved and wished to think us.

It was a gay light comedy, and Kay Francis wore long-sleeved white silk shirts with big cuff links. Her bedroom was all satin and flowers in vases, and her maid, who was Black, went around saying "Lawsy, missy" all the time. There was a Negro chauffeur too, who rolled his eyes and scratched his head, and I wondered how on earth an idiot like that could be trusted with her beautiful cars.

The whitefolks downstairs laughed every few minutes, throwing the discarded snicker up to the Negroes in the buzzards' roost. The sound would jag around in our air for an indecisive second before the balcony's occupants accepted it and sent their own guffaws to riot with it against the walls of the theater.

I laughed, too, but not at the hateful jokes made on my people. I laughed because, except that she was white, the big movie star looked just like my mother. Except that she lived in a big mansion with a thousand servants, she lived just like my mother. And it was funny to think of the whitefolks' not knowing that the woman they were adoring could be my mother's twin, except that she was white and my mother was prettier. Much prettier.

The movie star made me happy. It was extraordinary good fortune to be able to save up one's money and go see one's mother whenever one wanted to. I bounced out of the theater as if I'd been given an unexpected present. But Bailey was cast down again, (I had to beg him not to stay for the next show). On the way home he stopped at the railroad track and waited for the night freight train. Just before it reached the crossing, he tore out and ran across the tracks.

I was left on the other side in hysteria. Maybe the giant wheels were grinding his bones into a bloody mush. Maybe he tried to catch a boxcar and got flung into the pond and drowned. Or even worse, maybe he caught the train and was forever gone.

When the train passed he pushed himself away from the pole where he had been leaning, berated me for making all that noise and said, "Let's go home."

One year later he did catch a freight, but because of his youth and the inscrutable ways of fate, he didn't find California and his Mother Dear—he got stranded in Baton Rouge, Louisiana, for two weeks.

18

Another day was over. In the soft dark the cotton truck spilled the pickers out and roared out of the yard with a sound like a giant's fart. The workers stepped around in circles for a few seconds as if they had found themselves unexpectedly in an unfamiliar place. Their minds sagged.

In the Store the men's faces were the most painful to watch, but I seemed to have no choice. When they tried to smile to carry off their tiredness as if it was nothing, the body did nothing to help the mind's attempt at disguise. Their shoulders drooped even as they laughed, and when they put their hands on their hips in a show of jauntiness, the palms slipped the thighs as if the pants were waxed.

"Evening, Sister Henderson. Well, back where we started, huh?"

"Yes, sir, Brother Stewart. Back where you started, bless the Lord." Momma could not take the smallest achievement for granted. People whose history and future were threatened each day by extinction considered that it was only by divine intervention that they were able to live at all. I find it interesting that the meanest life, the poorest existence, is attributed to God's will, but as human beings become more affluent, as their living standard and style begin to ascend the material scale, God descends the scale of responsibility at a commensurate speed.

"That's just who get the credit. Yes, ma'am. The blessed Lord." Their overalls and shirts seemed to be torn on purpose and the cotton lint and dust in their hair gave them the appearance of people who had turned gray in the past few hours.

The women's feet had swollen to fill the discarded men's shoes they wore, and they washed their arms at the well to dislodge dirt and splinters that had accrued to them as part of the day's pickings.

I thought them all hateful to have allowed themselves to be worked like oxen, and even more shameful to try to pretend that things were not as bad as they were. When they leaned too hard on the partly glass candy counter, I wanted to tell them shortly to stand up and "assume the posture of a man," but Momma would have beaten me if I'd opened my mouth. She ignored the creaks of the counter under their weight and moved around filling their orders and keeping up a conversation. "Going to put your dinner on, Sister Williams?" Bailey and I helped Momma, while Uncle Willie sat on the porch and heard the day's account.

"Praise the Lord, no, ma'am. Got enough left over from last night to do us. We going home and get cleaned up to go to the revival meeting."

Go to church in that cloud of weariness? Not go home and lay those tortured bones in a feather bed? The idea came to me that my people may be a race of masochists and that not only was it our fate to live the poorest, roughest life but that we liked it like that.

"I know what you mean, Sister Williams. Got to feed the soul just like you feed the body. I'm taking the children, too, the Lord willing. Good Book say, 'Raise a child in the way he should go and he will not depart from it.' "

"That's what it say. Sure is what it say."

The cloth tent had been set on the flatlands in the middle of a field near the railroad tracks. The earth was carpeted with a silky layer of dried grass and cotton stalks. Collapsible chairs were poked into the still-soft ground and a large wooden cross was hung from the center beam at the rear of the tent. Electric lights had been strung from behind the pulpit to the entrance flap and continued outside on poles made of rough two-by-fours.

Approached in the dark the swaying bulbs looked lonely and purposeless. Not as if they were there to provide light or anything meaningful. And the tent, that blurry bright three-dimensional A, was so foreign to the cotton field, that it might just get up and fly away before my eyes.

People, suddenly visible in the lamplight, streamed toward the temporary church. The adults' voices relayed the serious intent of their mission. Greetings were exchanged, hushed.

"Evening, sister, how you?"

"Bless the Lord, just trying to make it in."

Their minds were concentrated on the coming meeting, soul to soul, with God. This was no time to indulge in human concerns or personal questions.

"The good Lord give me another day, and I'm thankful. "Nothing personal in that. The credit was God's, and there was no illusion about the Central Position's shifting or becoming less than Itself.

Teenagers enjoyed revivals as much as adults. They used the night outside meetings to play at courting. The impermanence of a collapsible church added to the frivolity, and their eyes flashed and winked and the girls giggled little silver drops in the dusk while the boys postured and swaggered and pretended not to notice. The nearly grown girls wore skirts as tight as the custom allowed and the young men slicked their hair down with Moroline Hairdressing and water.

To small children, though, the idea of praising God in a tent was confusing, to say the least. It seemed somehow blasphemous. The lights hanging slack overhead, the soft ground underneath and the canvas wall that faintly blew in and out, like cheeks puffed with air, made for the feeling of a country fair. The nudgings and jerks and winks of the bigger children surely didn't belong in a church. But the tension of the elders—their expectation, which weighted like a thick blanket over the crowd—was the most perplexing of all.

Would the gentle Jesus care to enter into that transitory setting? The altar wobbled and threatened to overturn and the collection table sat at a rakish angle. One leg had yielded itself to the loose dirt. Would God the Father allow His only Son to mix with this crowd of cotton pickers and maids, washerwomen and handymen? I knew He sent His spirit on Sundays to the church, but after all that was a church and the people had had all day Saturday to shuffle off the cloak of work and the skin of despair.

Everyone attended the revival meetings. Members of the hoity-toity Mount Zion Baptist Church mingled with the intellectual members of the African Methodist Episcopal and African Methodist Episcopal Zion, and the plain working people of the Christian Methodist Episcopal. These gatherings provided the one time in the year when all of those good village people associated with the followers of the Church of God in Christ. The latter were looked upon with some suspicion because they were so loud and raucous in their services. Their explanation that "the Good Book say, 'Make a joyful noise unto the Lord, and be exceedingly glad'" did not in the least minimize the condescension of their fellow Christians. Their church was far from the others, but they could be heard on Sunday, a half mile away, singing and dancing until they sometimes fell down in a dead faint. Members of the other churches wondered if the Holy Rollers were going to heaven after all their shouting. The suggestion was that they were having their heaven right here on earth.

This was their annual revival.

Mrs. Duncan, a little woman with a bird face, started the service. "I know I'm a witness for my Lord... I know I'm a witness for my Lord, I know I'm a witness..."

Her voice, a skinny finger, stabbed high up in the air and the church responded. From somewhere down front came the jangling sound of a tambourine. Two beats on "know," two beats on "I'm a" and two beats on the end of "witness."

Other voices joined the near shriek of Mrs. Duncan. They crowded around and tenderized the tone. Handclaps snapped in the roof and solidified the beat. When the song reached its peak in sound and passion, a tall, thin man who had been kneeling behind the altar all the while stood up and sang with the audience for a few bars. He stretched out his long arms and grasped the platform. It took some time for the singers to come off their level of exaltation, but the minister stood resolute until the song unwound like a child's playtoy and lay quieted in the aisles.

"Amen." He looked at the audience.

"Yes, sir, amen." Nearly everyone seconded him.

"I say, Let the church say 'Amen.' "

Everyone said, "Amen."

"Thank the Lord. Thank the Lord."

"That's right, thank the Lord. Yes, Lord. Amen."

"We will have prayer, led by Brother Bishop."

Another tall, brown-skinned man wearing square glasses walked up to the altar from the front row. The minister knelt at the right and Brother Bishop at the left.

"Our Father"—he was singing—"You who took my feet out the mire and clay—"

The church moaned, "Amen."

"You who saved my soul. One day. Look, sweet Jesus. Look down, on these your suffering children—"

The church begged, "Look down, Lord."

"Build us up where we're torn down... Bless the sick and the afflicted..."

It was the usual prayer. Only his voice gave it something new. After every two words he gasped and dragged the air over his vocal chords, making a sound like an inverted grunt. "You who"—grunt—"saved my"—gasp—"soul one"—inhalation—"day"—humph.

Then the congregation, led again by Mrs. Duncan, flew into "Precious Lord, take my hand, lead me on, let me stand." It was sung at a faster clip than the usual one in the C.M.E. Church, but at that tempo it worked. There was a joy about the tune that changed the meaning of its sad lyrics. "When the darkness appears, and the night draweth near and my life is almost gone..." There seemed to be an abandon which suggested that with all those things it should be a time for great rejoicing.

The serious shouters had already made themselves known, and their fans (cardboard advertisements from Texarkana's largest Negro funeral home) and lacy white handkerchiefs waved high in the air. In their dark hands they looked like small kites without the wooden frames.

The tall minister stood again at the altar. He waited for the song and the revelry to die.

He said, "Amen. Glory."

The church skidded off the song slowly. "Amen. Glory."

He still waited, as the last notes remained in the air, staircased on top of each other. "At the river I stand—" "I stand, guide my feet—" "Guide my feet, take my hand." Sung like the last circle in a round. Then quiet descended.

The Scripture reading was from Matthew, twenty-fifth chapter, thirtieth verse through the forty-sixth.

His text for the sermon was "The least of these."

After reading the verses to the accompaniment of a few Amens he said, "First Corinthians tells me, 'Even if I have the tongue of men and of angels and have not charity, I am as nothing. Even if I give all my clothes to the poor and have not charity, I am as nothing. Even if I give my body to be burned and have not charity it availeth me nothing. Burned, I say, and have not charity, it availeth nothing.' I have to ask myself, what is this thing called Charity? If good deeds are not charity—"

The church gave in quickly. "That's right, Lord."

"—if giving my flesh and blood is not charity?"

"Yes, Lord."

"I have to ask myself what is this charity they talking so much about."

I had never heard a preacher jump into the muscle of his sermon so quickly. Already the humming pitch had risen in the church, and those who knew had popped their eyes in anticipation of the coming excitement. Momma sat tree-trunk still, but she had balled her handkerchief in her hand and only the corner, which I had embroidered, stuck out.

"As I understand it, charity vaunteth not itself. Is not puffed up." He blew himself up with a deep breath to give us the picture of what Charity was not. "Charity don't go around saying 'I give you food and I give you clothes and by rights you ought to thank me.' "

The congregation knew whom he was talking about and voiced agreement with his analysis. "Tell the truth, Lord."

"Charity don't say, 'because I give you a job, you got to bend your knee to me.' " The church was rocking with each phrase. "It don't say, 'because I pays you what you due, you got to call me master.' It don't ask me to humble myself and belittle myself. That ain't what Charity is."

Down front to the right, Mr. and Mrs. Stewart who only a few hours earlier had crumbled in our front yard, defeated by the cotton rows, now sat on the edges of their rickety-rackety chairs. Their faces shone with the delight of their souls. The mean whitefolks was going to get their comeuppance. Wasn't that what the minister said, and wasn't he quoting from the words of God Himself? They had been refreshed with the hope of revenge and the promise of justice.

"Aaagh. Raagh. I said... Charity. Wooooooo, a Charity. It don't want nothing for itself. It don't want to be bossman... Waah... It don't want to be headman... Waah... It don't want to be foreman... Waah... It... I'm talking about Charity... It don't want... Oh Lord... help me tonight... It don't want to be bowed to and scraped at..."

America's historic bowers and scrapers shifted easily and happily in the makeshift church. Reassured that although they might be the lowest of the low they were at least not uncharitable, and "in that great Gettin' Up Morning, Jesus was going to separate the sheep (them) from the goats (the whitefolks)."

"Charity is simple." The church agreed, vocally.

"Charity is poor." That was us he was talking about.

"Charity is plain." I thought, that's about right. Plain and simple.

"Charity is... Oh, Oh, Oh. Cha–ri–ty. Where are you? Wooo... Charity... Hump."

One chair gave way and the sound of splintering wood split the air in the rear of the church.

"I call you and you don't answer. Woooh, oh Charity."

Another holler went up in front of me, and a large woman flopped over, her arms above her head like a candidate for baptism. The emotional release was contagious. Little screams burst around the room like Fourth of July firecrackers.

The minister's voice was a pendulum. Swinging left and down and right and down and left and—"How can you claim to be my brother, and hate me? Is that Charity? How can you claim to be my sister and despise me? Is that supposed to be Charity? How can you claim to be my friend and misuse and wrongfully abuse me? Is that Charity? Oh, my children, I stopped by here—"

The church swung on the end of his phrases. Punctuating. Confirming. "Stop by here, Lord."

"—to tell you, to open your heart and let Charity reign. Forgive your enemies for His sake. Show the Charity that Jesus was speaking of to this sick old world. It has need of the charitable giver." His voice was falling and the explosions became fewer and quieter.

"And now I repeat the words of the Apostle Paul, and 'now abideth faith, hope and charity, these three; but the greatest of these is charity.' "

The congregation lowed with satisfaction. Even if they were society's pariahs, they were going to be angels in a marble white heaven and sit on the right hand of Jesus, the Son of God. The Lord loved the poor and hated those cast high in the world. Hadn't He Himself said it would be easier for a camel to go through the eye of a needle than for a rich man to enter heaven? They were assured that they were going to be the only inhabitants of that land of milk and honey, except of course a few whitefolks like John Brown who history books said was crazy anyway. All the Negroes had to do generally, and those at the revival especially, was bear up under this life of toil and cares, because a blessed home awaited them in the far-off bye and bye.

"Bye and bye, when the morning come, when all the saints of God's are gathering home, we will tell the story of how we overcome and we'll understand it better bye and bye."

A few people who had fainted were being revived on the side aisles when the evangelist opened the doors of the church. Over the sounds of "Thank you, Jesus," he started a long-meter hymn:

> "I came to Jesus, as I was,
> worried, wounded and sad,
> I found in Him a resting place,
> And He has made me glad."

The old ladies took up the hymn and shared it in tight harmony. The humming crowd began to sound like tired bees, restless and anxious to get home.

"All those under the sound of my voice who have no spiritual home, whose hearts are burdened and heavy-ladened, let them come. Come before it's too late. I don't ask you to join the Church of God in Christ. No. I'm a servant of God, and in this revival, we are out to bring straying souls to Him. So if you join this evening, just say which church you want to be affiliated with, and we will turn you over to a representative of that church body. Will one deacon of the following churches come forward?"

That was revolutionary action. No one had ever heard of a minister taking in members for another church. It was our first look at Charity among preachers. Men from the A.M.E., A.M.E.Z., Baptist and C.M.E. churches went down front and assumed stances a few feet apart. Converted sinners flowed down the aisles to shake hands with the evangelist and stayed at his side or were directed to one of the men in line. Over twenty people were saved that night.

There was nearly as much commotion over the saving of the sinners as there had been during the gratifying melodic sermon.

The Mothers of the Church, old ladies with white lace disks pinned to their thinning hair, had a service all their own. They walked around the new converts singing,

"Before this time another year,
I may be gone,
In some lonesome graveyard,
Oh, Lord, how long?"

When the collection was taken up and the last hymn given to the praise of God, the evangelist asked that everyone in his presence rededicate his soul to God and his life's work to Charity. Then we were dismissed.

Outside and on the way home, the people played in their magic, as children poke in mud pies, reluctant to tell themselves that the game was over.

"The Lord touched him tonight, didn't He?"

"Surely did. Touched him with a mighty fire."

"Bless the Lord. I'm glad I'm saved."

"That's the truth. It make a whole lot of difference."

"I wish them people I works for could of heard that sermon. They don't know what they letting theyselves in for."

"Bible say, 'He who can hear, let him hear. He who can't, shame on 'em.'"

They basked in the righteousness of the poor and the exclusiveness of the downtrodden. Let the whitefolks have their money and power and segregation and sarcasm and big houses and schools and lawns like carpets, and books, and mostly—mostly—let them have their whiteness. It was better to be meek and lowly, spat upon and abused for this little time than to spend eternity frying in the fires of hell. No one would have admitted that the Christian and charitable people were happy to think of their oppressors' turning forever on the Devil's spit over the flames of fire and brimstone.

But that was what the Bible said and it didn't make mistakes. "Ain't it said somewhere in there that 'before one word of this changes, heaven and earth shall fall away?' Folks going to get what they deserved."

When the main crowd of worshipers reached the short bridge spanning the pond, the ragged sound of honky-tonk music assailed them. A barrelhouse blues was being shouted over the stamping of feet on a wooden floor. Miss Grace, the good-time woman, had her usual Saturday-night customers. The big white house blazed with lights and noise. The people inside had forsaken their own distress for a little while.

Passing near the din, the godly people dropped their heads and conversation ceased. Reality began its tedious crawl back into their reasoning. After all, they were needy and hungry and despised and dispossessed, and sinners the world over were in the driver's seat. How long, merciful Father? How long?

84

A stranger to the music could not have made a distinction between the songs sung a few minutes before and those being danced to in the gay house by the railroad tracks. All asked the same questions. How long, oh God? How long?

19

The last inch of space was filled, yet people continued to wedge themselves along the walls of the Store. Uncle Willie had turned the radio up to its last notch so that youngsters on the porch wouldn't miss a word. Women sat on kitchen chairs, dining-room chairs, stools and upturned wooden boxes. Small children and babies perched on every lap available and men leaned on the shelves or on each other.

The apprehensive mood was shot through with shafts of gaiety, as a black sky is streaked with lightning.

"I ain't worried 'bout this fight. Joe's gonna whip that cracker like it's open season."

"He gone whip him till that white boy call him Momma."

At last the talking was finished and the string-along songs about razor blades were over and the fight began.

"A quick jab to the head." In the Store the crowd grunted. "A left to the head and a right and another left." One of the listeners cackled like a hen and was quieted.

"They're in a clench, Louis is trying to fight his way out."

Some bitter comedian on the porch said, "That white man don't mind hugging that niggah now, I betcha."

"The referee is moving in to break them up, but Louis finally pushed the contender away and it's an uppercut to the chin. The contender is hanging on, now he's backing away. Louis catches him with a short left to the jaw."

A tide of murmuring assent poured out the doors and into the yard.

"Another left and another left. Louis is saving that mighty right..." The mutter in the Store had grown into a baby roar and it was pierced by the clang of a bell and the announcer's "That's the bell for round three, ladies and gentlemen."

As I pushed my way into the Store I wondered if the announcer gave any thought to the fact that he was addressing as "ladies and gentlemen" all the Negroes around the world who sat sweating and praying, glued to their "master's voice."

There were only a few calls for R. C. Colas, Dr. Peppers, and Hire's root beer. The real festivities would begin after the fight, Then even the old Christian ladies who taught their children and tried themselves to practice turning the other cheek would buy soft drinks, and if the Brown Bomber's victory was a particularly bloody one they would order peanut patties and Baby Ruths also.

Bailey and I lay the coins on top of the cash register. Uncle Willie didn't allow us to ring up sales during a fight. It was too noisy and might shake up the atmosphere. When the gong rang for the next round we pushed through the near-sacred quiet to the herd of children outside.

"He's got Louis against the ropes and now it's a left to the body and a right to the ribs. Another right to the body, it looks like it was low... Yes, ladies and gentlemen, the referee is signaling but the contender keeps raining the blows on Louis. It's another to the body, and it looks like Louis is going down."

My race groaned. It was our people falling. It was another lynching, yet another Black man hanging on a tree. One more woman ambushed and raped. A Black boy whipped and maimed. It was hounds on the trail of a man running through slimy swamps. It was a white woman slapping her maid for being forgetful.

The men in the Store stood away from the walls and at attention. Women greedily clutched the babes on their laps while on the porch the shufflings and smiles, flirtings and pinching of a few minutes before were gone. This might be the end of the world. If Joe lost we were back in slavery and beyond help. It would all be true, the accusations that we were lower types of human beings. Only a little higher than the apes. True that we were stupid and ugly and lazy and dirty and, unlucky and worst of all, that God Himself hated us and ordained us to be hewers of wood and drawers of water, forever and ever, world without end.

We didn't breathe. We didn't hope. We waited.

"He's off the ropes, ladies and gentlemen. He's moving towards the center of the ring." There was no time to be relieved. The worst might still happen.

"And now it looks like Joe is mad. He's caught Carnera with a left hook to the head and a right to the head. It's a left jab to the body and another left to the head. There's a left cross and a right to the head. The contender's right eye is bleeding and he can't seem to keep his block up. Louis is penetrating every block. The referee is moving in, but Louis sends a left to the body and it's the uppercut to the chin and the contender is dropping. He's on the canvas, ladies and gentlemen."

Babies slid to the floor as women stood up and men leaned toward the radio.

"Here's the referee. He's counting. One, two, three, four, five, six, seven... Is the contender trying to get up again?"

All the men in the store shouted, "NO."

"—eight, nine, ten." There were a few sounds from the audience, but they seemed to be holding themselves in against tremendous pressure.

"The fight is all over, ladies and gentlemen. Let's get the microphone over to the referee... Here he is. He's got the Brown Bomber's hand, he's holding it up... Here he is..."

Then the voice, husky and familiar, came to wash over us—"The winnah, and still heavyweight champeen of the world... Joe Louis."

Champion of the world. A Black boy. Some Black mother's son. He was the strongest man in the world. People drank Coca-Colas like ambrosia and ate candy bars like Christmas. Some of the men went behind the Store and poured white lightning in their soft-drink bottles, and a few of the bigger boys followed them. Those who were not chased away came back blowing their breath in front of themselves like proud smokers.

It would take an hour or more before the people would leave the Store and head for home. Those who lived too far had made arrangements to stay in town. It wouldn't do for a Black man and his family to be caught on a lonely country road on a night when Joe Louis had proved that we were the strongest people in the world.

20

"Acka Backa, Sody Cracka
Acka Backa, Boo
Acka Backa, Sody Cracka
I'm in love with you."

The sounds of tag beat through the trees while the top branches waved in contrapuntal rhythms. I lay on a moment of green grass and telescoped the children's game to my vision. The girls ran about wild, now here, now there, never here, never was, they seemed to have no more direction than a splattered egg. But it was a shared if seldom voiced knowledge that all movements fitted, and worked according to a larger plan. I raised a platform for my mind's eye and marveled down on the outcome of "Acka Backa." The gay picnic dresses dashed, stopped and darted like beautiful dragonflies over a dark pool. The boys, black whips in the sunlight, popped behind the trees where their girls had fled, half hidden and throbbing in the shadows.

The summer picnic fish fry in the clearing by the pond was the biggest outdoor event of the year. Everyone was there. All churches were represented, as well as the social groups (Elks, Eastern Star, Masons, Knights of Columbus, Daughters of Pythias), professional people (Negro teachers from Lafayette County) and all the excited children.

Musicians brought cigar-box guitars, harmonicas, juice harps, combs wrapped in tissue paper and even bathtub basses.

The amount and variety of foods would have found approval on the menu of a Roman epicure. Pans of fried chicken, covered with dishtowels, sat under benches next to a mountain of potato salad crammed with hard-boiled eggs. Whole rust-red sticks of bologna were clothed in cheese-cloth. Homemade pickles and chow-chow, and baked country hams, aromatic with cloves and pineapples, vied for prominence. Our steady customers had ordered cold watermelons, so Bailey and I chugged the striped-green fruit into the Coca-Cola box and filled all the tubs with ice as well as the big black wash pot that Momma used to boil her laundry. Now they too lay sweating in the happy afternoon air.

The summer picnic gave ladies a chance to show off their baking hands. On the barbecue pit, chickens and spareribs sputtered in their own fat and a sauce whose recipe was guarded in the family like a scandalous affair. However, in the ecumenical light of the summer picnic every true baking artist could reveal her prize to the delight and criticism of the town. Orange sponge cakes and dark brown mounds dripping Hershey's chocolate stood layer to layer with ice-white coconuts and light brown caramels. Pound cakes sagged with their buttery weight and small children could no more resist licking the icings than their mothers could avoid slapping the sticky fingers.

Proven fishermen and weekend amateurs sat on the trunks of trees at the pond. They pulled the struggling bass and the silver perch from the swift water. A rotating crew of young girls scaled and cleaned the catch and busy women in starched aprons salted and rolled the fish in corn meal, then dropped them in Dutch ovens trembling with boiling fat.

On one corner of the clearing a gospel group was rehearsing. Their harmony, packed as tight as sardines, floated over the music of the county singers and melted into the songs of the small children's ring games.

"Boys, don'chew let that ball fall on none of my cakes, you do and it'll be me on you."

"Yes, ma'am," and nothing changed. The boys continued hitting the tennis ball with pailings snatched from a fence and running holes in the ground, colliding with everyone.

I had wanted to bring something to read, but Momma said if I didn't want to play with the other children I could make myself useful by cleaning fish or bringing water from the nearest well or wood for the barbecue.

I wandered into a retreat by accident. Signs with arrows around the barbecue pit pointed MEN, WOMEN, CHILDREN toward fading lanes, grown over since last year. Feeling ages old and very wise at ten, I couldn't allow myself to be found by small children squatting behind a tree. Neither did I have the nerve to follow the arrow pointing the way for WOMEN. If any grownup had caught me there, it was possible that she'd think I was being "womanish" and would report me to Momma, and I knew what I could expect from her. So when the urge hit me to relieve myself, I headed toward another direction. Once through the wall of sycamore trees I found myself in a clearing ten times smaller than the picnic area, and cool and quiet. After my business was taken care of, I found a seat between two protruding roots of a black walnut tree and leaned back on its trunk. Heaven would be like that for the deserving. Maybe California too. Looking straight up at the uneven circle of sky, I began to sense that I might be falling into a blue cloud, far away. The children's voices and the thick odor of food cooking over open fires were the hooks I grabbed just in time to save myself.

Grass squeaked and I jumped at being found. Louise Kendricks walked into my grove. I didn't know that she too was escaping the gay spirit. We were the same age and she and her mother lived in a neat little bungalow behind the school. Her cousins, who were in our age group, were wealthier and fairer, but I had secretly believed Louise to be the prettiest female in Stamps, next to Mrs. Flowers.

"What you doing sitting here by yourself, Marguerite?" She didn't accuse, she asked for information, I said that I was watching the sky. She asked, "What for?" There was obviously no answer to a question like that, so I didn't make up one. Louise reminded me of Jane Eyre. Her mother lived in reduced circumstances, but she was genteel, and though she worked as a maid I decided she should be called a governess and did so to Bailey and myself. (Who could teach a romantic dreamy ten-year-old to call a spade a spade?) Mrs. Kendricks could not have been very old, but to me all people over eighteen were adults and there could be no degree given or taken. They had to be catered to and pampered with politeness, then they

89

had to stay in the same category of lookalike, soundalike and beingalike. Louise was a lonely girl, although she had plenty of playmates and was a ready partner for any ring game in the schoolyard.

Her face, which was long and dark chocolate brown, had a thin sheet of sadness over it, as light but as permanent as the viewing gauze on a coffin. And her eyes, which I thought her best feature, shifted quickly as if what they sought had just a second before eluded her.

She had come near and the spotted light through the trees fell on her face and braids in running splotches. I had never noticed before, but she looked exactly like Bailey. Her hair was "good"—more straight than kinky—and her features had the regularity of objects placed by a careful hand.

She looked up—"Well, you can't see much sky from here." Then she sat down, an arm away from me. Finding two exposed roots, she laid thin wrists on them as if she had been in an easy chair. Slowly she leaned back against the tree. I closed my eyes and thought of the necessity of finding another place and the unlikelihood of there being another with all the qualifications that this one had. There was a little peal of a scream and before I could open my eyes Louise had grabbed my hand. "I was falling"—she shook her long braids—"I was falling in the sky."

I liked her for being able to fall in the sky and admit it. I suggested, "Let's try together. But we have to sit up straight on the count of five." Louise asked, "Want to hold hands? Just in case?" I did. If one of us did happen to fall, the other could pull her out.

After a few near tumbles into eternity (both of us knew what it was), we laughed at having played with death and destruction and escaped.

Louise said, "Let's look at that old sky while we're spinning." We took each other's hands in the center of the clearing and began turning around. Very slowly at first. We raised our chins and looked straight at the seductive patch of blue. Faster, just a little faster, then faster, faster yet. Yes, help, we were falling. Then eternity won, after all. We couldn't stop spinning or falling until I was jerked out of her grasp by greedy gravity and thrown to my fate below—no, above, not below. I found myself safe and dizzy at the foot of the sycamore tree. Louise had ended on her knees at the other side of the grove.

This was surely the time to laugh. We lost but we hadn't lost anything. First we were giggling and crawling drunkenly toward each other and then we were laughing out loud uproariously. We slapped each other on the back and shoulders and laughed some more. We had made a fool or a liar out of something, and didn't that just beat all?

90

In daring to challenge the unknown with me, she became my first friend. We spent tedious hours teaching ourselves the Tut language. You (Yak oh you) know (kack nug oh wug) what (wack hash a tut). Since all the other children spoke Pig Latin, we were superior because Tut was hard to speak and even harder to understand. At last I began to comprehend what girls giggled about. Louise would rattle off a few sentences to me in the unintelligible Tut language and would laugh. Naturally I laughed too. Snickered, really, understanding nothing. I don't think she understood half of what she was saying herself, but, after all, girls have to giggle, and after being a woman for three years I was about to become a girl.

In school one day, a girl whom I barely knew and had scarcely spoken to brought me a note. The intricate fold indicated that it was a love note. I was sure she had the wrong person, but she insisted. Picking the paper loose, I confessed to myself that I was frightened. Suppose it was somebody being funny? Suppose the paper would show a hideous beast and the word YOU written over it. Children did that sometimes just because they claimed I was stuck-up. Fortunately I had got permission to go to the toilet—an outside job—and in the reeking gloom I read:

Dear Friend, M.J.

Times are hard and friends are few
I take great pleasure in writing you
Will you be my Valentine?

Tommy Valdon

I pulled my mind apart. Who? Who was Tommy Valdon? Finally a face dragged itself from my memory. He was the nice-looking brown-skinned boy who lived across the pond. As soon as I had pinned him down, I began to wonder, Why? Why me? Was it a joke? But if Tommy was the boy I remembered he was a very sober person and a good student. Well, then, it wasn't a joke. All right, what evil dirty things did he have in mind? My questions fell over themselves, an army in retreat. Haste, dig for cover. Protect your flanks. Don't let the enemy close the gap between you. What did a Valentine do, anyway?

Starting to throw the paper in the foul-smelling hole, I thought of Louise. I could show it to her. I folded the paper back in the original crease, and went back to class. There was no time during the lunch period since I had to run to the Store and wait on customers. The note was in my sock and every time Momma looked at me, I feared that her church gaze might have turned into X-ray vision and she could not only see the note and read its message but would interpret it as well. I felt myself slipping down a sheer cliff of guilt, and a second time I nearly detroyed the note but there was no opportunity. The take-up bell rang and Bailey raced me to school, so the note was forgotten. But serious business is serious, and it had to be attended to. After classes I waited for Louise. She was talking to a group of girls, laughing. But when I gave her our signal (two waves of the left hand) she said goodbye to them and joined me in the road. I didn't give her the chance to ask what was on my mind (her favorite question); I simply gave her the note. Recognizing the fold she stopped smiling. We were in deep waters. She opened the letter and read it aloud twice. "Well, what do you think?"

I said, "What do I think? That's what I'm asking you? What is there to think?"

"Looks like he wants you to be his valentine."

"Louise, I can read. But what does it mean?"

"Oh, you know. His valentine. His love."

There was that hateful word again. That treacherous word that yawned up at you like a volcano.

"Well, I won't. Most decidedly I won't. Not ever again."

"Have you been his valentine before? What do you mean never again?"

I couldn't lie to my friend and I wasn't about to freshen old ghosts.

"Well, don't answer him then, and that's the end of it." I was a little relieved that she thought it could be gotten rid of so quickly. I tore the note in half and gave her a part. Walking down the hill we minced the paper in a thousand shreds and gave it to the wind.

Two days later a monitor came into my classroom. She spoke quietly to Miss Williams, our teacher. Miss Williams said, "Class, I believe you remember that tomorrow is Valentine's Day, so named for St. Valentine, the martyr, who died around A.D. 270 in Rome. The day is observed by exchanging tokens of affection, and cards. The eighth-grade children have completed theirs and the monitor is acting as mailman. You will be given cardboard, ribbon and red tissue paper during the last period today so that you may make your gifts. Glue and scissors are here at the work table. Now, stand when your name is called."

She had been shuffling the colored envelopes and calling names for some time before I noticed. I had been thinking of yesterday's plain invitation and the expeditious way Louise and I took care of it.

We who were being called to receive valentines were only slightly more embarrassed than those who sat and watched as Miss Williams opened each envelope. "Helen Gray." Helen Gray, a tall, dull girl from Louisville, flinched. "Dear Valentine"—Miss Williams began reading the badly rhymed childish drivel. I seethed with shame and anticipation and yet had time to be offended at the silly poetry that I could have bettered in my sleep.

"Margue-you-reete Anne Johnson. My goodness, this looks more like a letter than a valentine. 'Dear Friend, I wrote you a letter and saw you tear it up with your friend Miss L. I don't believe you meant to hurt my feelings so whether you answer or not you will always be my valentine. T.V."

"Class"—Miss Williams smirked and continued lazily without giving us permission to sit down—"although you are only in the seventh grade, I'm sure you wouldn't be so presumptuous as to sign a letter with an initial. But here is a boy in the eighth grade, about to graduate—blah, blah, blooey, blah. You may collect your valentines and these letters on your way out."

It was a nice letter and Tommy had beautiful penmanship. I was sorry I tore up the first. His statement that whether I answered him or not would not influence his affection reassured me. He couldn't be after you-know-what if he talked like that. I told Louise that the next time he came to the Store I was going to say something extra nice to him. Unfortunately the situation was so wonderful to me that each time I saw Tommy I melted in delicious giggles and was unable to form a coherent sentence. After a while he stopped including me in his general glances.

21

Bailey stuck branches in the ground behind the house and covered them with a worn-through blanket, making a tent. It was to be his Captain Marvel hideaway. There he initiated girls into the mysteries of sex. One by one, he took the impressed, the curious, the adventurous into the gray shadows, after explaining that they were going to play Momma and Poppa. I was assigned the role of Baby and lookout. The girls were commanded to pull up their dresses and then he lay on top and wiggled his hips.

I sometimes had to lift the flap (our signal that an adult was approaching) and so I saw their pathetic struggles even as they talked about school and the movies.

He had been playing the game for about six months before he met

Joyce. She was a country girl about four years older than Bailey (he wasn't quite eleven when they met) whose parents had died and she along with her brothers and sisters had been parceled out to relatives. Joyce had come to Stamps to live with a widowed aunt who was even poorer than the poorest person in town. Joyce was quite advanced physically for her age. Her breasts were not the hard little knots of other girls her age; they filled out the tops of her skimpy little dresses. She walked stiffly, as if she were carrying a load of wood between her legs. I thought of her as being coarse, but Bailey said she was cute and that he wanted to play house with her.

In the special way of women, Joyce knew she had made a conquest, and managed to hang around the Store in the late afternoons and all day Saturdays. She ran errands for Momma when we were busy in the Store and sweated profusely. Often when she came in after running down the hill, her cotton dress would cling to her thin body and Bailey would glue his eyes on her until her clothes dried.

Momma gave her small gifts of food to take to her aunt, and on Saturdays Uncle Willie would sometimes give her a dime for "show fare."

During Passover week we weren't allowed to go to the movies (Momma said we all must sacrifice to purify our souls), and Bailey and Joyce decided that the three of us would play house. As usual, I was to be Baby.

He strung the tent and Joyce crawled in first. Bailey told me to sit outside and play with my doll baby, and he went in and the flap closed.

"Well, ain't you going to open your trousers?" Joyce's voice was muffled.

"No. You just pull up your dress."

There were rustling sounds from the tent and the sides pooched out as if they were trying to stand up.

Bailey asked, "What are you doing?"

"Pulling off my drawers."

"What for?"

"We can't do it with my drawers on."

"Why not?"

"How are you going to get to it?"

Silence. My poor brother didn't know what she meant. I knew. I lifted the flap and said, "Joyce, don't you do that to my brother." She nearly screamed, but she kept her voice low, "Margaret, you close that door." Bailey added," Yes. Close it. You're supposed to be playing with our doll baby." I thought he would go to the hospital if he let her do that to him, so I warned him, "Bailey, if you let her do that to you, you'll be sorry." But he threatened that if I didn't close the door he wouldn't speak to me for a month, so I let the end of the blanket fall and sat down on the grass in front of the tent.

Joyce poked her head out and said in a sugary, whitewoman-in-the-movies voice, "Baby, you go get some wood. Daddy and I going to light a fire, then I'm going to make you some cake." Then her voice changed as if she was going to hit me. "Go. Git."

Bailey told me after that Joyce had hairs on her thing and that she had gotten them from "doing it" with so many boys. She even had hair under her arms. Both of them. He was very proud of her accomplishments.

As their love affair progressed, his stealing from the Store increased. We had always taken candy and a few nickels and of course the sour pickles, but Bailey, now "called upon to feed Joyce's ravening hunger, took cans of sardines and greasy Polish sausage and cheese and even the expensive cans of pink salmon that our family could seldom afford to eat.

Joyce's willingness to do odd jobs slackened about this time. She complained that she wasn't feeling all that well. But since she now had a few coins, she still hung around the Store eating Planter's peanuts and drinking Dr. Pepper.

Momma ran her off a few times. "Ain't you said you wasn't feeling well, Joyce? Hadn't you better get home and let your aunty do something for you?"

"Yes, ma'am." Then reluctantly she was off the porch, her stiff-legged walk carrying her up the hill and out of sight.

I think she was Bailey's first love outside the family. For him, she was the mother who let him get as close as he dreamed, the sister who wasn't moody and withdrawing, and teary and tender-hearted. All he had to do was keep the food coming in and she kept the affection flowing out. It made no difference to him that she was almost a woman, or possibly it was just that difference which made her so appealing.

She was around for a few months, and as she had appeared, out of limbo, so she disappeared into nothingness. There was no gossip about her, no clues to her leaving or her whereabouts. I noticed the change in Bailey before I discovered that she was gone. He lost his interest in everything. He mulled around and it would be safe to say "he paled." Momma noticed and said that he was feeling poorly because of the change in seasons (we were nearing fall), so she went to the woods for certain leaves, made him a tea and forced him to drink it after a heaping spoonful of sulfur and molasses. The fact that he didn't fight it, didn't try to talk his way out of taking the medicine, showed without a glimmer of doubt he was very sick.

If I had disliked Joyce while she had Bailey in her grasp, I hated her for leaving. I missed the tolerance she had brought to him (he had nearly given up sarcasm and playing jokes on the country people) and he had taken to telling me his secrets again. But now that she was gone he rivaled me in being uncommunicative. He closed in upon himself like a pond swallowing a stone. There was no evidence that he had ever opened up, and when I mentioned her he responded with "Joyce who?"

Months later, when Momma was waiting on Joyce's aunt, she said, "Yes ma'am, Mrs. Goodman, life's just one thing right after the other."

Mrs. Goodman was leaning on the red Coca-Cola box. "That's the blessed truth, Sister Henderson." She sipped the expensive drink.

"Things change so fast, it make your head swim. "That was Momma's way of opening up a conversation. I stayed mouse-quiet so that I'd be able to hear the gossip and take it to Bailey.

"Now, you take little Joyce. She used to be around the Store all the time. Then she went up just like smoke. We ain't seed hide nor hair of her in months."

"No'm. I shamed to tell you... what took her off." She settled in on a kitchen chair. Momma spied me in the shadows. "Sister, the Lord don't like little jugs with big ears. You ain't got something to do, I'll find something for you."

The truth had to float to me through the kitchen door.

"I ain't got much, Sister Henderson, but I give that child all I had."

Momma said she bound that was true. She wouldn't say "bet."

"And after all I did, she run off with one of those railroad porters. She was loose just like her mammy before her. You know how they say 'blood will tell'?"

Momma asked, "How did the snake catch her?"

"Well, now, understand me, Sister Henderson, I don't hold this against you, I knows you a God-fearing woman. But it seems like she met him here."

Momma was flustered. Such goings on at the Store? She asked, "At the Store?"

"Yes, ma'am. 'Member when that bunch of Elks come over for their baseball game?" (Momma must have remembered. I did.) "Well, as it turned out, he was one of them. She left me a teenincy note. Said people in Stamps thought they were better than she was, and that she hadn't only made one friend, and that was your grandson. Said she was moving to Dallas, Texas, and gone marry that railroad porter."

Momma said, "Do, Lord."

Mrs. Goodman said, "You know, Sister Henderson, she wasn't with me long enough for me to get the real habit of her, but still I miss her. She was sweet when she wanted to be." Momma consoled her with,

"Well, we got to keep our mind on the words of the Book. It say, 'The Lord giveth and the Lord taketh away.'"

Mrs. Goodman chimed in and they finished the phrase together, "Blessed be the name of the Lord."

I don't know how long Bailey had known about Joyce, but later in the evening when I tried to bring her name into our conversation, he said, "Joyce? She's got somebody to do it to her all the time now." And that was the last time her name was mentioned.

22

The wind blew over the roof and ruffled the shingles. It whistled sharp under the closed door. The chimney made fearful sounds of protest as it was invaded by the urgent gusts.

A mile away ole Kansas City Kate (the train much admired but too important to stop in Stamps) crashed through the middle of town, blew its *wooo-wee* warnings, and continued to an unknownglamorous destination without looking back.

There was going to be a storm and it was a perfect night for rereading *Jane Eyre*. Bailey had finished his chores and was already behind the stove with Mark Twain. It was my turn to close the Store, and my book, half read, lay on the candy counter. Since the weather was going to be bad I was sure Uncle Willie would agree, in fact, encourage, me to close early (save electricity) and join the family in Momma's bedroom, which functioned as our sitting room. Few people would be out in weather that threatened a tornado (for though the wind blew, the sky was as clear and still as a summer morning). Momma agreed that I might as well close, and I went out on the porch, closed the shutters, slipped the wooden bar over the door and turned off the light.

Pots rattled in the kitchen where Momma was frying corn cakes to go with vegetable soup for supper, and the homey sounds and scents cushioned me as I read of Jane Eyre in the cold English mansion of a colder English gentleman. Uncle Willie was engrossed in the *Almanac*, his nightly reading, and my brother was far away on a raft on the Mississippi.

I was the first to hear the rattle on the back door. A rattle and knock, a knock and rattle. But suspecting that it might have been the mad wife in the tower, I didn't credit it. Then Uncle Willie heard it and summoned Bailey back from Huck Finn to unlatch the bolt.

Through the open door the moonshine fell into the room in a cold radiance to rival our meager lamplight. We all waited—I with a dread expectancy—for no human being was there. The wind alone came in, struggling with the weak flame in the coal-oil lamp. Pushing and bunting about the family warmth of our pot-bellied stove. Uncle Willie thought it must have been the storm and told Bailey to close the door. But just before he secured the raw wooden slab a voice drifted through the crack; it wheezed, "Sister Henderson? Brother Willie?"

Bailey nearly closed the door again, but Uncle Willie asked, "Who is it?" and Mr. George Taylor's pinched brown face swam out of the gray and into view. He assured himself that we hadn't gone to bed, and was welcomed in. When Momma saw him she invited him to stay for supper and told me to stick some sweet potatoes in the ashes to stretch the evening meal. Poor Brother Taylor had been taking meals all over town, ever since he buried his wife in the summer. Maybe due to the fact that I was in my romanticist period, or because children have a built-in survival apparatus, I feared he was interested in marrying Momma and moving in with us.

Uncle Willie cradled the *Almanac* in his divided lap. "You welcome here anytime, Brother Taylor, anytime, but this is a bad night. It say right here"—with his crippled hand he rapped the *Almanac*—"that November twelfth, a storm going to be moving over Stamps out of the east. A rough night." Mr. Taylor remained exactly in the same position he had taken when he arrived, like a person too cold to readjust his body even to get closer to the fire. His neck was bent and the red light played over the polished skin of his hairless head. But his eyes bound me with a unique attraction. They sat deep in his little face and completely dominated the other features with a roundness which seemed to be outlined in dark pencil, giving him an owlish appearance. And when he sensed my regarding him so steadily his head hardly moved but his eyes swirled and landed on me. If his look had contained contempt or patronage, or any of the vulgar emotions revealed by adults in confrontation with children, I would have easily gone back to my book, but his eyes gave off a watery nothing—a nothingness which was completely unbearable. I saw a glassiness, observed before only in new marbles or a bottle top embedded in a block of ice. His glance moved so swiftly from me it was nearly possible to imagine that I had in fact imagined the interchange.

"But, as I say, you welcome. We can, always make a place under this roof. "Uncle Willie didn't seem to notice that Mr. Taylor was oblivious to everything he said. Momma brought the soup into the room, took the kettle off the heater and placed the steaming pot on the fire. Uncle Willie continued, "Momma, I told Brother Taylor he is welcome here anytime." Momma said, "That's right, Brother Taylor. You not supposed to sit around that lonely house feeling sorry for yourself. The Lord giveth and the Lord taketh away."

I'm not sure whether it was Momma's presence or the bubbling soup on the stove which influenced him, but Mr. Taylor appeared to have livened up considerably. He shook his shoulders as if shaking off a tiresome touch, and attempted a smile that failed. "Sister Henderson, I sure appreciate... I mean, I don't know what I'd do if it wasn't for everybody... I mean, you don't know what it's worth to me to be able to... Well, I mean I'm thankful." At each pause, he pecked his head over his chest like a turtle coming out of its shell, but his eyes didn't move.

Momma, always self-conscious at public displays of emotions not traceable to a religious source, told me to come with her and we'd bring the bread and bowls. She carried the food and I trailed after her, bringing the kerosene lamp. The new light set the room in an eerie, harsh perspective. Bailey still sat, doubled over his book, a Black hunchbacked gnome. A finger forerunning his eyes along the page. Uncle Willie and Mr. Taylor were frozen like people in a book on the history of the American Negro.

"Now, come on, Brother Taylor." Momma was pressing a bowl of soup on him. "You may not be hungry, but take this for nourishment." Her voice had the tender concern of a healthy person speaking to an invalid, and her plain statement rang thrillingly true: "I'm thankful." Bailey came out of his absorption and went to wash his hands.

"Willie, say the blessing." Momma set Bailey's bowl down and bowed her head. During grace, Bailey stood in the doorway, a figure of obedience, but I knew his mind was on Tom Sawyer and Jim as mine would have been on Jane Eyre and Mr. Rochester, but for the glittering eyes of wizened old Mr. Taylor.

Our guest dutifully took a few spoonfuls of soup and bit a semicircle in the bread, then put his bowl on the floor. Something in the fire held his attention as we ate noisily.

Noticing his withdrawal, Momma said, "It don't do for you to take on so, I know you all was together a long time—"

Uncle Willie said, "Forty years."

"—but it's been around six months since she's gone to her rest... and you got to keep faith. He never gives us more than we can bear." The statement heartened Mr. Taylor. He picked up his bowl again and raked his spoon through the thick soup.

Momma saw that she had made some contact, so she went on, "You had a whole lot of good years. Got to be grateful for them. Only thing is, it's a pity you all didn't have some children."

If my head had been down I would have missed Mr. Taylor's metamorphosis. It was not a change that came by steps but rather, it seemed to me, of a sudden. His bowl was on the floor with a thud, and his body leaned toward Momma from the hips. However, his face was the most striking feature of all. The brown expanse seemed to darken with life, as if an inner agitation played under his thin skin. The mouth, opened to show the long teeth, was a dark room furnished with a few white chairs.

"Children." He gum-balled the word around in his empty mouth, "Yes, sir, children." Bailey (and I), used to be addressed so, looked at him expectantly.

"That's what she want." His eyes were vital, and straining to jump from the imprisoning sockets. "That's what she said. Children."

The air was weighted and thick. A bigger house had been set on our roof and was imperceptibly pushing us into the ground.

Momma asked, in her nice-folks voice, "What who said, Brother Taylor?" She knew the answer. We all knew the answer.

"Florida." His little wrinkled hands were making fists, then straightening, then making fists again. "She said it just last night."

Bailey and I looked at each other and I hunched my chair closer to him. "Said 'I want some children.' " When he pitched his already high voice to what he considered a feminine level, or at any rate to his wife's, Miz Florida's, level, it streaked across the room, zigzagging like lightning.

Uncle Willie had stopped eating and was regarding him with something like pity. "Maybe you was dreaming, Brother Taylor. Could have been a dream."

Momma came in placatingly. "That's right. You know, the children was reading me something th'other day. Say folks dream about whatever was on their mind when they went to sleep."

Mr. Taylor jerked himself up. "It wasn't not no dream. I was as wide awake as I am this very minute." He was angry and the tension increased his little mask of strength.

"I'll tell you what happened."

Oh, Lord, a ghost story. I hated and dreaded the long winter nights when late customers came to the Store to sit around the heater roasting peanuts and trying to best each other in telling lurid tales of ghosts and hants, banshees and juju, voodoo and other anti-life stories. But a real one, that happened to a real person, and last night. It was going to be intolerable. I got up and walked to the window.

Mrs. Florida Taylor's funeral in June came on the heels of our final exams. Bailey and Louise and I had done very well and were pleased with ourselves and each other. The summer stretched golden in front of us with promises of picnics and fish frys, blackberry hunts and croquet games till dark. It would have taken a personal loss to penetrate my sense of well-being. I had met and loved the Bronte sisters, and had replaced Kipling's "If" with "Invictus." My friendship with Louise was solidified over jacks, hopscotch and confessions, deep and dark, exchanged often after many a "Cross your heart you won't tell?" I never talked about St. Louis to her, and had generally come to believe that the nightmare with its attendant guilt and fear hadn't really happened to me. It happened to a nasty little girl, years and years before, who had no claim on me at all.

At first the news that Mrs. Taylor was dead did not strike me as a particularly newsy bit of information. As children do, I thought that since she was very old she had only one thing to do, and that was to die. She was a pleasant enough woman, with her steps made mincing by age and her little hands like gentle claws that liked to touch young skin. Each time she came to the Store, I was forced to go up to her, while she raked her yellow nails down my cheeks. "You sure got a pretty complexion." It was a rare compliment in a world of very few such words of praise, so it balanced being touched by the dry fingers.

"You going to the funeral, Sister." Momma wasn't asking a question.

Momma said, "You going 'cause Sister Taylor thought so much of you she left you her yellow brooch." (She wouldn't say "gold," because it wasn't). "She told Brother Taylor, 'I want Sis Henderson's grandbaby to have my gold brooch.' So you'll have to go."

I had followed a few coffins up the hill from the church to the cemetery, but because Momma said I was tenderhearted I had never been forced to sit through a funeral service. At eleven years old, death is more unreal than frightening. It seemed a waste of a good afternoon to sit in church for a silly old brooch, which was not only not gold but was too old for me to wear. But if Momma said I had to go it was certain that I would be there.

The mourners on the front benches sat in a blue-serge, black-crepe-dress gloom. A funeral hymn made its way around the church tediously but successfully. It eased into the heart of every gay thought, into the care of each happy memory. Shattering the light and hopeful: "On the other side of Jordan, there is a peace for the weary, there is a peace for me." The inevitable destination of all living things seemed but a short step away. I had never considered before that dying, death, dead, passed away, were words and phrases that might be even faintly connected with me.

But on that onerous day, oppressed beyond relief, my own mortality was borne in upon me on sluggish tides of doom.

No sooner had the mournful song run its course than the minister took to the altar and delivered a sermon that in my state gave little comfort. Its subject was, "Thou art my good and faithful servant with whom I am well pleased." His voice enweaved itself through the somber vapors left by the dirge. In a monotonous tone he warned the listeners that "this day might be your last," and the best insurance against dying a sinner was to "make yourself right with God" so that on the fateful day He would say, "Thou art my good and faithful servant with whom I am well pleased."

After he had put the fear of the cold grave under our skins, he began to speak of Mrs. Taylor, "A godly woman, who gave to the poor, visited the sick, tithed to the church and in general lived a life of goodliness." At this point he began to talk directly to the coffin, which I had noticed upon my arrival and had studiously avoided thereafter.

"I hungered and you gave me to eat. I was thirsty and you gave me to drink. I was sick and you visited me. In prison, and you left me not. Inasmuch as you have done it unto the least of one of these, you have done it unto Me. "He bounded off the dais and approached the velvet gray box. With an imperious gesture, he snatched the gray cloth off the open flap and gazed downward into the mystery.

"Sleep on, thy graceful soul, till Christ calls you to come forth into His bright heaven."

He continued speaking directly to the dead woman, and I half wished she would rise up and answer him, offended by the coarseness of his approach. A scream burst from Mr. Taylor. He stood up suddenly and lengthened his arms toward the minister, the coffin and his wife's corpse. For a long minute he hovered, his back to the church as the instructive words kept falling around the room, rich with promise, full with warnings. Momma and other ladies caught him in time to bring him back to the bench, where he quickly folded upon himself like a Br'er Rabbit rag doll.

Mr. Taylor and the high church officials were the first to file around the bier to wave farewell to the departed and get a glimpse of what lay in store for all men. Then on heavy feet, made more ponderous by the guilt of the living viewing the dead, the adult church marched up to the coffin and back to their seats. Their faces, which showed apprehension before reaching the coffin, revealed, on the way down the opposite aisle, a final confirmation of their fears. Watching them was a little like peeping through a window when the shade is not drawn flush. Although I didn't try, it was impossible not to record their roles in the drama.

102

And then a black-dressed usher stuck her hand out woodenly toward the children's rows. There was the shifty rustling of unreadiness but finally a boy of fourteen led us off and I dared not hang back, as much as I hated the idea of seeing Mrs. Taylor. Up the aisle, the moans and screams merged with the sickening smell of woolen black clothes worn in summer weather and green leaves wilting over yellow flowers. I couldn't distinguish whether I was smelling the clutching sound of misery or hearing the cloying odor of death.

It would have been easier to see her through the gauze, but instead I looked down on the stark face that seemed suddenly so empty and evil. It knew secrets that I never wanted to share. The cheeks had fallen back to the ears and a solicitous mortician had put lipstick on the black mouth. The scent of decay was sweet and clasping. It groped for life with a hunger both greedy and hateful. But it was hypnotic. I wanted to be off but my shoes had glued themselves to the floor and I had to hold on to the sides of the coffin to remain standing. The unexpected halt in the moving line caused the children to press upon each other, and whispers of no small intent reached my ears.

"Move along, Sister, move along." It was Momma. Her voice tugged at my will and someone pushed from the rear, so I was freed.

Instantly I surrendered myself to the grimness of death. The change it had been able to effect in Mrs. Taylor showed that its strength could not be resisted. Her high-pitched voice, which parted the air in the Store, was forever stilled, and the plump brown face had been deflated and patted flat like a cow's ordurous dropping.

The coffin was carried on a horse-drawn wagon to the cemetery, and all the way I communed with death's angels, questioning their choice of time, place and person.

For the first time the burial ceremony had meaning for me.

"Ashes to ashes and dust to dust." It was certain that Mrs. Taylor was returning to the earth from whence she came. In fact, upon considering, I concluded that she had looked like a mud baby, lying on the white satin of her velvet coffin. A mud baby, molded into form by creative children on a rainy day, soon to run back into the loose earth.

The memory of the grim ceremony had been so real to me that I was surprised to look up and see Momma and Uncle Willie eating by the stove. They were neither anxious nor hesitant, as if they knew a man has to say what he has to say. But I didn't want to hear any of it, and the wind, allying itself with me, threatened the chinaberry tree outside the back door.

"Last night, after I said my prayers, I lay down on the bed. Well, you know it's the same bed she died on." Oh, if he'd shut up. Momma said, "Sister, sit down and eat your soup. Cold night like this you need something hot in your stomach. Go on, Brother Taylor. Please." I sat down as near Bailey as possible.

"Well, something told me to open my eyes."

"What kind of something?" Momma asked, not laying down her spoon.

"Yes, sir," Uncle Willie explained, "there can be a good something and there can be a bad something."

"Well, I wasn't sure, so I figured better open 'em, 'cause it could have been, well, either one. I did, and the first thing, I saw little baby angel. It was just as fat as a butterball, and laughing, eyes blue, blue, blue."

Uncle Willie asked, "A baby angel?"

"Yes, sir, and it was laughing right in my face. Then I heard this long moan, 'Agh–h–h–' Well, as you say, Sister Henderson, we been together over forty years. I know Florida's voice. I wasn't scared right then. I called 'Florida?' Then that angel laughed harder and the moan got louder."

I set my bowl down and got closer to Bailey. Mrs. Taylor had been a very pleasant woman, smiling all the time and patient. The only thing that jarre and bothered me when she came in the Store was her voice. Like near-deaf people, she screamed, half not hearing what she was saying and partly hoping her listeners would reply in kind. That was when she was living. The thought of that voice coming out of the grave and all the way down the hill from the cemetery and hanging over my head was enough to straighten my hair.

"Yes, sir." He was looking at the stove and the red glow fell on his face. It seemed as if he had a fire going inside his head. "First I called, 'Florida, Florida. What do you want?' And that devilish angel kept on laughing to beat the band." Mr. Taylor tried to laugh and only succeeded in looking frightened. " 'I want some...' That's when she said 'I want some.' " He made his voice sound like the wind, if the wind had bronchial pneumonia. He wheezed," 'I want some chi–il–dren.' "

Bailey and I met halfway on the drafty floor.

Momma said, "Now, Brother Taylor, could be you was dreaming. You know, they say whatever you goes to bed with on your mind..."

"No, ma'am, Sister Henderson, I was as wide awake as I am right now."

"Did she let you see her?" Uncle Willie had a dreamy look on his face.

"No, Willie, all I seed was that fat little white baby angel. But wasn't no mistaking that voice... 'I want some children.' "

The cold wind had frozen my feet and my spine, and Mr. Taylor's impersonation had chilled my blood.

Momma said, "Sister, go bring the long fork to take the potatoes out."

"Ma'am?" Surely she didn't mean the long fork that hung on the wall behind the kitchen stove—a scary million miles away.

"I said, go get the fork. The potatoes are burning."

I unwound my legs from the gripping fear and almost tripped onto the stove. Momma said, "That child would stumble over the pattern in a rug. Go on, Brother Taylor, did she say any more?"

I didn't want to hear it if she did, but I wasn't eager to leave the lighted room where my family sat around the friendly fire.

"Well, she said 'Aaah' a few more times and then that angel started to walk off the ceiling. I tell you I was purt' near scared stiff."

I had reached the no man's ocean of darkness. No great decision was called for. I knew it would be torturous to go through the thick blackness of Uncle Willie's bedroom, but it would be easier than staying around to hear the ghoulish story. Also, I couldn't afford to aggravate Momma. When she was displeased she made me sleep on the edge of the bed and that night I knew I needed to be close to her.

One foot into the darkness and the sense of detachment from reality nearly made me panic. The idea came to me that I might never get out into the light again. Quickly I found the door leading back to the familiar, but as I opened it the awful story reached out and tried to grab my ears. I closed the door.

Naturally, I believed in hants and ghosts and "thangs." Having been raised by a super-religious Southern Negro grandmother, it would have been abnormal had I not been superstitious.

The trip to the kitchen and back could not have taken more than two minutes, yet in that time I tramped through swampy cemeteries, climbed over dusty gravestones and eluded litters of night-black cats.

Back in the family circle, I remarked to myself how like a cyclopean eye was the belly of the red-hot stove.

"It reminded me of the time when my daddy died. You know we're very close." Mr. Taylor had hypnotized himself into the eerie world of horrors.

I broke into his reminiscences. "Momma, here's the fork." Bailey had lain down on his side behind the stove and his eyes were shining. He was more fascinated with Mr. Taylor's morbid interest in his story than with the tale itself.

Momma put her hand on my arm and said, "You shaking, Sister. What's the matter?" My skin still rippled from the experience of fear.

Uncle Willie laughed and said, "Maybe she was scared to go in the kitchen."

His high little laugh didn't fool me. Everyone was uneasy at being beckoned into the unknown.

"No sir, I ain't never seen nothing so clear as that little angel baby." His jaws were scissoring mechanically on the already mushy sweet potatoes. "Just laughing like a house on fire. What you reckon it mean, Sister Henderson?"

Momma had reared back in her rocking chair, a half smile on her face, "If you sure you wasn't dreaming, Brother Taylor..."

"I was as wide awake as I am"—he was becoming angry again—"as I am right now."

"Well, then, maybe it means—"

"I ought to know when I'm asleep and when I'm awake."

"—maybe it mean Sister Florida wants you to work with the children in the church."

"One thing I always used to tell Florida, people won't let you get your words in edgewise—"

"Could be she's trying to tell you—"

"I ain't crazy, you know. My mind's just as good as it was."

"—to take a Sunday school class—"

"Thirty years ago. If I say I was awake when I saw that little fat angel, then people ought to—"

"Sunday school need more teachers. Lord knows that's so."

"—believe me when I say so."

Their remarks and responses were like a Ping-Pong game with each volley clearing the net and flying back to the opposition. The sense of what they were saying became lost, and only the exercise remained. The exchange was conducted with the certainty of a measured hoedown and had the jerkiness of Monday's wash snapping in the wind —now cracking east, then west, with only the intent to whip the dampness out of the cloth.

Within a few minutes the intoxication of doom had fled, as if it had never been, and Momma was encouraging Mr. Taylor to take in one of the Jenkins boys to help him with his farm. Uncle Willie was nodding at the fire, and Bailey had escaped back to the calm adventures of Huckleberry Finn. The change in the room was remarkable. Shadows which had lengthened and darkened over the bed in the corner had disappeared or revealed themselves as dark images of familiar chairs and such. The light which dashed on the ceiling steadied, and imitated rabbits rather than lions, and donkeys instead of ghouls.

I laid a pallet for Mr. Taylor in Uncle Willie's room and crawled under Momma, who I knew for the first time was so good and righteous she could command the fretful spirits, as Jesus had commanded the sea. "Peace, be still."

106

23

The children in Stamps trembled visibly with anticipation. Some adults were excited too, but to be certain the whole young population had come down with graduation epidemic. Large classes were graduating from both the grammar school and the high school. Even those who were years removed from their own day of glorious release were anxious to help with preparations as a kind of dry run. The junior students who were moving into the vacating classes' chairs were tradition-bound to show their talents for leadership and management. They strutted through the school and around the campus exerting pressure on the lower grades. Their authority was so new that occasionally if they pressed a little too hard it had to be overlooked. After all, next term was coming, and it never hurt a sixth grader to have a play sister in the eighth grade, or a tenth-year student to be able to call a twelfth grader Bubba. So all was endured in a spirit of shared understanding. But the graduating classes themselves were the nobility. Like travelers with exotic destinations on their minds, the graduates were remarkably forgetful. They came to school without their books, or tablets or even pencils. Volunteers fell over themselves to secure replacements for the missing equipment. When accepted, the willing workers might or might not be thanked, and it was of no importance to the pregraduation rites. Even teachers were respectful of the now quiet and aging seniors, and tended to speak to them, if not as equals, as beings only slightly lower than themselves. After tests were returned and grades given, the student body, which acted like an extended family, knew who did well, who excelled, and what piteous ones had failed.

Unlike the white high school, Lafayette County Training School distinguished itself by having neither lawn, nor hedges, nor tennis court, nor climbing ivy. Its two buildings (main classrooms, the grade school and home economics) were set on a dirt hill with no fence to limit either its boundaries or those of bordering farms. There was a large expanse to the left of the school which was used alternately as a baseball diamond or a basketball court. Rusty hoops on the swaying poles represented the permanent recreational equipment, although bats and balls could be borrowed from the P. E.

teacher if the borrower was qualified and if the diamond wasn't occupied.

Over this rocky area relieved by a few shady tall persimmon trees the graduating class walked. The girls often held hands and no longer bothered to speak to the lower students. There was a sadness about them, as if this old world was not their home and they were bound for higher ground. The boys, on the other hand, had become more friendly, more outgoing. A decided change from the closed attitude they projected while studying for finals. Now they seemed not ready to give up the old school, the familiar paths and classrooms. Only, a small percentage would be continuing on to college—one of the South's A & M (agricultural and mechanical) schools, which trained Negro youths to be carpenters, farmers, handymen, masons, maids, cooks and baby nurses. Their future rode heavily on their shoulders, and blinded them to the collective joy that had pervaded the lives of the boys and girls in the grammar school graduating class.

Parents who could afford it had ordered new shoes and ready-made clothes for themselves from Sears and Roebuck or Montgomery Ward. They also engaged the best seamstresses to make the floating graduating dresses and to cut down secondhand pants which would be pressed to a military slickness for the important event.

Oh, it was important, all right. Whitefolks would attend the ceremony, and two or three would speak of God and home, and the Southern way of life, and Mrs. Parsons, the principal's wife, would play the graduation march while the lower-grade graduates paraded down the aisles and took their seats below the platform. The high school seniors would wait in empty classrooms to make their dramatic entrance.

In the Store I was the person of the moment. The birthday girl. The center. Bailey had graduated the year before, although to do so he had had to forfeit all pleasures to make up for his time lost in Baton Rouge.

My class was wearing butter-yellow piqué dresses, and Momma launched out on mine. She smocked the yoke into tiny crisscrossing puckers, then shirred the rest of the bodice. Her dark fingers ducked in and out of the lemony cloth as she embroidered raised daisies around the hem. Before she considered herself finished she had added a crocheted cuff on the puff sleeves, and a pointy crocheted collar.

I was going to be lovely. A walking model of all the various styles of fine hand sewing and it didn't worry me that I was only twelve years old and merely graduating from the eighth grade. Besides, many teachers in Arkansas Negro schools had only that diploma and were licensed to impart wisdom.

The days had become longer and more noticeable. The faded beige of former times had been replaced with strong and sure colors. I began to see my classmates' clothes, their skin tones, and the dust that waved off pussy willows. Clouds that lazed across the sky were objects of great concern to me. Their shiftier shapes might have held a message that in my new happiness and with a little bit of time I'd soon decipher. During that period I looked at the arch of heaven so religiously my neck kept a steady ache. I had taken to smiling more often, and my jaws hurt from the unaccustomed activity. Between the two physical sore spots, I suppose I could have been uncomfortable, but that was not the case. As a member of the winning team (the graduating class of 1940) I had out-distanced unpleasant sensations by miles. I was headed for the freedom of open fields.

Youth and social approval allied themselves with me and we trammeled memories of slights and insults. The wind of our swift passage remodeled my features. Lost tears were pounded to mud and then to dust. Years of withdrawal were brushed aside and left behind, as hanging ropes of parasitic moss.

My work alone had awarded me a top place and I was going to be one of the first called in the graduating ceremonies. On the classroom blackboard, as well as on the bulletin board in the auditorium, there were blue stars and white stars and red stars. No absences, no tardinesses, and my academic work was among the best of the year. I could say the preamble to the Constitution even faster than Bailey. We timed ourselves often: "WethepeopleoftheUnited-Statesinordertoformamoreperfectunion..." I had memorized the Presidents of the United States from Washington to Roosevelt in chronological as well as alphabetical order.

My hair pleased me too. Gradually the black mass had lengthened and thickened, so that it kept at last to its braided pattern, and I didn't have to yank my scalp off when I tried to comb it.

Louise and I had rehearsed the exercises until we tired out ourselves. Henry Reed was class valedictorian. He was a small, very black boy with hooded eyes, a long, broad nose and an oddly shaped head. I had admired him for years because each term he and I vied for the best grades in our class. Most often he bested me, but instead of being disappointed I was pleased that we shared top places between us. Like many Southern Black children, he lived with his grandmother, who was as strict as Momma and as kind as she knew how to be. He was courteous, respectful and soft-spoken to elders, but on the playground he chose to play the roughest games. I admired him. Anyone, I reckoned, sufficiently afraid or sufficiently dull could be polite. But to be able to operate at a top level with both adults and children was admirable.

His valedictory speech was entitled "To Be or Not to Be." The rigid tenth-grade teacher had helped him write it. He'd been working on the dramatic stresses for months.

The weeks until graduation were filled with heady activities. A group of small children were to be presented in a play about buttercups and daisies and bunny rabbits. They could be heard throughout the building practicing their hops and their little songs that sounded like silver bells. The older girls (nongraduates, of course) were assigned the task of making refreshments for the night's festivities. A tangy scent of ginger, cinnamon, nutmeg and chocolate wafted around the home economics building as the budding cooks made samples for themselves and their teachers.

In every corner of the workshop, axes and saws split fresh timber as the woodshop boys made sets and stage scenery. Only the graduates were left out of the general bustle. We were free to sit in the library at the back of the building or look in quite detachedly, naturally, on the measures being taken for our event.

Even the minister preached on graduation the Sunday before. His subject was, "Let your light so shine that men will see your good works and praise your Father, Who is in Heaven." Although the sermon was purported to be addressed to us, he used the occasion to speak to backsliders, gamblers and general ne'er-do-wells. But since he had called our names at the beginning of the service we were mollified.

Among Negroes the tradition was to give presents to children going only from one grade to another. How much more important this was when the person was graduating at the top of the class. Uncle Willie and Momma had sent away for a Mickey Mouse watch like Bailey's. Louise gave me four embroidered handkerchiefs. (I gave her three crocheted doilies.) Mrs. Sneed, the minister's wife, made me an underskirt to wear for graduation, and nearly every customer gave me a nickel or maybe even a dime with the instruction "Keep on moving to higher ground," or some such encouragement.

Amazingly the great day finally dawned and I was out of bed before I knew it. I threw open the back door to see it more clearly, but Momma said, "Sister, come away from that door and put your robe on."

I hoped the memory of that morning would never leave me. Sunlight was itself still young, and the day had none of the insistence maturity would bring it in a few hours. In my robe and barefoot in the backyard, under cover of going to see about my new beans, I gave myself up to the gentle warmth and thanked God that no matter what evil I had done in my life, He had allowed me to live to see this day. Somewhere in my fatalism I had expected to die, accidentally, and

110

never have the chance to walk up the stairs in the auditorium and gracefully receive my hard-earned diploma. Out of God's merciful bosom I had won reprieve.

Bailey came out in his robe and gave me a box wrapped in Christmas paper. He said he had saved his money for months to pay for it. It felt like a box of chocolates, but I knew Bailey wouldn't save money to buy candy when we had all we could want under our noses.

He was as proud of the gift as I. It was a soft-leather-bound copy of a collection of poems by Edgar Allan Poe, or, as Bailey and I called him, "Eap." I turned to "Annabel Lee" and we walked up and down the garden rows, the cool dirt between our toes, reciting the beautifully sad lines.

Momma made a Sunday breakfast although it was only Friday. After we fnished the blessing, I opened my eyes to find the watch on my plates. It was a dream of a day. Everything went smoothly and to my credit. I didn't have to be reminded or scolded for anything. Near evening I was too jittery to attend to chores, so Bailey volunteered to do all before his bath.

Days before, we had made a sign for the Store, and as we turned out the lights Momma hung the cardboard over the doorknob. It read clearly: CLOSED. GRADUATION.

My dress fitted perfectly and everyone said that I looked like a sunbeam in it. On the hill, going toward the school, Bailey walked behind with Uncle Willie, who muttered, "Go on, Ju." He wanted him to walk ahead with us because it embarrassed him to have to walk so slowly. Bailey said he'd let the ladies walk together, and the men would bring up the rear. We all laughed, nicely.

Little children dashed by out of the dark like fireflies. Their crepe-paper dresses and butterfly wings were not made for running and we heard more than one rip, dryly, and the regretful "uh uh" that followed.

The school blazed without gaiety. The windows seemed cold and unfriendly from the lower hill. A sense of ill-fated timing crept over me, and if Momma hadn't reached for my hand I would have drifted back to Bailey and Uncle Willie, and possibly beyond. She made a few slow jokes about my feet getting cold, and tugged me along to the now-strange building.

Around the front steps, assurance came back. There were my fellow "greats," the graduating class. Hair brushed back, legs oiled, new dresses and pressed pleats, fresh pocket handkerchiefs and little handbags, all homesewn. Oh, we were up to snuff, all right. I joined my comrades and didn't even see my family go in to find seats in the crowded auditorium.

The school band struck up a march and all classes filed in as had been rehearsed. We stood in front of our seats, as assigned, and on a signal from the choir director, we sat. No sooner had this been accomplished than the band started to play the national anthem. We rose again and sang the song, after which we recited the pledge of allegiance. We remained standing for a brief minute before the choir director and the principal signaled to us, rather desperately I thought, to take our seats. The command was so unusual that our carefully rehearsed and smooth-running machine was thrown off. For a full minute we fumbled for our chairs and bumped into each other awkwardly. Habits change or solidify under pressure, so in our state of nervous tension we had been ready to follow our usual assembly pattern: the American national anthem, then the pledge of allegiance, then the song every Black person I knew called the Negro National Anthem. All done in the same key, with the same passion and most often standing on the same foot.

Finding my seat at last, I was overcome with a presentiment of worse things to come. Something unrehearsed, unplanned, was going to happen, and we were going to be made to look bad. I distinctly remember being explicit in the choice of pronoun. It was "we," the graduating class, the unit, that concerned me then.

The principal welcomed "parents and friends" and asked the Baptist minister to lead us in prayer. His invocation was brief and punchy, and for a second I thought we were getting back on the high road to right action. When the principal came back to the dais, however, his voice had changed. Sounds always affected me profoundly and the principal's voice was one of my favorites. During assembly it melted and lowed weakly into the audience. It had not been in my plan to listen to him, but my curiosity was piqued and I straightened up to give him my attention.

He was talking about Booker T. Washington, our "late great leader," who said we can be as close as the fingers on the hand, etc... Then he said a few vague things about friendship and the friendship of kindly people to those less fortunate than themselves. With that his voice nearly faded, thin, away. Like a river diminishing to a stream and then to a trickle. But he cleared his throat and said, "Our speaker tonight, who is also our friend, came from Texarkana to deliver the commencement address, but due to the irregularity of the train schedule, he's going to, as they say, 'speak and run.'" He said that we understood and wanted the man to know that we were most grateful for the time he was able to give us and then something about how we were willing always to adjust to another's program, and without more ado—"I give you Mr. Edward Donleavy."

Not one but two white men came through the door offstage. The

112

shorter one walked to the speaker's platform, and the tall one moved over to the center seat and sat down. But that was our principal's seat, and already occupied. The dislodged gentleman bounced around for a long breath or two before the Baptist minister gave him his chair, then with more dignity than the situation deserved, the minister walked off the stage.

Donleavy looked at the audience once (on reflection, I'm sure that he wanted only to reassure himself that we were really there), adjusted his glasses and began to read from a sheaf of papers.

He was glad "to be here and to see the work going on just as it was in the other schools."

At the first "Amen" from the audience I willed the offender to immediate death by choking on the word. But Amens and Yes, sir's began to fall around the room like rain through a ragged umbrella.

He told us of the wonderful changes we children in Stamps had in store. The Central School (naturally, the white school was Central) had already been granted improvements that would be in use in the fall. A well-known artist was coming from Little Rock to teach art to them. They were going to have the newest microscopes and chemistry equipment for their laboratory. Mr. Donleavy didn't leave us long in the dark over who made these improvements available to Central High. Nor were we to be ignored in the general betterment scheme he had in mind.

He said that he had pointed out to people at a very high level that one of the first-line football tacklers at Arkansas Agricultural and Mechanical College had graduated from good old Lafayette County Training School. Here fewer Amen's were heard. Those few that did break through lay dully in the air with the heaviness of habit.

He went on to praise us. He went on to say how he had bragged that "one of the best basketball players at Fisk sank his first ball right here at Lafayette County Training School."

The white kids were going to have a chance to become Galileos and Madame Curies and Edisons and Gauguins, and our boys (the girls weren't even in on it) would try to be Jesse Owenses and Joe Louises.

Owens and the Brown Bomber were great heroes in our world, but what school official in the white-goddom of Little Rock had the right to decide that those two men must be our only heroes? Who decided that for Henry Reed to become a scientist he had to work like George Washington Carver, as a bootblack, to buy a lousy microscope? Bailey was obviously always going to be too small to be an athlete, so which concrete angel glued to what country seat had decided that if my brother wanted to become a lawyer he had to first pay penance for his skin by picking cotton and hoeing corn and studying correspondence books at night for twenty years?

The man's dead words fell like bricks around the auditorium and too many settled in my belly. Constrained by hard-learned manners I couldn't look behind me, but to my left and right the proud graduating class of 1940 had dropped their heads. Every girl in my row had found something new to do with her handkerchief. Some folded the tiny squares into love knots, some into triangles, but most were wadding them, then pressing them flat on their yellow laps.

On the dais, the ancient tragedy was being replayed. Professor Parsons sat, a sculptor's reject, rigid. His large, heavy body seemed devoid of will or willingness, and his eyes said he was no longer with us. The other teachers examined the flag (which was draped stage right) or their notes, or the windows which opened on our now-famous playing diamond.

Graduation, the hush-hush magic time of frills and gifts and congratulations and diplomas, was finished for me before my name was called. The accomplishment was nothing. The meticulous maps, drawn in three colors of ink, learning and spelling decasyllabic words, memorizing the whole of *The Rape of Lucrece*—it was for nothing. Donleavy had exposed us.

We were maids and farmers, handymen and washerwomen, and anything higher that we aspired to was farcical and presumptuous.

Then I wished that Gabriel Prosser and Nat Turner had killed all whitefolks in their beds and that Abraham Lincoln had been assassinated before the signing of the Emancipation Proclamation, and that Harriet Tubman had been killed by that blow on her head and Christopher Columbus had drowned in the *Santa Maria*.

It was awful to be Negro and have no control over my life. It was brutal to be young and already trained to sit quietly and listen to charges brought against my color with no chance of defense. We should all be dead. I thought I should like to see us all dead, one on top of the other. A pyramid of flesh with the whitefolks on the bottom, as the broad base, then the Indians with their silly tomahawks and teepees and wigwams and treaties, the Negroes with their mops and recipes and cotton sacks and spirituals sticking out of their mouths. The Dutch children should all stumble in their wooden shoes and break their necks. The French should choke to death on the Louisiana Purchase (1803) while silkworms ate all the Chinese with their stupid pigtails. As a species, we were an abomination. All of us.

Donleavy was running for election, and assured our parents that if he won we could count on having the only colored paved playing field in that part of Arkansas. Also—he never looked up to acknowledge the grunts of acceptance—also, we were bound to get some new equipment for the home economics building and the workshop.

He finished, and since there was no need to give any more than the most perfunctory thank-you's, he nodded to the men on the stage, and the tall white man who was never introduced joined him at the door. They left with the attitude that now they were off to something really important. (The graduation ceremonies at Lafayette County Training School had been a mere preliminary.)

The ugliness they left was palpable. An uninvited guest who wouldn't leave. The choir was summoned and sang a modern arrangement of "Onward, Christian Soldiers," with new words pertaining to graduates seeking their place in the world. But it didn't work. Elouise, the daughter of the Baptist minister, recited "Invictus," and I could have cried at the impertinence of "I am the master of my fate, I am the captain of my soul."

My name had lost its ring of familiarity and I had to be nudged to go and receive my diploma. All my preparations had fled. I neither marched up to the stage like a conquering Amazon, nor did I look in the audience for Bailey's nod of approval. Marguerite Johnson, I heard the name again, my honors were read, there were noises in the audience of appreciation, and I took my place on the stage as rehearsed.

I thought about colors I hated: ecru, puce, lavender, beige and black.

There was shuffling and rustling around me, then Henry Reed was giving his valedictory address, "To Be or Not to Be." Hadn't he heard the whitefolks? We couldn't be, so the question was a waste of time. Henry's voice came out clear and strong. I feared to look at him. Hadn't he got the message? There was no "nobler in the mind" for Negroes because the world didn't think we had minds, and they let us know it. "Outrageous fortune"? Now, that was a joke. When the ceremony was over I had to tell Henry Reed some things. That is, if I still cared. Not "rub," Henry, "erase." "Ah, there's the erase." Us.

Henry had been a good student in elocution. His voice rose on tides of promise and fell on waves of warnings. The English teacher had helped him to create a sermon winging through Hamlet's soliloquy. To be a man, a doer, a builder, a leader, or to be a tool, an unfunny joke, a crusher of funky toadstools. I marveled that Henry could go through with the speech as if we had a choice.

I had been listening and silently rebutting each sentence with my eyes closed; then there was a hush, which in an audience warns that something unplanned is happening. I looked up and saw Henry Reed, the conservative, the proper, the A student, turn his back to the audience and turn to us (the proud graduating class of 1940) and sing, nearly speaking,

> "Lift ev'ry voice and sing
> Till earth and heaven ring
> Ring with the harmonies of Liberty..."

It was the poem written by James Weldon Johnson. It was the music composed by J. Rosamond Johnson. It was the Negro national anthem. Out of habit we were singing it.

Our mothers and fathers stood in the dark hall and joined the hymn of encouragement. A kindergarten teacher led the small children onto the stage and the buttercups and daisies and bunny rabbits marked time and tried to follow:

> "Stony the road we trod
> Bitter the chastening rod
> Felt in the days when hope, unborn, had died.
> Yet with a steady beat
> Have not our weary feet
> Come to the place for which our fathers sighed?"

Every child I knew had learned that song with his ABC's and along with "Jesus Loves Me This I Know." But I personally had never heard it before. Never heard the words, despite the thousands of times I had sung them. Never thought they had anything to do with me.

On the other hand, the words of Patrick Henry had made such an impression on me that I had been able to stretch myself tall and trembling and say, "I know not what course others may take, but as for me, give me liberty or give me death."

And now I heard, really for the first time:

> "We have come over a way that with tears
> has been watered,
> We have come, treading our path through
> the blood of the slaughtered."

While echoes of the song shivered in the air, Henry Reed bowed his head, said "Thank you," and returned to his place in the line. The tears that slipped down many faces were not wiped away in shame.

We were on top again. As always, again. We survived. The depths had been icy and dark, but now a bright sun spoke to our souls. I was no longer simply a member of the proud graduating class of 1940; I was a proud member of the wonderful, beautiful Negro race.

Oh, Black known and unknown poets, how often have your auctioned pains sustained us? Who will compute the lonely nights made less lonely by your songs, or the empty pots made less tragic by your tales?

If we were a people much given to revealing secrets, we might raise monuments and sacrifice to the memories of our poets, but slavery cured us of that weakness. It may be enough, however, to have it said that we survive in exact relationship to the dedication of our poets (include preachers, musicians and blues singers).

24

The Angel of the candy counter had found me out at last, and was exacting excruciating penance for all the stolen Milky Ways, Mounds, Mr. Goodbars and Hersheys with Almonds. I had two cavities that were rotten to the gums. The pain was beyond the bailiwick of crushed aspirins or oil of cloves. Only one thing could help me, so I prayed earnestly that I'd be allowed to sit under the house and have the building collapse on my left jaw. Since there was no Negro dentist in Stamps, nor doctor either, for that matter, Momma had dealt with previous toothaches by pulling them out (a string tied to the tooth with the other end looped over her fist), pain killers and prayer. In this particular instance the medicine had proved ineffective; there wasn't enough enamel left to hook a string on, and the prayers were being ignored because the Balancing Angel was blocking their passage.

I lived a few days and nights in blinding pain, not so much toying with as seriously considering the idea of jumping in the well, and Momma decided I had to be taken to a dentist. The nearest Negro dentist was in Texarkana, twenty-five miles away, and I was certain that I'd be dead long before we reached half the distance. Momma said we'd go to Dr. Lincoln, right in Stamps, and he'd take care of me. She said he owed her a favor.

I knew there were a number of whitefolks in town that owed her favors. Bailey and I had seen the books which showed how she had lent money to Blacks and whites alike during the Depression, and most still owed her. But I couldn't aptly remember seeing Dr. Lincoln's name, nor had I ever heard of a Negro's going to him as a patient. However, Momma said we were going, and put water on the stove for our baths. I had never been to a doctor, so she told me that after the bath (which would make my mouth feel better) I had to put on freshly starched and ironed underclothes from inside out. The ache failed to respond to the bath, and I knew then that the pain was more serious than that which anyone had ever suffered.

Before we left the Store, she ordered me to brush my teeth and then wash my mouth with Listerine. The idea of even opening my clamped jaws increased the pain, but upon her explanation that when you go to a doctor you have to clean yourself all over, but most especially the part that's to be examined, I screwed up my courage and unlocked my teeth. The cool air in my mouth and the jarring of my molars dislodged what little remained of my reason. I had frozen to the pain, my family nearly had to tie me down to take the toothbrush away. It was no small effort to get me started on the road to the dentist. Momma spoke to all the passers-by, but didn't stop to chat. She explained over her shoulder that we were going to the doctor and she'd "pass the time of day" on our way home.

Until we reached the pond the pain was my world, an aura that haloed me for three feet around. Crossing the bridge into whitefolks' country, pieces of sanity pushed themselves forward. I had to stop moaning and start walking straight. The white towel, which was drawn under my chin and tied over my head, had to be arranged. If one was dying, it had to be done in style if the dying took place in whitefolks' part of town.

On the other side of the bridge the ache seemed to lessen as if a whitebreeze blew off the whitefolks and cushioned everything in their neighborhood—including my jaw. The gravel road was smoother, the stones smaller and the tree branches hung down around the path and nearly covered us. If the pain didn't diminish then, the familiar yet strange sights hypnotized me into believing that it had.

But my head continued to throb with the measured insistence of a bass drum, and how could a toothache pass the calaboose, hear the songs of the prisoners, their blues and laughter, and not be changed? How could one or two or even a mouthful of angry tooth roots meet a wagonload of powhitetrash children, endure their idiotic snobbery and not feel less important?

Behind the building which housed the dentist's office ran a small path used by servants and those tradespeople who catered to the butcher and Stamps' one restaurant. Momma and I followed that lane to the backstairs of Dentist Lincoln's office. The sun was bright and gave the day a hard reality as we climbed up the steps to the second floor.

Momma knocked on the back door and a young white girl opened it to show surprise at seeing us there. Momma said she wanted to see Dentist Lincoln and to tell him Annie was there. The girl closed the door firmly. Now the humiliation of hearing Momma describe herself as if she had no last name to the young white girl was equal to the physical pain. It seemed terribly unfair to have a toothache and a headache and have to bear at the same time the heavy burden of Blackness.

It was always possible that the teeth would quiet down and maybe drop out of their own accord. Momma said we would wait. We leaned in the harsh sunlight on the shaky railings of the dentist's back porch for over an hour.

He opened the door and looked at Momma. "Well, Annie, what can I do for you?"

He didn't see the towel around my jaw or notice my swollen face.

Momma said, "Dentist Lincoln. It's my grandbaby here. She got two rotten teeth that's giving her a fit."

She waited for him to acknowledge the truth of her statement. He made no comment, orally or facially.

"She had this toothache purt' near four days now, and today I said, 'Young lady, you going to the Dentist.'"

"Annie?"

"Yes, sir, Dentist Lincoln."

He was choosing words the way people hunt for shells. "Annie, you know I don't treat nigra, colored people."

"I know, Dentist Lincoln. But this here is just my little grandbaby, and she ain't gone be no trouble to you..."

"Annie, everybody has a policy. In this world you have to have a policy. Now, my policy is I don't treat colored people."

The sun had baked the oil out of Momma's skin and melted the Vaseline in her hair. She shone greasily as she leaned out of the dentist's shadow.

"Seem like to me, Dentist Lincoln, you might look after her, she ain't nothing but a little mite. And seems like maybe you owe me a favor or two."

He reddened slightly. "Favor or no favor. The money has all been repaid to you and that's the end of it. Sorry, Annie." He had his hand on the doorknob. "Sorry." His voice was a bit kinder on the second "Sorry," as if he really was.

Momma said, "I wouldn't press on you like this for myself but I can't take No. Not for my grandbaby. When you come to borrow my money you didn't have to beg. You asked me, and I lent it. Now, it wasn't my policy. I ain't no moneylender, but you stood to lose this building and I tried to help you out."

"It's been paid, and raising your voice won't make me change my mind. My policy..." He let go of the door and stepped nearer Momma. The three of us were crowded on the small landing. "Annie, my policy is I'd rather stick my hand in a dog's mouth than in a nigger's."

He had never once looked at me. He turned his back and went through the door into the cool beyond. Momma backed up inside herself for a few minutes. I forgot everything except her face which was almost a new one to me. She leaned over and took the doorknob, and in her everyday soft voice she said, "Sister, go on downstairs. Wait for me. I'll be there directly."

Under the most common of circumstances I knew it did no good to argue with Momma. So I walked down the steep stairs, afraid to look back and afraid not to do so. I turned as the door slammed, and she was gone.

Momma walked in that room as if she owned it. She shoved that silly nurse aside with one hand and strode into the dentist's office. He was sitting in his chair, sharpening his mean instruments and putting extra sting into his medicines. Her eyes were blazing like live coals and her arms had doubled themselves in length. He looked up at her just before she caught him by the collar of his white jacket.

"Stand up when you see a lady, you contemptuous scoundrel." Her tongue had thinned and the words rolled off well enunciated. Enunciated and sharp like little claps of thunder.

The dentist had no choice but to stand at R.O.T.C. attention. His head dropped after a minute and his voice was humble. "Yes, ma'am, Mrs. Henderson."

"You knave, do you think you acted like a gentleman, speaking to me like that in front of my granddaughter?" She didn't shake him, although she had the power. She simply held him upright.

"No, ma'am, Mrs. Henderson."

"No, ma'am, Mrs. Henderson, what?" Then she did give him the tiniest of shakes, but because of her strength the action set his head and arms to shaking loose on the ends of his body. He stuttered much worse than Uncle Willie. "No, ma'am, Mrs. Henderson, I'm sorry."

With just an edge of disgust showing, Momma slung him back in his dentist's chair. "Sorry is as sorry does, and you're about the sorriest dentist I ever laid my eyes on." (She could afford to slip into the vernacular because she had such eloquent command of English.)

"I didn't ask you to apologize in front of Marguerite, because I don't want her to know my power, but I order you, now and herewith. Leave Stamps by sundown."

"Mrs. Henderson, I can't get my equipment..." He was shaking terribly now.

"Now, that brings me to my second order. You will never again practice dentistry. Never! When you get settled in your next place, you will be a vegetarian caring for dogs with the mange, cats with the cholera and cows with the epizootic. Is that clear?"

The saliva ran down his chin and his eyes filled with tears. "Yes, ma'am. Thank you for not killing me. Thank you, Mrs. Henderson."

Momma pulled herself back from being ten feet tall with eight-foot arms and said, "You're welcome for nothing, you varlet, I wouldn't waste a killing on the likes of you."

On her way out she waved her handkerchief at the nurse and turned her into a crocus sack of chicken feed.

Momma looked tired when she came down the stairs, but who wouldn't be tired if they had gone through what she had. She came close to me and adjusted the towel under my jaw (I had forgotten the toothache; I only knew that she made her hands gentle in order not to awaken the pain). She took my hand. Her voice never changed. "Come on, Sister."

I reckoned we were going home where she would concoct a brew to eliminate the pain and maybe give me new teeth too. New teeth that would grow overnight out of my gums. She led me toward the drugstore, which was in the opposite direction from the Store. "I'm taking you to Dentist Baker in Texarkana."

I was glad after all that that I had bathed and put on Mum and Cashmere Bouquet talcum powder. It was a wonderful surprise. My toothache had quieted to solemn pain, Momma had obliterated the evil white man, and we were going on a trip to Texarkana, just the two of us.

On the Greyhound she took an inside seat in the back, and I sat beside her. I was so proud of being her granddaughter and sure that some of her magic must have come down to me. She asked if I was scared. I only shook my head and leaned over on her cool brown upper arm. There was no chance that a dentist, especially a Negro dentist, would dare hurt me then. Not with Momma there. The trip was uneventful, except that she put her arm around me, which was very unusual for Momma to do.

The dentist showed me the medicine and the needle before he deadened my gums, but if he hadn't I wouldn't have worried. Momma stood right behind him. Her arms were folded and she checked on everything he did. The teeth were extracted and she bought me an ice cream cone from the side window of a drug counter. The trip back to Stamps was quiet, except that I had to spit into a very small empty snuff can which she had gotten for me and it was difficult with the bus humping and jerking on our country roads.

At home, I was given a warm salt solution, and when I washed out

121

my mouth I showed Bailey the empty holes, where the clotted blood sat like filling in a pie crust. He said I was quite brave, and that was my cue to reveal our confrontation with the peckerwood dentist and Momma's incredible powers.

I had to admit that I didn't hear the conversation, but what else could she have said than what I said she said? What else done? He agreed with my analysis in a lukewarm way, and I happily (after all, I'd been sick) flounced into the Store. Momma was preparing our evening meal and Uncle Willie leaned on the door sill. She gave her version.

"Dentist Lincoln got right uppity. Said he'd rather put his hand in a dog's mouth. And when I reminded him of the favor, he brushed it off like a piece of lint. Well, I sent Sister downstairs and went inside. I hadn't never been in his office before, but I found the door to where he takes out teeth, and him and the nurse was in there thick as thieves. I just stood there till he caught sight of me. "Crash bang the pots on the stove." He jumped just like he was sitting on a pin. He said, 'Annie, I done tole you, I ain't gonna mess around in no niggah's mouth.' I said, 'Somebody's got to do it then,' and he said, 'Take her to Texarkana to the colored dentist' and that's when I said, 'If you paid me my money I could afford to take her.' He said, 'It's all been paid.' I tole him everything but the interest been paid. He said "Twasn't no interest.' I said "Tis now. I'll take ten dollars as payment in full.' You know, Willie, it wasn't no right thing to do, 'cause I lent that money without thinking about it.

"He tole that little snippity nurse of his'n to give me ten dollars and make me sign a 'paid in full' receipt. She gave it to me and I signed the papers. Even though by rights he was paid up before, I figger, he gonna be that kind of nasty, he gonna have to pay for it."

Momma and her son laughed and laughed over the white man's evilness and her retributive sin.

I preferred, much preferred, my version.

25

Knowing Momma, I knew that I never knew Momma. Her African-bush secretiveness and suspiciousness had been compounded by slavery and confirmed by centuries of promises made and promises broken. We have a saying among Black Americans which describes Momma's caution. "If you ask a Negro where he's been, he'll tell you where he's going." To understand this important information, it is necessary to know who uses this tactic and on whom it works. If an unaware person is told a part of the truth (it is imperative that the answer embody truth), he is satisfied that his query has been answered. If an aware person (one who himself uses the stratagem) is given an answer which is truthful but bears only slightly if at all on the question, he knows that the information he seeks is of a private nature and will not be handed to him willingly. Thus direct denial, lying and the revelation of personal affairs are avoided.

Momma told us one day that she was taking us to California. She explained that we were growing up, that we needed to be with our parents, that Uncle Willie was, after all, crippled, that she was getting old. All true, and yet none of those truths satisfied our need for The Truth. The Store and the rooms in back became a going-away factory. Momma sat at the sewing machine all hours, making and remaking clothes for use in California. Neighbors brought out of their trunks pieces of material that had been packed away for decades in blankets of mothballs (I'm certain I was the only girl in California who went to school in water-marked moiré skirts and yellowed satin blouses, satin-back crepe dresses and crepe de Chine underwear).

Whatever the real reason, The Truth, for taking us to California, I shall always think it lay mostly in an incident in which Bailey had the leading part. Bailey had picked up the habit of imitating Claude Rains, Herbert Marshall and George McCready. I didn't think it at all strange that a thirteen-year-old boy in the unreconstructed Southern town of Stamps spoke with an Englishy accent. His heroes included D'Artagnan and the Count of Monte Cristo and he affected what he thought were their swashbuckling gallantries.

On an afternoon a few weeks before Momma revealed her plan to take us West, Bailey came into the Store shaking. His little face was no longer black but a dirty, colorless gray. As was our habit upon entering the Store, he walked behind the candy counter and leaned on the cash register. Uncle Willie had sent him on an errand to whitsfolks' town and he wanted an explanation for Bailey's tardiness. After a brief moment our uncle could see that something was wrong, and feeling unable to cope, he called Momma from the kitchen.

"What's the matter, Bailey Junior?"

He said nothing. I knew when I saw him that it would be useless to ask anything while he was in that state. It meant that he had seen or heard of something so ugly or frightening that he was paralyzed as a result. He explained when we were smaller that when things were very bad his soul just crawled behind his heart and curled up and

123

went to sleep. When it awoke, the fearful thing had gone away. Ever since we read *The Fall of the House of Usher*, we had made a pact that neither of us would allow the other to be buried without making "absolutely, positively sure" (his favorite phrase) that the person was dead. I also had to swear that when his soul was sleeping I would never try to wake it, for the shock might make it go to sleep forever. So I let him be, and after a while Momma had to let him alone too.

I waited on customers, and walked around him or leaned over him and, as I suspected, he didn't respond. When the spell wore off he asked Uncle Willie what colored people had done to white people in the first place. Uncle Willie, who never was one for explaining things because he took after Momma, said little except that "colored people hadn't even bothered a hair on whitefolks' heads." Momma added that some people said that whitefolks had come over to Africa (she made it sound like a hidden valley on the moon) and stole the colored people and made them slaves, but nobody really believed it was true. No way to explain what happened "blows and scores" ago, but right now they had the upper hand. Their time wasn't long, though. Didn't Moses lead the children of Israel out of the bloody hands of Pharaoh and into the Promised Land? Didn't the Lord protect the Hebrew children in the fiery furnace and didn't my Lord deliver Daniel? We only had to wait on the Lord.

Bailey said he saw a man, a colored man, whom nobody had delivered. He was dead. (If the news hadn't been so important, we would have been visited with one of Momma's outbursts and prayers. Bailey was nearly blaspheming.) He said, "The man was dead and rotten. Not stinking but rotten."

Momma ordered, "Ju, watch your tongue."

Uncle Willie asked, "Who, who was it?"

Bailey was just tall enough to clear his face over the cash register. He said, "When I passed the calaboose, some men had just fished him out of the pond. He was wrapped in a sheet, all rolled up like a mummy, then a white man walked over and pulled the sheet off. The man was on his back but the white man stuck his foot under the sheet and rolled him over on the stomach."

He turned to me. "My, he had no color at all. He was bloated like a ball." (We had had a running argument for months. Bailey said there was no such thing as colorlessness, and I argued that if there was color there also had to be an opposite and now he was admitting that it was possible. But I didn't feel good about my win.) "The colored men backed off and I did too, but the white man stood there, looking down, and grinned. Uncle Willie, why do they hate us so much?"

Uncle Willie muttered, "They don't really hate us. They don't know us. How can they hate us? They mostly scared."

Momma asked if Bailey had recognized the man, but he was caught in the happening and the event.

"Mr. Bubba told me I was too young to see something like that and I oughta hightail it home, but I had to stay. Then the white man called us closer. He said, 'O.K., you boys, stretch him out in the calaboose and when the Sheriff comes along he'll notify his people. This here's one nigger nobody got to worry about no more. He ain't going nowhere else.' Then the men picked up corners of the sheet, but since nobody wanted to get close to the man they held the very ends and he nearly rolled out on the ground. The white man called me to come and help too."

Momma exploded. "Who was it?" She made herself clear. "Who was the white man?"

Bailey couldn't let go of the horror. "I picked up a side of the sheet and walked right in the calaboose with the men. I walked in the calaboose carrying a rotten dead Negro." His voice was ancient with shock. He was literally bug-eyed.

"The white man played like he was going to lock us all up in there, but Mr. Bubba said 'Ow, Mr. Jim. We didn't do it. We ain't done nothing wrong.' Then the white man laughed and said we boys couldn't take a joke, and opened the door." He breathed his relief. "Whew, I was glad to get out of there. The calaboose, and the prisoners screaming they didn't want no dead nigger in there with them. That he'd stink up the place. They called the white man 'Boss.' They said, 'Boss, surely we ain't done nothing bad enough for you to put another nigger in here with us, and a dead one at that.' Then they laughed. They all laughed like there was something funny."

Bailey was talking so fast he forgot to stutter, he forgot to scratch his head and clean his fingernails with his teeth. He was away in a mystery, locked in the enigma that young Southern Black boys start to unravel, start to try to unravel, from seven years old to death. The humorless puzzle of inequality and hate. His experience raised the question of worth and values, of aggressive inferiority and aggressive arrogance. Could Uncle Willie, a Black man, Southern, crippled moreover, hope to answer the questions, both asked and unuttered? Would Momma, who knew the ways of the whites and the wiles of the Blacks, try to answer her grandson, whose very life depended on his not truly understanding the enigma? Most assuredly not.

They both responded characteristically. Uncle Willie said something like he didn't know what the world was coming to, and Momma prayed, "God rest his soul, poor man." I'm sure she began piecing together the details of our California trip that night.

Our transportation was Momma's major concern for some weeks.

125

She had arranged with a railroad employee to provide her with a pass in exchange for groceries. The pass allowed a reduction in her fare only, and even that had to be approved, so we were made to abide in a kind of limbo until white people we would never see, in offices we would never visit, signed and stamped and mailed the pass back to Momma. My fare had to be paid in "ready cash." That sudden drain on the nickel-plated cash register lopsided our financial stability. Momma decided Bailey couldn't accompany us, since we had to use the pass during a set time, but that he would follow within a month or so when outstanding bills were paid. Although our mother now lived in San Francisco, Momma must have felt it wiser to go first to Los Angeles where our father was. She dictated letters to me, advising them both that we were on our way.

And we were on our way, but unable to say when. Our clothes were washed, ironed and packed, so for an immobile time we wore those things not good enough to glow under the California sun. Neighbors, who understood the complications of travel, said goodbye a million times.

"Well, if I don't see you before your ticket comes through, Sister Henderson, have a good trip and hurry back home." A widowed friend of Momma's had agreed to look after (cook, wash, clean and provide company for) Uncle Willie, and after thousands of arrested departures, at last we left Stamps.

My sorrow at leaving was confined to a gloom at separating from Bailey for a month (we had never been parted), the imagined loneliness of Uncle Willie (he put on a good face, though at thirty-five he'd never been separated from his mother) and the loss of Louise, my first friend. I wouldn't miss Mrs. Flowers, for she had given me her secret word which called forth a djinn who was to serve me all my life: books.

26

The intensity with which young people live demands that they "blank out" as often as possible. I didn't actually think about facing Mother until the last day of our journey. I was "going to California." To oranges and sunshine and movie stars and earthquakes and (finally I realized) to Mother. My old guilt came back to me like a much-missed friend. I wondered if Mr. Freeman's name would be mentioned, or if I would be expected to say something about the situation myself. I certainly couldn't ask Momma, and Bailey was a zillion miles away.

The agony of wonder made the fuzzy seats hard, soured the boiled eggs, and when I looked at Momma she seemed too big and too black and very old-fashioned. Everything I saw shuttered against me. The little towns, where nobody waved, and the other passengers in the train, with whom I had achieved an almost kinfolk relationship, disappeared into a common strangeness.

I was as unprepared to meet my mother as a sinner is reluctant to meet his Maker. And all too soon she stood before me, smaller than memory would have her but more glorious than any recall. She wore a light-tan suede suit, shoes to match and a mannish hat with a feather in the band, and she patted my face with gloved hands. Except for the lipsticked mouth, white teeth and shining black eyes, she might have just emerged from a dip in a beige bath. My picture of Mother and Momma embracing on the train platform has been darkly retained through the coating of the then embarrassment and the now maturity. Mother was a blithe chick nuzzling around the large, solid dark hen. The sounds they made had a rich inner harmony. Momma's deep, slow voice lay under my mother's rapid peeps and chirps like stones under rushing water.

The younger woman kissed and laughed and rushed about collecting our coats and getting our luggage carted off. She easily took care of the details that would have demanded half of a country person's day. I was struck again by the wonder of her, and for the length of my trance, the greedy uneasinesses were held at bay.

We moved into an apartment, and I slept on a sofa that miraculously transformed itself at night into a large comfortable bed. Mother stayed in Los Angeles long enough to get us settled, then she returned to San Francisco to arrange living accommodations for her abruptly enlarged family.

Momma and Bailey (he joined us a month after our arrival) and I lived in Los Angeles about six months while our permanent living arrangements were being concluded. Daddy Bailey visited occasionally, bringing shopping bags of fruit. He shone like a Sun God, benignly warming and brightening his dark subjects.

Since I was enchanted with the creation of my own world, years had to pass before I reflected on Momma's remarkable adjustment to that foreign life. An old Southern Negro woman who had lived her life under the left breast of her community learned to deal with white landlords, Mexican neighbors and Negro strangers. She shopped in supermarkets larger than the town she came from. She dealt with accents that must have struck jarringly on her ears. She, who had never been more than fifty miles from her birthplace, learned to traverse the maze of Spanish-named streets in that enigma that is Los Angeles.

She made the same kinds of friends she had always had. On late Sunday afternoons before evening church services, old women who were carbon copies of herself came to the apartment to share leftovers from the Sunday meal and religious talk of a Bright Hereafter.

When the arrangements for our move north were completed, she broke the shattering news that she was going back to Arkansas. She had done her job. She was needed by Uncle Willie. We had our own parents at last. At least we were in the same state.

There were foggy days of unknowing for Bailey and me. It was all well and good to say we would be with our parents, but after all, who were they? Would they be more severe with our didoes than she? That would be bad. Or more lax? Which would be even worse. Would we learn to speak that fast language? I doubted that, and I doubted even more that I would ever find out what they laughed about so loudly and so often.

I would have been willing to return to Stamps even without Bailey. But Momma left for Arkansas without me with her solid air packed around her like cotton.

Mother drove us toward San Francisco over the big white highway that would not have surprised me had it never ended. She talked incessantly and pointed out places of interest. As we passed Capistrano she sang a popular song that I'd heard on the radio: "When the swallows come back to Capistrano."

She strung humorous stories along the road like a bright wash and tried to captivate us. But her being, and her being our mother, had done the job so successfully that it was a little distracting to see her throwing good energy after good.

The big car was obedient under her one-hand driving, and she pulled on her Lucky Strike so hard that her cheeks were sucked in to make valleys in her face. Nothing could have been more magical than to have found her at last, and have her solely to ourselves in the closed world of a moving car.

Although we were both enraptured, neither Bailey nor I was unaware of her nervousness. The knowledge that we had the power to upset that goddess made us look at each other conspiratorially and smile. It also made her human.

We spent a few dingy months in an Oakland apartment which had a bathtub in the kitchen and was near enough to the Southern Pacific Mole to shake at the arrival and departure of every train. In many

128

ways it was St. Louis revisited—along with Uncles Tommy and Billy—and Grandmother Baxter of the pince-nez and strict carriage was again In Residence, though the mighty Baxter clan had fallen into hard times after the death of Grandfather Baxter some years earlier.

We went to school and no family member questioned the output or quality of our work. We went to a playground which sported a basketball court, a football field and Ping Pong tables under awnings. On Sundays instead of going to church we went to the movies.

I slept with Grandmother Baxter, who was afflicted with chronic bronchitis and smoked heavily. During the day she stubbed out half-finished cigarettes and put them in an ashtray beside her bed. At night when she woke up coughing she fumbled in the dark for a butt (she called them "Willies") and after a blaze of light she smoked the strengthened tobacco until her irritated throat was deadened with nicotine. For the first weeks of sleeping with her, the shaking bed and scent of tobacco woke me, but I readily became used to it and slept peacefully through the night.

One evening after going to bed normally, I awoke to another kind of shaking. In the blunted light through the window shade I saw my mother kneeling by my bed. She brought her face close to my ear.

"Ritie," she whispered, "Ritie. Come, but be very quiet." Then she quietly rose and left the room. Dutifully and in a haze of ponderment I followed. Through the half-open kitchen door the light showed Bailey's pajamaed legs dangling from the covered bathtub. The clock on the dining-room table said 2:30. I had never been up at that hour.

I looked Bailey a question and he returned a sheepish gaze. I knew immediately that there was nothing to fear. Then I ran my mind through the catalogue of important dates. It wasn't anybody's birthday, or April Fool's Day, or Halloween, but it was something.

Mother closed the kitchen door and told me to sit beside Bailey. She put her hands on her hips and said we had been invited to a party.

Was that enough to wake us in the middle of the night! Neither of us said anything.

She continued, "I am giving a party and you are my honored and only guests."

She opened the oven and took out a pan of her crispy brown biscuits and showed us a pot of milk chocolate on the back of the stove. There was nothing for it but to laugh at our beautiful and wild mother. When Bailey and I started laughing, she joined in, except that she kept her finger in front of her mouth to try to quiet us.

We were served formally, and she apologized for having no orchestra to play for us but said she'd sing as a substitute. She sang and did the Time Step and the Snake Hips and the Suzy Q. What child can resist a mother who laughs freely and often, especially if the child's wit is mature enough to catch the sense of the joke?

Mother's beauty made her powerful and her power made her unflinchingly honest. When we asked her what she did, what her job was, she walked us to Oakland's Seventh Street, where dusty bars and smoke shops sat in the laps of storefront churches. She pointed out Raincoat's Pinochle Parlor and Slim Jenkins' pretentious saloon. Some nights she played pinochle for money or ran a poker game at Mother Smith's or stopped at Slim's for a few drinks. She told us that she had never cheated anybody and wasn't making any preparations to do so. Her work was as honest as the job held by fat Mrs. Walker (a maid), who lived next door to us, and "a damn sight better paid." She wouldn't bust suds for anybody nor be anyone's kitchen bitch. The good Lord gave her a mind and she intended to use it to support her mother and her children. She didn't need to add "And have a little fun along the way."

In the street people were genuinely happy to see her. "Hey, baby. What's the news?"

"Everything's steady, baby, steady."

"How you doing, pretty?"

"I can't win, 'cause of the shape I'm in." (Said with a laugh that belied the content.)

"You all right, momma?"

"Aw, they teli me the whitefolks still in the lead." (Said as if that was not quite the whole truth.)

She supported us efficiently with humor and imagination. Occasionally we were taken to Chinese restaurants or Italian pizza parlors. We were introduced to Hungarian goulash and Irish stew. Through food we learned that there were other people in the world.

With all her jollity, Vivian Baxter had no mercy. There was a saying in Oakland at the time which, if she didn't say it herself, explained her attitude. The saying was, "Sympathy is next to shit in the dictionary, and I can't even read." Her temper had not diminished with the passing of time, and when a passionate nature is not eased with moments of compassion, melodrama is likely to take the stage. In each outburst of anger my mother was *fair*. She had the impartiality of nature, with the same lack of indulgence or clemency.

Before we arrived from Arkansas, an incident took place that left the main actors in jail and in the hospital. Mother had a business partner (who may have been a little more than that) with whom she ran a restaurant cum gambling casino. The partner was not shouldering his portion of the responsibility, according to Mother, and when she confronted him he became haughty and domineering, and he unforgivably called her a bitch. Now, everyone knew that although she cursed as freely as she laughed, no one cursed around her, and certainly no one cursed her. Maybe for the sake of business arrangements she restrained a spontaneous reaction. She told her partner, "I'm going to be one bitch, and I've already been that one." In a foolhardy gesture the man relieved himself of still another "bitch"—and Mother shot him. She had anticipated some trouble when she determined to speak to him and so had taken the precaution to slip a little .32 in her big skirt pocket.

Shot once, the partner stumbled toward her, instead of away, and she said that since she had intended to shoot him (notice: shoot, not kill) she had no reason to run away, so she shot him a second time. It must have been a maddening situation for them. To her, each shot seemed to impel him forward, the reverse of her desire; and for him, the closer he got to her, the more she shot him. She stood her ground until he reached her and flung both arms around her neck, dragging her to the floor. She later said the police had to untwine him before he could be taken to the ambulance. And on the following day, when she was released on bail, she looked in a mirror and "had black eyes down to here." In throwing his arms around her, he must have struck her. She bruised easily.

The partner lived, though shot twice, and although the partnership was dissolved they retained admiration for each other. He had been shot, true, but in her fairness she had warned him. And he had had the strength to give her two black eyes and then live. Admirable qualities.

World War II started on a Sunday afternoon when I was on my way to the movies. People in the streets shouted, "We're at war. We've declared war on Japan."

I ran all the way home. Not too sure I wouldn't be bombed before I reached Bailey and Mother. Grandmother Baxter calmed my anxiety by explaining that America would not be bombed, not as long as Franklin Delano Roosevelt was President. He was, after all, a politician's politician and he knew what he was doing.

Soon after, Mother married Daddy Clidell, who turned out to be the first father I would know. He was a successful businessman, and he and Mother moved us to San Francisco. Uncle Tommy, Uncle Billy and Grandmother Baxter remained in the big house in Oakland.

27

In the early months of World War II, San Francisco's Fillmore district, or the Western Addition, experienced a visible revolution. On the surface it appeared to be totally peaceful and almost a refutation of the term "revolution." The Yakamoto Sea Food Market quietly became Sammy's Shoe Shine Parlor and Smoke Shop. Yashigira's Hardware metamorphosed into La Salon de Beauté owned by Miss Clorinda Jackson. The Japanese shops which sold products to Nisei customers were taken over by enterprising Negro businessmen, and in less than a year became permanent homes away from home for the newly arrived Southern Blacks. Where the odors of tempura, raw fish and *cha* had dominated, the aroma of chitlings, greens and ham hocks now prevailed.

The Asian population dwindled before my eyes. I was unable to tell the Japanese from the Chinese and as yet found no real difference in the national origin of such sounds as Ching and Chan or Moto and Kano.

As the Japanese disappeared, soundlessly and without protest, the Negroes entered with their loud jukeboxes, their just-released animosities and the relief of escape from Southern bonds. The Japanese area became San Francisco's Harlem in a matter of months.

A person unaware of all the factors that make up oppression might have expected sympathy or even support from the Negro newcomers for the dislodged Japanese. Especially in view of the fact that they (the Blacks) had themselves undergone concentration-camp living for centuries in slavery's plantations and later in sharecroppers' cabins. But the sensations of common relationship were missing.

The Black newcomer had been recruited on the dessicated farm lands of Georgia and Mississippi by war-plant labor scouts. The chance to live in two- or three-story apartment buildings (which became instant slums), and to earn two- and even three-figured weekly checks, was blinding. For the first time he could think of himself as a Boss, a Spender. He was able to pay other people to work for him, i.e. the dry cleaners, taxi drivers, waitresses, etc. The shipyards and ammunition plants brought to booming life by the war let him know that he was needed and even appreciated. A completely alien yet very pleasant position for him to experience. Who could expect this man to share his new and dizzying importance with concern for a race that he had never known to exist?

Another reason for his indifference to the Japanese removal was more subtle but was more profoundly felt. The Japanese were not whitefolks. Their eyes, language and customs belied the white skin and proved to their dark successors that since they didn't have to be feared, neither did they have to be considered. All this was decided unconsciously.

No member of my family and none of the family friends ever mentioned the absent Japanese. It was as if they had never owned or lived in the houses we inhabited. On Post Street, where our house was, the hill skidded slowly down to Fillmore, the market heart of our district. In the two short blocks before it reached its destination, the street housed two day-and-night restaurants, two pool halls, four Chinese restaurants, two gambling houses, plus diners, shoeshine shops, beauty salons, barber shops and at least four churches. To fully grasp the never-ending activity in San Francisco's Negro neighborhood during the war, one need only know that the two blocks described were side streets that were duplicated many times over in the eight- to ten-square-block area.

The air of collective displacement, the impermanence of life in wartime and the gauche personalities of the more recent arrivals tended to dissipate my own sense of not belonging. In San Francisco, for the first time, I perceived myself as part of something. Not that I identified with the newcomers, nor with the rare Black descendants of native San Franciscans, nor with the whites or even the Asians, but rather with the times and the city. I understood the arrogance of the young sailors who marched the streets in marauding gangs, approaching every girl as if she were at best a prostitute and at worst an Axis agent bent on making the U.S.A. lose the war. The undertone of fear that San Francisco would be bombed which was abetted by weekly air raid warnings, and civil defense drills in school, heightened my sense of belonging. Hadn't I, always, but ever and ever, thought that life was just one great risk for the living?

Then the city acted in wartime like an intelligent woman under siege. She gave what she couldn't with safety withhold, and secured those things which lay in her reach. The city became for me the ideal of what I wanted to be as a grownup. Friendly but never gushing, cool but not frigid or distant, distinguished without the awful stiffness.

To San Franciscans "the City That Knows How" was the Bay, the fog, Sir Francis Drake Hotel, Top o' the Mark, Chinatown, the Sunset District and so on and so forth and so white. To me, a thirteen-year-old Black girl, stalled by the South and Southern Black life style, the city was a state of beauty and a state of freedom. The fog wasn't simply the steamy vapors off the bay caught and penned in by hills, but a soft breath of anonymity that shrouded and cushioned the bashful traveler. I became dauntless and free of fears, intoxicated by the physical fact of San Francisco. Safe in my protecting arrogance, I was certain that no one loved her as impartially as I. I walked around the Mark Hopkins and gazed at the Top o' the Mark, but (maybe sour grapes) was more impressed by the view of Oakland from the hill than by the tiered building or its fur-draped visitors. For weeks, after the city and I came to terms about my belonging, I haunted the points of interest and found them empty and un-San Francisco. The naval officers with their well-dressed wives and clean white babies inhabited another time-space dimension than I. The well-kept old women in chauffeured cars and blond girls in buckskin shoes and cashmere sweaters might have been San Franciscans, but they were at most gilt on the frame of my portrait of the city.

Pride and Prejudice stalked in tandem the beautiful hills. Native San Franciscans, possessive of the city, had to cope with an influx, not of awed respectful tourists but of raucous unsophisticated provincials. They were also forced to live with skin-deep guilt brought on by the treatment of their former Nisei schoolmates.

Southern white illiterates brought their biases intact to the West from the hills of Arkansas and the swamps of Georgia. The Black ex-farmers had not left their distrust and fear of whites which history had taught them in distressful lessons. These two groups were obliged to work side by side in the war plants, and their animosities festered and opened like boils on the face of the city.

San Franciscans would have sworn on the Golden Gate Bridge that racism was missing from the heart of their air-conditioned city. But they would have been sadly mistaken.

A story went the rounds about a San Franciscan white matron who refused to sit beside a Negro civilian on the streetcar, even after he made room for her on the seat. Her explanation was that she would not sit beside a draft dodger who was a Negro as well. She added that the least he could do was fight for his country the way her son was fighting on Iwo Jima. The story said that the man pulled his body away from the window to show an armless sleeve. He said quietly and with great dignity, "Then ask your son to look around for my arm, which I left over there."

28

Although my grades were very good (I had been put up two semesters on my arrival from Stamps), I found myself unable to settle down in the high school. It was an institution for girls near my house, and the young ladies were faster, brasher, meaner and more prejudiced than any I had met at Lafayette County Training School. Many of the Negro girls were, like me, straight from the South, but they had known or claimed to have known the bright lights of Big D (Dallas) or T Town (Tulsa, Oklahoma), and their language bore up their claims. They strutted with an aura of invincibility, and along with some of the Mexican students who put knives in their tall pompadours they absolutely intimidated the white girls and these Black and Mexican students who had no shield of fearlessness. Fortunately I was transferred to George Washington High School.

The beautiful buildings sat on a moderate hill in the white residential district, some sixty blocks from the Negro neighborhood. For the first semester, I was one of three Black students in the school, and in that rarefied atmosphere I came to love my people more. Mornings as the streetcar traversed my ghetto I experienced a mixture of dread and trauma. I knew that all too soon we would be out of my familiar setting, and Blacks who were on the streetcar when I got on would all be gone and I alone would face the forty blocks of neat streets, smooth lawns, white houses and rich children.

In the evenings on the way home the sensations were joy, anticipation and relief at the first sign which said BARBECUE or DO DROP INN or HOME COOKING or at the first brown faces on the streets. I recognized that I was again in my country.

In the school itself I was disappointed to find that I was not the most brilliant or even nearly the most brilliant student. The white kids had better vocabularies than I and, what was more appalling, less fear in the classrooms. They never hesitated to hold up their hands in response to a teacher's question; even when they were wrong they were wrong aggressively, while I had to be certain about all my facts before I dared to call attention to myself.

George Washington High School was the first real school I attended. My entire stay there might have been time lost if it hadn't been for the unique personality of a brilliant teacher. Miss Kirwin was that rare educator who was in love with information. I will always believe that her love of teaching came not so much from her liking for students but from her desire to make sure that some of the things she knew would find repositories so that they could be shared again.

She and her maiden sister worked in the San Francisco city school system for over twenty years. My Miss Kirwin, who was a tall, florid, buxom lady with battleship-gray hair, taught civics and current events. At the end of a term in her class our books were as clean and the pages as stiff as they had been when they were issued to us. Miss Kirwin's students were never or very rarely called upon to open textbooks.

She greeted each class with "Good day, ladies and gentlemen." I had never heard an adult speak with such respect to teenagers. (Adults usually believe that a show of honor diminishes their authority.) "In today's *Chronicle* there was an article on the mining industry in the Carolinas [or some such distant subject]. I am certain that all of you have read the article. I would like someone to elaborate on the subject for me."

After the first two weeks in her class, I, along with all the other excited students, read the San Francisco papers, *Time* magazine, *Life* and everything else available to me. Miss Kirwin proved Bailey right. He had told me once that "all knowledge is spendable currency, depending on the market."

There were no favorite students. No teacher's pets. If a student pleased her during a particular period, he could not count on special treatment in the next day's class, and that was as true the other way around. Each day she faced us with a clean slate and acted as if ours were clean as well. Reserved and firm in her opinions, she spent no time in indulging the frivolous.

She was stimulating instead of intimadating. Where some of the other teachers went out of their way to be nice to me—to be a "liberal" with me—and others ignored me completely, Miss Kirwin never seemed to notice that I was Black and therefore different. I was Miss Johnson and if I had the answer to a question she posed I was never given any more than the word "Correct," which was what she said to every other student with the correct answer.

Years later when I returned to San Francisco I made visits to her classroom. She always remembered that I was Miss Johnson, who had a good mind and should be doing something with it. I was never encouraged on those visits to loiter or linger about her desk. She acted as if I must have had other visits to make. I often wondered if she knew she was the only teacher I remembered.

136

I never knew why I was given a scholarship to the California Labor School. It was a college for adults, and many years later I found that it was on the House Un-American Activities list of subversive organizations. At fourteen I accepted a scholarship and got one for the next year as well. In the evening classes I took drama and dance, along with white and Black grownups. I had chosen drama simply because I liked Hamlet's soliloquy beginning, "To be, or not to be." I had never seen a play and did not connect movies with the theater. In fact, the only times I had heard the soliloquy had been when I had melodramatically recited to myself. In front of a mirror.

It was hard to curb my love for the exaggerated gesture and the emotive voice. When Bailey and I read poems together, he sounded like a fierce Basil Rathbone and I like a maddened Bette Davis. At the California Labor School a forceful and perceptive teacher quickly and unceremoniously separated me from melodrama.

She made me do six months of pantomime.

Bailey and Mother encouraged me to take dance, and he privately told me that the exercise would make my legs big and widen my hips. I needed no greater inducement.

My shyness at moving clad in black tights around a large empty room did not last long. Of course, at first, I thought everyone would be staring at my cucumber-shaped body with its knobs for knees, knobs for elbows and, alas, knobs for breasts. But they really did not notice me, and when the teacher floated across the floor and finished in an arabesque my fancy was taken. I would learn to move like that. I would learn to, in her words, "occupy space." My days angled off Miss Kirwin's class, dinner with Bailey and Mother, and drama and dance.

The allegiances I owed at this time in my life would have made very strange bedfellows: Momma with her solemn determination, Mrs. Flowers and her books, Bailey with his love, my mother and her gaiety, Miss Kirwin and her information, my evening classes of drama and dance.

29

Our house was a fourteen-room typical San Franciscan post-Earthquake affair. We had a succession of roomers, bringing and taking their different accents, and personalities and foods. Shipyard workers clanked up the stairs (we all slept on the second floor except Mother and Daddy Clidell) in their steel-tipped boots and metal hats, and gave way to much-powdered prostitutes, who giggled through their make-up and hung their wigs on the doorknobs. One couple (they were college graduates) held long adult conversations with me in the big kitchen downstairs, until the husband went off to war. Then the wife who had been so charming and ready to smile changed into a silent shadow that played infrequently along the walls. An older couple lived with us for a year or so. They owned a restaurant and had no personality to enchant or interest a teenager, except that the husband was called Uncle Jim, and the wife Aunt Boy. I never figured that out.

The quality of strength lined with tenderness is an unbeatable combination, as are intelligence and necessity when unblunted by formal education. I was prepared to accept Daddy Clidell as one more faceless name added to Mother's roster of conquests. I had trained myself so successfully through the years to display interest, or at least attention, while my mind skipped free on other subjects that I could have lived in his house without ever seeing him and without his becoming the wiser. But his character beckoned and elicited admiration. He was a simple man who had no inferiority complex about his lack of education and, even more amazing, no superiority complex because he had succeeded despite that lack. He would say often, "I been to school three years in my life. In Slaten, Texas, times was hard, and I had to help my daddy on the farm."

No recriminations lay hidden under the plain statement, nor was there boasting when he said, "If I'm living a little better now, it's because I treats everybody right."

He owned apartment buildings and, later, pool halls, and was famous for being that rarity "a man of honor." He didn't suffer, as many "honest men" do, from the detestable righteousness that diminishes their virtue. He knew cards and men's hearts. So during the age when Mother was exposing us to certain facts of life, like personal hygiene, proper posture, table manners, good restaurants and tipping practices, Daddy Clidell taught me to play poker, blackjack, tonk and high, low, Jick, Jack and the Game. He wore expensively tailored suits and a large yellow diamond stickpin. Except for the jewelry, he was a conservative dresser and carried himself with the unconscious pomp of a man of secure means. Unexpectedly, I resembled him, and when he, Mother and I walked down the street his friends often said, "Clidell, that's sure your daughter. Ain't no way you can deny her."

Proud laughter followed those declarations, for he had never had children. Because of his late-arriving but intense paternal sense, I was introduced to the most colorful characters in the Black underground. One afternoon, I was invited into our smoke-filled dining room to make the acquaintance of Stonewall Jimmy, Just Black, Cool Clyde, Tight Coat and Red Leg. Daddy Clidell explained to me that they were the most successful con men in the world, and they were going to tell me about some games so that I would never be "anybody's mark."

To begin, one man warned me, "There ain't never been a mark yet that didn't want something for nothing." Then they took turns showing me their tricks, how they chose their victims (marks) from the wealthy bigoted whites and in every case how they used the victims' prejudice against them.

Some of the tales were funny, a few were pathetic, but all were amusing or gratifying to me, for the Black man, the con man who could act the most stupid, won out every time over the powerful, arrogant white.

I remember Mr. Red Leg's story like a favorite melody.

"Anything that works against you can also work for you once you understand the Principle of Reverse.

"There was a cracker in Tulsa who bilked so many Negroes he could set up a Negro Bilking Company. Naturally he got to thinking, Black Skin means Damn Fool. Just Black and I went to Tulsa to check him out. Come to find out, he's a perfect mark. His Momma must have been scared in an Indian massacre in Africa. He hated Negroes only a little more than he despised Indians. And he was greedy.

"Black and I studied him and decided he was worth setting up against the store. That means we were ready to put out a few thousand dollars in preparation. We pulled in a white boy from New York, a good con artist, and had him open an office in Tulsa. He was supposed to be a Northern real estate agent trying to buy up valuable land in Oklahoma. We investigated a piece of land near Tulsa that had a toll bridge crossing it. It used to be part of an Indian reservation but had been taken over by the state.

"Just Black was laid out as the decoy, and I was going to be the fool. After our friend from New York hired a secretary and had his cards printed, Black approached the mark with a proposition. He told him that he had heard that our mark was the only white man colored people could trust. He named some of the poor fools that had been taken by that crook. It just goes to show you how white folks can be deceived by their own deception. The mark believed Black.

"Black told him about his friend who was half Indian and half colored and how some Northern white estate agent had found out that he was the sole owner of a piece of valuable land and the Northerner wanted to buy it. At first the man acted like he smelled a rat, but from the way he gobbled up the proposition, turns out what he thought he smelled was some nigger money on his top lip.

"He asked the whereabouts of the land but Black put him off. He told his cracker that he just wanted to make sure that he would be interested. The mark allowed how he was being interested, so Black said he would tell his friend and they'd get in touch with him. Black met the mark for about three weeks in cars and in alleys and kept putting him off until the white man was almost crazy with anxiety and greed and then accidentally it seemed Black let drop the name of the Northern real estate agent who wanted the property. From that moment on we knew we had the big fish on the line and all we had to do was to pull him in.

"We expected him to try to contact our store, which he did. That cracker went to our setup and counted on his whiteness to ally him with Spots, our white boy, but Spots refused to talk about the deal except to say the land had been thoroughly investigated by the biggest real estate concern in the South and that if our mark did not go around raising dust he would make sure that there would be a nice piece of money in it for him. Any obvious inquiries as to the rightful ownership of the land could alert the state and they would surely push through a law prohibiting the sale. Spots told the mark he would keep in touch with him. The mark went back to the store three or four times but to no avail, then just before we knew he would crack, Black brought me to see him. That fool was as happy as a sissy in a C.C.C. camp. You would have thought my neck was in a noose and he was about to light the fire under my feet. I never enjoyed taking anybody so much.

"Anyhow, I played scary at first but Just Black told me that this was one white man that our people could trust. I said I did not trust no white man because all they wanted was to get a chance to kill a Black man legally and get his wife in the bed. (I'm sorry, Clidell.) The mark assured me that he was the only white man who did not feel like that. Some of his best friends were colored people. In fact, if I didn't know it, the woman who raised him was a colored woman and he still sees her to this day. I let myself be convinced and then the mark began to drag the Northern whites. He told me that they made Negroes sleep in the street in the North and that they had to clean out toilets with their hands in the North and even things worse than that. I was shocked and said, 'Then I don't want to sell my land to that white man who offered seventy-five thousand dollars for it.' Just Black said, 'I wouldn't know what to do with that kind of money,' and I said that all I wanted was to have enough money to buy a home for my old mom, to buy a business and to make one trip to Harlem. The mark asked how much would that cost and I said I reckoned I could do it on fifty thousand dollars."

"The mark told me no Negro was safe with that kind of money. That white folks would take it from him. I said I knew it but I had to have at least forty thousand dollars. He agreed. We shook hands. I said it would do my heart good to see the mean Yankee go down on some of 'our land.' We met the next morning and I signed the deed in his car and he gave me the cash."

"Black and I had kept most of our things in a hotel over in Hot Springs, Arkansas. When the deal was closed we walked to our car, drove across the state line and on to Hot Springs."

"That's all there was to it."

When he finished, more triumphant stories rainbowed around the room riding the shoulders of laughter. By all accounts those storytellers, born Black and male before the turn of the twentieth century, should have been ground into useless dust. Instead they used their intelligence to pry open the door of rejection and not only became wealthy but got some revenge in the bargain.

It wasn't possible for me to regard them as criminals or be anything but proud of their achievements.

The needs of a society determine its ethics, and in the Black American ghettos the hero is that man who is offered only the crumbs from his country's table but by ingenuity and courage is able to take for himself a Lucullan feast. Hence the janitor who lives in one room but sports a robin's-egg-blue Cadillac is not laughed at but admired, and the domestic who buys forty-dollar shoes is not criticized but is appreciated. We know that they have put to use their full mental and physical powers. Each single gain feeds into the gains of the body collective.

Stories of law violations are weighed on a different set of scales in the Black mind than in the white. Petty crimes embarrass the community and many people wistfully wonder why Negroes don't rob more banks, embezzle more funds and employ graft in the unions. "We are the victims of the world's most comprehensive robbery. Life demands a balance. It's all right if we do a little robbing now." This belief appeals particularly to one who is unable to compete legally with his fellow citizens.

My education and that of my Black associates were quite different from the education of our white schoolmates. In the classroom we all learned past participles, but in the streets and in our homes the Blacks learned to drop s's from plurals and suffixcs from past-tense verbs. We were alert to the gap separating the written word from the colloquial. We learned to slide out of one language and into another without being conscious of the effort. At school, in a given situation, we might respond with "That's not unusual." But in the street, meeting the same situation, we easily said, "It be's like that sometimes."

30

Just like Jane Withers and Donald O'Connor I was going on a vacation. Daddy Bailey invited me to spend the summer with him in southern California and I was jumpy with excitement. Given our father's characteristic air of superiority, I secretly expected him to live in a manor house surrounded by grounds and serviced by a liveried Staff.

Mother was all cooperation in helping me to shop for summer clothes. With the haughtiness San Franciscans have for people who live in the warmer climate, she explained that all I needed were lots of shorts, pedal pushers, sandals and blouses because "southern Californians hardly ever wear anything else."

Daddy Bailey had a girl friend, who had begun corresponding with me some months before, and she was to meet me at the train. We had agreed to wear white carnations to identify each other, and the porter kept my flower in the diner's Frigidaire until we reached the small hot town.

On the platform my eyes skimmed over the whites and searched among the Negroes who were walking up and down expectantly. There were no men as tall as Daddy, and no really glamorous ladies (I had decided that given his first choice, all his succeeding women would be startlingly beautiful). I saw a little girl who wore a white flower, but dismissed her as improbable. The platform emptied as we walked by each other time after time. Finally she stopped me with a disbelieving "Marguerite?" Her voice screeched with shock and maturity. So, after all, she wasn't a little girl. I too, was visited with unbelief.

She said, "I'm Dolores Stockland."

Stunned but trying to be well mannered, I said, "Hello. My name is Marguerite."

Daddy's girl friend? I guessed her to be in her early twenties. Her crisp seersucker suit, spectator pumps and gloves informed me that she was proper and serious. She was of average height but with the unformed body of a girl and I thought that if she was planning to marry our father she must have been horrified to find herself with a nearly six-foot prospective stepdaughter who was not even pretty. (I found later that Daddy Bailey had told her that his children were eight and nine years old and cute as buttons. She had such a need to believe in him that even though we corresponded at a time when I loved the multisyllabic words and convoluted sentences she had been able to ignore the obvious.)

I was another link in a long chain of disappointments. Daddy, had promised to marry her but kept delaying until he finally married a woman named Alberta, who who was another small tight woman from the South. When I met Dolores she had all the poses of the Black bourgeoisie without the material basis to support the postures. Instead of owning a manor house and servants, Daddy, lived in a trailer park on the outskirts of a town that was itself the outskirts of town. Dolores lived there with him and kept the house clean with the orderliness of a coffin. Artificial flowers reposed waxily in glass vases. She was on close terms with her washing machine and ironing board. Her hairdresser could count on absolute fidelity and punctuality. In a word, but for intrusions her life would have been perfect. And then I came along.

She tried hard to make me into something she could reasonably accept. Her first attempt, which failed utterly, concerned my attention to details. I was asked, cajoled, then ordered to care for my room. My willingness to do so was hampered by an abounding ignorance of how it should be done and a fumbling awkwardness with small objects. The dresser in my room was covered with little porcelain white women holding parasols, china dogs, fat-bellied cupids and blown-glass animals of every persuasion. After making the bed, sweeping my room and hanging up the clothes, if and when I remembered to dust the bric-a-brac, I unfailingly held one too tightly and crunched off a leg or two, or too loosely and dropped it, to shatter it into miserable pieces.

143

Daddy wore his amused impenetrable face constantly. He seemed positively diabolic in his enjoyment of our discomfort. Certainly Dolores adored her outsize lover, and his elocution (Daddy Bailey never spoke, he orated), spiced with the rolling *ers* and *errers*, must have been some consolation to her in their less-than-middle-class home. He worked in the kitchen of a naval hospital and they both said he was a medical dietician for the United States Navy. Their Frigidaire was always stocked with newly acquired pieces of ham, half roasts and quartered chickens. Dad was an excellent cook. He had been in France during World War I and had also worked as doorman at the exclusive Breakers' Hotel; as a result he often made Continental dinners. We sat down frequently to coq au vin, prime ribs au jus, and cotelette Milanese with all the trimmings. His speciality, however, was Mexican food. He traveled across the border weekly to pick up condiments and other supplies that graced our table as pollo en salsa verde and enchilada con carne.

If Dolores had been a little less aloof, a little more earthy, she could have discovered that those ingredients were rife in her town proper, and Dad had no need to travel to Mexico to buy provisions. But she would not be caught so much as looking into one of the crusty Mexican *mercados*, let alone venturing inside its smelliness. And it also sounded ritzy to say, "My husband, Mr. Johnson, the naval dietician, went over to Mexico to buy some things for our dinner." That goes over large with other ritzy people who go to the white area to buy artichokes.

Dad spoke fluent Spanish, and since I had studied for a year we were able to converse slightly. I believe that my talent with a foreign language was the only quality I had that impressed Dolores. Her mouth was too taut and her tongue too still to attempt the strange sounds. Admittedly, though, her English, like everything else about her, was absolutely perfect.

We indulged in a test of strength for weeks as Dad stood figuratively on the sidelines, neither cheering nor booing but enjoying himself greatly. He asked me once if I "er liked errer my mother." I thought he meant my mother, so I answered yes—she was beautiful and gay and very kind. He said he wasn't talking about Vivian, he meant Dolores. Then I explained that I didn't like her because she was mean and petty and full of pretense. He laughed, and when I added she didn't like me because I was so tall and arrogant and wasn't clean enough for her, he laughed harder and said something like "Well, that's life."

One evening he announced that on the next day he was going to Mexico to buy food for the weekend. There was nothing unusual about his pronouncement until he added that he was taking me along. He filled the shocked silence with the information that a trip to Mexico would give me an opportunity to practice Spanish.

Dolores' silence might have been brought on by a jealous reaction, but mine was occasioned by pure surprise. My father had not shown any particular pride in me and very little affection. He had not taken me to his friends or to southern California's few points of interest. It was incredible that I was to be included in something as exotic as a trip to Mexico. Well, I quickly reasoned, I deserved it "After all, I was his daughter and my vacation fell far short of what I had expected a vacation to be. Had I protested that I would like Dolores to go along, we might have been spared a display of violence and near tragedy.

But my young mind was filled with self, and my imagination shivered at the prospect of seeing sombreros, rancheros, tortillas and Pancho Villa. We spent a quiet night. Dolores mended her perfect underwear, and I pretended to read a novel. Dad listened to the radio with a drink in his hand and watched what I now know was a pitiful spectacle.

In the morning, we set out on the foreign adventure. The dirt roads of Mexico fulfilled all my longing for the unusual. Only a few miles from California's slick highways and, to me, tall buildings, we were bumping along on gravel streets that could have competed in crudeness with the worst paths in Arkansas, and the landscape boasted adobe huts or cabins walled with corrugated metal. Dogs, lean and dirty, slunk around the houses, and children played innocently in the nude or near nude with discarded rubber tires. Half the population looked like Tyrone Power and Dolores Del Rio, and the other half like Akim Tamiroff and Katina Paxinou, maybe only fatter and older.

Dad gave no explanation as we drove through the border town and headed for the interior. Although surprised, I refused to indulge my curiosity by questioning him. After a few miles we were stopped by a uniformed guard. He and Dad exchanged familiar greetings and Dad got out of the car. He reached back into the pocket of the door and took a bottle of liquor into the guard's kiosk. They laughed and talked for over a half hour as I sat in the car and tried to translate the muffled sounds. Eventually they came out and walked to the car. Dad still had the bottle but it was only half full. He asked the guard if he would like to marry me. Their Spanish was choppier than my school version but I understood. My father added as an inducement the fact that I was only fifteen years old. At once the guard leaned into the car and caressed my cheek. I supposed that he thought before that I was not only ugly but old, too, and that now the knowledge that I was probably unused attracted him. He told Dad that he would marry me and we would have "many babies." My father found that promise the

145

funniest thing he had heard since we left home. (He had laughed uproariously when Dolores didn't answer my goodbye and I explained as we drove away that she hadn't heard.) The guard was not discouraged by my attempts to get away from his probing hands and I would have squirmed to the driver's seat had not Dad opened the door and got in. After many *adiós*'s and *bonitas* and *espositas* Dad started the car, and we were on our grimy way again.

Signs informed me that we were headed for Ensenada. In those miles, along the twisted roads beside the steep mountain, I feared that I would never get back to America, civilization, English and wide streets again. He sipped from the bottle and sang snatches of Mexican songs as we climbed the tortuous mountain road. Our destination turned out not to be the town of Ensenada, after all, but about five miles out of the city limits. We pulled up in the dirt yard of a *cantina* where half-clothed children chased mean-looking chickens around and around. The noise of the car brought women to the door of the ramshackle building but didn't distract the single-minded activity of either the grubby kids or the scrawny fowls.

A woman's voice sang out, "Baylee, Baylee." And suddenly a claque of women crowded to the door and overflowed into the yard. Dad told me to get out of the car and we went to meet the women. He explained quickly that I was his daughter, which everyone thought to be uncontrollably funny. We were herded into a long room with a bar at one end. Tables sat lopsidedly on a loose-plank floor. The ceiling caught and held my attention. Paper streamers in every possible color waved in the near-still air, and as I watched a few fell to the floor. No one seemed to notice, or if they did, it was obviously unimportant that their sky was falling in. There were a few men on stools at the bar, and they greeted my father with the ease of familiarity. I was taken around and each person was told my name and age. The formal high school "*Cómo está usted?*" was received as the most charming utterance possible. People clapped me on the back, shook Dad's hand and spoke a rat-a-tat Spanish, that I was unable to follow. Baylee was the hero of the hour, and as he warmed under the uninhibited show of affection I saw a new side of the man. His quizzical smile disappeared and he stopped his affected way of talking (it would have been difficult to wedge *ers* into that rapid Spanish).

It seemed hard to believe that he was a lonely person, searching relentlessly in bottles, under women's skirts, in church work and lofty job titles for his "personal niche," lost before birth and unrecovered since. It was obvious to me then that he had never belonged in Stamps, and less to the slow-moving, slow-thinking Johnson family. How maddening it was to have been born in a cotton field with aspirations of grandeur.

146

In the Mexican bar, Dad had an air of relaxation which I had never seen visit him before. There was no need to pretend in front of those Mexican peasants. As he was, just being himself, he was sufficiently impressive to them. He was an American. He was Black. He spoke Spanish fluently. He had money and he could drink tequila with the best of them. The women liked him too. He was tall and handsome and generous.

It was a fiesta party. Someone put money in the jukebox and drinks were served to all the customers. I was given a warm Coca-Cola. The music poured out of the record machine as high-tenored voices wavered and held, wavered and held for the passionate rancheros. Men danced, at first alone, then with each other and occasionally a woman would join the foot-stomping rites. I was asked to dance. I hesitated because I wasn't sure I'd be able to follow the steps, but Dad nodded and encouraged me to try. I had been enjoying myself for at least an hour before I realized it. One young man had taught me how to put a sticker on the ceiling. First, all the sugar must be chewed out of Mexican gum, then the bartender gives a few slips of paper to the aspirant, who writes either a proverb or a sentimental remark on the strip. He takes the soft gum from his mouth and sticks it to the end of the streamer. Choosing a less densely covered area of the ceiling he aims at the spot, and as he throws he lets out a bloodcurdling scream which would not be out of place in a bronco-busting rodeo. After a few squeaky misses, I overcame my reserve and tore my tonsils loose with a yell that would have been worthy of Zapata. I was happy, Dad was proud and my new friends were gracious. A woman brought *chicharrones* (in the South they're called cracklings) in a greasy newspaper. I ate the fried pig skins, danced, screamed and drank the extra-sweet and sticky Coca-Cola with the nearest approach to abandonment I had ever experienced. As new revelers joined the celebration I was introduced as la niña de Baylee, and as quickly, accepted. The afternoon sun failed in its attempt to light the room through the single window, and the press of bodies and scents and sounds melted to give us an aromatic and artificial twilight. I realized that I hadn't seen my father for some time. "*Dónde está mi padre?*" I asked my dancing partner. My formal Spanish must have sounded as pretentious to the ears of the paisano as "Whither goeth my sire?" would have sounded to a semi-literate Ozark mountaineer. In any case it brought on a howl of laughter, a bear-crushing embrace and no answer. When the dance was finished, I made my way through the squeeze of the people as unobtrusively as possible. A fog of panic nearly suffocated me. He wasn't in the room. Had he made an arrangement with the guard back at the pass? I would not put it beyond him. My drink had been spiked. The certainty made my knees weak, and dancing couples blurred before my eyes. Dad was gone. He was probably halfway back home with the money from my sale in his pocket. I had to get to the door, which seemed miles and mountains away. People stopped me with "*Dónde vas?*" My response was something as stiff and double meaning as "*Yo voy por ventilarme,*" or "I am going to air out." No wonder I was a big hit.

Seen through the open door Dad's Hudson sat in lonely splendor. He hadn't left me, after all. That meant, of course, that I hadn't been drugged. I immediately felt better. No one followed me into the yard where the late afternoon sun had tenderized the midday harshness. I decided to sit in his car and wait for him since he couldn't have gone far. I knew he was with a woman, and the more I thought about it, it was easy to figure which one of the gay señoritas he had taken away. There had been a small neat woman with very red lips who clung to him avidly when we first arrived. I hadn't thought of it at the time but had simply recorded her pleasure. In the car, in reflection, I played the scene back. She had been the first to rush to him, and that was when he quickly said "This is my daughter" and "She speaks Spanish." If Dolores knew, she would crawl up in her blanket of affectations and die circumspectly. The thought of her mortification kept me company for a long time, but the sounds of music and laughter and Cisco Kid screams broke into my pleasant revengeful reveries. It was, after all, getting dark and Dad must have been beyond my reach in one of the little cabins out back. An awkward fear crept up slowly as I contemplated sitting in the car all night alone. It was a fear distantly related to the earlier panic. Terror did not engulf me wholly, but crawled along my mind like a tedious paralysis. I could roll up the windows and lock the door. I could lie down on the floor of the car and make myself small and invisible. Impossible! I tried to staunch the flood of fear. Why was I afraid of the Mexicans? After all, they had been kind to me and surely my father wouldn't allow his daughter to be ill treated. Wouldn't he? Would he? How could he leave me in that raunchy bar and go off with his woman? Did he care what happened to me? Not a damn, I decided, and opened the flood gates for hysteria. Once the tears began, there was no stopping them. I was to die, after all, in a Mexican dirt yard. The special person that I was, the intelligent mind that God and I had created together, was to depart this life without recognition or contribution. How pitiless were the Fates and how helpless was this poor Black girl.

I made out his shadow in the near gloom and was about to jump out and run to him when I noticed that he was being propelled by the small woman I had seen earlier and a man. He wobbled and lurched but they held him up firmly and guided his staggering toward the door of the *cantina*. Once he got inside we might never leave. I got out of the car and went to them. I asked Dad if he wouldn't like to get into the car and rest a little. He focused enough to recognize me and answered that that was exactly what he wanted; he was a little tired and he'd like to rest before we set out for his place. He told his friends his wishes in Spanish and they steered him to the car. When I opened the front door he said No, he'd lie down on the back seat for a little while. We got him into the car and tried to arrange his long legs comfortably. He began snoring even as we tugged at him. It sounded like the beginning of a deep and long sleep, and a warning that, after all, we were to spend the night in the car, in Mexico.

I thought fast as the couple laughed and jabbered at me in incomprehensible Spanish. I had never driven a car before, but I had watched carefully and my mother was declared to be the best driver in San Francisco. *She* declared it, at least. I was superbly intelligent and had good physical coordination. Of course I could drive. Idiots and lunatics drove cars, why not the brilliant Marguerite Johnson? I asked the Mexican man to turn the car around, again in my exquisite high school Spanish, and it took about fifteen minutes to make myself understood. The man must have asked me if I could drive, but I didn't know the Spanish for the verb "to drive," so I kept repeating "*Sí, sí*" and "*Gracias*" until he got in and headed the car toward the highway. He showed his understanding of the situation by his next action. He left the motor running. I put my foot on the accelerator and clutch, jiggled the gearshift and raised both feet. With an ominous roar we leaped out of the yard.

As we shook onto the shelf of the road the car nearly stalled and I stamped both feet again on the pedal and clutch. We made no progress and an awful amount of noise, but the motor didn't stop. I understood then that in order to go forward I would have to lift my feet off the pedals, and if I did so abruptly the car would shake like a person with St. Vitus Dance. With that complete understanding of the principle of motor locomotion, I drove down the mountainside toward Calexico, some fifty miles away. It is hard to understand why my vivid imagination and tendency toward scariness didn't provide me with gory scenes of bloody crashes on a *risco de Mexico*. I can only think that my every sense was concentrated on steering the bucking car.

When it became totally dark, I fumbled over knobs, twisting and pulling until I succeeded in finding the lights. The car slowed down as I centered on that search, and I forgot to step on the pedals, and the motor gurgled, the car pitched and the engine stopped. A bumbling sound from the back told me that Dad had fallen off the seat (I had been expecting this to happen for miles). I pulled the hand brake and carefully considered my next move. It was useless to think of asking Dad. The fall on the floor had failed to stir him, and I would be unable to do so. No car was likely to pass us—I hadn't seen any motor vehicles since we passed the guard's house early in the day. We were headed downhill, so I reasoned that with any luck we might coast right up to Calexico—or at least to the guard. I waited until I formulated an approach to him before releasing the brake. I would stop the car when we reached the kiosk and put on my siddity air. I would speak to him like the peasant he was. I would order him to start the car and then tip him a quarter or even a dollar from Dad's pocket before driving on.

With my plans solidly made, I released the brake and we began coasting down the slope. I also pumped the clutch and the accelerator, hoping that the action would speed our descent, and wonder of wonders the motor started again. The Hudson went crazy on the hill. It was rebelling and would have leaped over the side of the mountain, to all our destruction, in its attempt to unseat me had I relaxed control for a single second. The challenge was exhilarating. It was me, Marguerite, against the elemental opposition. As I twisted the steering wheel and forced the accelerator to the floor I was controlling Mexico, and might and aloneness and inexperienced youth and Bailey Johnson, Sr., and death and insecurity, and even gravity.

After what seemed like one thousand and one nights of challenge the mountain began to level off and we started passing scattered lights on either side of the road. No matter what happened after that I had won. The car began to slow down as if it had been tamed and was going to give up without grace. I pumped even harder and we finally reached the guard's box. I pulled on the hand brake and came to a stop. There would be no need for me to speak to the guard since the motor was running, but I had to wait until he looked into the car and gave me the signal to continue. He was busy talking to people in a car facing the mountain I had just conquered. The light from his hut showed him bent from the waist with his upper torso completely swallowed by the mouth of the open window. I held the car in instant readiness for the next lap of our journey. When the guard unfolded himself and stood erect I was able to see he was not the same man of the morning's embarrassment. I was understandably taken aback at the discovery and when he saluted sharply and barked *"Pasa"* I released the brake, put both feet down and lifted them a bit too sharply. The car outran my intention. It leaped not only forward but left as well, and with a few angry spurts propelled itself onto the side of the car just pulling off. The crash of scraping metal was

150

followed immediately by a volley of Spanish hurled at me from all directions. Again, strangely enough, fear was absent from my sensations. I wondered in this order: was I hurt, was anyone else hurt, would I go to jail, what were the Mexicans saying, and finally, had Dad awakened? I was able to answer the first and last concern promptly. Buoyed by the adrenalin that had flooded my brain as we careened down the mountainside, I had never felt better, and my father's snores cut through the cacophony of protestations outside my window. I got out of the car, intending to ask for the *policías*, but the guard beat me to the punch. He said a few words, which were strung together like beads, but one of them was *policías*. As the people in the other car fumbled out, I tried to recover my control and said loudly and too graciously, *"Gracias, señor."* The family, some eight or more people of every age and size, walked around me, talking heatedly and sizing me up as if I might have been a statue in a city park and they were a flock of pigeons. One said *"Joven,"* meaning I was young. I tried to see which one was so intelligent. I would direct my conversation to him or her, but they shifted positions so quickly it was impossible to make the person out. Then another suggested *"Borracho."* Well, certainly, I must have smelled like a tequila farm, since Dad had been breathing out the liquor in noisy respirations and I had kept the windows closed against the cold night air. It wasn't likely that I would explain that to these strangers even if I could. Which I couldn't. Someone got the idea to look into the car, and a scream brought us all up short. People—they seemed to be in the hundreds—crowded to the windows and more screams erupted. I thought for a minute that something awful might have happened. Maybe at the time of the crash... I, too, pushed to the window to see, but then I remembered the rhythmic snores, and coolly walked away. The guard must have thought he had a major crime on his hands. He made moves and sounds like "Watch her" or "Don't let her out of your sight." The family came back, this time not as close but more menacing, and when I was able to sort out one coherent question, *"Quién es?"* I answered dryly and with all the detachment I could summon, *"Mi padre."* Being a people of close family ties and weekly fiestas they suddenly understood the situation. I was a poor little girl thing who was caring for my drunken father, who had stayed too long at the fair. *Pobrecita.*

The guard, the father and one or two small children began the herculean job of waking Dad. I watched coolly as the remaining people paraded, making figure eights around me and their badly bruised automobile. The two men shook and tugged and pulled while the children jumped up and down on my father's chest. I credit the children's action for the success of the effort. Bailey Johnson, Sr., woke up in Spanish. "*Qué tiene? Qué pasa? Qué quiere*" Anyone else would have asked, "Where am I?" Obviously, this was a common Mexican experience. When I saw he was fairly lucid I went to the car, calmly pushed the people away, and said from the haughty level of one who has successfully brought to heel a marauding car and negotiated a sneaky mountain, "Dad, there's been an accident." He recognized me by degrees and became my pre-Mexican-fiesta father.

"An accident, huh? Er, who was at fault? You, Marguerite? Errer was it you?"

It would have been futile to tell him of my mastering his car and driving it nearly fifty miles. I didn't expect or even need, now, his approbation.

"Yes, Dad, I ran into a car."

He still hadn't sat up completely, so he couldn't know where we were. But from the floor where he rested, as if that was the logical place to be, he said, "In the glove compartment. The insurance papers. Get them and er give them to the police, and then come back."

The guard stuck his head in the other door before I could form a scathing but polite response. He asked Dad to get out of the car. Never at a loss, my father reached in the glove compartment, and took out the folded papers and the half bottle of liquor he had left there earlier. He gave the guard one of his pinch-backed laughs, and descended, by joints, from the car. Once on the ground he towered over the angry people. He took a quick reading of his location and the situation, and then put his arm around the other driver's shoulder. He kindly, not in the least condescendingly, bent to speak to the guard, and the three men walked into the hut. Within easy minutes, laughter burst from the shack and the crisis was over, but so was the enjoyment.

Dad shook hands with all the men, patted the children and smiled winsomely at the women. Then, and without looking at the damaged cars, he eased himself behind the steering wheel. He called me to get in, and as if he had not been helplessly drunk a half hour earlier, he drove unerringly toward home. He said he didn't know I could drive, and how did I like his car? I was angry that he had recovered so quickly and felt let down that he didn't appreciate the greatness of my achievement. So I answered yes to both the statement and the question. Before we reached the border he rolled down the window, and the fresh air, which was welcome, was uncomfortably cold. He told me to get his jacket from the back seat and put it on. We drove into the city in a cold and private silence.

31

Dolores was sitting, it seemed, in the same place as the night before. Her pose was so similar it was hard to believe she had gone to sleep, eaten breakfast or even patted her firm hairdo. Dad said sportily, "Hello, kid," and walked toward the bathroom. I greeted her: "Hello, Dolores" (we had long dropped the pretense of familial relationship). She responded, briefly but politely, and threaded her attention through the eye of her needle. She was now prudently making cute kitchen curtains, which would soon starchily oppose the wind. Having nothing more to say, I went to my room. within minutes an argument ensued in the living area that was as audible to me as if the separating walls were muslin sheets.

"Bailey, you've let your children come between us."

"Kid, you're too sensitive. The children, er, my children, can't come between us, unless you let them."

"How can I stop it?"—she was crying—"They're doing it" Then she said, "You gave your daughter your jacket."

"Was I supposed to let her freeze to death? Is that what you'd like, kid? "He laughed. "You would, wouldn't you?"

"Bailey, you know I wanted to like your children, but they..." She couldn't bring herself to describe us.

"Why the hell don't you say what you mean? You're a pretentious little bitch, aren't you? That's what Marguerite called you, and she's right."

I shivered to think how that revelation would add to her iceberg of hate for me.

"Marguerite can go to hell, Bailey Johnson. I'm marrying you, I don't want to marry your children."

"More pity for you, you unlucky sow. I am going out. Goodnight."

The front door slammed. Dolores cried quietly and broke the piteous whimpers with sniffles and a few dainty nose blows into her handkerchief.

In my room, I thought my father was mean and cruel. He had enjoyed his Mexican holiday, and still was unable to proffer a bit of kindness to the woman who had waited patiently, busying herself with housewifely duties. I was certain that she knew he'd been drinking, and she must have noticed that although we were away over twelve hours, we hadn't brought one tortilla into the house.

I felt sorry and even a little guilty. I had enjoyed myself, too. I had been eating *chicharrones* while she probably sat praying for his safe return. I had defeated a car and a mountain as she pondered over my father's fidelity. There was nothing fair or kind about the treatment, so I decided to go out and console her. The idea of spreading mercy, indiscriminately, or, to be more correct, spreading it on someone I really didn't care about, enraptured me. I was basically good. Not understood, and not even liked, but even so, just, and better than just. I was merciful. I stood in the center of the floor but Dolores never looked up. She worked the thread through the flowered cloth as if she were sewing the torn ends of her life together. I said, in my Florence Nightingale voice, "Dolores, I don't mean to come between you and Dad. I wish you'd believe me." There, it was done. My good deed balanced the rest of the day.

With her head still bent she said, "No one was speaking to you, Marguerite. It is rude to eavesdrop on other people's conversations."

Surely she wasn't so dumb as to think these paper walls were made of marble. I let just the tiniest shred of impudence enter my voice. "I've never eavesdropped in my life. A deaf person would have been hard put not to hear what you said. I thought I'd tell you that I have no interest in coming between you and my father. That's all."

My mission had failed and succeeded. She refused to be pacified, but I had shown myself in a favorable and Christian light. I turned to go.

"No, that's not all." She looked up. Her face was puffy and her eyes swollen red. "Why don't you go back to your mother? If you've got one." Her tone was so subdued she might have been telling me to cook a pot of rice. If I've got one? Well, I'd tell her.

"I've got one and she's worlds better than you, prettier, too, and intelligent and—"

"And"—her voice keened to a point—"she's a whore." Maybe if I had been older, or had had my mother longer, or understood Dolores' frustration more deeply, my response would not have been so violent. I know that the awful accusation struck not so much at my filial love as at the foundation of my new existence. If there was a chance of truth in the charge, I would not be able to live, to continue to live with Mother, and I so wanted to.

I walked to Dolores, enraged at the threat. "I'm going to slap you for that, you silly, old bitch." I warned her and I slapped her. She was out of the chair like a flea, and before I could jump back she had her arms around me. Her hair was under my chin and she wrapped her arms, it seemed two or three times, around my waist. I had to push her shoulders with all my strength to unlock the octopus hold. Neither of us made a sound until I finally shoved her back onto the sofa. Then she started screaming. Silly old fool. What did she expect if she called my mother a whore? I walked out of the house. On the steps I felt something wet on my arm and looked down to find blood. Her screams still sailed through the evening air like skipping stones, but I was bleeding. I looked carefully on my arm, but there was no cut. I put my arm back to my waist and it brought fresh blood as I pulled it away. I was cut. Before I could fully understand, or comprehend enough to respond, Dolores opened the door, screaming still, and upon seeing me, instead of slamming the door she ran like a mad woman down the stairs. I saw a hammer in her hand, and without wondering if I would be able to take it from her, I fled. Dad's car sat in a yard twice in one day offering magnificent refuge. I jumped in, rolled up the windows and locked the door. Dolores flitted around the car, screaming like a banshee, her face bedizened with fury.

Daddy Bailey and the neighbors he was visiting responded to the screams and crowded around her. She shouted that I had jumped on her and tried to kill her and Bailey had better not bring me back in the house. I sat in the car, feeling the blood slip down to my buttocks as the people quieted and cooled her rage. My father motioned to me to open the window, and when I did he said he would take Dolores inside but I should stay in the car. He would be back to attend to me.

The events of the day swarmed over me and made my breathing difficult. After all the decisive victories of the day my life was to end in sticky death. If Dad stayed a very long time in the house, I was too afraid to go to the door and ask for him, and besides, my feminine training would not allow me to walk two steps with blood on my dress. As I had always feared, no, known, the trials had been for nothing. (The dread of futility has been my lifelong plague.) Excitement, apprehension, release and anger had drained me of mobility. I waited for Fate, the string puller, to dictate my movements.

My father came down the steps in a few minutes and angrily slammed into the car. He sat in a corner of blood and I gave no warning. He must have been pondering what to do with me when he felt the damp on his trousers.

"What the hell is this?" He hunched himself up on a hip and brushed the pants. His hand showed red in the porch's cast-off light. "What is this, Marguerite?"

I said with a coldness that would have done him proud, "I've been cut."

"What do you mean, cut?"

155

It only lasted a precious minute, but I managed once to see my father perplexed.

"Cut." It was so delicious. I didn't mind draining away into the plaid seat cushions.

"When? By whom?"

Daddy, even in a critical moment, wouldn't say "By who?"

"Dolores cut me." The economy of words showed my contempt for them all.

"How badly?"

I would have reminded him that I was no doctor and therefore was ill equipped to do a thorough examination, but impudence would have diminished my lead.

"I don't know."

He put the car in gear, smoothly, and I enviously realized that although I had driven his car I didn't know how to drive.

I thought we were en route to an emergency hospital, and so with serenity I made plans for my death and will. As I faded into time's dateless night, I would say to the doctor, "The moving finger writes and having writ, moves on..." and my soul would escape gracefully. Bailey was to have my books, my Lester Young records and my love from the next world. I had groggily surrendered myself to oblivion when the car stopped.

Dad said, "O.K., kid, errer let's go."

We were in a strange driveway, and even before I got out of the car he was on the steps of a typical southern California ranch-type house. The doorbell chimed, and he beckoned me up the steps. When the door opened he signaled me to stand outside. After all, I was dripping, and I could see the living room was carpeted. Dad went in but didn't quite close the door, and a few minutes later a woman called to me in a whisper from the side of the house. I followed her into a recreation room, and she asked me where I was hurt. She was quiet and her concern seemed sincere. I pulled off my dress and we both looked into the open flesh on my side. She was as pleased as I was disappointed that the edges of the wound had begun to clot. She washed witch hazel over the rupture and taped me tightly with extra-long Band-Aids. Then we went into the living room. Dad shook hands with the man he'd been talking to and thanked my emergency nurse and we left.

In the car he explained that the couple were his friends and he had asked the wife to look at me. He said he told her if the laceration wasn't too deep he would be grateful if she treated it. Otherwise he'd have to take me to a hospital. Could I imagine the scandal if people found out that his, Bailey Johnson's, daughter had been cut by his lady friend? He was after all a Mason, an Elk, a naval dietician and the first Negro deacon in the Lutheran church. No Negro in the city would be able to hold his head up if our misfortune became common knowledge. While the lady (I never knew her name) dressed my wound he had telephoned other friends and made arrangements for me to spend the night with them. At another strange trailer, in yet another mobile park, I was taken in and given night clothes and a bed. Dad said he'd see me around noon the next day.

I went to bed and slept as if my death wish had come true. In the morning neither the empty and unfamiliar surroundings nor the stiffness of my side bothered me. I made and ate a big breakfast and sat down with a slick magazine to wait for Dad.

At fifteen life had taught me undeniably that surrender, in its place, was as honorable as resistance, especially if one had no choice.

When my father came, with a jacket thrown over the striped cotton uniform he wore as a naval dietician, he asked how I felt, gave me a dollar and a half and a kiss, and said he'd drop by late in the evening. He laughed as usual. Nervous?

Alone, I imagined the owners returning to find me in their house, and realized that I didn't even remember what they looked like. How could I bear their contempt or their pity? If I disappeared Dad would be relieved, not to mention Dolores. I hesitated nearly too long. What would I do? Did I have the nerve to commit suicide? If I jumped in the ocean wouldn't I come up all bloated like the man Bailey saw in Stamps? The thought of my brother made me pause. What would he do? I waited a patience and another patience and then he ordered me to leave. But don't kill yourself. You can always do that if things get bad enough.

I made a few tuna sandwiches, lumpy with pickles, put a Band-Aid supply in my pocket, counted my money (I had over three dollars plus some Mexican coins) and walked out. When I heard the door slam I knew the decision had jelled. I had no key and nothing on earth would induce me to stand around until Dad's friends returned to pityingly let me back in.

Now that I was out free, I set to thinking of my future. The obvious solution to my homelessness concerned me only briefly. I could go home to Mother, but I couldn't. I could never succeed in shielding the gash in my side from her. She was too perceptive not to notice the crusty Band-Aids and my favoring the wound. And if I failed to hide the wound we were certain to experience another scene of violence. I thought of poor Mr. Freeman, and the guilt which lined my heart, even after all those years, was a nagging passenger in my mind.

32

I spent the day wandering aimlessly through the bright streets. The noisy penny arcades with their gaggle-giggle of sailors and children and the games of chance were tempting, but after walking through one of them it was obvious that I could only win more chances and no money. I went to the library and used a part of my day reading science fiction, and in its marble washroom I changed my bandage.

On one flat street I passed a junkyard, littered with the carcasses of old cars. The dead hulks were somehow so uninviting that I decided to inspect them. As I wound my way through the discards a temporary solution sprang to my mind. I would find a clean or cleanish car and spend the night in it. With the optimism of ignorance I thought that the morning was bound to bring a more pleasant solution. A tall-bodied gray car near the fence caught my eye. Its seats were untorn, and although it had no wheels or rims it sat evenly on its fenders. The idea of sleeping in the near open bolstered my sense of freedom. I was a loose kite in a gentle wind floating with only my will for an anchor. After deciding upon the car, I got inside and ate the tuna sandwiches and then searched the floorboards for holes. The fear that rats might scurry in and eat off my nose as I slept (some cases had been recently reported in the papers) was more alarming than the shadowed hulks in the junkyard or the quickly descending night. My gray choice, however, seemed rat-tight, and I abandoned my idea of taking another walk and decided to sit steady and wait for sleep.

My car was an island and the junkyard a sea, and I was all alone and full of warm. The mainland was just a decision away. As evening became definite the street lamps flashed on and the lights of moving cars squared my world in a piercing probing. I counted the headlights and said my prayers and fell asleep.

The morning's brightness drew me awake and I was surrounded with strangeness. I had slid down the seat and slept the night through in an ungainly position. Wrestling with my body to assume an upward arrangement, I saw a collage of Negro, Mexican and white faces outside the windows. They were laughing and making the mouth gestures of talkers but their sounds didn't penetrate my

158

refuge. There was so much curiosity evident in their features that I knew they wouldn't just go away before they knew who I was, so I opened the door, prepared to give them any story (even the truth) that would buy my peace.

The windows and my grogginess had distorted their features. I had thought they were adults and maybe citizens of Brobdingnag, at least. Standing outside, I found there was only one person taller than I, and that I was only a few years younger than any of them. I was asked my name, where I came from and what led me to the junkyard. They accepted my explanation that I was from San Francisco, that my name was Marguerite but that I was called Maya and I simply had no place to stay. With a generous gesture the tall boy, who said he was Bootsie, welcomed me, and said I could stay as long as I honored their rule: No two people of opposite sex slept together. In fact, unless it rained, everyone had his own private sleeping accommodations. Since some of the cars leaked, bad weather forced a doubling up. There was no stealing, not for reasons of morality but because a crime would bring the police to the yard; and since everyone was underage, there was the likelihood that they'd be sent off to foster homes or juvenile delinquent courts. Everyone worked at something. Most of the girls collected bottles and worked weekends in greasy spoons. The boys mowed lawns, swept out pool halls and ran errands for small Negro-owned stores. All money was held by Bootsie and used communally.

During the month that I spent in the yard I learned to drive (one boy's older brother owned a car that moved), to curse and to dance. Lee Arthur was the only boy who ran around with the gang but lived at home with his mother. Mrs. Arthur worked nights, so on Friday evening all the girls went to his house for a bath. We did our laundry in the Laundromat, but those things that required ironing were taken to Lee's house and the ironing chore was shared, as was everything else.

On Saturday night we entered the jitterbug contest at the Silver Slipper, whether we could dance or not. The prizes were tempting ($25 to first couple, $10 to second and $5 to third), and Bootsie reasoned that if all of us entered we had a better chance. Juan, the Mexican boy, was my partner, and although he couldn't dance any better than I, we were a sensation on the floor. He was very short with a shock of straight black hair that swished around his head when he pivoted, and I was thin and black and tall as a tree. On my last weekend at the yard, we actually won the second prize. The dance we performed could never be duplicated or described except to say that the passion with which we threw each other around the small dance area was similar to the zeal shown in honest wrestling matches and hand-to-hand combat.

After a month my thinking processes had so changed that I was hardly recognizahle to myself. The unquestioning acceptance by my peers had dislodged the familiar insecurity. Odd that the homeless children, the silt of war frenzy, could initiate me into the brotherhood of man. After hunting down unbroken bottles and selling them with a white girl from Missouri, a Mexican girl from Los Angeles and a Black girl from Oklahoma, I was never again to sense myself so solidly outside the pale of the human race. The lack of criticism evidenced by our ad hoc community influenced me, and set a tone of tolerance for my life.

I telephoned Mother (her voice reminded me of another world) and asked her to send for me. When she said she was going to send my air ticket to Daddy, I explained that it would be easier if she simply sent my fare to the airline, then I'd pick it up. With the easy grace characteristic of Mother when she was given a chance to be magnanimous she agreed.

The unrestrained life we had led made me believe that my new friends would be undemonstrative about my leaving. I was right. After I picked up my ticket I announced rather casually that I would be leaving the following day. My revelation was accepted with at least the equal amount of detachment (only it was not a pose) and everyone wished me well. I didn't want to say goodbye to the junkyard or to my car, so I spent my last night at an all-night movie. One girl, whose name and face have melted into the years, gave me "an all-enduring friendship ring," and Juan gave me a black lace handkerchief just in case I wanted to go to church sometime.

I arrived in San Francisco, leaner than usual, fairly unkempt, and with no luggage. Mother took one look and said, "Is the rationing that bad at your father's? You'd better have some food to stick to all those bones." She, as she called it, turned to, and soon I sat at a clothed table with bowls of food, expressly cooked for me.

I was at a home, again. And my mother was a fine lady. Dolores was a fool and, more important, a liar.

33

The house seemed smaller and quieter after the trip south, and the first bloom of San Francisco's glamour had dulled around the edges. Adults had lost the wisdom from the surface of their faces. I reasoned that I had given up some youth for knowledge, but my gain was more valuable than the loss.

Bailey was much older too. Even years older than I had become. He had made friends during that youth-shattering summer with a group of slick street boys. His language had changed. He was forever dropping slangy terms into his sentences like dumplings in a pot. He may have been glad to see me, but he didn't act much like it. When I tried to tell him of my adventures and misadventures, he responded with a casual indifference which stilled the tale on my lips. His new companions cluttered the living room and halls wearing zoot suits and wide-brimmed hats and dangling long snaky chains hooked at their belts. They drank sloe gin secretly and told dirty jokes. Although I had no regrets, I told myself sadly that growing up was not the painless process one would have thought it to be. In one area my brother and I found ourselves closer. I had gotten the knack of public dancing. All the lessons with Mother, who danced so effortlessly, had not borne immediate fruit. But with my newly and dearly bought assurance I could give myself up to the rhythms and let them propel me where they willed.

Mother allowed us to go to the big band dances in the crowded city auditorium. We danced the jitterbug to Count Basie, the Lindy and the Big Apple to Cab Calloway, and the Half Time Texas Hop to Duke Ellington. In a matter of months cute Bailey and his tall sister were famous as those dancing fools (which was an apt description).

Although I had risked my life (not intentionally) in her defense, Mother's reputation, good name and community image ceased, or nearly ceased, being of interest to me. It was not that I cared for her less but that I concerned myself less about everything and everyone. I often thought of the tedium of life once one had seen all its surprises. In two months, I had become blasé.

Mother and Bailey were entangled in the Oedipal skein. Neither could do without or do with the other; yet the constrictions of conscience and society, morality and ethos dictated a separation. On some flimsy excuse, Mother ordered Bailey out of the house. On an equally flimsy excuse he complied. Bailey was sixteen, small for his age, bright for any and hopelessly in love with Mother Dear. Her heroes were her friends and her friends were big men in the rackets. They wore two-hundred-dollar Chesterfield coats, Busch shoes at fifty dollars a pair, and Knox hats. Their shirts were monogrammed and their fingernails manicured. How could a sixteen-year-old boy hope to compete with such overshadowing rivals? He did what he had to do. He acquired a withered white prostitute, a diamond ring on his little finger and a Harris tweed coat with raglan sleeves. He

161

didn't consciously consider the new possessions the open sesame to Mother Dear's vault of acceptance. And she had no idea that her preferences prodded him to such excesses.

From the wings I heard and watched the pavane of tragedy move steadily toward its climax. Interception and even the thought of it was impossible. Easier to plan an obstruction to a sunrise or a hurricane. If Mother was a beautiful woman who exacted the tribute of obeisance from all men, she was also a mother, and "a damn good one." No son of hers was going to be exploited by a used-up white whore, who wanted to milk him of his youth and spoil him for adulthood. Hell, no.

Bailey, for his part, was her son as she was his mother. He had no intention of taking low even from the most beautiful woman in the world. The fact that she happened to be his mother did nothing to weaken his resolve.

Get out? Oh, hell, yes. Tomorrow? What's wrong with today? Today? What about right now? But neither could move until all the measured steps had been negotiated.

During the weeks of bitter wrangling I sat in hopeless wonder. We were not allowed profanity or even obvious sarcasm, but Bailey looped his language around his tongue and issued it out to Mother in alum drops. She threw her "ing bings" (passionate explosions guaranteed to depilate the chest of the strongest man) and was sweetly sorry (only to me) after.

I had been left out of their power/love struggle. It would be more correct to say that since neither needed a claque I was forgotten on the sidelines.

It was a little like Switzerland in World War II. Shells were bursting all around me, souls were tortured and I was powerless in the confines of imposed neutrality—hopes were dying. The confrontation, which brought relief, had come on an ordinary unheralded evening. It was after eleven o'clock, so I left my door ajar, hoping to hear Mother go out, or the creak of Bailey easing up the stairs.

The record player on the first floor volumed up Lonnie Johnson singing, "Tomorrow night, will you remember what you said tonight?" Glasses clinked and voices rubbed each other. A party was shimmering below and Bailey had defied Mother's eleven o'clock curfew. If he made it in before midnight, she might be satisfied with slapping him across the face a few times with her lashing words.

Twelve o'clock came and went at once, and I sat up in bed and laid my cards out for the first of many games of solitaire.

"Bailey!"

My watch hands made the uneven V of one o'clock.

162

"Yes, Mother Dear?" En garde. His voice thrust sweet and sour, and he accented the "dear."

"I guess you're a man... Turn down that record player." She shouted the last to the revelers.

"I'm your son, Mother Dear." A swift parry.

"Is it eleven o'clock, Bailey?" That was a feint, designed to catch the opponent offguard.

"It's after one o'clock, Mother Dear." He had opened up the game, and the strokes from then on would have to be direct.

"Clidell is the only man in this house, and if you think you're so much of a man..." Her voice popped like a razor on a strap.

"I'm leaving now, Mother Dear." The deferential tone heightened the content of his announcement. In a bloodless coup he had thrust beneath her visor.

Now, laid open, she had no recourse but to hurry along the tunnel of her anger, headlong.

"Then Goddammit, get your heels to clicking." And her heels were clicking down the linoleum hall as Bailey tap-danced up the stairs to his room.

When rain comes finally, washing away a low sky of muddy ocher, we who could not control the phenomenon are pressed into relief. The near-occult feeling: The fact of being witness to the end of the world gives way to tangible things. Even if the succeeding sensations are not common, they are at least not mysterious.

Bailey was leaving home. At one o'clock in the morning, my little brother, who in my lonely days of inferno dwelling had protected me from goblins, gnomes, gremlins and devils, was leaving home.

I had known all along the inevitable outcome and that I dared not poke into his knapsack of misery, even with the offer to help him carry it.

I went to his room, against my judgment, and found him throwing his carefully tended clothes into a pillowcase. His maturity embarrassed me. In his little face, balled up like a fist, I found no vestige of my brother, and when, not knowing what to say, I asked if I could help, he answered, "Leave me the shit alone."

I leaned on the doorjamb, lending him my physical presence but said no more.

"She wants me out, does she? Well, I'll get out of here so fast I'll leave the air on fire. She calls herself a mother? Huh! I'll be damned. She's seen the last of me. I can make it. I'll always make it."

At some point he noticed me still in the doorway, and his consciousness stretched to remember our relationship.

"Maya, if you want to leave now, come on. I'll take care of you."

He didn't wait for an answer, but as quickly went back to speaking to his soul. "She won't miss me, and I sure as hell won't miss her. To hell with her and everybody else."

He had finished jamming his shoes on top of his shirts and ties, and socks were wadded into the pillowcase. He remembered me again.

"Maya, you can have my books."

My tears were not for Bailey or Mother or even myself but for the helplessness of mortals who live on the sufferance of Life. In order to avoid this bitter end, we would all have to be born again, and born with the knowledge of alternatives. Even then?

Bailey grabbed up the lumpy pillowcase and pushed by me for the stairs. As the front door slammed, the record player downstairs mastered the house and Nat King Cole warned the world to "straighten up and fly right." As if they could, as if human beings could make a choice.

Mother's eyes were red, and her face puffy, the next morning, but she smiled her "everything is everything" smile and turned in tight little moons, making breakfast, talking business and brightening the corner where she was. No one mentioned Bailey's absence as if things were as they should be and always were.

The house was smudged with unspoken thoughts and it was necessary to go to my room to breathe. I believed I knew where he headed the night before, and made up my mind to find him and offer him my support. In the afternoon I went to a bay-windowed house which boasted ROOMS, in green and orange letters, through the glass. A woman of any age past thirty answered my ring and said Bailey Johnson was at the top of the stairs.

His eyes were as red as Mother's had been, but his face had loosened a little from the tightness of the night before. In an almost formal manner I was invited into a room with a clean chenille-covered bed, an easy chair, a gas fireplace and a table.

He began to talk, covering up the unusual situation that we found ourselves in.

"Nice room, isn't it? You know it's very hard to find rooms now. The war and all... Betty lives here [she was the white prostitute] and she got this place for me... Maya, you know, it's better this way... I mean, I'm a man, and I have to be on my own..."

I was furious that he didn't curse and abuse the Fates or Mother or at least act put upon.

"Well"—I thought to start it—"If Mother was really a mother, she wouldn't have——"

He stopped me, his little black hand held up as if I were to read his palm. "Wait, Maya, she was right. There is a tide and time in every man's life——"

"Bailey, you're sixteen."

"Chronologically, yes, but I haven't been sixteen for years. Anyway, there comes a time when a man must cut the apron strings and face life on his own... As I was saying to Mother Dear, I've come to—"

"When were you talking to Mother...?"

"This morning, I said to Mother Dear—"

"Did you phone her?"

"Yes. And she came by here. We had a very fruitful discussion"— he chose his words with the precision of a Sunday school teacher— "She understands completely. There is a time in every man's life when he must push off from the wharf of safety into the sea of chance... Anyway, she is arranging with a friend of hers in Oakland to get me on the Southern Pacific. Maya, it's just a start. I'll begin as a dining-car waiter and then a steward, and when I know all there is to know about that, I'll branch out... The future looks good. The Black man hasn't even begun to storm the battlefronts. I'm going for broke myself."

His room smelled of cooked grease, Lysol and age, but his face believed the freshness of his words, and I had no heart nor art to drag him back to the reeling reality of our life and times.

Whores were lying down first and getting up last in the room next door. Chicken suppers and gambling games were rioting on a twenty-four-hour basis downstairs. Sailors and soldiers on their doom-lined road to war cracked windows and broke locks for blocks around, hoping to leave their imprint on a building or in the memory of a victim. A chance to be perpetrated. Bailey sat wrapped in his decision and anesthetized by youth. If I'd had any suggestion to make I couldn't have penetrated his unlucky armor. And, most regrettable, I had no suggestion to make.

"I'm your sister, and whatever I can do, I'll do it."

"Maya, don't worry about me. That's all I want you to do. Don't worry. I'll be okey-dokey."

I left his room because, and only because, we had said all we could say. The unsaid words pushed roughly against the thoughts that we had no craft to verbalize, and crowded the room to uneasiness.

34

Later, my room had all the cheeriness of a dungeon and the appeal of a tomb. It was going to be impossible to stay there, but leaving held no attraction for me, either. Running away from home would be anticlimactic after Mexico, and a dull story after my month in the car lot. But the need for change bulldozed a road down the center of my mind.

I had it. The answer came to me with the suddenness of a collision. I would go to work. Mother wouldn't be difficult to convince; after all, in school I was a year ahead of my grade and Mother was a firm believer in self-sufficiency. In fact, she'd be pleased to think that I had that much gumption, that much of her in my character. (She liked to speak of herself as the original "do-it-yourself girl.")

Once I had settled on getting a job, all that remained was to decide which kind of job I was most fitted for. My intellectual pride had kept me from selecting typing, shorthand or filing as subjects in school, so office work was ruled out. War plants and shipyards demanded birth certificates, and mine would reveal me to be fifteen, and ineligible for work. So the well-paying defense jobs were also out. Women had replaced men on the streetcars as conductors and motormen, and the thought of sailing up and down the hills of San Francisco in a dark-blue uniform, with a money changer at my belt, caught my fancy.

Mother was as easy as I had anticipated. The world was moving so fast, so much money was being made, so many people were dying in Guam, and Germany, that hordes of strangers became good friends overnight. Life was cheap and death entirely free. How could she have the time to think about my academic career?

To her question of what I planned to do, I replied that I would get a job on the streetcars. She rejected the proposal with: "They don't accept colored people on the streetcars."

I would like to claim an immediate fury which was followed by the noble determination to break the restricting tradition. But the truth is, my first reaction was one of disappointment. I'd pictured myself, dressed in a neat blue serge suit, my money changer swinging jauntily at my waist, and a cheery smile for the passengers which would make their own work day brighter.

From disappointment, I gradually ascended the emotional ladder

166

to haughty indignation, and finally to that state of stubbornness where the mind is locked like the jaws of an enraged bulldog.

I would go to work on the streetcars and wear a blue serge suit. Mother gave me her support with one of her usual terse asides, "That's what you want to do? Then nothing beats a trial but a failure. Give it everything you've got. I've told you many times, 'Can't do is like Don't Care.' Neither of them have a home."

Translated, that meant there was nothing a person can't do, and there should be nothing a human being didn't care about. It was the most positive encouragement I could have hoped for.

In the offices of the Market Street Railway Company, the receptionist seemed as surprised to see me there as I was surprised to find the interior dingy and the décor drab. Somehow I had expected waxed surfaces and carpeted floors. If I had met no resistance, I might have decided against working for such a poor-mouth-looking concern. As it was, I explained that I had come to see about a job. She asked, was I sent by an agency, and when I replied that I was not, she told me they were only accepting applicants from agencies.

The classified pages of the morning papers had listed advertisements for motorettes and conductorettes and I reminded her of that. She gave me a face full of astonishment that my suspicious nature would not accept.

"I am applying for the job listed in this morning's *Chronicle* and I'd like to be presented to your personnel manager." While I spoke in supercilious accents, and looked at the room as if I had an oil well in my own backyard, my armpits were being pricked by millions of hot pointed needles. She saw her escape and dived into it.

"He's out. He's out for the day. You might call tomorrow and if he's in, I'm sure you can see him." Then she swiveled her chair around on its rusty screws and with that I was supposed to be dismissed.

"May I ask his name?"

She half turned, acting surprised to find me still there.

"His name? Whose name?"

"Your personnel manager."

We were firmly joined in the hypocrisy to play out the scene.

"The personnel manager? Oh, he's Mr. Cooper, but I'm not sure you'll find him here tomorrow. He's... Oh, but you can try."

"Thank you."

"You're welcome."

And I was out of the musty room and into the even mustier lobby. In the street I saw the receptionist and myself going faithfully through paces that were stale with familiarity, although I had never encountered that kind of situation before and, probably, neither had

167

she. We were like actors who, knowing the play by heart, were still able to cry afresh over the old tragedies and laugh spontaneously at the comic situations.

The miserable little encounter had nothing to do with me, the me of me, any more than it had to do with that silly clerk. The incident was a recurring dream, concocted years before by stupid whites and it eternally came back to haunt us all. The secretary and I were like Hamlet and Laertes in the final scene, where, because of harm done by one ancestor to another, we were bound to duel to the death. Also because the play must end somewhere.

I went further than forgiving the clerk, I accepted her as a fellow victim of the same puppeteer.

On the streetcar, I put my fare into the box and the conductorette looked at me with the usual hard eye of white contempt. "Move into the car, please move on in the car." She patted her money changer.

Her Southern nasal accent sliced my meditation and I looked deep into my thoughts. All lies, all comfortable lies. The receptionist was not innocent and neither was I. The whole charade we had played out in that crummy waiting room had directly to do with me, Black, and her, white.

I wouldn't move into the streetcar but stood on the ledge over the conductor, glaring. My mind shouted so energetically that the announcement made my veins stand out, and my mouth tighten into a prune.

I WOULD HAVE THE JOB. I WOULD BE A CONDUCTORETTE AND SLING A FULL MONEY CHANGER FROM MY BELT. I WOULD.

The next three weeks were a honeycomb of determination with apertures for the days to go in and out. The Negro organizations to whom I appealed for support bounced me back and forth like a shuttlecock on a badminton court. Why did I insist on that particular job? Openings were going begging that paid nearly twice the money. The minor officials with whom I was able to win an audience thought me mad. Possibly I was.

Downtown San Francisco became alien and cold, and the streets I had loved in a personal familiarity were unknown lanes that twisted with malicious intent. Old buildings, whose gray rococo façades housed my memories of the Forty-Niners, and Diamond Lil, Robert Service, Sutter and Jack London, were then imposing structures viciously joined to keep me out. My trips to the streetcar office were of the frequency of a person on salary. The struggle expanded. I was no longer in conflict only with the Market Street Railway but with the marble lobby of the building which housed its offices, and elevators and their operators.

During this period of strain Mother and I began our first steps on the long path toward mutual adult admiration. She never asked for reports and I didn't offer any details. But every morning she made breakfast, gave me carfare and lunch money, as if I were going to work. She comprehended the perversity of life, that in the struggle lies the joy. That I was no glory seeker was obvious to her, and that I had to exhaust every possibility before giving in was also clear.

On my way out of the house one morning she said, "Life is going to give you just what you put in it. Put your whole heart in everything you do, and pray, then you can wait." Another time she reminded me that "God helps those who help themselves." She had a store of aphorisms which she dished out as the occasion demanded. Strangely, as bored as I was with clichés, her inflection gave them something new, and set me thinking for a little while at least. Later when asked how I got my job, I was never able to say exactly. I only knew that one day, which was tiresomely like all the others before it, I sat in the Railway office, ostensibly waiting to be interviewed. The receptionist called me to her desk and shuffled a bundle of papers to me. They were job application forms. She said they had to be filled in triplicate. I had little time to wonder if I had won or not, for the standard questions reminded me of the necessity for dexterous lying. How old was I? List my previous jobs, starting from the last held and go backward to the first. How much money did I earn, and why did I leave the position? Give two references (not relatives).

Sitting at a side table my mind and I wove a cat's ladder of near truths and total lies. I kept my face blank (an old art) and wrote quickly the fable of Marguerite Johnson, aged nineteen, former companion and driver for Mrs. Annie Henderson (a White Lady) in Stamps, Arkansas.

I was given blood tests, aptitude tests, physical coordination tests, and Rorschachs, then on a blissful day I was hired as the first Negro on the San Francisco streetcars.

Mother gave me the money to have my blue serge suit tailored, and I learned to fill out work cards, operate the money changer and punch transfers. The time crowded together and at an End of Days I was swinging on the back of the rackety trolley, smiling sweetly and persuading my charges to "step forward in the car, please."

For one whole semester the street cars and I shimmied up and scooted down the sheer hills of San Francisco. I lost some of my need for the Black ghetto's shielding sponge quality, as I clanged and cleared my way down Market Street, with its honky-tonk homes for homeless sailors, past the quiet retreat of Golden Gate Park and along closed undwelled-in-looking dwellings of the Sunset District.

My work shifts were split so haphazardly that it was easy to believe that my superiors had chosen them maliciously. Upon mentioning my suspicions to Mother, she said, "Don't worry about it. You ask for what you want, and you pay for what you get. And I'm going to show you that it ain't no trouble when you pack double."

She stayed awake to drive me out to the car barn at four thirty in the mornings, or to pick me up when I was relieved just before dawn. Her awareness of life's perils convinced her that while I would be safe on the public conveyances, she "wasn't about to trust a taxi driver with her baby."

When the spring classes began, I resumed my commitment with formal education. I was so much wiser and older, so much more independent, with a bank account and clothes that I had bought for myself, that I was sure that I had learned and earned the magic formula which would make me a part of the gay life my contemporaries led.

Not a bit of it. Within weeks, I realized that my schoolmates and I were on paths moving diametrically away from each other. They were concerned and excited over the approaching football games, but I had in my immediate past raced a car down a dark and foreign Mexican mountain. They concentrated great interest on who was worthy of being student body president, and when the metal bands would be removed from their teeth, while I remembered sleeping for a month in a wrecked automobile and conducting a streetcar in the uneven hours of the morning.

Without willing it, I had gone from being ignorant of being ignorant to being aware of being aware. And the worst part of my awareness was that I didn't know what I was aware of. I knew I knew very little, but I was certain that the things I had yet to learn wouldn't be taught to me at George Washington High School.

I began to cut classes, to walk in Golden Gate Park or wander along the shiny counter of the Emporium Department Store. When Mother discovered that I was playing truant, she told me that if I didn't want to go to school one day, if there were no tests being held, and if my school work was up to standard, all I had to do was tell her and I could stay home. She said that she didn't want some white woman calling her up to tell her something about her child that she didn't know. And she didn't want to be put in the position of lying to a white woman because I wasn't woman enough to speak up. That put an end to my truancy, but nothing appeared to lighten the long gloomy day that going to school became.

To be left alone on the tightrope of youthful unknowing is to experience the excruciating beauty of full freedom and the threat of eternal indecision. Few, if any, survive their teens. Most surrender to the vague but murderous pressure of adult conformity. It becomes easier to die and avoid conflicts than to maintain a constant battle with the superior forces of maturity.

Until recently each generation found it more expedient to plead guilty to the charge of being young and ignorant, easier to take the punishment meted out by the older generation (which had itself confessed to the same crime short years before). The command to grow up at once was more bearable than the faceless horror of wavering purpose, which was youth.

The bright hours when the young rebelled against the descending sun had to give way to twenty-four-hour periods called "days" that were named as well as numbered.

The Black female is assaulted in her tender years by all those common forces of nature at the same time that she is caught in the tripartite crossfire of masculine prejudice, white illogical hate and Black lack of power.

The fact that the adult American Negro female emerges a formidable character is often met with amazement, distaste and even belligerence. It is seldom accepted as an inevitable outcome of the struggle won by survivors and deserves respect if not enthusiastic acceptance.

35

The Well of Loneliness was my introduction to lesbianism and what I thought of as pornography. For months the book was both a treat and a threat. It allowed me to see a little of the mysterious world of the pervert. It stimulated my libido and I told myself that it was educational because it informed me of the difficulties in the secret world of the pervert. I was certain that I didn't know any perverts. Of course I ruled out the jolly sissies who sometimes stayed at our house and cooked whopping eight-course dinners while the perspiration made paths down their made-up faces. Since everyone accepted them, and more particularly since they accepted themselves, I knew that their laughter was real and that their lives were cheerful comedies, interrupted only by costume changes and freshening of make-up.

But true freaks, the "women lovers," captured yet strained my imagination. They were, according to the book, disowned by their families, snubbed by their friends and ostracized from every society. This bitter punishment was inflicted upon them because of a physical condition over which they had no control.

After my third reading of *The Well of Loneliness* I became a bleeding heart for the downtrodden misunderstood lesbians. I thought "lesbian" was synonymous with hermaphrodite, and when I wasn't actively aching over their pitiful state, I was wondering how they managed simpler body functions. Did they have a choice of organs to use, and if so, did they alternate or play favorite? Or I tried to imagine how two hermaphrodites made love, and the more I pondered the more confused I became. It seemed that having two of everything other people had, and four where ordinary people just had two, would complicate matters to the point of giving up the idea of making love at all.

It was during this reflective time that I noticed how heavy my own voice had become. It droned and drummed two or three whole tones lower than my schoolmates' voices. My hands and feet were also far from being feminine and dainty. In front of the mirror I detachedly examined my body. For a sixteen-year-old my breasts were sadly undeveloped. They could only be called skin swellings, even by the kindest critic. The line from my rib cage to my knees fell straight without even a ridge to disturb its direction. Younger girls than I boasted of having to shave under their arms, but my armpits were as smooth as my face. There was also a mysterious growth developing on my body that defied explanation. It looked totally useless.

Then the question began to live under my blankets: How did lesbianism begin? What were the symptoms? The public library gave information on the finished lesbian—and that woefully sketchy—but on the growth of a lesbian, there was nothing. I did discover that the difference between hermaphrodites and lesbians was that hermaphrodites were "born that way." It was impossible to determine whether lesbians budded gradually, or burst into being with a suddenness that dismayed them as much as it repelled society.

I had gnawed into the unsatisfying books and into my own unstocked mind without finding a morsel of peace or understanding. And meantime, my voice refused to stay up in the higher registers where I consciously pitched it, and I had to buy my shoes in the "old lady's comfort" section of the shoe stores.

I asked Mother.

Daddy Clidell was at the club one evening, so I sat down on the side of Mother's bed. As usual she woke completely and at once. (There is never any yawning or stretching with Vivian Baxter. She's either awake or asleep.)

"Mother, I've got to talk to you..." It was going to kill me to have to ask her, for in the asking wouldn't it be possible that suspicion would fall on my own normality? I knew her well enough to know that if I committed almost any crime and told her the truth about it she not

172

only wouldn't disown me but would give me her protection. But just suppose I was developing into a lesbian, how would she react? And then there was Bailey to worry about too.

"Ask me, and pass me a cigarette." Her calmness didn't fool me for a minute. She used to say that her secret to life was that she "hoped for the best, was prepared for the worst, so anything in between didn't come as a surprise." That was all well and good for most things but if her only daughter was developing into a...

She moved over and patted the bed, "Come on, baby, get in the bed. You'll freeze before you get your question out."

It was better to remain where I was for the time being. "Mother... my pocketbook..."

"Ritie, do you mean your vagina? Don't use those Southern terms. There's nothing wrong with the word 'vagina.' It's a clinical description. Now, what's wrong with it?"

The smoke collected under the bed lamp, then floated out to be free in the room. I was deathly sorry that I had begun to ask her anything.

"Well?... Well? Have you got crabs?"

Since I didn't know what they were, that puzzled me. I thought I might have them and it wouldn't go well for my side if I said I didn't. On the other hand, I just might not have them, and suppose I lied and said I did?

"I don't know, Mother."

"Do you itch? Does your vagina itch?" She leaned on one elbow and jabbed out her cigarette.

"No, Mother."

"Then you don't have crabs. If you had them, you'd tell the world."

I wasn't sorry or glad not to have them, but made a mental note to look up "crabs" in the library on my next trip.

She looked at me closely, and only a person who knew her face well could have perceived the muscles relaxing and interpreted this as an indication of concern.

"You don't have a venereal disease, do you?"

The question wasn't asked seriously, but knowing Mother I was shocked at the idea. "Why, Mother, of course not. That's a terrible question." I was ready to go back to my room and wrestle alone with my worries.

"Sit down, Ritie. Pass me another cigarette." For a second it looked as if she was thinking about laughing. That would really do it. If she laughed, I'd never tell her anything else. Her laughter would make it easier to accept my social isolation and human freakishness. But she wasn't even smiling. Just slowly pulling in the smoke and holding it in puffed cheeks before blowing it out.

"Mother, something is growing on my vagina."

There, it was out. I'd soon know whether I was to be her ex-daughter or if she'd put me in hospital for an operation.

"Where on your vagina, Marguerite?"

Uh-huh. It was bad all right. Not "Ritie" or "Maya" or "Baby." "Marguerite."

"On both sides. Inside." I couldn't add that they were fleshy skin flaps that had been growing for months down there. She'd have to pull that out of me.

"Ritie, go get me that big *Webster's* and then bring me a bottle of beer."

Suddenly, it wasn't all that serious. I was "Ritie" again, and she just asked for beer. If it had been as awful as I anticipated, she'd have ordered Scotch and water. I took her the huge dictionary that she had bought as a birthday gift for Daddy Clidell and laid it on the bed. The weight forced a side of the mattress down and Mother twisted her bed lamp to beam down on the book.

When I returned from the kitchen and poured her beer, as she had taught Bailey and me beer should be poured, she patted the bed.

"Sit down, baby. Read this." Her fingers guided My eyes to VULVA. I began to read. She said, "Read it out loud."

It was all very clear and normal-sounding. She drank the beer as I read, and when I had finished she explained it in every-day terms. My relief melted the fears and they liquidly stole down my face.

Mother shot up and put her arms around me.

"There's nothing to worry about, baby. It happens to every woman. It's just human nature."

It was all right then to unburden my heavy, heavy heart I cried into the crook of my arm. "I thought maybe I was turning into a lesbian."

Her patting of my shoulder slowed to a still and she leaned away from me.

"A lesbian? Where the hell did you get that idea?"

"Those things growing on my... vagina, and my voice is too deep and my feet are big, and I have no hips or breasts or anything. And my legs are so skinny."

Then she did laugh. I knew immediately that she wasn't laughing at me. Or rather that she was laughing at me, but it was something about me that pleased her. The laugh choked a little on the smoke in its way, but finally broke through cleanly. I had to give a small laugh too, although I wasn't tickled at all. But it's mean to watch someone enjoy something and not show your understanding of their enjoyment.

When she finished with the laughter, she laid it down a peal at a time and turned to me, wiping her eyes.

"I made arrangements, a long time ago, to have a boy and a girl. Bailey is my boy and you are my girl. The Man upstairs, He don't make mistakes. He gave you to me to be my girl and that's just what you are. Now, go wash your face, have a glass of milk and go back to bed."

I did as she said but I soon discovered my new assurance wasn't large enough to fill the gap left by my old uneasiness. It rattled around in my mind like a dime in a tin cup. I hoarded it preciously, but less than two weeks later it became totally worthless.

A classmate of mine, whose mother had rooms for herself and her daughter in a ladies' residence, had stayed out beyond closing time. She telephoned me to ask if she could sleep at my house. Mother gave her permission, providing my friend telephoned her mother from our house.

When she arrived, I got out of bed and we went to the upstairs kitchen to make hot chocolate. In my room we shared mean gossip about our friends, giggled over boys and whined about school and the tedium of life. The unusualness of having someone sleep in my bed (I'd never slept with anyone except my grandmothers) and the frivolous laughter in the middle of the night made me forget simple courtesies. My friend had to remind me that she had nothing to sleep in. I gave her one of my gowns, and without curiosity or interest I watched her pull off her clothes. At none of the early stages of undressing was I in the least conscious of her body. And then suddenly, for the briefest eye span, I saw her breasts. I was stunned.

They were shaped like light-brown falsies in the five-and-ten- cent store, but they were real. They made all the nude paintings I had seen in museums come to life. In a word they were beautiful. A universe divided what she had from what I had. She was a woman.

My gown was too snug for her and much too long, and when she wanted to laugh at her ridiculous image I found that humor had left me without a promise to return.

Had I been older I might have thought that I was moved by both an esthetic sense of beauty and the pure emotion of envy. But those possibilities did not occur to me when I needed them. All I knew was that I had been moved by looking at a woman's breasts. So all the calm and casual words of Mother's explanation a few weeks earlier and the clinical terms of Noah Webster did not alter the fact that in a fundamental way there was something queer about me.

I somersaulted deeper into my snuggery of misery. After a thorough self-examination, in the light of all I had read and heard about dykes and bulldaggers, I reasoned that I had none of the obvious traits—I didn't wear trousers, or have big shoulders or go in for sports, or walk like a man or even want to touch a woman. I wanted to be a woman, but that seemed to me to be a world to which I was to be eternally refused entrance.

What I needed was a boyfriend. A boyfriend would clarify my position to the world and, even more important, to myself. A boyfriend's acceptance of me would guide me into that strange and exotic land of frills and femininity.

Among my associates, there were no takers. Understandably the boys of my age and social group were captivated by the yellow- or light-brown-skinned girls, with hairy legs and smooth little lips, and whose hair "hung down like horses' manes." And even those sought-after girls were asked to "give it up or tell where it is." They were reminded in a popular song of the times, "If you can't smile and say yes, please don't cry and say no." If the pretties were expected to make the supreme sacrifice in order to "belong," what could the unattractive female do? She who had been skimming along on life's turning but never-changing periphery had to be ready to be a "buddy" by day and maybe by night. She was called upon to be generous only if the pretty girls were unavailable.

I believe most plain girls are virtuous because of the scarcity of opportunity to be otherwise. They shield themselves with an aura of unavailableness (for which after a time they begin to take credit) largely as a defense tactic.

In my particular case, I could not hide behind the curtain of voluntary goodness. I was being crushed by two unrelenting forces: the uneasy suspicion that I might not be a normal female and my newly awakening sexual appetite.

I decided to take matters into my own hands. (An unfortunate but apt phrase.)

Up the hill from our house, and on the same side of the street, lived two handsome brothers. They were easily the most eligible young men in the neighborhood. If I was going to venture into sex, I saw no reason why I shouldn't make my experiment with the best of the lot. I didn't really expect to capture either brother on a permanent basis, but I thought if I could hook one temporarily I might be able to work the relationship into something more lasting.

I planned a chart for seduction with surprise as my opening ploy. One evening as I walked up the hill suffering from youth's vague malaise (there was simply nothing to do), the brother I had chosen came walking directly into my trap.

"Hello, Marguerite." He nearly passed me.

I put the plan into action. "Hey." I plunged, "Would you like to have a sexual intercourse with me?" Things were going according to the chart. His mouth hung open like a garden gate. I had the advantage and so I pressed it.

"Take me somewhere."

His response lacked dignity, but in fairness to him I admit that I had left him little chance to be suave.

He asked, "You mean, you're going to give me some trim?"

I assured him that that was exactly what I was about to give him. Even as the scene was being enacted I realized the imbalance in his values. He thought I was giving him something, and the fact of the matter was that it was my intention to take something from him. His good looks and popularity had made him so inordinately conceited that they blinded him to that possibility.

We went to a furnished room occupied by one of his friends, who understood the situation immediately and got his coat and left us alone. The seductee quickly turned off the lights. I would have preferred them left on, but didn't want to appear more aggressive than I had been already. If that was possible.

I was excited rather than nervous, and hopeful instead of frightened. I had not considered how physical an act of seduction would be. I had anticipated long soulful tongued kisses and gentle caresses. But there was no romance in the knee which forced my legs, nor in the rub of hairy skin on my chest.

Unredeemed by shared tenderness, the time was spent in laborious gropings, pullings, yankings and jerkings.

Not one word was spoken.

My partner showed that our experience had reached its climax by getting up abruptly, and my main concern was how to get home quickly. He may have sensed that he had been used, or his disinterest may have been an indication that I was less than gratifying. Neither possibility bothered me.

Outside on the street we left each other with little more than "Okay, see you around."

Thanks to Mr. Freeman nine years before, I had had no pain of entry to endure, and because of the absence of romantic involvement neither of us felt much had happened.

At home I reviewed the failure and tried to evaluate my new position. I had had a man. I had been had. I not only didn't enjoy it, but my normalcy was still a question.

What happened to the moonlight-on-the-prairie feeling? Was there something so wrong with me that I couldn't share a sensation that made poets gush out rhyme after rhyme, that made Richard Arlen brave the Arctic wastes and Veronica Lake betray the entire free world?

There seemed to be no explanation for my private infirmity, but being a product (is "victim" a better word?) of the Southern Negro upbringing, I decided that I "would understand it all better by-and-by." I went to sleep.

Three weeks later, having thought very little of the strange and strangely empty night, I found myself pregnant.

36

The world had ended, and I was the only person who knew it. People walked along the streets as if the pavements hadn't all crumbled beneath their feet. They pretended to breathe in and out while all the time I knew the air had been sucked away in a monstrous inhalation from God Himself. I alone was suffocating in the nightmare.

The little pleasure I was able to take from the fact that if I could have a baby I obviously wasn't a lesbian was crowded into my mind's tiniest corner by the massive pushing in of fear, guilt, and self-revulsion.

For eons, it seemed, I had accepted my plight as the hapless, put-upon victim of fate and the Furies, but this time I had to face the fact that I had brought my new catastrophe upon myself. How was I to blame the innocent man whom I had lured into making love to me? In order to be profoundly dishonest, a person must have one of two qualities: either he is unscrupulously ambitious, or he is unswervingly egocentric. He must believe that for his ends to be served all things and people can justifiably be shifted about, or that he is the center not only of his own world but of the worlds which others inhabit. I had neither element in my personality, so I hefted the burden of pregnancy at sixteen onto my own shoulders where it belonged. Admittedly, I staggered under the weight.

I finally sent a letter to Bailey, who was at sea with the merchant marine. He wrote back, and he cautioned me against telling Mother of my condition. We both knew her to be violently opposed to abortions, and she would very likely order me to quit school. Bailey suggested that if I quit school before getting my high school diploma I'd find it nearly impossible to return.

The first three months, while I was adapting myself to the fact of pregnancy (I didn't really link pregnancy to the possibility of my having a baby until weeks before my confinement), were a hazy period in which days seemed to lie just below the water level, never emerging fully.

Fortunately, Mother was tied up tighter than Dick's hatband in the weave of her own life. She noticed me, as usual, out of the corner of her existence. As long as I was healthy, clothed and smiling she felt no need to focus her attention on me. As always, her major concern was to live the life given to her, and her children were expected to do the same. And to do it without too much brouhaha.

Under her loose scrutiny I grew more buxom, and my brown skin smoothed and tight-pored, like pancakes fried on an unoiled skillet. And still she didn't suspect. Some years before, I had established a code which never varied. I didn't lie. It was understood that I didn't lie because I was too proud to be caught and forced to admit that I was capable of a less than Olympian action. Mother must have concluded that since I was above out-and-out lying I was also beyond deceit. She was deceived.

All my motions focalized on pretending to be that guileless schoolgirl who had nothing more wearying to think about than mid-term exams. Strangely enough, I very nearly caught the essence of teenage capriciousness as I played the role. Except that there were times when physically I couldn't deny to myself that something very important was taking place in my body.

Mornings, I never knew if I would have to jump off the streetcar one step ahead of the warm sea of nausea that threatened to sweep me away. On solid ground, away from the ship-motioned vehicle and the smell of hands coated with recent breakfasts, I regained my balance and waited for the next trolley.

School recovered its lost magic. For the first time since Stamps, information was exciting for itself alone. I burrowed myself into caves of facts, and found delight in the logical resolutions of mathematics.

I credit my new reactions (although I didn't know at the time that I had learned anything from them) to the fact that during what surely must have been a critical period I was not dragged down by hopelessness. Life had a conveyor-belt quality. It went on unpursued and unpursuing, and my only thought was to remain erect, and keep my secret along with my balance.

Midway along to delivery, Bailey came home and brought me a spun-silver bracelet from South America, Thomas Wolfe's *Look Homeward, Angel*, and a slew of new dirty jokes.

As my sixth month approached, Mother left San Francisco for Alaska. She was to open a night club and planned to stay three or four months until it got on its feet. Daddy Clidell was to look after me but I was more or less left on my own recognizance and under the unsteady gaze of our lady roomers.

Mother left the city amid a happy and cheerful send-off party (after all how many Negroes were in Alaska?), and I felt treacherous allowing her to go without informing her that she was soon to be a grandmother.

Two days after V-Day, I stood with the San Francisco Summer School class at Mission High School and received my diploma. That evening, in the bosom of the now-dear family home I uncoiled my fearful secret and in a brave gesture left a note on
Daddy Clidell's bed. It read: *Dear Parents, I am sorry to bring this disgrace on the family, but I am pregnant. Marguerite.*

The confusion that ensued when I explained to my stepfather that I expected to deliver the baby in three weeks, more or less, was reminiscent of a Molière comedy. Except that it was funny only years later. Daddy Clidell told Mother that I was "three weeks gone." Mother, regarding me as a woman for the first time, said indignantly, "She's more than any three weeks." They both accepted the fact that I was further along than they had first been told but found it nearly impossible to believe that I had carried a baby, eight months and one week, without their being any the wiser.

Mother asked, "Who is the boy?" I told her. She recalled him, faintly.

"Do you want to marry him?"

"No."

"Does he want to marry you?" The father had stopped speaking to me during my fourth month.

"No."

"Well, that's that. No use ruining three lives." There was no overt or subtle condemnation. She was Vivian Baxter Jackson. Hoping for the best, prepared for the worst, and unsurprised by anything in between.

Daddy Clidell assured me that I had nothing to worry about. That "women been gittin' pregnant ever since Eve ate that apple." He sent one of his waitresses to I. Magnin's to buy maternity dresses for me. For the next two weeks I whirled around the city going to doctors, taking vitamin shots and pills, buying clothes for the baby, and except for the rare moments alone, enjoying the imminent blessed event.

After a short labor, and without too much pain (I decided that the pain of delivery was overrated), my son was born. Just as gratefulness was confused in my mind with love, so possession became mixed up with motherhood. I had a baby. He was beautiful and mine. Totally mine. No one had bought him for me. No one had helped me endure the sickly gray months. I had had help in the child's conception, but no one could deny that I had had an immaculate pregnancy.

Totally my possession, and I was afraid to touch him. Home from the hospital, I sat for hours by his bassinet and absorbed his mysterious perfection. His extremities were so dainty they appeared unfinished. Mother handled him easily with the casual confidence of a baby nurse, but I dreaded being forced to change his diapers. Wasn't I famous for awkwardness? Suppose I let him slip, or put my fingers on that throbbing pulse on the top of his head?

Mother came to my bed one night bringing my three-week-old baby. She pulled the cover back and told me to get up and hold him while she put rubber sheets on my bed. She explained that he was going to sleep with me.

I begged in vain. I was sure to roll over and crush out his life or break those fragile bones. She wouldn't hear of it, and within minutes the pretty golden baby was lying on his back in the center of my bed, laughing at me.

I lay on the edge of the bed, stiff with fear, and vowed not to sleep all night long. But the eat-sleep routine I had begun in the hospital, and kept up under Mother's dictatorial command, got the better of me. I dropped off.

My shoulder was shaken gently. Mother whispered, "Maya, wake up. But don't move."

I knew immediately that the awakening had to do with the baby. I tensed. "I'm awake."

She turned the light on and said, "Look at the baby." My fears were so powerful I couldn't move to look at the center of the bed. She said again, "Look at the baby," I didn't hear sadness in her voice, and that helped me to break the bonds of terror. The baby was no longer in the center of the bed. At first I thought he had moved. But after closer investigation I found that I was lying on my stomach with my arm bent at a right angle. Under the tent of blanket, which was poled by my elbow and forearm, the baby slept touching my side.

Mother whispered, "See, you don't have to think about doing the right thing. If you're for the right thing, then you do it without thinking."

She turned out the light and I patted my son's body lightly and went back to sleep.

Gather Together in My Name

This book is dedicated to my blood brother
BAILEY JOHNSON
and to the other real brothers who encouraged me to be
bodacious enough to invent my own life daily:
JAMES BALDWIN
KWESI BREW
DAVID DU BOIS
SAMUEL FLOYD
JOHN O. KILLENS
VAGABOND KING
LEO MAITLAND
VUSUMZI MAKE
JULIAN MAYFIELD
MAX ROACH

A special thanks to my friend
DOLLY MCPHERSON

It was a "come as you are" party and "all y'all come." If you bring your own bottle, you'll be expected to share; if you don't it's all right, somebody will share with you. It was triumph and brotherhood. Everybody was a hero. Hadn't we all joined together to kick the hell out of *der Gruber*, and that fat Italian, and put that little rice-eating Tojo in his place?

Black men from the South who had held no tools more complicated than plows had learned to use lathes and borers and welding guns, and had brought in their quotas of war-making machines. Women who had only known maid's uniforms and mammy-made dresses donned the awkward men's pants and steel helmets, and made the ship-fitting sheds hum some buddy. Even the children had collected paper, and at the advice of elders who remembered World War I, balled the tin foil from cigarettes and chewing gum into balls as big as your head. Oh, it was a time.

Soldiers and sailors, and the few black Marines fresh from having buried death on a sandy South Pacific beach, stood around looking proud out of war-wise eyes.

Black-marketeers had sped around a million furtive corners trying to keep the community supplied with sugar, cigarettes, rationing stamps and butter. Prostitutes didn't even take the time to remove their seventy-five dollar shoes when they turned twenty-dollar tricks. Everyone was a part of the war effort.

And at last it had paid off in spades. We had won. Pimps got out of their polished cars and walked the streets of San Francisco only a little uneasy at the unusual exercise. Gamblers, ignoring their sensitive fingers, shook hands with shoeshine boys. Pulpits rang with the "I told you so" of ministers who knew that God was on the side of right and He would not see the righteous forsaken, nor their young beg bread. Beauticians spoke to the shipyard workers, who in turn spoke to the easy ladies. And everybody had soft little preparation-to-smile smiles on their faces.

I thought if war did not include killing, I'd like to see one every year. Something like a festival.

All the sacrifices had won us victory and now the good times were coming. Obviously, if we earned more than rationing would allow us to spend during wartime, things were really going to look up when restrictions were removed.

There was no need to discuss racial prejudice. Hadn't we all, black and white, just snatched the remaining Jews from the hell of concentration camps? Race prejudice was dead. A mistake made by a young country. Something to be forgiven as an unpleasant act committed by an intoxicated friend.

During the crisis, black people had often made more money in a month than they had seen in their whole lives. Black men did not leave their wives, driven away by an inability to provide for their families. They rode in public transport on a first-come/first-seated basis. And more times than not were called Mister/Missus at their jobs or by sales clerks.

Two months after V-Day, war plants began to shut down, to cut back, to lay off employees. Some workers were offered tickets back to their Southern homes. Back to the mules they had left tied to the tree on ole Mistah Doo hickup farm. No good. Their expanded understanding could never again be accordioned into these narrow confines. They were free or at least nearer to freedom than ever before and they would not go back.

Those military heroes of a few months earlier, who were discharged from the Army in the city which knows how, began to be seen hanging on the ghetto corners like forgotten laundry left on a backyard fence. Their once starched khaki uniforms were gradually bastardized. An ETO jacket, plus medals, minus stripes, was worn with out-of-fashion zoot pants. The trim army pants, creases trained in symmetry, were topped by loud, color-crazed Hawaiian shirts. The shoes remained. Only the shoes. The Army had made those shoes to last. And dammit, they did.

Thus we lived through a major war. The question in the ghettos was, Can we make it through a minor peace?

I was seventeen, very old, embarrassingly young, with a son of two months, and I still lived with my mother and stepfather.

They offered me a chance to leave my baby with them and return to school. I refused. First, I reasoned with the righteous seriousness of youth, I was not Daddy Clidell Jackson's blood daughter and my child was his grandchild only as long as the union between Daddy and Mother held fast, and by then I had seen many weak links in their chain of marriage. Second, I considered that although I was Mother's child, she had left me with others until I was thirteen and why should she feel more responsibility for my child than she had felt for her own. Those were the pieces that made up the skin of my refusal, but the core was more painful, more solid, truer. A textured guilt was my familiar, my bedmate to whom I had turned my back. My daily companion whose hand I would not hold. The Christian teaching dinned into my ears in the small town in Arkansas would not be quieted by the big-city noise.

My son had no father—so what did that make me? According to the Book, bastards were not to be allowed into the congregation of the righteous. There it was. I would get a job, and a room of my own, and take my beautiful son out into the world. I thought I might even move to another town and change our names.

During the months when I was tussled with my future and that of my son, the big house we lived in began to die. Suddenly jobless roomers, who lined their solemn trunks with memories before they packed in folds of disappointment, left San Francisco for Los Angeles, Chicago, Detroit, where "they say" jobs were begging for workers. The loud slams of the front doors were heard more seldom, and the upstairs kitchen, where the roomers exercised their cooking privileges, gave fewer and fewer of the exotic aromas which used to send me running to our kitchen for snacks.

The gamblers and prostitutes, black-marketeers and boosters, all those suckerfish who had gotten fat living on the underbelly of the war, were the last to feel the pinch. They had accumulated large masses of money, which never went into a bank, but circulated among their tribe like promiscuous women, and by the nature of their professions, they were accustomed to the infidelity of Lady Luck and the capriciousness of life. I was sorry to see the dancers go—those glamorous women, only slightly older than I, who wore pounds of Max Factor No. 31, false eyelashes and talked out of the sides of their mouths, their voices sliding around cigarettes which forever dangled from their lips. They had often practiced their routines in the downstairs kitchen. The B.S. Chorus. Time steps, slides, flashes and breaks, smoking all the time. I was fairly certain that in order to be a chorus dancer, one would have to smoke.

By no amount of agile exercising of a wishful imagination could my mother have been called lenient. Generous she was; indulgent, never. Kind, yes; permissive, never. In her world, people she accepted paddled their own canoes, pulled their own weight, put their own shoulders to their own plows and pushed like hell, and here I was in her house, refusing to go back to school. Not giving a thought to marriage (admittedly, no one asked me) and working at nothing. At no time did she advise me to seek work. At least not in words. But the strain of her nights at the pinochle table, the responsibility of the huge sums which were kept in the bedroom closet, wore on her already short temper.

In earlier, freer days I might have simply noted and recorded her

189

grumpiness, but now my guilt, which I carried around like a raw egg, fed my paranoia, and I became sure that I was a nuisance. When my baby cried I rushed to change him, feed him, coddle him, to in fact shut him up. My youth and shuddering self-doubt made me unfair to that vital woman.

She took great joy in her beautiful grandchild, and as with most egocentric people, saw his every virtue as a mirror for her own. He had pretty hands... "Well, look at mine." His feet were absolutely straight with high insteps; so were hers. She was not annoyed with me; she was playing the hand life had dealt her as she had always done. And she played it masterfully.

The mixture of arrogance and insecurity is as volatile as the much-touted alcohol and gasoline. The difference is that with the former there is a long internal burning usually terminating in self-destroying implosion.

I would quit the house, take a job and show the whole world (my son's father) that I was equal to my pride and greater than my pretensions.

1

I was mortified. A silly white woman who probably counted on her toes looked me in the face and said I had not passed. The examination had been constructed by morons for idiots. Of course I breezed through without thinking much about it.

REARRANGE THESE LETTERS: ACT · ART · AST

Okay. CAT. RAT. SAT. Now what?

She stood behind her make-up and coiffed hair and manicured nails and dresser-drawers of scented angora sweaters and years of white ignorance and said that I had not passed.

"The telephone company spends thousands of dollars training operators. We simply cannot risk employing anyone who made the marks you made. I'm sorry."

She was sorry? I was stunned. In a stupor I considered that maybe my outsized intellectual conceit had led me to take the test for granted. And maybe I deserved this high-handed witch's remarks.

190

"May I take it again?" That was painful to ask.

"No, I'm sorry." If she said she was sorry one more time, I was going to take her by her sorry shoulders and shake a job out of her.

"There is an opening, though"—she might have sensed my unspoken threat—"for a bus girl in the cafeteria."

"What does a bus girl do?" I wasn't sure I could do it. "The boy in the kitchen will tell you."

After I filled out forms and was found uninfected by a doctor, I reported to the cafeteria. There the boy, who was a grandfather, informed me, "Collect the dishes, wipe the tables, make sure the salt and pepper shakers are clean, and here's your uniform."

The coarse white dress and apron had been starched with concrete and was too long. I stood at the side of the room, the dress hem scratching my calves, waiting for the tables to clear. Many of the trainee operators had been my classmates. Now they stood over laden tables waiting for me or one of the other dumb bus girls to remove the used dishes so that they could set down their trays.

I lasted at the job a week, and so hated the salary that I spent it all the afternoon I quit.

2

"Can you cook Creole?"

I looked at the woman and gave her a lie as soft as melting butter. "Yes, of course. That's all I know how to cook."

The Creole Café had a cardboard sign in the window which bragged: COOK WANTED. SEVENTY-FIVE DOLLARS A WEEK. As soon as I saw it I knew I could cook Creole, whatever that was.

Desperation to find help must have blinded the proprietress to my age or perhaps it was the fact that I was nearly six feet and had an attitude which belied my seventeen years. She didn't question me about recipes and menus, but her long brown face did trail down in wrinkles, and doubt hung on the edges of her questions.

"Can you start on Monday?"

"I'll be glad to."

"You know it's six days a week. We're closed on Sunday."

"That's fine with me. I like to go to church on Sunday." It's awful to think that the devil gave me that lie, but it came unexpectedly and worked like dollar bills. Suspicion and doubt raced from her face, and she smiled. Her teeth were all the same size, a small white picket fence semicircled in her mouth.

"Well, I know we're going to get along. You a good Christian. I like that. Yes, ma'am, I sure do."

My need for a job caught and held the denial.

"What time on Monday?" Bless the Lord!

"You get here at five."

Five in the morning. Those mean streets before the thugs had gone to sleep, pillowing on someone else's dreams. Before the streetcars began to rattle, their lighted insides like exclusive houses in the fog. Five!

"All right, I'll be here at five, Monday morning."

"You'll cook the dinners and put them on the steam table. You don't have to do short orders. I do that."

Mrs. Dupree was a short plump woman of about fifty. Her hair was naturally straight and heavy. Probably Cajun Indian, African and white, and naturally, Negro.

"And what's your name?"

"Rita." Marguerite was too solemn, and Maya too rich-sounding. "Rita" sounded like dark flashing eyes, hot pepper and Creole evenings with strummed guitars. "Rita Johnson."

"That's a right nice name." Then, like some people do to show their sense of familiarity, she immediately narrowed the name down. "I'll call you Reet. Okay?"

Okay, of course. I had a job. Seventy-five dollars a week. So I was Reet. Reet, poteet and gone. All Reet. Now all I had to do was learn to cook.

3

I asked old Papa Ford to teach me how to cook. He had been a grown man when the twentieth century was born, and left a large family of brothers and sisters in Terre Haute, Indiana (always called the East Coast), to find what the world had in store for a "good-looking colored boy with no education in his head, but a pile of larceny in his heart." He traveled with circuses "shoveling elephant shit." He then shot dice in freight trains and played koch in back rooms and shanties all over the Northern states.

192

"I never went down to Hang'em High. Them crackers would have killed me. Pretty as I was, white women was always following me. The white boys never could stand a pretty nigger."

By 1943, when I first saw him, his good looks were as delicate as an old man's memory, and disappointment rode his face bareback. His hands had gone. Those gambler's fingers had thickened during the Depression, and his only straight job, carpenting, had further toughened his "money-makers." Mother rescued him from a job as a sweeper in a pinochle parlor and brought him home to live with us.

He sorted and counted the linen when the laundry truck picked it up and returned it, then grudgingly handed out fresh sheets to the roomers. He cooked massive and delicious dinners when Mother was busy, and he sat in the tall-ceilinged kitchen drinking coffee by the pots.

Papa Ford loved my mother (as did nearly everyone) with a childlike devotion. He went so far as to control his profanity when she was around, knowing she couldn't abide cursing unless she was the curser.

"Why the sheeit do you want to work in a goddam kitchen?"

"Papa, the job pays seventy-five dollars a week."

"Busting some goddam suds." Disgust wrinkled his face. "Papa, I'll be cooking and not washing dishes."

"Colored women been cooking so long, thought you'd be tired of it by now."

"If you'll just tell me—"

"Got all that education. How come you don't get a goddam job where you can go to work looking like something?"

I tried another tack. "I probably couldn't learn to cook Creole food, anyway. It's too complicated."

"Sheeit. Ain't nothing but onions, green peppers and garlic. Put that in everything and you got Creole food. You know how to cook rice, don't you?"

"Yes." I could cook it till each grain stood separately.

"That's all, then. Them geechees can't live without swamp seed." He cackled at his joke, then recalled a frown. "Still don't like you working as a goddam cook. Get married, then you don't have to cook for nobody but your own family. Sheeit."

4

The Creole Café steamed with onion vapor, garlic mists, tomato fogs and green-pepper sprays. I cooked and sweated among the cloying odors and loved being there. Finally I had the authority I had always longed for. Mrs. Dupree chose the daily menu, and left a note on the steam table informing me of her gastronomic decisions. But, I, Rita, the chef, decided how much garlic went into the baked short ribs à la Creole, how many bay leaves would flavor the steamed Shreveport tripe. For over a month I was embroiled in the mysteries of the kitchen with the expectancy of an alchemist about to discover the secret properties of gold.

A leathered old white woman, whom Mother found, took care of my baby while I worked. I had been rather reluctant to leave him in her charge, but Mother reminded me that she tended her white, black and Filipino children equally well. I reasoned that her great age had shoved her beyond the pale of any racial differences. Certainly anyone who lived that long had to spend any unused moments thinking about death and the life to come. She simply couldn't afford the precious time to think of prejudices. The greatest compensation for youth's illness is the utter ignorance of the seriousness of the affliction.

Only after the mystery was worn down to a layer of commonness did I begin to notice the customers. They consisted largely of light-skinned, slick-haired Creoles from Louisiana, who spoke a French patois only a little less complicated than the contents of my pots and equally spicy. I thought it fitting and not at all unusual that they enjoyed my cooking. I was following Papa Ford's instructions loosely and adding artistic touches of my own.

Our customers never ate, paid and left. They sat on the long backless stools and exchanged gossip or shared the patient philosophy of the black South.

"Take it easy, Greasy, you got a long way to slide."

With the tolerance of ages they gave and accepted advice. "Take it easy, but take it."

One large ruddy man, whose name I never knew, allowed his elbows to support him at the twelve-stool counter, and told tales of

194

the San Francisco waterfront: "They got wharf rats who fight a man flat-footed."

"No?" A voice wanted to believe.

"Saw one of those suckers the other night backed a cracker up 'gainst a cargo crate. Hadn't been for me and two other guys, colored guys"—naturally—"he'd of run down his throat and walked on his liver."

Near the steam counter, the soft sounds of black talk, the sharp reports of laughter, and the shuffling feet on tiled floors mixed themselves in odorous vapors and I was content.

5

I had rented a room (with cooking privileges) in a tall, imposing San Francisco Victorian and had bought my first furniture and a white chenille bedspread. God, but it looked like a field of tiny snow roses. I had a beautiful child, who laughed to see me, a job that I did well, a baby-sitter whom I trusted, and I was young and crazy as a road lizard. Surely this was making it.

One foggy evening on my day off, I had picked up my son and was carrying him home along the familiar streets with the casual ease of an old mother. He snoozed in the angle of my arm, and I thought of dinner, and the radio and a night of reading. Two ex-schoolmates came up the hill toward me. They were of that rare breed, black born San Franciscans. I, cushioned in my maturity, didn't think to further arm myself. I had the arrowproof vest of adult confidence, so I let them approach—easy.

"Let us look at the baby... I hear he's cute." She was fat with small covetous eyes and was known for having a tiny but pugnacious wit. Her friend, Lily, even as a teenager, was old beyond knowing and bored beyond wisdom.

"Yes. They say you made a pretty baby."

I lifted the flap of light blanket from my son's face and shifted myself so that they might see my glory.

"My God, you did that?" The fat one's face broke open into a wounded grin.

Her somber friend intoned, "Jesus, he looks like he's white. He could pass." Her words floated into my air on admiration and wonder. I shriveled that she could say such a terrible thing about my baby, but I had no nerve to cover my prize and walk away. I stood dumfounded, founded in dumbness.

The short one laughed a crackly laugh and pushed the point between my ribs. "He's got a little nose and thin lips." Her surprise was maddening. "As long as you live and troubles rise, you ought to pay the man for giving you that baby, huh. A crow gives birth to a dove. The bird kingdom must be petrified."

There's a point in fury when one becomes abject. Motionless. I froze, as Lot's wife must have done, having caught a last glimpse of concentrated evil.

"And what did you name him? 'Thank God A-mighty'?"

I could have laid him down there, bunting and all, and left him for someone who had more grace, more style and beauty. My own pride of control would not allow me to show the girls what I was feeling, so I covered my baby and headed home. No good-byes—I left them as if I were planning to walk off the edge of the world. In my room I lay my five months of belongingness on the chenilleed bed and sat beside him to look over his perfection. His little head was exactly round and the soft hair curled up in black ripples. His arms and legs were plump marvels, and his torso as straight as a look between lovers. But it was his face with which I had to do.

Admittedly, the lips were thin and traced themselves sparely under a small nose. But he was a baby, and as he grew, these abnormalities would flesh out, become real, imitate the regularity of my features. His eyes, even closed, slanted up toward his throbbing temples. He looked like a baby Buddha. And then I examined his hairline. It followed mine in every detail. And that would not grow away or change, and it proved that he was undeniably mine.

6

Butter-colored, honey-brown, lemon- and olive-skinned. Chocolate and plum-blue, peaches-and-cream. Cream. Nutmeg. Cinnamon. I wondered why my people described our colors in terms of something good to eat. Then God's prettiest man became a customer at my restaurant.

He sat beside the light-skinned Creoles, and they thinned and paled and disappeared. His dark-brown skin glistened, and the reflected light made it hard to look into my mysterious pots. His voice to the waitress was a thumb poking in my armpits. I hated his being there because his presence made me jittery, but I loathed his leaving and could hardly bear waiting for him to return.

The waitress and Mrs. Dupree called him, "Curly," but I thought whoever named him little used their imagination. When he opened the steamy door to the restaurant, surely it was the second coming of Christ.

His table manners pleased me. He ate daintily and slowly as if he cared what he put in his muth. He smiled at me, but the nervous grimaces I gave him in return couldn't even loosely be called smiles. He was friendly with the customers, the waitress and me, since he always came alone. I wondered why he didn't have girl friends. Any woman would give a pretty to go out with him or rush to sit and talk to him. I never thought he would find me interesting, and if he did, it would be just to tease me.

"Reet." There it was. I acted as if I hadn't heard him. "Reet. You hear me. Come here."

I have seen bitch dogs in heat sidle sinuously along the ground, tempting, luring. I would like to be able to say I went to him so naturally. Unfortunately not. I draped myself in studied indifference and inched out my voice in disdainful measures.

"Were you speaking to me?"

"Come here, I won't bite." Looking down upon his request, I conceded. If he was beautiful from a distance, up close he was perfection. His eyes were deep-black and slow-lidded. His upper lip arched and fell over white teeth held together in the middle by the merest hint of yellow gold.

"How long you been knowing to cook like that?"

"All my life." I could hardly make the lie leave my tongue.

"You married?"

"No."

"You be careful, somebody's gonna come here and kidnap you."

"Thank you." Why didn't he? Of course he would have had to knock me down, bind and gag me, but I would have liked nothing better.

"You want a soda?"

"No thanks." I turned and went back to the steam table, sweat nibbling above my top lip and under my arms. I wished him away but could feel his gaze on my back. I had spent so many years being people other than myself that I continued to stir and mix, raise and lower burners as if every nerve in my body were not attached to the third stool of the lunch counter.

The door opened and closed and I turned to watch his retreating back, only to find that another customer had left. Automatically I looked for him and met his eyes, solemn on me. I burned at giving myself away.

He nodded me over.

"What time you get off?"

"One o'clock."

"Want me to take you home?"

"I usually go out to see my baby."

"You've got a baby? Somebody must of give it to you for Christmas. A doll baby. How old are you?"

"Nineteen." Sometimes I was twenty, or eighteen. It depended on my mood.

"Nineteen going on seventeen." His smile held no ridicule. Just a smidgen of indulgence.

"Okay. I'll take you to see your baby."

He drove his 1941 Pontiac without seeming to think about it. I sat in the corner pushed against the door trying desperately not to watch him.

"Where's the baby's Daddy?"

"I don't know."

"He wouldn't marry you, huh?" His voice hardened in the question.

"I didn't want to marry him." Partly true.

"Well, he's a low-down bastard in my book and needs his ass kicked." I began to love him at that moment.

I shifted to look at him. My avenging angel. Mother and my brother had been so busy being positive and supportive, neither had given any thought to the possibility that I might want revenge. I don't think I had even thought about it before. Now anger was an injection that flooded my body, making me warm and excited.

That's true, he was a low-life bastard. He should have given me a chance to refuse his proposal. Out of my head and into forgetfulness went the memory that I had wilfully initiated my one sexual tryst. My personal reasons and aggressive tactics were conveniently obliterated. Self-pity in its early stage is as snug as a feather mattress. Only when it hardens does it become uncomfortable.

Curly stood in the center of the baby-sitter's living room and said all the mother-liking things: "Sure is a fine baby... Looks just like you... He's gonna be a big one... Check those feet."

Back in the car it never occured to me to put up resistance when he said we were going to his hotel. I wanted to do what he wanted, so I sat quiet.

198

As we passed through the hotel lobby, I felt the first stirring of reluctance. Now, wait a minute. What was I doing here? What did he think I was? He hadn't even said he loved me. Where was the soft music that should be playing as he kissed my ear lobe?

He sensed the hesitation and took my hand to guide me down the carpeted hallway. His touch and confidence rushed my doubts. Obviously I couldn't stop now.

"Make yourself comfortable."

He removed his coat and I sat quickly in the one large chair. On the dresser, amid cards and toiletries, stood a bottle of whiskey.

"May I have a drink?" I had never drunk anything stronger than Dubonnet.

"No. I don't think so. But I'll have one." He poured the liquor into a glass he took down from above the face bowl. Water sloshed around and he gulped it down. Then in a moment he stood over me. I wanted to look up at him but my head refused.

"Come here, Reet. Get up." I wanted to, but my muscles had atrophied. I didn't want him to think of me as a dick teaser. A cheat. But my body wouldn't obey.

He bent and took both hands and pulled me upright. He enclosed me in his arms.

"You nearly 'bout as tall as me. I like tall girls." Then he kissed me, softly. And slowly. When he stopped, my body had gone its own way. My heart raced and my knees were locked. I was embarrassed at my trembling.

"Come over to the bed." He patiently pulled me away from the chair.

We both sat on the bed and I could hardly see him, although he was a breath away. He held my face in his large dark hands.

"I know you're scared. That's natural. You're young. But we're going to have a party. Just think of it like that. We're having a love party."

My previous brushes with sex had been just that. Brushes. One violent. The other indifferent, and now I found myself in the hands and arms of a tender man.

He stroked and talked. He kissed me until my ears rang, and he made me laugh. He interrupted his passion to make some small joke, and the second I responded he resumed lovemaking.

I lay crying in his arms, after.

"You happy?" The gold in his mouth glinted like a little star.

I was so happy that the next day I went to a jewelers and bought him an onyx ring with a diamond chip. I charged it to my stepfather's account.

7

Love was what I had been waiting for. I had done grown-up things out of childish ignorance or juvenile bravado, but now I began to mature. I became pleased with my body because it gave me such pleasure. I shopped for myself carefully for the first time. Searching painstakingly for just the right clothes instead of buying the first thing off the rack. Unfortunately my taste was as new as my interest. Once when Curly was to take me out to dinner, I bought a smart yellow crepe dress with black roses, black baby-doll shoes, whose straps sank a full inch into my ankles, and an unflattering wide coolie hat with veil. I pinned a small cluster of yellow rose buds on my bosom and was ready for the fray.

He only asked me to remove the corsage.

Curly had said at the beginning of our affair that he had a girl who worked in a San Diego shipyard and her job would be up soon. Then they'd go back to New Orleans and get married. I hastily stored the information in that inaccessible region of the mind where one puts the memory of pain and other unpleasantries. For the while it needn't bother me, and it didn't.

He was getting out of the Navy and only had a couple of months before all his papers would be cleared. Southern upbringing and the terror of war made him seem much older than his thirty-one years.

We took my son for long walks through parks; when people complimented us on our child, he played the proud papa and accepted. At playland on the beach we rode the Ferris wheel and loop-the-loop and gooed ourselves with salt-water taffy. Late afternoons we took the baby back to the sitter and then went to his hotel and one more, or two more, or three more love parties. I never wanted it to end. I bought things for him. A watch (he already had one), a sports coat (too small), another ring, and paid for them myself. I couldn't hear his protestations. I wasn't buying things. I was buying time.

One day after work he took me to the sitter's. He sat and held the baby. His silence should have told me something. Maybe it did, but again I didn't want to know. We left in a quiet mood. He only said, "I want me a boy like that. Just like that."

Since we weren't heading for the hotel, I asked where we were going.

"I'm taking you to your house."

"Why?"

No answer.

He found a parking space a half-block away. The street-lights were just coming on and a soft fog dimmed the world. He reached in the back seat and took out two large boxes. He handed them to me and said, "Give me a kiss."

I tried to laugh, to pretend that the kiss was payment for the gifts, but the laugh lied. He kissed me lightly and looked at me long.

"Reet. My girl friend is here and I'll be checking out of the hotel tonight."

I didn't cry because I couldn't think.

"You're going to make some man a wonderful wife. I mean it. These things are for you and the baby. I hate to say goodbye, but I gotta."

He probably said more, but all I remember is walking from the car to my front door. Trying for my life's sake to control the angry lurchings of my stomach. Trying to walk upright carrying the awkward boxes. I had to set down the boxes to find the door key, and habit fitted it into the lock. I entered the hall without hearing him start the car.

Because he had not lied, I was forbidden anger. Because he had patiently and tenderly taught me love, I could not use hate to ease the pain. I had to bear it.

I am certain, with the passage of time, that he loved me. Maybe for the loveless waif I was. Maybe he felt pity for the young mother and fatherless child, and so decided to give us what we both needed for two months. I don't know. I'm only certain that for some reason he loved me and that he was a good man.

The loss of young first love is so painful that it borders on the ludicrous.

I even embarrassed myself. Weeks after Charles left, I stumbled around San Francisco operating in the familiar. The lovely city disappeared in my fog. Nothing I did to food made it interesting to me. Music became a particular aggravation, for every emotional lyric had obviously been written for me alone.

> Gonna take a sentimental journey
> gonna set my heart at ease...

Charles had taken that journey and left me all alone. I was one emotional runny sore. To be buffeted about emotionally was not new, only the intensity and reason were. The new pain and discomfort was physical. My body had been awakened and fed, and suddenly I discovered I had a ravenous appetite. My natural reticence and habit of restraint prevented me from seeking other satisfaction even if it could be found.

I began to lose weight, which, with my height and thinness, I could ill afford to do. The burst of energy which had propelled me into beauty salons and dress shops was now as absent as my gone lover. I longed and pined, sighed and yearned, cried and generally slouched around feeling dismal and bereaved. By eighteen I managed to look run down if not actually run over.

My brother Bailey again was my savior, a role he fulfilled most of my early years.

He returned to the city after some months on an ammunition ship, and came to the restaurant to see me.

"My. What the hell's happened to you?" The way I looked seemed to anger rather than worry him. I introduced him to my employer. She said, "Your brother. He awful little, ain't he? I mean, to be your brother?"

Bailey thanked her smoothly, allowing just the tail of his sarcasm to flick in her face. She never noticed.

"I said, what's the matter with you? Have you been sick?" I held in the tears that wanted to pour into my brother's hands.

"No. I'm okay."

I thought at the time that it was noble to bear the ills one had silently. But not so silently that others didn't know one was bearing them.

"What time do you get off?"

"One o'clock. I'm off tomorrow, so I'm going out to get the baby."

"I'll be back and take you. Then we can talk."

He turned to Mrs. Dupree. "And a good day to you, too, madam." Bailey did little things with such a flourish. He might have been the Count of Monte Cristo, or Cyrano saying farewell to fair Roxanne.

After he had gone, Mrs. Dupree grinned her lips into a pucker. "He's as cute as a little bug."

I busied myself amid the pots. If she thought likening my big brother to an insect would please me, she had another think coming.

The baby crawled around the floor of my room as I told Bailey of my great love affair. Of the pain of discovery of pain. He nodded understanding and said nothing.

I thought that while I had his attention I might as well throw in my other sadness. I told him that because my old schoolmates laughed at me, I felt more isolated than I had in Stamps, Arkansas.

202

He said, "He sounds like a nice guy" and "I think its time for you to leave San Francisco. You could try Los Angeles or San Diego."

"But I don't know where I'd live. Or get a job." Although I was miserable in San Francisco, the idea of any other place frightened me. I thought of Los Angeles and it was a gray vast sea without ship or lighthouse.

"I can't just tear Guy away. He's used to the woman who looks after him."

"But she's not his mother."

"I've got a good job here."

"But surely you don't mean to make cooking Creole food your life's work."

I hadn't thought about it. "I have a nice room here. Don't you think its nice?"

He looked at me squarely, forcing me to face my fears. "Now, My, if you're happy being miserable, enjoy it, but don't ask me to feel sorry for you. Just get all down in it and wallow around. Take your time to savor all its subtleties, but don't come to me expecting sympathy."

He knew me too well. It was true. I was loving the role of jilted lover. Deserted, yet carrying on. I saw myself as the heroine, solitary, standing under a streetlight's soft yellow glow. Waiting. Waiting. As the fog comes in, a gentle rain falls but doesn't drench her. It is just enough to make her shiver in her white raincoat (collar turned up). Oh, he knew me too well.

"If you want to stay around here looking like death eating a soda cracker, that's your business. There are some rights no one has the right to take from you. That's one. Now, what do you want to do?"

That evening I decided to go to Los Angeles. At first I thought I'd work another month, saving every possible penny. But Bailey said, "When you make up your mind to make a change you have to follow through on the wave of decision." He promised me two hundred dollars when his ship paid off and suggested that I tell my boss that I'd be leaving in a week.

I had never had two hundred dollars of my own. It sounded like enough to live on for a year.

The prospect of a trip to Los Angeles returned my youth to me.

My mother heard my plans without surprise. "You're a woman. You can make up your own mind." She hadn't the slightest idea that not only was I not a woman, but what passed for my mind was animal instinct. Like a tree or a river, I merely responded to the winds and the tides.

She might have seen that, but her own mind was misted with the knowledge of a failing marriage, and the slipping away of the huge sums of money which she had enjoyed and thought her due. Her fingers still glittered with diamonds and she was a weekly customer at the most expensive shoe store in town, but her pretty face had lost its carefree adornment and her smile no longer made me think of day breaking.

"Be the best of anything you get into. If you want to be a whore, it's your life. Be a damn good one. Don't chippy at anything. Anything worth having is worth working for."

It was her version of Polonius' speech to Laertes. With that wisdom in my pouch, I was to go out and buy my future.

8

The Los Angeles Union Railway Terminal was a marvel of Moorish Spanish glamour. The main waiting room was vast and the ceiling domed its way up to the clouds. Long curved benches sat in dark wooden splendor, and outside its arched doors, palm trees waved in lovely walks. Inlaid blue and yellow tiles were to be found on every wall, arranged in gay and exotic design.

It was easy to distinguish San Franciscans detraining amid the crowd. San Franciscan women always, but always, wore gloves. Short white snappy ones in the day, and long black or white kid leather ones at night. The Southern Californians and other tourists were much more casual. Men sported flowered shirts, and women ambled around or lounged on the imposing seats in cotton dresses which could have passed for brunch coats in San Francisco.

Being from The City, I had dressed for the trip. A black crepe number which pulled and pleated, tucked and shirred, in a warp all its own. It was expensive by my standards and dressy enough for a wedding reception. My short white gloves had lost their early-morning crispness during the ten-hour coach trip, and Guy, whose immensity matched his energy, had mashed and creased and bungled the dress into a very new symmetry. Less than a year old, he had opinions. He definitely wanted to get down and go to that smiling stranger across the aisle, and immediately wanted to be in my lap pulling on the rhinestone brooch which captured and brought light to the collar of my dress.

In spite of the wrinkled dress and in spite of the cosmetic case full to reeking with dirty diapers, I left the train with my son a picture of controlled dignity. I had over two hundred dollars rolled in scratchy ten-dollar bills in my brassiere, another seventy in my purse, and two bags of seriously selected clothes. Los Angeles was going to know I was there.

My aunt answered my telephone call.

"Ritie, where are you?"

"We're at the station."

"What we?"

Like all the family she had heard about my pregnancy, but she hadn't seen the result.

"My son and I."

A tiny hesitation, then: "Get a taxi and come out here. I'll pay the cab fare." Her voice didn't ooze happiness at hearing from me, but then, the Baxters were not known to show any emotions. Except violent ones.

Wilshire Boulevard was wide and glossy. Large buildings sat back on tiny little lawns in a privacy that projected money and quiet voices and white folks.

The house on Federal Avenue had a no-nonsense air about it. It was a model of middle-class decorum. A single-story, solidly made building with three bedrooms, good meant-to-last furniture, and samplers on the wall which exhorted someone to "Bless This Home" and warned that "Pride Goeth before a Fall."

The clan had met, obviously called by my aunt, to check out my new addition to the family and give me the benefit of their conglomerate wisdom. My Uncle Tommy sat, wide-spraddled as usual, and grumbled. "Hey, Ritie. Got a baby, I see."

Guy was in my arms and talking, pointing, laughing, so the meaning in his statement was not in the words. He was simply greeting me and saying that although I had a child without benefit of marriage, he for one was not going to ignore either me or the baby.

My family spoke its own mysterious language. The wives and husbands of my blood relatives handed my son around as if they were thinking of adding him to their collection. They removed his bootees and pulled his toes.

"Got good feet."

"Uh huh. High arches."

One aunt ran her hand around his head and was satisfied. "His head is round."

"Got a round head, huh?"

"Sure does."

"That's good."

"Uh huh."

This feature was more than a symbol of beauty. It was an indication of the strength of the bloodline. Every Baxter had a round head.

"Look a lot like Bibbi, doesn't he?" "Bibbi" was the family name for my mother. Guy was handed around the circle again.

"Sure does."

"Yes. I see Bibbi right here."

"Well... but he's mighty fair, isn't he?"

"Sure is."

They all spoke without emotion, except for my Aunt Leah. Her baby voice rose and fell like music played on a slender reed.

"Reetie, you're a woman now. A mother and all that. You'll have two to think of from now on. You'll have to get a job—"

"I've been working as a cook." She shouldn't think I had come to be taken care of.

"—and learn to save your money."

Tommy's wife, Sarah, wrapped my son carefully in his blanket and handed him to me. Aunt Leah stood, a signal that the inspection was over. "What time is your train? Charlie can drive you to the station."

My brain reeled. Had I given the impression that I was going on? Did they say something I missed? "In a few hours. I should be getting back."

We were all shaking hands. Their relief was palpable. I was, after all, a Baxter and playing the game. Being independent. Expecting nothing and if asked, not giving a cripple crab a crutch.

Tom asked, "Need some money, Reet?"

"No thanks. I've got money. "All I needed was to get away from that airless house.

My uncles and aunts were childless, except for my late Uncle Tuttie, and they were not equipped to understand that an eighteen-year-old mother is also an eighteen-year-old girl. They were a close-knit group of fighters who had no patience with weakness and only contempt for losers.

I was hurt because they didn't take me and my child to their bosom, and because I was a product of Hollywood upbringing and my own romanticism. On the silver screen they would have vied for me. The winner would have set me up in a cute little cottage with frangipani and roses growing in the front yard. I would always wear pretty aprons and my son would play in the Little League. My husband would come home (he looked like Curly) and smoke his pipe in the den as I made cookies for the Boy Scouts meeting.

I was hurt because none of this would come true. But only in part. I was also proud of them. I congratulated myself on having absolutely the meanest, coldest, craziest family in the world.

Uncle Charlie, Aunt Leah's husband, never talked much, and on the way back to that station he broke the silence only a few times.

"You sure got yourself a cute baby."

"Thank you."

"Going on to San Diego, huh?"

I guessed so.

"Well, your father's down there. You won't be by yourself."

My father, who spent his time drinking tequila in Mexico and putting on high-toned airs in San Diego, would give me a colder reception than the one I'd just received.

I would be by myself. I thought how nice it would be.

I decided that one day I would be included in the family legend. Someday, as they sat around in the closed circle recounting the fights and feuds, the prides and prejudices of the Baxters, my name would be among the most illustrious. I would become a hermit. I would seal myself off from the world, just my son and I.

I had written a juicy melodrama in which I was to be the star. Pathetic, poignant, isolated. I planned to drift out of the wings, a little girl martyr. It just so happened that life took my script away and upstaged me.

9

"Are you in the life?"

The big black woman could have been speaking Russian. She sat with her back to the window and the sunlight slid over her shoulders, making a pool in her lap.

"I beg pardon?"

"The life. You turn tricks?"

The maid at the hotel had given me the woman's address and said she took care of children. "Just ask for Mother Cleo."

She hadn't asked me to sit, so I just stood in the center of the cluttered room, the baby resting on my shoulder.

"No. I do not." How could she ask me such a question?

"Well, you surely look like a trickster. Your face and everything."

"Well, I assure you, I'm not a whore. I have worked as a chef." How the lowly have become mighty. Ole Creole Kitchen would hitch up its shoulders to know that it once had had a chef—not just a garden-variety cook.

"Well." She looked at me as if she'd soon be able to tell if I was lying.

"How come you got so much powder and lipstick?" That morning I had bought a complete cosmetic kit and spent over an hour pasting my face into a mask with Max Factor's Pancake No. 31. I didn't really feel I had to explain to Mother Cleo, but on the other hand I couldn't very well be rude. I did need a baby-sitter.

"Maybe I put on too much."

"Where do you work?"

It was an interrogation. She had her nerve. Did she think that being called Mother Cleo gave her maternal privileges?

"The Hi Hat Club needs a waitress. I'm going to apply." The make-up was supposed to make me look older. Maybe it only succeeded in making me look cheap.

"That's a good job. Tips can make it a real good job. Let me see the baby."

She got up with more ease than I had expected. When she stretched out her hands a cloud of talcum powder was released. She took the baby and adjusted him down in the crook of her arm. "He's pretty. Still sleeping, huh?"

Mother Cleo metamorphosed in front of me. She was no longer the ugly fat ogre who threatened from her deep chair. Looking down on the infant, she had become the prototype of mother. Her face softened and her voice blurred. She ran stubbly fat fingers around his cap and slid it off.

"I don't usually take them this young. Too much trouble. But he's cute as can be, ain't he?"

"Well, you know—"

"Don't do for you to say so, but still it's true. And you're almost too young to have a baby. I guess your folks put you out, huh?"

She had noticed I wore no wedding ring. I decided to let her think I was homeless. Then I thought, "Let her think nothing. I was homeless."

"Well, I'm going to give you a hand. I'll keep him and I'm going to charge you less than the white ones." I was shocked that she kept white babies. "Lots of white women trust their babies with me rather than they own mothers. There lot of them from the South and they like the idea that they still got a mammy for they children. Can't you just see them? Snotty-nosed little things growing up talking about 'I had a colored mammy.' Huh?" She uglied her face with wrinkles. "But I naturally like children and I make they mommas pay. They pay me good. Don't care how much I like they young 'uns, they don't pay they have to go."

I agreed to her terms and paid her for the first week. Before I left, the baby struggled awake in her arms. She began a rocking motion which didn't lull him. His large black eyes took in the strange face and he began to look around for me. A small cry found its way to the surface before I came into his vision. Once he had assured himself that indeed I was there, he hollered in earnest, angry that I had allowed him to be held by this unknown person, and maybe even a little afraid that I'd given him away. I moved to take him.

"Let him cry." Mother Cleo increased her rocking and bouncing. "He got to get used to it."

"Just let me hold him a second." I couldn't bear his loneliness. I took his softness and kissed him and patted his back and he quieted immediately, as a downpour of rain cuts off.

"You too soft. They all do that till they get used to me." She stood near me and held out her arms. "Give him to me and you go on and get your job. I'll feed him. You bring diapers?"

I nodded to the bag I had dropped beside the door.

"Hush baby, hush baby, hush baby, hush." She had started to croon. I handed the baby to her and right away he began to cry.

"Go on. He'll be all right."

He yelled louder, splitting the air with screams. She contrived a wordless song. His screams were lightning, piercing the dark cloud of her music. I closed the door.

10

The night club sat on the corner, a one-story building whose purple stucco façade was sprinkled with glitter dust. Inside the dark square room, a bar dimly curved its way from the door to a small dance floor in the rear. Minuscule round tables and chairs jammed against one another, and red bulbs shone down, intensifying the gloom.

The Hi Hat Club had almost too much atmosphere.

Music blared and trembled, competing with the customers' voices for domination of the air. Neither won, except that for a few seconds during the lull between records, the jukebox sat quiet up against the wall, its green and red and yellow lights flickering like an evil robot from a Flash Gordon film.

The customers came mostly from the underworld, though there was a scattering of young sailors among them. They all jockeyed and shifted, lifting glasses and voices in the thick air, which smelled of Lysol and perfume and bodies, and cigarettes and stale beer. The women were mistresses of decorum. They sat primly at the bar, skirts tucked in, voices quick or silent altogether. On the street they had been as ageless as their profession, but near the posturing, flattering men, they became modest girls. Kittens purring under the strokes.

I watched them and understood. I saw them and envied. They had men of their own. Of course they bought them. They laid open their bodies and threw away their dignity upon a heap of come-filled rubbers. But they had men.

In the late evenings, boosters and thieves wove their paths among the night people, trading, bartering, making contacts and taking orders.

"Got two Roos Bros. suits. Thirty-eight. Black. Pinstripe and nigger-brown. Tag says one-ninety dollars... they both yours for an ace fifty."

"Gelman shoes. I. Magnin dresses. Your woman'll catch if she wear these threads. For you, four dresses for a deuce."

Depending on the evening's take and the sweet man's mood, the thieves were given money by the pimps which had been given them by the girls which they had saved by lying down first and getting up last.

The waitresses, in a block, were the least interesting of the club's inhabitants. They were for the most part dull married women, who moved among the colorful patrons like slugs among butterflies. The men showed no interest in them, leading me to believe that virtue is safest in a den of iniquity.

I was younger but no more interesting than my colleagues, so the pretty men lumped me with them and ignored us all.

I had no chance to show them how clever I was because wit is communicated by language and I hadn't yet learned theirs. I understood their lack of interest to imply that smart women were prostitutes and stupid ones were waitresses. There were no other categories.

I worked cleaning ashtrays, serving drinks and listening for over a month. My tips were good because I was fast and had a good memory.

"Scotch and milk for you, sir?"

"That's right, little girl, you got a good memory." Though he never saw me, he'd leave a dollar tip.

My first week in San Diego, Mother Cleo had told me she had a room for rent. "I see you a good girl coming over here to see your baby ever day and all, so my husband and me, we ready to let you live here with us. Room'll be fifteen dollars a week. Got a new bedroom suite in it and if you put a rubber sheet on the bed, your baby can sleep with you." So I became a roomer in the home of Mr. Henry and Mrs. Cleo Jenkins.

My life began to move at a measured tempo. I found a modern dance studio where a long-haired white woman gave classes to a motley crew of Navy wives.

I went to work at six (five-thirty to set up tables, get change, arrange my tray with napkins and matches) and was off at two. I shared a ride with a waitress whose husband picked her up every night. I slept late, woke to fix my breakfast around noon and play with my baby.

He amused me. I could not and did not consider him a person. A real person. He was my baby, rather like a pretty living doll that belonged to me. I was myself too young and unformed a human being to think of him as a human being. I loved him. He was cute. He laughed a lot and gurgled and he was mine.

11

I had begun to look forward to two women coming in every night. They were both just under thirty, and separately they would not have attracted much attention. Johnnie Mae was thin, taller than average, dark-brown-skinned. Her long jaw sagged down, giving her a look of sadness even when she laughed. She wore fuchsia lipstick and most often showed pink smudges on her long white teeth.

Beatrice was plump to ripening. A short yellow woman whose role seemed to be straight man to Johnnie Mae's unfunny but loud humor.

The fact that the pimps and panderers didn't harass them, bespoke the tolerance in the black community for people who chose to lead lives different from the norm. Although they were obviously not sisters, they dressed identically and never spoke to anyone except each other and me.

"Good evening, ladies. Two Tom Collins, I presume." I was a democrat and treated every lady the same.

"Evening, Rita. That's right." They must have spent their free time practicing before mirrors. They sounded alike and even the looks on one face were reflected on the other.

"Got you running this evening, ain't they?" The question did not

211

really need answering. My tray was always filled with fresh drinks, dirty ashtrays or empty glasses.

"When you going to come over to our house?" They smiled at each other, then gave me their sly glances.

"Well, I work all the time, you know."

"Yes, but you have a day off. You say you don't have any friends here."

"I'm thinking about it. That'll be two dollars, please."

Lesbians still interested me, but I no longer felt tenderly protective of them: when I was fifteen I had spent nearly a year concerning myself with society's gross mistreatment of hermaphrodites. I was anxious over the plight of lesbians during the time I was consumed with fear that I might be an incipient one. Their importance to me had diminished in direct relationship to my assurance that I was not.

"Johnnie Mae got something nice for you yesterday."

"Sure did."

"It's a birthday surprise."

"But you don't know my birthday."

"That's how come it's a surprise."

They laughed into each other's laugh and I was forced to join them. Customers at other tables needed my attention, but the two women stayed on the fringes of my mind as I laced myself around the room. They weren't frightening, and they were funny.

"We'll get a bottle of Dubonnet"—Beatrice pronounced it doo bonnet—"for you and I'll cook. You're off on Sunday. Come over and I'll fry a Sunday bird."

"And we can have a ham."

"Just the three of us? Chicken and ham?" That was a lot of food.

"Nigger ham. A watermelon." Their laughter, crackling, met in the air above the table.

"I take my baby out on Sundays."

They thought about that while I waited on the other customers.

"You can bring him over."

"I'll think about it."

At the bar a thick-waisted waitress who had never invited me to her house curled her upper lip.

"You'd better be careful." She sent a hostile glance to Johnnie Mae's table.

"Why?" I wanted to hear her say it.

"Those women. You know what they are?" Her voice had taken on a sinister depth.

"What?"

"Bull daggers." She smirked her satisfaction at saying the word.

"Oh, really?" I put no surprise in my voice.

212

"You know about bull daggers, don't you?" Her face showed how her tongue relished the words.

"They dag bulls?" For a second she wasn't sure if I was being smart.

"They love women."

"Oh, is that all? That's all right then. They don't scare me. They can't eat me up." I flounced away, leaving my tray on the bar, and went directly to the table.

"Listen. I'm not a... not... not a lesbian, and I don't want to be one. Is that all right?"

Their faces closed. Johnnie Mae asked, "Is what all right?" Suddenly I was ashamed. "I mean, I'd like to come to your house on Sunday. But... I mean, I wanted you to know that... I don't go that way."

They were silent, wind-up toys whose springs had broken. I wished I could catch the words and swallow them whole.

"I'd like your address." I held out my pencil. Johnnie Mae took it and handed it to Beatrice."

"What time on Sunday?" I had to put something into the emptiness. Beatrice was writing.

"Two o'clock. When we come from church," said Johnnie Mae, handing me the paper.

"Okee dokee. See you then." I wanted to be flippant, to be funny, to say something that would erase the sadness, but I could think of nothing. I got my tray and went back to work.

12

On the blocks where Saturday-night revelers rambled, Sunday afternoons were given over to the godly. They filled the streets with a mighty thronging, vestiges of a recent contact with God, the Father, lying brightly on a few faces. Most gossiped, shared confidences, checked others' Sunday go-to-meeting clothes, and then spun from the crowd to head homeward.

Growing up, becoming responsible, having to think ahead and assuming the postures of adulthood had certain compensations for me. One that I weekly appreciated was the freedom to sleep late on Sundays. (Somehow the bed was more sensual on that morning than weekdays.) I loved the soul-stirring songs and heartily approved of the minister's passions, but being penned shoulder to shoulder with a rocking crowd of strangers for three hours or more did nothing for my soul.

I maneuvered through the churchgoers, listening for and hearing:

"The Reverend sure spoke today."

"That's the truth, child. He did it today."

"Reverend was talking to my soul this morning."

"Bless your heart. Mine too."

"It's a wonderful thing to go into the house of the Lord. That's the truth."

The sounds waved like pretty ribbons and belonged to me.

I understood them all. I was a part of that crowd. The fact of my Southern upbringing, the fact of my born blackness meant that I was for the rest of my life a member of that righteous band, and would be whether or not I ever went to church again.

The small white house sat squarely in a dirt yard. A few roses tried vainly to grow along a wire fence.

Johnnie Mae opened the door and from her taut smile I knew my blunt words of the other night might have been forgiven, but they were not forgotten.

Beatrice came from the rear of the house and stood beside Johnnie Mae. Both of them talked at once.

"You made it. We didn't think you were going to. We just got back from church. Just changed our clothes." They had changed into matching white T-shirts and pedal pushers.

In Southern towns, the people my grandmother called "worldly" socialized on Saturday night, while the "godly" entertained and were entertained in cool parlors on Sunday. The black people brought that custom north along with their soft speech and remembered recipes. Since my hostesses and I were Southern, I expected to sit at an overloaded table giving fulsome compliments while they plied me with "just one more helping."

"Come in. Take the weight off. Hope you're not starving. I'm just starting to cook." They were as nervous as I. I moved into the tiny room and immediately felt too big for it.

"Thought you were going to bring the baby."

"He was asleep. I'll go back early and take him for a walk." That was going to be my excuse to get away.

"Well, what do you think of our house?" I hadn't had a chance to look around before. I noticed that the walls were bare and there were no books, but furniture they had plenty. A fat, overstuffed rust sofa pressed its matching chair into a corner. Two large chairs, more accidental than incidental, stood pompous against the other wall. Little clear glass lamps, topped with white frilly shades, sat on two end tables. Things took up all the air.

"Come on, see the rest before you sit down." Johnnie Mae's pride carried us into a bedroom while Beatrice went back to the kitchen.

"Have you ever slept in a round bed before?" I hadn't and I hadn't seen one either. It didn't seem appealing, although it was covered with a blue satin spread which matched its curves.

"When Beatrice has her flowers she sleeps in here." I followed her into a monastic cell. A small cot and an old dresser were the room's only furnishings. No lamps, no doilies.

"Her flowers?" I wasn't really so curious as I was uncomfortable.

Johnnie Mae said, "Her monthlies. I don't get them any more. I had an operation. If she wasn't so scared of hospitals, she'd have one too."

"An operation?" I was young, but I was also stupid.

"Had my ovaries and all that mess taken out; Bee ought to get it done too. After all, I'm not about to give her any babies, am I?" She hunched me and winked. I must have returned the wink. I don't know. But I was thinking of the stupidity which got me in the predicament. The big generous unprejudiced spirit which had got me hooked up with two lesbians of heavy humor.

"It's nice. Your house is really very nice. I mean, it reflects your taste and your personalities. I always say, if you want to know a woman, I mean a person, go to their house. It will tell you..." I knew that words, despite the old saying, never fail. And my reading had given me words to spare. I could, and often did to myself or my baby, recite whole passages of Shakespeare, Paul Lawrence Dunbar poems, Kipling's "If," Countee Cullen, Langston Hughes, Longfellow's *Hiawatha*, Arna Bontemps. Surely I had enough words to cover a moment's discomfort. I had enough for hours if need be.

Back on the prickly sofa, Johnnie Mae offered me Dubonnet. I held the glass of thick sweet wine as protection. Thinking she would hesitate to pounce on me if there was a chance I would spill the wine on her furniture, I kept it in front of me like a shield.

"Beatrice, come out here. You're not chained to the stove." She looked at me and raised thick eyebrows. Johnnie Mae had the infuriating habit of making anyone she spoke to into a fellow conspirator. I raised my eyebrows back at her as if I understood her meaning. Beatrice came into the room, a sprinkling of perspiration dotting her face.

"Now, baby, you don't want no black chicken do you?" Beatrice was teasing. Flirting.

"If that chicken gets any darker than you, I'll have to whip your rusty dusty." They were a comedy team. If I had heard that exchange at the club I would have joined their laughter, but perched guarded in the cluttered room, I couldn't find anything funny. I laughed.

"Come here, you sweet thing." Beatrice obeyed and stood like a little chubby girl in front of Johnnie Mae.

"Bend down." Johnnie Mae raised her face and the two women's lips met. I watched and saw their tongues snaking in and out. Except in movies I had never even seen men and women kiss passionately. They pulled apart and looked at me in a practiced gesture. For a second I was too embarrassed to have been caught watching, and in the next second I knew they had wanted me to see. Even after I told them I had no interest in lesbianism, they thought the sight of women kissing would excite me.

I hated their stupidity, but more than that I hated being underestimated. If they only knew, they could strip buck naked and do the Sassy Sue wiggle and I would continue to sit, with my legs crossed, sipping the Dubonnet.

Beatrice's laughter floated over her shoulder as she headed back to the kitchen. Johnnie Mae looked at me and by leering tried to include me in her appreciation.

"Beatrice would make a rabbit hug a hound." She grunted like a pig.

Because laughter seemed to be the safest sport in the house, I laughed and said, "Where do you work? I mean both of you?"

"Right here. Flat on our backs." Nothing embarrassed the woman. "We both take two all-night tricks apiece once a week. Comes to two hundred dollars. We more than get by." She indicated the sofa and chairs. "As you can see."

Lesbian prostitutes! Did they trick with women? I ached to know. How did they pick them up? I had never heard of women hustling other women, but surely they didn't go to bed with men. I fished for a way to put my question.

Johnnie Mae looked around the room, her eyes counting and loving the many pieces of furniture. Her head finished its semicircle and I was back in her vision.

"We're going to have to move, you know?" The question was foolish. Not only did I not know, I didn't care. And if I'd had the chance to think about it, I'd have thought it was a good thing, too.

"The landlord doesn't like us. He's a church deacon, he says. But the real reason is that his son is a faggot. Goes around wearing women's clothes, so the old bastard can't stand gay people." She was happy to grin, thinking of the man's unhappiness. "I told the old bastard so, too." She shrugged her shoulders against the fates. "We'll find another place. I hate to move, though. I mean, we painted this place ourselves." The walls were pea-yellow in the living room. "We called this our honeymoon cottage. Beatrice planted the roses."

I felt there was something I was supposed to say. Something like

216

"You have my deepest sympathy." For some reason, at that moment I thought about Curly and did in fact feel sorry for the two women.

"Niggers make me sick. And nigger men make me sicker than that." She might have been thinking of her landlord, but it seemed she was reading my mind and had the audacity to mean Curly. She would have lost my sympathy, anyway. I hated the word "nigger" and never believed it to be a term of endearment, no matter who used it.

"Now you tell me. We been wondering about you. How come you working as a waitress? You speak such good English, you must have a diploma."

"Yes, I do." Shock pushed my voice; out.

"You mean you graduated from high school?"

"Yes."

"And work as a waitress?"

"Well, I can't type or take shorthand or—"

"You remind me of Beatrice." She shouted, "Beatrice. Come here." I feared I was going to have to sit through the kissing again.

Beatrice stood at the door leading to the living room. "What's on your mind?"

Johnnie Mae didn't have time for fun. "Bee, Rita's just like you. She finished high school."

Beatrice, knowing that wasn't such a grand feat said, "Really. Got your diploma, huh?"

Johnnie Mae answered for me. "Sure she got it. And works as a waitress." I started to explain, but she stopped me. "Beatrice was a WAC. A corporal." It was hard to believe that all that soft-looking flesh had been contained in an army uniform. "And when she got out she went to work. That's where we met. At some rich old woman's house. Bee was the cook and I was the housekeeper. I took one look at Bee and I have been keeping her ever since."

Break for peals of laughter.

13

"Let's have a little grifa before dinner." Johnnie Mae gave an order, not an invitation. She turned to me.

"You like grifa?"

"Yes. I smoke." The truth was I had smoked cigarettes for over a year, but never marijuana. But since I had the unmitigated gall to sit up cross-legged in a lesbian apartment sipping wine, I felt I had the stamina to smoke a little grifa. Anyway, I was prepared to refuse anything else they offered me, so I didn't feel I could very well refuse the pot.

Beatrice laid down a Prince Albert can on the table with cigarette papers.

"Do you want to roll it?" Johnnie Mae was being gracious.

"No thanks. I don't roll very well." I hadn't seen loose tobacco and cigarette papers since I'd left the South, five years earlier. My brother and I used to roll lumpy cigarettes for my uncle on a small hand-cranking machine when he'd run out of ready rolls.

She took the papers and deftly began to sift marijuana. I tried not to appear too curious as the grains of tobacco fell into the cupped paper.

"I'd like to use your bathroom."

"Sure. You know where it is."

I talked to the bathroom mirror. "You have nothing to be nervous about. You'll get out of this. Don't you always get out of everything? Marijuana is not habit-forming. Thousands of people have smoked it. The Indians and Mexicans and it didn't send them mad. Just wash your hands"—which were damp—"and go back to the living room. Keep your cool. Cool."

I inhaled the smoke as casually as if the small brown cigarette I held were the conventional commercial kind.

"No. No. Don't waste the grifa. Hand it here." She dragged the cigarette and made the sound of folks slurping tea from a saucer.

"But I like it my way." Stubborn to the end.

"Well, try it like this." Again the rattling sound.

"All right. I will." I opened my throat and kept my tongue flat so that the smoke found no obstacle in its passage from my lips to my throat. It tore the lining off my tonsils, made my nasal passages burn like red pepper and choked me. While I coughed, gagging, those silly bitches laughed. They would be sitting there with those vapid wrinkles on their faces while I choked to death. Wouldn't they do anything for me? No. Beatrice rescued the joint and sucked in the smoke, puffing out her already fat cheeks to bursting, while her lady love was busily engaged in rolling another stick of tearing fire.

Before the cough stopped shaking me, I had decided I would get even with them. They were lesbians, which was sinful enough, but they were also inconsiderate, stupid bitches. I reached again for the marijuana.

The food was the best I'd ever tasted. Every morsel was an experience of sheer delight. I lost myself in a haze of sensual pleasure, enjoying not only the tastes but the feel of the food in my mouth, the smells, and the sound of my jaws chewing.

"She's got a buzz. That's her third helping."

I looked up to see the two women looking at me and laughing. Their faces seemed to be mostly teeth. White teeth staggering inside dark lips. They were embarrassingly ugly, and yet there was something funny about it. They had no idea that they were so strange-looking. I laughed at their ignorance, and they, probably thinking themselves to be laughing at mine, joined me. When I remembered how they were ready to let me choke to death and how I vowed to get them, the tears rolled down my cheeks. That was really funny. They didn't know what I was thinking and I didn't know what form my revenge would take.

"Let's have some sounds." Beatrice got up from the table. We were by magic back in the murky living room. Johnnie Mae stood putting records on the player. She turned to me as the first record began to play. "You said you're studying how to dance. Do us a dance." Lil Green's voice whined out the sadful lyrics:

"In the dark, in the dark, I get such a thrill
when you press your fingertips upon my lils."

I couldn't explain that I didn't do dancing alone to music like that. At the studio I did stretches, extensions, pliés and relevés to Prokofiev, Tchaikovsky and Stravinsky.

It was considered normal in gatherings to ask a child or even an adult to entertain. The talented person was expected to share his gift. The singer was asked to "Sing us a little song!" and the person with a gift of memorizing was asked to "Render us a poem!" In my mother's house I had often been called to show what I was studying at dance school. The overstuffed chairs were pulled back and I would dance in the cleared living-room space. I hummed inaudibly and moved precisely from ballet position one straight into a wobbling arabesque. Mother's company would set their highballs down to applaud.

I decided to dance for my hostesses. The music dipped and swayed, pulling and pushing. I let my body rest on the sound and turned and bowed in the tiny room. The shapes and forms melted until I felt I was in a charcoal sketch, or a sepia watercolor.

When the record finished I stopped. The two women sat on the sofa. Made solemn.

"That was good. Wasn't it, baby?"

"Sure was."

"Dance with Beatrice. I don't mind. Go on. Beatrice, dance with Rita."

Again, order was in her voice. The last thing in the world I wanted to do was dance with another woman. Johnnie Mae got up and started the Lil Green song again and Beatrice moved up close to me. She put her arm around my waist and took my left hand as if we were going to waltz. It was crushing. Not only was she fat and soft and a head shorter than I, her big breasts rubbed against my stomach. She stuck her thigh between my knees and we wobbled around the room.

This was the ultimate insult. I would vent my spleen on those thick-headed lecherous old hags. They couldn't do me this way and get away with it.

"That's right, Beatrice, do the dip." The woman did a fancy step and bent back, pulling me with her. I nearly toppled over. Mercifully, the record finished after what seemed one thousand hours and I was allowed to return to the sofa.

"You all look good together. Beatrice can sure dance, can't she? Come here, baby, and give me a kiss."

I got up and made room for Beatrice.

"No. You can stay." She encircled Beatrice, whose face was heavy with submission.

"Have to go to the toilet again." Let the mental machine do its work. In the bathroom an idea bloomed. They were whores. Why not encourage them in their chosen profession? From what I understood, whores can never get enough money, and since they had so little, I dressed my newborn creation carefully and took it back to the living room. I asked if we could turn down the music because I wanted to talk.

"Rita wants to talk." They broke out of their embrace. Nasty things.

"I just thought I might be able to help you keep this place. You like it so much and you've made it so cute, it'd be a shame if you lost it."

They nearly became maudlin in their agreement.

"Well, I could rent it, and you could continue to stay."

"You mean you pay the rent and we pay you back."

"No. I'll rent the place in my name, I'll have the lights and gas put in my name. And pay everything. And three nights a week or four nights a week, you all stay here and turn tricks."

Beatrice's silly little voice complained: "You mean to turn our home into a whorehouse?"

Well, whores lived in it and it was a house. "Do you realize if the trade builds up, you can buy a place of your own and fix it just like this?" And they probably would.

"Where would we get the tricks? "Ever-practical Johnnie Mae.

"We'd get white taxi drivers and give them a percentage." My brain was clicking along like a Santa Fe train. A-hooting and a-

GATHER TOGETHER IN MY NAME

howling. "They could be told the hours, like between ten and two. Then if every trick is twenty dollars, they get five and we split the fifteen. Seven-fifty for you. Seven-fifty for me."

"We don't want to be whores. I mean, full time." Old big little Beatrice already scared. What did she do in the WACS? Seduce young girls?

"Tricking four days a week isn't full time," I said. "And anyway, if you're successful, you can quit it in six months. Go and buy you a little place. Fact is, you could even get a bigger house." And get even more junk in it.

Johnnie Mae looked at me with suspicion. "When did you figure all that out?"

"Well, I've been wanting to go into business. So I'd been saving my money. I had been thinking in terms of a hamburger stand, but this place is so perfect." And so were they. "If all three of us save, do you realize we could open a restaurant in a year? Beatrice as the chef. You and I as managers."

I was getting to them. "I had a little operation up the coast. A three-girl deal, but I had to close down." Admiration and a little fear showed in their faces. They hadn't bargained for what they were getting.

Johnnie Mae, not wanting to believe what she already believed, asked, "Why were you working as a waitress?"

Should I tell them in order to eat and pay for my son's keep, so they'd throw me down on that uncomfortable sofa and rape me? "I needed a front. Cops after me."

"Cops!" Both of them screamed. Like many weak people they wanted to milk the cow, at the same time denying the smell of bullshit. I saw immediately that I had gone too far.

"Not after me myself. One of my girls, but I wanted to lay a cover for myself."

Beatrice said, "You're awfully young to be in the rackets."

"I've been around, baby." I rolled my eyes to indicate distant and mysterious places." Well, how does it sound? Say we say Wednesday, Thursday, Friday and Saturday. Then you're free for church on Sunday and—"

"We'd better talk about it."

"I'm off tomorrow and I can get all the business taken care of. No time like the present."

"We only have the two bedrooms. Where will *you* work?"

I almost shouted at the tall woman. Me, turn tricks? What did she think I was? "I'm going to stay on at the restaurant. Shouldn't call attention to myself, you understand. But you won't be alone. I'll have somebody here to watch out for you. Just leave it to me."

I became pompously professional, which was never hard for me, being my father's daughter. "If you'll let me have a tablet and a pen, I'll take the landlord's address."

"Beatrice. Get some paper."

I moved over to the table, shifting the dinner dishes and crumbs out of my way as Johnnie Mae dictated.

"What's this address again?"

She gave it to me and I wrote it over and over on slips of paper.

"What you doing now?" Johnnie Mae wasn't bright, but she'd always be too clever to just go for the okey-doke. I put it in my mind that I'd better keep that in my mind.

"When I leave here, I'm going to start drumming up business," I said. "In a few weeks we'll be thousandaires."

"What?"

"That's just a step from millionaire. Let's have a drink on it" Beatrice poured. The first mouthful nearly sent me reeling. It made contact with the grifa in my brain. For a lightning second I was sober with a clear recollection of what I had done, then blissfully I was high again. An authority in charge of affairs.

I said good-bye, alluded again to the wonderful food and the wonderful future we had in store, and walked out of the house.

I was certain that my heartlessness regarding the women stemmed from a natural need for revenge. After all my soggy sentimentality for the misunderstood, no one could have convinced me that I was merely acting out society's hate for the "other ones."

However, an irony struck me before I reached the little one-foot wire fence that guarded the pavement from the yard. In a successful attempt to thwart a seduction I had ended up with two whores and a whorehouse. And I was just eighteen.

14

"Good evening, driver."

"Yeah."

"Are there enough houses of ill repute to service the naval personnel?"

"Whaat?"

"I know you're generally paid four dollars on a twenty-dollar customer (I guessed, I didn't know), but if, after Thursday night ten o'clock, you bring clients to this address, you'll be remunerated to the tune of five dollars per head."

You had to be very careful in speaking to whites, and especially white men. My mother said that when a white man sees your teeth he thinks he sees your underclothes.

I had managed in a few tense years to become a snob on all levels, racial, cultural and intellectual. I was a madam and thought myself morally superior to the whores. I was a waitress and believed myself cleverer than the customers I served. I was a lonely unmarried mother and held myself to be freer than the married women I met.

Hank was the club's erratic bouncer. Erratic because sometimes he didn't show up, and other times, when his habits hit him, he bounced people onto the sidewalk who had done no more than offend his sensibilities. He spent a few nights monthly in the drunk tank, and was always taken back on his release.

The other waitresses hinted that Hank did a few private jobs for the boss. Secretly I believed the man was afraid of Hank, rightly, for there was no way to anticipate him. He might see in a stranger qualities of great worth, or he might develop an active hate for a person's color.

He had kind of adopted me on my arrival, and at the earliest opportunity I approached him. "Hank, I want to know if you'd look after some business for me?"

In another century that face would have so frightened a slave owner that he would have been compelled to lash the broad back and shackle the wide hands.

"Yeah, li'l sister. What's the matter?"

"You know the two les—bull daggers who come in here?"

"They ain't been messing with you, is they?"

"Oh no." The reverse. "They've asked me to back them in a business. Whorehouse, to be exact. Wednesday to Saturday. And you're the only person I can trust to watch out for my end. I figure to pay you one third of my take."

His mouth hung open. "You're going to be turning tricks?"

"Not me, I'm going to keep on working, but they will. Could you manage the place for me? Watch out for the police and keep track of the money?"

After much repeating myself, he agreed. I created an elaborate system of chits, which would be given to the women and the cabdrivers. At around two-thirty in the morning Hank was to put on a porch light denoting a clear coast, and I would go in and pay off the workers.

223

I had a vague worry—that a sudden large bank account would put the vice squad on my trail. I wasn't afraid of the police, since I wasn't turning tricks myself, but I was terrified of how a police investigation would influence Mother Cleo. She'd toss me and my baby out of the house with much damning me to the depths of hell. There were other places to live of course, and with the money piling up in secret places I could afford anyone to tend my child, but the fact was that I cared for the Jenkinses and what they thought of me was important.

Their home and their ways reminded me of the grandmother who raised me and whom I idolized. I wouldn't have them offended. When my illicit business reached its peak, I joined their church, and stood in the choir singing the old songs with great feeling.

One afternoon Mother Cleo remarked, "I know something." And smiled a leer. Panic set in.

"What?"

"You doing something." She sang the accusation like schoolchildren promising to tell.

"What? I'm not doing anything." The ready lie at my tongue.

"You got yourself a fella."

Of all things, how could she come up with that? However wrong she was, I perceived she wasn't angry, and it would be safer to lie again.

I asked, "How did you know?" Pleased now that she had caught me.

"'Cause you're coming in later than you used to. Me, I'm a light sleeper. Mr. Henry can sleep till the cows come home, but taking care of children makes me a light sleeper. I hear every footfall. You used to be in around two twenty-five, two-thirty. Now you get in sometimes its three-thirty. Am I right?"

"Yes."

"Well, is he a nice boy? Work where you work, don't he?"

"How do you know so much, Mother Cleo?"

"'Cause anybody else couldn't stay up every night till you get off. If you want to, he can come 'round here to see you."

I started. "Not at night. But in the daytime, I don't mind." That was more like it. With so many unexpected things happening I would be very unhappy to see Mother Cleo's morals slip.

For two and a half months I operated at the points of a stylistic triangle, braggadocio (in front of the women) and modest servitude (at the club), and kept wondering what to do with all the cash.

I bought a car which was a model of Detroit genius. A pale-green Chrysler, '39 vintage, convertible. It sported wooden doors and highly polished wooden dashboards. Knobs and buttons were a yellow material like the handles of old-fashioned flatware. I fashioned a sling made out of belts and secured my son, who had begun to walk. We drove around the monotonous streets of San Diego in my beautiful chariot. I had paid cash for it from a dresser drawer of money.

Mother Cleo asked charily "And where in the world...?"

I had my answer molded. "My boyfriend gave it to me!"

"What'd he do? Steal it?"

"Oh no. He paid cash."

"How come he don't come around?"

"He's going to. I invited him." In fact, I had thougnt of palming Hank off as the hard-working boyfriend but decided he'd never be able to carry it off.

"Listen here. He ain't a married man, is he?" She began to draw away from me as if I might be a carrier of a loathsome disease.

"No, ma'am. He's not even divorced. I mean, he's never been married."

She calmed down gradually, then her face hardened. "He ain't a white man, is he? I don't 'low white men."

I had to laugh. Of all the tricks who came and went in my establishment, I hadn't even seen one. "No, Mother Cleo, he's not even light-skinned."

Reluctantly she smiled. "One thing I don't hold with is women messing 'round with married mens. The other is messing 'round with white men. First one the Bible don't like, second one the law don't like."

She could have put her time to greater use concerning herself with my lack of morals rather than with my sexual involvements. Since coming to San Diego I let no attraction penetrate the invisible widow's weeds I had donned. My love was dead, my love was gone, married to some stupid shipfitter and living in the mosquito-ridden swamps of Louisiana. Long die, and stay dead, my love.

15

During this time when my life hinged melodramatically on intrigue and deceit, I discovered the Russian writers. One title caught my eye. Not because I felt guilty raking in money from the doings of prostitutes but because of the title's perfect balance. Life, as far as I had deduced it, was a series of opposites: black/white, up/down, life/death, rich/poor, love/hate, happy/sad, and no mitigating areas in between. It followed Crime/Punishment.

The heavy opulence of Dostoevsky's world was where I had lived forever. The gloomy, lightless interiors, the complex ratiocinations of the characters, and their burdensome humors, were as familiar to me as loneliness.

I walked the sunny California streets shrouded in Russian mists. I fell in love with the Karamazov brothers and longed to drink from a samovar with the lecherous old father. Then Gorki became my favorite. He was the blackest, most dear, most despairing. The books couldn't last long enough for me. I wished the writers all alive, turning out manuscripts for my addiction. I took to the Chekov plays and Turgenev, but always returned in the late night's, after I had collected my boodle, to the Maxim Gorki and his murky, unjust world.

My dance teacher, who took no personal interest, wore the most outlandish clothes. Her long dark skirt, gathered, fell to just above her ankles. The blouses were of Mexican persuasion and were worn off her thin shoulders. Ropes of colorful beads and thong sandals completed her costume. She looked odd enough for admiration. I copied her clothes, and when not dressed in the white-blouse, black-skirt waitress uniform, I could be seen haunting the libraries, a tall thin black girl in too-long skirts and señorita blouses, which might have been sexy had I had the figure and/or attiude to complement them. Alas, I didn't.

Upon reflection, I marvel that no one saw through me enough to bundle me off to the nearest mental institution. The fact that it didn't happen depended less on my being a good actress than the fact that I was surrounded, as I had been all my life, by strangers. The world of waitress, dreamer, madam and mother might have continued indefinitely, except for another of life's unexpected surprises.

I didn't insist on any rules in my little whorehouse by the side of the road, except one: no all-night dates, no matter what the temptation. I wanted the money without name, the ease without strain. I never wanted any tricks to be in the house after I arrived, hence the signal with Hank.

One evening I sat in a taxi on the darkened street (I never took my automobile to the whorehouse) and waited for the light to go off on the porch. The driver, who also brought trade, and I walked into the house.

I stood in the center of the tiny living room, which smelled of Lysol and smoke and incense, hemmed in by the driver, the women

226

and Hank, and by the furniture, which threatened to oust us all at any moment. Beatrice and Johnnie Mae erased any budding aspirations I had for owning things. Now that they had money, their acquisitive natures came into their own. The total filling up of the living room was so gradual that it was as if the existing furniture gave birth nightly to smaller and even larger images of itself.

Hank passed me the cigar box of money.

"Damn. Turn the damned radio off till we get business settled. You can't hear a shitting thing." I had taken to cursing to round out my image. The two women no longer took any interest in me, except possibiy to hate my arrogance and envy my authority. I couldn't care less.

I had not finished recovering their chits and was about to turn to the cabdriver when a drunk, half-dressed white sailor stumbled through the bedroom door. He had nothing on below the blue middy. There was a moment's hush when the women and Hank looked at me. I was hypnotized at the man's nudity and couldn't take my eye's from his white, soft, dangling penis.

Beatrice ran to him. "Honey. I told you to stay—"

"What's going on? Who are all these folks?" His accent was lower Mississippi, and he looked as naked and white and ugly and drunk and nasty as anything I could think of.

Beatrice herded him back to the room.

In those seconds I became a child again. Unreasoning rage consumed me. The low-down sneaky bitches—I had told them to have the place cleared before I got there. They had probably had tricks there every night and I hadn't even questioned them. I could have gone to jail or worse. After all I'd done for them, their whorish hearts were so ungrateful that I had been subjugated to looking at the sickening aspect of a white man's penis.

I turned to Hank, and lumbering toward me, he said, "Rita, swear to God, I thought they was all gone."

Johnnie Mae allowed a little of her jealousy to.show. "I don't see nothing wrong myself. You come over here every night collecting money, acting like you somebody's pimp. But you too good to turn a trick. And you keep this big rough sonofabitch watching us all the time. Well, you can kiss my black ass."

Her rudeness didn't surprise me. I would not have moved an eyebrow at anything any more. The drivers stood mesmerized by the event.

I gave the cigar box to Hank. "Hank. Do you want a whorehouse, complete with whores? You've just been given one." I turned to the women, gathering all my injured dignity. "And, ladies, you decided in the beginning that you were going to screw me one way or the other. Look at us now. Who did the screwing?"

227

Beatrice's voice keened, sharpened and moved through the room like a swinging razor. "If it hadn't been for you, we'd be living like we always did."

"Yes, in the street, or back in some white woman's kitchen."

Johnnie Mae swelled up as if she had taken in more air than it was possible to release. "Be goddam careful how you talk to her, you big-nose bitch."

It was time to go. These lying heathens were not above attacking me. And after all I'd done for them.

"Hank, if you want this place, it's all yours." And one parting shot to the traitors: "At least I'm leaving you better off than I found you. You've got enough secondhand furniture to start you own Goodwill store." And to the cabdriver: "Will you please take me home."

I stood straighter, separating myself from the stench of my present environment, and started out. Johnnie Mae's rage propelled her after me. I reached the door just as she stretched her hand for me. I put on a little speed, not wanting to appear to be running, and escaped down the steps as she and the cabdriver collided in the doorway. He extricated himself in a hurry, more than a little terrified of getting caught between two restless tribes. Johnnie Mae, thwarted, for I had gained the sidewalk, screamed out into the quiet darkness, "You bitch! You think the police don't want to know how you bought that car. You better not drive it again. I'll have the vice squad on your ass."

I don't know how I continued walking to the cab. Her threat and the sound of her screech had stabbed me to the quick as surely as it had pierced the night. The wretch would put the cops on my trail and I'd lose my car, go to jail and be put out of Mother Cleo's. I was sitting in the back of the taxi when a numbing thought sidled across my brain like a poisonous snake. I might be declared an unfit mother and my son would be made a ward of the court. There were cases like that. In the cool early-morning air I began to sweat. The tiny glands in my armpits opened and closed to the pricking of a thousand straight pins.

"Please take me home, and I'm sorry for that terrible outburst." Fear still rode the front seat with the driver and he lost no time depositing me at my destination. I paid him, tipped him grandly and inundated him with praise for his reliability and courtesy, and lack of familiarity. I don't think he heard a word, and before I reached the front door, his tail lights had turned winking around the corner.

During the exotic buying sprees I hadn't thought to get luggage to hold my new acquisitions. I heaped piles of my clothes and my son's into the suitcases Bailey had given me in San Francisco. I had made up my mind that come daybreak, my son and I were going to make a run for it. If the police caught me, they'd catch me at the railway station or on the train, not a sitting duck waiting passively to be arrested. When I had finished cramming as many things as possible into the bags, I sat down to read until daybreak.

Since childhood I had often read until the gray light entered my room, but on that tense night it seemed sleep had allied itself with my enemies, and along with them was determined to overpower me, do me down. I tried sitting in a chair and sitting cross-legged on the bed. A knock awoke me. It was Mother Cleo.

"Rita, you left your light on again. You going to start helping me with the electricity. You don't know how much it cost..." She was moving away from the door, and her words reached down the hall.

I came to full attention and checked my luggage, my money and my story again.

"Mother Cleo, my mother is sick in San Francisco. She telephoned me at the club last night, so I have to go home." I had followed her into the kitchen. She put down her cup and looked at me with such sympathy I almost wished I wasn't lying.

"Oh, you poor thing. She ain't bad off, is she?"

"Oh no, nothing serious." I wanted to calm her fears.

"Well then, you won't be long. You'll leave the baby?"

"Oh no. She wants to see him. And I'll tell you the truth"—as if I could—"I'm not coming back soon."

"Aw. Don't tell me that. I've come to look on your as family."

"Mother Cleo, I appreciate everything you've done for us. And I want you to have this." I laid fifty dollars on the table. "My boyfriend sent it to you as a present."

She beamed and I saw the tears start to form.

"Now, don't cry. We'll come back sometime. I wish you'd bathe the baby while I'm taking a bath, and then we'll hit the highway."

Her last words to me as she and Mr. Henry helped me to the car were attributes to my acting and successful deceit.

"You're just what I wanted for a daughter. You smart and mannerable and truthful. That's what I like most. You living a Christian life. Keep up the good work. God bless you and the child. And your mother."

I tore down the morning streets as if the hounds of hell were coming to collect my soul. The baby responded to the two-wheel curve-taking by giving out air-splitting screams. My "Hush, baby" and "It's all right, baby" could have been unheard whispers. He felt my panic and seemed to want the world to know that he was just as afraid as his mother.

At the train station I wiped the steering wheel and unstrapped the baby. I left the car parked in a No Parking zone, and as far as I know, it is there to this day.

I was racing away with my son on my hip and sheer fright in my heart. My general destination was the little village in Arkansas where I had grown up. But the particular goal of the journey was the protective embrace of Mrs. Annie Henderson, the grandmother who had raised me. Momma, as we called her, was a deliberately slow-speaking, right-thinking woman. And above all, she had what I lacked most at the moment. Courage.

16

There is a much-loved region in the American fantasy where pale white women float eternally under black magnolia trees, and white men with soft hands brush wisps of wisteria from the creamy shoulders of their lady loves. Harmonious black music drifts like perfume through this precious air, and nothing of a threatening nature intrudes.

The South I returned to, however, was flesh-real and swollen-belly poor. Stamps, Arkansas, a small hamlet, had subsisted for hundreds of years on the returns from cotton plantations, and until World War I, a creaking lumbermill. The town was halved by railroad tracks, the swift Red River and racial prejudice. Whites lived on the town's small rise (it couldn't be called a hill), while blacks lived in what had been known since slavery as "the Quarters."

After our parents' divorce in California, our father took us from Mother, put identification and destination tags on our wrists, and sent us alone, by train, to his mother in the South. I was three and my brother four when we first arrived in Stamps. Grandmother Henderson accepted us, asked God for help, then set about raising us in His way. She had established a country store around the turn of the century, and we spent the Depression years minding the store, learning Bible verses and church songs, and receiving her undemonstrative love.

We lived a good life. We had some food, some laughter and Momma's quiet strength to lean against. During World War II the armed services drew the town's youth, black and white, and Northern war plants lured the remaining hale and hearty. Few, if any, blacks or poor whites returned to claim their heritage of terror and poverty. Old men and women and young children stayed behind to tend the gardens, the one paved block of stores and the long-accepted way of life.

In my memory, Stamps is a place of light, shadow, sounds and entrancing odors. The earth smell was pungent, spiced with the odor of cattle manure, the yellowish acid of the ponds and rivers, the deep pots of greens and beans cooking for hours with smoked or cured pork. Flowers added their heavy aroma. And above all, the atmosphere was pressed down with the smell of old fears, and hates, and guilt.

On this hot and moist landscape, passions clanged with the ferocity of armored knights colliding. Until I moved to California at thirteen I had known the town, and there had been no need to examine it. I took its being for granted and now, five years later, I was returning, expecting to find the shield of anonymity I had known as a child.

Along with other black children in small Southern villages, I had accepted the total polarization of the races as a psychological comfort. Whites existed, as no one denied, but they were not present in my everyday life. In fact, months often passed in my childhood when I only caught sight of the thin hungry po' white trash (sharecroppers), who lived sadder and meaner lives than the blacks I knew. I had no idea that I had outgrown childhood's protection until I arrived back in Stamps.

Momma took my son in one arm and folded the other around me. She held us for one sweet crushing moment. "Praise God Almighty you're home safe."

She was already moving away to keep her crying private.

"Turned into a little lady. Sure did." My Uncle Willie examined me with his quiet eyes and reached for the baby. "Let's see what you've got there."

He had been crippled in early childhood, and his affliction was never mentioned. The right side of his body had undergone severe paralysis, but his left arm and hand were huge and powerful. I laid the baby in the bend of his good arm.

"Hello, baby. Hello. Ain't he sweet?" The words slurred over his tongue and out of the numb lips. "Here, take him." His healthy muscles were too strong for a year-old wriggler.

Momma called from the kitchen, "Sister, I made you a little something to eat."

We were in the Store; I had grown up in its stronghold. Just seeing the shelves loaded with weenie sausages and Brown Plug chewing tobacco, salmon and mackerel and sardines all in their old places softened my heart and tears stood at the ready just behind my lids. But the kitchen, where Momma with her great height bent to pull

231

cakes from the wood-burning stove and arrange the familiar food on well-known plates, erased my control and the tears slipped out and down my face to plop onto the baby's blanket.

The hills of San Francisco, the palm trees of San Diego, prostitution and lesbians and the throat hurting of Curly's departure disappeared into a never-could-have-happened land. I was home.

"Now what you crying for?" Momma wouldn't look at me for fear my tears might occasion her own. "Give the baby to me, and you go wash your hands. I'm going to make him a sugar tit. You can set the table. Reckon you remember where everything is."

The baby went to her without a struggle and she talked to him without the cooing most people use with small children. "Man. Just a little man, ain't you? I'm going to call you Man and that's that."

Momma and Uncle Willie hadn't changed. She still spoke softly and her voice had a little song in it.

"Bless my soul, Sister, you come stepping up here looking like your daddy for the world."

Christ and Church were still the pillars of her life.

"The Lord my God is a rock in a weary land. He is a great God. Brought you home, all in one piece. Praise His name."

She was, as ever, the matriarch. "I never did want you children to go to California. Too fast that life up yonder. But then, you all's their children, and I didn't want nothing to happen to you, while you're in my care. Jew was getting a little too big for his britches."

Five years before, my brother had seen the body of a black man pulled from the river. The cause of death had not been broadcast, but Bailey (Jew was short for Junior) had seen that the man's genitals had been cut away. The shock caused him to ask questions that were dangerous for a black boy in 1940 Arkansas. Momma decided we'd both be better off in California where lynchings were unheard of and a bright young Negro boy could go places. And even his sister might find a niche for herself.

Despite the sarcastic remarks of Northerners, who don't know the region (read Easterners, Westerners, North Easterners, North Westerners, Midwesterners), the South of the United States can be so impellingly beautiful that sophisticated creature comforts diminish in importance.

For four days I waited on the curious in the Store, and let them look me over. I was that rarity, a Stamps girl who had gone to the fabled California and returned. I could be forgiven a few siditty airs. In fact, a pretension to worldliness was expected of me, and I was too happy to disappoint.

When Momma wasn't around, I stood with one hand on my hip and my head cocked to one side and spoke of the wonders of the

West and the joy of being free. Any listener could have asked me: if things were so grand in San Francisco, what had brought me back to a dusty mote of Arkansas? No one asked, because they all needed to believe that a land existed somewhere, even beyond the Northern Star, where Negroes were treated as people and whites were not the all-powerful ogres of their experience.

For the first time the farmers acknowledged my maturity. They didn't order me back and forth along the shelves but found subtler ways to make their wants known.

"You all have any long-grain rice, Sister?"

The hundred-pound sack of rice sat squidged down in full view.

"Yes, ma'am, I believe we do."

"Well then, I'll thank you for two pounds."

"Two pounds? Yes, ma'am."

I had seen the formality of black adult equals all my youth but had never considered that a time would come when I, too, could participate. The customs are as formalized as an eighteenth-century minuet, and a child at the race's knee learns the moves and twirls by osmosis and observation.

Values among Southern rural blacks are not quite the same as those existing elsewhere. Age has more worth than wealth, and religious piety more value than beauty.

There were no sly looks over my fatherless child. No cutting insinuations kept me shut away from the community. Knowing how closely my grandmother's friends hewed to the Bible, I was surprised not to be asked to confess my evil ways and repent. Instead, I was seen in the sad light which had been shared and was to be shared by black girls in every state in the country. I was young, yes, unmarried, yes—but I was a mother, and that placed me nearer to the people.

I was flattered to receive such acceptance from my betters (seniors) and strove mightily to show myself worthy.

Momma and Uncle Willie noted my inclusion into the adult stratum, and on my fourth day they put up no resistance when I said I was going for a night on the town. Since they knew Stamps, they knew that any carousing I chose to do would be severely limited. There was only one "joint" and the owner was a friend of theirs.

Age and travel had certainly broadened me and obviously made me more attractive. A few girls and boys with whom I'd had only generalities in common, all my life, asked me along for an evening at Willie Williams' café. The girls were going off soon to Arkansas Mechanical and Technical College to study Home Economics and the boys would be leaving for Tuskegee Institute in Alabama to learn how to farm. Although I had no education, my California past and having a baby made me equal to an evening with them.

When my escorts walked into the darkened Store, Momma came from the kitchen, still wearing her apron, and joined Uncle Willie behind the counter.

"Evening, Mrs. Henderson. Evening, Mr. Willie."

"Good evening, children." Momma gathered herself into immobility.

Uncle Willie leaned against the wall. "Evening, Philomena, and Harriet and Johnny Boy and Louis. How you all this evening?"

Just by placing their big still bodies in the Store at that precise time, my grandmother and uncle were saying, "Be good. Be very very good. Somebody is watching you."

We squirmed and grinned and understood.

The music reached out for us when we approached the halfway point. A dark throbbing bass line whonked on the air lanes, and our bodies moved to tempo. The steel guitar urged the singer to complain

> "Well, I ain't got no
> special reason here.
> No, I ain't got no
> special reason here.
> I'm going leave
> 'cause I don't feel welcome here..."

The Dew Drop In café was a dark square outline, and on its wooden exterior, tin posters of grinning white women divinely suggested Coca-Cola, R.C. Cola and Dr Pepper for complete happiness. Inside the one-room building, blue bulbs hung down precariously close to dancing couples, and the air moved heavily like stagnant water.

Our entrance was noted but no one came rushing over to welcome me or ask questions. That would come, I knew, but certain formalities had first to be observed. We all ordered Coca-Cola, and a pint bottle of sloe gin appeared by magic. The music entered my body and raced along my veins with the third syrupy drink. Hurray, I was having a good time. I had never had the chance to learn the delicate art of flirtation, so now I mimicked the other girls at the table. Fluttering one hand over my mouth, while laughing as hard as I could. The other hand waved somewhere up and to my left as if I and it had nothing to do with each other.

"Marguerite?"

I looked around the table and was surprised that everyone was gone. I had no idea how long I had sat there laughing and smirking behind my hand. I decided they had joined the dancing throng and looked up to search for my, by now, close but missing friends.

"Marguerite." L. C. Smith's face hung above me like the head of a bodyless brown ghost.

"L.C., how are you?" I hadn't seen him since my return, and as I waited for his answer a wave of memory crashed in my brain. He was the boy who had lived on the hill behind the school who rode his own horse and at fifteen picked as much cotton as the grown men. Despite his good looks he was never popular. He didn't talk unless forced. His mother had died when he was a baby, and his father drank moonshine even during the week. The girls said he was womanish, and the boys that he was funny that way.

I commenced to giggle and flutter and he took my hand.

"Come on. Let's dance."

I agreed and caught the edge of the table to stand. Half erect, I noticed that the building moved. It rippled and buckled as if a nest of snakes were mating beneath the floors. I was concerned, but the sloe gin had numbed my brain and I couldn't panic. I held on to the table and L.C.'s hand, and tried to straighten myself up.

"Sit down. I'll be right back." He took his hand away and I plopped back into the chair. Sometime later he was back with a glass of water.

"Come on. Get up." His voice was raspy like old corn shucks. I set my intention on getting up and pressed against the iron which had settled in my thighs.

"We're going to dance?" My words were thick and cumbersome and didn't want to leave my mouth.

"Come on." He gave me his hand and I stumbled up and against him and he guided me to the door.

Outside, the air was only a little darker and a little cooler, but it cleared one corner of my brain. We were walking in the moist dirt along the pond, and the café was again a distant outline. With soberness came a concern for my virtue. Maybe he wasn't what they said.

"What are you going to do?" I stopped and faced him, readying myself for his appeal.

"It's not me. It's you. You're going to throw up." He spoke slowly. "You're going to put your finger down your throat and tickle, then you can puke."

With his intentions clear, I regained my poise.

"But I don't want to throw up. I'm not in the least—"

He closed a hand on my shoulder and shook me a little. "I say, put your finger in your throat and get that mess out of your stomach."

I became indignant. How could he, a peasant, a nobody, presume to lecture me? I snatched my shoulder away.

"Really, I'm fine. I think I'll join my friends," I said and turned toward the café.

"Marguerite." It was no louder than his earlier tone but had more force than his hand.

"Yes?" I had been stopped.

"They're not your friends. They're laughing at you." He had misjudged. They couldn't be laughing at me. Not with my sophistication and city ways.

"Are you crazy?" I sounded like a San Francisco-born debutante.

"No. You're funny to them. You got away. And then you came back. What for? And with what to show for your travels?" His tone was as soft as the Southern night and the pond lapping. "You come back swaggering and bragging that you've just been to paradise and you're wearing the very clothes everybody here wants to get rid of."

I hadn't stopped to think that while loud-flowered skirts and embroidered white blouses caused a few eyebrows to be raised in San Diego, in Stamps they formed the bulk of most girls' wardrobes.

L.C. went on, "They're saying you must be crazy. Even people in Texarkana dress better than you do. And you've been all the way to California. They want to see you show your butt outright. So they gave you extra drinks of sloe gin."

He stopped for a second, then asked, "You don't drink, do you?"

"No." He had sobered me.

"Go on, throw up. I brought some water so you can rinse your mouth after."

He stepped away as I began to gag. The bitter strong fluid gurgled out of my throat, burning my tongue. And the thought of nausea brought on new and stronger contractions.

After the cool water we walked back past the joint, and the music, still heavy, throbbed like gongs in my head. He left the glass by the porch and steered me in the direction of the Store.

His analysis had confused me and I couldn't understand why I should be the scapegoat.

He said, "They want to be free, free from this town, and crackers, and farming, and yes-sirring and no-sirring. You never were very friendly, so if you hadn't gone anywhere, they wouldn't have liked you any more. I was born here, and will die here, and they've never liked me." He was resigned and without obvious sorrow.

"But, L.C., why don't you get away?"

"And what would my poppa do? I'm all he's got." He stopped me before I could answer, and went on, "Sometimes I bring home my salary and he drinks it up before I can buy food for the week. Your grandmother knows. She lets me have credit all the time."

We were nearing the Store and he kept talking as if I weren't there. I knew for sure that he was going to continue talking to himself after I was safely in my bed.

236

"I've thought about going to New Orleans or Dallas, but all I know is how to chop cotton, pick cotton and hoe potatoes. Even if I could save the money to take Poppa with me, where would I get work in the city? That's what happened to him, you know? After my mother died he wanted to leave the house, but where could he go? Sometimes when he's drunk two bottles of White Lightning, he talks to her. 'Reenie, I can see you standing there. How come you didn't take me with you, Reenie? I ain't got no place to go, Reenie. I want to be with you, Reenie.' And I act like I don't even hear him."

We had reached the back door of the Store. He held out his hand.

"Here, chew these Sen-sen. Sister Henderson ought not know you've been drinking. Good night, Marguerite. Take it easy."

And he melted into the darker darkness. The following year I heard that he had blown his brains out with a shotgun on the day of his father's funeral.

17

The midmorning sun was deceitfully mild and the wind had no weight on my skin. Arkansas summer mornings have a feathering effect on stone reality.

After five days in the South my quick speech had begun to drag, and the clipped California diction (clipped in comparison) had started to slur. I had to brace myself properly to "go downtown." In San Francisco, women dressed particularly to shop in the Geary and Market streets' big-windowed stores. Short white gloves were as essential a part of the shopping attire as girdles, which denied cleaved buttocks. and deodorant, which permitted odorless walkings up and down the steep hills.

I dressed San Francisco style for the nearly three-mile walk and proceeded through the black part of town, past the Christian Methodist Episcopal and African Methodist Episcopal churches and the proud little houses that sat above their rose bushes in grassless front yards, on toward the pond and the railroad tracks which separated white town from black town. My postwar Vinylite high heels, which were see-through plastic, crunched two inches into the resisting gravel, and I tugged my gloves all the way up to my wrist. I had won over the near-tropical inertia, and the sprightly walk made a bit jerky by the small grabbing stones, the neat attire and the high headed position, was bound to teach the black women watching behind lace curtains how they should approach a day's downtown shopping. It would prove to the idle white women, once I reached their territory, that I knew how things should be done. And if I knew, well, didn't that mean that there were legions of Black women in other parts of the world who knew also? Up went the Black Status.

When I glided and pulled into White Town, there was a vacuum. The air had died and fallen down heavily. I looked at the white windows expecting to see curtains lose strained positions and resume their natural places. But the curtaills on both sides of the street remained fixed. Then I realized that the white women were missing my halting but definitely elegant advance on their town. I then admitted my weariness, but urged my head higher and my shoulders squarer than before.

What Stamps' General Merchandise Store missed in class it made up in variety. Cheap grades of thread and chicken feed, farming implements and hair ribbons, fertilizer, shampoo, women's underwear, and B.V.D.s. Socks, face powder, school supplies and belly-wrenching laxatives were shoved on and under the shelves.

I pitied the poor storekeeper and the shop attendants. When I thought of the wide aisles of San Francisco's Emporium and the nearly heard, quiet conversations in the expensive City of Paris, I gave the store a patronizing smile.

A young, very blond woman's mournful countenance met me in the middle of a crowded aisle. I gave her, "Good morning," and let a benign smile lift the corners of my lips.

"What can I do for you?" The thin face nodded at me like a sharp ax descending slowly. I thought, "The poor shabby dear." She didn't even form her words. Her question floated out like a hillbilly song, "Whakin I dew fer yew?"

"I'd like a Simplicity pattern, please." I could afford to be courteous. I was the sophisticate. When I gave her the pattern number out of my head and saw her start at my Western accent, regained for the moment, I felt a rush of kindness for the sorrowful cracker girl. I added, "If you please."

She walked behind a counter and riffled through a few aging sewing patterns, her shoulders rounding over the drawer as if its contents were in danger. Although she was twenty, or more likely eighteen, her stance and face spoke of an early surrender to the poverty of poor-white Southern life. There was no promise of sex in her hip span, nor flight in her thin short fingers.

"We ain't got it here. But I can put in a order to Texarkana for it for you."

238

She never looked up and spoke of the meager town twenty five miles away as if she meant Istanbul.

"I would so much appreciate that." I did feel grateful and even more magnanimous.

"It'll be back in three days. You come in on Friday."

I wrote my name, Marguerite A. Johnson, without flourishes on the small pad she handed me, smiled encouragement to her and walked back into the now-serious noon sunshine. The heat had rendered the roads empty of pedestrians, and it assaulted my shoulders and the top of my head as if it had been lying in wait for me.

The memory of the insensate clerk prodded me into exaggerated awareness and dignity. I had to walk home at the same sprightly clip, my arms were obliged to swing in their same rhythm, and I would not under any circumstances favor the shade trees which lined the road. My head blurred with deep pains, and the rocky path swam around me, but I kept my mind keen on the propriety of my position and finally gained the Store.

Momma asked from the cool, dark kitchen, "What'd you buy, Sister?"

I swallowed the heat-induced nausea and answered, "Nothing, Momma."

The days eased themselves around our lives like visitors in a sickroom. I hardly noticed their coming and going. Momma was as engrossed as she'd allow herself in the wonder of my son. Patting, stroking, she talked to him and never introduced in her deep voice the false humor adults tend to offer babies. He, in turn, surrendered to her. Following her from kitchen to porch to store to the backyard.

Their togetherness came to be expected. The tall and large dark-brown woman (whose movement never seemed to start or stop) was trailed one step by the pudgy little butter-yellow baby lurching, falling, now getting himself up, at moments rocking on bowed legs, then off again in the wave of Momma. I never saw her turn or stop to right him, but she would slow her march and resume when he was steady again.

My pattern had arrived from old exotic Texarkana. And I dressed for the trek downtown, and checked my hair, which was straightened to within an inch of its life and greased to desperation. From within the Store, I felt the threat of the sun but walked out into the road impelled by missionary zeal.

By the time I reached the pond and Mr. Willie Williams' Dew Drop In, the plastic seemed to have melted to the exact shape of my feet, and sweat had popped through the quarter inch of Arrid in my armpits.

Mr. Williams served me a cold drink. "What you trying to do? Fry your brains?"

"I'm on my way to the General Merchandise Store. To pick up an order."

His smile was a two-line checkerboard of white and gold. "Be careful they don't pick you up. This sun ain't playing."

Arrogance and stupidity nudged me out of the little café and back on the white hot clay. I drifted under the shade trees, my face a mask of indifference. The skin of my thighs scudded like wet rubber as I walked deliberately by the alien white houses and on to my destination.

In the store the air lay heavily on the blades of two sluggish overhead fans, and a sweet, thick odor enveloped me at the cosmetic counter. Still, I was prepared to wander the aisles until the sun forgave our sins and withdrew its vengeance.

A tall saleswoman wearing a clerk's smock confronted me. I tried to make room for her in the narrow corridor. I moved to my left, she moved to her right. I right, she left, we jockeyed a moment's embarrassment and I smiled. Her long face answered with a smile. "You stand still and I'll pass you." It was not a request for cooperation. The hard mountain voice gave me an order.

To whom did she think she was speaking? Couldn't she see from my still-white though dusty gloves, my starched clothes, that I wasn't a servant to be ordered around? I had walked nearly three miles under a sun on fire and was neither gasping nor panting, but standing with the cool decorum of a great lady in the tacky, putrid store. She should have considered that.

"No, you stand still and I'll pass around you," I commanded.

The amazement which leaped upon her face was quickly pushed aside by anger. "What's your name? Where you from?"

A repetition of "You stand still and I'll pass around you" was ready on my tongue, when the pale woman who had taken my order slack-butted down the aisle toward us. The familiar face brought back the sympathy I had felt for her and I explained the tall woman into limbo with "Excuse me, here comes my salesgirl."

The dark-haired woman turned quickly and saw her colleague approach. She put herself between us, and her voice rasped out in the quiet store: "Who is this?"

Her head jerked back to indicate me. "Is this that sassy Ruby Lee you was telling me about?"

The clerk lifted her chin and glanced at me, then swirled to the older woman. "Naw, this ain't her." She flipped the pages of a pad in her hand and continued, "This one's Margaret or Marjorie or something like that."

240

Her head eased up again and she looked across centuries at me. "How do you pronounce your name, gal? Speak up."

In that moment I became rootless, nameless, pastless. The two white blurs buoyed before me.

"Speak up," she said. "What's your name?"

I clenched my reason and forced their faces into focus. "My name"—here I drew myself up through the unrevenged slavery—"is Miss Johnson. If you have occasion to use my name, which I seriously doubt, I advise you to address me as Miss Johnson. For if I need to allude to your pitiful selves, I shall call you Miss Idiot, Miss Stupid, Miss Fool or whatever name a luckless fate has dumped upon you."

The women became remote even as I watched them. They seemed actually to float away from me down the aisle; and from watching their distant faces, I knew they were having trouble believing in the fact of me.

"And where I'm from is no concern of yours, but rather where you're going. I'll slap you into the middle of next week if you even dare to open your mouths again. Now, take that filthy pattern and stick it you-know-where."

As I strode between the two women I was sheathed in satisfaction. There had been so few critical times when my actions met my approval that now I congratulated myself. I had got them told and told correctly. I pictured the two women's mouths still open in amazement. The road was less rocky and the sun's strength was weakened by my pleasure. Congratulations were in order.

There was no need to stop at Mr. Williams' for a refreshing drink. I was as cool as a fountain inside as I headed home.

Momma stood on the porch facing the road. Her arms hung at her sides and she made no motions with her head. Yet something was wrong. Tension had distorted the statue straightness and caused her to lean leftward. I stopped patting myself on the back and ran to the Store.

When I reached the one-step porch, I looked up in her face. "Momma, what's the matter?"

Worry had forced a deep line down either side of her nostrils past her stiffly held lips.

"What's wrong?"

"Mr. Coleman's granddaughter, Miss June, just called from the General Merchandise Store." Her voice quaked a little. "She said you was downtown showing out."

So that's how they described my triumph to her. I decided to explain and let her share in the glory. I began, "It was the principle of the thing, Momma—"

I didn't even see the hand rising, and suddenly it had swung down hard against my cheek.

"Here's your principle, young miss."

I felt the sting on my skin and the deep ache in my head. The greatest hurt was that she didn't ask to hear my side.

"Momma, it was a principle." My left ear was clogged, but I heard my own voice fuzzily.

The hand didn't surprise me the second time, but the same logic which told me I was right at the white store told me I was no less right in front of Momma. I couldn't allow myself to duck the blow. The backhand swing came down on my right cheek.

"Here's your principle." Her voice had a far-away-tunnel sound.

"It was a principle, Momma." Tears poured down my burning face, and ache backed up in my throat.

The hand came again and again each time I mumbled "principle," and I found myself in the soft dust in front of the porch. I didn't want to move. I never wanted to get up again.

She stepped off the porch and caught my arms. "Get up. Stand up, I say."

Her voice never allowed disobedience. I stood, and looked at her face. It glistened as if she had just dashed a pan of water over her head.

"You think 'cause you've been to California these crazy people won't kill you? You think them lunatic cracker boys won't try to catch you in the road and violate you? You think because of your all-fired principle some of the men won't feel like putting their white sheets on and riding over here to stir up trouble? You do, you're wrong. Ain't nothing to protect you and us except the good Lord and some miles. I packed you and the baby's things, and Brother Wilson is coming to drive you to Louisville."

That afternoon I climbed into a horse-drawn wagon, and took my baby from Momma's arms. The baby cried as we pulled away, and Momma and Uncle Willie stood waving and crying good-bye.

18

Momma's intent to protect me had caused her to hit me in the face, a thing she had never done, and to send me away to where she thought I'd be safe. So again, the South and I had parted and again I was

242

headed for the cool gray hills of San Francisco. I raged on the train that white stupidity could so dictate my movements and looked unsheathed daggers at every white face I saw.

If the tables could have turned at that instant, I would gladly have consigned every white person living and the millions dead to a hell where the devil was blacker than their fears of blackness and more cruel than forced starvation. But, powerless, I spent the time on the train entertaining the baby when I thought of it, and wondering if I would be met by a warrant for my arrest when I returned to California.

The city didn't even know I had been away, and Mother took me and the baby to a room in her new fourteen-room house as if I had just returned from a long-intended holiday.

I found a job as a short-order cook in a tiny greasy spoon. The men who ate there were defeated leftovers from the now-closed war plants. They slouched into the fifth-rate dingy diner hugging their distress.

The job paid very little and the atmosphere of despair that never lifted depressed me. I left the restaurant each afternoon feeling that the rancid cooking oil and the old men's sadness had seeped into my pores and were crawling through my body.

One afternoon I went into a record shop across the street from the diner and found a woman who was friendly and warm behind the counter. She was white and thirtyish, and didn't condescend to either my color or my youth. When I told her that I liked blues, she pulled out some old Columbia Blue Labels. I said that I also liked jazz, and she suggested recent Charlie "Bird" Parker releases. I let the music wash away the odors and moods of the restaurant, and I left the shop with more records than I could afford. I had agreed with her that I should start collecting the Dial records featuring Bird, Max Roach, Al Haig, Bud Powell, Dizzy Gillespie and others who she said were going to be the "masters." Each payday I kept out enough money to pay my own way at Mother's, and spent the rest on records and books.

Mother was unhappy that my job made me unhappy. She always knew her "daughter had great potential" and was determined that if she had anything to do with it, I was going to realize it.

Weeks later she and I sat in the dining room and picked and poked through the classifieds for my future.

I was nearly nineteen, had a baby, responsibilities and no real profession. I could cook Creole and was a fast, friendly cocktail waitress. Also I was qualified as an absentee madam, but I somehow felt that I simply had not yet "found out my niche" (I had just discovered that phrase and yo-yo'ed it around with frequent and gay abandon).

243

"Private secretary. If you could type fast enough and do shorthand." Mother was serious. Her pretty face was lined with concentration. "Telephone operator, pays pretty good."

I reminded her that we'd already been through that.

"Key punch. Stenographer. You need training, baby."

She looked at me spot on and added, "Anything worth doing is worth doing well."

I didn't dare remind her that everything I had done had been well done.

"What is Alice doing? What about Jean Mae, and the twins? What are they all doing? Going to college?" Her voice and round black eyes worried me for answers.

Jean Mae, the neighborhood's sepia Betty Grable, had a job hopping cars at a popular drive-in. I hardly had the face, figure or sexuality to be taken in at that restaurant. Alice could be seen nightly whistling down Post Street and up Sutter, her young walk exaggerated, her thin voice insinuating the lone sailor into following three paces behind her to the nearest transient hotel.

The twins married twins, which seemed as appalling to me as streetwalking. I felt there was a closet incest about the whole thing.

The small percentage of classmates who went on to college had become unbearably stuck-up and boring. So I found no inspiration among my peers.

"Companion, Chauffeurette." That I could do. I immediately set a film to flickering on my mind screen. In a snappy uniform, no cap, gray serge and British walker shoes, I drove a man around who was the spitting image of Lionel Barrymore. He always addressed me as "Johnson" and while we liked and respected each other, we took pains never to show it. Late nights, he would call me into the drawing room and I would stand at attention, easily.

"Johnson. Tomorrow's a beaut."

"Yes, sir?"

"We go up to the city, then back to the country club, then the city, then the farm. A little hard on you, I fear."

"It's my job, sir."

"I could count on you to say that, Johnson."

"Yes, sir."

"Good night."

"Good night, sir."

Mother's gaze followed her ringed fingers up and down the page.

"You'd have to live in and it doesn't really pay enough for you to afford a full-time baby-sitter." She flipped the paper closed.

"Take anything that looks like something. You can always quit. Or there's a chance that you won't rise to the challenge and you'll be

244

fired. But the only thing to remember is that 'you were looking for a job when you found that one.' So whoever fires you ain't getting no cherry." She got up and went into the kitchen.

"How about a Dubonnet"—ice already clucked against the sides of glasses—"with a twist of lemon? I'm going to fix myself a Scotch."

When I was around ten in Arkansas, I saw a glamorous actress play a jaunty chauffeurette in a movie. She maneuvered an Oldsmobile with one hand and was as chic as a model. I looked at the paper again and thought about the chauffeuring job. A wisp of nostalgia floated in my heart. The uniform, the easy camaraderie with the staff, the asexuality with my boss, and peace. Just like the Army. Routine, honorable work, hail-fellows well met, good-hearted companions and fair-minded officers. The Army! Just the thing. The idea snap-saluted in my brain. The Army!

I bounded into the kitchen and nearly collided with Mother and her tray of gold and purple drinks. I had developed some grace, quite a lot when I kept my mind on being graceful, but in unguarded moments my body tended to respond giraffe-like to stimuli.

"Mother!" She had righted the threatened glasses and pushed past me for the dining room. "I'm going in the Army!"

She set down the Dubonnet. "You as a sergeant and the baby as a private?"

Her tongue was sharper than the creases in zoot pants and I knew better than to try to best her. I said nothing.

"What would be the value of becoming a WAC?" she asked.

"The Army has all those side benefits and I could learn a trade. There's the G.I. Bill, and when you get out you can go back to school and buy a home at the same time."

"Side benefits" had caused a glint in Mother's eyes.

"Now"—she pushed the wine toward me—"now you have to consider if you're serious. Because if you are, it would be like volunteering for jail. People tell you when to sleep, eat, wake up, work. Personally, I couldn't do it in a million years." Her face frowned revulsion. "But in a way the country would be helping you get a start in life."

Behind her smooth beige forehead, deep thoughts were being turned over, examined and replaced or discarded.

"If you are serious and get in, we'll talk to Mrs. Peabody about taking care of the baby. You could sign up for a two-year tour, save your money, and study languages and advanced typing."

She was talking my future into shape.

"Try out for Officer Candidate School or Officers' Training Corps. Nothing they could say to you but yes or no. And when you go down there, remember they need you as much as you need them." She saw my disbelief and explained. "The U.S. Army needs nice colored girls, well raised from good families. That's what I meant." She reached for her lipstick tube (never far away). "Government is going to give you an education and a start in life and you're going to give class to that uniform."

"Mother, they would examine me, physically, and find out about the baby."

"You don't have stretch marks and because you breast-fed, your breasts never got out of shape." Her words nudged past indifference. "That's not what you ought to be thinking of. No. Decide if you want the Army for two years. Away from your baby and family. Taking orders, and keeping your temper under wraps. That's a decision no one can make for you nor help you make."

She got up from the table and visited one of her flashiest smiles on me.

"I have a date now. We can talk more when you're ready. Remember if you decide for the Army, I'll support you. If you decide to be a whore, all I can say is, be the best. Don't be a funky chippie. Go with class."

She pasted a waxy kiss on my forehead and draped her Kolinsky over her shoulders.

"How do I look?"

"Beautiful."

She tugged the furs into a more casual drape and laughed. "You only say it 'cause it's true."

Her high heels tapped toward the door in drumming rhythm.

19

The U.S. Recruitment Center hadn't tried hard. The offices were at the foot of San Francisco's Market Street, near the glamorous Ferry Building, but none of the latter's exotica strayed to the prefab whitewash walls of the Center.

A uniformed woman offered me a Dagwood sandwich of brochures and applications and I sat down to read.

Indeed, it sounded like what I needed. Food, shelter, training and comradeship. Two years and I could buy a house for myself and my son. Might find a man, too. After all, there was a conglomeration of men in the Army. All I had to do now was maneuver between outrageous lies and delicate untruths to pass the various tests. (I wasn't concerned about the I.Q., but about the Rorschach.) Had I just wanted to join the regular Women's Army it would have taxed my creative lying skills, but I had gone one further. Mother had said, "Start at the top," so I decided to try out for Officer Candidate School. I thought daily trips to the Center would help my case.

The war's end had left the skeletal WAC staff with little to do except file papers in triplicate and dress up in privilege. For nearly a month I provided diversion. Naturally, the clerks couldn't enjoy my artful dodging as much as I, because they weren't privy to my secrets.

I sidled over the questionnaires and applications, double-checking, doubly-lying. Married... check one. No. Children... check one. No.

My cavorting brain was of no use to me at the medical examination, though. There the doctors opened my mouth wide (I needed dental work; the Army would pay), thudded and tapped and listened to my strong lungs and courageous heart. All was well.

The gynecologist's table was my Armageddon. There on the cold table, gray steel instruments would probe between my legs and into the unknown territory where my deepest guilts had lodged. I had no more idea of the construction of a woman's regenerative organs than I had of the structure of the moon. Surely, I thought, there would be some scars visible from my son's birth. Some leftover tube hanging down which would signal to the knowledgeable that I was a mother and therefore unfit to serve my country (which by this time I had come to love with a maudlin sentimentality).

"We'll take a few slides." The nurse's face was stony, and the doctor ignored my face, acting as if I was nothing but a thin chest, flat belly and long black legs.

I asked why.

"These are venereal-disease tests." She spoke as if she were weather-watching. I'd gladly have settled for syphilis and gonorrhea. If the Army could take care of my teeth, a couple of injections would cure the diseases.

"The tests will be back in a few days."

I tried to scrape from their faces any information they had gathered. But those faces were trained in suppression. I wanted to shout at their closed ears, "I'll wait. I'll sit in the outer office and wait for the results. "But I too had some training—that is, "Never let white folks know what you really think. If you're sad, laugh. If you're bleeding inside, dance."

"I'll be away for a few days," I lied, "but I'll phone as soon as I return." I tried to make it sound as if I would be doing them a favor.

Three or four days jittered by with no pretense at flowing, and then the phone call came.

"Miss Johnson?" I recognized the voice with echoes of starched uniforms and drill squadrons.

"Yes, I'm Miss Johnson." I tried to put "I'm Miss Johnson, so what?" into my own response and failed.

"Sergeant Matthews at the Induction Center."

I know. I know. Go on, dammit.

"I'm calling to tell you you've passed all your tests and have been included in the March–April quota of personnel to enter Officer Candidate School. Is that all right with you?"

I suddenly had dirigible-sized air pockets in my cheeks which prevented me from making any sound except a loud explosion. I nodded into the telephone.

"Will you be prepared to leave the San Francisco area at the beginning of May for Fort Lee, Virginia?"

The air plopped out of my mouth and I jerked the phone away. God knows I didn't want to frighten the sergeant and give her a reason to re-examine my dossier of lies. I turned the sound into a fake cough and brought the mouthpiece back.

"Excuse me. A little spring cough. Oh yes, I can certainly be ready for May first." I was in a little more control, so I added, "I'm most happy to have this opportunity to serve my country and I shall—"

She interrupted, "Yes, well, come down in the next few days and sign the loyalty oath. Good-bye." And hung up.

Now I was ready. Things had arranged themselves in my favor at last. For the next two years I would have the security of purpose and the dignity of being a soldier in good standing in the Army of the United States of America.

Natural restraint and the conceit of sophistication kept me from rushing down immediately to sign the loyalty oath. I was able to keep myself away for two days before I surrendered.

I stood in front of the flag, one hand on the Bible, the other clasped to my breast, and swore I would defend this land from her enemies, etc., etc. The deep motives, the noble intent so moved me that with the least encouragement I would have dissolved in a flood of patriotic tears.

Mother was happy but not surprised at my success story. When I told Bailey that I would soon be going into the Army, he turned a cold stare on me and asked without relishing curiosity, "What the shit for? Men are trying like hell to get out and my sister is dying to get in. You dumb bunny." The air between Bailey and me had coarsened with our growing up and thickened with his cynicism. He could no longer see me clearly and I could not distinguish his black male disappointment in life.

It could not be said that Bailey was living at home, but more accurately that he was based there. He worked as a waiter on the Southern Pacific trains running from San Francisco to Chicago or Los Angeles or Houston.

Few black families are without ties to the U.S. railroads. The early-twentieth-century Negro aristocrats were the families of ministers, morticians, teachers and railroad men. Passes to ride the trains were traded in Southern black areas as easily as legitimate money. And many poor black families ate their beans and greens from good china and used heavy silver from the Union Pacific, Southern Pacific and New York Central.

Bailey was still the plum pretty black color and his teeth shone white like promises. His hair was glossy and his small hands delicate and graceful. But all the gentle reminders of his love for me through our childhood stopped at his eyes. It seemed some confrontation, which he had kept secret, dulled their shine and left them flat and unseeing.

His fast speech, which used to stumble into a stutter with excitement, had slowed, and a songless monotone rasped out his meanings. When he was home from a trip, he never sat around with Mother and me, playing pinochle or coon can, as we used to do, but hurriedly put down his gear and left the house for some mysterious destination. He successfully blocked my prying by saying, "Take care of yourself and your baby and your own business and that'll take all your time."

When I tried to involve Mother in discussion of his whereabouts and how abouts, she said nearly the same thing but generally added, "He's a man. He's got a job and his health and strength. Some people have to make it through life with less." And that was that.

Papa Ford, who had been brought to the new house, sat bowed over his coffee in the warm kitchen.

I asked him, "Papa, what's Bailey doing? Why is he changing so?"

He lifted his head and relished a toothless mouth. Smack. Smack.

"Uh. Uh, girl. Uh, uh." He lowered his head, loving the doom he hinted.

"Papa, what does that mean? Say something."

The passage of years had ground away his emotional-transition apparatus. He would often shift in a moment from a dozing indifference to a fighting fury. He did so then.

"Don't ask so many goddam questions. Keep your goddam big eyes open. You're no shitty-ass baby." A slurp from his mug and he was nearly asleep again.

249

20

I had to make arrangements for my personal belongings. I told mother that when I got out of the Army I would dress in suits, and my cashmere-sweater sets would match kick-pleated Scotch-plaid skirts. I wouldn't be needing the old clothes. Mother had decided they were good enough to be given to charity. I remembered the large St. Vincent de Paul's trucks, backing down our driveway once a year during my teens, collecting Mother's unwanted items. After a brief but pointed sermon when Mother spoke of "those less fortunate than you," I chose the Salvation Army as my beneficiary. Those fresh clean faces in their absurd regalia playing their uninspired music, unheeded, had always depressed me. They had to be the most deserving.

The records would stay in the house. Mother enjoyed Lester Young, Billie Holiday, Louis Jordan, Buddy Johnson and Arthur "Big Boy" Crudup as much as I. She'd play them at her parties and think of me.

I found it hard to think of leaving my books. They had been my elevators out of the midden, and to whom could I entrust such close friends?

The benevolent act of giving away my clothes, however, spilled over into that decision making. Hospitals were the answer. I was certain that lean and lonely tubercular patients would have their spirits lifted reading the *Topper* stories of Thorne Smith, and I had proved it possible to read Robert Benchley's essays and short stories over a hundred times and still laugh. Ann Petry's *The Street*, all Thomas Wolfe, Richard Wright and Hemingway would be given to an old-folks home. But the Russian writers would be packed away in mothballs and stored in our basement. I would savor the idea of Dostoevsky's Tolstoy's and Gorki's volumes molding in the dank cellar, wisps of camphor and odors of wet earth floating above them.

I quit my job to spend more time with Guy, to record his cherubic smile and be amazed at the beauty of his coordination. He seldom cried and seemed a budding introvert, for although he never thrust himself from company, he appeared to be equally amused alone. A baby's love for his mother is probably the sweetest emotion we can

250

savor. When my son heard my voice at the downstairs door he'd begin to sing, and when I arrived in his view he'd fall back on his fat legs, his behind would thud to the floor and he'd laugh, his big head rocking up and down.

I knew it would be hard to leave him. Hard on me, but harder on him, for he had no way of understanding that I was gone to prepare a place for us. I hugged his sweetness to me and squeezed my love into his pores. If we were to have a decent life, a small but neat house, good neighborhood and schools, bulky knit sweaters and the expensive tennis shoes I saw large boys wearing, I'd have to get some kind of training and I needed help. Uncle Sam was going to be more a friend to me than any of my bad blood uncles.

With my clothes gone to the Salvation Army and my books packed in wooden boxes downstairs, I spent my remaining time gazing at the training manual and familiarizing myself with creases and salutes and drill formations, how a bunk should be made and how officers were to be addressed.

A week before I was to be inducted, a military voice over the telephone ordered me down to the Recruitment Center.

"I can come this morning or this afternoon."

"This morning! And that's an order, soldier."

"It sounds urgent." Maybe our departure date had been moved up.

"It's more urgent than that. It's about some discrepancy on your documents. We'll see you this morning." Click.

Dammit, dammit and double damn. Probably some ruthless, relentless doctor had re-examined my charts and found that I'd had a baby. And I had sworn that everything I had written was God's own truth. There were laws to punish criminals who lied ("perjury" it was called) on oath. And it must have been worse to lie on oath *and* the flag.

Mother had taken Guy out for the morning, to leave me alone with my army books. I had no one to accompany me. I dressed as I wondered. I shook as I planned. It was pretty certain I wasn't going into the Army, but I might go to jail if the Army wanted to press charges. I should have known better than to lie to the government. People always said Uncle Sam would spend a thousand dollars to get you if you stole a three-cent stamp from him. He was more revengeful than God.

I couldn't run, I couldn't hide. I went to the government building.

On the bus I soft-conned myself. I had done so well on the examinations that if I came clean and explained that I had made solid arrangements for my son's care for two years, they might make an exception. It could be simple, if only I got a kind interviewer and could stop shaking.

"Marguerite Johnson?"

The woman's long thin neck rose out of wide sloping shoulders and her voice skidded like a fire alarm. I would have liked her face softer.

"Yes." Er... "Yes, ma'am." She was an officer. Oh hell, I mean... "Yes, sir."

"Did you or did you not sign the loyalty oath?"

"I did." Did I? I had gone down a few weeks before and sworn to uphold the flag, defend the country and protect my fellow Americans with my life, if need be. I had been so moved by my sincerity that I added to myself, "My country may she always be right but right or wrong, my country." Off we go into the wild blue yonder and the caissons go rolling along.

"Were you or were you not asked if you had ever been a member of the Communist party?"

"I was asked, and I said no." Well, if that was all it was! I felt the blood pushing to open up its old passages and start to flow again.

"You lied, Johnson." The voice sirened up to a screech. "Lied, sir? No, sir. I've never—"

"This is your signature, Johnson?" She produced the loyalty oath by slight of hand. I didn't need to peer to see the large curving Marguerite Johnson.

"Yes, sir. That is my signature."

She flipped the paper over and grinned her pleasure. "The California Labor School is on the House Un-American Activities list, Johnson. Do you know why?"

"No, sir. I only studied dance and drama there."

"Oh, come now. Don't be stupid. It's a Communist organization and you know it."

"Maybe so, but I have never been a member."

"You went to the school for two years." She had regained her composure, her stiffness.

"But that was when I was fourteen and fifteen. I had just come from the South, and a playground teacher got me a scholarship. It was because I had trouble talking—"

"Communists are ungodly, Johnson. And this man's army fights under God."

I felt as if I were drowning in straw. The light was still visible but no amount of struggling brought me nearer to it.

"Because you were young and, I hope, you're still innocent, the Army is not going to bring charges of falsification against you. But we definitely cannot risk you as a soldier in our army, Johnson. Dismissed."

I was suspended, physically and mentally, for a second. "Dismissed."

I know I'd have made a good soldier because without the benefit of habit or training, my body turned sharply and walked out into the sunshine.

Mother and the baby were still out when I returned to the big house. Papa Ford was away on his noonday constitutional. The rooms were all dark and cool. I sat at the ornate dining-room table and tried to sort things out.

My clothes were gone, I had no job and I had been rejected by the Army. That damn institution, which accepts everybody (to tell from its soldiers), had turned me down. My life had no center, no purpose. I had to admit, though, that I had lied. Not on the issue they charged against me (hell, I wouldn't have recognized Stalin if he'd been in my class when I was fourteen. Literally, all white folks still looked alike to me: pale and similar), but I had lied about Guy's birth. I wondered if justice was served. If maybe I should just shut up and take my punishment. I needed Bailey. I longed for the old days when I could speak to him and work out my problems.

I got up from the table and opened the door to his room. It had a strange emptiness. Not as if the occupant had just stepped out and was expected back, but as if it had never been occupied and expected nothing. There was a deadness in the air. I turned on the overhead light, went to the windows and pulled up the shades. The gray spring light dared only to enter a yard or so. I decided to change his linen, clean up and put fresh flowers in his room. Meanwhile I would think over my problem.

I stripped the blankets and folded them, then I tugged at the linen. For a moment I was so amazed I forgot my whereabouts. This couldn't be Bailey's bed. He was the model of cleanliness, neatness, decorum. Every member of my family had said at one time or other, "Maya should have been a boy and Bailey a girl. She's so sloppy and he's so neat"—and more to that effect.

The sheets were gray and black with dirt. An odor of perfumed hair oil and musk lifted heavily. I tugged at the edges and let the sheets slide to the floor. The pillows rode along on the end of the sheet. As they tumbled, a small round bundle wrapped in brown paper bounced down at my feet.

I opened it without needing to. Thin brown cigarettes were held together with three rubber bands.

Even in his absence, Bailey had helped me. I lighted one of the cigarettes and in minutes was snickering over the stupidity of the Establishment. The U.S. Army with its corps of spies had been fooled by a half-educated black girl. I sat down on Bailey's bed and laughed until I had to fight for my breath.

253

21

I took a job as swing-shift waitress in a day-and-night restaurant called the Chicken Shack. The record player blared the latest hits incessantly and the late-night clientele spent their overflow energy loudly in the brightly lighted booths.

Smoking grass eased the strain for me. I made a connection at a restaurant nearby. People called it Mary Jane, hash, grass, gauge, weed, pot, and I had absolutely no fear of using it. In the black ghetto of the forties, marijuana, cocaine, hop (opium) and heroin were only a little harder to obtain than rationed whiskey. Although my mother didn't use anything but Scotch (Black & White), she often sang a song popular in the thirties that at its worst didn't condemn grass, and at its best extolled its virtues.

> Dream about a reefer five foot long
> Vitamin but not too strong
> You'll be high but not for long
> If you're a viper.
>
> I'm the queen of everything
> I got to get high before I can swing
> Light some tea and let it be
> If you're a viper.
>
> Now when your throat gets dry
> you know you're high
> Everything is dandy
> You truck on down to the candy store
> And bust your conk on peppermint candy
>
> Then you know your brown body scent
> You don't give a damn if you don't pay your rent
> Light some tea and let it be
> If you're a viper.

I learned new postures and developed new dreams. From a natural stiffness I melted into a grinning tolerance. Walking on the streets became high adventure, eating my mother's huge dinners an opulent entertainment, and playing with my son was side-cracking hilarity. For the first time, life amused me.

Positive dreaming was introduced on long, slow drags of the narcotic. I was going to do all right in the world, going to have it made—and no doubt through the good offices of a handsome man who would love me to distraction.

My charming prince was going to appear out of the blue and offer me a cornucopia of goodies. I would only have to smile to have them brought to my feet.

R. L. Poole was to prove my dreams at least partially prophetic. When I opened the door to his ring and informed him that I was Rita Johnson, his already long face depressed another inch.

"The... uh... dancer?" His voice was slow and cloudy.

Dancer? Of course. I had been a cook, waitress, madam, bus girl— why not a dancer? After all, it was the only thing I had studied.

"Yes, I'm a dancer." I looked at him boldly. "Why?"

"I'm looking for a dancer, to work with me."

I thought he might be a talent scout for a chorus line or maybe the big stage show, featuring colored dancers, called "Change Your Luck."

"Come in."

We sat at the dining-room table and I offered a coffee. He looked me over, one feature at a time. My legs (long), my hips (spare), my breasts (nearly nonexistent). He drank the coffee slowly.

"I've studied since I was fourteen," I said.

If the U.S. Army was going to penalize me for having gone to the California Labor School, it was just possible that someone else would find the time spent there valuable. I was right. His eyes moved from an examination of my body back to my face.

"I'm Poole. From Chicago." His announcement held no boast, and I was sure that represented sophistication rather than false modesty. "I do rhythm tap and I want a girl partner. She doesn't have to do much but flash. Are you agva?" ("Flash" and "A.G.V.A." were words unknown to me.)

I sat quietly and looked at him. Let him figure it out for himself.

"I met the woman at the record shop and she told me about you. Said all you talked about was dancing. She gave me your address."

"Some cats from the Local, musicians, straightened me out with the contacts for a few gigs. Scale is twenty-two fifty, but I'll do a few under scale to get some ends together."

I hadn't the slightest notion of what he was talking about. Scale. Agva. Gigs. Local. Ends.

"More coffee?" I went into the kitchen, walking like a model, chin down and sternum up, and my tail bone tucked under like white women.

I put on a fresh pot of coffee and tried desperately to decide on a role for myself. Should I be mysterious and sultry, asking nothing, answering all questions with a knowing smirk, or should I be the open, friendly, palsy every-boy's-sister girl-next-door type? No decision came to my mind, so I went back into the dining room, my legs stuck together with fine decorum.

"What did you study?"

"Ballet. Modern Ballet and the Theory of Dance." I made it sound like Advanced Thermonuclear Propulsion.

His face fell again.

"Any tap-dancing?"

"No."

"Jazz?"

"No."

"Acrobatics?"

"No." I was losing him, so I jumped in the gap. "I used to win every jitterbug contest. I can do the Texas Hop. The Off Time. The boogie-woogie. The Camel Walk. The new Coup de Grâce. And I can do the split."

With that I stood up, straddle-legged, and looked down into his sad face, then I began to slide down to the floor.

I was unprepared for the movement (I had on a straight skirt), but R.L. was less ready than I. As my legs slipped apart and down, I lifted my arms in the graceful ballet position number 1 and watched the impresario's face race from mild interest to incredulous. My hem caught mid-thigh and I felt my equilibrium teeter. With a quick sleight of hand I jerked up my skirt and continued my downward glide. I hummed a little snatch of song during the last part of the slither, and kept my mind on Sonja Henie in her cute little tutus.

Unfortunately, I hadn't practiced the split in months, so my pelvic bones resisted with force. I was only two inches from the floor, and I gave a couple of little bounces. I accomplished more than I planned. My skirt seams gave before my bones surrendered. Then my left foot got caught between the legs of Mother's heavy oak table, and the other foot jumped at the gas heater and captured the pipe that ran from the jets into the wall. Pinned down at my extremities with the tendons in my legs screaming for ease, I felt as if I were being crucified to the floor, but in true "show must go on" fashion I kept my back straight and my arms uplifted in a position that would have made Pavlova proud. Then I looked at R.L. to see what impression I was making. Pity at my predicament was drawing him up from his chair, and solicitude was written over his face with a brush wider than a kitchen mop.

My independence and privacy would not allow me to accept help. I lowered my arms and balanced my hands on the floor and jerked my right foot. It held on to the pipe, so I jerked again. I must have been in excellent shape. The pipe came away from the stove, and gas hissed out steadily like ten fat men resting on a summer's day.

R.L. stepped over me and looked down into the gas jet. "Goddam." He swiveled over to the window and opened it as wide as it would go, then back down to the stove. Near the wall at the end of the pipe, he found a tap and turned it. The hissing died and the thick sweetish odor diluted.

I had still to extricate my other leg from the avaricious table.

R.L. lifted an edge of the table, and my ankle was miraculously free. I could have gotten up, but my feelings were so hurt by the stupid clumsiness that I just rolled over on my stomach, beat my hands on the floor and cried like a baby.

There was no doubt that R.L. Poole had just witnessed his strangest audition. He could have walked down the hall and out the door, leaving me breathing in the dust of the ancient rug, but he didn't. I heard the chair creak, announcing that he had sat back down.

I was sure he was doing his best to hold in his laughter. I tried for more tears, to irritate him and force him to leave, but the tear ducts had closed and the sound I made was as false as a show girl's eyelashes. Nothing for it but to get up.

I dried my face with dusty hands and lifted my head. R.L. was sitting at the table in the same chair, his head propped up with his hand. The dark-brown face was somber and he said quietly, "Well, anyway, you've got nice legs."

When we went to a nearby rehearsal hall I was amazed to see R.L. Poole move. The wind seemed to make him dance. I pictured his lean bony legs as being attached directly to his sharp shoulders with skeletal pins. For he would hunch his shoulders and glide across the rehearsal-hall floor, his heels and toes tapping below him in a fusillade of small explosions, his arms dangling at his side, his face a pockmarked oval.

He tried to simplify the intricate tap rhythms by singing them to me in a rough, low voice. "Boom, boom, boo rah, boo rah, boo rah,

257

boo rah, brah, brah." Sharp slaps on the floor, dust rising from the old wood.

With the polish of a professional, R.L. made it all appear easy. I telescoped my energy on the gliding steps of the flash, with no less purpose than a ballet student mastering a tour jeté. I would raise my arms shoulder-high, then open them out slowly, take two sliding steps, bend one knee and hold the position. An accomplished flash partner frames and highlights the principal dancer when he is tapping out complex rhythms. To be able to let my body swing free over the floor and the crushing failures in my past was freedom. I thanked R.L. for my liberation and fell promptly in love with him.

22

I committed myself to a show-business career, and dancing and studying dance swallowed me. Charlie Parker's "Cool Breeze" was my practice piece. Flash, slide through the opening riff, then stash during Bird's solo; keeping soft-shoe time by dusting the boards with the soles of my feet, then break during Bud Powell's piano wizardry. Break, cross step. Chicago. Fall. Fall. Break, crossover. Apple. Break. Time step. Slap crossover. Then break and Fall off the Log, going out on the closing riff.

I practiced until my ankles ached, without complaint, and was more than rewarded when R.L. told me one day, "After we break in our act out here, I think we'll go East. Big Time. Join Duke's or Basie's road show."

My concern was not how I'd manage with my son on the Big-time Circuit, but how I could perfect my flash so that R.L. wouldn't go looking for a prettier partner. I used my time at the Chicken Shack to strengthen my ankles. When I was behind the counter I stood on tiptoe, letting one heel down, then raising it, and pressing the other to the floor.

When R.L. decided we were ready to try out our act, I sprang my homemade costume on him. I had gone to a theatrical store and bought a wig, coke feathers, a padded bra and a G-string. I sewed the shiny black feathers on the scanty outfit, then added a few sequins

258

and a little sparkle for show. My costume could be held in one balled fist, and the G-string barely covered my pubic hair and the cleavage of my buttocks.

"Er... no." He lowered his head and searched painfully for the words he wanted. "Uh... Rita... no. That won't... uh... get it... That's... wh... a shake dancer's rig... I mean, I'll show you... Something like a bathing suit... with spangles..."

I stood before him, my oiled skin gleaming, the fluffy wig trembling with ringlets on my head, withering with disappointment. My costume was a faithful copy of L'Tanya's, the popular interpretive dancer who was a current favorite at the Champagne Supper Club.

"You'l look... I mean, tap shoes are gonna look... I mean, they don't go together..."

I remembered. L'Tanya danced barefoot, with a string of little bells around her ankles and rings on her toes. I reluctantly agreed that my creation didn't fit a rhythm tap routine but put it away for future use.

R.L. rented a red, white and blue costume for me that was cut like a one-piece bathing suit. I added a top hat and cane, and we were ready for our first gig in a small night club down the peninsula. Ah, the smell of grease paint!

Our routine was honed to a fine point, our flashes and stashes and hand movements coordinated in machinelike precision. My costume fit pasably well, my hair was done beautifully, and I had on enough make-up to stave off a winter cold.

The orchestra struck up our music and I led "Poole and Rita" out on the dance floor.

Dum dum te dum dum dum.

"And now, breaking in their new act, from way out Chicago way— Poole and Rita!"

I was miraculously in the center of an empty floor, with lights blazing down and I felt nearly naked. Just out of the glare I saw what appeared like a thousand knees and legs around small tables. I couldn't make out faces in the gloom, but I was sure they were there and probably all staring at me.

R.L. glided onto the floor, tap-tap-tapping away, flashed by me and I wanted to grab his hand. He pulled away to anywhere, but I was frozen in the spotlight.

Boom boom boom rah boom rah, boom rah brah, brah.

I realized that I was frightened and I nearly panicked. My God, what was going to happen? I'd never be able to leave this place. A stake had been driven down through my head and body, rooting me forever to this spot.

R.L. flashed by again.

Boom rah boom rah.

If he would only stop that silly tap-dancing and take my hand, we could leave.

He marched up and spoke to me under the music.

"Come on, Rita. Break. Break!"

Break what? I looked at him as if I had never seen him before.

He put his arm around my shoulder like Astaire did Rogers in one of their military parodies.

He looked at me and gave me a push that almost sent me into one of the tables, and hissed, "Break, goddammit, break!"

I broke.

I started dancing all over the place. Tapping, flashing, stashing up and down the floor. I threw in a little Huckle Buck, Suzie Q and trucking. Our routine had completely disappeared, but I was the world's dancing fool. Boogie-woogie, the Charleston. When the band was moving into the last chorus, I was just getting warmed up.

R.L. pursued me across the floor. He finally put his arm around my shoulder again, and by brute force led me off the floor, flashing to the end.

The audience clapped and I pulled away and raced back, booming and boom-rahing. R.L. joined me and again pulled me back to the wings.

I loved it. I was a hungry person invited to a welcome table for the first time in her life.

The costume rental and transportation had diminished our take to fifteen dollars apiece, I was exhausted and had the long bus ride ahead back to the city. But all was better than well. It was supercolossal. I had broken in. I was in show business. The only way up was up.

23

As I scrambled around the foot of the success ladder, Mother's life flowed radiant. Fluorescent-tipped waves on incoming tides. Men with exotic names, slick hair and attitudes of bored wisdom came into Vivian Baxter's large dark house, stayed awhile and went, making room for their successors.

Good-Doing David, with his silky black skin (Mother always preferred very black men, saying they were the cleanest folks in the world) and silk foulard tie, sat around the kitchen table for a few months. His eyes monitored her movements carefully, and when it was nearly too late she repaid him with a sultry look, thrown over her shoulder, and a smile that promised secret delight. Good-Doing forfeited his tenancy because of a misjudgment in logic. He thought since he was her man, it followed that she was his woman. He shouldn't have been so wrong.

One afternoon a seaman friend called her from the dock, and she invited him over. They maintained a brother/sister relationship.

"John Thomas is coming," she said to me. "Please go get a couple of chickens from the kosher poultry store. Tell them to cut them up." She had pulled out the wooden bowl, and laid her diamond rings in an ashtray. "I'll whip up a few biscuits and give him some fried chicken."

I knew that although the store was only two blocks away, she would have the bread in the oven and the oil heating for the chicken before I returned.

When they said cooking, they called Vivian Baxter's middle name.

When I rushed back into the house, the smell of hot grease met me, and the mixing bowl was washed and draining on the sink. Mother was setting the table for two.

"You have to pick up the baby? Make me a little drink, honey. And see if there's bourbon. John Thomas drinks bourbon. I'll put your chicken on the back of the stove." Her smile was partly for me, partly for the coming visitor and partly for the chicken seasoned, floured and dropping into the boiling skillet.

"You know there's always some in the kitchen for 'grandma 'n de chillun'." Her favorite old-folks line slid into whitefolks vulgarity of the black accent.

I answered the door for Mr. Thomas, and took his herringbone raglan coat and hat.

"Hey, baby, still growing, huh? Where your old ugly mama?" He walked down the hall laughing.

"Let him in, he may be a gambler." Mother's voice clinked like good glass from the kitchen.

Their welcoming laughter mixed as I left the house.

The ambulance screamed as it two-wheel-turned the corner from our block. I picked Guy up, not noticing his weight, and ran to our house, where two police cars sat empty, their red eyes turning faintly in the afternoon sunlight.

For the passionate, joy and anger are experienced in equal proportions and possibly with equal anticipation. My mother's capacity to enjoy herself was vast and her rages were legendary.

Mother never instigated violence; but she was known not to edge an inch out of the way of its progress. The sound of police and ambulance sirens whine through my childhood memory with dateless frequency. The red lights whirring on top of official cars and the heavy disrespectful footsteps of strange authority in our houses can be brought back clearly in my mind at a beckon.

Inside, Mother was slipping into her suede coat, a quiet smile on her face. She saw me and turned to the brace of policemen who waited for her.

"This is my daughter, Officers. That's who I was waiting for. Baby..." Now for the instructions that I already knew well. "Call the bail bondsman, Boyd Puccinelli. Tell him to meet me at Central Station."

I knew better than to ask what happened. I held the baby tighter.

"It's just a little business with David. Now, don't you worry. I'll be back in an hour."

She checked her make-up in her compact mirror, gave me and the baby a peck on our lips and walked down the steps with the police. Separate and dignified.

Then from the bottom: "Your dinner's in the oven. On low. Oh, and baby, clean up in the bedroom before that stuff dries, please."

There was no sign of Mr. John Thomas in the kitchen. After my son and I had eaten, and I put him down for an afternoon nap, I opened her bedroom door. One chair was on its side, but elsewhere things were in order. As I walked in, the weak winter sunshine paled over dark rust blotches on the rug and showed the lighter red splashes down the sides of the mantel.

Lukewarm soap suds are best to remove bloodstains from furniture. I had nearly finished cleaning up when Mother returned.

"Hi, baby. Any phone calls?"

"No."

"Here, leave that, I'll do the rest. Come on in the kitchen and let me tell you what happened."

Over a fresh drink she gave me what she called a "blow by blow" description.

"John Thomas and I were up to our elbows in fried chicken (I made a gravy longer than I been away from St. Louis for the biscuits) when Good-Doing rang the bell. I let him in and brought him back to the kitchen. He saw John Thomas and stopped shorter than a show horse. Said no, he didn't want to eat. Didn't want a drink, didn't want a chair, so I sat back down and started tending to business. Every time I looked up, I saw he was getting fuller than I was. Finally he said he wanted a few words with me and would I come to the bedroom. I told him to go on, I'd be there. I excused myself from John Thomas and went up the hall.

" 'What's that nigger doing here?' He got ugly in the face and jumped around like a tail on a kite."

"I said, 'You know John Thomas. He's my friend. He's like a brother to me.'

" 'Well, I don't like him eating here. Get him out of the house.' "

"I said, 'Good-Doing, don't get it twisted. This is my house and my chicken, and he's my friend.' "

"He said, 'Bitch, you supposed to be so bad. You need a good ass-kicking.' "

She looked at me, puzzlement wrinkling her pretty face.

"Baby, I swear to you, I don't know what sent him off, but before I could say anything, he reached in his pocket and pulled out a knife. You know he's got something wrong with the fingers on his left hand, so he bent his head over and was trying to open the knife with his teeth. Now, you can see by that, that he's a fool. Instead of moving away from him I just stepped over to the mantel. I put Bladie Mae in my pocket before I went up to the room. When he came up with his knife half open, I slapped him cross the face with ole Bladie."

"He jumped faster than the blood. Screamed, 'Goddammit, Bibbie, you cut me!' "

"I said, 'You goddam right, and you lucky I don't shoot you on top of it.' "

"He was holding his face, blood dripping down his hands on to his Hart Schaffner and Marx suit. I gave him a pillow off my bed and told him to sit down. I told him moving around makes the blood pump faster. I came back to the kitchen and told John Thomas to make himself scarce—no point in him being involved—then I called the police and the ambulance."

Mother inspected the contents of her glass, then she took my large hand in her smaller, plump one and ordered my close attention.

"Baby, Mother Dear's going to tell you something about life."

Her face was beautifully calm, all traces of violence lost.

"People will take advantage of you if you let them. Especially Negro women. Everybody, his brother and his dog thinks he can walk a road in a colored woman's behind. But you remember this, now. Your mother raised you. You're full-grown. Let them catch it like they find it. If you haven't been trained at home to their liking tell them to get to stepping." Here a whisper of delight crawled over her face. "Stepping. But not on you."

"You hear me?"

"Yes, Mother. I hear you."

There had been some changes at home. Bailey had found his first great love. Eunice was a small, smiling brown-skinned girl who had been our classmate. They had met again, and over the protests of her family, rushed to marry. Bailey, the airy false charmer, had drifted to earth and was happy. He laughed and joked again.

They invited me to their Turk Street apartment, where large Gauguin and Van Gogh prints enlivened the walls and fresh flowers sparkled on waxed tables.

He told funny dirty stories and the three of us laughed into the cheap wine and congratulated ourselves on being smart enough to be young and intelligent. We could see the plateaus of success in our futures. Plateaus where we would wait and rest awhile before climbing higher. When he looked at my 8″ by 10″ professional glossies, he said I had the "biggest nose in show business" but it was prettier than Jimmy Durante's and I ought to be proud.

I tried to punch him, but he laughed and swerved out of the way. "You'll be the tallest dancer on Broadway. Ha ha." He ran around the table escaping my outstretched hand. "You'll make a million with each leg and a zillion with your nose."

Relief made me laugh out of proportion. Later I kissed them both good night and wished I knew how to thank Eunice for helping Bailey find his sense of humor again.

I walked the dark streets toward home and shivered at Bailey's close escape. Most of his friends, funny and bright during our schooldays, now leaned in nighttime doorways, nodding as their latest shot of heroin raced in their veins. Sparkling young men who were hopes of the community had thrown themselves against the sealed doors set up by a larger community, and not only hadn't opened them, but hadn't even shaken the bolts. The potential sharp-tongued lawyer, keen-eyed scientist and cool-hand surgeon changed his mind about jimmying the locks and took to narcotics so that he could float through the key hole.

Eunice's happy love and soft laughter had come just in time. My brother was saved.

24

Poole and Rita were booked into the Champagne Supper Club. Pride made me go beserk. I quit my job. How could I exchange the glittering sequined bathing suit and purple satin tap shoes for a waitress apron and old-lady comforts? I wouldn't insult my muse, Terpsichore, by letting even the idea of the Chicken Shack enter into my thoughts.

A two-week engagement in Big Time, and I was ready.

My lights in stars, my name in lights, my name in stars.

For a few months before the opening we worked for whatever money was offered and practiced daily. R.L. showed me increasingly complicated steps. As soon as I learned, he laced them into our routines. When I had no cash, I asked Mother for a loan. I explained that I was investing my time in career preparation, and when the investment paid off she would be with me, holding hands and laughing and reaping the returns.

With characteristic talent, she enlarged my skit into a full-length revue. And she was the star. She reminded me that during the war years, when she had had lots of money and could have afforded to sit back idle, she had studied barbering, cosmetology, ship-fitting, welding, tool-and-dye making, and that the diplomas attesting to her perseverance hung on the walls of her den. She said she had no intention of ever going to work in an airplane factory or barber shop, but if push came to shove (she snapped her fingers), she was qualified. She approved of sticking to an idea until it was definitely proven bad or good.

She lent me the money without further preachments, and Poole and Rita continued to practice.

Although I lived and ate at home, the small savings I kept in a jar under my bed diminished. My son always seemed to need new clothes; on Sundays I traditionally bought fresh flowers for the house; and then there were the tap shoes. Rehearsing wore out more taps than dancing three times a night in a cabaret.

I approached Bailey for a small advance. He sat, stubble-jawed, on his corduroy sofa, and looked at the adjacent wall.

"I've put Eunice in the hospital. She's very sick."

"What's wrong with her?" I made my voice soft.

"She just had a cold. That's all." But he didn't believe that was all.

"Well, come on. She's young. Nobody dies from a cold." If only I could get him to look at me. I went on making a joke. "They only wish they could."

"Yeah." He put his feet on the cluttered coffee table, leaned back on the sofa and closed his eyes.

"Good-bye, Maya."

"Bailey, it's not that serious." He didn't try to hear me and I could not intrude further by repeating myself.

The apartment stank of dead flowers and dirty dishes. His voice blurred but didn't rise or fall. "I've cut out all the runs except Los Angeles so I can be with her."

The room was oppressive as if a large hand had squeezed the gaiety out of it drop by drop and then released it to resume its former shape.

I was getting so I could fairly fly through the routine. My romance with R.L. was danced out in the rehearsal hall, because he made few sexual demands. I gave no arguments to his monthly requests for lovemaking. After all, he was my teacher and my transportation to Broadway. But I was grateful that they didn't come with greater frequency. An artist, I was certain, protected and preserved his instrument. Pianists, drummers, horn players, saxists all look after their instruments. As a dancer, my instrument was my body. I couldn't just allow a person, anyone, to screw my instrument.

Opening night arrived. Mother had taken a large table for her friends, and Bailey miraculously didn't have to be on the road or at the hospital. The night club, which was large and bedizened with glittering spinning lights, was full.

Excitement made me glow and the lights backstage rubbed away R.L.'s pockmarks. We looked at ourselves in the large mirror. He was absolutely dashing in his powder-blue tuxedo, and I was as glamorous as Esther Williams in my swimsuit. And could dance better, too.

The M.C. called our names, and the band swung into our introduction.

R.L. said in his slow voice, "Okay, Rita, break a leg." Show-business talk. I grinned. "You, too."

And we hit the stage.

The first moment's unreality was caused by the lights. I couldn't see the audience, and I thought about the first time when I panicked and froze to the stage. Maybe this was happening again. Maybe I had frozen, I couldn't tell if I was moving. But suddenly I heard the clap of taps breaking, exploding through the band's arrangement, and I found I was on the far side of the stage and it was time for me to break. I was dancing, my feet and body were doing the right things. With that I let go, just let the orchestra push, prod and pull me. I surrendered every memory I had to oblivion and let myself dance. Each time I danced near R.L., I laughed out loud at the perfect glory of it all. The music was my friend, my lover, my famiiy. It was a pretty day on a San Francisco hill with just enough high to remark on details. It was my son laughing when I entered his room. Great poetry that I had memorized and recited to myself in a warm bath.

The band was playing the closing riffs and R.L. took my hand. We

266

danced to the edge of the stage and bowed. The audience applauded moderately, except for Mother's table and a bravo from where Bailey sat near the door. I never knew whether the great disappointment came from having to stop dancing or from the fact that the audience didn't jump up, run screaming for the stage to touch my victory. But in the dressing room I began to drown in a depression sea. Neither the flowers Bailey sent nor Mother's smile saved me. Two more shows to do that night and by the last one I was questioning whether I was cut out for show biz... whether or not it was too coarse for my pure and delicate nature, too commercial for my artistic soul.

All the area's drunks and sporting people caught the last show and I was again intoxicated. They shouted, "Shake it, baby," "Dance, baby, dance," made noise, stumbled around from table to table, and the sense of gay activity helped Poole and Rita and the orchestra to re-create the earlier magic.

The patrons may not really have noticed the very tall, big-nosed dancing fool up there, but their vitality locked me into a love of performing that continued for many years.

Except for a few "casuals" (one-night performances in convention halls), the talent of Poole and Rita was going largely unappreciated. We refused the itinerant offers to perform at stags. I said I would never dance nude for a bunch of white men to gape at me. R.L. agreed and tried to appear possessive, but probably the larger truth was that we couldn't work up a "Beauty and Beast" routine. Neither did I have the attributes to portray Beauty, nor did he have the body to dance Beast. We would have been ludicrous.

The gigs at the Elks were bright splatches in the dull landscape. In black communities there is a counterpart to the white segregated secret society, B.P.O.E. (Benevolent and Protective Order of Elks). We call ours the Improved Benevolent and Protective Order of Elks of the World. I had been initiated into the mysterious organization as a teenager and had once won prizes in its oratorical contest, and now our dance team was hired at the hilarious and good-fun *dansants*.

The middle-aged ladies, usually stout and dressed more attractively than the women whose houses they cleaned, patted me after the shows and admired my leanness.

"Honey, you sure know how to shake that thing." A big pretty laugh. "I used to shake it like that, but them days is gone forever."

Then they would run their palms down my side.

"Bet your momma is proud of you. I bet you she is." And she was. And I was proud of myself.

"Blue Flame" and "Caravan" were my favorite dance arrangements because R.L. laid out most of the time and I danced barefoot in little balls of blue ostrich feathers and Indian bells at my ankles. I tried to imitate Frances Nealy, a beautiful black woman who had played an Egyptian dancer in a forties technicolor movie. A few Dorothy Lamour hand movements and Ann Miller's leg kicks just added spice.

Then Cotton Candy Adams came to town.

> "Let me be your little dog
> till your big dog come
> Let me be your little dog
> till your big dog come
> And when your big dog come,
> tell him what your little dog done."

R.L.'s words stumbled when he started to tell me about his ex-girl friend and former dancer. "Oh, Rita... she—Candy and I—I mean, she was my old lady... and she, uh, left me. That is, we used to dance together. She came out here—I mean, she said if... When she left me... uh, if I... if she... ever changed her mind, she'd, uh, find me."

"Okay, R.L. She came. Are you all going back together?" I was as snappy as I thought a chorus dancer would be.

"See, Rita, she's a, uh, dancer. I mean, she's great. She used to dance with Parker and Johnson. And she's worked the Orpheum Circuit." He had stopped stuttering. "She brought her costumes. Really flash. Feather fans with rhinestones. See, most of what I taught you—I mean..." Shyness tripped his tongue and he began to stutter again. "Wait till you meet her. She's... You're going to... I think you'll like each other."

"Sure thing, Bozo." I had never called a living soul Bozo. "I'd be delighted to meet her."

Cotton Candy was the picture of every "Daddy's little girl." Her real hair hung down in black waves and dimples punctured her light-brown cheeks. She had a cute walk, which wavered between a wanton strut and a little-girl mince. And then she opened her mouth. "Hi, Rita. R.L. told me about you. You're a dancer."

I didn't know how to hold the shock. Her teeth were rotten and her lips refused to help mold her words. I looked at her eyes and understood. They shone feverishly, yet seemed lifeless. Cotton Candy was a user.

Certainly R.L. knew. After all, he was from Chicago. I couldn't grasp why he would want to get reconciled with her, and I knew from the enchanted way he watched her that that was exactly what he wanted.

"Yes, I'm a dancer. Are you planning to dance in San Francisco?" Might as well have it out in the open.

"Oh yes." Although R.L. was feet from her, she cuddled in his direction. "R.L. and I are going to brush up our old act and get started

268

again." She closed her mouth and dimpled. Her eyes slowly moved to R.L. "Isn't that what you said, Boogie?"

"Yeah. Uh-huh. Yeah. We'll do all the stuff we used to do."

I had to get away immediately. "Well, good luck to you both. Break a leg." I walked away from the lovers before they could see the life leaking out of me.

At home, I paced the floors. Mother had taken my son out and Papa Ford snored in the small back bedroom. I cursed Cotton Candy for coming to San Francisco and consigned R.L. to hell for being stupid enough to take her back. My career was over before it began. My tears came hot and angry. I had dared so many things and failed. There was to be nothing left to do. I had given Curly my young love; he had gone away to marry another woman. The self-defense tactics with the lesbians had gained me a whorehouse, which I had neither the skill nor the courage to keep. I had fled to the home of my youth and had been sent away. The Army and now my dance career, the one thing I wanted beyond all others (needed, in fact) for my son but mostly for myself, had been plucked right out of my fingers. All the doors had slammed shut, and I was locked into a too-tall body, with an unpretty face, and a mind that bounced around like a ping-pong ball. I gave in to sadness because I had no choice.

A few days passed and R.L. didn't come to the house. I telephoned him. He was distracted but promised to drop by and talk about it. I waited past the afternoon hour he mentioned, and long into the night. He never came; he didn't call.

If we had had the opportunity to talk about it, laboriously and painfully, I might have been forever lost in the romance of romance lost. But with no sounding board except my own ears and honest thoughts, I had to stop weeping (it was too exhausting) and admit that Cotton Candy had dibs on him and maybe R.L. felt more loyal to her because she was a user and needed him.

There was nothing about me to bind anyone to me in sympathy. No limp, no habit, crossed eyes or attitude of helplessness. I decided I'd try to sort out my life. I tried to crush the thoughts of self-pity that needled into my brain and told myself that it was time to roll up my costumes, which would eternally have the odor of grease paint in their seams, and put away the tap shoes, which hurt my feet anyway. For, after all, only poets care about what happened to the snows of yesteryear. And I hadn't time to be a poet, I had to find a job, get my grits together and take care of my son. So much for show biz, I was off to live real life.

25

A friend of Mother's who had a restaurant in Stockton needed a fry cook. I packed the clothes I thought we might need and set out for the eighty-mile journey. I wasn't sure that I'd find pot in the little town, so I stashed a Prince Albert can full, and papers, in the bottom of my suitcase. I refused to cry all the way in the back seat of a Greyhound bus.

Stockton had an unusual atmosphere. Situated in the agricultural San Joaquin Valley, it had long been a center for the itinerant workers, Southerners drawn from depleted farms, Mexicans and Filipinos from their poverty-stricken countries who had raised large families on meager incomes since the early 1900s. World War II had enriched the town's blood by attracting blacks from the South to work at the local dry dock, the shipyards and defense plants in nearby Pittsburg.

When I arrived, there was Wild West rhythm in the streets. Since some of the plants were still running and the police hadn't yet cracked down on crime, prostitutes and gamblers came from San Francisco and Los Angeles on weekends to fleece the willing local yokels.

The restaurant was large, seating seventy-five, and had a steady and regular clientele. But because it was two blocks from Center Street, we got little of the sophisticated walk-in trade. My shift began at four in the afteenoon, and I fried hamburgers, pork chops and eggs and ham steaks until midnight. Then, to add juice to my dry life, I would wash up, exchange the sweaty uniform for a clinging one-shoulder deal and high-heeled shoes that hurt my already swollen feet. A slow saunter to Center Street, and a perch at the crowded bar gave me a chance to watch the fascinating city folks, and at the same time haughtily explain to any man fresh enough to approach me that I worked for a living. I wasn't a whore. I told myself that the fact that I might have been mistaken for one, because of my flagrant way of dressing or clinging to a bar alone in a small town at one in the morning, was simply evidence of men trying to read a book by its cover.

270

Big Mary was a large-boned, rough woman from Oklahoma whose husband had died in the tomato fields surrounding Stockton. She was the neighborhood's surrogate mother. She tended children on a daily basis, but when I explained that I needed a weekly arrangement because of my hours, she agreed to let my son live in her house; I could pick him up on my day off. The blood of Indian ancestors pushed her cheekbones up so high that her eyes appeared to be closed, and her skin was the black brown of old polished wood. Mary drank once a month and other arrangements had to be made for all children on that one day. She would dress herself in a clean, loose-fitting cotton dress, and her dead husband's shoes cut out to ease the strain. Sitting at the bar, she'd pull a coffee cup from her purse and order the bartender, "Fill it up!" After drinking the contents, she'd ask the bartender to wash the cup and fill it up again. She would sit, sipping, staring straight ahead, until she had drunk three cups of bourbon. Then she would pay, and without having passed the time of day with anyone, leave the bar as straight as she had entered it.

Her way with children was to feed them well and coddle them. She fell into baby talk whenever children were mentioned, even if none were present.

Her thick Oklahoma accent slurred and her tongue protruded through the evenly shaped, full black lips. I figured that such a display of affection couldn't hurt my son, so I worked without great concern, and devoted myself to the serious business of accumulating a wardrobe.

Boys seem to think that girls hold the keys to all happiness, because the female is supposed to have the right of consent and/or dissent. I've heard older men reflect on their youth, and an edge of hostile envy drags across their voices as they conjure up the girls who whetted but didn't satisfy their sexual appetites. It's interesting that they didn't realize in those yearning days past, nor even in the present days of understanding, that if the female had the right to decide, she suffered from her inability to instigate. That is, she could only say yes or no if she was asked.

She spends half her time making herself attractive to men, and the other half trying to divine which of the attracted are serious enough to marry her, and which wish to ram her against the nearest wall and jab into her recklessly, then leave her leaning, legs trembling, cold wet evidence running down her inner thigh. Which one will come to her again, proud to take her to his friends, and which will have friends who only know of her as the easy girl with good (or even bad) poontang?

The crushing insecurity of youth, and the built-in suspicion between the sexes, militate against the survival of the species, and yet, men do legalize their poking, and women do get revenge their whole lives through for the desperate days of insecurity and bear children so that the whole process remains in process.

Alas.

The Poole-Rita partnership, with a little romance on the side, had left me yearning more for the stage and music and bravos of audiences than for a lover's arms.

But as fry cook in a small restaurant in the farm community, my fantasies were little different from any other girl of my age. He would come. He would. Just walk into my life, see me and fall everlastingly in love. I had the affliction suffered by most young women. The sexual excitement of my teens had abated, and I looked forward to a husband who would love me ethereally, spiritually, and on rare (but beautiful) occasions, physically.

He would be a little younger than my father, and handsome in that casual way. His conservative clothes would fit well, and he'd talk to me softly and look at me penetratingly. He'd often pat me and tell me how proud he was of me and I'd strain to make him even prouder. We would live quietly in a pretty little house and I'd have another child, a girl, and the two children (whom he'd love equally) would climb over his knees and I would make three-layer caramel cakes in my electric kitchen until they went off to college.

L.D. Tolbrook was my father's age, my father's color, and was as conservative as a black Episcopalian preacher. He wore tailor-made clothes and his rare smile showed teeth so anxious they clambered over each other. His hands were dainty and his long brown fingers ended with natural-polish manicured nails.

One night he was with a party who had come to the restaurant for a midnight breakfast. I had changed into evening clothes but my replacement hadn't yet come. When the waitress explained the situation to L.D.'s party, he came to the door of the kitchen and said, "Excuse me. I wanted a word with the chef." His voice was soft.

"I'm the swing-shift cook, but I'm off now." I didn't really look at him.

"Well, I understand that." His smile came from a deep well of understanding. "But my party is especially hungry. And we'd take anything you'd give us." He looked at my dress. "I'd make it worth your while to be late to your party."

"I'm not going to a—" Before my mouth could close.

He peeled a ten-dollar bill off his money roll. "Give us bacon and eggs, or ham and eggs. Or anything and any way you fix them. We'll be happy."

I needed the money, so I took it and turned to go back to the dressing room and change my clothes.

272

"What's your name?"

"Rita."

"All right, Miss Rita. Thank you. We all thank you." He pushed his way through the door.

Though I prided myself on tender sensitivity, I have never known when a great love affair was beginning. Some barricade lies midway my mind, and I'm usually on my back scrutinizing a ceiling before it is borne in on me that this is the man I fantasized in my late-night fingering.

L.D. (Louis David) came the next night a half-hour before midnight, had breakfast and asked for me by name. The waitress brought the message and I went out uniformed and shining with sweat.

He stood. "Miss Rita." He pulled out a chair. "Can you have a seat with me?"

I told him I was still working.

"If you're not busy after, I'd like to invite you for a ride... er, I guess you wouldn't want breakfast." His lips pulled back a little to let me know he'd made a joke.

"No thanks, no breakfast." And, I thought, no ride either. This dry little man couldn't compete with the bar on Center Street.

"I'll tell you how I happened to be here."

He was still standing. My eyes looked straight into his forehead where curly black hair retreated from the advance of scalp.

"After I dropped those people off last night, I went to the gambling shack. Something happened to me. I couldn't keep my mind on the game. Kept forgetting what I was doing. I kept on thinking how sweet it was of you to get out of your nice clothes and fix us something to eat."

His head dropped and his eyes lifted shyly. "I knew it wasn't for the tenner. Something about you told me that." It was time for my eyes to drop.

"So I sat around awhile, then I went on home. This afternoon I got up and went back and cleaned the house out. I won six hundred playing Koch. Then I thought I might pick up that nice lady and spend some of this money on her."

Here he pulled out a roll of money that looked the same as the one he had stripped the night before, but this time I noticed the big diamond ring and his manicured nails. I looked down and was certain the glistening pointed shoes were expensive Florsheims, and the hat lying in the next chair was a Dobbs. Here was the real thing. No loud-talking, door-popping shucker from the Center Street bar, but an established gambler who had Southern manners and city class.

"I thought we might drop in on some of my friends in Sacramento."

273

The glorious feeling of having caught the big one gently massaged me and diffused in my mind and body. I was lovely when I changed into something sleek and appealing, and said good night to the waitress and the relief cook.

The silver-blue Lincoln struck me as perfect for L.D. It wasn't large or brand-new, but it was rubbing-clean and shining with polish. When we drove away from the lights of Stockton, he found music on the radio and turned it down to a touching purr.

> "I want a Sunday kind of love
> A love to last past Saturday night
> I want to know it's more than
> love at first sight..."

He asked if I was married. Law or common-law? I said no, neither. (I pronounced it 'n eye ther). He said almost to himself, "I must have got my lucky break. At last."

I leaned back into the real leather seat and grinned for my own enjoyment.

"I have to take care of some business. And I wanted you to come with me. I have to see a lady friend named Clara."

His words never rushed but were selected, chewed over, released into the air as if the best choice possible had been made.

For once being young was fortunate. Everyone had heard the stories about young girls and older men. How older men were good to and generous to and crazy about young girls. I thought to myself, I'd rather be an old man's darling than a young man's slave.

"Clara is a real square shooter. Four square, Rita, like I think you are. Yes sir, honest as the day is long."

Even his idiom was old.

When we drove up to the three-shaded house, he started to get out of the car. "Come on. I'd like you to meet Clara. She's sure to like you..."

I followed him.

The heavy odor of disinfectant in the house was as telltale as a red light over the door. Although memories of my San Diego experience rushed me, I kept my face straight, giving no hint that I knew where we were.

Clara was a small, well-built woman in her thirties. Her heavy make-up mask cracked into seams at her delight.

"Lou!" She backed away from the door and we were right-handed into a dully furnished living room.

L.D. said he had some business to talk over with Clara and excused himself. He offered me a drink but I explained that I didn't drink and received an approving smile for my information.

274

No sounds reached me from the back of the house. I began wondering: suppose L.D. was renting a room and instead of coming back himself sent Clara to get me. If she said, "Rita, Lou wants to see you in the back," I wouldn't know how to answer. I wasn't stupid enough to say, "Please tell him that I never go to bed with a man on the first date." She'd laugh me out of the place. There was nothing for it but to submit. But submit in such a way that he'd feel badly and I'd feel nothing. That was my plan.

They were laughing as they came back into the room.

"Clara, you're still ace-high in my book," said L.D. "But we have to get a move-on."

"Aw, Lou, let's sit down for a while. Let me and Rita get acquainted." Her smile wrinkled her whole face and she looked like a rubber doll won at playland.

"This lady worked hard all night and I know she'd like to get home and rest." He looked at me. "I'm sorry. Maybe the next time I'll let you sit around talking women's talk with her. Come on, Rita, we'd better head back to Stockton."

I shook hands with Clara and said, "Thank you, I'm sure... See you again... I had a very nice time... 'Bye."

In the car I hastily discarded my unnecessary defense plans and tried to figure what to expect next. He probably wanted to take me to his place. But as soon as we reached the outskirts of Stockton I was going to ask to be taken home because I had a fearful headache. If he was a real gentleman, he would acquiesce.

We were as quiet on the return drive as the black trees outside the windows. The lights of the town flashed faintly and I prepared my spiel.

"Rita, I've sure appreciated you making this ride with me. I have to go to Sacramento twice a week and it's lonely at night by yourself. I knew you were tired when I asked you, but just like the other night, you showed what a big heart you had. I really appreciate it."

He swung the car into the black area.

"Where do you live?"

Again I had girded myself for no reason. "I have a room at Kathryn's."

"Cooking privileges?" He knew the place.

"Yes."

"Well, sometimes maybe you'll cook me a meal. If you're not too tired."

We were in front of my door and he made no attempt to even kiss me good night.

"Good night, L.D."

"Good night, Rita. I'll see you soon."

The blue car eased down the street and I wondered if in my ignorance I had lost my chance for a life of tender loving being cared for.

The next evening when I left work he was parked outside. He flashed the lights.

"Rita. Good evening. I hope you don't mind, but I wanted to see you again."

Glorious day.

I sat back in the already familiar seat and breathed in his perfume.

"You're so young and fresh. And I sure like the way you talk. So young." He laughed a little. I couldn't remember what I'd talked about the night before, and felt the terrible burden of trying to think up something useful to entertain him.

Young talk to me was silly vacant chatter. I couldn't imagine the drivel of young girls coming out of my head and mouth, but I wanted to amuse, so I decided to tell him one story of my life.

"You know, I love to dance. I've studied since I was fourteen and I've been in show business. I was part of the Poole and Rita dance team."

We had left Stockton streetlights and were on the highway before I noticed.

"We're going down to Tulare; it's not far. Go on, tell me about your dancing. I knew you weren't all that graceful for nothing."

I unreeled imaginary stories of the night clubs I had worked in and the steps I learned and my glamorous costumes. As I talked my career sparkled with success and I was a star of the brightest magnitude, bowing and smiling to a vast audience which would never be satisfied.

In Tulare we visited Minnie, whose house was identical with Clara's, down to the disinfectant and artificial flowers. Minnie lacked Clara's pixie charm and regarded me with the hard eyes of a buyer at a horse auction.

L.D. and Minnie went into a side bedroom and stayed only a few minutes. "Okay, Minnie, see you soon. Let's go, Rita." He had no smile for her and no small talk. I was glad. It was obvious that she wasn't a very nice person. (Nice persons meaning people who tried to draw me out and who found my stolid face and ungiving attitude charming.)

He was either running a lottery or selling the whores dope, and the fact that he never mentioned what his "business" was told me that he thought I was square. It never occurred to me that he might have liked that, so I decided at just the proper time I would tell him that once I had a house in San Diego employing two whores.

That night, I told him about my baby and that he was three years

276

old and how pretty and smart he was. L.D. said nothing until we parked in front of my house.

He twisted in the dark and pulled his roll of money from a side pocket.

"Rita, I don't want you to get me wrong. I'm not trying to buy your affections. But you are alone and have a baby to raise. I'd be less than a man if I didn't try to help you." He folded a bill and pressed it into my hand. "Now, don't say anything. Just use it for yourself and the baby."

"All right, get out now. I won't be able to see you for a few days. There's a big game down in the city. I'll come to the restaurant as soon as I get back."

I wanted to lean over and kiss him, but his aloofness didn't encourage me.

"Good night, L.D., and good luck."

"Thank you, Rita."

I turned the lamp on in my room and looked down at the fifty-dollar bill crumpled in my palm.

It was the first time any man other than Bailey had given me money.

I bought an outfit worthy of a Hollywood siren and toys for my son.

26

For the next three weeks I rode the California highways with L.D. I met Dimples in Fresno and Helen in Merced and Jackie and Lil in Mendota and Firebaugh, and a few women who had cabins along the road with access to the transient field workers. L.D. continued making generous gifts, saying business was good. I never asked him what business it was and he never offered any information. I didn't have to fend off his advances, since he didn't make any.

Desire for him grew in direct proportion to his indifference. I experimented with every ploy I could dream up. He had revealed to me that he didn't read books, so I tried to impress him with my great love of learning. He liked straight shooters, so one night I told him how much I cared. He had pity for me, an unmarried mother. I cried out my aching loneliness. Nothing fazed him or prodded him into taking me in his arms.

The restaurant had become a larger bore than a lifetime in the Gobi Desert, and I found no enjoyment in my books or playing with my son. All life funneled down to one smile, one man's soft, quiet "Good evening, Rita. How you doing tonight?"

"Here's a hundred dollars." The bills fanned out from his fingers.

"Oh, I couldn't take that much."

"I want you to go shopping and buy some different clothes. You dress too old. You ought to dress your age. You're young. Buy some low shoes and anklets. Some blouses and pretty colored skirts. And put a bow ribbon in your hair."

I hadn't worn socks in years and had hated them then. They made my already long legs look longer. But L.D. asked.

When he saw me in the schoolgirl outfit he said I was his "Bobby Sock Baby" and he was going to give me a special gift. On my next day off he took me to the city.

"This is not business this time. It's just for you. I'm going to give you what you've been wanting."

He smiled and patted my cheek and I would have thought it a privilege to die for him.

San Francisco's South of Market area was a mystery land where homeless drunks loitered before the dirty windows of liquor stores. Pawnshops' glaring signs promised to exchange money out of proportion for goods. People I knew only went South of Market to reach the S.P. railway station or to pay bills at some of the location's loan offices.

L.D. guided his car down the dark streets and I, snuggled at his side, wished the ride would never end. On the highway he had said I was the sweetest little thing he'd ever seen and praised me for wearing the high school clothes that he preferred. I was his Bobby Sock Baby, and he was going to make me so happy I'd cry.

I held precariously to the grateful tears that gathered behind my lids.

When he stopped the car and kissed me gently, long and loving my body pressed to be rid of the prison of skin.

Skid Row's broken glass might have been rose petals, and the arid smell of secondhand alcohol was India's most hypnotizing incense.

L.D. rang the bell at a grille door and called out his name. The door opened automatically and I followed him up dim, carpeted stairs. When he nodded to me I heeled in the shadows. He walked down the hall where a light gleamed over a half door. I heard whispers, then he came back to me jangling a key. The energy of passion carried me over the room's threshold and threw me across the bed.

L.D. sat patiently beside me and spoke quietly.

"You know I'm much older than you. I'm an old man, so don't

expect the same things from me that you get from your young beaus."

Beaus? R.L.? I couldn't matt my allure by telling him there were no beaus, or scream at him to undress or I'd tear his clothes in shreds. I forced my eyes closed and waited.

He kissed me and the tears I had held in the car came unfastened. L.D. held me as if I were made of feather.

"Daddy's baby is scared, huh? Well, Daddy won't hurt his baby. Get undressed and wash up so we can lie down."

"I had a bath before we left Stockton."

He whispered, "Wash over there in that face bowl. Daddy's going to love his baby."

I spent the next month metamorphosizing from Miss Insecure to Bobby Sock Baby. Being loved by an older married man gave me a youth I'd never known. I giggled into my Kleenex, fluttered my eyelashes and fairly gamboled over the greensward. At midnight when I doffed the cook's apron and washed my face and arms, I flew, anklets sparking white, into the arms of my garbardined lover. We went to chicken suppers in San Francisco, where I hoped and feared the stubble-bearded gamblers in the back room would recognize me as Vivian's daughter, who made good.

The grass I'd brought from San Francisco was holding out. I disciplined myself. One joint on Sunday and one on the morning of my day off. The weed always had an intense and immediate effect. Before the cigarette was smoked down to roach length, I had to smother my giggles. Just to see the falling folds of the curtains or the sway of a chair was enough to bring me to audible laughter. After an hour the hysteria of the high would abate and I could trust myself in public.

One day off, L.D. took me and my son for a picnic in the country. He had arrived early at my house, but I got ready quickly and we went to pick up the baby.

From the car windows I watched the farm rows. They ran toward the road as if to intercept it. It amused me that the neat lines marched up and fell away, to be replaced by others which in turn were themselves replaced. They had the show business precision of a drill team on parade. The thought of cotton rows practicing routines at night when everyone was asleep tickled my funny bone. A small blob of laughter curdled in the back of my throat and rolled over my tongue. I wanted to explain the joke to L.D., but there was no time. The chuckle was out. My laughter triggered the baby's and he joined me. The whole thing was getting funnier. I tried to control myself, but each time I looked at L.D.'s disapproving face I climbed to a new height of hilarity. When he stopped the car, the contractions were beginning to ease.

We unloaded the car silently and spread a blanket I'd taken from my bed.

When we settled, he said, "You've been smoking gauge, haven't you?"

"Yes." I wasn't ashamed to admit it.

"How long have you been smoking?"

"About a year."

He took my hand and held it tightly. "Do you know that junk can kill your nature?"

I had never heard that. "No."

"Well, let me tell you something. It's gauge that's breaking up my marriage. He stroked my hand. "My silly dilly wife stopped letting me have any and she goes around laughing and giggling all the time. I've told her that I can't go on much longer. I'd hate to lose you too, Rita. Just after I've found you." I thought he was sincere and I was sorry I'd upset him.

I didn't need to think long. The pot had been important when I was alone and lonely, when my present was dull and the future uncertain. Now I had a man, who talked sweet to me, made excruciatingly good love to me, considered my baby, and was going to make me his wife.

"L.D., when you take me home, I'll throw the rest in the toilet."

He grinned and touched my face. "You're my Bobby Sock Baby. Now let's see what we have to eat."

As we picnicked he continued talking about his wife (I hadn't expected to find My Prince without encumbrances). "She's a millstone around my neck. Sometimes I stay all night in the gambling house just to keep away from her evil mind and sharp tongue."

"Why do you stay with her, L.D.?"

"She's older than I am, and she was good to me once. I never once forget a favor. Can't afford to. Now she's sickly. When I get on my feet, I'm going to send her back home to her folks." He waited a minute, then took my face in his hands. "You're such a sweet baby, Rita. Let's don't talk about it any more." I admired his restraint.

The naturally lonely person does not look for comfort in love, but accepts the variables as due course.

I thought I was making him happy. In any case I would have done anything to win a smile or hear him laugh and pat my cheek. The job had become so very tiresome. If I didn't have to work, we could spend more time together. I loved the movies and we'd never been; also I wanted to get into a dance class so I wouldn't get rusty. I knew it was a matter of time before he'd catch on to my hints about the job and order me to quit. I would get an apartment and furnish it with the ragingly popular blond furniture. My bedroom was to tremble with pink frills and lacy ruffles. My son's would be painted yellow and white, with decals of happy animals climbing the walls, expensive toys stacked neatly in a corner, and he would sit at a cute little table learning from clever educative books. Home-baked breads would give the kitchen a solid country air, and after my family had eaten and the baby was fast asleep, I would lie on my scented bed as L.D. loved his baby in the darkness.

Three days passed and L.D. didn't come to the restaurant. I was jittery with worry. He told me where he lived when he told me how hateful and lacking in understanding his wife was, but I didn't know the telephone number. Gamblers protect themselves from borrowers by having unlisted telephones. Before and after work I walked by the gambling joints looking for his car, then past his two-story house, which sat back in a yard of tended rose bushes. Ideas of all sizes and degrees of madness plagued me. He might have had an accident, fatal. Or he might have had a heart attack. Fatal. He might have tired of me and found someone else. I hastily discarded that one. It was better to picture him in a lovely coffin, "his small face narrowed by death and his thin lips at peace."

"Baby, Daddy didn't mean to worry you." Although his face was lined with exhaustion and he hadn't shaved, he looked beautiful. He had driven up just as I walked out of the café, and told me to get in the car.

"Things have been going badly for me. Very badly."

I had no idea how a juvenile bride was to console her man. Should I pinch him and giggle or stroke him like a sister?

"I've been gambling for three days and I lost everything."

Now I could say it. "You've got *me*, L.D."

He didn't hear me.

"I lost over five thousand dollars."

I nearly screamed. There wasn't that much money anywhere except in banks. He could have bought me a house with five thousand dollars.

"And I'm up to my neck. I was trying to win enough money"—he turned away—"to divorce that old hag I'm married to and send her back to Louisiana. Then you and I could be together forever."

I knew it. He did want to marry me. I put my hand on his cheek and pulled him back to face me.

"I don't mind waiting, darling." I had to reassure him, to erase his deep worry. "As long as I know you care."

"But you see, I may have to go away. I owe the big boys over two thousand dollars. And they don't play."

My God. The mob. I read the papers and had seen enough movies to know they'd take him for a ride and blow his brains out.

"Where would you go?" Anything but to see him killed.

"I used to work for some white folks in Shreveport. Rich ones. I telephoned them and asked for a loan. They said all right, but the wife said I'd have to come back to work for them. Old hot-tailed bitch. I know what she wants."

"What does she want?" I knew and hated her immediately.

"She nearly got me lynched. Says she's in love with me and don't care who knows it. You know how Southern women are."

I didn't know about the women, but I knew L.D. was the greatest lover in the world and if white men were as sad as I'd heard, I could believe the old bitch was in love with him.

"How old is she?"

"Be about twenty-five now, I guess. I haven't seen her for three years."

Old? I thought he had meant wrinkled, yellow-fingernailed old. Why, that bitch probably tried to make him enjoy having sex with her. She probably wriggled and moaned under him just as I did.

"You can't go back there, L.D. You might get killed."

"I've got to do something. This is the time I need a good woman." He had leaned back against the door.

"But I'm a woman, L.D."

"You're a little girl. Sweet as sugar, but a little girl. I mean somebody who can make some money, and in a hurry."

My salary was sixty a week and I paid twenty for the babysitter, fifteen for my room, five extra for the baby's milk and laundry. I had the right to take all my meals in the restaurant and that would save cutting into the twenty left. I had enough clothes, thanks to L.D. but what good was twenty dollars against five thousand?

"When Head Up had a little trouble with the Big Boys last month, his wife went to a house in Santa Barbara and made five hundred dollars the first week. In a month he was clear."

"Doing what?"

He still thought I was a square. "But I don't know if I could let anybody I love do that kind of business. I don't think my life is worth a nice woman, my woman, giving up that much of herself."

"L.D., if a woman loves a man, there is nothing too precious for her to sacrifice and nothing too much for him to ask." I had to make him know that I was as capable of doing him a favor as his aging wife. He said nothing.

"Love is blind and hides a multitude of faults. I know what you're talking about, and prostitution is like beauty. It is in the eye of the beholder. There are married women who are more whorish than a street prostitute because they have sold their bodies for marriage licenses, and there are some women who sleep with men for money who have great integrity because they are doing it for a purpose."

"Do you really think that, baby?" His face was beginning to look better.

"Yes, and I'd do it to help you."

He leaned forward and folded me in his arms.

"You sweet child. No, that's wrong. Sweet woman." He pulled away and saw the tears sliding down my face. "What's that for? I didn't ask you to do anything."

"No, I'm just crying out of joy. That you'll let me help you."

"I heard of women like you, but I never thought I'd have one to call my own. My own." He patted me and kissed away my tears.

"Clara. You remember Clara? I think she took to you. I would trust her with you. Clara runs a straight house. No three-way girls and no freak parties." His voice ordered angrily, "I don't want you to get in no freak parties, you understand?"

"Yes, Lou, I understand."

"When this is all over, I want us to be able to get married and I don't want you remembering nothing that I don't do to you. I always want to be able to make you happy, I want you to keep on being my little Bobby Sock Baby."

27

"You sure are starting at a good time. The radio said rain today."

I sat in an uncomfortable chair and watched the two women.

Clara looked up at me and explained, "Tricks walk in the rain." She laughed. "I'm sure I don't know why. If I was them, I'd rather stay in my own bed." She laughed again. "By myself." Chuckle.

Bea's voice interrupted Clara's amusement. "Goddam. Don't say nothing like that, you'll put the bad mouth on the day. I want to be in bed with ten tricks by noon. It's already nine o'clock and I haven't even broke luck yet."

Carefully applied make-up did not disguise the woman's hard features. When I met her the night before, I had decided she wasn't nearly as nice as Clara, and although I would work with her, we'd never become friends.

"New girl gets to break luck." Clara laid on a little authority. "You know how it goes."

The language was new but its meaning was clear, and I wanted above all things not to appear stupid and not to display my immoblizing nervousness. I tried to concentrate on what the women were doing. Their fingers darted making knots in long strings of heavy white twine.

Bea looked up at me, disdain a mist across her face. "You a cherry, ain't you?"

"Yes." Lying would get me nothing.

"Well, that's a thirty-second business. When you turn the first trick, you'll be a 'ho. A stone 'ho. I mean for life." She grinned sourer than a rotten lemon, but her make-up and jewelry and air of abandoned sex gave her a glint of glamour.

Clara wedged in a peacemaker's tone, "Well, that won't be so bad will it? I mean you're a whore."

"Hell, yes, I'm a damn good one. I'm a mud kicker. In the streets I make more money by accident than most bitches make on purpose." She rolled her head and twisted her body. "And it's more action, too. I mean the lights and tricking all night till the sun comes up."

I wondered why she left the streets.

"I just got too hot. I was getting busted two, three times a week. So my daddy brought me down to this crib. Let the heat get off. Then I'll be back switching and bitching and getting merry like Christmas."

They both stood up and shook out strings in their hands. Clara walked to the living-room door and attached two strings to tacks over the lintel. She took matches from her robe pocket and lighted the ends that swung lazily near the floor.

"You burn string in the morning for luck, Rita. When it reaches the first knot the tricks begin to walk."

Bea had left the room to place string over the other doors. Clara went back to her uneasy chair.

"Now, Rita, let's have a little talk. You were so tired when L.D. brought you in last night, I thought I'd wait till morning to tell you how I run this place." I pulled my attention from the little red mouths that were nibbling up the string.

"L.D. said your work name was Sugar. I think that goes with you. You so young and quiet. Now, here's how it goes. In your room you have a tablet, and when you take a trick he pays me; and after, I sign your book. If you didn't have a man of your own, I'd give you your money at the end of the day and you could leave. But what'll happen is, at the end of the week Lou will come and I'll give it to him. He'll straighten out your bills, room rent, board and liquor." She caught herself. "'Course you don't drink and soft drinks are free. Then you get your day off and get to stay all night with your man."

"All my tricks are Mexican. They're fast but not too clean. Each girl has her own trick pan and towels. You wash them first and after. Then you take fresh water and wash yourself good. Since you're a cherry, I have to tell you Mexicans aren't built very large, but don't open your legs wide. They are tricks, not your old man, so don't try making love to them. That's why they call them tricks."

Clara's superstition about the burning string had already disenchanted me, and her conversation on deception of customers erased any respect I had for her. The only way I could be in the business was to give due service for the money paid. I decided privately that I would make each trick (each man) happy and forget the unbearable loneliness that sent him out in the rain searching for love.

"They walk in here," she continued, "and take their choice of you or Bea. L.D. said you shouldn't use make-up and ought to keep on wearing those junie flip clothes. That's all right with me. When you get regulars, Bea is not allowed to pull them, unless you're busy and they can't wait. That's the same with her steadies. Anything you want to know, ask me."

The doorbell rang.

"See, Rita! Look at the string." The red dot had reached a knot on one of the strings. "Trick time."

Bea came running into the room, and the sound of her footsteps was a little more audible than my heartbeat. The moment of truth had gotten stuck in my throat and saliva refused to go around it.

Clara went to open the door.

"Hello, Papa, come in. I've got something special for you today." She stage-whispered, "A school girl."

My God, she was lying. I was already going to be a whore. Take this man's hard-earned money, go to bed with him without love. Why add lying to it?

They came in view. Clara had her arm around the shoulders of a short little fat man who wore matching gray khaki pants and shirt. He looked Indian.

"Sugar, come over and say hello to Papa Pedro."

I walked over as if I were being introduced in my mother's living room.

"*Buenos dias, Señor Pedro.*"

His eyes left my flat chest and narrow hips. "*Oh. Hablas español?*"

My mind flinched at his use of the familiar. It should only be used between family members, close friends and lovers, according to my high school teacher.

"*Si. Yo lp puedo hablar.*"

"Okay, Sugar. Take him in the back and show him a good time."

Bea's voice hacked through from the corner. "Yea, Pedro. If she don't give you enough, you can see me after. Remember the last time?"

His glance didn't stay two seconds in her direction.

Clara took us both by the hand. "Come on, you two. You're wasting time." And drew us to my bedroom door. "Get in there and have fun."

I found my voice. *"Viene con migo, señor."*

He stood in the middle of the floor, looking like a bemused Akim Tamiroff. I had to say something but didn't know how to say "take you clothes off" in Spanish, so I asked how he was. He said well. I pulled off all my clothes during the long pause and he opened his pants. Dignity rode his face bareback.

I washed him and all I remember of my first great slide down into the slimy world of mortal sin is the scratching of the man's zipper on my upper thighs.

At sundown Bea washed her face and spent a few minutes in Clara's bedroom. She came out clicking her purse shut.

"I'm nearly shamed to show this little money to my daddy. I've spoiled that man." She looked at me, and without the cosmetic she was ten years younger. "How you feel?"

I didn't know how I felt. I said, "All right, thank you."

"Clara, you ought to get the news over to the camp. Tell them that you got a cherry. Maybe that'll stir up some tricks." She walked to the door, shaking her hips from side to side. "You won't be a cherry long, little girl. Better git it while the gittin's good. See you all in the morning." She slammed the door behind her.

Clara followed and snapped a double lock, then drew a chain across the door.

"Sugar, you better take a long bath. Put some Epsom salts in the water. Take out the soreness."

I said nothing because I thought nothing.

"Don't worry, you didn't do so good today, but then, you're just starting. I'll give you a few tips. Don't take off all your clothes. It takes too long. And remember, the men come here to trick, not to get married. Talk to them dirty but soft. And play with them."

She hmphed to herself.

"You got it easy. I was turned out with white men. They want to talk all the time. They tell you how beautiful you are and how much they love you. And wonder what you're doing being a whore all the time they're jugging in you and paying for it. Then when they get finished they got the nerve to ask you how you liked it. And talk about your freaks! White men can really think of some nasty things to do."

She started to her room and turned. "One thing I can say about my daddy"—her lips prissed and she lifted her nose and wiggled it—"he doesn't want me to do anything freakish. No matter how much money is involved. I like that." She rubbed her hands down her sides complimenting herself. "Better get your bath. Dinner'll be ready soon."

I sat thinking about the spent day. The faces, bodies and smells of the tricks made an unending paisley pattern in my mind. Except for the Tamiroffish first customer, the others had no individual characteristics. The strong Lysol washing water stung my eyes and a film of the vapor coated my adenoids.

I had expected the loud screams of total orgasmic release and felt terribly inadequate when the men had finished with grunts and yanked up their pants without thanks. I decided that being black, I had a different rhythm from the Latinos and all I had to do was let myself learn their tempos.

Clara gave me salts and bath oil and I continued examining the day in fingernailfuls. I was intelligent and I was young. I could teach myself the craft and make loads of money. L.D. might be able to settle his debts before the month was up.

The woman who came in daily at five o'clock to cook reminded me of my grandmother and I had to avert my eyes when she placed dinner on the table.

I reassured myself. I was helping my man. And, after all, there was nothing wrong with sex. I had no need for shame. Society dictated that sex was only licensed by marriage documents. Well, I didn't agree with that. Society is a conglomerate of human beings, and that's just what I was. A human being.

For the next week I vied with Bea for the attentions of Pedros, Josés, Pablos and Ramóns. I brushed up on my Spanish and tried with little success to include *tú* in my enticing come-ons. The women's conversations interested me more than the tricks' visits. Men came to Clara's house singly, and rather than having an air of celebration, they all seemed to be ashamed of their own presence and at the same time resigned to be there. I never found one man who considered how I might or might not enjoy those three-minute sojourns in the cell-like room. And for my part, I accepted Clara's signature on my tablet as a symbol of being paid in full.

Bea made an attempt at friendliness one morning. She came into the house early and settled on a stiff chair opposite me.

"Sugar, how do you like it?"

Her voice was kinder than usual, which surprised me, and as I had no ready answer, I muttered, "Well, it's...a new—"

"New? Screwing ain't new, is it?" She slipped back into sarcasm easily.

"No. That's not what I meant."

"Well, don't worry about it. You'll break in."

"I won't be doing this long." I had to separate myself from the insinuation.

"Like hell. Wait till you make a nice piece of money. Then your daddy will give you a little white girl."

"A what? What would I do with a white girl?"

She laughed a tight little laugh. "Not 'a' white girl. You don't know what 'white girl' is?"

"I don't know' what you mean." I was trying to withdraw.

"They call cocaine 'white girl.' Some people call horse 'white girl,' too. I don't mess with heroin, though. It makes me sick. But wait till your daddy gives you some coke. Kiss the baby!" Hugging herself, she coasted away for a second on her thought.

I wouldn't tell her that L.D. didn't even want me to smoke pot, but she seemed to pick the thought out of my mind.

"They won't let you smoke hemp, though. They say it makes a 'ho too frisky. 'Hos get their heads bad and forget about tending to business."

Clara came in bringing coffee, and Bea plunged into conversation with her.

"You know what we did last night? Daddy took me down to a gambling game in Firebaugh... You know who I saw?... Haven't seen that bitch in a month of Sundays..."

I didn't know the people she was talking about and couldn't have cared less what she did the night before, but she had given me something to think about. Since she spoke from experience, she was probably right. But she was talking about pimps and I knew L.D. wasn't a pimp. He was a gambler. I couldn't allow myself to entertain corrosive thoughts. All I had to do was do my best to help him and keep my thoughts clear and unpolluted. I decided I wouldn't even mention the conversation to L.D.

In the long waits between customers, Bea and Clara talked about money, their old men, other whorehouses and their old men and travel to nearby towns and their old men. They both called their men "Daddy," and when speaking of them even when relating the beatings they had received from "Daddy," their voices tightened into lurid imitations of baby talk. Their faces softened and their lips pouted (Clara could wrinkle her nose and wiggle it like a bunny).

I wondered if prostitutes as one suffered from an Electra complex and were motivated by a need to have a daddy, please a daddy and finally make love to a daddy.

"My daddy said he's going to take me to Hot Springs 'for the season.'" Bea sat in her chair by the door and shook her delight.

"Daddy and I went to the Kentucky Derby last year. We had a ball." Clara began to shake her nose. "Everybody was there. I met sports from New York City and Detroit and Chicago."

"My daddy says those Eastern pimps are colder than a whore's heart in Nome. I believe him too. Look at their faces. They chilly. If they don't kill their whores, they make them wish they were dead."

"Well, my daddy didn't never hit me except when I needed it. Oh, he whip my ass then. Better believe it. But no scars. He ain't never left a scar on me."

Bea grinned as if she had outwitted the men. "They ain't crazy. They wouldn't hurt their little moneymakers."

Their conversations were tightly choreographed measures, and since I didn't know the steps, I sat on the sidelines and watched. They would hardly be interested in my dance career, or my son, or the books I'd read. And I flatly, on principle, refused to call L.D. "Daddy." I mean, I protested to myself, my father, Bailey Johnson, Sr., was in San Diego, posturing and er'rering his pretentious butt off. Daddy Clidell was my one-time stepfather, but he and Mother had signed divorce papers. Mother's men, whom I had called Daddy Jack, Uncle Bob or Hanover Daddy, came and went with such regularity that whatever name I tacked on after the paternal title escaped me after a few months. I decided I wouldn't discuss L.D. at all. They were too cynical to understand that we were in love and that after I had helped him out of trouble, after he had a divorce, we were going to be married and live in a dream house with my son and lots of flowers. I would not share my plan with hard-hearted whores.

Despite my youth and high school clothes and stilted Spanish, I wasn't popular at Clara's. The men preferred Bea. She had a swing to her hips and a knowing smile that I couldn't imitate. Then, Mexican farm workers obviously had no erotic fantasies starring black teenage girls; they came to a whorehouse for a whore, and Bea answered their needs.

"Have a good time, you all." Clara waved to L.D. and me from the steps. He didn't acknowledge her but I turned and waved.

In the car he wore the same sour face he'd had when he returned from talking with Clara in her bedroom. Fear that he didn't love me any more iced my bare arms. When I first went to Clara's he had assured me, "Don't worry about going to bed with other men. It'll just make me love you more. You're doing it to help Daddy." He hugged me too. Now I remembered and supposed he had thought so at the time. But when face to face with the reality, he found me disgusting. For the first time since I went to Clara's, I began to feel unclean. I was Lady Macbeth. All the waters in the world wouldn't wash away the fingerprints of the men who had mauled me. I had been stupid to let him talk me into doing something that would turn him from me. He needed love. He needed a good woman to love him, especially now while he was in trouble with the big boys. But instead of using the brain I was inordinately proud of, I had let him down. His life was so unstable (the big diamond ring and expensive car were symbols of insecurity), and when I had a chance to introduce some order into his world I had fluffed it. It was clear I'd never see him again, since waves of hate radiated from him as rhythmically as the heat trembled up from the highway. We rode in silence until we reached Stockton.

"Where do you want to go?" His question popped like a whip.

"To pick up the baby."

The steering wheel almost came off in his hand.

When he parked the car, he made no move toward getting out, so I opened my door and had to ask, "Will you take us for a ride?"

"Close the door, Rita. I better talk to you."

Now it would come. The bad words, the insults, and all rightly placed. I closed the door.

"I talked to Clara. And there wasn't hardly any money at all. I don't think you tried."

"L.D., I did. I tried with all my heart." Relief flooded my brain. If that was all he worried about.

"Clara says you sit around like a judge, never saying anything to them. And that you talk to the tricks in Spanish like a goddam schoolteacher."

"L.D., I'm sorry. I just don't know what to do. But I promise, I'll try harder. Don't be angry, Lou."

"Another thing, you haven't called me Daddy. All the—I'm supposed to be your daddy." He was fierce suddenly. "Remember that."

I said, "Yes, Daddy," and hated it. Later on I'd be able to tell him the Electra story and explain why I hated my own father, and expand my theory about prostitutes and their men. I knew he wouldn't appreciate being thought a pimp and we'd be able to lose "Daddy" from our vocabulary, unless he allowed my son the right to so address him.

"I can't take you all out today, but here, pay the woman, and here's ten dollars. You all go to a picture show, but don't keep him all night. Take him back to her and I'll come over to your place this evening."

"Yes, Lou." He wasn't angry any longer.

"Daddy?" he prompted.

"Daddy." I smiled and bided my time.

28

My baby's joy at seeing me instantly erased the odor of disinfectant that had clung to the lining of my nostrils. Clara's house and its inhabitants and its visitors were a puff of smoke sliding behind the farthest hill. I paid Big Mary, and gave no answers to her blunt questions about my new job.

I gathered my son in my arms, and told Mary I'd bring him back in the early evening.

"Ain't you got time for him to spend one night with you? How come you all of a sudden so busy?"

I couldn't explain the tenderness of a great love. And under no pressures could I confide to her the month I planned to spend at Clara's. She'd simply make the common moral judgment, totally missing the finer point of sacrifice and purpose.

The baby, beautiful as a China doll, chattered all the way to the movie, in the movie house and all the way back to my room. He had picked up Big Mary's run-over-shoes accent. I kept repeating the proper pronunciations as he dropped past tenses and plurals. L.D. was right. I had to try harder. My son needed to be with me. I would read to him every day and get the long-playing albums for children of "The Little Prince" and "The Ugly Duckling."

I turned down the path leading to my house, my arms numb to aching with the weight of my son.

"Home, James."

"My name ain't no James."

"My name isn't James."

"No. Yo' name Mother."

"Your name is Mother."

"No, my name ain't no Mother."

When I tried to put him down he folded his legs up under his body and held on to my neck.

"I'm not going to leave you." His heart was thudding on my shoulder, so I carried him into the house.

"Rita." The landlord met me in the hall. "You got lots of long-distance phone calls. From San Francisco. You better call home."

I forced the baby's legs and arms from my side and put him on the floor. He set up an alarm of screaming and I stood at the pay phone waiting for someone to answer.

Papa Ford accepted my collect call. "Girl, I been trying to get you."

Maybe Mother's aim had been good to the extreme and the bail bondsman's magic wouldn't work. I would be very little help, with my own man in trouble at the same time. Of course, there was no contest. Mother came first.

"Your mother's in the hospital."

My Lord. For once she wasn't quick enough. "For what? And how is she?" My calm voice was a lie.

"Operation. Pretty goddam serious. She keeps asking for you. You'd better come home."

I took my son back to Big Mary and told her I had to leave town for a few days. Baxters never tell family business to outsiders, so I left her with no explanation, and my son screaming his motherlessness out, shut up in a back room.

I thought about L.D., but I had no phone number for him, so I asked the landlord to tell him that I had to go to San Francisco... trouble in the family.

I turned my thoughts with the Greyhound, toward San Francisco.

My mother's head dipped into the pillow like a yellow rose embedded in a pan of ice. Her forefinger stood sentinel over her red lips.

"Sh. Bailey's over there." A small figure, semaphored on a chaise longue in the corner of the hospital room.

"Eunice died today. He's completely broken up. Today is their one-year anniversary. I got a sedative for him, so he's been asleep for an hour."

Her face and voice showed the strain of worry and illness. "How are you?"

She dismissed her illness. "Just a female operation. The things I had removed have been used and I wouldn't be needing them again." She still whispered. "I'm glad you came home, though. Bailey needs us. I don't think he'll pull through without one of us around. And I'm going to be in the hospital at least a week. Can you take off from your job?"

"Yes." Sure could.

"Try and wake Bailey up and take him to the house. Have you got somebody good taking care of the baby?"

"Yes, Mother."

"And make him something hot. He hasn't eaten all day. Remember, he's the only brother you've got."

I sat on the seat beside my only brother and gently shook him. He came out of sleep reluctantly. I called his name and he opened his eyes, sat up, looked around. His eyes found Mother, examined the room, came back to me, stunned. He couldn't grasp who he was or where he was.

"My?" His childhood name for me was nearly a cry. His eyes knew something was very wrong, but for the first seconds couldn't remember. The recall split his face open and tears poured down his cheeks.

"Oh my God, My. My. It's Eunice. They've... oh, My."

I took him in my arms and cradle-rocked his body. The sounds of Mother's crying mingled with his muffled moans.

"Let's go home, Bail. Let's just get to the house and we can talk. Let's go home, Bail."

He was eight years old again and trusting. His big wet black eyes looked at me wanting to believe I could do something for his grief. I knew I had no magic, when he most needed me.

"Let's go home, Bail." I could hide the shame of my inadequacy in a skillet, and drown out his sobs in the rattle of pans.

We hugged Mother and they cried together for a moment, but he freed himself without my prodding and came with me to the old high-ceilinged house as obedient as a penitent child.

Grief works its way on people differently. Some sulk, or become morose, or weep and scream a vengeance at the gods. Bailey cried for two hours, unintelligible human sounds growled and gurgled from his throat. Then his face was dry. All tears wasted. And he began to talk.

He ate the food I gave him, automatically, greedily, never stopping or slowing the string of chatter that ran from his mouth.

He told me about Eunice's illness, double pneumonia and tuberculosis, the details of her treatment. The small talk of their sickroom visits. His voice didn't lower and become dramatic when he related how she began to fail. He spoke of the nurse, new on the floor, who barred his way to Eunice's room. "Mrs. Johnson? Mrs. Johnson? Oh, she died this morning. They've taken her away."

He rattled about his new tennis rackets and the better courts in San Francisco. The Southern Pacific dining cars and how hot Arizona was.

I let him talk and didn't try to answer. By morning he began to run down and finally noticed that he was repeating himself. "Oh, My, I told you about that, didn't I?" He drew words around as protection against his news. I gave him a sleeping pill.

"My, you're not leaving me, are you?"

"No."

He balled himself up in Mother's bed and was asleep in minutes.

I awakened to the splash of water and the sound of Bailey singing in the bathroom.

"Jelly, Jelly, Jelly, Jelly stays on my mi-i-nd." He could imitate the bass baritone of Billy Eckstine.

"Jelly Roll killed my pappy, and ran my mammy stone blind."

His voice rolled over joyously in waves. My instant response of elation lasted seconds. He couldn't have made such a quick adjustment. I joined Papa at the kitchen table and waited.

"Hey, Maya. Fresh coffee? Good morning, Papa Ford." His face was no wider than my outstretched hand, and the usual rich brown color was dusty like an old chocolate bar exposed to the light. A smile struggled free and limped across his lips.

"Boy, I sure was upset last night. I hope I didn't worry you too much. And Mom. Goddam, that was inconsiderate of me to go to her hospital room screaming and crying."

"It wasn't inconsiderate, Bail, you were upset. You went to your mother. Where else could you go?"

"Yes, but she's sick herself. And, after all, I'm a man. A man. A man takes his knocks. He doesn't go running to his mother."

He poured coffee and drank standing, refusing the chair I pulled out for him.

"Shall I make breakfast for you?" His grin was a little scary, something more that impish, and not yet satanic. "I've learned how to make Eggs Benedict." He turned to Papa.

"Papa, can you make Eggs Benedict? That's what rich white people eat."

Papa growled, "I never cooked for white folks, rich or not."

Bailey poked in the refrigerator, and took out eggs and bacon. He nearly ran to the kitchen closet and was back in a flash with pots, pans, skillets.

"I'll cook for you, Bailey." Not knowing how to console him. "I think you need turkey and ham for Eggs Benedict."

He turned on me in red anger. "Will you please leave me alone? I'm no fucking invalid. I wasn't the one who died, you know."

I liked it better when he cried. I could pet him and talk softly and feel as if I were effectively coping with his grief.

"I'm Cuban Pete." He started singing in a bad Latin accent, "Oh, I'm Cuban Pete." He Cesar Romeroed around the table, to the sink, over to the stove, his grin awful. In a few minutes he placed burned bacon, scrambled eggs and lopsided stacks of hot cakes on the table.

"Get your own silverware. I'm the chef, I'm not the waiter." He straightened up the pancakes with his hands and broke off the ragged edges, trying desperately to make them uniform.

"Sit down, I'll get your plate, Bailey."

"I'm not going to eat right now. But you all enjoy yourself. *Bon appétit.*" He walked out of the kitchen. "I want to hear some music."

In moments, the sound of water splashing in the bathtub mixed with Lester Young's mellow sax reached the kitchen.

Papa Ford frowned. "He's had one bath today, ain't he? He ain't dirty enough for two baths."

"There's nothing wrong with him. He's just nervous." I slammed the sentence out, a barrier against further conversation.

In two days Bailey lost pounds from his already skinny frame and gained in degrees of deception.

Only once did we speak of Eunice.

"If I could have afforded it, I'd have taken her out of San Francisco General and put her in St. Joseph's. People lie who say you die when it's your time to die." He quoted Robert Benton, his favorite at the time. "Hate can be legislated too."

He opened his face by dint of will. "My, I want a favor."

"Anything."

"Eunice's funeral is tomorrow. After that, I never want to hear her name again." He waited.

"All right, Bailey."

"Thank you, My." He closed in upon himself and smiled the new grimace. I lost part of my brother forever.

I didn't report to Mother that the next morning he put on fresh white tennis shorts and shirt, thick white socks and tennis shoes, and walked into the church carrying his new tennis racket.

Papa Ford frowned his disapproval. "Your brother sounds crazy to me. He said he's going to quit his job. This ain't no time to leave the road. Get his meals free. Tips. He can bring home butter and stuff, can't he? Nigger men ain't got but two outs now, as I see it. Keep on sleeping with Old Lady Southern Pacific, or start sleeping in the streets." He smirked. "And he crazy, but he ain't crazy enough for the streets. Shit. He remind me of them Jew boys. He's smart like them. But them Jew boys git some backing to open up some kind of little business. That's how they get their start. Any kind of business he try to start going to be against the law, and he have to be sharper than mosquito shit, too. Keep out of jail. He better stay on the road."

Bailey started staying out all night long, and when he came in, his eyelids were puffy and his movements slow. He walked in pushing before him an odor of unwashed clothes. His eyes were half shut on his secrets. In the afternoons Bobby Wentworth, a former schoolmate now unrecognizable in his thinness and color change, came to the house. He went into Bailey's bedroom walking like a defeated old man and closed the door.

One morning I stood in his empty room over the unmade bed and wondered how I could save my brother. If L.D. and I married soon, he would get us a house large enough for Bailey to have a room. I would nurse him back to health and buy him books and records. Maybe he'd like to go back to school and study law. With his quick brain and silver tongue, he'd be an ace criminal lawyer.

I thought of Grandmother Henderson, who prayed every tribulation into manageable size. I prayed.

Around noon Bailey came home, the unslept night dragging his shoulders down.

I faced him in the hall. "Bailey, what's the matter with Little Bobby?"

His tired face tried to shut me out. "Nothing's the matter with him. Why?"

"He's about the color of mustard and he's got so thin."

"He's just getting down to his fighting weight. Anyway, when are you going back to Stockton? How long can you take off from your job?"

I wasn't sure how much I should tell him. "I'll stay till Mother comes out of the hospital."

"Why?"

"Well, you... I mean, I want to be with you."

"I don't need anything. I have told you I'm not an invalid. You'd better get back to Stockton and take care of your own business." It was an order.

I wanted to be sure about his future before I left. "Papa Ford says you're going to quit your job."

"Not going to. I did."

"But what will you do? To live?"

"I'll live." He wasn't bragging, just making a statement.

"But, Bailey, it pays well, doesn't it? I mean, pretty well."

"You're not the one to talk to me about slinging hash. You might be a fry cook the rest of your life, if you're that stupid, but not me."

I refused to bear the insult. "I'm not cooking now, if you want to know. I'm working in a house on the outskirts of Sacramento."

"A what?" He sat up and leaned over to me. "Doing what?"

I knew I had gone too far. I was a boulder rolling down a steep hill and couldn't stop myself.

"What do women do in houses?" The best defense was to be uppity.

"You goddam silly ass. You silly little ass. Turning tricks, huh? My baby goddam sister."

His new temper was cold and sneering. His rages used to be full of fire and crackling; now his diction sharpened and his neck was stiff and he looked down his nose at me. "Who is the nigger?"

296

"Bailey, it's not like you think."

"Who is the smartass nigger who turned you out?"

"Bailey, he's in trouble and I'm just helping him for a month."

"What's his name?" Although he continued sneering he seemed to thaw a little. "Tell me his name."

"L.D. Tolbrook. And he's old."

"How old?"

"About forty-five."

"What kind of drugs has he given you?"

"You don't understand. He's even stopped me from smoking pot. He's straight and—"

"No pot? Then it's a matter of time before he gives you a noseful of cocaine."

"Bailey." I couldn't bear Bailey's thinking evil about L.D. "He's a... He's a gambler and he's in trouble with the big boys. So I offered to help him for a month, then we're going to be married."

He leaned into me and spoke gray steel, "You're not going to get married."

"Yes, I am. Yes..."

"I'll tell you what you're going to do. You are going to go to Stockton and get your baby. Then you're going to find L.D. You're going to tell him he's not to worry about the big boys any more. That he can start worrying about one little boy. Just one. And tell him how little I am. Also tell him that you are my baby goddam sister. Then you're going to get back on the bus and come home. Is that clear, Marguerite?"

I knew the old Bailey could be as violent as Mother, and this new one seemed even more lethal.

"Clear?"

"Yes." That was all I could say. When I arrived in Stockton, I could explain to L.D. that Bailey had misunderstood everything, so for a while I'd go back to San Francisco. When Bailey cooled down, I'd return to him. My absence would make him fonder and I'd have more chance to help my brother pull himself together.

Bailey gave me money for the round trip, and to pay the baby-sitter. I took the afternoon bus to Stockton.

29

Big Mary's house was near the corner of a typical small-town block, and in the late-afternoon sun the clapboard cottages seemed to be dreaming. I concluded that I must have passed the house when I reached the farthest intersection. My mind was busy with other things, so when I turned and didn't see the house, I decided I was on the wrong street. Another glance at the street names on a sign post assured me that this was the street. Then where was the house? I started back. Here was the little white railroad house. Here was the house with a fenced yard. Here was... but it couldn't be Mary's house. The windows were boarded up and large planks had been nailed in an X across the door.

The two houses flanking Big Mary's were empty. I might have stopped breathing as I walked up and down the creaking steps and tried to peer into windows. The world had suddenly spun off its familiar axis and the rhythm of life slowed to quarter time. The streets and houses, broken toys that lay in overgrown weeds, were monotone in color like objects in an old sepia photograph.

"Who you looking for?"

I turned to face a woman on a porch across the street. Time was in such strange process that I had the opportunity to examine her in minute point. She was fat and white and wore a flowery loose housecoat. From a distance I made out her friendly countenance and the sweat that already dampened semicircles under her arms.

"My baby." But the words wouldn't come. I tried again and the words refused again. I had become paralyzed, literally struck dumb. I stared at the woman in horror.

"Come over here, lady."

She ordered and I had no resistance.

"I know you're looking for Big Mary, aren't you?"

I nodded.

"She moved three days ago. A big truck pulled up and took everything away."

She must have waited for me to question her. After seconds, she continued, "You're the mother, aren't you?"

I nodded.

"There was a big coming and going of the other parents, but I noticed you didn't come for your little boy. Mary and I haven't spoken since she called me a meddling bitch three years ago—she used foul language. But I broke the silence and asked where she was taking the boy. She said you had given him to her. Said you were too busy. I asked where she was going and she told me none of my business. But I know she's got a brother in Bakersfield."

It was a rattling tale told on a radio and I couldn't make it have to do with my life.

"If you want to call the police, come in. I'll give you some lemonade... while you're waiting for them."

The word "police" shook me awake. My brain moved sluggishly. Big Mary had left with my baby and lied as well. Then she kidnapped him. If the police came, they'd question me about my job. A whore (well, I had to admit it) wasn't a fit mother and they'd take him from me and put me in jail.

"I'll call them for you." The woman turned and an oblong of perspiration was dripping down the back of her dress.

Before she reached the door, I forced my voice out. "No thank you. I know where she is, everything's all right."

"Where is he?" The woman's suspicion was nasty.

"I'm going there now. It's over on the south side. By the sloughs." I waved at her. "Thanks anyway," I said and marched down the street.

L.D.'s car was parked in front of his house. My scheme was to ring his bell and if his wife answered, tell her I was an old friend and had a message for him from a friend. I'd quickly tell him about Big Mary and the baby and he'd decide what to do. I was proud that I hadn't cried and that I wasn't afraid of his naggish wife.

A pretty, thirtyish, light-brown-skinned woman opened the door. Her long black hair curled around her shoulders, reminding me of a beige Hedy Lamarr.

"You want to see L.D.? What's your name?"

She had the same soft slur that made me love to hear L.D. talk. "My name is Rita."

"Oh." Her lips firmed on the edge. "So you're Rita. Well, just wait a minute, I'll get Lou."

She closed the door and I waited on the landing, wondering how we'd find my baby.

"Rita." L.D. had opened the door and held it just wide enough for me to see half of his body. "What put it in your head to come to my house?"

I whispered, "I told her I was a friend, L.D. My baby's—"

"Don't you have better sense than to come to my house?"

"I need some help, L.D. I have to talk to you."

He stepped out on the porch and pulled the door closed behind him. His face was inches from me and he spoke through uneven teeth.

"Let me pull your coat, you silly little bitch. This is my house. No 'ho goes to a man's house. You talked to my wife. No 'ho opens her mouth to speak to a man's wife." He curled his mouth and snarled, "Clara's never even met my wife and Clara's been my woman three years. You've been gone a week and you got the nerve... Go to your place. I'll be there when I get time."

He walked back in the house and slammed the door.

I wanted desperately to cry.

I had been stupid, again. And stupidity had led me into a trap where I had lost my baby. I tried to erase L.D. Tolbrook from my mind. Obviously he wasn't very bright. He had had a good woman who would have done anything to help him. And he was too dumb to even have the courtesy to listen to my troubles. And he had lied to me by not telling me that Clara was his woman.

Pity. That he thought outsmarting a young girl, living off the wages of women was honorable. He obviously had been doing it for years. He probably started in the South with white women, thinking that by taking their bodies and their money, he was getting revenge on the white men, who were free to insult him, ignore him and keep him at the bottom of the heap.

Clara must have wriggled her nose off in laughing at my stupidity with her "daddy." And L.D.'s wife probably bought the white pique dress she wore with money I had made. I detested him for being a liar and a pimp, but more, I hated him for being such an idiot that he couldn't value my sterling attributes enough to keep me for himself alone.

There was no thought of the greed which coerced me to agree with L.D.'s plans in the hope that I'd win, in the end, a life of ease and romance. Like most young women, I wanted a man, any man, to give me a June Allyson screen-role life with sunken living room, and cashmere-sweater sets, and I, for one, obviously would have done anything to get that life.

I couldn't telephone Bailey or Mother. Even if they had been in the best of shape, I couldn't admit to them that out of ignorance I'd lost the baby.

As I walked, my rage at L.D. diminished and I regained some steadying peripheral vision. Had I melted down on the pavement in tears of frustration, the action would not have changed the fact that my baby was still missing. Or the fact that with this latest loss, I was shatteringly lonely for my baby and his arms hugging my neck. The weight was on me.

300

I decided to sleep the night in my old room and leave the next morning for Bakersfield. The idea that Big Mary might have taken him on to Oklahoma was squashed over and over in my mind like a buzzing fly.

The small Southern California town on those midnight rides with L.D. had seemed fanciful and unreal; now from the bus windows it was drab and seemed overpopulated with mean-faced whites straight out of my Arkansas past.

A black man gave me a ride to Cottonwood Road.

"If her brother is farming, he got to be living around here somewhere. And you say you don't know his name?"

"No, but I'll find him."

He stopped his old car in front of a café that claimed "Home Cooking."

"Well, I wish you Godspeed. Try in there. But be careful. These is some rough folks."

I thanked him and he drove away.

The young waitress shouted over the noisy jukebox and talk, "Anybody here know Mary Dawson?"

Conversation dimmed but no one answered.

She went on, "This woman's looking for her baby."

The Faces became friendlier, but still there were no answers.

"Nobody knows her, honey. Try down at Buckets." She directed me to a dirt-floor joint a couple of blocks away.

Old-timey blues whined in the artificial darkness, and one stout bartender walked up and down behind the bar setting up and taking away beer bottles. Every stool was taken by men and women who laughed and talked with the easy familiarity of regulars.

"Mary Dawson? Mary Dawson." The bartender digested the name as he filed my face in his memory bank. "Naw, baby, I don't know no Mary Dawson."

"They call her Big Mary."

"Big Mary. Naw, I don't know no Big Mary."

"She's got my baby. Took him away from Stockton." I felt as if I were blowing my breath against a tornado.

His face softened as suspicion left it. "What she look like?"

"She's as tall as I. As me"—"as I" sounded too dickty—"but bigger, and she has a brother who farms around here. They're from Oklahoma."

A little light winked in his eyes. "Does she drink?"

"Not often, but they say she drinks a lot when she does."

"In a coffee cup?" The smile was abundant.

301

"Yes." I wanted to hug him.

"That's old John Peterson's sister. Yeah, baby. He lives bout three miles from here."

In the past, whenever I had slipped free of Fate's pressing heel, I gave thanks. This time I promised God a regular church attendance.

"Can you direct me?"

"Aw, you can't walk it. Wait a minute."

He called to a man over at the jukebox. "Buddy."

The man turned and came over to the bar.

"Little lady, Buddy runs a cab service... Buddy, you know where John Peterson's place is?"

Buddy nodded.

"Take her out there, will you?"

Buddy nodded again.

"He'll treat you right, little lady, good luck."

I thanked the bartender and followed Buddy to a dilapidated car. He said nothing on the ride, but my heart beat so that I wouldn't have been able to answer in any case.

He stopped the car on a lonely road surrounded by overturned farmland. A graying clapboard house set deep in a plot of muddy ground.

Buddy nodded toward the house. "That's it. You want me to come back to get you?"

I looked at the house, which seemed left alone, and thought that maybe its occupants had gone to Oklahoma. Then I noticed some movement a few hundred yards from the house. I focused on the movement, trying to determine if the action was caused by a pet or farm animal rooting in the mud.

In a second, my heart squeezed and I screamed. "My baby! That's my baby." One thought shot my legs out of the car and in two steps I was ankle-deep in muck, a new thought sluicing in my mind. Where does he think his mother is?

I picked him up and pressed him close. I felt his body throb and pound with excitement. He stiffened his arms and pushed himself away to see my face. He kissed me and then started crying. The restraint which had held through the long night and the bus trip began to disintegrate. He took a fistful of my hair and twisted and pulled, crying all the time. I couldn't untangle the hair or pull my head away. I stood holding him while he raged at being abandoned. My sobs broke free on the waves of my first guilt. I had loved him and never considered that he was an entire person. Separate from my boundaries, I had not known before that he had and would have a life beyond being my son, my pretty baby, my cute doll, my charge. In

302

the plowed farmyard near Bakersfield, I began to understand that uniqueness of the person. He was three and I was nineteen, and never again would I think of him as a beautiful appendage of myself.

Big Mary leaned against the rickety kitchen table. "I didn't mean no harm. I just love him. I take good care of him. You know that."

Her big face crumbled like pastry dough and she trembled. "Why don't you let him stay with me awhile?"

She looked at Guy in my arms and her voice pinched into baby talk. "Pretty, don't you want to stay with Big Mary? Tell your momma you want to stay."

His arms scissored around my neck.

"I'm taking him, Mary."

She couldn't control the tears. "Can't you all stay one night—just one?"

"I have a taxi waiting." I started to the door.

"Well, wait and I'll get his things together."

"No, that's all right, we have to leave."

She made a lunge but stopped before she reached me.

"You don't hate me, do you, Rita? I pray God you don't hate me."

"I don't hate you, Mary."

"He was the prettiest of them all. And you was always going somewhere."

"I understand, Mary. Good-bye. Say good-bye, Guy."

"Good-bye."

Buddy took us to the bus station and my muddy baby and I headed for San Francisco again.

30

At home, life stumbled on. Mother was again in residence. The record player spun disks ceaselessly, cooking odors wafted through every room, and ice jiggled in glasses like snow bells.

Bailey had given up his apartment and had moved his belongings back into his old room. He told Mother he was job hunting, and paid her room rent "out of savings." He now wore one-button roll suits in dun and charcoal-gray; the modified pegged pants and colorful jerkins were given away. And his smiles were less frequent and different. When Papa Ford said something too ribald or old-fashioned, Bailey seemed not to notice. He never lifted his eyes to check with me, and the teasings about my height and arrogance had stopped.

Since I was job hunting too, I asked where he was looking and for what.

"In the streets. I'm looking for a bank roll, then I'm heading for New York City."

What could he do except wait tables and sing for the family's enjoyment?

"I can use my brain. I've told you 'all knowledge is spendable currency depending upon the market.' There's money to be had, and I intend to have some."

"Bailey, you're not going to pimp, are you?"

"Let me straighten you out. Pimps are men who hate women or fear them. I respect women, and how can I fear a woman when the baddest one I've ever heard of is my mother?"

He looked at me sharply. "And let me tell you another thing, a whore is the saddest and silliest broad walking. All she hopes is to beat somebody out of something, by lying down first and getting up last."

I didn't want to be included in that company, yet I had lived at Clara's.

"I'm not talking about you. There is such a thing as a whore mentality. You can find it in a housewife who will only go to bed with her husband if he buys a new washing machine. Or a secretary who'll sleep with the boss for a raise. Hell, you're both too smart and not smart enough to be a whore. Never. But I don't want you trying it again."

He was seven inches shorter and one year older than I, but as always, he had the last and loudest word. Afterward, as I thought about him, he became even larger in my mind.

He had endured the death of his love and was still going on. Certainly he was limping and using a crutch I didn't approve of, but he hadn't atrophied. He had plans for his future. I reasoned that hard drugs might not be as bad as the people who used them. It was possible that the dirty, ragged, smelly hypes, who were so frightening and repulsive, were naturally slouchy and low-class. There were probably many people who took drugs and never lowered their living standards. I knew from experience that weed wasn't dangerous, so it could follow that heroin and cocaine were victims of rumors spread by the self-righteous. Anyway, man had always needed something to help him through this vale of tears. Fermented berries, corn, rice and potatoes. Scotch or magic mushrooms. Why not the residue of poppies?

The maids and doormen, factory workers and janitors who were able to leave their ghetto homes and rub against the cold-shouldered white world, told themselves that things were not as bad as they seemed. They smiled a dishonest acceptance at their mean servitude and on Saturday night bought the most expensive liquor to drown their lie. Others, locked in the unending maze of having to laugh without humor and scratch without agitation, foisted their hopes on the Lord. They shouted loudly on Sunday morning at His goodness and spent the afternoon preparing the starched uniforms to meet a boss's unrelenting examination. The timorous and the frightened held tightly to their palliatives. I was neither timid nor afraid.

I applied for work along Fillmore Street. Neither the local beauty shop nor record store needed a manageress. The realtor said his friend, an Oakland businessman, wanted a cool-headed person to run his restaurant. I bristled with the big-city disdain for small towns; it was generally accepted in San Francisco that Oakland was placed on the other side of the Bay Bridge to accept snide remarks from city sophisticates. But the chance to rise in the business world to manageress was too tempting to ignore. I didn't entertain the thought that I wouldn't do the job well. After all, although my experience had not included managing a restaurant, I had successfully lived through some harrowing events and considered myself mature and adult enough for responsibility.

I took the train to Oakland.

James Cain was impressed with what he thought of as my college vocabulary, and the half-carat diamonds flashing in his two front teeth enchanted me. He didn't ask for references and offered seventy-five dollars a week and all my meals.

He was a large, gentle man who smiled a lot at life and kept all the details of his many business affairs in his head. He owned a dry cleaners, a shoe-repair shop, and next door to the restaurant, a gambling house. His clothes were tailor-made, and he wore them with a casual flair. If he had tightened his lips over the diamonds, and if he had lived in another world, he'd have passed for an erudite broker who regularly made killings on Wall Street.

"Cain's" served well-cooked Southern dishes in ample proportions and was popular with the area regulars. Cain had bought three unknown prize fighters and was pushing them toward championship. He wanted to upgrade the restaurant and extend dinner invitations to the successful white fight promoters he met at the gym.

He sat in a red leatherette booth and talked to me. "Ought to have a soup. And a salad. Ought to have a menu, too." When I went to

305

work for him, the day's choices were printed on a child's blackboard near the door.

NECK BONES
SHORT RIBS
HOG MAWS
PORK CHOP
RED SNAPPER

As determined as I was to make good at the job, I couldn't decide what soup or salad would complement those entrées. Soup had been for me, in my Southern youth, an entrée in itself, and salad was mostly potato or slaw. I suggested bouillon. Cain smiled at the sound and told the cook to fix it.

"Tossed salad. Roquefort dressing."

Cain gave the signal to the cook.

I also told him that I had seldom seen hog maws or neck bones featured in white cafés.

The chef was told to cut down on his orders.

"They eat a lot of omelettes, and liver and bacon. I would suggest you stock Chicken à la King."

Cain's keen intelligence had won for him the position of tycoon in Oakland, and he operated on the theory of an equal distribution of labor. He left the menu design and plan to me.

Within a month customers were delivered large menus which offered, in Old English print,

Chicken à la King
Irish Stew
Veal Cutlet
T-bone Steak
Peach Cobbler—Sweet Potato Pie
Ham Hocks and Mustard Greens (a sop which was always sold out an hour after opening)

As dining business slackened, I had the opportunity to examine the gamblers carefully. They straggled into the restaurant during the high California mornings, well-cut pants bagging away from their knees; hand-painted silk ties undone and hanging, flapping, forgotten, down their shirt fronts. When their hands shook coffee onto the tablecloths, the waiters brought fresh coffee without condemnation.

The winners and losers looked equally disordered but were distinguishable by their company. Beggars, grifters and petty losers hung on their words, pulled, chairs out for them, and shouted at slow-moving waiters for faster service.

The street women who met their men at the dining tables (Cain didn't allow hustling in the restaurant, and no women at all in the gambling room) were of particular interest to me. They came in tired, the night's glamour gone from their faces and the swing from their hips.

The men who drank whiskey for steadiness or diversion took their women's money in the open, counting it out bill by bill, then ordering a flunky to run to the liquor store and quickly bring "a taste." The women's faces surged with pride and defeat. They had proved they were successful and trustworthy whores, but they also knew the men would return to the gambling tables to chance the night's earnings, and the women would be sent home exhausted to empty beds.

A man who got his highs from heavier narcotics never treated his woman so carelessly. He would wait impatiently, drinking heavily sugared coffee. As soon as his woman passed the window, he stood up and paid the small check. The woman waited at the door and the couple walked away eagerly and together. I knew they were hurrying to the fix. I knew that the woman had already made the connection before she came to pick up her man. I knew, and could see nothing wrong. At least they were a couple and depended on each other.

Cain had little time to notice that all was not well at the restaurant, since he spent his days engrossed with his fighters. The operators of his cleaning shop and gambling house were hewing to the traditional lines, and their businesses were booming.

I had to speak to him.

"Mr. Cain, I'm afraid this month we, er, slid back a little."

He thought. "Lost money, huh?"

"Yes. Actually, the menu doesn't seem to appeal to the regulars and there aren't enough of the others to equalize the loss of patronage."

"I see what you mean." And he did. "Let's keep it like you got it for another month. Give those backward Negroes a chance for something better."

He tucked up a large fork of greens, and crumbled corn bread in the pot liquor. "Some people don't appreciate the better things in life."

The second month showed the restaurant deeper in the red, and although I brought Guy to the restaurant daily and fed him T-bone steak while I ate veal cutlet, the chef complained that his refrigerator was jammed with spoiled food.

Mr. Cain told me not to worry. "They scared to go down-town and eat, and when I bring them the same food to their own neighborhood

they won't even eat it. That's all right with me. I did my best." He told
the cook to clean out the refrigerator and go back to the old menu.

"Can you drive?"

"Yes."

"I want you to take the car and pick up my boxers in the mornings.
You drive them to Lake Merrit. They'll get out and run while you
follow them. When they go clear around the lake, you pick them up
and take them to the gym. Then you pick me up and I'll take you
home, then I'll go back to the gym."

Hooray! At last! A chauffeurette.

I guided the Cadillac slowly around the dark curves, and the sounds
of the three men panting mixed with the soft slaps of the waves. Two
boxers were large, muscular heavyweights who gave me unsmiling
grunts when I picked them up at the run-down hotel. They sat like
huge black monoliths in the back seat, while Billy, a cute little
flyweight, joked in the front seat with me.

"Baby, I'll burn 'em up... with the uppercut. I'll cut their flab... with
a little jab."

Billy reminded me of the old Bailey and I determined to see him
fight.

Cain bought me a brown suede suit, and a matching snapbrim hat.
My shoes, gloves and purse were suede, and I knew I was as sharp as
anyone had a right to be.

I sat up front with him and four other fat old men who smoked
cigars and passed fistfuls of money in the glaring lights. The whoosh
of sound in the auditorium, and the frenetic activity of people rising
and sitting, walking, running, the faces turning like cardboard
cutouts, made me think I had been stupid not to have attended a fight
before.

The lights dimmed and Billy in white shorts ran down an aisle
toward the arena. Another small boxer wearing black trunks kneed
his way through the ropes from another aisle.

I turned to Cain, who was negotiating money business with his
cronies.

"It's Billy. Why aren't you watching?"

He glanced up at the lighted square and turned back to the sheaf of
money in his hands.

He mumbled, "That's just the prelims."

The referee held up both men's hands, and the gong rang. The
boxers crouched with their arms tucked into their sides. They began
to inch a circle on the floor leaning in and over as if they were trying
to identify the different brands of aftershave lotion. Black Shorts, with
a rude immediacy, thrust his left fist into Billy's ribs.

308

Whump.

He withdrew, and while Billy was adjusting, shot his right fist against Billy's cheek.

My scream lofted high and made no indentation on the room's boisterousness.

Billy wobbled for a second, looking for a wall or shoulder to lean against.

"Hit him, Billy." I was standing and ready to climb in the ring.

Black Shorts bounded away and then moved in close. As if responding to a public announcement, the fight fans began to give their attention to the action. Their low thunder diminished and I could hear the boxers' feet sliding across the mat. *Sh-h-h, sh-h-h-whomp.* There is no sound in the world like that of a man storing his fist in the chest of another man. Lions may roar, and coyotes howl, but the vibrations of two human beings struggling for physical superiority introduced to me a nauseating and new terror.

Whump! Whomp! Sh! Sh! Sh! Ooo!

The breath was being pounded out of Billy's little body and I knew it could have been Bailey up there dancing his waltz under the cold eyes of gamblers.

"Stop them, Cain." I turned and leaned over my boss and Billy's owner.

He regarded me as if I were a stranger just gone mad before his eyes.

"What? What? Sit down and cool off." The edges of his teeth showed and his fat face glimmered in the dark.

"Stop them, I said. That man is beating Billy to death."

"Shut up." I was embarrassing him in front of his friends. "Shut up and sit down."

"You dog. You sadistic dog freak!" The words were accented by the *whomps* and *shs* from the ring. "Freak!" I screamed it and turned to run.

Cain grabbed at my arm but I had moved away. The other men were questioning:

"What's the matter with her?"

"She go crazy or what?"

Cain ordered, "Sit down, dizzy bitch."

I was nearly out into the aisle, but I turned and straddled a patron who was by now more interested in our row than in the public contest above.

"Marquis de Sade son of a bitch." I threw my suede purse at Cain and lifted a leg over the patron, freeing myself to reach the aisle. I ran up the corridor to the front door, expecting at any moment to be caught and dragged back to be forced to watch poor little Billy be whomped to death.

I paused to catch my breath and consider the number of pursuers on my trail. The divisions between the rows were empty and the faces, which I expected to have swiveled in my departing direction, still faced forward.

I noticed that the roar was growing and from where I stood I saw the figure in white shorts fold down, knees first, to the canvas. Black Shorts' feet might have been mired in concrete, he stood so certain.

Billy's head crashed forward and the audience screamed its approval. I was right and wrong. Cain was a sadistic bastard. But he wasn't alone. All the bloodthirsty fans were sadistic, too. And so was Billy.

I walked the streets to my house and comforted myself with the knowledge that although my brother was small and agile enough to be a featherweight fighter, no one would ever sit eating hot dogs while he was beaten to death. He shadow-boxed and danced down cruel streets, and his opponents made Black Shorts look less threatening than Papa Ford. I was proud that my brother was living a dangerous life and didn't bow his knee to a living soul.

I knew the job was gone, and even if an apology rectified things with Cain, I couldn't apologize. To hell with him, the job and the fighters. Hooray for my brother.

Cain's letter the next day was as stiff as a short jab: "Rita Johnson, your services will no longer be necessary."

I was in a state again that was blood line familiar. Up a tree, out on a limb, in a pickle, in a mess but I didn't pack my bags (or leave them) and go back to Mother.

Survival was all around me but it didn't take hold. Women nearly as young as I, with flocks of children, were creating their lives daily. A few hustled (I had obviously little aptitude for that); some worked as housemaids (becoming one of a strange white family was impossible. I would keep my negative Southern exposures to whites before me like a defensive hand); some wrestled with old lady Welfare (my neck wouldn't bend for that).

While the total trust of a child can mold a parent into a new form, Guy's big smile (Mother said he laughed an awful lot for a baby) and happy disposition lost its magic to make me happy. He believed in me, but he was a child and I had lost belief in myself.

My head stayed high from habit, but my last hope was gone. Every way out of the maze had proved to be a false exit. My once lively imagination would not come up with one more fantasy. My courage was dwindling. Unfortunately, fortitude was not like the color of my skin, given to me once and mine forever. It needed to be resurrected each morning and exercised painstakingly. It also had to be fed with at least a few triumphs. My strength had fallen away from me as the pert features fade from an aging beauty. I didn't drink and had run out of pot. For the first time in my life I sat down defenseless to await life's next assault.

31

I had often noticed Troubadour Martin at Cain's. He was extremely tall and dangerously thin. When I used to see him, he reminded me of the phrase often used to describe me, "A long drink of water." He came to my house a week after my job ran out. That was how I'd begun to think of it. His movements were slow and his speech a long time coming. We sat in my living room.

"Hello, Rita."

"Hi, Troub."

Pause.

"Heard you not working for Cain."

"No. The job ran out."

Wait.

"Well, you find anything yet?"

"No, I'm taking a rest."

Hesitation.

"Of course."

Delay.

"Maybe you can help me."

I demurred. This time I didn't intend to jump at the first persuasion. He was black and handsome, and when the light fell right across his face he looked like a thin Paul Robeson. I also knew he wasn't one of the men who sent out for drinks.

"Maybe you know I deal in clothes?"

I knew he was a gambler.

"No."

"I have a connection for ladies' dresses and suits. New." He shook his head before my question. "They're not hot. I run sort of like a catalog business. I'll tell you what I need. See, you won't have to do nothing. I'll bring the things, and ladies can come over here to try them on."

He smiled slowly, and dropped his eyes. I saw the Southern shyness of the man and knew the clothes were stolen.

311

"You know how you ladies are. Wouldn't like to undress unless there's another lady around."

I didn't know about that. I said nothing.

"And you don't have to sell, I'll do that. I'll give you a percentage of the money. How's that?"

There was nothing to think about. I agreed.

I'd have money coming in and my time would be my own. I could read all day, and take Guy to the park and to movies. I would have the time to teach him to read. And I'd be beholden to no one. Troubadour wasn't interested in me romantically, so I didn't have to concern myself about getting involved with him.

"All right, Troub. When do we start?"

"I'll bring some things around tonight." His words lingered in his mouth. "Uh, Rita, uh, I'm glad to be working with you. Every time I used to see you, I thought to myself, 'That's a real nice lady.' Sure did."

He left me a demure smile.

After two months my closets were filled with expensive two- and three-piece suits. Dresses, sweaters and stockings crammed my drawers, and I spent my days reading Thomas Wolfe and going to the movies with Guy. I had cut down my visits to San Francisco. Mother's house was dim with foreboding tragedy and Bailey still hadn't got his "bankroll together." He was thinner and the new clothes didn't fit. The shirt sleeves slid down to cover half his hands, and his stomach couldn't resist the belt's descent. His color seemed to have faded and his once fast speech had slowed nearly to Troub's rhythm. For her part, Mother talked faster and popped her fingers louder, but her laughter shattered out of her mouth. Unreal.

There was no happiness in the house.

In Oakland, my fantasy settled upon becoming Mrs. Troubadour Martin. He was kind, generous and quiet, and although we made a desultory kind of love a few times, he had never asked for more. The ideal husband.

Troub was definitely strung out on heavy narcotics. Even when I smoked grass, he would take only one or two drags and let me have the rest. I had waited to see when he would try to introduce me to heroin and hadn't been quite sure how I'd respond. Order him out of my house or consider that he made enough money to be able to keep us both high for life? One hit of heroin wouldn't make me an addict. And maybe if I shot it once, he'd know I didn't disapprove and our relationship would be closer. Since he never answered my direct questions about heroin, I schemed to bring about a confrontation.

"Troubadour, I think you'll have to find someone else."

"Why, Rita?" Even shock didn't scurry across his face.

"I think you're keeping something from me. Or have an old lady. And... and I'm beginning to fall for you." It wasn't difficult to make myself cry. All I had to do was think about losing my soft perch, or my brother, or my mother, or old L.D. or the long-lost Curly.

"Rita, I've told you, I don't have any woman."

Tears flowed. "But you never take me with you. I'm not a girl. I want to be your woman. And share everything with you. You don't care about me."

"Yes, I do, Rita. I like you. You're just fine."

"But you don't want me, is that it?"

"No. That's not it." At least he was speaking a little faster.

"Then if you want me, stop hiding what you do. I can take it."

I dried my tears enough to look at him. His eyes squinched together and his jaws clenched. He looked straight at me. "Can you leave the baby for a while? Come for a ride with me."

Here it was. I had to leave Guy alone. Nothing ventured... Troub pointed the car toward San Francisco.

"Where are we going?" I had expected he was taking me to his room, which was in Oakland near my house. He didn't answer. The Bay Bridge amber lights washed out his brown-earth color and he was a cold, sallow stranger. I couldn't show panic.

"Oh, to the city, huh? That's nice." ("Did I ever tell you I have only a little while to live? I have a brain tumor and the doctors give me six months." I had planned the speech years before to be used if I encountered a rapist or murderer. "They can't operate. Too near the cerebellum.")

Troubadour stared at the streets and chose one. I was dismayed to see that we were on the waterfront. My God, he was a freak of some kind and this was going to be the last few minutes of my life. I still couldn't scream.

He stopped the car on the wharf.

"Come on, Rita."

"But where are we going?"

"I'm going to show you something."

There was an absoluteness about the way he spoke and nodded his head toward the opposite side of the street. A pale sign said "Hotel." I was glad I hadn't screamed. A hotel. Maybe his house was hot and he was bringing me to a hotel to show me the ropes. I followed him through the fog, across four sets of railroad tracks to the hotel.

He walked straight to the desk and told a chalky-white clerk. "Give me the key."

The clerk didn't hesitate and I still followed, a little shaken. Did he keep a room here to act out some extravagant fantasy?

He turned the key in a lock and I went sheeplike into the room.

313

My first impression was that I was in a city bus station very early in the morning. People sat and lounged on every available place. Three bodies were draped over a bed, men and women sat on the floor, backed by the wall. Two women sat in one chair and all, black and white, were dozing off or waking up or fast asleep. No one noticed our entrance.

Troubadour reached back for me in the dim lamplight.

"Come on." I reeled and tried to shake my sluggish brain awake but it couldn't compute the situation.

It seemed a slow whole minute before the scene registered. This was a hit joint for addicts. Fear flushed my face and neck and made the room tremble before me. I had been prepared to experiment with drugs, but I hadn't counted on this ugly exposure. As I watched the wretched nod and scratch, I felt my own innocence as real as a grain of sand between my teeth. I was pure as moonlight and had only begun to live. My escapades were the fumblings of youth and to be forgiven as such.

I twisted for the door behind me and tried to snatch my hand away, but Troub held on.

"Come on. I want you to see something."

I was afraid to scream and alarm the addicts in their dreaming. If I pulled free and reached the lobby, would the desk clerk know I wasn't going to the police and allow me to go?

Troub tugged at me and we stumbled over outstretched legs toward an open bathroom door.

In the bathroom, Troub removed his jacket and gave it to me. He rolled up his shirt sleeve. Time for Troub and me moved as if we were swimming under water. He took a tablespoon from the sink and a small square of paper from his pocket.

The senses of sound, taste and touch had disappeared, but I had never seen so clearly or smelled so acutely.

The powder was dusted into the spoon and he dribbled a little water over it. He held three matches under the belly of the spoon while the mixture simmered. The sweet smell went into my nose and unlocked my tongue. "Don't do it, Troub. Please don't."

"Shut up and watch me." He tied his arm above the elbow with his tie and tightened it with his teeth. Then he took a syringe from the grimy face bowl and filled it with the hot clear liquid. High-standing keloid scars ran down his inner arm, and the black flesh was purple and yellow in a place, with fresh sores. He pushed the needle into a scar and wiggled it around, then took it out and tried another.

"Please, Troub."

"Shut up and watch this."

314

The needle pricked one of the soft scabs and rich yellow pus flowed out and down his arm to the wrist.

My tears, which had been terror-frozen, thawed at the sight of the man who had been so nice to me, jabbing and picking in his own flesh, oblivious to the pain and the ugliness.

The needle found its place and blood, mixed with a few drops of heroin, had snaked across his upheld arm. He loosened the tie with his teeth, and as if I had x-ray vision, I watched the narcotic reach his brain. His face muscles slackened and he leaned heavily against the wall.

"Now, you want some?" Slow lips, slow question.

"No."

"You sure? I can cook up for you." His head lolled, but he kept his eyes on me.

"I'm sure. I don't want it."

"Then I want you to promise me you won't use shit. That's why they call it shit. It is. You a nice lady, Rita. I don't want to see you change. Promise me you'll stay like I found you. Nice."

"I promise."

"Let me rest a little in the car, then I'll take you home."

He slumped behind the steering wheel for a half-hour and I watched him.

I thought about the kindness of the man. I had wanted him before for the security I thought he'd give me. I loved him as he slouched, nodding, his mouth open and the saliva sliding down his chin as slowly as the blood had flowed down his arm. No one had ever cared for me so much. He had exposed himself to me to teach me a lesson and I learned it as I sat in the dark car inhaling the odors of the wharf. The life of the underworld was truly a rat race, and most of its inhabitants scurried like rodents in the sewers and gutters of the world. I had walked the precipice and seen it all; and at the critical moment, one man's generosity pushed me safely away from the edge.

He finally awakened and we headed back to Oakland. In front of my house I told him he should take his clothes. I explained that I planned to move back to the city.

He said, "Sell them, you need the money. You've got a baby. There's plenty more stores and plenty more clothes."

The next day I took the clothes, my bags and Guy back to Mother's. I had no idea what I was going to make of my life, but I had given a promise and found my innocence. I swore I'd never lose it again.

Singin' and Swingin' and Gettin' Merry Like Christmas

ACKNOWLEDGEMENTS

Thanks to the
BELLAGIO STUDY AND CONFERENCE CENTER
of the
ROCKEFELLER FOUNDATION
particularly
BILL AND BETSY OLSEN
A special thanks to my friend and secretary,
SEL BERKOWITZ

For
MARTHA and LILLIAN,
NED and BEY,
for the laughter,
the love and the music

1

"Don't the moon look lonesome shining through
the trees?
Ah, don't the moon look lonesome shining through
the trees?
Don't your house look lonesome when your baby
pack up to leave?"

Music was my refuge. I could crawl into the spaces between the notes and curl my back to loneliness.

In my rented room (cooking privileges down the hall), I would play a record, then put my arms around the shoulders of the song. As we danced, glued together, I would nuzzle into its neck, kissing the skin, and rubbing its cheek with my own.

The Melrose Record Shop on Fillmore was a center for music, musicians, music lovers and record collectors. Blasts from its loudspeaker poured out into the street with all the insistence of a false mourner at a graveside. Along one wall of its dark interior, stalls were arranged like open telephone booths. Customers stood playing their selections on turntables and listening through earphones. I had two hours between jobs. Occasionally I went to the library or, if the hours coincided, to a free dance class at the YWCA. But most often I directed myself to the melodious Melrose Record Store, where I could wallow, rutting in music.

Louise Cox, a short blonde who was part owner of the store, flitted between customers like a fickle butterfly in a rose garden. She was white, wore perfume and smiled openly with the Negro customers, so I knew she was sophisticated. Other people's sophistication tended to make me nervous and I stayed shy of Louise. My music tastes seesawed between the blues of John Lee Hooker and the bubbling silver sounds of Charlie Parker. For a year I had been collecting their records.

On one visit to the store, Louise came over to the booth where I was listening to a record.

"Hi, I'm Louise. What's your name?"

I thought of "Puddin' in tame. Ask me again, I'll tell you the same." That was a cruel childhood rhyme meant to insult.

The last white woman who had asked me anything other than "May I help you?" had been my high school teacher. I looked at the little woman, at her cashmere sweater and pearls, at her slick hair and pink lips, and decided she couldn't hurt me, so I'd give her the name I had given to all white people.

"Marguerite Annie Johnson." I had been named for two grand-mothers.

"Marguerite? That's a pretty name."

I was surprised. She pronounced it like my grandmother. Not Margarite, but Marg-you-reet.

"A new Charlie Parker came in last week. I saved it for you." That showed her good business sense.

"I know you like John Lee Hooker, but I've got somebody I want you to hear." She stopped the turntable and removed my record and put on another in its place.

"Lord I wonder, do she ever think of me,
Lord I wonder, do she ever think of me,
I wonder, I wonder, will my baby come back to me?"

The singer's voice groaned a longing I seemed to have known my life long. But I couldn't say that to Louise. She watched my face and I forced it still.

"Well, I ain't got no special reason here,
No, I ain't got no special reason here,
I'm gonna leave 'cause I don't feel welcome here."

The music fitted me like tailor-made clothes.

She said, "That's Arthur Crudup. Isn't he great?"; excitement lighted her face.

"It's nice. Thank you for letting me hear it."

It wasn't wise to reveal one's real feelings to strangers. And nothing on earth was stranger to me than a friendly white woman.

"Shall I wrap it for you? Along with the Bird?"

My salary from the little real estate office and the dress shop downtown barely paid rent and my son's baby-sitter.

"I'll pick them both up next week. Thank you for thinking of me." Courtesy cost nothing as long as one had dignity. My grandmother, Annie Henderson, had taught me that.

She turned and walked back to the counter, taking the record with her. I counseled myself not to feel badly. I hadn't rejected an

offer of friendship, I had simply fielded a commercial come-on."
I walked to the counter.

"Thank you, Louise. See you next week." When I laid the record on the counter, she pushed a wrapped package toward me.

"Take these, Marg-you-reet. I've started an account for you." She turned to another customer. I couldn't refuse because I didn't know how to do so gracefully.

Outside on the evening sreet, I examined the woman's intention. What did I have that she wanted? Why did she allow me to walk away with her property? She didn't know me. Even my name might have been constructed on the spot. She couldn't have been seeking friendship; after all she was white, and as far as I knew, white women were never lonely, except in books. White men adored them, Black men desired them and Black women worked for them. There was no ready explanation for her gesture of trust.

At home I squeezed enough from the emergency money I kept in a drawer to repay her. Back at the store, she accepted the money and said, "Thanks, Marg-you-reet. But you didn't have to make a special trip. I trust you."

"Why?" That ought to get her. "You don't know me."

"Because I like you."

"But you don't know me. How can you like someone you don't know?"

"Because my heart tells me and I trust my heart."

For weeks I pondered over Louise Cox. What could I possibly have that she could possibly want? My mind, it was certain, was a well-oiled mechanism which worked swiftly and seminoiselessly. I often competed with radio contestants on quiz programs and usually won hands down in my living room. Oh, my mental machine could have excited anyone. I meant anyone interested in a person who had memorized the Presidents of the United States in chronological order, the capitals of the world, the minerals of the earth and the generic names of various species. There weren't too many callers for those qualifications and I had to admit that I was greatly lacking in the popular attractions of physical beauty and womanly wiles.

All my life, my body had been in successful rebellion against my finer nature. I was too tall and raw-skinny. My large extroverted teeth protruded in an excitement to be seen, and I, attempting to thwart their success, rarely smiled. Although I lathered Dixie Peach in my hair, the thick black mass crinkled and kinked and resisted the smothering pomade to burst free around my head like a cloud of angry bees. No, in support of truth, I had to admit Louise Cox was not friendly to me because of my beauty.

Maybe she offered friendship because she pitied me. The idea was a string winding at first frayed and loose, then tightening, binding into my consciousness. My spirit started at the intrusion. A white woman? Feeling sorry for me? She wouldn't dare. I would go to the store and show her. 1 would roll her distasteful pity into a ball and throw it in her face. I would smash her nose deep into the unasked-for sympathy until her eyes dribbled tears and she learned that I was a queen, not to be approached by peasants like her, even on bended knees, and wailing.

Louise was bent over the counter talking to a small Black boy. She didn't interrupt her conversation to acknowledge my entrance.

"Exactly how many boxes have you folded, J.C.?" Her intonation was sober.

"Eighteen." The boy's answer matched her seriousness. His head barely reached the counter top. She took a small box from a shelf behind her.

"Then here's eighteen cents." She pushed the coins around counting them, then pouted them into his cupped palms.

"O.K." He turned on unsure young legs and collided with me. He mumbled "Thank you."

Louise rounded the counter, following the little voice. She ran past me and caught the door a second after he slammed it.

"J.C." She stood, arms akimbo on the sidewalk, and raised her voice. "J.C., I'll see you next Saturday." She came back into the store and looked at me.

"Hi, Marg-you-reet. Boy, am I glad to see you. Excuse that scene. I had to pay off one of my workers."

I waited for her to continue. Waited for her to tell me how precious he was and how poor and wasn't it all a shame. She went behind the counter and began slipping records into paper jackets.

"When I first opened the shop, all the neighborhood kids came in. They either demanded that I 'gi' them a penny' "— I hated whites' imitation of the Black accent—"or play records for them. I explained that the only way I'd give them anything was if they worked for it and that I'd play records for their parents, but not for them until they were tall enough to reach the turntables."

"So I let them fold empty record boxes for a penny apiece." She went on, "I'm glad to see you because I want to offer you a job."

I had done many things to make a living, but I drew the line at cleaning white foiks' houses. I had tried that and lasted only one day. The waxed tables, cut flowers, closets of other people's clothes totally disoriented me. I hated the figured carpets, tiled kitchens and refrigerators filled with someone else's dinner leftovers.

"Really?" The ice in my voice turned my accent to upper-class Vivien Leigh (before *Gone With the Wind*).

324

"My sister has been helping me in the shop, but she's going back to school. I thought you'd be perfect to take her place."

My resolve began to knuckle under me like weak knees.

"I don't know if you know it, but I have a large clientele and try to keep in stock a supply, however small, of every record by Negro artists. And if I don't have something, there's a comprehensive catalog and I can order it. What do you think?"

Her face was open and her smile simple. I pried into her eyes for hidden meaning and found nothing. Even so, I had to show my own strength.

"I don't like to hear white folks imitate Negroes. Did the children really ask you to 'gi' them a penny'? Oh, come now."

She said, "You are right—they didn't ask. They demanded that I 'gi' them a penny.'" The smile left her face. "You say it."

"Give me a penny." My teeth pressed my bottom lip, stressing the *v*.

She reached for the box and handed me a coin. "Don't forget that you've been to school and let neither of us forget that we're both grown-up. I'd be pleased if you'd take the job." She told me the salary, the hours and what my duties would be.

"Thank you very much for the offer. I'll think about it." I left the shop, head up, back straight. I tried to exude indifference, like octopus ink, to camouflage my excitement.

I had to talk to Ivonne Broadnax, the Realist. She was my closest friend. Ivonne had escaped the hindrance of romantic blindness, which was my lifelong affliction. She had the clear, clean eyes of a born survivor. I went to her Ellis Street house, where she, at twenty-five, was bringing up an eight-year-old daughter and a fifteen-year-old sister.

"Vonne, you know that woman that runs the record store?"

"That short white woman with the crooked smile?" Her voice was small and keen and the sound had to force itself past white, even teeth.

"Yes."

"Why?"

"She offered me a job."

"Doing what?" I knew I could count on her cynicism.

"Salesgirl."

"Why?"

"That's what I've been trying to figure out. Why? And why me?"

Ivonne sat very still, thinking. She possessed a great beauty which she carried nonchalantly. Her cupid's-bow lips pursed, and when she raised her head her face was flushed pink and cream from the racing blood.

325

"Is she funny that way?"

We both knew that was the only logical explanation.

"No. I'm sure that she's not."

Ivonne bent her head again. She raised it and looked at me.

"Did you ask her?"

"No."

"I mean did you ask her for the job?"

"No. She offered it." I added just a little indignation to my answer.

Ivonne said, "You know white people are strange. I don't even know if they know why they do things." Ivonne had grown up in a small Mississippi town, and I, in a smaller town in Arkansas. Whites were as constant in our history as the seasons and as unfamiliar as affluence.

"Maybe she's trying to prove something," She waited, "What kind of pay she offering?"

"Enough so I can quit both jobs and bring the baby home."

"Well, take it."

"I'll have to order records and take inventories and all that." The odor of an improvement in my life had barely touched my nostrils and it made me jittery.

"Come on, Maya" (she called me by the family name). "If you could run a hook shop, you can run a record shop."

Once when I was eighteen in San Diego I had managed a house of prostitution, where two qualified workers entertained and I, as financial backer, took a percentage. I had since layered that experience over and over in my mind with forgiveness and a conscious affectation of innocence. But it was true, I did have a certain talent for administration.

"Tell her you'll take the job and then watch her like a hawk. You know white women. They pull off their drawers, lay down first, then scream rape. If you're not careful, she'll get weak and faint on you, then before you know it you'll be washing windows, and scrubbing the floor." We cackled like two old crones, remembering a secret past. The laughter was sour and not really directed at white women. It was a traditional ruse that was used to shield the Black vulnerability; we laughed to keep from crying.

I took the job, but kept Louise under constant surveillance. None of her actions went unheeded, no conversation unrecorded. The question was not if she would divulge her racism but when and how the revelation would occur. For a few months I was a character in a living thriller plot. I listened to her intonations and trailed her glances.

On Sundays, when the older people came in after church services to listen to the Reverend Joe May's sermons on 78 rpm records, I trembled with the chase's excitement. Large, corseted women gathered around the record players, their bosoms bloated with religious fervor, while their dark-suited husbands leaned into the music, faces blank in surrender to the spirit, their black and brown fingers restive on clutched Bibles.

Louise offered folding chairs to the ladies and moved back behind the counter to her books. I waited for one smirk, one roll of her eyes to the besieged heavens and I would have my evidence that she thought her whiteness was a superior quality which she and God had contrived for their own convenience.

After two months, vigilance had exhausted me and I had found no thread of prejudice. I began to relax and enjoy the wealth of a world of music. Early mornings were given over to Bartok and Schoenberg. Midmorning I treated myself to the vocals of Billy Eckstine, Billie Holiday, Nat Cole, Louis Jordan and Bull Moose Jackson. A piroshki from the Russian delicatessen next door was lunch and then the giants of bebop flipped through the air. Charlie Parker and Max Roach, Dizzy Gillespie, Sarah Vaughan and Al Haig and Howard McGhee. Blues belonged to late afternoons and the singers' lyrics of lost love spoke to my solitude.

I ordered stock and played records on request, emptied ashtrays and dusted the windows' cardboard displays. Louise and her partner, David Rosenbaum, showed their pleasure by giving me a raise, and although I was grateful to them for the job and my first introduction to an amiable black-white relationship, I could exhibit my feelings only by being punctual in coming to the shop and being efficient at work and coolly, grayly respectful.

At home, however, life shimmered with beautiful colors. I picked up my son from the baby-sitter's every evening. He was five years old and so beautiful his smile could break the back of a brute.

For two years we had spun like water spiders in a relentless eddy. I had to be free to work for our support, but the babysitters were so expensive I had to have two jobs to pay their fees and my own rent. I boarded him out six days and five nights a week.

On the eve of my day off, I would go to the baby-sitter's house. First he'd grab the hem of my dress, then wrap his arms around my legs and hold on screaming as I paid the weekly bill. I would pry his arms loose, then pick him up and walk down the street. For blocks, as I walked, he would scream. When we were far enough away, he'd relax his strangle hold on my neck and I could put him down. We'd spend the evening in my room. He followed my every turn and didn't trust me to go to the bathroom and return. After dinner, cooked in the communal kitchen, I would read to him and allow him to try to read to me.

The next day was always spent at the park, the zoo, the San Francisco Museum of Art, a cartoon movie house or any cheap or free place of entertainment. Then, on our second evening he would fight sleep like an old person fighting death. By morning, not quite awake, he would jerk and make hurtful noises like a wounded animal. I would still my heart and wake him. When he was dressed, we headed back to the sitter's house. He would begin to cry a few blocks from our destination. My own tears stayed in check until his screams stabbed from behind the closed doors and stuck like spearheads in my heart.

The regularity of misery did nothing to lessen it. I examined alternatives. If I were married, "my husband" (the words sounded as unreal as "my bank account") would set me up in a fine house, which my good taste would develop into a home. My son and I could spend whole days together and then I could have two more children who would be named Deirdre and Craig, and I would grow roses and beautiful zinnias. I would wear too-large gardening gloves so that when I removed them my hands would look dainty and my manicure fresh. We would all play chess and Chinese checkers and twenty questions and whist. We would be a large, loving, hilarious family like the people in *Cheaper by the Dozen*.

Or I could go on welfare.

There wasn't a shadow of a husband-caliber man on my horizon. Indeed, no men at all seemed attracted to me. Possibly my façade of cool control turned them away or just possibly my need, which I thought well disguised, was so obvious that it frightened them. No, husbands were rarer than common garden variety unicorns.

And welfare was absolutely forbidden. My pride had been starched by a family who assumed unlimited authority in its own affairs. A grandmother, who raised me, my brother and her own two sons, owned a general merchandise store. She had begun her business in the early 1900's in Stamps, Arkansas, by selling meat pies to saw men in a lumber mill, then racing across town in time to feed workers in a cotton-gin mill four miles away.

My brother, Bailey, who was a year older than I and seven inches shorter, had drummed in my youthful years: "You are as intelligent as I am"—we both agreed that he was a genius—"and beautiful. And you can do anything."

My beautiful mother, who ran businesses and men with autocratic power, taught me to row my own boat, paddle my own canoe, hoist my own sail. She warned, in fact, "If you want something done, do it yourself."

I hadn't asked them for help (I couldn't risk their refusal) and they loved me. There was no motive on earth which would bring me, bowed, to beg for aid from an institution which scorned me and a government which ignored me. It had seemed that I would be locked in the two jobs and the weekly baby-sitter terror until my life was done. Now with a good salary, my son and I could move back into my mother's house.

A smile struck her face like lightning when I told her I had retrieved my son and we were ready to come home. There was a glaze over her eyes. It was unnerving: My mother was anything, everything, but sentimental. I admired how quickly she pulled her old self back in charge. Typically she asked only direct questions.

"How long will you all stay this time?"

"Until I can get a house for us."

"That sounds good. Your room is pretty much as you left it and Clyde can have the little room in back."

I decided that a little bragging was in order. "I've been working at the record shop on Fillmore and the people down there gave me a raise. I'll pay rent to you and help with the food."

"How much are they paying you?"

When I told her, she quickly worked out a percentage. "O.K. You pay me that amount and buy a portion of food every week."

I handed her some cash. She counted it carefully. "All right, this is a month's rent. I'll remember."

She handed the money back to me. "Take this downtown and buy yourself some clothes."

I hesitated.

"This is a gift, not a loan. You should know I don't do business slipshod."

To Vivian Baxter business was business, and I was her daughter; one thing did not influence the other.

"You know that I'm no baby-sitter, but Poppa Ford is still with me looking after the house. He can keep an eye on Clyde. Of course you ought to give him a little something every week. Not as much as you pay the baby-sitters, but something. Remember, you may not always get what you pay for, but you will definitely pay for what you get."

"Yes, Mother." I was home.

For months life was a pleasure ring and we walked safely inside its perimeter. My son was in school, reading very well, and encouraged by me, drifting into a love affair with books. He was healthy. The old fears that I would leave him were dissolving. I read Thorne Smith to him and recited Paul Laurence Dunbar's poems in a thick Black Southern accent.

On an evening walk along Fillmore, Clyde and I heard loud shouting and saw a group of people crowded around a man on the corner across the street. We stopped where we were to listen.

329

"Lord, we your children. We come to you just like newborn babies. Silver and gold have we none. But O Lord!"

Clyde grabbed my hand and started to pull me in the opposite direction.

"Come on, Mom. Come on."

I bent down to him. "Why?"

"That man is crazy." Distaste wrinkled his little face.

"Why do you say that?"

"Because he's shouting in the street like that."

I stooped to my son giving no attention to the passers-by. "That's one of the ways people praise God. Some praise in church, some in the streets and some in their hearts."

"But Mom, is there really a God? And what does He do all the time?"

The question deserved a better answer than I could think of in the middle of the street. I said, "We'll talk about that later, but now let's go over and listen. Think of the sermon as a poem and the singing as great music."

He came along and I worked my way through the crowd so he could have a clear view. The antics of the preacher and the crowd's responses embarrassed him. I was stunned. I had grown up in a Christian Methodist Episcopal Church where my uncle was superintendent of Sunday School, and my grandmother was Mother of the Church. Until I was thirteen and left Arkansas for California, each Sunday I spent a minimum of six hours in church. Monday evenings Momma took me to Usher Board Meeting; Tuesdays the Mothers of the Church met; Wednesday was for prayer meeting; Thursday, the Deacons congregated; Fridays and Saturdays were spent in preparation for Sunday. And my son asked me if there was a God. To whom had I been praying all my life?

That night I taught him "Joshua Fit the Battle of Jericho."

2

My life was an assemblage of strivings and my energies were directed toward acquiring more than the basic needs. I was as much a part of the acquisitive, security-conscious fifties as the quiet young white girls who lived their pastel Peter Pan-collared days in clean, middle-class neighborhoods. In the Black communities, girls, whose clothes struck with gay colors and whose laughter crinkled the air, flashed streetwise smirks and longed for one picket fence. We startled with our overt flirtations and dreamed of being "one man's woman." We found ourselves too often unmarried, bearing lonely pregnancies and wishing for two and a half children each who would gurgle happily behind that picket fence while we drove our men to work in our friendly-looking station wagons.

I had loved one man and dramatized my losing him with all the exaggerated wailing of a wronged seventeen-year-old. I had wanted others in a ferocious desperation, believing that marriage would give me a world free from danger, disease and want.

In the record store, I lived fantasy lives through the maudlin melodies of the forties and fifties.

"You'd be so nice to come home to."

Whoever you were.

"I'm walking by the river
'cause I'm meeting someone there tonight."

Anyone—that is, anyone taller than I and who wanted to get married. To me. Billy Eckstine sang,

"Our little dream castle with everything gone
Is lonely and silent, the shades are all drawn
My heart is heavy as I gaze upon
A cottage for sale."

That was my house and it was vacant. If Mr. Right would come along right now, soon we could move in and truly begin to live.

Louise Cox and her mother were practicing Christian Scientists. I accepted an invitation to visit their church. The interior's severity, the mass of quiet, well-dressed whites and the lack of emotion unsettled me. I took particular notice of the few Blacks in the congregation. They appeared as soberly affluent and emotionally reserved as their fellow white parishioners. I had known churches to be temples where one made "a joyful noise unto the Lord" and quite a lot of it.

In the First Church of Christ, Scientist, the congregation wordlessly praised the Almighty. No stamping of feet or clapping of hands accompanied the worship. For the whole service, time seemed suspended and reality was just beyond the simple and expensive heavy doors.

"Did you like it?"

We sat in Louise's kitchen, eating her mother's homemade-from-scratch biscuits.

"I don't know. I didn't understand it."

After a year of relentless observation, I trusted her to think me unexposed, rather than ignorant.

Her mother gave me a copy of Mary Baker Eddy's *Science and Health*. I began to wrestle with new concepts.

The tough texture of poverty in my life had been more real than sand wedged between my teeth, yet Mary Baker Eddy encouraged me to think myself prosperous. Every evening I went home to a fourteen-room house where my son and seventy-five-year-old Poppa Ford awaited my arrival. Mother usually was out dining with friends, drinking with acquaintances or gambling with strangers. Had she been there, her presence would not have greatly diminished my loneliness. My brother, who had been my ally, my first friend, had left home and closed himself to me. We had found safety in numbers when we were young, but adulthood had severed the bonds and we drifted apart over deep and dangerous seas, unanchored.

In Mother's house, after dinner, I would read my son to sleep and return to the kitchen. Most often, the old man dreamt over an outsized cup of heavily sugared coffee. I would watch his aged ivory face, wrinkled under ghostly memories, then go to my room where solitude gaped whale-jawed wide to swallow me entire.

Science and Health told me I was never alone. "There is no place God is not." But I couldn't make the affirmation real for me.

The sailor wandered around the store. He was reading the bulletins and scanning the posters. His dark hair and oval, sensual face reminded me of Italian Renaissance paintings. It was strange to see a white military man in the Black area in broad daylight. I decided that he had gotten lost. He walked to the counter.

"Good morning."

"Have you got 'Cheers'?"

Maybe he wasn't lost, just found himself in our neighborhood and decided to buy some records. "Cheers"? I thought of all the white singers—Jo Stafford, Helen O'Connell, Margaret Whiting, Dinah Shore, Frank Sinatra, Bob Crosby, Bing Crosby and Bob Eberle. Tex Beneke. None had recorded a song entitled "Cheers." I ran my mind over Anita O'Day, Mel Tormé, June Christy. No "Cheers" there. He had looked like a vocal man, but then maybe he was looking for a white Big Band instrumental. Stan Kenton, Neal Hefti, Billy May. No "Cheers" in their catalogs.

"I don't know if we have it. Who cut it?" I smiled. "Cut it" showed that I was so much a part of the record business that I wouldn't say "Who recorded it?"

The man looked at me and said dryly, "Charlie Parker."

Although I lived in a large city, in truth I lived in a small town within that city's preserves. The few whites I knew who were aware of Charlie Parker were my brother's friends and were wrapped away from me in a worldly remoteness. I stumbled to get the record. When I shucked the jacket off he said, "You don't have to play it." He went on, "I'll take 'Well You Needn't' by Thelonius Monk and 'Night in Tunisia' by Dizzy Gillespie."

My brain didn't want to accept the burden of my ears. Was that a white man talking? I looked to see if maybe he was a Creole. Many Negroes from the bayou country could and did pass for white. They, too, had hank-straight black hair, dark eyes and shell-cream skin.

There was nothing like a straight question: "Are you from Louisiana?"

"No, I'm from Portland."

There is a textured grain that colors the Black voice which was missing when he spoke. I wrapped his selections and he paid for them and left. I wondered that he had been neither amiable nor rude and that he didn't remind me of anyone I'd ever met.

My two employers and Louise's handsome friend, Fred E. Pierson, cabdriver and painter, were the only whites I knew, liked and partially understood. When I met Fred, his friendliness had caused my old survival apparatus to begin meshing its gears. I suspected him (perhaps hopefully) of being personally (which meant romantically) interested in me. He helped me to paint the seven downstairs rooms at Mother's house and told me of his great and sad and lost love affair and that he liked having me for a friend.

The next weekend the sailor returned. He browsed for a while, then came to the counter and interrupted my preoccupation with papers.

"Hi."

I looked up as if startled. "Hello."

"Have you any Dexter Gordon?"

"Yes, 'Dexter's Blues'." Another Negro musician.

"I'll take that."

I asked, "How about a Dave Brubeck?"

"No. Thanks, anyway." Brubeck was white. "But anything by Prez? Do you have 'Lester Leaps In'?"

"Yes."

He waited. "Do you know of any jam sessions around here?"

"Oh, you're a musician." That would explain it. Members from the large white jazz orchestras visited Black after-hours joints. They would ask to sit in on the jam sessions. Black musicians often refused, saying, "The white boys come, smoke up all the pot, steal the chord changes, then go back to their good paying jobs and keep us Black musicians out of the union."

He said, "No, I just like jazz. My name is Tosh. What's yours?"

"Marguerite. What kind of name is Tosh?"

"It's Greek for Thomas—Enistasious. The short of it is Tosh. Are there any good jazz clubs here? Any place to meet some groovy people?"

There was Jimbo's, a blue-lighted basement where people moved in the slow-motion air like denizens of a large aquarium, floating effortlessly in their own element.

Ivonne and I went to the night spot as often as possible. She would take money from her catering business and I from my savings; we would put on our finest clothes, and hiding behind dignified façades, enter the always crowded room. Unfortunately, our attitudes were counterproductive. We projected ourselves as coolly indifferent and distant, but the blatant truth was we were out to find any handsome, single, intelligent, interested men.

I told Tosh I didn't know of any places like that in my neighborhood. When he left the store, I was certain he'd find his way to the downtown area, where he would be more welcome.

Louise continued encouraging me toward Christian Science. I gingerly poked into its precepts, unwilling to immerse myself in the depths because, after all, Christian Science was an intellectual religion and the God its members worshiped seemed to me all broth and no bones. The God of my childhood was an old, white, Vandyck-bearded Father Time, who roared up thunder, then puffed out His cheeks and blew down hurricanes on His errant children. He could be placated only if one fell prostrate, groveled and begged for mercy. I didn't like that God, but He did seem more real than a Maker who was just thought and spirit. I wished for a Someone in between.

Louise's partner was Jewish, so I spoke to him of my need and asked him about Judaism. He smiled until he sensed my seriousness, then said he attended Beth Emanu-El. He told me that there was a new rabbi who was very young and extremely modern. A Black singer had recorded "Eli Eli" and I listened to the song carefully. The beautiful high melodies and the low moaning sounded very close to the hymns of my youth. It was just possible that Judaism was going to answer my need. The Torah couldn't be as foreign as *Science and Health*.

334

For hundreds of years, the Black American slaves had seen the parallels between their oppression and that of the Jews in Biblical times.

> Go down Moses
> Way down in Egypt land
> Tell old Pharoah
> To let my people go.

The Prophets of Israel inhabited our songs:

> Didn't my Lord deliver Daniel?
> Then why not every man?
>
> Ezekiel saw the wheel, up in the middle
> of the air.
>
> Little David play on your harp.

The Hebrew children in the fiery furnace elicited constant sympathy from the Black community because our American experience mirrored their ancient tribulation. With that familiarity, I figured Judaism was going to be a snap!

Beth Emanu-El looked like a Tyrone Power movie set. Great arches of salmon-pink rose over a Moorish courtyard. Well-dressed children scuttled from shul and down the wide stairs.

I explained to a receptionist that I wanted to speak to Rabbi Fine.

"Why?" Her question really was, What are you doing within my hallowed halls? She repeated, "Why?"

"I want to talk to him about Judaism."

She picked up the phone and spoke urgently.

"This way." Stiff-legged and stiff-backed, she guided me to the end of a hall. Her gaze rested on me for a still second before she opened the door.

Rabbi Alvin I. Fine looked like a young physical education teacher dressed up for an open house at school. I had thought all rabbis had to be old and bearded, just as all priests were Irish, collared and composites of Bing Crosby and Barry Fitzgerald. He invited me in and offered a seat.

"You want to discuss Judaism?" There wasn't a hint of a snicker in his voice. He could have been asking a question of a fellow rabbi. I liked him.

"I don't know anything about it, so I can't discuss it."

"Do you want to become a Jew?"

335

"I don't know. I'd just like to read up on your faith, but I don't know the titles of any books."

"What is the faith of your fathers?"

"Methodist."

"And what is it not giving you that you think Judaism would provide?"

"I don't know what Judaism's got."

"Can you say you have applied yourself to a careful study of the Methodist tenets?"

"No."

"Would you say you have totally applied the dictates of the Methodist church?"

"No."

"But you want to study Judaism, an ancient faith of a foreign people?"

He was systematically driving me to defense. If he wanted debate, I'd give him debate.

I said, "I want to read about it, I didn't say I wanted to join your church. I like the music in the C.M.E. Church and I like the praying, but I don't like the idea of a God so frightening that I'd be afraid to meet Him."

"Why does your God frighten you?"

It would sound too childish to say that when my minister threatened fire and brimstone, I could smell my flesh frying and see my skin as crisp as pork cracklings. I told him a less personal truth. "Because I'm afraid to die."

I expected the bromide: If a person lived a good life free of sin, he or she can die easy.

Rabbi Fine said, "Judaism will not save you from death. Visit a Jewish cemetery."

I looked at him and felt the full force of my silliness in being there.

He said, "I'll give you a list of books. Read them. Think about them. Argue with the writers and the ideas, then come back to see me." He bent over his desk to write. I knew I would enjoy talking with him about Life, Love, Hate and mostly Death. He gave me the paper and smiled for the first time and looked even more boyish. I thanked him and left, certain that we would continue our discussion soon. I took a year to buy or borrow and read the books, but twenty years were to pass before I would see Rabbi Fine again.

3

Tosh became such a regular in the store that his arrivals raised no eyebrows and Black customers even began saying hello to him, although he only nodded a response. He had been discharged from the Navy and found a job in an electrical appliance shop. He had taken a room in the Negro neighborhood and came to the record store every day. We talked long over the spinning records. He said he liked to talk to me because I didn't lie.

I asked how he had come to like Black people so much.

"I don't like Black people," he said, dead serious. "And I don't like Italians or Jews or Irish or Orientals. I'm Greek and I don't like them either."

I thought he was crazy. It was one thing to be introverted, but another to admit to me that he disliked Black people.

"Why do you dislike people?"

"I didn't say I disliked people. Not to like people isn't the same as to dislike them."

He sounded profound and I needed time to mull over that idea.

I asked if he liked children. He said he liked some children.

I told him about my son, how bright he was and pretty and funny and sweet.

"Does he play baseball?"

I hadn't thought about the physical games Clyde could share with a father. A new world appeared with the question. In my next castle-building session, I would dream about a husband who would take our sons to the park to play baseball, football, basketball and tennis, while our daughter and I made cookies and other refreshments ready for their return.

"No, he doesn't play ball yet."

"Let's go to the park on your day off. I'll teach him what I know."

I had not really examined Tosh before. He had thick black hair and the slow, sloe eyes of Mediterranean people. His face was gentle and had an air of privacy. He was handsome, but he fell some distance from the mark I had set for a husband. He was two inches shorter than I and White. My own husband was going to come handsome, six feet three inches and Black. I snatched myself away from the vague

337

reflection and set a date for the three of us to go to Golden Gate Park.

My son and Tosh liked each other. They played handball, and after a picnic lunch, Tosh took a portable set from a package and began to teach my son chess. The day ended at my house, where I introduced Tosh to my mother. She was hospitable, just.

"How did you come to meet Maya? Where are you from?" and "When are you going back?" Tosh held his own before that whirlwind of a woman. He looked directly at her, ignored the implied queries, answering only what he was asked outright. When he left, Mother asked me my intentions.

"He's just a friend."

She said, "Well, remember that white folks have taken advantage of Black people for centuries."

I reminded her: "You know a lot of white people. There's Aunt Linda and Aunt Josie and Uncle Blackie. Those are your friends. And Bailey has those friends Harry and Paul, the table tennis expert."

"That's what I'm saying to you. They are friends. And that's all. There's a world of difference between laughing together and loving together."

A few days later I agreed to allow Tosh to take Clyde out alone. They came to the store as I was leaving and Clyde was full of his afternoon.

"We rode on the cable cars and went to Fisherman's Wharf. I'm going to be a ship's captain or a cable car conductor." His eyes jumped like targets in a game of marbles. "Mr. Angelos is going to take me to the zoo next week. I'm going to feed the animals. I might become a lion tamer." He examined my face and added, "He said I could."

Although Tosh had said nothing romantic to me, I realized that through my son he was courting me as surely as Abelard courted Héloïse. I couldn't let him know I knew. The knowledge had to remain inside me, unrevealed, or I would have to make a decision, and that decision had been made for me by the centuries of slavery, the violation of my people, the violence of whites. Anger and guilt decided before my birth that Black was Black and White was White and although the two might share sex, they must never exchange love. But the true nature of the human heart is as whimsical as spring weather. All signals may aim toward a fall of rain when suddenly the skies will clear.

Tosh grew up in a Greek community, where even Italians were considered foreign. His contact with Blacks had been restricted to the Negro sailors on his base and the music of the bebop originators.

I would never forget the slavery tales, or my Southern past, where all whites, including the poor and ignorant, had the right to speak

338

rudely to and even physically abuse any Negro they met. I knew the ugliness of white prejudice. Obviously there was no common ground on which Tosh and I might meet.

I began to await his visits to the shop with an eagerness held in close control. We went to parks, the beach and dinners together. He loved W.C. Fields and adored Mae West, and the three of us howled our laughter into the quiet dark air of art movie houses.

One night, after I had put my son to bed, we sat having coffee in the large kitchen. He asked me if I could read fortunes and put his hand in mine.

I said, "Of course, you are going to be a great musician and be very wealthy and live a long, rich life." I laid his hand on the table, palm open.

He asked, "Do you see where I'm going to be married?" I was thrust through with disappointment. While I hadn't ever seen him in the "my husband" role, his attention had been a balm for my loneliness. Now he was saying he was planning marriage. Some childhood sweetheart would arrive on the scene. I would be expected to be kind to her, and gracious.

I looked at the shadowy lines in his hand and spitefully said, "Your love line is very faint. I don't see a happy marriage in your future."

He caught my hand and squeezed it. "I am going to be married, and I'm going to marry you."

The sounds refused to come together and convey meaning, I am going to marry you. He had to be talking about me, since he was addressing me, yet the two words "you" and "marry" had never been said to me before.

Even after I accepted the content of his statement, I found nothing to say.

"A white man? A poor white man? How can you even consider it?" Disbelief struggled across her face. My mother's diamond winked at me as her hand flew about in the air. "A white man without a pot to piss in or a window to throw it out."

She was famous for temperamental explosions but she had never been angry enough at me to hurl her full thunderbolt of rage. Now, when I told her of Tosh's proposal, she was accelerating from an "ing bing" (her phrase for a minor riot) to a full-out tantrum. With alarming speed her pretty buttercolored face became tight and reddened.

"Think of your life. You're young. What's going to happen to you?"

I hoped not much more than had happened already. At three years old I had been sent by train from California to Arkansas, accompanied only by my four year-old brother; raped at seven and returned to

California at thirteen. My son was born when I was sixteen, and determined to raise him, I had worked as a shake dancer in night clubs, fry cook in hamburger joints, dinner cook in a Creole restaurant and once had a job in a mechanic's shop, taking the paint off cars with my hands.

"Think ahead. What the hell is he bringing you? The contempt of his people and the distrust of your own. That's a hell of a wedding gift."

And, of course, I was bringing him a mind crammed with a volatile mixture of insecurities and stubbornness, and a five-year-old son who had never known a father's discipiine.

"Do you love him? I admit I'd find that hard to believe. But then I know love goes where it's sent, even in a dog's behind. Do you love him? Answer me."

I didn't answer.

"Then tell me why. Just why are you going to marry him?"

I knew Vivian Baxter appreciated honesty above all other virtues. I told her, "Because he asked me, Mother."

She looked at me until her eyes softened and her lips relaxed. She nodded, "All right. All right." She turned on her high heels and strutted up the hall to her bedroom.

Bailey came to the house at my invitation. He sat in the kitchen with Tosh as I made an evening meal. They spoke about jazz musicians and the literary virtues of Philip Wylie and Aldous Huxley. Tosh had studied literature at Reed College in Oregon and Bailey had dropped out of high school in the eleventh grade. My brother had continued to read, however, spending his days on the Southern Pacific run waiting table in the dining cars and his nights with Thomas Wolfe, Huxley and Wylie. After dinner, Bailey wished Tosh a good night and asked to speak to me. We stood in the dim doorway.

"You invited me over for something more than dinner, didn't you?"

I had never been successful in keeping anything from Bailey.

"I guess so."

"He's in love with you. Did you know that?"

I said he hadn't told me.

Bailey leaned against the door; his dark, round face in the shadow was broken open by a white smile. "A smart man only tells half of what he thinks. He's a nice cat, Maya."

Bailey had been my protector, guide and guard since we were tots, and I knew, despite the disparity in our sizes, that he would remain my big brother as long as we lived.

"Bail, do you think it's all right if I marry him?"

"Did he ask you?"

"Yes."

"Do you want to?"

"Yes."

"What are you waiting for?"

"People will talk about me."

"Marry him, Maya. Be happy and prove them all fools and liars."

He gave me a typically sloppy Bailey kiss on the cheek and left.

Tosh and I were married in the Courthouse on a clear Monday morning. To show her displeasure, Mother moved her fourteen rooms of furniture to Los Angeles three days before the ceremony.

We rented a large flat, and on Tosh's orders I quit my job. At last I was a housewife, legally a member of that enviable tribe of consumers whom security made fat as butter and who under no circumstances considered living by bread alone, because their husbands brought home the bacon. I had a son, a father for him, a husband and a pretty home for us to live in. My life began to resemble a Good Housekeeping advertisement. I cooked well-balanced meals and molded fabulous jello desserts. My floors were dangerous with daily applications of wax and our furniture slick with polish.

Clyde was sprouting with independence and opinions. Tosh told him often and with feeling that he was absolutely the most intelligent child in the world. Clyde began calling Tosh "Daddy," although I had concocted and given him a dramatic tale during his younger years. The story told how his own father had died on the sands of some Pacific island fighting for his life and his country. I would cry at the telling of the fiction, wishing so hard it had been true.

Tosh was a better husband than I had dared to dream. He was intelligent, kind and reliable. He told me I was beautiful (I decided that he was blinded by my color) and a brilliant conversationalist. Conversation was easy. He brought flowers for me and held my hand in the living room. My cooking received his highest praise and he laughed at my wit.

Our home life was an Eden of constant spring, but Tosh was certain the serpent lay coiled just beyond our gate. Only two former Navy friends (white), one jazz pianist (Black) and Ivonne were allowed to visit our domestic paradise. He explained that the people I liked or had known or thought I liked were all stupid and beneath me. Those I might meet, if allowed to venture out alone, beyond our catacomb, couldn't be trusted. Clyde was the brightest, most winning boy in the world, but his friends weren't welcome in our house because they were not worthy of his time. We had tickets to silent movies and the early talkies, and on some Sundays, took our trash to the town dump. I came to love Tosh because he wrapped us in a

341

cocoon of safety, and I made no protest at the bonds that were closing around my existence.

After a year, I saw the first evidence of a reptilian presence in my garden. Tosh told Clyde that there was no God. When I contradicted him, he asked me to prove His presence. I countered that we could not discuss an Entity which didn't exist. He had been a debater at his univesity and told me that he could have argued either side with the same power; however, he knew for a fact there was no God, so I should surrender the discussion.

I knew I was a child of a God who existed but also the wife of a husband who was angered at my belief. I surrendered.

I tucked away the memory of my great-grandmother (who had been a slave), who told me of praying silently under old wash pots, and of secret meetings deep in the woods to praise God ("For where two or three are gathered together in my name, there am I in the midst of them"). Her owner wouldn't allow his Negroes to worship God (it might give them ideas) and they did so on pain of being lashed.

I planned a secret crawl through neighborhood churches. First I took a nice dress to Ivonne's house and left it, explaining my intent. Then, on at least one Sunday a month, I would prepare a good breakfast for my family and an equally good lie in order to get out of the house. Leaving Clyde at home (he hadn't the experience to lie), I would hurry to Ivonne's, put on the Sunday dress and rush to church. I changed sites each month, afraid that too many repeated visits would familiarize my face and that on some promenade with Tosh I would be stopped by a church member and possibly asked about last week's sermon.

The spirituals and gospel songs were sweeter than sugar. I wanted to keep my mouth full of them and the sounds of my people singing fell like sweet oil in my ears. When the polyrhythmic hand-clapping began and the feet started tapping, when one old lady in a corner raised her voice to scream "O Lord, Lordy Jesus," I could hardly keep my seat. The ceremony drove into my body, to my fingers, toes, neck and thighs. My extremities shook under the emotional possession. I imposed my will on their quivering and kept them fairly still. I was terrified that once loose, once I lifted or lost my control, I would rise from my seat and dance like a puppet, up and down the aisles. I would open my mouth, and screams, shouts and field hollers would tear out my tongue in their rush to be free.

I was elated that I could wallow in the ceremonies and never forsake control. After each service I would join the church, adding

342

my maiden name to the roster in an attempt to repay the preacher and parishioners for the joyful experience. On the street I felt cleansed, purged and new. Then I would hurry to Ivonne's, change clothes and go back to my own clean house and pretty, though ungodly, family.

After watching the multicolored people in church dressed in their gay Sunday finery and praising their Maker with loud voices and sensual movements, Tosh and my house looked very pale. Van Gogh and Klee posters which would please me a day later seemed irrelevant. The scatter rugs, placed so artfully the day before, appeared pretentious. For the first few hours at home I kept as tight a check on my thoughts as I had held over my body in church. By the evening meal, I was ready again for cerebral exercises and intellectual exchange.

4

During the first year of marriage I was so enchanted with security and living with a person whose color or lack of it could startle me on an early-morning waking, and I was so busy keeping a spotless house, teaching myself to cook and serve gourmet meals and managing a happy, rambunctious growing boy that I had little time to notice public reactions to us. Awareness gradually grew in my mind that people stared, nudged each other and frowned when we three walked in the parks or went to the movies. The distaste on their faces called me back to a history of discrimination and murders of every type. Tosh, I told myself, was Greek, not white American; therefore I needn't feel I had betrayed my race by marrying one of the enemy, nor could white Americans believe that I had so forgiven them the past that I was ready to love a member of their tribe. I never admitted that I made the same kind of rationalization about all the other non-Blacks I liked. Louise was white American (but she was a woman). David was white (but he was Jewish). Jack Simpson, Tosh's only friend, was plain white (but he was young and shy). I stared back hard at whites in the street trying to scrape the look of effrontery off their cruel faces. But I dropped my eyes when we met Negroes. I couldn't explain to all of them that my husband had not been a part of our degradation. I fought against the guilt which was slipping into my closed life as insidiously as gas escaping into a sealed room.

I clung to Tosh, surrendering more of my territory, my independence. I would ignore the straightness of his hair which worried my fingers. I would be an obedient, dutiful wife, restricting our arguments to semantic differences, never contradicting the substance of his views.

Clyde stood flinching as I combed his thick snarled hair. His face was screwed into a frown.

"Mom—ouch—when am I going to grow up—ouch-and have good hair like Dad's?"

The mixed marriage bludgeoned home. My son thought that the whites' straight hair was better than his natural abundant curls.

"You are going to have hair like mine. Isn't that good?" I counted on his love to keep him loyal.

"It's good for you, but mine hurts. I don't like hurting hair."

I promised to have the barber give him a close cut on our next visit and told him how beautiful and rich he looked with his own hair. He looked at me, half disbelieving, so I told him about a little African prince named Hannibal, who had hair just like his. I felt a dislike for Tosh's hair because of my son's envy.

I began scheming. There was only one way I could keep my marriage balanced and make my son have a healthy respect for his own looks and race: I had to devote all my time and intelligence to my family. I needed to become a historian, sociologist and anthropologist. I would begin a self-improvement course at the main library. Just one last church visit, then I would totally dedicate myself to Tosh and Clyde and we would all be happy.

The Evening Star Baptist Church was crowded when I arrived and the service had begun. The members were rousing a song, urging the music to soar beyond all physical boundaries.

> "I want to be ready
> I want to be ready
> I want to be ready
> To walk in Jerusalem, just like John."

Over and over again the melodies lifted, pushed up by the clapping hands, kept aloft by the shaking shoulders. Then the minister stepped out away from the altar to stand at the lip of the dais. He was tall and ponderous as befitted a person heavy with the word of God.

"The bones were dry." The simple statement sped through my

344

mind. "Dry Bones in the Valley" was my favorite sermon. The song that whites had come to use in mimicry of the Negro accent, "Dem Bones" was inspired by that particular portion of the Old Testament. Their ridicule—"De toe bone connected to de foot bone, foot bone connected to de ankle bone, ankle bone connected to de..."—in no way diminished my reverence for the sermon. I knew of no teaching more positive than the legend which said that will and faith caused a dismembered skeleton, dry on the desert floor, to knit back together and walk. I also knew that that sermon, properly preached, could turn me into a shouting, spinning dervish. I tried for the first few minutes to rise and leave the church, but the preacher swung his head to look at me each time I poised myself to leave. I sat again. He told the story simply at first, weaving a quiet web around us all, binding us into the wonder of faith and the power of God. His rhythm accelerated and his volume increased slowly, so slowly he caught me off guard. I had sat safe in my own authority in so many churches and waited cautiously for the point in the service when the ignition would be sparked, when "the saints" would be fired with the spirit and jump in the aisles, dancing and shaking and shouting their salvation. I had always resisted becoming a part of that enchanted band.

The minister's voice boomed, "These bones shall walk. I say these bones shall walk again."

I found myself in the aisle and my feet were going crazy under me—slithering and snapping like two turtles shot with electricity. The choir was singing "You brought my feet out the mire and clay and you saved my soul one day." I loved that song and the preacher's voice over it measured my steps. There was no turning back. I gave myself to the spirit and danced my way to the pulpit. Two ushers held me in gloved hands as the sermon fell in volume and intensity around the room.

"I am opening the doors of the Church. Let him come who will be saved." He paused as I trembled before him.

"Jesus is waiting." He looked at me. "Won't somebody come?"

I was within arm's reach. I nodded. He left the altar and took my hand.

"Child, what church were you formerly affiliated with?" His voice was clear over the quiet background music. I couldn't tell him I had joined the Rock of Ages Methodist Church the month before and the Lily of the Valley Baptist the month before that.

I said, "None."

He dropped my hand, turned to the congregation and said, "Brothers and sisters, the Lord has been merciful unto us today. Here is a child that has never known the Lord. A young woman

345

trying to make her way out here in this cruel world without the help of the ever-loving Jesus." He turned to four old ladies who sat on the front row. "Mothers of the Church, won't you come? Won't you pray with her?"

The old women rose painfully, the lace handkerchiefs pinned in their hair shook. I felt very much in need of their prayers, because I was a sinner, a liar and a hedonist, using the sacred altar to indulge my sensuality. They hobbled to me and one in a scratchy voice said, "Kneel, child."

Four right hands overlapped on my head as the old women began to pray. "Lord, we come before you today, asking for a special mercy for this child."

"Amens," and "Yes, Lords" sprang around the room like bouncing balls in a cartoon sing-along.

"Out, Devil," one old lady ordered.

"She has come to you with an open heart, asking you for your special mercy."

"Out of this baby, Devil."

I thought about my white atheist husband and my son, who was following in his nonbelieving footsteps, and how I had lied even in church. I added, "Out, Devil."

The raspy voice said, "Stretch out, child, and let the Devil go. Make room for the Lord."

I lay flat on the floor as the congregation prayed for my sins. The four women commenced a crippled march around my body.

They sang,

> "Soon one morning when death comes walking
> in my room,
> Soon one morning when death comes walking
> in my room,
> Oh, my Lord,
> Oh, my Lord,
> What shall I do?"

They were singing of their own dread, of the promise of death whose cool hand was even then resting on their frail shoulders. I began to cry. I wept for their age and their pain. I cried for my people, who found sweet release from anguish and isolation for only a few hours on Sunday. For my fatherless son, who was growing up with a man who would never, could never, understand his need for manhood; for my mother, whom I admired but didn't understand; for my brother, whose disappointment with life was drawing him relentlessly into the clutches of death; and, finally, I cried for myself, long and loudly.

When the prayer was finished I stood up, and was enrolled into the church roster. I was so purified I forgot my cunning. I wrote down my real name, address and telephone number, shook hands with members, who welcomed me into their midst and left the church.

Midweek, Tosh stood before me, voice hard and face stony. "Who the hell is Mother Bishop?"

I said I didn't know.

"And where the hell is the Evening Star Baptist Church?"

I didn't answer.

"A Mother Bishop called here from the Evening Star Baptist Church. She said Mrs. Angelos had joined their church last Sunday. She now must pay twelve dollars for her robe, since she will be baptized in the Crystal Pool plunge next Sunday."

I said nothing.

"I told her no one who lived here was going to be baptized. Anywhere. At any time."

I made no protest, gave no confession—just stood silent. And allowed a little more of my territory to be taken away.

5

The articles in the women's magazines did nothing to help explain the deterioration of my marriage. We had no infidelity; my husband was a good provider and I was a good cook. He encouraged me to resume my dance classes and I listened to him practice the saxophone without interruption. He came directly home from work each afternoon and in the evening after my son was asleep I found as much enjoyment in our marital bed as he.

The form was there, but the spirit had disappeared.

A bizarre sensation pervades a relationship of pretense. No truth seems true. A simple morning's greeting and response appear loaded with innuendo and fraught with implications.

"How are you?" Does he/she really care?

"Fine." I'm not really. I'm miserable, but I'll never tell you.

Each nicety becomes more sterile and each withdrawal more permanent.

Bacon and coffee odors mingled with the aseptic aroma of Lifebuoy soap. Wisps of escaping gas, which were as real a part of a fifty-year-old San Francisco house as the fourteen-foothigh ceilings and the cantankerous plumbing, solidified my reality. Those were natural morning mists. The sense that order was departing my life was refuted by the daily routine. My family would awaken. I would shower and head for the kitchen to begin making breakfast. Clyde would then take over the shower as Tosh read the newspaper. Tosh would shower while Clyde dressed, collected his crayons and lunch pail for school. We would all sit at breakfast together. I would force unwanted pleasantries into my face. (My mother had taught me: "If you have only one smile in you, give it to the people you love. Don't be surly at home, then go out in the street and start grinning 'Good morning' at total strangers.")

Tosh was usually quiet and amiable. Clyde gabbled about his dreams, which had to do with Roy Rogers as Jesus and Br'er Rabbit as God. We would finish breakfast in a glow of family life and they would both leave me with kisses, off to their separate excitements.

One new morning Tosh screamed from the bathroom, "Where in the hell are the goddamn dry towels?" The outburst caught me as unexpectedly as an upper cut. He knew that I kept the linen closet filled with towels folded as I had seen them photographed in the *Ladies Home Journal*. More shocking than his forgetfulness, however, was his shouting. Anger generally rendered my husband morose and silent as a stone.

I went to the bathroom and handed him the thickest towel we owned.

"What's wrong, Tosh?"

"All the towels in here are wet. You know I hate fucking wet towels."

I didn't know because he had never told me. I went back to the kitchen, not really knowing him, either.

At breakfast, Clyde began a recounting of Roy Rogers on his horse and Red Ryder, riding on clouds up to talk to God about some rustlers in the lower forty.

Tosh turned, looking directly at him, and said, "Shut up, will you. I'd like a little fucking peace and quiet while I eat."

The staterrent slapped Clyde quiet; he had never been spoken to with such cold anger.

Tosh looked at me. "The eggs are like rocks. Can't you fry a decent goddamn egg? If not, I'll show you."

I was too confounded to speak. I sat, not understanding the contempt. Clyde asked to be excused from the table. I excused him and followed him to the door.

He whispered, "Is Dad mad at me?"

I picked up his belongings, saw him jacketed and told him, "No, not at you. You know grownups have a lot on their minds. Sometimes they're so busy thinking they forget their manners. It's not nice, but it happens."

He said, "I'll go back and tell him 'bye."

"No, I think you should just go on to school. He'll be in a better mood this evening."

I held the front door open.

He shouted, " 'Bye, Dad."

There was no answer as I kissed him and closed the door. Fury quickened my footsteps. How could he scream at my son like that? Who the hell was he? A white-sheeted Grand Dragon of the Ku Klux Klan? I wouldn't have a white man talk to me in that tone of voice and I'd slap him with a coffeepot before he could yell at my child again. The midnight murmuring of soft words was forgotten. His gentle hands and familiar body had become in those seconds the shelter of an enemy.

He was still sitting over coffee, brooding. I went directly to the table.

"What do you mean, screaming at us that way?"

He said nothing.

"You started, first with the towels, then it was Clyde's dream. Then my cooking. Are you going crazy?"

He said, "I don't want to talk about it," still looking down into a half-filled cup of near-cold coffee.

"You sure as hell will talk about it. What have I done to you? What's the matter with you?"

He left the table and headed for the door without looking at me. I followed, raising my protest, hoping to puncture his cloak of withdrawal.

"I deserve and demand an explanation."

He held the door open and turned at last to face me. His voice was soft again and tender. "I think I'm just tired of being married." He pulled the door closed.

There is a shock that comes so quickly and strikes so deep that the blow is internalized even before the skin feels it. The strike must first reach bone marrow, then ascend slowly to the brain where the slowpoke intellect records the deed.

I went about cleaning my kitchen. Wash the dishes, sweep the floor, swipe the sputtered grease from the stove, make fresh coffee, put a fresh starched cloth on the table. Then I sat down. A sense of loss suffused me unt l I was suffocating within the vapors.

What had I done? I had placed my life within the confines of my marriage. I was everything the magazines said a wife should be. Constant, faithful and clean. I was economical. I was compliant, never offering headaches as excuses for not sharing the marital bed.

I had generously allowed Tosh to share my son, encouraging Clyde to think of him as a permanent life fixture. And now Tosh was "tired of being married."

Experience had made me accustomed to make quick analyses and quick if often bad decisions. So I expected Tosh, having come to the conclusion that marriage was exhausting, to ask me for a divorce when he returned from work. My tears were for myself and my son. We would be thrown again into a maelstrom of rootlessness. I wept for our loss of security and railed at the brutality of fate. Forgotten were my own complaints of the marriage. Unadmitted was the sense of strangulation I had begun to feel, or the insidious quality of guilt for having a white husband, which surrounded me like an evil aura when we were in public.

At my table, immersed in self-pity, I saw my now dying marriage as a union made in heaven, officiated over by St. Peter and sanctioned by God. It wasn't just that my husband was leaving me, I was losing a state of perfection, of grace.

My people would nod knowingly. Again a white man had taken a Black woman's body and left her hopeless, helpless and alone. But I couldn't expect their sympathy. I hadn't been ambushed on a dark country lane or raped by a group of randy white toughs. I had sworn to obey the man and had accepted his name. Anger, first at injustice, then at Tosh, stopped my tears. The same words I had used to voice my anguish I now used to fan the fires of rage. I had been a good wife, kind and compliant. And that wasn't enough for him? It was better than he deserved. More than he could reasonably have expected had he married within his own race. Anyway, had he planned to leave me from the first? Had he intended in the beginning to lure me into trust, then break up our marriage and break my heart? Maybe he was a sadist, scheming to inflict pain on poor, unsuspecting me. Well, he didn't know me. I would show him. I was no helpless biddy to be beckoned, then belittled. He was tired of marriage; all right, then I would leave him.

I got up from the table and cooked dinner, placed the food in the refrigerator and dressed in my best clothes. I left the dinner pots dirty and my bed unmade and hit the streets.

The noontime bar in the popular hotel on Eddy Street was filled with just-awakened petty gamblers and drowsy whores. Pimps not yet clad in their evening air of exquisite brutality spent the whores' earnings on their fellow parasites. I was recognized by a few drinkers, because I was Clydell and Vivian's daughter, because I had worked at the popular record shop or because I was that girl who had married the white man. I knew nothing about strong liquor except the names of some cocktails. I sat down and ordered a Zombie.

I clung to the long, cold drink and examined my predicament. My marriage was over, since I believed the legal bonds were only as good as the emotional desire to make them good. If a person didn't want you, he didn't want you. I could have thrown myself and my son on Tosh's mercy; he was a kind man, and he might have tolerated us in his home and on the edges of his life. But begging had always stuck, resisting, in my throat. I thought women who accepted their husbands' inattention and sacrificed all their sovereignty for a humiliating marriage more unsavory than the prostitutes who were drinking themselves awake in the noisy bar.

A short, thickset man sat down beside me and asked if he could pay for my second Zombie. He was old enough to be my father and reminded me of a kindly old country doctor from sepia-colored B movies. He asked my name and where I lived. I told his soft, near-feminine face that my name was Clara. When I said "No, I'm not married," he grinned and said, "I don't know what these young men are waiting for. If I was a few years younger, I'd give them a run for they money. Yes siree bob." He made me feel comfortable. His Southern accent was as familiar to me as the smell of baking cornbread and the taste of wild persimmons. He asked if I was "a, uh, a ah a fancy lady?"

I said, "No." Desperate, maybe. Fanciful, maybe. Fancy? No.

He told me he was a merchant marine and was staying in the hotel and asked would I like to come upstairs and have a drink with him.

I would.

I sat on the bed in the close room, sipping the bourbon diluted with tap water. He talked about Newport News and his family as I thought about mine. He had a son and daughter near my age and they were "some kinda good children" and the girl was "some kinda pretty."

He noticed that I was responding to the whiskey, and came near the bed. "Why don't you just stretch out and rest a little while? You'll feel better. I'll rest myself. Just take off your shoes and your clothes. To keep them from wrinkling up on you."

My troubles and memories swam around, then floated out the window when I laid my head on the single pillow.

When I awakened, the dark room didn't smell familiar and my head throbbed. Confusion panicked me. I could have been picked up by an extraterrestrial being and teleported into some funky rocket ship. I jumped out of bed and fumbled along the walls, bumping until I found the light switch. My clothes were folded neatly and my shoes peeked their tidy toes from under the chair. I remembered the room

351

and the merchant marine. I had no idea what had happened since I passed out. I examined myself and found no evidence that the old man had misused my drunkenness.

Dressing slowly, I wondered over the next move. Night had fallen on my affairs, but the sharp edges of rejection were not softened. There was a note on the dresser. I picked it up to read under the naked bulb that dangled from the ceiling; it said in effect:

> Dear Clara,
>   I tell you like I tell my own daughter. Be careful of strangers. Everybody smile at you don't have to mean you no good. I'll be back in two months from now. You be a good girl, hear? You'll make some boy a good wife.
>
> Abner Green

I walked through the dark streets to Ivonne's house. After I explained what had happened, she suggested I telephone home.

"Hello, Tosh?"

"Marguerite, where are you?" The strain in his voice made me smile.

He asked, "When are you coming home? Clyde hasn't eaten."

I knew that was a lie.

"Nor have I. I can't eat," he said. I wasn't concerned about his appetite.

I said, "You're tired of being married. Yes? Well, I'll be home when I get there." I hung up before he could say more.

Ivonne said, "Maya, you're cold. Aren't you worried about Clyde?"

"No. Tosh loves Clyde. He'll look after him. He loves me too, but I gave up too much and gave in too much. Now we'll see."

The thought of his loneliness in the large apartment made my own less acute. I slept badly on Ivonne's sofa.

I went home the next day and we resumed a sort of marriage, but the center of power had shifted. I was no longer the dutiful wife ready with floors waxed and rugs beaten, with my finger between the pages of a cookbook and my body poised over the stove or spread-eagled on the bed.

One day my back began to hurt with a sullen ache, the kind usually visited only on the arthritic aged. My head pulsed and my side was punished by short, hot stabs of pain. The doctor advised immediate hospitalization. A simple appendectomy developed complications and it was weeks before I was released. The house was weary with failure—I told my husband that I wanted to go to Arkansas. I would stay with my grandmother until I had fully recovered. I meant in mind, as well as body.

He came close and in a hoarse whisper said, "Marguerite. Your grandmother died the day after your operation. You were too sick. I couldn't tell you."

Ah, Momma. I had never looked at death before, peered into its yawning chasm for the face of a beloved. For days my mind staggered out of balance. I reeled on a precipice of knowledge that even if I were rich enough to travel all over the world, I would never find Momma. If I were as good as God's angels and as pure as the Mother of Christ, I could never have Momma's rough slow hands pat my cheek or braid my hair.

Death to the young is more than that undiscovered country; despite its inevitability, it is a place having reality only in song or in other people's grief.

6

When our marriage ended completely, a year later, I was a saner, healthier person than the young, greedy girl who had wanted a man to belong to and a life based on a Hollywood film, circa 1940.

Clyde was heartbroken by the separation. He acted as if I were the culprit and he and Tosh the injured parties. His once cheerful face was a muddle of solemnity. He grumbled and whined, asked again and again, "Why did Dad leave us?"

My direct answer of "Because he and I didn't love each other anymore" frightened him, and when he looked at me his eyes held the wonder: Will you stop loving me, too?

I tried to soothe him by explaining that he was my son, my child, my baby, my joy. But his good sense told him that Tosh had been my husband, my love and his father, and I had been able to sever those bonds. What safety was there for him?

A few months before the separation my mother and her close friend, Lottie Wells, returned to San Francisco from Los Angeles. They opened a café with ten tables and a ten-stool counter where they shared soul-food cooking chores. Lottie was a strong, powerfully built woman the color of freshly made coffee. She spoke softly, hardly above a whisper and was so tender it was impossible to resist loving her. She folded Clyde and me into her care and became our beloved Aunt Lottie.

At first Mother had exhibited no change in her attitude to my marriage, but when she observed my faithful husband, the good provider, and Clyde's love for Tosh, she had said, "O.K., so I was wrong. He's good. I'm big enough to admit my mistake; are you big enough to understand that I only wanted the best for you?" When I told her later that the marriage was at an end, she only said, "Well, as I always say, 'No matter how good a fellow seems on the outside, you have to take him home to know him.'"

Now that I was trying to mend the rift between me and Clyde I appreciated her indifference.

There are few barriers more difficult to breach or more pitiable to confront than that of a child's distrust. I used every wile in the mother's little homemaker kit to win my way back into my son's good graces. I paid attention to his loss and sympathized with him. I taught myself to skate so that we could go to the rink together. At home, I cooked his favorite foods, in portions that would please a cowpuncher and surrendered my reading time to play scrabble and twenty questions and any other diversion he chose. In the street we skipped over cracks in the pavement in a sport he called "no stepping on the lines."

Gradually we rebuilt our friendship.

As that emotional worry diminished, a practical one assumed importance. My pride had not allowed me to ask Tosh for money, but he had left me the small bank account and it was dwindling fast. I had to get a job and one that paid enough so I could afford a baby-sitter. I started looking.

Four dingy strip joints squatted cheek by jowl in San Francisco's International Settlement. The exteriors of the Garden of Allah and the Casbah were adorned with amateur drawings of veiled women, their dark eyes sultry with promise and their navels crammed with gems. The Pirates Cave and Captain's Table advertised lusty wenches and busy serving girls with hitched-up skirts and crowded cleavages, all sketched by the same wishful artist.

I stood on the pavement across from the Garden of Allah. A papier-mâché sultan with a lecherous grin winked atop the one-floor building. Around the doorway old photographs of near-nude women curled under a dirty glass façade. Large letters proclaimed BEAUTIFUL GIRLS! CONTINUOUS ENTERTAINMENT! The advertisement had read: Female Dancers Wanted. Good take-home pay."

The interior was dimly lighted and smelled of beer and disinfectant. A large man behind the bar asked if I had come to audition. Most of his attention was centered on checking the bottles.

I said, "Yes."

He said, "Dressing rooms downstairs. Go that way."

I followed the path of his arm and descended a narrow stairwell. Women's voices floated up to meet me.

"Eddie's a nice Joe. I used to work here before."

"Yeah. He don't hassle the girls."

"Hey, Babe, who made that costume?"

"Francis."

"Frances?"

"Nah, Fran*cis*. He male, but he's more twat than you."

I allowed the light and sound from an open doorway to direct me. A floor-to-ceiling mirror made the four women seem like forty. They were older than I expected and all white. They were taken aback by my presence. I said hello and received hi's and hello's and then a heavy silence.

They busied themselves professionally, gluing on eyelashes and adjusting wigs and attaching little sequined cones to their nipples. Their costumes were exotic, complicated and expensive. Rhinestones twinkled, sequins shone, nets and feathers and chiffon wafted at each movement. I had brought a full leotard, which left only my hands, head and feet exposed. Obviously I couldn't compete with these voluptuous women in their glamorous clothes. I turned to go. Wrong place, wrong time.

"Hey, where ya going? This is the only dressing room."

I turned back to see a short redhead looking at me.

She said, "My name's Babe, what's yours?"

I stammered. I ran through all my names, Marguerite, Maya, Ritie, Sugar, Rita. The first three were too personal and the others too pretentious, but since I felt least like Rita, I said "Rita."

Babe said, "You'd better get changed. The band will start soon. What's your routine?"

I had no routine. When I read the ad I had expected to audition for a revue and thought a choreographer would give me steps to do, rather like a teacher asking questions in an examination. I said defiantly, "I do modern, rhythm, tap and flash."

Babe looked at me as if I had answered in Latin.

"I mean what's your routine? I'm little Red Riding Hood, see?" She posed offering her costume for my observation. She wore a red gathered see-through net skirt with folds of the same material draped across her shoulders. Clearly visible beneath the yards of cloth were a red brassiere and a red sequined belt low on her hips; panels of red satin hung from the belt to cover her crotch and the cleavage of her buttocks. A precious little poke bonnet sat on her red curls and at her feet was a cute wicker basket.

I said, "I see." And did.

She pointed to an older blonde, whose breasts hung heavy and uncovered.

"That's Rusty. She's Salome" (she pronounced it "salami") "She does the Dance of the Seven Veils. That's Jody, she's the Merry Widow. See? Kate is the only one who's not somebody. She does acrobatics. You know? Flips and splits and things like that. So you gotta have a routine."

None of the women looked up.

I said, "Well, I don't have one, so I'd better go home." She said, "Let me see your costume. Maybe we can make one up."

I was unable to resist Babe's friendliness. Reluctantly I took the balled-up black leotard from my handbag.

"That's it?" Astonishment narrowed her voice into a shriek. The other women looked up for the second time since I'd entered the dressing room.

As usual when I was embarrassed, I responded with an angry stiffness. I said, "Well, I *am* a *dancer*. I might not have a fancy costume, and I may not have a routine, but I can dance. So don't try to make me look small." I looked around at each woman as I fought back mortification. The dancers resumed picking at their flesh privately, like cats licking their fur.

Babe said, "Wait a minute. Don't get your ass on your shoulders. They've never had a colored girl work here. Why don't you try it? I used to work at the Pirates Cave down the street and my best friend was Pat Thomas. She's colored, too."

I thought I am expected to stand here embarrassed and listen to that old "colored best friend" lie again. I rolled my leotard and put it in my bag.

Babe said, "I got an idea. What size are you?"

I told her.

She said, "I've got a G-string and bra made out of rabbit fur. I'll let you wear it, just for the audition, and you can be Jungle Bunny."

That was out, and I told her so emphatically.

She said, "Boy, you sure are sensitive. I didn't mean no harm."

I said, "I didn't mean to scream at you." After all, she had been kind.

"Well, let me think." Her face worked as she looked at me. She shouted, "I know, I know." She bent quickly and began fumbling in an open suitcase on the floor. She pulled out a blue satin set of panties and brassiere. Both pieces were studded with rhinestones and trimmed with blue-dyed feathers. "Try these on."

I undressed while the other women finished their make-up, their faces averted from me. I looked closely at the seat of the panties, and although they seemed clean I didn't pull it too close.

356

Babe said, "Boy, you got yourself a pretty figure," then she draped yards of blue tulle over me that floated and fell to the floor. "Now you're Alice Blue Gown. That's your routine. You know the song? It's a waltz."

The first tuning-up notes of a rhythm band reached the dressing room and the dancers started like robots jerking to attention. They picked up their purses and rushed to the stairs. Babe trailed them.

She whispered, "They only want four girls and we are five. I hope you get the job. Be real sexy. And don't leave your purse in the dressing room." She turned and raced for the stairs.

The figure in the mirror was strange to me. A long, mostly straight brown body clothed in a cloud of blue gauze. I would never be able to dance with all that material playing around. I took it off, folded it and laid it on Babe's tote bag. I tried to bring the lyrics of "Alice Blue Gown" out of my memory. I couldn't remember and I knew I couldn't waltz without a partner. I went upstairs wearing the bra and G-string.

Four white men sat murmuring in the shadows in the back of the club and four black men were playing "Tea for Two" on the bandstand. Rusty moved across the square polished floor, ridding her body of veils and indifferent to the music. Finally, as the music stopped, she was still as a statue and almost as pale. No hint of sexuality touched her body. And no applause appreciated her performance. She left the stage.

The acrobat took over next as the band began "Smoke Gets in Your Eyes." She wore a tasseled green G-string and brassiere and somersaulted, double-somersaulted, back-flipped, held one leg up over her head, showing the green patch that covered her vagina. As the last notes faded in the air she spun and jumped, ending in a perfect split. She jiggled short rises and allowed the floor to kiss her. There was no response from either the men watching or the men playing.

Jody walked onto the stage to the strains of "Besame Mucho." She wore black tulle, corseted to her body by a sparkling black waist cincher. Her black-stockinged legs and black patent shoes raced across the floor. She rushed from one side to the other, throwing wicked come-hither looks and tossing her wisps of clothes into the audience. When she finished, clad only in a black G-string and bra, she turned her back, pooched her behind up and looked over her shoulder with a pout. The music had ended, but she waited to her own drummer, then went around collecting the discarded clothing and went downstairs.

When Babe walked onto the stage, the four men fell silent. She nodded to the musicians, put one hand on her hip and held her basket aloft with the other.

357

The band played "All of Me" and the woman became a sexy, taunting twelve-year-old. She pranced about the stage offering illicit sex. She stuck out her tongue in a juvenile tease, then changed the purpose by sliding it around her lips insinuatingly, curling it over the corners. Her eyes were hard and wise and her body ample and rounded. Her breasts jiggled and her hips quivered with promise. She stripped to the red G-string and cones which covered her nipples.

When the music stopped, she stood still, looking out toward the men. Her face wrinkled in a strange smile. She had been sexually exciting and knew it. Within seconds, they began their murmuring again, and Babe collected her discarded clothes and waved at the musicians, who grinned in response. She passed me saying nothing.

I waited in the dark, not quite knowing if I should introduce myself or just go up and start dancing, or be sensible, race downstairs, put my clothes on and go home.

A voice shouted, "Where's the colored girl?"

I nearly answered "Present." I said, "Here."

"Well, let's go," the voice ordered.

I walked onto the stage and the musicians stared their surprise. The drummer beckoned to me.

"Hi, honey. What's your routine?"

Certainly not "Alice Blue Gown."

I said, "I don't know." And added, "I can dance, but I need something fast to dance to."

He nodded. "How about 'Caravan'?"

"That's fine."

He spoke to the other players, counted down four and the music began. I started dancing, rushing into movement, making up steps and changing direction. There was no story, no plan; I simply put every dance I had ever seen or known into my body and onto the stage. A little rhumba, tango, jitterbug, Susy-Q, trucking, snake hips, conga, Charleston and cha-cha-cha. When the music was finished I had exhausted my repertoire and myself. Only after the low talking resumed in the rear did I realize the men had stopped to watch me and that the other women had dressed and were sitting at a small table in the dark.

The drummer said, "Baby, you didn't lie, you can dance." All the brown and black faces smiled in agreement.

I thanked them and went downstairs with pride to change clothes. Babe passed me on the stairs, carrying her bag.

She asked, "How did it go?"

I said, "O.K. What about these things?" meaning her G-string and bra.

She said, "Bring them up with you. I'll just put them in my purse."

358

They would have fit comfortably in a cigarette package.

I said, "O.K. In a minute."

The big bartender stood over the table after I joined the other dancers.

He said, "Rusty, you, and Jody and Kate and—" He turned to me. "What's your name?"

I said, "Rita."

"—and Rita. Start tomorrow." He looked at Babe. "Babe, try again. We had you here last year. The customers like new faces."

He went back to the bar. The three women got up silently and walked over to him. I was embarrassed for Babe, and when I handed the costume to her I wanted to say something kind.

She said, "Congrats. You've got a job. You'd better go over and talk to Eddie. He'll explain everything. How much, hours and the drinks."

I said, "I'm sorry you didn't make it."

She said, "Aw, I expected it. All these guys are down on me since last year."

I asked, "Why?"

She said, "I got married. My old man is colored."

I went to join the others, and the bartender said, "O.K., Kate, you and the other girls know the routine. See you tomorrow night. You." Although he didn't look at any of us, he meant me. The bartender was a fleshy man with large hands and a monotone voice. His thin, pink skin barely covered a network of broken veins.

"You worked around here before, Rita?" His eyes were focused on the edge of the bar.

"No."

"You been a B-girl?"

"No." I had no idea what he was talking about.

"Salary is seventy-five a week and you work the bar."

I began to get nervous, wondering if I should tell him I knew nothing about mixing drinks.

He continued, "If you hustle you can clear ten, fifteen bucks a night. You get a quarter for every champagne cocktail a customer buys for you and two dollars off every eight-dollar bottle of champagne."

Eddie had given the spiel so often he no longer listened to himself. I began to pick meaning from his litany. I was expected to get men to buy drinks for me and I would get a percentage. Ten extra dollars a night sounded like riches, fur coats and steaks. I rattled around twenty-five cents into ten dollars and choked on the idea of forty cocktails per night. If I told the man I didn't drink, I'd lose the job.

"We use ginger ale and sometimes 7-Up with a lemon twist. And we got the fastest waitresses on the street. Show time is eight o'clock.

Six shows a night, six times a week each one of you girls dance fifteen minutes a show." He shifted his head, the spiel was over. I backed away, but he stopped me. "Uh, Rita, you belong to the union?"

"No." I had never heard of a dancers' union or a B-girls' union.

"Soon as we reopen, the AGVA representative'll be down here. Every girl has to belong to the union or we get blackballed. If you want to, we'll advance your initiation fee and you can pay it back in two weekly payments."

"Thank you." I was beginning to like this man who talked like a villainous Edward G. Robinson, yet was too withdrawn to look directly at my face.

"I'm only the manager, but the boss thinks that you shouldn't strip. The other girls are strippers. You just dance. And wear costumes like you wore today. "The costume I had borrowed made stripping absolutely unnecessary." Most girls buy their materials from Lew Serbin's Costume Company down on Ellis Street. Last thing is this, Rita: we've never had a colored girl here before, so people might say something. Don't get upset. If a customer gets out of line with any of the girls in a coming-on way, I take care of that, but uh, if they say something about your color, I can't help that. 'Cause you *are* colored. Right?" He nearly looked at me. "And don't go home with any guy or else the police'll be down and close us up." He turned his back and began typing on the cash register keys.

"See you at seven-thirty tomorrow."

"Thank you."

A showgirl. I was going to be a star shining in the firmamemt of show biz. Once more adventure had claimed me as its own, and the least I could do was show bravery in my strut and courage in the way I accepted the challenge. It was time to celebrate. No bus could take me back fast enough to Ivonne's house, where I had left my son. I stopped a taxi and gave the driver her address.

Ivonne grinned when I told her of my new profession and laughed outright at the salary.

"Seventy-five bones a week. What are you going to do with all that money? Buy a yacht?"

"It's going to be more than seventy-five." I told her about the drinks and the percentage. Ivonne had the talent of forcing her face absolutely still and looking so intently at an object that her eyes seemed to telescope. She sat a few moments registering my information.

"My. I know you'll try anything once, but be careful. How many Negroes are working down there?"

"Only the guys in the band, as far as I can see. I'm the first Negro dancer they've had."

360

"That makes it a little different, doesn't it?" Her voice had descended to a tone just above a whisper.

"I don't see that, Vonne."

I had always wanted to believe that things were exactly as they seemed, that secrets and furtive acts and intents always made themselves known somehow. So I acted easily or uneasily on the face rather than the hidden depth of things. "I'm going there to dance and to make some money."

She got up from the sofa and walked toward the kitchen. Our children's laughter floated out from a back bedroom.

"Aleasar made some spaghetti. Let's eat."

We sat down at the wrought-iron dinette table.

I asked, "What worries you about my working down there?"

"I'm not worried, you can take care of yourself." A smile widened her small mouth as much as it could. "All I want to say is what the old folks say, 'If you don't know, ask.' But, don't let anybody make you do something you don't think is right. Your mother already raised you. Stay steady. And if that makes somebody mad, they can scratch their mad place and get glad."

We laughed together. Our friendship was possible because Ivonne was wise without glitter, while I, too often, glittered without wisdom.

7

The costume store gave me the sense of being in a zoo of dead animals. Rusty bear skins hung on one corner rack; their heads flopped on deflated chests and their taloned paws dragged the floor. Ostrich feathers and peacock plumes in tall bottles were swept in a confined arc by each gust of wind. Tiger skins were pinned flat against the walls and lengths of black feather boa lay curled in a glass-topped counter.

I explained to a heavily made up quick-moving black man that I needed some G-strings and net bras and rhinestones. He flounced around the counter with a feather's grace and scanned my body as if I had offered to sell it and he was in the market.

"Who are you, dear?"

I wondered if it was against the store's policy to trade with just anybody.

"I'm Rita. I'm starting to work tomorrow night at the Casbah."

"Oh no, dear. I mean what's your act? Who are you?"

There it was again. I thought of glamorous Black women in history.

"I'm Cleopatra and... Sheba."

He wiggled and grinned. "Oh, goody. Two queens."

"And Scheherazade." If I felt distant from the first two, the last one fitted me like a pastie. She also was a teller of tall tales.

"Then you'll need three changes, Right?"

He had begun to jot notes on a pad. I thought of Ivonne's advice and decided that since I really didn't know what I was doing, I'd better ask somebody.

"Listen, excuse me. I've never danced in a strip joint and in fact, the owners don't even want me to strip. They just want me to wear brief costumes and dance."

The man's jerky movements calmed, and when he spoke, some of the theatricality had disappeared from his voice.

"You're new?"

I hadn't thought of myself as new since I was seven years old. "Well, I'm new in the sense that—"

"I mean, you have no act?"

"Yes. I have no act."

His body took on a stillness as he looked at me. "I will create your costumes. You will be gorgeous."

He brought out beige net bras and G-strings and told me how to dye them the color of my skin by soaking them in coffee grounds. I was to sew brown shiny coq feathers on one set for the Sheba dance, red sequins on another for Scheherazade and gold lame panels on a G-string for my Cleopatra number. He selected a stuffed cobra, which I was to carry when I portrayed the Egyptian Queen, and ankle bells for Sheherazade. Sheba was to be danced with no frills—a brown doe upon the hills.

He seemed to know so much about show business, I asked if he used to dance.

"I was a female impersonator in New York for years, dear. Just years. When I came out here and found I had gotten older, I got this job, and now I sell pretty things to the pretty young boys."

I paid for the purchases and was grateful that the man hadn't laced sadness in his sad story.

"If you need anything, come back or call me. Ask for Gerry." He flipped away to another customer, then turned his head over his shoulder in my direction and said, "Gerry with a 'G.'" His laughter snapped in the dusty air.

The first shows were anticlimactic. No crowds threw flowers at my bare feet, no deafening bravos exploded when I bowed after dancing for fifteen strenuous minutes. When I realized that I was the only person in the entire night club embarrassed by my near nudity, my embarrassment increased.

My body was all I had to offer and few of the serious-faced men in the audience seemed to notice. There had been scattered applause as the other dancers floated across the stage, flirting with their bodies and snuggling up to the soon-to-be-discarded bits of chiffon. My only applause for the first three performances were the desultory claps from Eddie, who, I decided, was programmed to automatically respond each time an orchestra beat out the closing chord.

The musicians encouraged me as I danced. "Yeah, baby. That's right, shake it!" Their union had ruled that they must have fifteen minutes off each hour, and Eddie arranged for another pianist to come in and play for the acrobat.

Before the next show, Jack, the drummer, came to the dressing room. He had close-set eyes and a sharp countenance, as if his features had run away from his ears to gather at the center of his face.

"Rita, me and the rest of the cats dig you. Just tell us what you want. We can play anything, but all anybody asks for is 'Tea for Two' and 'Lady in Red' and 'Blue Moon' and everything slow. I play so much draggy music, my butt is dragging. One thing I like about you is you don't drag your butt." Then he smiled. His lips parted and a million white teeth gleamed. The abrupt change startled me away from my defenses. I stood watching that sparkling smile, unable to think of an appropriate response. His lips suddenly withdrew from the smile with the finality of a door being slammed.

"Here's the rundown. We'll do 'Caravan' first. Then, 'Night in Tunisia' and 'Babalu.' Then we go back to 'Caravan.' Okay?"

I managed an "O.K." and Jack left the dank dressing room. I had once fallen in desperate love at first sight when I was seventeen. He was a handsome, cocoa-bean-colored man, whose voice was as soft as mink. He had loved me in return and treated me gently. Now, again, there was a dull whirr in my ears and a tightness around my chest and the man wasn't even handsome, might be a brute or happily married and I didn't even know his last name. I only knew he was a drummer and that the sun rose when he smiled.

When Eddie announced my last turn, "Here is Rita as the Arabian princess, Scheherazade," and I went on stage, Jack became the blasé Sultan for whom I danced beautifully. When I finished, there was scattered applause. I turned first to Jack, but he was talking to the pianist. Hastily I remembered my manners, and spun around to bow to the audience. The solemn old men still leaned, hands occupied with diluted drinks. I looked over the audience and found Ivonne sitting alone at one of the tray-sized tables. She smiled and nodded. I smiled back and walked off the stage. Another patter of hands came from a table by the door. I saw two men at a table lighted yellow by the outside amber neons. One looked like a false eye-lashed mannequin; the other was Gerry—spelled with a "G."

For the first week after each show, I raced down the concrete stairs and put on my street clothes. Fully dressed, I tried to disregard the contemptuous looks of the strippers who clattered into the room, flung provocative garments over their naked bodies, then without sitting once, went back to the bar and the clients. I was afraid that I would be speechless if a customer spoke and mortified if he didn't. Furthermore, Jack, whose last name I still didn't know, continued to excite my imagination. I couldn't allow him to see me planted on a barstool guzzling down the fraudulent drinks. So when I danced I refused to look at the audience and kept my eyes half shut and my mind centered on Jack.

"Rita." The bar was empty, except for the musicians packing down their instruments and the strippers waiting for their nightly take. "Rita." Eddie's voice caught me with my hand on the door. I turned.

"Come over here."

I walked back to the bar, the air conditioner had stopped its hum and the room had settled in silence. The women seemed to lean toward me in slow motion and the men on the stage might have been dolls handled by a drowsy puppeteer.

"Rita, we didn't pay your union dues for you to sit downstairs on your can. Do you think that's why we hired you?" He sounded like a teacher admonishing a mischievous child.

"I thought you hired me to dance." My voice would not follow my urging and it came out nearly whining.

A woman snickered in the prurient dark.

"To dance? Dance?" His cough could have been a chuckle. "This here's no concert hall. This ain't the San Francisco Ballet Company."

The pianist laughed out loud. "Lord, ain't that the truth."

Eddie continued, "You want the job?"

Yes. Desperately. I needed the money and I wanted to be near Jack and I loved to dance. I said nothing.

"Tomorrow night, you bring your fanny up here as soon as you change and sit at the bar. First joker that comes in here alone, you ask him for a drink. Or..." The unnamed threat hung in my ears. Teacher was brandishing his whipping cane.

"Tomorrow night. One more chance." He began to count bills, thudding his hand on the bar. "Okay, Kate. Here's yours."

Last chance? He didn't know me. There was no chance, absolutely no chance that I'd be there the next night. I went to the door and fumbled at the lock.

"I'll help you, Rita." I turned to see Jack's sharp face cutting through the gloom. My prince, my sultan.

"Thank you."

He opened the door easily. The mustard light from the exterior neon sign robbed him of his own color. He slanted toward me and whispered, "Wait for me. I'll just be a minute."

Standing in the amber doorway, I decided I would call the sitter and tell her I'd be late. Jack would probably take me to breakfast at one of the popular after-hours places and we could talk softly over the loud music. He would smile his break-of-day smile and I would say how much he meant to me. The job was forgotten.

The musicians came out of the club together. Jack was the only one not surprised to find me at the entrance. He said, "You cats go on. I'll meet you at the club. I'm going to walk Rita to a cab." He took my elbow and steered me toward the corner.

"I understand you, Rita." I knew he did. "You think taking B drinks makes you cheap. Well, let me tell you it doesn't. These old guys come in strip joints because they went to look at pretty women. Pretty naked women. Some of them are married, but their wives are old and fat or young and mean. They're not trying to get you to go to bed or anything like that. If they wanted prostitutes, they'd go to whorehouses. They just want to see you and talk to you. Personally, I feel sorry for them. Don't you?" We stopped in front of another darkened night club. If he felt sorry for them, I pitied them to pieces. All I wanted from Jack was to know what he thought I ought to be thinking.

"My wife and I talk about them all the time. She's a waitress in a club like the Garden of Allah and every night she's got some story. I pick her up downtown and she right away starts talking about the guys she's waited on."

A smile began to pull at his face. "Philomena—pretty name, ain't it? She can tell a story that would break your heart. Or else she can make you split your sides. Anyway..." He forced his thoughts back to me. "It's just life, Rita. Just life. Don't be afraid. You're in that joint to make money. So make it." He put his hand on my cheek. "See you tomorrow night." As he turned I caught a side glimpse of his smile. It was all for Philomena and not a wrinkle of it for me.

I spent the next day girding my mind for battle. I loved to dance and I needed to work. I could create steps and develop new choreographies. If men wanted to buy my drinks, I would accept and tell them that the drinks they were paying for were 7-Up or ginger ale. That, along with imaginative dancing, would erase the taint of criminality. Art would be my shield and honesty my spear, and to hell with Jack and his close-set eyes.

365

The next night Eddie's face moved slowly in surprise when I appeared at the bar. I gave a smile to encourage him.

"Rita. Well. Decided to join the gang, huh?"

I said, "I want the job, Eddie." And kept the grin easy.

"All right. You understand what I told you. Twenty-five cents off every drink and two dollars on a bottle of champagne. There's not many customers yet, but it's early. More'll be coming in soon. You stand a better chance sitting at the bar than at one of the tables. It's too dark for them to see you."

I couldn't afford to ask if he was making a slur at my color. I grinned and waited.

"Want a little drink to warm you up?"

"No, thanks. I'll wait for a customer to buy me something."

I looked around the club. A few men had come in, but the other dancers had already fanned out to sit at their tables. There was a dense romance to the room I hadn't noticed before. The white faces hovered like dully lighted globes and the gloom was fired by glinting rhinestone jewelry. The musicians' stands glittered under red, orange and blue revolving spotlights."

Eddie announced, "And now the Garden of Allah proudly presents Rusty dancing 'Salome and the Seven Veils.'"

Rusty got up from her chair and shrugged off her filmy wrap. She draped it over the customer's lap and stepped up onstage. Her body angled stiffly across the floor in contradiction to the floating chiffon veils.

I hadn't watched any of the women perform since that first day of audition, and so I sat fascinated with Rusty's conception of what was erotically exciting. She glided and stopped, glided and stopped, while her long, lethargic hands draped to the cups of her bra, promising to remove it, then a better idea motivated them to float away and descend to the chiffon at her crotch where they arrived with the same intent. Miraculously a veil would drift off her figure and slowly onto the floor. Rusty's face seemed divorced from the actions of her body. It wore the resignation of a tired traveler on a cross-country bus ride. I knew that that wasn't carnal, but when I turned to get confirmation from the customers, their eyes were focused on the indifferent dancer. They were using her feinting body to erase their present and catapult themselves into a fantasy where sex-starved women lay submissive and split open like red, ripe watermelons.

If I was going to be a success, I had to elicit if not the quality then the same quantity of response.

I had heard all my life that white males, from boyhood to senility, dreamed of slipping into the slave cabin of young "hot mommas" and "ripping off a piece of black tail." My arrogance and my hatred of slavery would not allow me to consciously batten on that image. I decided during Rusty's dance that I would interest the customers in my movements and hold them in the present, even as a tightrope walker hypnotizes an audience.

Eddie announced, "Rita dancing Scheherazade." I stepped upon the stage and into a thousand and one nights. The musicians were forgotten behind me as I moved to the edge of the stage. And the furtive men with their lonely longings became the sultans whom I had to entertain. I watched their faces come alive to me as I pointed and gyrated and swept my arms over my head and out and down to my sides as if I might fly offstage straight to a camel caravan waiting. I convinced myself that I was dancing to save my life, and without knowing why, the audience responded to my predicament. The amount of applause startled me, and even Eddie pursed his lips and nodded as I walked by the bar, headed for the stairs.

The dressing room was empty. I stood amid the costumes and wigs and hair rats considering my success and the next move. There was no time to waste. The men had liked my dance and surely one would buy me a drink. While I toweled my body I planned my strategy. Unlike the other dancers, I would not sit around the bar with kimono or peignoir thrown over my costume. I put on street clothes and went up to the bar.

Eddie showed his pleasure at seeing me by introducing a customer. "Rita, here is Tom. He wants to buy you a drink."

The first conversation was repeated so often, all customers might have been handed questions on slips of paper at the door and been forced to memorize the questions.

"Where'd you learn to dance like that?"

"In school."

"Did you ever make love to a white man?"

"No."

"Would you like to?"

"No. No, I don't think so." Leave room for them to hope. Leave space for me to ask for another drink. "May I have another drink?"

"Sure. Where're you from?"

"N.Y." N.O.Y.B. None of Your Business.

"Long way from home. Don't you get lonely?"

"This drink is called a champagne cocktail and I get twenty-five cents for every one you buy, but really it's only 7-Up. If you buy a bottle of champagne, it'll cost you eight dollars and I'll get two of that. But at least it'll be real champagne and I can sit with you as long as it lasts."

The ploy worked, but my interest was never aroused. The men awoke no curiosity in me. I did not follow them in my mind to their

367

hotel rooms or their loveless homes. They were like markers on a highway, to be used without gratitude and to be forgotten without guilt.

The other dancers did not warm to me, nor I to them. They chatted to each other and kept their conversations and their glances to themselves. They had not forgiven me for that first week when I sat haughtily in the dressing room as they hustled around the bar soliciting drinks. And since they had the toughness without the tenderness I had found in Babe, I ignored them completely. Success at cadging drinks changed my public personality. I became sassy to the customers. Quick, brittle words skipped off my tongue like happy children in a game of tag. Some men liked the flippancy and began to come back to the club not only to watch me dance but to buy drinks, listen to me and talk.

8

Two months after I began working in the Garden of Allah the composition of the patronage changed. The lonely men whose hands played with their pocketed dreams slowly gave way to a few laughing open-faced couples who simply came in to watch the show.

Occasionally I would be invited to join a table of admirers. They had been told a good dancer was working in a strip joint. I answered their overused question by telling the truth. "I'm here because I have to work and because I love to dance." I also explained about the drinks.

Being so close to the tawdry atmosphere titillated the square couples. I decided they were the fifties version of whites slumming in Harlem's Cotton Club during Prohibition, and while their compliments pleased me, I was not flattered.

Away from the bar my days were cheerful. I was making real money. Enough to buy smart, understated clothes for myself and matching ensembles for Clyde. We spent Saturday afternoons at horror movies, which I loathed. He adored the blood and popping eyes of "the Wolf Man," the screams of "vampire victims" and the menacing camel walk of Frankenstein's monster. He yelled and jumped and hid behind my arm or peeked through his fingers at the grisly scenes.

I asked him why he liked the fearful stories if they frightened him. His reply was a nonsequitur. "Well, Mom, after all, I'm only eight years old."

Three months passed and I freely spent my salary and commissions in dining at good restaurants, buying new furniture and putting a small portion away for a trip—Ivonne and I had discussed taking our children on a vacation to Hawaii or New York or New Orleans.

I was young, in good health, and my son was happy and growing more beautiful daily.

One night Eddie paid off the other girls first, saying he wanted to talk to me. After they left, he bellied up to the bar and cast his glance on the bandstand where the musicians were stowing away their instruments. When he didn't look at me, I knew it had to be serious.

"Rita, you're making more money than the other girls."

I hoped so.

"... and they say they have a complaint."

"What's the complaint, Eddie?"

"They say you must be promising to sleep with the clients. Otherwise why do you end up every night with four or five bottles of champagne and ten dollars or more in cocktails?"

"Eddie, I don't care whether they like it or not. I haven't promised anybody anything. I've just made more money. Let's leave it at that, O.K.?"

"It's not O.K., Rita. They can bring you up on charges with the union, or even get the club in Dutch. You must be doing something. No new girl makes this kind of money." His hand covered some dollars on the bar.

My protested innocence was forceful but without explanation. I could not reveal to him that I told all my customers about the ginger ale and that they knew the percentage I made from the champagne.

"Please believe me, Eddie. When I leave here, I go straight to my house and let the baby-sitter take my cab so she can go home. I have a child at home."

"Rita, it's not me. Far as I'm concerned, you're a straight shooter. Good people. But these other broads. They, uh, what I mean is they can give us a bad time. If they want to make real trouble all they have to do is hint to the right people that girls here accept B drinks." He wiped at a long-dried spill on the bar and my ears began to burn. "The State Board of Equalization suspended our license once before."

I had ignored the fact that officers from the Board visited the club in plain clothes. I told each man who offered me a drink the composition of the drinks and the percentage I would receive. So I had been dense before, but if I thought fast I could recover.

369

"Eddie, if they do that—I mean, tell the wrong person—they'll lose their jobs, too."

He found another spot to rub. "They don't care, not if they get mad enough. They'll just go to work down the street or around the corner. These joints are always looking for experienced girls. And that's what I want to tell you. I'm putting you on notice. Two weeks. You start looking for another place. I'll tell the girls tomorrow night that you're on notice. That ought to make them happy. If you haven't found something in two weeks, I'll try to keep you on a week at a time, but you won't have no trouble finding another job."

Shock made me patient. I stood silent and sheeplike as he counted out my night's money. In the taxi I gathered his words together and poked at them dully. Two weeks' notice. Fourteen days before the good life faded and my son and I would be cut loose to scud again without anchor. The dancers didn't like me and the disaffection was mutual. If they envied the money I made, I was jealous of the whiteness of their skin that allowed them to belong anywhere they chose to go. They could pick up their tassels and pack up their G-strings and go to another job without hesitation, but I remembered Babe. She was as white as they, but just because she slept side by side with her black husband, she was banned from the street. And what about me? I was black all over. No—the strippers felt nothing for me that I didn't feel for them.

I was always tired after the six shows, but this night sleep did not rush to float me out of exhaustion.

The next evening the dressing room was filled with electricity. The women were costumed, but had not made their customary dash upstairs. When I entered, they all turned to look at me. Sour little grins played on their faces. Rusty said, "So, you're leaving, huh, Rita?"

I gaped, surprised for a second. Eddie had told them already. I offered them my most gracious smile, looking into each woman's eyes.

"Good evening, ladies. Jody"—turn—"Kate"—turn—"Rusty."

Jody said, "Lovely evening, isn't it?"

My grandmother would have been proud of me. She had purred into my ears since babyhood, "Three things no person worth a hill of beans won't do. One is eat in the street and another is cry in the street. And never let a stranger get your goat." If they were going to lick their chops over my distress, they would find their tongues stuck to a cake of salt.

Upstairs I greeted Eddie as if he was simply a bartender. I looked away from him quickly and around the club. A few women sat at the tables with male companions. Their two-piece knit dresses and bouffant hairdos were strikingly out of place in the musty club.

I sucked in my breath and followed the opening bars of my music to the stage. Since I was on notice, I could forget the audience and go for myself.

Three fashionably dressed men and a young Marlene Dietrich-looking woman huddled over a table in the center of the room. The woman had a shock of sunlight-yellow hair and brooded over a cigarette holder. The red-haired man had been in before, but had not spoken. Now the four sat watching me as if they were French couturiers and I was wearing the latest creation from Jacques Fath. The more I tried to ignore them, the more they intruded into my mind. Who were they? Some slumming socialites looking for thrills? I tried to give myself to the music, but the group stared so intently that for once the music wouldn't have me, and I stumbled around the floor creating no continuity in my movement and no story in my dance. It occurred to me that they might be talent scouts and maybe I was going to be discovered. I threw that silly thought out of my mind before it could take hold. Lana Turner and Rita Hayworth got discovered, Black girls got uncovered.

I changed downstairs in the empty dressing room and half expected, half wished that the quartet would be gone when I went back upstairs.

"Hello, I'm Don." The redhead grinned and a map of freckles wiggled across his face. "This is Barry."

Barry was a tall, graying man whose smile was distant and distinguished. Don, obviously the major-omo of the group, waved his hand toward a pretty young man whose eyes were beautifully deep.

"This is Fred Kuh, and this"—he gestured like a circus announcer who had saved the lion tamer for the last—"this is Jorie!"

She shook her head and her hair fell back from her face, heavily as if in slow motion. She spoke in a low, theatrical voice.

"Hello. My dear, you dance divinely. Just divine."

Not Marlene Dietrich, I was wrong; she was Veronica Lake with substance, a young Tallulah Bankhead. "And you're so refreshingly young." Her perfume was thick, like the air in Catholic churches.

I said, "I'm twenty-one."

Barry asked if I would have a drink with them and I began my spiel about the B drinks, the percentages and the bad champagne.

Jorie said, "It's true. My Gawd, it's true. You're right on cue. We were told that you'd say that."

"What?"

You're kind of famous, you know."

Don grinned, "You must be the only open-faced B-girl on the Barbary Coast."

"In San Francisco," said Barry.

Jorie corrected: "In captivity."

They approved of me and I warmed to them. I allowed myself their flattery. It was easy to suppose they liked me because I was honest. I did not want to pry into their acceptance for fear that what I found would be unacceptable to me. Suppose they thought me a clown?

Barry explained that Jorie was a chanteuse, currently starring at the Purple Onion, a nearby night club. He managed the place and was the emcee. Don Curry and Fred Kuh were bartenders and I was welcome anytime I could get away.

These beautiful people and their friends began dropping in each evening and I awaited their arrival. I danced indifferently until I caught a glimpse of their party near the back of the room, then I offered them the best steps I had and as soon as the dance was finished I hurried over. There was no need to butter up the manager or hustle the customers. It gave me a delicious sense of luxury to be sitting with such well-dressed, obviously discriminating people, while the strippers roamed among the tables looking for the odd drink and the lone man.

9

One evening I was invited to a wine party at Jorie's apartment after closing time. The house sat on a hilly street. A stranger opened the door and took no more notice of me, so I entered and sat on a floor pillow and watched the guests spin around one another in minuet patterns. There were glamorous young men with dyed hair who rustled like old cellophane. Older men had airs of sophistication and cold grace, giving the impression that if they were not so terribly tired they would go to places (known only to a select few) where the conversation was more scintillating and the congregation more interesting.

There were young women who had the exotic sheen of recently fed forest animals. Although they moved their fine heads languorously this way and that, nothing in the room excited their appetites. Unfashionable red lips cut across their white faces, and the crimson fingernails, as pointed as surgical instruments, heightened the predatory effect. Older, sadder women were more interesting to me. Voluminous skirts and imported shawls did not hide their heavy bodies, nor was their unattractiveness shielded by the clanks of chains and ribbons of beads, or by pale pink lips and heavily drawn doe eyes. Their presence among the pretty, people enchanted me. It was like seeing frogs buzzed by iridescent dragonflies. The young men, whose names were Alfie, Reggie and Roddy and Fran, hovered around these fat women, teasing them, tickling them, offering to share a portion of their svelte beauty. None of the company spoke to me. That I was one of the three Negroes in the room, the only Negro woman and a stranger as well, was not a sufficiently exotic reason to attract attention.

I sipped the wine and listened to the concert of gossip and bon mots, repartee and non sequiturs.

Don stooped beside me and asked if I was all right and had I met everyone. I told him I was and I had, and added a sincere smile. His high pink color, green eyes and fire-red hair made him the prettiest person at the party, and he had a sense of humor I found missing in the other blades, despite their clacking laughter.

He looked into my eyes an found the lie. He stood and turned quickly. "Everybody!" He spoke just below a shout. "Everybody!" Voices quieted. When the room was still, he spread his arms and fanned his fingers away from his wrists and nodded toward me. "Everybody, this is Rita. She's an artist, a truly tremendous dancer. She is absolutely the world's greatest. I thought you should know."

People peered at me. Most found nothing remarkable about the announcement and, indeed, if at that moment I had executed a tour jeté from a sitting position, it would not have pried them away from their indifference. Only the plum-soft women marked the statement and cared. Each round face softened and smiled on me.

Don dropped his arms and said rather weakly, "Well, I just thought you ought to know." To me he said, "Don't mind these people, Rita. They're only pretending to be blasé because they don't know what else to pretend to be. I'll get you some wine."

One large woman came over to me carrying a pillow. She gracefully settled on the floor at my side, denying her bulk.

"I'm Marge." Then she told me, "And you're Rita."

"That's right."

"And what kind of dancing do you do, Rita?"

"Modern ballet and interpretive." (I knew a shake dancer named L'Tanya who could quiver her hips so fast they disappeared in a blur and she called her performance interpretive.)

Marge's mouth made an O. One young boy who had been courting her wafted over to us. He folded down beside Marge and arched an arm over her round shoulders, his hand dropping on the rise of her breast.

"And what have we here, Mother dear?"

She nearly suppressed a giggle. "Reggie, you're too naughty."

He turned to me, holding his lips tight. "How now, brown cow?"

I knew or should have known it would be a matter of time before some racial remark would be made. Here this chit was calling me a brown cow.

"Rita, this is Reggie. Isn't he a naughty boy? Naughty, naughty." She nearly kitchy-kooed his chin.

I made my diction as prudish as the young man's was prissy. "I haven't the faintest idea whether he's naughty or not. I do know that if he's your son, at least one of you has something to be ashamed of."

Reggie blanched and tightened. "You have a nasty mind to go with that nasty mouth." His voice sharpened with indignation. "What are you doing here, anyway? Who asked you?" He began to tremble.

Marge said, "There's no reason to get excited, Reggie baby. Calm down, hear? Just consider the source." She slipped out of his embrace and put both arms around his back and pulled him over into her lap. "There now, baby, there, there." She pressed chunky fingers on his hair and then looked up at me distraught.

I was thoroughly displeased with myself. I murmured "Sorry" and rose to go, but a door opened behind me and I turned. Jorie stood in the doorway. She wore a long black dress and lights leaped in her hair.

"Well, darlings, aren't you kind. You started without me." She laughed at her own good humor. I liked her more at that moment than I had before. She didn't appear to take herself too seriously. When she saw me she gave a little shriek of delight.

"How marvelous, Rita! You didn't forget. Has everyone met this most divine dancer?"

She came toward me as if she was going to take my hand like a referee and proclaim me champion. She stopped and patted my shoulder. "Have you had wine? Are they treating you all right?"

I told her that they were and, satisfied, she walked on to meet the other guests.

I was in a quandary. Obviously I couldn't leave the moment the hostess made her appearance, and just as obviously I couldn't sit back down on the floor near Marge and Reggie, who had finished ministering to each other's sorrow and were watching Jorie's movements keenly.

I wandered into the kitchen and claimed a drink. I had not drunk

374

much dry wine before that night, but if white people could drink wine like Kool-aid, then there was no reason on God's green earth I could not do the same. The second glass went down smoother than the first and the third more swiftly than the second. Alone, seated in a strange house filled with strangers, I felt as if I were in dangerous waters, swimming badly and out of my depth. I was plankton in an ocean of whales. The image was so good I toasted it with another glass of wine. Loud laughter penetrated the closed door and I wondered how people became so poised, so at ease. Sophistication was not an inherent trait, nor was it the exclusive property of whites. My mother's snappy-fingered, head-tossing elegance would have put every person in the room to shame. If she walked in the house uninvited, even unexpected, in seconds she would have the party clustered around her, filling her glass, listening to her stories and currying for one of her brilliant smiles. My mother was more elegant than Kay Francis and Greer Garson put together, prettier than Claudette Colbert (who I secretly thought was the prettiest white woman in the world) and funnier than Paulette Goddard. Oh, yes. I drank a glass of wine to my mother.

When I found the door leading from the kitchen, I walked back into a near-empty living room. I would have sworn that I had spent no more than fifteen minutes over the wine, but it would have been impossible for the room to clear in that time.

Jorie, Don, Barry and Fred sat in easy chairs listening intently to a record. Gertrude Lawrence or Bea Lillie sang shakily in a reedy voice.

I interrupted, "Oh, hello."

They jumped up, startled into speaking all at once. "Where have you been?"

"I thought you had gone."

"What were you doing?"

"Where have you been?"

I told them I'd been in the kitchen drinking wine.

Jorie collected herself. "Well, my dear, it's awfully late, but do come and sit a minute."

My progress across the room was not as steady as I wanted, but I proceeded in what I hoped was a dignified manner.

Don got up and led me to a chair.

Barry said, "We're listening to some songs for Jorie's act. She's going to open in New York at the Blue Angel."

Jorie shook out her hair. "My God, I've got to make New Yorkers laugh. That's what I call a challenge. What have New Yorkers got to laugh about?"

I said, "But I thought you were a singer."

Don said, "She's a singer-comedienne. And"—he became protective—"she's bloody brilliant."

Jorie touched Don lightly and smiled, "You don't need to defend me. She didn't say I wasn't bloody brilliant."

Don caught her affectionate tone. "Sorry, Rita, but of course you've never seen Jorie perform, have you?"

Barry said, "And she won't, either. Her working hours, remember? Jorie leaves in three weeks."

At that moment I thought about my job and covered my fear by blurting out, "I'll be able to see you next week. I'm on notice at the club."

"You mean you've been fired?" Disbelief raised Don's voice and widened his eyes.

Jorie said, "But, darling, you're the only talent they've got. I mean. Surely they don't think people come there to see those awful strippers in their awful sequins. I mean."

I explained why I was fired, putting the blame on jealousy.

Barry asked what I'd do next and I could not answer. Only a small savings account stood between me and poverty.

"It's a pity you don't sing," Barry said in his clipped accent, "The Purple Onion needs someone to take Jorie's place."

I had not told them I could sing.

"What about folk songs?" Jorie said. "My dear, everyone, but every single soul today, knows at least one folk song. Of course, it has one thousand verses and lasts for two hours without intermission. I mean."

Everyone laughed and I joined in. Not because I agreed, but because I was pleased to be in such clever company.

I said, "I know a calypso song."

The men exchanged knowing looks with Jorie, then turned to me, straight-faced for a minute, and broke into a mean laughter.

"That's a good one. Oh, Rita, you're good."

They were laughing at me and I was expected to join them. Only the secure can bear the weight of a joke and only the very secure can share in the laughter.

"Do you think calypso music isn't folk music? Folks sing it. Or do you believe because the folks are Negroes their music doesn't count, or that because they're Negroes they aren't folks?"

It was obvious that my anger was unexpected. A pale shock registered on their features. Don's eyebrows rose, making him look like a leprechaun tricked out of his burrow. Barry, having found my loss of control distasteful, averted his eyes. Jorie blinked and winked her false eyelashes. Fred Kuh, who had said little, quietly offered: "No one meant to hurt your feelings, Rita. Jorie has a passion against calypso. That's all there is to it."

376

"What's wrong with calypso?" I had so strongly pulled anger to me as a defense that I could not shoo it away merely because it was no longer needed.

Fred said, "I think it's because the singers rely more on the beat than on storytelling. And Jorie's concerns are just the opposite."

"Oh, my dear"—Jorie was back with us—"It's the god-Awful thump, thump, thump. It's the 'de man,' 'de girl,' 'de boat.' My God, haven't we got beyond 'dis' and 'dat'? Really."

It was a question of how I was to show that I was mollified without seeming to surrender my advantage.

"When you or any white person says 'dis' or 'dat,' it is certain that you intend to ridicule. When a Black person says it, it is because that's the way he speaks. There's a difference." There was a delicious silence. For the moment, I had them and their uneasiness in the palm of my hand. The sense of power was intoxicating.

"You say you dislike calypso and that the songs have no story line. Do you know 'Run Joe' by Louis Jordan?"

Their heads shook, which showed they were not totally immobilized.

"It goes like this." I stood.

> "Moe and Joe ran a candy store
> Telling fortunes behind the door
> The police came in and as Joe ran out
> Brother Moe, he began to shout
> 　　Run Joe
> 　　　　Hey, the man at the do'
> 　　Run Joe
> 　　　　The man he won't let me go
> 　　Run Joe
> 　　　　Run as fast as you can
> 　　Run Joe
> 　　　　The police holding me hand."

I had played Louis Jordan's record until it was gun-metal gray, so I knew every rest and attack of the song. I stretched my arms and waved my hands and body in a modified hula, indicating how fast Joe made his getaway. I tugged away from an imaginary policeman showing the extent of restraint imposed on Moe. I spun in place in the small area, kneeled and bowed and swayed and swung, always in rhythm.

When I finished the song, which seemed to consist of fifty verses, the assembly applauded loudly and their smiles were brilliant.

Jorie lifted a handful of hair and said, "But I mean, pet, you can sing. Have you ever sung before?"

377

Don said, "It's obvious you have. But professionally?"

When I was growing up in Stamps, Arkansas, Momma used to take me to some church service every day of the week. At each gathering we sang. So I knew I could sing. I did not know how well. Our church was bare because the parishioners were poor and our only musical instruments were tambourines and our voices. I had never sung to piano accompaniment, and although my sense of rhythm was adequate, I had not the shadow of an understanding of meter.

Jorie said, "But, my dear, if you can sing like that you should take my place at the Purple Onion. You'll be a smashing success. I mean they will simply adore you."

"How many songs like that do you know?"

"How many musicians will you need?"

"What about gowns?"

"Can you have an act together in three weeks?"

My God. My world was spinning off its axis, and there was nothing to hold on to. Anger and haughtiness, pride and prejudice, my old back-up team would not serve me in this new predicament. These whites were treating me as an equal, as if I could do whatever they could do. They did not consider that race, height, or gender or lack of education might have crippled me and that I should be regarded as someone invalided.

The old habits of withdrawing into righteous indignation or lashing out furiously against insults were not applicable in this circumstance.

Oh, the holiness of always being the injured party. The historically oppressed can find not only sanctity but safety in the state of victimization. When access to a better life has been denied often enough, and successfully enough, one can use the rejection as an excuse to cease all efforts. After all, one reckons, "they" don't want me, "they" accept their own mediocrity and refuse my best, "they" don't deserve me. And, finally, *I* am better, kinder, truer than "they," even if I behave badly and act shamefully. And if I do nothing, I have every right to my idleness, for, after all, haven't I tried?

Jorie said, "Of course you won't get the mint or probably half of what you're making now. But, my dear, if you're not working after next week, you may as well take this on. For the time being."

They began to make me up. I had to change my name. And wouldn't it be super duper if I had another origin? Something more exotic than tired old Southern Negro. People were tired of the moss hanging from the magnolia trees and the corn pone and the lynchings and all that old stuff. Anyway, I couldn't compete with Josh White, or Odetta, who I thought was the greatest singer of American Negro folk songs, and who worked nearby.

Couldn't we come up with something gayer, less guilt-awakening?

Jorie, Don and Barrie, along with quick assists from Fred, poked around in their imaginations as I sat watching. It was three o'clock in the morning and they were like children amusing themselves with play dough on a rainy day.

Because I was tall, I should be very grand, possibly from a long line of African kings. And could I speak any African?

I had studied African dance with Pearl Primus, but I had never met an African face-to-face. In fact, in the Negro community of 1953 the phrase used to describe a loud and uncaring person was "as uncouth as an African." I had lost a job in a leading dance school in Cleveland because I promised to teach "African primitive dance" to the children of the Black middle class.

No, I did not know any African. But I did speak Spanish. Jorie announced that she had an idea: I could be Cuban. That was it. I could be a Cuban who spoke little English, although I sang in the language. I should be torrid and passionate on-stage, but haughty and distant offstage: "Rita, the Cuban Bombshell," the Latin señorita whose father was a Watusi chieftain sold in Cuba.

They were casting me as the star in a drama and I had no real desire to refuse the role. I feebly wondered aloud what would happen if I was discovered a phony. Herb Caen, the acerbic columnist, was a Janus creature, who guarded the local past while guiding the locals' future. He liked Jorie and Stan Wilson and Mort Sahl. But, what if he found that I was a fraud? He could make me the laughingstock of San Francisco.

My new friends countered, "Why should he care? If he did find out and mentioned it, San Franciscans would be amused." People would laugh *with* me, rather than at me. After all, the city had more eccentrics than lights on the Golden Gate Bridge.

I not only agreed to the charade but began adding my own touches. My father, the Watusi chieftain, had not been a slave (ah, to rid myself of that stigma) but was the son of a chief who had sailed to Cuba to retrieve his sister, who had been stolen from Africa. Once there, he had fallen in love with a dark-eyed Spanish girl. He had won her after a bloody duel, married her and she had given birth to my father. They, my very well-to-do parents, had sent me to the United States so that I could see some of the world before I married and settled down in my own well-staffed hacienda.

My audience listened, mouths agape, as I reeled my story before them. Their imaginations had been good, but mine was better. They had been amusing themselves, but I was motivated by the desire to escape.

Ivonne sat watching me as I talked. She nodded to indicate not so much that she agreed with me but, rather, that she comprehended what I was saying.

"So I'm going to sing at the Purple Onion. I'll sing calypso songs. Jorie Remus, who is the star there now, and the manager and bartenders are fixing it all up." I sipped the beer I had brought for a celebration. "They're all white, but they're nice. Sort of like foreigners."

She inclined her head.

"I mean they are Americans, but Jorie has lived in Paris. In France. And I guess that's why she's kind of different."

Ivonne drank beer and waited. Our friendship had brought us so close, she sensed that I had something more to say and that what I was saving until last was the most pertinent of my news.

"They remind me of Hemingway and Gertrude Stein and that group that lived in France, you know?"

Because she had not read the books I had read, the names I mentioned did not bring to her visions of the Left Bank and Montmartre. She made no connections with a gay time when America's good white writers sat in places like the Deux Magots dreaming up a literature which would enthrall the world for decades.

My friend was at ease in her silence.

"So they suggested I change my name and..." What had been easy to accept in the company of strangers was almost unspeakable now in Ivonne's familiar living room.

I had thought only that an attempt to pass was an acceptance of that which was not true. As I searched for words, it occurred to me that what I was about to do was to deny that which was true.

"They suggested that I say I came from Cuba."

Her black eyes and voice were equally cold and hard.

"Oh, Ivonne. For the romance. Just because it'll make me more exotic."

"They want you to stop being Negro..."

"Oh no, come on."

"And you say these people are free? Free of what? And free for what?"

"You don't understand." I was exasperated with her. She and my mother had more in common than I had with either of them. "And I'm going to sing. I'm going to have a new career."

"You're going to sing Cuban songs? Like Carmen Miranda? With bananas on your head going 'Chi chi boom boom?" Sarcasm syruped in her voice.

"Listen, Vonne, I'm going to sing calypsos. And I'm going to be good." I didn't relish having to defend myself. She was my friend. We

380

shared secrets and woes and each other's money. We had keys to each other's houses and together watched our children grow.

"Just listen to this." I got up and took a place in front of the coffee table.

> "He's stone cold dead in de market
>   Stone cold dead in de market
>   Stone cold dead in de market
> I kill nobody but me husband."

My voice faltered and fell. I lifted it into a shout. When it sharpened into a screech I softened it. I fled between and over the notes like a long-distance runner on a downhill patch. When it was all over, I had sung in about three keys and Ivonne leaned back on the nearly paid-for sofa. A small resigned smile played hide-and-seek on her face.

She said, "I'll say this for you, Marguerite Johnson"—no one had called me by that name in years—"You've got a lot of nerve."

And she was right.

10

North Beach bubbled as noisily and colorfully as the main street in a boom town. Heavy drumbeats thudded out of the doors of burlesque houses. Italian restaurants perfumed the air for blocks while old white-shirted men loudly discussed their bocce games in Washington Square. Pagoda signs jutted from tenements in Chinatown and threatened the upturned faces of milling tourists. One block away on Columbus Avenue, Vesuvio's bar was an international center for intellectuals, artists and young beats who were busily inventing themselves. Next door, Allen Ginsberg and Lawrence Ferlinghetti read their new poetry at the City Lights Bookstore. Two hundred yards down Columbus, the Black Cat bar was a meeting place for very elegant homosexuals who draped themselves dramatically beside the bar and spoke loudly and familiarly of "culture."

The Purple Onion was a basement cabaret which Jorie called *la Boîte* (Don translated that into "the sardine can"). Its walls were painted a murky purple, and although it was supposed to accommodate two hundred people, well over that number crowded into the room the first night I went to catch the show, and the air was claustrophobically close. Jorie in a simply cut, expensive black dress leaned her back against the curve of the piano. She partly sang and partly talked a torch song, waving a cigarette holder in one hand and languorously moving a long chiffon scarf in the other. Her voice scratched lightly over the notes.

> "He's just my Bill
>   An ordinary guy
>   you'd see him on the street
>   [*pause*]
>   And never notice him.

She looked at the audience directly, shrugging her thin shoulders. Her look said that Bill really was quite awful and she had little understanding of why she herself had noticed Bill. Before our eyes she changed from the worldly-wise woman, disillusioned by a burnt-out love affair, into a "regular" girl who was just one of the folks. The audience howled at the transformation, delighted by having been taken in.

I sat in the rear enthralled. It was hard to believe I was being asked to move into this brilliant woman's place, although my audition had gone well enough. The Rockwell family, led by the elder son, Keith, owned the club, and without much enthusiasm had signed a six-month contract with a three-month option for my services.

Jorie drooped over the piano dripping chiffon, and delivering accented witticisms. Or she would stand still, her shoulders down and her hands at ease and speak/sing a song that so moved her listeners that for a few seconds after she finished, people neither applauded nor looked at one another.

When I went to my first rehearsal, Jorie brought her drama coach to meet me. He was a tall, thin, black-haired man named Lloyd Clark, who spoke elegantly out of pursed lips and threw his fingers out as if he was constantly shooting his cuffs. He was accompanied by a handsome Dutch Amazon, whose blond hair was pulled back and hung in a two-foot ponytail. Her little girl's smile seemed incongruous on a face that could have modeled for a ship's prow.

And she spoke softly. "I'm Marguerite Clark. I'm his wife." There was so much pride in her statement that I would not have been surprised had she hooked her fingers in her armpits and stalked around the room. Lloyd took her adoration as his due and asked me if I had ever worked with a drama coach. I told him that I had not, but that I had studied drama and that I was a dancer.

"Well, first, my dear, you must sing for me." He held a cigarette between his third and fourth fingers, reminding me of a European movie actor. He puffed fastidiously. There was a neatness about the man which showed most prominently in his diction.

"I can't know if I can help you until I have"—each beloved word chosen carefully and handed out graciously, like choice pieces of fruit—"seen you perform."

The piano player, who was white and experienced, intimidated me nearly as much as the drama coach. Earlier in the afternoon he had asked for my sheet music, and when I told him that the songs I intended to sing had hardly been published, he slammed the piano lid down and stood up.

"Do you mean I'm supposed to play without music? Just vamp till ready?' "

I did not understand his indignation, nor the sarcasm in his last question. "I've signed a contract and I'm supposed to open in two weeks. What can I do?" I had found that direct questions brought direct answers if they brought answers at all.

"Have some lead sheets written for you," he said indifferently.

"Can you do it? May I pay you to write the lead sheets? Whatever they are."

He gave me a thin smile and, partially pacified, said, "If I can find the time."

He sat again on the bench and opened the piano. "What do you sing?"

I said, "Calypso. 'Stone Cold Dead in the Market.' 'Run Joe,' 'Babalu.' Things like that."

He asked, "What key for 'Stone Cold Dead'?" His fingers ran over the keyboard and I thought of my pervasive ignorance.

"I don't know." The music stopped and the musician leaned his head an the piano. He was so dramatic I thought he should have been the star.

I said, "I'm sorry to be a bother." Usually when one throws oneself at another's feet, one should be prepared to do a fast roll to avoid being stepped on. "But I'd appreciate your help—I'm new."

The pianist rose to the occasion, which, given his sardonic expression earlier, might have come as a bigger surprise to him than to me.

"O.K." He straightened away from the keyboard. "Try this." He started to play and I recognized the tune.

"Yes, that's it."

"I know that's it," he said dryly. "Now how about singing so I can find your key."

I listened carefully, squinting my eyes and tried to find where in all the notes he played I should insert my voice.

383

"Sing." It was an order.

I started: "He's stone cold dead in de market."

"No, that's wrong. Listen." He played, I listened. I started to sing. He said, "No, wrong again."

Finally by chance I hit the right note. The pianist grudgingly nodded and I sang the song through.

He stood up and bounced a glance off me as he turned toward the bar. "You need music. You really need it."

I watched him order and then gulp down a drink greedily. And here was Lloyd Clark, tended by his adoring Brünnhilde, telling me to repeat the awkward performance.

Whenever I had danced non-angelically on the point of a pin, I always knew I might slip and break my neck. It could be fatal, but at least all anxiety would cease. Because of that, I often rushed toward holocausts with an abandon that caused observers to think of me as courageous. The truth was, I simply wanted an end to uncertainty.

The pianist responded to my nod and with visible resignation sat at the piano and began to play the song we had tried earlier.

I looked beyond my audience and decided to ignore the musician and his snide attitude. I fastened my mind on the plot. A poor West Indian woman had been threatened by her brutal husband (my mother's father was Trinidadian, and although he was kind he was very severe) and she struck back in self-defense. My sympathies rested with the mistreated woman. So I told the story from her point of view.

Don said, "Great, just great."

Jorie asked Lloyd and the world at large, "Didn't I say she's marvy?"

Lloyd rose smiling, he came toward me offering his hands "Fab, fab, darling, you're going to be fab. You're marvelously dramatic." He turned to his wife, who was like a tall, white shadow following him. "Isn't she, Marg? Just fab?"

Marguerite gave him a loving smile "Yes, Lloyd darling." Then to me she said softly, "You're good. So very good. And after you work with Lloyd... Oh, I can hardly wait." Her voice belied impatience.

"Now, dear, do sit down. Come, we must do some serious talking." Lloyd took my hands. He leaned around me and said to the musician who was beelining for the bar, "Thank you, young man, thank you. And you did it without lead sheets. Brilliant!"

"Now, my dear, sit." He pulled me along to Jorie's table. She patted my cheek and lowered one long-lashed eye slowly, meaning I was in, and hadn't she said so, and I had nothing to worry about and weren't we all so awfully smart. I winked back and grinned.

Marguerite sat so close to Lloyd she was nearly in his lap and Don made congratulatory little noises to me and to himself.

384

"First, dear, your name," Lloyd said.

"Rita."

"Is that your name? The name you were born with?" Disbelief was evident.

"No, my name is Marguerite."

Marguerite Clark complimented us both. "Oh, isn't that nice?"

"It's all right for you, Marguerite, but it doesn't do anything for her." I had been named for my maternal grandmother, who would not have taken kindly to that statement.

"She needs something more exotic. More glamorous." Lloyd turned to Jorie and Don. "Don't you agree?"

They did indeed.

"A really good name," Don said, "is half the act."

I thought about the popular entertainers who were mentioned in the newspapers weekly. I didn't know if their names were created for show business or if the entertainers had simply been lucky. I said nothing.

"Let's think. Think up some names "

Don went to the bar and brought over a bottle of wine and some glasses.

Thaïs, Sappho, Diana, Lana, Bette, names of heroines from Greek history, world literature and Hollywood were bandied about, but none seemed to please my inventors.

I said, "My brother has always called me Maya For 'Marguerite.' He used to call me 'My sister,' then he called me 'My,' and finally, 'Maya.' Is that all right?"

Jorie said, "Di-vine. Di-vine, darling."

Don was ecstatic. "It suits you, my dear, oh God, it suits you."

Marguerite waited for Lloyd. He thought, looking at me pointedly, trying to find the name in my face. After a minute, he said, "Yes, you're Maya," as if he was christening me.

Marguerite said, "Lloyd, you're right, darling. She *is* Maya."

Don passed the wine around.

"Maya what?" Jorie looked at Lloyd. "Do deliver us from performers with one name. Hildegarde, Liberace. No, she must have at least two names."

I said, "My married name is Angelos."

Don chewed the words around, tasting them.

"Maya Angelos." Jorie took the name over, weighing it on her tongue. "That's not bad."

Lloyd said, "It sounds too Spanish. Or Italian. No, it won't do." An idea broke his face wide open. "I've got it. Drop the *s* and add a *u*. Maya Angelou." He pronounced it Angeloo. "Of course! That's it!"

Jorie said it was too divine. Don said it was perfection. Marguerite beamed her approval of Lloyd and then of the name.

We all drank wine to toast our success. I had a job, a drama coach, a pianist who was going to provide me with lead sheets, and I had a new name (I wondered if I'd ever feel it described the me myself of me).

We began to prepare for my debut. For three hours each day Lloyd coached me. His instructions included how to stand, how to walk, how to turn and offer my best profile to an audience. He worked over my act as busily as a couturier creating a wedding gown for royalty.

"My dear, but you *must* stand still. Glide out onstage like the *Queen Mary* slipping out of her berth, reach the piano and then stand absolutely, but absolutely, still. After a few seconds look around at your audience and then, only then, at your pianist. Nod your head to him and then you will begin your music. When he finishes his intro, then you will begin to sing."

I found standing still the most difficult of all his instructions. During rehearsal when I was introduced my nerves shivered and the swallows in my stomach did nose dives. I would hear "... and now Miss Maya Angelou," and I would race from the dressing room, down the narrow aisle to the stage and, immediately, without waiting for the music, begin: "Moe and Joe ran a candy store."

"No, my dear. Still. Be totally still. Think of a deep pool."

Again and again I tried until I was able to walk on stage, and, thinking of nothing at all—neither deep pools nor sailing ships— stand absolutely still.

Lloyd said I had to learn at least twelve songs before opening night. I plundered the memories of every acquaintance. Mornings found me in the sheet music shops and record stores, ferreting for material. By midday, I hurried to the pianist's apartment, where we practiced songs over and over until they began to have less meaning than words in a children's game. Afternoons I worked with Lloyd in my house. When he left, I selected some songs to practice in front of Clyde. Although I sang the cute, the humorous songs for his enjoyment and would prance around this way and that, he always watched me with a seriousness that would have impressed a judge. When I finished he would remove his horn-rimmed glasses and look at me speculatively and ask, "Gee, Mom, how can you remember all those words?"

Clyde had become a talker. He talked to me, to the family, to strangers and had long, involved conversations with himself. His discourses ranged over the subjects of his life. He had become a voracious reader, consuming books whole at nearly one sitting, then reliving the plot in his conversations. He read science fiction (he loved Ray Bradbury) and western pulp, his Sunday School lessons, Paul Laurence Dunbar's poems and animal stories and explained to all who would listen that he, Red Ryder and Fluke were going to ride their horses to the moon and talk to God, who was an old Black man who played the guitar. Red Ryder was a Western character from books and Fluke was Clyde's invisible miscreant friend. Fluke made him laugh aloud with his mischievousness. He was able to do things Clyde could not do, and Fluke did them with impunity. If a lamp was overturned and broken, it was because Fluke was walking around on the lampshade. When the bathtub ran over and turned the tiled floor into a shallow pool, Fluke had gone to the bathroom after Clyde left and turned the spigot on.

Vainly I tried to explain the difference between lying and making up a story, but decided it was more important that Clyde keep his nonexistent buddy to lessen the loneliness of an only child. I liked to listen from the kitchen when he told Fluke good-night stories and when, in his morning bath, he laughed outright as he warned his friend against indulging in some troublemaking antic.

Francis, the dressmaker, took Gerry's (with a G) ideas and fashioned long, snug dresses out of bolts of raw silk and white corduroy. The gowns were slit on both sides from floor to hip, and underneath 1 wore one-legged pants of gay batik. When I stood still, the dress material fell gracefully, giving an impression of sober elegance, but when I moved the panels would fiy up and it seemed as if one leg was bare and the other tattooed. I wore no shoes. The total effect was more sensational than attractive, but having no illusions about my ability to sing, I reasoned that if I could startle the audience with my costumes and my personality, they might be so diverted that they wouldn't notice.

Opening night, I longed for one of two things. To be dead—dead and forgotten—or to have my brother beside me. Life had made some strenuous demands on me, and although I had never ruled out suicide, no experience so far had shattered me enough to make me consider it seriously. And my brother, Bailey, who could make me laugh at terror or allow me the freedom to cry over sentimental things, was in New York State, grappling with his own bitter reality. So, despite my wishes, I was alive and I was alone.

I watched through a peephole as Barry Drew walked to the stage. He claimed that he was descended from two great theatrical families and had to live up to his heritage.

"And now, ladies and gentlemen"—he rubbed his hands together—"this evening, making her debut at the Purple Onion"—he turned his best side to the light and opened his arms for the world—"Miss Maya Angelou!"

There was some applause, not enough to hearten but not so little I could deny that people were waiting for me.

387

I counted three and walked slowly down the aisle and onto the stage. I stood still as I had at rehearsal, and a dead calm surrounded me. One second later fear plummeted to my stomach and made my knees weak. I realized that I could not see the people. No one had warned me that a combination of spotlights and nerves would cause blindness. The aisle down which I had walked still lay open and unobstructed. I looked at it once, longingly, then turned to the pianist and nodded. And although I did not know it, another career for me had begun.

Popularity was an intoxicant and I swayed drunkenly for months. Newspaper reporters began to ask for interviews and I gave them in an ersatz accent, which was a mélange of the speech of Ricardo Montalban, Jorie Remus and Akim Tamiroff. I was invited to talk on radio and sing on television. Fans began to recognize me in the street and one well-to-do woman organized a ten-member Maya Angelou fan club.

Later I met people who said, "I saw you dance at the Purple Onion." I graciously withheld the information that in fact I was hired at the club as a singer, but the songs had many refrains and such complex rhythms that often I got lost in the plot and forgot the lyrics. So, when the words eluded me, I would admit my poor memory and add that if the audience would bear with me I would dance. The first few times I owned up to a weak memory, Lloyd Clark and Barry Drew frowned disapprovingiy, but after the audiences applauded loudly Barry accepted it and Lloyd said, "Wonderful, dear, wonderful. Keep it in. In fact, you should dance more."

I shared the bill with a strange and talented couple. Jane Connell sang scatterbrained ditties, while her sober-side husband Gordon dryly played piano. Their patter was sharp and displayed their Berkeley university background. When they left to join Jorie in New York's Blue Angel, a frowzy blond housewife from Alameda auditioned and was accepted at the club. She brought a wardrobe of silly flowered hats and moth-eaten boas which she flung around her thin neck. Her laugh, which she shared often, was a cross between a donkey's braying and a foghorn. She said she would not change her name because when she became successful she wanted everyone to know it was, indeed, her herself. The name was painted in large white letters outside the club: Phyllis Diller.

11

Without a father in the house and no other male authority figure in his world, Clyde fell under the spell of uniforms. He began to adore policemen and daydream about becoming a bomber pilot.

"I'll zoom down like this, Mom, brrr and blow their heads off. Boom, boom, boom." He marched and clumped around the house in a poor parody of Gestapo goose-stepping. He saluted walls and chairs and ordered doors to be "at rest, Sergeant Door." He had become enamored of the Air Force and every evening at bedtime he waited in his room for me to hear his prayers and then to sing (he would join in):

> "off we go into the wild blue yonder
> Singing songs into the blue..."

Each evening as I left for work, the baby-sitter would say, "Our little soldier is bedded down in his bunk, huh?" I wished I could have cashiered her out of my service with dishonorable discharge.

I was dismayed, but I left him alone until I could decide on the best way to counter his sudden affection for violence. I hoped for divine intercession and bided my time. As his birthday approached he began spending time after school in the local five-and-dime store. He wanted a machine gun or a tank or a pistol that shot real plastic bullets or a BB gun. I took him to the local S.P.C.A. pound and told him he could have an animal. A small dog or any cat he wanted. He wandered around the cages, choosing one dog and then rejecting it when he saw a lonelier-looking cat. He finally settled on a small black kitten with rheumy eyes and a dull, dusty coat. I asked the attendant if the cat was healthy. He said it was, but that it had been taken from its mother too early and abandoned. It needed personal care or the pound would have to destroy it. Clyde was shocked. I could barely get him and his ragged cat out of the building before rage broke through. "Mom, did he mean he would have to kill my cat?"

He was clutching the small animal so tightly I thought he himself might put an end to its miserable life.

"Yes, if no one wanted it, they'd do away with it."

"But Mom, isn't that place called a place for the protection of animals?"

"Yes."

"Well." He thought for a few minutes. "Wow! What sort of person would have a job like that? Going around killing animals all the time."

I saw my opening. "Of course, some people have jobs that order them to go around killing human beings."

The earlier shock was nothing to the sensation that caught and held him. He nearly squeezed the breath out of the kitten. "What? Who? Who kills human beings?"

"Oh, soldiers, sailors. Pilots who use machine guns and bombs. You know. That's mainly what they're hired for."

He leaned back in the car, stroking the kitten. Silent, thinking.

I never mentioned killing again and he never asked for another weapon.

Leonard Sillman's Broadway hit *New Faces of 1953* came West in 1954. San Francisco, already the home of irreverent comedians, political folk singers, expensively dressed female impersonators, beat poets and popular cabaret singers, took the witty revue to its heart. Don Curry and I attended an early matinée. When Eartha Kitt sang "Monotonous" in her throaty vibrato and threw her sleek body on a sleek chaise longue, the audiences loved her. Alice Ghostly, with "Boston Beguine," created a picture of a hilarious seduction scene in a seedy hotel lobby where "even the palms seemed to be potted." Paul Lynde, as a missionary newly returned from a three-day tour of the African continent, and Robert Clary, as the cup-sized Frenchman rolling his saucer eyes, turned farce into a force that was irresistible. Ronnie Graham shared the writing and performed in skits with June Carrol.

I left the theater nearly numb. The quality of talent and quantity of energy had drained me of responses.

My family made plans to come to the Onion for an early show. Mother was coming with Aunt Lottie, and they were bringing a few old-time gamblers from the Fillmore district who never left the Negro neighborhood except to buy expensive suits from white tailors. Ivonne was bringing her daughter, Joyce, and Clyde. I reserved front-row seats and then spent a nervous thirty minutes waiting for them to arrive.

The adults had a loud, happy reunion in the front row. A stranger could easily have deduced that they had not seen each other in months or more probably years.

Mother's friends examined Clyde and complimented him on growing so fast. He beamed and threw back his already wide

390

shoulders. Lottie praised Joyce for "turning into a fine young lady" and the conservatively dressed men who generally dealt the poker at the legally illegal gambling houses smiled at everyone and politely ordered drinks for the party. Ketty Lester, a great beauty who hailed from a small Arkansas town thirty miles north of my home, always opened the show. She sang good songs and sang them well. Phyllis Diller followed her and spread her aura of madness over the stage and onto the audience, and then I closed the round's entertainment. The older people were transfixed by Ketty's singing. She sang "Little Girl from Little Rock" and the black people who all had Southern roots acted as if the song had been written expressly for Ketty to sing to them. From the rear of the club, I watched as they smiled and nodded to one another and didn't have to be in hearing distance to know they were exchanging "That's right" and "Sure is" and "Ain't that the truth?"

There was only a minute between the last notes of her encore and Phyllis Diller's introduction. Curiosity kept me standing against the back wall, for I wanted to see how my family would take to the frumpy comedienne. Black people rarely forgave whites for being ragged, unkempt and uncaring. There was a saying which explained the disapproval: You been white all your life. Ain't got no further along than this? What ails you?"

When Phyllis came out onstage, Clyde almost fell off the chair and Joyce started giggling so she nearly knocked over her Shirley Temple. The comedienne, dressed outrageously and guffawing like a hiccoughing horse and a bell clapper, chose to play to the two children (she had four of her own). They were charmed and so convulsed with laughter they gasped for breath, but being well-brought-up Negro youngsters who were told nice children do not laugh loudly, they put their hands over their mouths.

I slipped into the dressing room, pleased that at last there was something in the show for everyone. Only Ivonne had appeared less than enchanted with the two acts. But then I knew she was waiting for me to sing.

I walked down the aisle to the stage, registering the applause and hoping that my family was not so busy clapping their hands that they were unable to note that other people were applauding as well. I stood quietly, looking out into the audience (I had enlarged on Lloyd's coaching and now took the time to select faces in the pale light). My breath caught audibly as I recognized Alice Ghostly and Paul Lynde at a table midway in the room. Their presence exhilarated me.

I nodded to the three musicians and began my song.

> "I put the peas in the pot to cook
> I got the paper and started to look
> My horse..."

I heard the "shush" and "hush" from somewhere around my kneecaps, but kept on singing.

> "... was running at twenty to one
> So me peas and me rice
> They get..."

The "tsk's" and the "sh's" were coming from my family. I looked down and saw everyone leaning in toward Clyde. His mouth was open and smiling, and then I heard his voice and knew why everyone was admonishing him. He was singing with me—after all, he had heard every song rehearsed a hundred times at home and now he decided to show me that he, too, could memorize the words. It might have been ignored if he had kept up with me, but his words lagged behind mine by at least one beat.

> "I put..."
> *"I"*
> "... the peas in..."
> *"...put the..."*
> "The pot to cook..."
> *"peas in..."*

Absolutely the first time I had a chance to sing for big-time stars and my son was messing it up, I looked at him, hard this time, and he laughed openly. His eyes nearly shut as his face gave way to his own private joke. He acted as if we were playing a game, like twenty questions or top this, and he was enjoying himself so much that I had to forget about the audience and settle for entertaining my son. I tried to slow down my delivery until he could catch up.

When we finished, still a beat apart, I thanked the audience and added that I had had some unexpected but very welcome help. I introduced my son, Mr. Clyde Bailey Johnson. He stood, turned to the audience and bowed, straight-faced, as he had seen his favorite Bud Abbott do in so many films. I gave Clyde a look that in parent/offspring language meant "That was nice, but now we've stopped playing." He translated aptly and was quiet through the rest of my performance.

In the dressing room my family clutched around me, talking in low voices, commending me, relieved that at least I was good enough to spare them embarassment. They saved their compliments for Ketty and Phyllis, paganly believing that too much praise attracted the gods' attention and might summon their powerful jealousy. They also thought I just might get a swelled head if given too many compliments, so instead they gave me sly looks and furtive pats and when no one was looking the slick old men encouraged me to "keep up the good work." They whispered that Ketty and I were the best on the bill but we had "better be careful" and "take it easy, 'cause white folks get jealous when they see Negroes gettin' ahead."

They left the club, taking with them the familiar nuances and I was somewhat relieved when they had gone. Insecurity can make us spurn the persons and traditions we most enjoy. I had always loved the gamblers when they sat in Mother's kitchen telling tales of the Texas Panhandle and reliving the excitement of boom towns in Oklahoma. But downtown, where educated whites might overhear the Negro grammar and think less of me because of it, I was uncomfortable.

Alice and Paul came to the dressing room and invited me out for a drink. I accepted immediately. We exchanged compliments and during the intermission we sat in an easy friendliness until the next show began. A few nights later Alice brought other members of the company down to catch my show. One singer told me that Eartha was leaving and Leonard Sillman and Ronnie Graham were auditioning dancer/singers to replace her. She had been bound by a contract which had run out at last and was going to open in one of the big-paying Las Vegas hotels. And would I like to try for the part? Naturally I wanted to audition and just as naturally I was petrified.

The theater stage jutted out aggressively into an empty darkness. Sillman sat erect on a straight-backed chair, apart from, yet fearfully a part of, the proceedings.

I was shivering in the wings, thinking of the excitement Eartha brought to her music when a stage manager asked me if I was going to sing "Monotonous." The play on words occurred to me and I did not find it funny. I said yes, but did not add that I would not be singing it like Eartha Kitt. She was overtly sexy and famously sensual. I was friendly, gangly and more the big-sister type. No, I would have no chance if I tried imitating the brown velvet kitten.

When I was called I went out onto the stage and put my hands on my hips and a foot on the chaise longue. I sang a few bars, then swirled around and put the other foot on the chaise longue. I sang and danced, skimming over the stage (a dance teacher had told me when I was fourteen years old that a good dancer "occupies space consciously"), always ending back at the seat with an attitude of haughty boredom. My plan was to capture attention by

393

displaying absolute contradiction. Hot dance and cool indifference.

I waited an interminable two days for Leonard Sillman's "reaction." The phone call came and my heart jumped against my breastbone. I had the job. The famous show-business break had come. Ivonne's friend Calvin bought champagne and we celebrated at her house. I also bought champagne (although I did not care very much for it) and went to Mr. Hot Dogs, where Mom and Lottie and the counter customers helped me to celebrate. I told them that I would join the company for the rest of its tour, then settle down in New York City. My only hesitation was caused by the question of what to do about Clyde. Mom and Lottie said they would take care of him. He could have his breakfast at home as usual and come directly to the restaurant after school, by which time one of them would be going home on the split shift. I accepted that solution, knowing that when I "made it," as I was sure to do, I would rent a large Manhattan apartment and hire a governess for my son. And when I traveled I would take him along with the governess and possibly a tutor.

My life was arranging itself as neatly as a marble staircase and I was climbing to the stars.

Barry Drew met my announcement with an apoplectic explosion. "Oh no, you're not. What? You can't close. What? We have you under contract, you can't walk out on a contract."

I countered that I had already accepted the role, that he had the Kingston Trio and Rod McKuen opening at the club and they were as good or better than I. "I will never have another chance like this again. I don't want to spend my life at the Purple Onion."

He was firm. "You didn't think that when we brought you in here. You're lucky we didn't offer you a year's contract. You'd have signed your life away to get a job like this."

I cried and begged and hated myself for doing so. He remained unmoved. I ranted about his cruelty, throwing curse words at him like blobs of hot tar, hoping at least to smear his surface.

Barry said coolly, "Sillman not only will not, but cannot, hire you if you break your contract. The union will have you up on charges and you will be blackballed."

He acted as if he himself had founded the union and written its bylaws just to keep restless and irresponsible singers in their places. His contempt was impenetrable. My anger calmed enough for me to see my predicament. I was totally hemmed in and I left the club and headed home, glowering at every passerby and wrapped up close in sullenness.

I expected sympathy from the rest of my family and received it in generous portions. My mother said she was shocked at Barry's behavior, but then as she always said, "The smallest insect makes the most noise," and I should keep that in mind. Aunt Lottie stroked me, gave me tea and as if I were sick, offered to make a nice pot of soup. Ivonne told me on the telephone that I was right to be angry, but to consider that the role in the play simply was not for me and as the saying goes, "You can't miss something you never had."

My pain yielded to the well-worn adages and soft consoling voices. In the absence of anguish I was able to think. It became clear that the roles had been exchanged. Once I had had a need of the Purple Onion facilities and now the Purple Onion had need of my services. The thought that irritated me and planted a seed of disdain was that the managers of the club had not noticed the reversal and had not the grace to appeal to my sense of "Turnabout is fair play."

I had heard the statement made by wistful whites (and had also made it in my youth myself, hoping to prove worthy of acceptance): "There's nothing as loyal as a Negro. Once you make a friend of one, you have a friend for life." Like making a pet of a grizzly bear.

My attitude at the club proved either that the statement was fallacious or that I was not a Negro. I withdrew my affection and kept only the shell of cool courtesy.

12

"Hello, Mrs. Angelos?"

The telephone had rung on a bleary morning. It was a woman's voice.

"Yes?"

"This is Tennessee Kent at Golden Gate School."

"Yes?" I suppose the wonder in my voice carried over the wires.

"Your son, Clyde, is a student here."

My son's name brought me immediately clear of sleep. "Yes, I know that." Suddenly a clear-headed, responsible mother.

"I think possibly you'd like to come to school and discuss something Clyde has said."

"Is he all right?"

"Oh, yes, don't worry about him."

I did just that as I dressed.

Since our brief period of estrangement, I had worked very hard impressing Clyde that I was reliable, that in any conflict I was on his side. I had not forgotten the importance of my brother's impartial love during my own lonely childhood, and since my son had no sibling, I had to make him know he had support.

I went to the school and found Clyde sitting forlornly on a straight chair in the corridor. I patted his shoulder and stooped to ask what had happened. His eyes were liquid with unshed tears.

He whispered, "I don't know, Mom. They said I said something bad."

"Did you?" He had learned some profanity at a day camp the year before and had been quite proud of it for a few weeks.

"I don't know," he still whispered.

The two women remained seated when I led Clyde into the office.

"Good morning, Mrs. Angelos," Miss Kent said. "This is Clyde's teacher, Miss Blum." A stout, middle-aged woman nodded to me seriously. Miss Kent went on, "And maybe it's better to let Clyde sit outside in the corridor while we..."

"No"—I still had my hand on his shoulder—"this concerns him. I want him to hear the discussion."

The teachers exchanged looks. I directed Clyde to a chair and sat beside him.

"Well, maybe Miss Blum will tell you what happened," Miss Kent said.

Clyde's little body was trembling. I patted his knee.

Miss Blum said, "Yesterday was Armed Forces Day and I asked all the children what branch of the service they admired. Some said Navy, others Air Force, others Seabees, but Clyde stood up on his turn and said he'd go to jail first." She looked at him with such venom I wanted to put my body between her look and my son.

Miss Kent said soothingly, "Now, Mrs. Angelos, we know Clyde didn't get that at home. So, we wanted you to know that somewhere, maybe among his friends, he's picking up dangerous thoughts."

I thought immediately about Joseph McCarthy. The witch hunt was in full stride and newspapers carried items about blacklists and jobs being jeopardized. Reputations had been ruined and some people imprisoned because they were suspected of harboring dangerous and treacherous thoughts. My own background was not without incident. When I was nineteen, I had enlisted in the Army and been given a date for induction, but had been summarily rejected because it was discovered that during my fourteenth and fifteenth years I had gone to a school which was on the list of un-American activities.

They said they knew he didn't pick up such thoughts at home.

"Yes, he got that at home, Miss Kent." Oh Lord, my career. What would the Rockwell family do if I was accused of Communist leanings?

"Oh, is that your religious belief?" She was being nice-nasty, giving me a cowardly way out. My son sat beside me, waiting. He had stopped trembling and was holding himself tight, listening to the exchange.

"If you mean do I believe in it religiously, I do."

"Oh, then Clyde was voicing your political views that you hold religiously?"

There was nothing for it but to agree. I said, "That's right."

And that was all Clyde had been waiting for. He bounced up out of his chair, arms stretched and flailing.

"Mom, isn't it true that just because U.S. Steel wants to sell more steel, I shouldn't go and kill some baby Koreans who never did anything to me?"

"Yes, that's true."

"And, Mom, isn't it true that capitalists just make the poor people go and bomb other poor people till they're all dead and live on dead people's money?"

I did not recognize that line, but I said "Yes."

He lifted his arms like a conductor asking a full orchestra for the last chord. "Well, that's all I said."

The teachers sat silent as I stood up.

"Miss Kent, and Miss Blum, I think the session has been emotionally very tiring for Clyde. I'll take him home now and he'll come back to school tomorrow."

They did nothing to hinder our departure.

That afternoon Clyde and I went to a movie that showed ten Disney shorts.

13

George Hitchcock was a playwright whose play *Princess Chan Chan* was being performed by the Interplayers at a little theater near North Beach. A tall, shambling man with large hands and a staccato laugh, he doubled as an aging character actor. His hair was always dusty because he did not effectively rinse out the white powder.

He watched my show and afterwards asked if he could see me

home. I wanted to accept, but wondered what he would think of my living arrangements. I was a glamorous night-club singer, or at least wanted to be considered glamorous, but I still lived at home with my mother. Late evenings I would find her sitting at the dining room table drinking beer and playing solitaire, and definitely not waiting up for me. I was a grown woman and had better know how to look after myself. Just to make sure, she played solitaire until I came home. Her voice would greet the sound of the opening front door. "Hi, baby, I'm in here."

I would say, "Good evening, Mom." And when she lifted her face for a kiss, she'd ask, "How'd it go this evening?" and I'd say, "O.K., Mom." That was what she wanted to hear, and all she wanted to know. Vivian Baxter could and would deal with grand schemes and large plots, but please, pray God, spare her the details.

I invited George home, and on the way, told him about my mother and my son. If he was surprised he didn't show it.

I countered Mom's "Hi, baby. I'm in here" with "I brought a friend home."

George would have had to know my mother to have recognized how startled she was when he walked in. She stopped her laying out of red and black and said, "Welcome," then "How are you tonight?" As if she knew how he had fared the night before.

George seemed at ease.

Mother looked at his worn tweed jacket, rumpled trousers and not quite clean hair and asked, "How long have you known my daughter?"

I knew where she was heading. I said, "We've just met tonight, Mom. George is a writer. That information held her steady for a while.

"He asked me out for a coffee and I thought maybe you'd have a pot on." Coffee was drunk by the potful at breakfast, but never served in my mother's house after morning. "But, of course, we can go down the street to the Booker T. Washington Hotel."

She bounced out of her chair. "Only takes a minute. How about some breakfast?"

I knew the idea of her daughter going into the then swankiest Negro hotel in town, escorted by a raggedy-looking white man would cause hospitality to flow like water.

She invited us into the kitchen.

"What about a little omelette and some bacon?" She turned on the oven and I held out my hand. Whenever she baked biscuits she removed her large diamond rings and put them on my fingers. "And just a few hot biscuits?"

She began the arrangement of bowls and pans and I excused myself and left George to his fate.

398

When I returned, changed out of evening clothes, the meal was nearly ready and she ordered me to set the table for two, and asked, "So, did you know that George makes a living as a gardener?"

"No, how do you know? Did George tell you that?"

George said, "Yes."

Mom was moving round the kitchen talking, cooking, singing little wisps of songs, the diamond earrings twinkling.

He was hypnotized.

"Put some butter on the table, Maya, please, and did you know he's unmarried and not thinking about getting married in the foreseeable future? Will the strawberry preserves be all right? Get that platter out of the cupboard, will you? Hum, hum..." She whipped up the eggs with a whisk.

"George, how did you come to tell my mother so much of your business?"

He shrugged his shoulders helplessly. "She asked me."

Mother said later that since he was white that was enough to make him unsuitable, but he was also much too old for me. Still I found his company easy and his intelligence exciting. He understood loving poetry, and although I would not show him my own poems, I recited Shakespearean sonnets and Paul Laurence Dunbar late at night in his house in Sausalito.

We shared long walks in Golden Gate Park and picnicked in John Muir woods. His mother was a well-known San Francisco journalist and he told me endless stories of the area and its colorful characters.

A gentle affection, devoid of romance, grew up between us and I enjoyed watching from his window as night faded over the Golden Gate Bridge. I was always back home before daybreak because Clyde expected me at the breakfast table while he chatted about his dreams or Fluke's misdoings.

I answered the telephone.

"Meez Angeloo?"

"Yes."

The voice was male and rich and the accent thick and poetic.

"My name is Yanko Varda. I am a painter." He was a well-known figure in San Francisco art circles.

"Yes, Mr. Varda." Why was he calling me?

"No, pleez—Yanko. Just Yanko."

"Yes, Yanko?" Yes, but why was he calling me?

"Meez Angeloo, I have heard so much about you, about your beauty and your talent and your grace. I have decided I must meet this wonderful woman with whom all the men are in love.

I could not think of a soul who was in love with me, but who can resist the suggestion that one has secret admirers?

"How nice of you to say that."

"Not atall. No, not atall. I have decided that I must give a dinner for you so that I myself may see this phenomenon: a beautiful woman with a great mind."

I knew I did not fit his description, but I would have torn my tongue out before I would have denied it.

He set Monday night for dinner and said he lived on a houseboat in Sausalito.

"George Hitchcock will bring you to my boat, which is called the *Vallejo*. I shall prepare, as only I can prepare, an ambrosia fit for a princess, but if you are in fact a queen, as I suspect, I hope you will condescend to take a sip from these humble hands. George will bring you to me. *Au revoir*."

He sounded like a character in a Russian novel. The embroidery of his language, complex and passionate, enchanted me.

What did one wear to an ambrosial dinner on a houseboat? I selected and rejected every outfit in my closet and finally settled on a flowered dress that belonged to my mother. It was gay but not frivolous, chic but not formal.

George and I drove across the Golden Gate Bridge through a swirling fog and he stopped the car near the water. I stepped out onto wet mud. He rushed around and took my hand. "Follow me, walk on the planks."

Thick boards extended to a small rickety bridge. Lights shone dimly in the mists, but I had to keep my attention on the walkway or I might fall into the sullen-looking water below.

There were turns and steps and more turns. Then George stopped, turned and moved around me in the short space. "Here's where I get off. You go on up these three steps and knock at the door."

I tried to see his face in the overcast night. "What are you talking about?" His features were indistinct.

"I'm not invited tonight. This dinner is just for you."

"Well, wait a minute, I'm not going to..." I reached for him.

He backed away, laughing, it seemed to me, sardonically. "I'll be back to pick you up at eleven. *Bon appétit*!"

During our short relationship, I had projected an air of independence, kindly but assured, and I could not scream at him or race down the flimsy walkway to clutch his retreating back.

I stood until George melted in the mist, then I turned and looked around. The shape of a large boat seemed to shiver in and out of a dark, misty sky, its windows beaming happily like lights in a giant jack-o'-lantern.

I walked up the remaining stairs wondering if I had been set up for an orgy—or perhaps I was to be an innocent participator in devil worship. I knew you could never tell about white people. Negroes had survived centuries of inhuman treatment and retained their humanity by hoping for the best from their pale-skinned oppressors but at the same time being prepared for the worst.

I looked through the porch door window at a short sturdy man quickly lighting candles in wine bottles, which he put on a long wooden table. No one else was visible, and although he looked strong, I decided I could probably take care of myself if he tried to take advantage of me.

I knocked sharply on the windowpane. The man looked up toward the door and smiled. His face was nearly as brown as mine and a sheaf of gray hair trembled when he moved. He came directly to the door, his smile broadening with each step.

"Rima," I thought I heard him say through the closed door. He pulled the door open and in the same movement stepped away from it and admired me.

"Ah, Rima, it ees you." He could not have been happier.

"No. Uh. My name is Maya."

He was expecting someone else. I quickly traced the days. This was Monday. Had I misunderstood him because of his accent or my excitement? But then, George must have made a mistake too.

"Don't stand there, my dear. Come in. Let me take your coat. Come in."

I walked into the warm kitchen, whose air was dense with the odor of cooking herbs. I looked at my host as he closed the door and hung my coat on a wall peg. His arms were thick and muscled and his neck broad and weather-roughened.

He turned. "Now, Rima, at last you've come to me. Let us drink wine to this meeting."

He seemed so happy, I was truly sorry to disappoint him. "I'm sorry, but I'm Maya Angelou. I'm the singer."

"My dear, I have known since I was a small boy on a hill in Greece that when I met you, you'd never tell me who you were, you would give another name. Equally beautiful and equally mystical. But I would know you by the music in your voice and the shadow of the forest on your beautiful face."

I was completely undone.

Over goblets of wine, he re-created his own version of the Rima legend for me. A creature, half girl and half bird, came periodically to earth assuming full womanly form, singing lilting birdlike melodies and lightening human hearts. Her stays were brief, then she became a bird and flew away to her beloved forest where she was happiest and free. While we ate a thick meat soup, he told me of W. H. Hudson's *Green Mansions* and the heroine, Rima, and said he would lend me the book, since its story was based on my magic.

"I shall address you as Maya in both public and private, for I fear if I continue calling you Rima, you may become annoyed and fly away. But you shall always know that in a small place in my heart I am thanking you for your visit."

The walls were adorned with delicately tinted pastels, and he guided me to each one, explaining, "In this collage I have tried to show a Carthaginian ship, swathed in grace moving from the harbor on its route to pillage another civilization. And here we have the King and Queen of Patagonia before the Feast of Stars." He talked about the beauty of Greece and the excitement of Paris. He was a close friend of Henry Miller and an acquaintance of Pablo Picasso. The time sped by as we ate fruit and cheese and I listened to the stories told in English as ornate as a Greek Orthodox ritual.

"I have a set of young friends who will be embellished by your presence. I beg you to be kind enough to come back to the *Vallejo* on a Sunday afternoon and meet them. We form a party each week and drink wine, eat soup and feast upon the riches of each other's thoughts. Please come—the men will surely worship you and the women will adore you."

George returned for me, and after a ceremonial glass of wine and an embrace from Yanko's leathery arms, he took me back to his house and patiently listened to my story of the evening. He stopped me: "Maya, I believe you're infatuated with Yanko."

"I most certainly am not."

"Many women find him irresistible."

"Probably." And I added without thinking, "but he is old and white."

George got up and turned on the record player.

One night at the Purple Onion I bowed to a full house and as I raised my head I heard "Bravo," "Bis," "Bravo." A group of people were standing in the middle of the room applauding, their hands over their heads like flamenco dancers. I bowed again and blew kisses as I had seen it done in movies. They continued applauding and shouting "More!" until the other patrons rose and, joining the group, implored me for another song. I always planned for at least two encores, so it was not the requests that embarrassed me but, rather, the overt display of appreciation which I had never received before. I sang another song and retreated to my dressing room. A waiter brought me a note which informed me: "We are friends." Please join us. Mitch."

I went to the table reluctantly, fearing they might be drunks, out for an evening's hilarity at anyone's expense.

As I approached, the group stood again and began applauding. I was ready to flee to the safety of my dressing room.

A large, dark-haired man offered me his hand.

"Maya, I am Mitch Lifton." He indicated the others individually. I shook hands with Victor Di Suvero and Henrietta, Francis and Bob Anshen, and Annette and Cyril March. "We are friends of Yanko and he suggested that we come to see you. You are absolutely wonderful."

We sat drinking wine and they gave me their particulars. Mitch Lifton's parents were Russian Jews, he was born in Paris, grew up in Mexico and was interested in film. Victor Di Suvero was a descendant of an Italian family that still had businesses in Italy and he was seriously courting the breath-taking Henrietta. Cyril March was a dermatologist from France, and architect Robert Anshen was a Frank Lloyd Wright devotee, whose wife, Frances Ney, gave great parties, kept a wonderful house and her own name. Annette March was an American who spoke French and was a blond, vibrating beauty. I took their cues and told them the things about myself that I thought it wise for them to know.

After my last performance they again stood and shouted their bravos and applauded as if Billie Holiday accompanied by Duke Ellington had just finished singing "I Cover the Waterfront." They left together after reminding me that we all had a date on Sunday, and because I was used to BYOB parties, I asked what I should bring.

"Imagine you're coming to Corfu," Victor said, "and remember that cheese and fruit have never been rejected in the Mediterranean."

Gaily colored pennants floated on posts attached to the boat. Cut-glass windows, oddly shaped, broke the monotony of weathered wood. Large pieces of sculpture stood sentinel in the area leading to the bridge in the sunlight. The boat looked like a happy child's dream castle.

Yanko greeted me warmly, but without surprise, allowing me to feel not only welcome but expected. Mitch came forward smiling, followed by Victor. They both embraced me and complimented George on his good luck. The three men fell into a private exchange and I wandered away to observe the gathering.

The party was in lingual swing. European classical music provided a background for tidbits of conversation that drifted clear from the general noise. In one corner Annette and Cyril spoke French to a wild-haired woman who never allowed one sentence to end before she interrupted. A thin, professorial man stroked his goatee and

403

spoke to Yanko in Greek. Bob Anshen waved me over and I stayed awhile listening to him discourse on the merits of solar heating systems. Victor joined the group who warbled in Italian as melodious as a concerto.

Other languages I could not recognize spattered and rattled around the room. One handsome Negro was talking to a group around the long table. When he saw me his face spread in a broad smile and he stood up. If he had started speaking to me in an African language, I would not have been surprised.

"Hello there. How are you?" Straight, university, Urban League, colored, NAACP middle-class Negro accent.

"Fine, thank you."

"My name is Jim, join us."

I had never been found attractive by middle-class Negro men, since I was neither pretty nor fair-skinned, well-off or educated, and since most were firmly struggling up Striver's Row they needed women who could either actually help them or at least improve their visual image.

I sat down and found myself in the middle of a discussion on the recent Supreme Court ruling in *Brown* vs. *Board of Education* that had banned racial segregation in education. Jim and I and a pretty blond woman on the other side of the table argued that not only was the ruling just, it was very late in coming. Our opponents contended for the legitimacy of states' rights. As voices were raised and the selection of words became keener, I noticed that I was less angry than interested. I knew many whites were displeased by the ruling, but I had never heard them discuss it.

One debater was called away; another, bored with the display of passion, said, "You people are too serious," and left to kibbitz a chess game.

Jim impressed me. Hearing his formal accent, I had not expected such resolve. "Where do you live?" Maybe I could invite him to Mother's for dinner.

"We live in Mill Valley. What about you?"

I heard the "we" and restrained myself from a new examination of the room. The place was so crowded I must have overlooked his wife.

"I live in San Francisco."

The blonde who had been on our side in the argument and had made perceptive points in the controversy edged forward on the bench. She leaned toward me.

"San Francisco's not far from Mill Valley. Why don't you come over for dinner?"

Jim said, "And meet our kids." He laughed a little self-consciously.

404

"Jenny is learning how to cook greens and she bakes a mean pan of cornbread."

Jenny blushed prettily.

I said, "Thank you, but I work nights." I had not quite accepted that white women were as serious in interracial marriages as white men.

A statement that had great currency in the Negro neighborhood warned: "Be careful of white women with colored men. They might marry and bear children, but when they get what they want out of the men, they leave their children and go back to their own people." We are all so cruelly and comprehensively educated by our tribal myths that it did not occur to me to question what it was that white women wanted out of the men. Since few Negro men in the interracial marriages I had seen had a substantial amount of money, and since the women could have had the sex without the marriage, and since mothers leave their children so rarely that an incident of child abandonment is cause for a newspaper story, it followed that the logic of the warning did not hold.

I excused myself from the table and went to stand on the deck. The small exclusive town of Tiburon glistened across the green-blue water and I thought about my personal history. Of Stamps, Arkansas, and its one paved street, of the segregated Negro school and the bitter poverty that causes children to become bald from malnutrition. Of the blind solitude of unwed motherhood and the humiliation of prostitution. Waves slapped at the brightly painted catamaran tied up below me and I pursued my past to a tardy marriage which was hastily broken. And the inviting doors to newer and richer worlds, where the sounds of happiness drifted through closed panels and the doorknobs came off in my hands.

Guests began to leave, waving at Yanko, who stood beside me at the rail: *"À tout à l'heure,"* *"Adiós,"* *"Ciao,"* *"Adieu,"* *"Au revoir,"* "Good-bye," "Ta." Yanko put his hand on my elbow and guided me back inside.

We had become a crowd of intimates around the table. Annette ladled the soup into large bowls and they all talked about sailing plans for next Sunday. If the weather was nice we would leave early so that we could have a full sail in before the Sunday crowd came for open house. Cyril wondered if I would like him and Annette to pick me up, since they also lived in San Francisco. Mitch said he wanted to talk to me about a short film he was going to do. Possibly I would like to narrate it. Victor said he and Henrietta were going to the Matador on Saturday for lunch and I should join them.

They did not question whether I wanted acceptance into their circle. I was chosen and my being a part of the group was a fact; the burden of choice was removed from me and I was relieved.

I told them I had a young son, and before I could ask, Yanko said, "Bring him. The sea is a female. And females desire young and masculine life. Bring him and we shall pacify the mother of us all. Bring him."

One morning we sailed out on a smooth sea. Cyril was at the helm and Victor was regaling us with a gallant tale of medieval conquest. A young Scandinavian was on board, and when Victor was finished he, in turn, told a Viking story of heroic deeds and exploration.

Yanko slapped his forehead and said, "Ah, yes. Now I know what we must do. We must all plan to go abroad and civilize Europe. We must get a large ship and sail down the Thames and cultivate Britain first because they need it most. Then we cross the Channel and bring culture to France. Cyril, you shall be the first mate because you have by nature and training the mechanical mind. Mitch, you shall be the boatswain because of your 'Samson strength'; Maya, you shall be the *cantante*, sitting in the prow singing us to victory. Victor, you shall be second mate because your talent is to organize. Annette, you shall be our figurehead, for your beauty will stun the commoners and enchant the aristocracy. I shall be captain and do absolutely nothing. *Allons, enfants!*"

Yanko allowed me to enter a world strange and fanciful. Although I had to cope daily with real and mundane matters, I found that some of the magic of his world stayed around my shoulders.

14

If *New Faces of 1957* excited the pulses of San Franciscans, *Porgy and Bess* set their hearts afire. Reviewers and colummsts raved about Leontyne Price and William Warfield in the title roles and praised the entire company. The troupe had already successfully toured other parts of the United States, Europe and South America.

The Purple Onion contract bound me inextricably, but it also held the management to the letter of the law—I could not be fired except after having committed the most flagrant abuses.

On *Porgy and Bess*'s second night I called Barry and said, "I'm off tonight. You may say I'm ill."

"Are you ill?"

"You may say so." And hung up.

I had matured into using a ploy of not quite telling the truth but not quite telling a lie. I experienced no guilt at all and it was clear that the appearance of innocence lay mostly in a complexity of implication.

I went to the theater ready to be entertained, but not expecting a riot of emotion. Price and Warfield sang; they threaded their voices with music and spellbound the audience with their wizardry. Even the chorus performed with such verve that a viewer could easily believe each singer was competing for a leading part.

By intermission I had been totally consumed. I had laughed and cried, exulted and mourned, and expected the second act to produce no new emotions. I returned to my seat prepared for a repetition of great music.

The curtain rose on a picnic in progress. The revelers were church members led by a pious old woman who forbade dancing, drinking and even laughing. Cab Calloway as Sportin' Life pranced out in a cream-colored suit and tried to paganize the Christians.

He sang "It Ain't Necessarily So," strutting as if he was speaking ex cathedra.

The audience applauded loudly, interrupting the stage action. Then a young woman broke away from a group of singers near the wings. She raced to the center of the stage and began to dance.

The sopranos sang a contrapuntal high-toned encouragement and the baritones urged the young woman on. The old lady tried to catch her, to stop the idolatrous dance, but the dancer moved out of her reach, flinging her legs high, carrying the music in her body as if it were a private thing, given into her care and protection. I nearly screamed with delight and envy. I wanted to be with her on the stage letting the music fly through my body. Her torso seemed to lose solidity and float, defying gravity. I wanted to be with her. No, I wanted to *be* her.

In the second act, Warfield, as the crippled Porgy, dragged the audience into his despair: Even kneeling, he was a large man, broad and thick-chested. His physical size made his affliction and his loss of Bess even sadder. The resonant voice straddled the music and rode it, controlling it.

I remained in my seat after the curtain fell and allowed people to climb over my knees to reach the aisle. I was stunned. *Porgy and Bess* had shown me the greatest array of Negro talent I had ever seen.

I took Clyde to the first matinée and he liked the dancing and "the little goat that pulled Porgy off the stage" at the end of the opera.

The Purple Onion had picked up my three-month option and I decided to develop my own material. I began making up music for poems I had written years before and writing new songs that fit the calypso form.

407

One night the club was filled and more people were waiting outside for the room to clear. I lifted my head from a bow and standing before me was a beautiful Black woman holding a long-stemmed rose. I bowed to her and she returned the bow, continuing to bend until she laid the flower at my feet. She blew a kiss and walked down the aisle to her table. Her friends began applauding again. I was not sure whether it was for me or for her, so I nodded to the musicians and started another encore. Halfway through I recognized the woman. She was the soprano who sang the "Strawberry Song" in *Porgy and Bess*. I almost bit my song in two; all the people at that table were probably from *Porgy and Bess*.

I went directly from the stage to the table and took the rose along.

The group stood and applauded again. I laid the flower on the table and applauded them. The audience, infected, began to applaud us.

"These are the great singers from *Porgy and Bess*," I shouted over the noise. People stood up to look, and soon the whole audience was standing and we were applauding ourselves for our good taste to be alive and in the right place at the right time.

We went to Pete's Pool Room, a large rambling restaurant on Broadway where the beats and artists and big-eyed tourists and burlesque queens went for a breakfast of hard rolls and maybe a game of pool. I wanted to call the whole room to order and present to them the singers from *Porgy and Bess*. We found seats and I heard the names again.

Ned Wright, a tall muscular man of about thirty, said I was excellent and "Don't run yourself down, darling, there are plenty of people in the world who will do that for you."

Lillian Hayman, the dramatic soprano, who was as plump as a pillow and biscuit-brown, laughed often, trilling like a bird and showing perfect white teeth. Chief Bey, the drummer, mumbled in a deep voice that seemed to shake his wiry black frame. Joseph Attles, a tenor, was at forty the oldest of the group. He was tall and very delicately made. A lemon-yellow man, he was understudy for Cab Calloway, who was Sportin' Life, and Joseph James, who sang the role of Jake.

And, of course, Martha Flowers, a great soprano and at that time a Bess understudy. Martha said, "My dear, you stand like an African queen holding off a horde of marauders. All alone." She was short, but as she talked and gestured, body erect, she grew tall before my eyes. I told them how their singing had affected me, and when the opportunity arose, I asked about the dancer.

Martha said, "Leesa Foster, Elizabeth Foster. She is also a soprano and I hear she is going to be one of our Besses." They promised to bring her to the club the next evening.

Martha bettered her promise by bringing not only Leesa Foster but even more people the next night. The voice teacher, Frederick Wilkerson, and two or three other cast members sat with the original group at two tables pushed together. Again they all said they enjoyed my singing, again I demurred, saying that I was really a dancer. Leesa was instantly interested and we spoke of dance schools, teachers and styles. Again we went to Pete's for breakfast. Wilkie, as the voice teacher was called, leaned forward and boomed, "You are singing totally wrong. Totally wrong. If you keep it up you'll lose your voice in five years." He leaned back in his chair and added, "Maybe three years, yes, yes. Maybe three."

His pronouncement pinched my budding confidence. I looked around the table, but no one seemed perturbed by his warning. I asked him what I could do to prevent disaster. He nodded and said in sonorous tones, "You are intelligent, yes I see that. You are intelligent. Get to a voice teacher, a good voice teacher. And study very hard. Apply yourself. That's all." He smacked his lips as if he had just tasted a favorite sweet.

"How can I find a good teacher?"

The singers were as curious about his answer as I. They looked at him.

"Now that's another intelligent question," his voice boomed. "As a matter of fact, I plan to leave *Porgy and Bess* and relocate myself in San Francisco. I am willing to take you as a student if, and only if, you work hard and listen to me. I don't have time for any more students; however, I want to help you. If you don't get help, you not only won't be able to sing, you'll hardly be able to talk."

Robert Breen, *Porgy and Bess*'s good-looking and balding producer, came to the Purple Onion the next evening accompanied by his wife, Wilva, a pleasant little blond woman; the business manager, Robert Dustin; and an attractive, well-built woman who was introduced to me as Ella Gerber, company drama coach. When we shook hands, her dark-lashed eyes studied me.

Breen said he had heard I was a professional dancer. I admitted that.

"We may have an opening soon for a dancer who sings. Would you come to the theater and audition for us?"

I thought about my contract. I would not be free to take the job for nearly three months. Should I tell them? It would be honest and fair to leave the job open for another dancer. I told myself that I loved honesty and openness, not so much for its own sake but for its simplicity—I would be free from apologies, recriminations and accusations. Then I thought of Leesa Foster dancing to the sound of great voices, tossing herself into music and movement as if within that marriage lay all human bliss.

"Would I have to audition to a record or could I work with the company?"

Breen turned his pink, baby-skinned face to Dustin.

"We have a full rehearsal scheduled," Dustin said, "and if you want Maya to try out, that could be arranged."

They looked at me, Ella Gerber's eyes computing the length of my legs, the size of my brain and the amount of my talent.

Breen suggested a date and I agreed. We drank a cold white wine to the audition and they left.

I went to the bar and told Ned about the conversation I had had with Breen. "Dance, darling." He raised his hands to eye level and snapped his fingers. "Dance until they see Nijinsky in a duet with Katherine Dunham." Snap!

All the singers were in street clothes, as if they had stopped by the theater en route for something more important. Some stood on the empty stage, others stood in the wings or lounged in the front row of the theater.

Billy Johnson, assistant conductor, waited while the musicians warmed up and tuned their instruments in the orchestra pit. Trills and arpeggios of voices came from backstage.

The stage manager, Walter Riemer, had a flashy smile and was as elegant as John Gielgud, whom he resembled. He took a position just off the stage. "Watch me, dear, when I do this"—he waved his hand like a flag in a high wind—"that's your cue." And he left me.

I sneaked around the curtain and watched as Billy lifted his arms as if he was trying to pull the orchestra out of the pit by invisible strings. The music began to swell, the singers poised.

At a casual indication from Johnson's right hand the voices exploded, ripping shreds in the air.

When Riemer's hand floated my cue, I was laughing and crying at the wonder of it all. I ran on stage, stepping lightly between the singers' notes. If I was supposed to portray a woman carried away by music, blinded and benumbed by her surroundings, enchanted so by the rhythm and melody that she fancied herself a large, gloriously colored bird free to fly rainbows and light up the winds, then I was she.

Three days later, Bob Dustin offered me the job.

I said, as if newly indignant, that the Purple Onion would not let me out of my contract. Dustin commiserated with me and added, "We'll be auditioning people for the next two months. We have to have a lead dancer before we go back to Europe."

Even my imagination had never dared to include me in Europe. Whenever I envisioned foreign countries, I saw them through other people's words or other people's pictures. London to me was as Dickens saw it, a folk song in a cockney accent, Churchill V-ing his fingers, saying, "We shall fight on the beaches," and so forth. Paris, in my mind, rang with the hoofbeats of horse-drawn carriages from the age of Guy de Maupassant. Germany was Hitler and concentration-camp horror or beery burghers in stiff white shirts sitting on benches photographed by Cartier-Bresson. Italy was the hungry streets of *Open City* or curly-haired people singing and eating pasta.

The images had been provided by movies, books and Pathé News, and none included a six-foot-tall Black woman hovering either in the back or in the foreground.

15

When *Porgy and Bess* left San Francisco I resigned myself to the night-club routine, and the burden of life was lightened only by twice-weekly sessions with Wilkie and Lloyd and the romping growth of Clyde.

Three days before my contract ran out I received a telephone call from Saint Subber, the Broadway producer, inviting me to come to New York City to try out for a new show called *House of Flowers*. He said Pearl Bailey would be starring and he had heard I was a great deal like her. If I satisfied him and got the role he had in mind, I would play opposite Miss Bailey.

New Yorkers may love their hometown loyally, but San Francis-cans believe that when good angels die they stay in northern California and hover over the Golden Gate Bridge. I appreciated the chance to try out for a Broadway show, but the invitation did not make me ecstatic. It meant leaving San Francisco, without the prospect of Europe with *Porgy and Bess*.

Mom and Lottie and Wilkie encouraged me to go. The voice teacher and my mother had found that they had much in common and Mother invited him to move into our house. He came bringing his piano, students, huge rumbling voice and his religious positivism. He could cook nearly as well as the two women and the kitchen rang and reeked with the attempts of three chefs to outtalk and outcook one another.

They would take care of Clyde until I found an apartment and then he could fly to me. Of course I was going to get the part. There was no question of that.

I arrived in New York and went to a midtown hotel which Willkie had suggested. The congested traffic and raucous voices, the milling crowds and towering buildings, made me think of my tiny fourth-floor room at the end of a dark corridor a sanctuary.

I telephoned Saint Subber, who said I must come to his apartment. I wriggled around his invitation, not wishing to face the street again so soon and hesitant about going to a strange man's apartment—especially a New York producer's apartment. Hollywood films had taught me that breed was dangerous: each one was fat, smoked large smelly cigars and all said, "All right, girlie, ya got talent, now lemme see ya legs."

"Mr. Saint Subber"—or was one supposed to call him Mr. Subber?—"I need to have my hair done. May I see you tomorrow?"

He blasted my excuse. "No, no matter, I won't be looking at your hair."

See, my legs. Just as I thought.

"I want to see what you look like." He gave me his address and hung up.

I had come three thousand miles, so surely I had the courage to go a few more blocks.

A uniformed doorman in front of a neat East Side apartment house raised his brows when I told him my destination, but he walked me into the lobby and reluctantly handed me over to a uniformed elevator operator. The operator pulled his face down as if to say "So, hot stuff, huh?" but he said "Penthouse," and we began our smooth ascent. When we stopped he rang a bell and the door opened.

A beautiful blond young man offered me his hand. "Miss Angelou?" He did not look as if my legs would interest him.

"Yes. Mr. Subber?"

The elevator door closed and we were in a beautifully furnished living room.

"No, I'm not Saint. My name is Tom. I'm helping on the production. Please have a seat." He led me to a sofa. "Saint will be with you in a few minutes. What can I get you to drink?"

While he was away I looked at the room and wondered about the tenant. Paintings adorned the walls and flowers were fresh and gay on little tables. A man's voice in argument came through a louvered door.

Tom returned with a gin and tonic in a very tall, extraordinarily thin glass. He asked about my trip and tried to reassure me when I told him I was nervous.

A man rushed through the shuttered door; he was small and thin and his dark hair was cut in a "Quo Vadis."

412

"Well, that's over. Oh, my God!" He threw himself on a chaise longue and gingerly put both hands to his head. "Oh, God! What do they want? Oh, my head. Virginia!"

A large Negro woman came through another door. She wore the kind of apron I had not seen since I had left the small country town in Arkansas. It was white, bibbed, starched and voluminous. She went directly to the man and began to massage his temples.

"That's all right, Saint honey, that's all right, you hear. Now don't think about it, honey. Everything's going to be all right."

I could not believe it.

Neither had taken notice of me and I was so enthralled I frankly stared, recording the scene.

Tom and I could have been an audience while two actors performed a scene in experimental theater.

It was decidedly too new, too strange. I started laughing. The man sat bolt upright. "Who are you?"

"I?" I held the laughter. "I'm Maya Angelou."

"You can't be." He was still sitting straight.

"But I am, I am Maya Angelou." I was willing to swear to it.

"Well, my God, how tall are you?"

"I'm six feet."

"But you can't be!" He seemed sure.

"I am, I am too."

"Stand up. I don't believe it."

I stood up, hoping I had not shrunk in the plane or in the taxi or in the elevator.

"My God, it's true, you're six feet tall."

I laughed because I was happy that at least my height had not betrayed me and because he was funny.

"And a great laugh, too. Oh, my God, I know, you're a Black Carol Channing."

That made me laugh again. He stood up and came to me.

"We'll do your hair red. Will that be all right? Red or blond?"

I said, "I don't think so."

"Oh, you wouldn't like that?" It was a sincere question.

"Noooo." I pictured myself with hair as red as Gwen Verdon's and started laughing again. "No, I don't think it would work."

"All right." He chuckled, too. "We'll think of something else."

I was still laughing.

"What's so funny?"

When I could catch my breath I told him. "I expected you to smoke a cigar and pinch my cheeks, to roll your eyes at me and make some lewd proposition. I've been dreading that all the way from California, and I get here"—the funny bone was struck again—"I get

413

here and... Tom and you and Virginia and my red hair." He, too, began to laugh at the absurd situation. Tom joined in.

Saint Subber said impulsively, "Stay for dinner. Virginia, we'll be another for dinner." For all his theatrics, or maybe because of them, I knew he was a strong man. I had always been more comfortable around strong people.

After a dinner of frogs' legs (I had never eaten them before and had to ask if they were eaten with a knife and fork or with the fingers like spare ribs), he told me to come to the theater the next morning and not to sing any special material, because Truman Capote was going to be at the theater and "Truman hates special material."

I thanked them both for their hospitality and went back to the hotel to telephone Mom. "Do your best tomorrow" she said, "and don't worry. Remember, you've got a home to come back to." I spoke to Clyde, who sounded fine, and hung up and went to bed.

The Alvin Theater was on Broadway and I had been asked to go to the stage door around the corner. I walked quite cheerfully among the crowds on the sidewalk. I had stopped at a music store and bought a copy of "Love for Sale," for no reason except that it had been on display and I had heard it sung so often. If Truman Capote did not like special material, I would sing a standard for him. I noticed only after I had turned the corner at the theater that a line of Negro people stretched around the block headed in the direction I was taking. I exchanged smiles with some of the young standees and gave good mornings to some of the older women with pleasant faces. The line stopped at the stage door. I had never auditioned in New York and thought maybe all Broadway shows had their tryouts in the same theater.

I knocked at the door and Tom opened it. I would not have been surprised if I had been given a number and told to take my place in line. Instead, he said, "Oh, Miss Angelou. Please come in. I'll tell Saint you're here."

He led me to a corner and excused himself. The blurred forms inside the theater became more visible. There were over a hundred Negro people lined up along the backstage wall, waiting, alert.

Tom waved me over and whispered, "Saint will hear you now. Have you your music?"

I said, "Yes."

"Give it to me," he said, "I'll take it to the pianist. Do you want to run over it with her?"

I did not think so—after all, it was only "Love for Sale."

"Just a minute and I'll call your name. Walk right through here." He showed me to the wings and an entrance stage left. "The pianist is in the pit. You nod to her and she'll begin." Just like the old Purple Onion days.

"And there's nothing to worry about." He added, "Truman Capote is out there and Saint and Yip Harburg and Peter Hall. Do your best."

I waited, trying not to think about trying out and thinking about New York. The Apple. I would make it and send for Clyde, then we would spend afternoons in Central Park, perhaps not as nice as Golden Gate Park, but then... I would find a lover, too; among all those millions of people there had to be a man who had been waiting for me to come along and cheer up his life. I would not think about trying out. Just wait until my name was called and then go out and sing.

"Miss Angelou, Maya Angelou."

I walked out in front of the velvet curtain. The lights were bright and hard and white, and the theater seats, only dimly lighted near the stage, darkened into oblivion, I saw a small clump of figures in the distance. On the right side of the orchestra pit a woman sat patiently at a grand piano.

I took my position, thinking of Lloyd Clark: "Stand still, stand perfectly still, darling, still." I stood. Wilkie's teaching ran in my thoughts: "Drop your jaw. Don't try to look pretty by grinning when you sing. Drop your jaw." I dropped my jaw, and then nodded to the pianist, moving nothing but my head.

She stroked out the first notes of my song and I began.

"Love for sale, appetizing young love—"

She stopped.

"Uh, no, uh, I'm playing the verse. If you don't want the verse I'll go right to the refrain."

I had read the verse when I bought the music, but I had never heard it sung.

"Just the 'love for sale' part, please." I thought I heard a titter from backstage, but I could not be sure. She played the first three notes and I began to sing. "Love for sale, appetizing young love for sale." I imagined I was a girl in a trench coat and a beret, standing under a streetlight in old Chinatown in a light rain. Men passed me by after looking me over and I continued my plaintive offer.

I was so engrossed in telling the story that I did not know when the music and I had parted company, or quite how we could get back together. I only knew I was in one key and the piano in another. I looked at the pianist. She began to strike the keys harder, and in a vain attempt to settle correctly I began to sing louder. She lifted her hands and pounded on the piano. I raised my voice and screamed, "If you want to buy my wares" a mile away from what she was playing.

She half rose, crouched over the keyboard. There was a frantic determination in the position of her body, in the bend of her neck. She would get me back on pitch or there would just be splinters left on the piano.

Plunk plunk—she was as loud as I—and I heard a low vocal grumble as she sought to overwhelm my voice into submission. I shouted, "Follow me and climb the stairs." A thin but definite screech slid through my nose. I dropped my jaw to try to force the sound down into the back of my mouth where I could control it. The pianist was standing. Her brow was knit and her teeth bared. She was about to attack the piano for the final chord. I barged in, overtook her and in a second outdistanced her as I yelled "Love for sale."

She flopped on the piano stool exhausted and in defeat.

I was just a little proud that I had gotten all the way through the song. Then I heard the sounds. There were gurgles and giggles from the theater and the muffled bubbling of outright disorderly laughter from backstage.

The flush of heat crawled up my face and spread through my body the instant I realized that I was the object of derision. But I was, I told myself, the person who'd had flowers put at her feet. And I was the entertainer asked to take Eartha Kitt's role in *New Faces*. I was the dancer *Porgy and Bess* wanted to follow the fabulous Lizabeth Foster. And I was being laughed away just because I could not sing "Love for Sale." Well, they need not.

"Excuse me," I said, and looked over the rows of seats toward the indistinct shadows. "I understand that Mr. Capote doesn't like special material. And you've asked me to come out here to show you what I do. I am willing to sing calypso for you or I'd be just as happy to go home."

Indeed, it would be nicer to go back to California. To my mother's big house and good food. To my son, who needed me, and Aunt Lottie, who loved me. Back to the wonderful Purple Onion where my friends would welcome me. The period between becoming a great Broadway star setting New York on its ear and returning to the family's bosom was shorter than the first intervals between the overheard laughter.

There was little sound from the audience. They clapped as if they were wearing furry gloves.

"Yes, Miss Angelou, sing whatever you like."

I said, "I'm going to sing 'Run Joe,' and since I was discouraged from bringing my sheet music, I'll have to sing it a cappella." Wilkie had told me that music sung without accompaniment was called "a cappella."

If I was going home, I had to show them what they were missing, and that I had some place to go.

I gave them the special Saturday-night standing-room-only encore version. The one where I spun around, my body taut. The one where I yelped small noises and sighed like breaking ocean waves.

When I finished, the first applause came from the pianist. She was smiling and clapping so energetically that I surmised that I had rescued her recently endangered belief in the human voice. There

416

was more applause from the audience, and this time it sounded fresh and sincere. I did not know what I was expected to do next. I stood still for a moment, then bowed and rather stiffly turned away.

"Will you wait backstage, Miss Angelou?" Tom's voice sprang through the void.

"Yes, thank you."

Whenever I was embarrassed or felt myself endangered, I relied on my body's training to deliver me. Grandmother Henderson and Grandmother Baxter had drilled my brother and me in the posture of "shoulders back, head up, look the future in the eye," and years of dance classes had compounded the education. I turned and walked to the wings like Cleopatra walking to the throne room (meanwhile clasping the asp in her bodice).

Backstage a few of the hopeful contenders tapped their hands together or snapped their fingers when they saw me. They grinned saucy compliments to me, probably as much for my own sassiness in standing up and talking back as for what they heard of my second song.

Saint Subber, Tom and Truman Capote came backstage and walked over to me.

Saint Subber said, "You've got a certain quality."

Tom's praise was as generous as his manner.

Truman Capote spoke, and I thought for a desperate moment that he was pulling my leg. He said in a faint falsetto, "Miss Angelou, honey, ah love yoah work." He sounded just like a rich old Southern white woman. He reminded me of a Countee Cullen poem:

> She even thinks that up in heaven
> Her class lies late and snores
> While poor Black cherubs rise at seven
> To do celestial chores.

Yet I could not detect a shread of superciliousness on his face or in his soft yielding manner. I thanked him. Tom said he would be in touch with me and I shook hands with the men and left the theater.

Outside I passed the line of people still waiting. They scanned my features intently, trying to read the outcome of my ordeal and thereby prophesy their own. If I was triumphant it meant that success was in the air and might come to them. On the other hand, it could mean that I had just filled the vacancy that they themselves might have taken.

Theirs was a grievous lot. Ten or twenty jobs for two thousand or more trained, talented and anxious aspirants. Another Countee Cullen poem stated that God, should he choose, could explain why

417

he gave the turtle such a strange yet lovely shell, why the spring follows winter, why the snake doffs its skin, "yet," said the poet, "do I marvel at this curious thing, to make a poet Black and bid him sing." And of all things, to bid him sing in New York City.

I thought of *Porgy and Bess*. Of the sixty people who sang and laughed and lived together, the camaraderie and the pride they had in one another's genius. Although I had not heard from the company administrators for three months, I had received cards from Martha Flowers and from Ned Wright. I waited around in my small hotel room and prowled my dingy lobby. I called Mother, who ordered me to keep my chin up, and Clyde, who missed me and gave me news of Fluke's latest adventures. Wilkie reminded me that "In God I live and have my being."

On a Thursday morning I received a note which read: "Miss Angelou, the *House of Flowers* company is happy to inform you that you have been chosen for the part in our production. Please come to the office Thursday afternoon at three to sign your contract."

I shared the news with my family immediately, and when I hung up, the telephone rang again. I thought it was probably Saint Subber calling to congratulate me.

It was Breen's Everyman's Opera Company. Bob Dustin said, "Maya Angelou?"

"Yes."

"This is *Porgy and Bess*. We called your San Francisco number and were told you were in New York."

"Yes."

"We want you for the role of Ruby."

How could there be so much of a good thing?

"But I've just got a part in a new show opening on Broadway."

"Really? Oh, that's too bad. The company is in Montreal now and we leave for Italy in four days."

There really was no contest. I wanted to travel, to try to speak other languages, to see the cities I had read about all my life, but most important, I wanted to be with a large, friendly group of Black people who sang so gloriously and lived with such passion.

"I don't have a passport."

"We are being sponsored by the State Department."

I thought about the school I had attended which was on the House Un-American Activities Committee list.

He said, "Don't worry about your passport. We can get a special dispensation. Do you want to join *Porgy and Bess*?"

"Yes, yes." Yes, indeed.

"Then come to the office and we'll get you straightened out. You'll leave tomorrow afternoon for Montreal."

418

I telephoned Saint Subber and explained that I had been offered another job. He asked me if I would give up a new Broadway show for a chorus part in a touring company.

I said "Yes."

16

My mind turned over and over like a flipped coin: Paris, then Clyde's motherless birthday party, Rome and my son's evening prayers said to Fluke, Madrid and Clyde struggling alone with his schoolwork.

I telephoned home again. Mother was pleased and gave me a load of phrases to live by. "Treat everybody right, remember life is a two-way street. You might meet the same people on your way down that you met going up." And "Look to the hills from whence cometh your help." Lottie said she was proud of me and that I had it in me to become great. Wilkie told me to hum a lot, place my voice in the mask and always drop my jaw. And to keep in my heart the knowledge that there was no place where God was not.

I asked to speak with Clyde. Using a tack I loathed, I talked to him as if he was a small child with faulty English. He asked when I was coming home and when was I sending for him. His voice became faint after I said I was not coming the next week but soon. Very soon.

Yes, he'd be a good boy. Yes, he would mind Grandmother and Aunt Lottie. And yes, he knew I loved him. He hung up first.

When I called Ivonne she told me to stop crying, that Clyde had no father, so it was up to me to make a place for both of us, and that that was what I was doing. She said she would go over to the house as usual and see him and take him out. After all, he was not with strangers but with his grandmother—why did I worry?

The past revisited. My mother had left me with my grandmother for years and I knew the pain of parting. My mother, like me, had had her motivations, her needs. I did not relish visiting the same anguish on my son, and she, years later, had told me how painful our separation was to her. But I had to work and I would be good. I would make it up to my son and one day would take him to all the places I was going to see.

I had been given a précis of the DuBose Heyward book on which George and Ira Gershwin had based their opera:

Porgy, a crippled beggar, lives in the Negro hamlet of Catfish Row,

419

North Carolina. He is loved by the town's inhabitants, who eke out their meager living by fishing and selling local produce.

When Crown, a tough stevedore, kills Robbin, Serena's husband, in a crap game, the white police descend upon the hamlet to find the culprit. Sportin' Life, who runs the gambling and other nefarious money-making schemes, escapes into Ruby's house, but Bess, Crown's beautiful and worldly woman, is rejected by the community's women and is nearly captured in the raid. Just as the police dragnet is about to close in on her, Porgy opens the door of his hut and Bess finds safety. Porgy falls in love with Bess and she accepts his love and protection, swearing that she will stay with him forever. Crown escapes from jail and comes to claim Bess at a picnic which Porgy does not attend. Bess is sexually attracted to her old lover and goes away with him for three days. Porgy goes to look for her. When she returns to Catfish Row, Porgy is away and the local women scorn her. Sportin' Life courts her, gives her cocaine and begs her to leave the small town and accompany him to New York, where "I'll give you the finest diamonds on upper Fifth Avenue."

> And through Harlem we'll go a struttin'
> > We'll go a struttin' and there'll be nuttin'
> > Too good for you."

She cannot resist his entreaty, his style and the drugs. She leaves with him.

Porgy returns and is told of Bess's journey, and against the pleas of his neighbors, calls for his goat, hitches the cart to the animal and sets out to travel to New York to find his Bess.

The naïve story is given dramatic pace by the birth of a longed-for child, a hurricane in which a member of the community is killed and a picnic where Sportin' Life tries to tempt the religious people away from their beliefs.

On Friday, breathless, excited and afraid, I arrived at dusk in Montreal.

I was met at the airport, and although it was too early for the cast to assemble, taken directly to the theater. Backstage, men shouted to one another in French and English and hustled around, pulling ropes and adjusting pieces of scenery. When I walked onto the empty set, all the shards of the last two days' tensions fell away. I was suddenly in the papier-mâché world of great love, passion and poignancy.

I was examining Porgy's cabin and the house where Robbin's widow, Serena, sings her mournful aria when the singers began to trickle into the back of the theater.

420

Ella Gerber saw me slouching upstage in the shadows.

"Oh, Maya, you've arrived!" She came forward. "Here's your script, your hotel and room number. A schedule for rehearsals. I suggest you watch this performance carefully and study your script tonight. You'll be rehearsing tomorrow."

She said I had no dressing room because I would not be performing until we arrived in Italy, but she would tell the cast that I had arrived.

My fears that I had been forgotten turned out to be baseless. When Ella led me down the dressing room corridor, she called out, "Maya's here!"

Martha Flowers ran out into the hall. "*La première danseuse, elle est ici!*"

Lillian Hayman followed smiling, saying "Welcome."

Barbara Ann Webb grinned, spread her arms and made "Hey, girl" sound like "Where have you been so long?" and "Why weren't you here sooner?"

The three women shared a cluttered dressing room and I sat amid the costumes and the disarray of make-up, watching them prepare for the show. Martha was as delicately made as a Stradivarius. Her complexion was the rich brown of polished mahogany and her hands fine and small. She had large bright eyes. Her lips, full and open, revealed even white teeth in the dark face. She called herself, and was called by her friends, "Miss Fine Thing." Rightly.

If Martha was a violin, Lillian Hayman was a cello. She was a medium-brown woman of heavy curves and deep arches. Her dignified posture caused her to be regarded as stout rather than fat, and she moved lightly as if her weight might be only in the eye of the beholder. She had a handsome face softened by a ready warm smile. She was a dramatic soprano and the description was apt.

Barbara Ann Webb, a lyric soprano, was the innocent when I joined the company, and so she remained until I left. She was nearly as large as Lillian, but her curves were younger and more conventionally arranged. A Texan, she had an openness that reminded me of sunshine in movies by Technicolor. Her skin was a shade lighter than a ripe peach, and had she been white, she could have been a stand-in for Linda Darnell. Throughout ten countries and fifteen cities, those three women became and remained my closest friends.

That first night the chatter in the dressing room wound down and there was a knock at the door.

"Fifteen minutes."

"O.K.," Lillian shouted.

I had heard the announcement of "Half-hour" earlier, but none of

421

the women responded. Now Martha turned away from the mirror and her eyes glazed, began to sing "Do re me fa sol la ti do." I didn't know whether I was expected to say something, then Lillian also dropped her interest in our conversation and an unseeing look came into her eyes, she stretched her lips in a taut, false smile and holding her teeth closed, yelped "Ye, ya, yo, you." Barbara Ann stood and began to sway slowly from side to side. She started to lower and raise her jaw and then sang "Woooo Woooooo."

They took no notice of me, but I couldn't do the same with them. I had never been so close to trained singers and the reverberations shook in my ears. I left the room and walked down the corridor to find my place in the wings. Sounds came out of each door I passed. One baritone roared like a wounded moose, another wailed like a freight train on a stormy night. The tenors yelped in high screeches. There were whines and growls and the siren of an engine on its way to a four-alarm fire. Grunts overlapped the high-pitched "ha ha ho ho's" and the total cacophony tickled me; I could have laughed outright. These exquisite singers who would soon stand on the stage delivering the most lovely and liquid tones had first to creak like rusty scissors and wail like banshees. I remembered that before I could lift my torso and allow my arms to wave as if suspended in water, I had to bend up and down, sticking my behind in the air, plié and relevé until my muscles ached, arch-roll and contract and release until my body begged for deliverance. The singers were not funny. They were working. Preparation is rarely easy and never beautiful. That was the first of many lessons *Porgy and Bess* taught me.

I sat on a stool in the wings and watched the singers respond to the stage manager's shouted "Places, please. Places." They moved directly to their positions in *Porgy*'s world. There were a few whispers as the lights began their slow descent to black.

There was applause from in front of the curtain and the lively overture of Gershwin's opera swelled onto the stage. The curtain began sliding open and pastel lights illuminated the set. A group of men, downstage left, were involved in a crap game; some knelt, others mimed throwing dice. Then Ned Wright, as Robbins, threw the dice and sang "Nine to Make, Come Nine." The pure tenor line lifted and held in the air for a second, and in a rush the pageant began.

The sopranos and tenors, bassos and baritones, acted as if they were indeed the poverty-stricken Southern Negroes whose lives revolved around the dirt road encampment of Catfish Row. They sang and listened, then harmonized with each other's tones so closely that the stage became a wall of music without a single opening unfilled.

Their self-hypnotism affected the audience and overwhelmed me. I cried for Robbin's poor widow, Serena, who sang the mournful aria "My Man's Gone Now." Helen Thigpen, a neat little quail of a woman, sang the role with a conviction that burdened the soul. Irene Williams sang Bess, sassily tossing her hips as effortlessly as she flung the notes into the music of the orchestra. Leslie Scott, handsome and as private as an African mask, sang Porgy and in a full, rich baritone. When the first act was over, the audience applauded long and loudly, and I found myself drenched with perspiration and exhausted.

The singers, on the other hand, seemed to step out of the roles as easily as one kicks off too large slippers. They passed me in the wings on their way to the dressing rooms chattering about packing and whether they ought to buy more clothes in Montreal for the European trip.

I didn't like their frivolity. It seemed as if they were being disloyal to the great emotions they had sung about and aroused in me. It wasn't pleasant to discover they were only playing parts. I wanted them to walk offstage wrapped in drama, trailing wisps of tragedy. Instead, Martha came through a parting in the backdrop curtain. Her dark face split in a smile.

"Hey, girl. How do you like it?"

She would not have understood had I said I loved the singing but felt betrayed by the singers.

I said, "I love it."

"Is this the first time you've watched an opera from backstage?"

I told her it was.

The final act was more astounding than the first. I knew now that the actors were not wholly involved in their roles because I had seen the alacrity with which they shuffled off their characters, and yet they caught me again and wove me deftly into the pattern of the play.

The audience jumped to their feet, shouting "Bravo" and clapping their hands, and the company bowed ensemble. Then the chorus members began to peel off the long double lines, leaving a neat arrangement of principal actors, and the audience thundered its approval.

Backstage after the final curtain, singers, stage hands, administrators acted as if the play had never been. The moods they had created, the tears they had wept so copiously and the joy they had reveled in were forgotten.

I wondered if I would make any real friendships or, to be more precise, I doubted that people who could be so emotionally casual had the ability, desire or need to make friendships.

Billy Johnson told me I was expected at the theater the next afternoon for rehearsal. He asked if I could sight-sing and I answered

423

no. Wilkie had encouraged me to study solfeggio so that I would be able to pick up a piece of sheet music and read it as naturally as one reads a newspaper, but I hadn't had the time. Johnson, a prematurely balding white man from Oklahoma, said we'd work it out. That I didn't really have much to learn.

I was assigned to the hotel where Martha and Lillian stayed and we sat late into the night telling our life stories. Martha was the daughter of a preacher in North Catolina. Lillian was choir director of a large church in Jamaica, Long Island. My grandmother had been Mother of the C.M.E. Church in Stamps, Arkansas, so we shared a common religious background.

Rehearsal wasn't as frightening as I had expected. Once Billy Johnson was convinced that the company administrators had actually hired a singer who couldn't read music, he took the situation in hand.

He sat at the piano and with one hand played my part. Having been surrounded by the group of highly trained, talented singers, it would be understandable if he had come to believe that not only could all Negroes sing, but they could all sing opera and had perfect pitch. He barely covered his shock at finding that I didn't have a good ear.

His accent was Southern and as refined as oil of wintergreen.

"Well, no, Maya, that's not quite it. Close, but not quite." He played the air again, his fingers stroking the keys daintily. "It's more like this."

After an hour, during which I sang the same tune over and over again, he surrendered gracefully.

"I think you're going to have to put in some work on this before you open with us in Venice."

In the dance sequence I was all right. The rhythmn was complex, but I seemed to hear it easily and I danced it freely. Robert Breen had explained that he didn't want the piece to look choreographed. The dancer had to appear so bewitched by the music that she abandoned herself in a glory of dance. I surrendered to the music and allowed it to fashion my performance.

17

For three days I rehearsed in the afternoons and observed the company from the wings at night. But mornings I spent walking the clean streets of Montreal and listening to the foreign accents and looking at the people.

Among the many perversities in American race relations is the fact that Blacks do not relish looking closely at whites. After hundreds of years of being the invisible people ourselves, as soon as many of us have achieved economic security we try to force whites into nonexistence by ignoring them.

Montreal provided me with my first experience of looking freely at whites. The underground railroad had had Canada as its final destination, and slaves had created a powerful liturgy praising Canada which was sung all over the world. Spirituals abounded with references to the Biblical body of water, the river Jordan. I had been told that Jordan, in our music, meant the Mississippi or the Arkansas or the Ohio River and the stated aim to get to Canaan land was the slave's way of saying he longed to go to Canada, and freedom.

Therefore, Canadians were exempt from many Blacks' rejection of whites. They were another people. I observed their clean streets and the fact that their faces did not tighten when they saw me. The atmosphere was comfortable enough to allow me to try my recently learned French words. Sometimes I was understood.

The hotel lobby looked like a train station. Two children, sixty adults with their suitcases, coats, umbrellas, hats and other paraphernalia were trying to check out and board the two buses that were to take them to the airport.

A scene was played out which I was to see repeated in the capitals of Europe and North Africa. Remaining hotel guests were astounded by the horde of colorful people queuing up to windows, shouting across lines to each other, laughing at the joy of travel and the promise of Europe.

The stars of the company sparkled and attracted. Earl Jackson, our second Sportin' Life, had just joined the troupe when I arrived in Montreal. His wardrobe was as new to the old members as it was to me. He was not a trained singer and the gossip was that he had been hired from the streets of Chicago because he had firsthand information of the role he was to play. He wore a snappy, flashy suit and his hair was as black and slick as his pointy shoes. He knew he was handsome, and because he did not yet belong to any clique, he stood aloof and haughty, as if he were the absolute center of the universe and we were inconsequential people on the periphery.

Leslie Scott dressed expensively and behaved like a classic baritone. His fitted coat had a Persian lamb collar, which was accented by a cashmere scarf. He was a star and made no attempt to play it down.

The women who sang Bess were unfailingly and dramatically attractive. Martha was perfectly made-up and dressed in her dainty coat of many colors; Gloria Davy, tall and Black, held her strangely

Oriental beauty contained in distant impassivity. Irene Williams, golden and cheerful, looked as much like Bess in a hotel lobby as she did on the stage. John McCurry, who sang the role of Crown, was six foot six, two hundred and fifty pounds—a booming bass-baritone and the color of a ripe Satsuma plum. His wife was little and as white as he was black. She spoke softly and seldom. Because of the disparity in size, and color, they were called secretly Jack and Jane Sprat.

Most of the tenors who had visited Europe on an earlier tour and had the temperament of their vocal range, wore their coats over their shoulders with a studied indifference and carried walking sticks.

Eloise Uggams and Ruby Green were among the quiet, self-effacing women who looked and acted more like pillars of a religious order than singing members of a flamboyant opera company. Their male counterparts, Joe Jones, Merritt Smith, could have been church deacons, small business owners or solid insurance collectors. They not only didn't seem to belong to the dramatic group but appeared a little ill-at-ease with them in public. The sober members always managed to stand a little apart from the vociferous group as if they were waiting for another train going to a different destination.

The company descended on the airport like an invading horde of Goths on ancient Rome. Some people hummed little airs from *Madame Butterfly* or *Cavalleria Rusticana*. Others continued the conversations they had started on the buses in loud voices to override the general noise. At least five bags were lost, searched for, bemoaned and then found with cries of welcome. After processing about only twenty passports and fifty suitcases, looks passed between the Canadian officials as if they had rehearsed the scene: they raised their eyebrows, shrugged, looked in another direction and waved *Porgy and Bess* company through the turnstile and out of their sight.

The airplane stewardesses found that their aloof manner designed to keep obstreperous passengers in check did not work with their cargo of singers. The sopranos complained that the plane was too cold; the baritones were certain that the overheating was detrimental to their vocal cords; the tenors asked for rock and rye, and said generously they would settle for clover honey and fresh lemon juice. Panic increased among the stewardesses in direct relation to the requests made by their passengers.

When the pilot informed us we were passing over Newfoundland, which meant one hour from Montreal and eight whole hours from Milan, our final destination, the cabin attendants looked dazedly wild-eyed. They withdrew to the front of the plane and remained there, refusing to answer the persistent demands for attention.

Ruby Green was terrified of flying, so I had asked to be her seat

SINGIN' AND SWINGIN' AND GETTIN' MERRY LIKE CHRISTMAS

companion. I knew that I was always at my best when I was near someone in a worse condition than I. When the plane took off she grabbed the seat arms, tensed her body and, by will alone, lifted the carrier safely in the air. I spoke to her of California, and thinking of Wilkie, reminded her (and myself) that "there was no place God was not." After a few hours she relaxed enough to join the conversation. She said that she had no doubts about God but had no previous knowledge of the pilot, and that throughout three years of traveling with *Porgy and Bess* her serious misgivings about airplane captains had not diminished in the least.

The stewardesses appeared near the front seats. They began hauling out tablecloths and silverware from right to left as fast as possible. Once all our tray tables were down and dressed, they raced back to the minute kitchen stand and grabbed the meals. They handed them rapidly from right to left as quickly and deftly as a Las Vegas gambler deals a deck of cards. When we were all served they returned to their retreat without a single backward glance.

The Milan airport hustle differed only in language from the cacophonous noise of other airports I had known. I busied myself gathering my luggage and staying as close to my friends as possible without appearing to do exactly what I was doing—that is, clinging to their coattails for safety's sake.

The first part of the bus trip from Milan to Venice gave me and my colleagues no time to contemplate the Italian countryside. The driver was determined to show that not only did he know his vehicle and the roads, he was an artist at keeping the two in conjunction even under the most hair-raising circumstances. The bus—extra long and loaded with the entire company and all our baggage, and a guide who thought the language he spoke was English—skidded into curves, screeching like a stuck factory whistle; aimed itself at smaller vehicles as, growling, it leaped and bucked and swung around hills, holding onto the road by two wheels, one wheel, and then simply by sheer memory.

The guide shouted and gesticulated, held his upturned hands away from his body and moved them up and down as if he were weighing two large grapefruit, his head rolling from side to side.

When the bus finally entered a small town, children and dogs became feathers blown out of its path; adults screamed at the driver, who, keeping his foot on the accelerator, turned his head and answered them shout for shout. We stopped at a square in the center of town and relief prevented us from cursing the driver, who stood by the open door, pride in his skill written on his face.

The guide led us to a restaurant and said, "blah, blah, Verona, blah blah." The word "Verona" hit my ears like a clap of remembered

427

thunder. Here was Verona, the home of Romeo and Juliet. The home of the Montagues and Capulets. I walked away from the crowd and looked at the buildings and up at the stone balconies. I placed Juliet above me, imagined her asking "Romeo, Romeo! wherefore art thou, Romeo?" I put her lover in a shadow across the square and allowed him to praise Juliet's beauty and to wish: "O that I were a glove upon that hand, that I might touch that cheek!"

I was really in Italy. Not Maya Angelou, the person of pretensions and ambitions, but me, Marguerite Johnson, who had read about Verona and the sad lovers while growing up in a dusty Southern village poorer and more tragic than the historic town in which I now stood.

I was so excited at the incredible turn of events which had brought me from a past of rejection, of slammed doors and blind alleys, of dead-end streets and culs-de-sac, into the bright sun of Italy, into a town made famous by one of the world's greatest writers. I ran to find Martha and Lillian.

They had saved a chair for me inside the café.

"Martha, did you know this is Verona?"

She looked up from the menu she was studying. "Yes, and it's only twenty miles to Venice."

Lillian said, "My God, if we don't get a different driver, we may never get there."

"Or if we keep this one we'll be there in five minutes." Martha laughed.

I said, "But I mean, this is Verona. Where the— This is the setting for Shakespeare's *Romeo and Juliet.*"

"We all heard it on the bus, Maya." Lillian smiled at me as if I were an excited child. "The guide told us. Weren't you listening?"

Martha pursed her lips, "The Everyman Opera Company goes to the tremendous expense of hiring a guide who speaks an unheard-of language and moves his arms like a semaphore in a strong wind, and our prima ballerina doesn't even listen to him. Alas." She went back to the menu.

Lillian looked at me and shook her head. "Maya, in the next year you'll probably be in the place where Hamlet died, where Othello killed Desdemona or where Cleopatra did herself in with an asp. You're not going to get this excited each time, are you?"

Martha said, "Dear, do let her have her day. After all, this is her first time in Europe." They had both traveled with Gertrude Stein's *Four Saints in Three Acts*, and they acted as if they had chalets in Switzerland and villas in Spain where they took weekend visits. Martha continued, "Let me help you with the menu."

I decided that day never again to let them know how I really felt. If they wanted to play it cool, then I'd show them how to play it cool. I asked for the menu and with my heart beating loud enough for them to hear it, gazed at the list of foods, written in Italian and in a script I'd never seen before. I recognized *uova* as eggs on the basis of my high school Latin and ordered. I knew that I must buy a dictionary the next day and start to teach myself Italian. I would speak the language of every country we visited; I would study nights and mornings until I spoke foreign languages, if not perfectly, at least coherently.

Neither books nor films had prepared me for Venice. I had seen *"Blood and Sand,"* the Tyrone Power movie, and felt I could walk easily among bullfighters and the beautiful señoritas of Spain. *The Bicycle Thief* and *Open City* gave clear if painful images of Italy after World War II. The Ali Baba and Aladdin's lamp stories, although portrayed by actors with heavy Central European accents, gave me some sense of the Moslem world. But Venice was a fantasia I had not experienced even secondhand. Our bus drove through narrow streets walled by tall buildings. Erratically we burst away from enclosures and saw open water where gondoliers plied their boats with as much élan as our driver conducted his vehicle. Balconies thrust above our heads; vegetable stalls and small shops jutted out beyond the pavement.

Across the square we stopped in a small plaza where there was a hotel. Tables sat out in front of a restaurant. As the company piled out of the bus and began the routine of sorting themselves and their baggage into individual lots, I stood looking at the black-coated waiters who were covering the tables with red checkered cloths.

A few had seen and heard the singers identifying their belongings in loud voices and they had rushed to the restaurant door to call to their fellow workers and Venetian customers. Men and women flowed out of the restaurant and onto the square, their eyes on the crowd of colorful Negroes who hadn't the time or the inclination to give them the slightest thought.

The ogling crowd who waved their hands in a kind of balletic concert were the first large group of native Italians I observed carefully. In Verona I had been too busy coping with my memories and the ancient romance and my own image to really look at the waiters or the other customers. But now, as I stood apart and had the opportunity to take in the whole scene, the Italian faces were contorted with what I took to be revulsion; I concluded that they had never seen so many Black people before and were frightened and repelled.

A tall, tub-chested man in a white coat, who had been standing with the gawkers, said something which brought laughter from the crowd and walked toward the bus. I headed back to where the guide was ineffectually standing guard over a raggle-taggle mound of suitcases and offering his arms and head and torso and garbled tongue as a sacrifice to the god who reclaimed lost luggage. The white-coated man searched among the teeming, shouting singers and settled on John McCurry, who was bent double talking to his wife.

The man stood as if at attention. He spoke to John in Italian, then shot his hand out from waist level. Understandably, John, who had grown up in New York, jumped. The man began to wave his arms, and John, like most of the group who knew Italian from singing Puccini, Rossini, Verdi and Bellini answered him in the poetic language of opera. The man beamed. He turned to the people who waited in the doorway of the restaurant and shouted. They clapped their hands and started toward the bus, talking loudly.

In general, Black Americans do not take kindly to being rushed by a crowd of strange white men. John McCurry was still talking to the man who had acted as scout, but the other singers saw the crowd advancing across the square, and we reacted as if choreographed. We drew in closer to each other, our bags and the bus. The movement was subtle, but it was made with a fair amount of haste. The two small children stood nearer their fathers, who began talking earnestly with their wives. Ned Wright and Joe Attles chose that time to put their arms into the coats which they had always thrown cape-like over their shoulders.

As the group of Italians neared us, their smiles became evident; they were welcoming us to Venice. Our tight group relaxed and the old breezy attitudes returned. We mingled and mixed with the Italians, laughing and shaking hands.

They crowded around John McCurry and shouted, thinking he was the star of the opera. Leslie Scott and Laverne Hutchinson, who alternated in the lead role, were not pleased: John kept saying, "*No, no, io sono* Crown." But because of his size, his wide smile, large bass-baritone voice and probably his impeccable Italian accent, the new fans were certain they were admiring the right person.

Rose Tobias, who handled public relations for *Porgy and Bess*, stepped in to clear up the matter. She was a bright, young New Yorker, confident and pretty. She took Leslie and Laverne by the arms and pulled them into the center of the fray. The Italians were pumping John's hand as if they were priming a well.

Rose, still holding on to her stars, wedged herself between the Italians and John. She shook her head rapidly, causing her heavy blond hair to swirl in the men's faces. She pointed her finger at Laverne and then at Leslie, saying loudly, "Porgy, Porgy." She repeated the action until she was sure that credit went where it was due. She was happy because she had accomplished the task set before her. Rose Tobias was a success as our publicist, even in Italy. It hardly mattered that she didn't speak a word of Italian.

18

After I registered at the hotel, handed over my passport to the desk clerk and was shown my room, I decided to see Venice on my own. The company manager advanced each singer a portion of salary in lira. I bought a map, a cheap guide to Italian which contained useful phrases and a small Italian-English dictionary, and began my exploration.

The ancient buildings sat closed and remote, holding dead glories within their walls. The canals fanned in every direction from the pavement edge, while red and black gondolas slid along on the water's surface like toy boats sailing on ice. The gondoliers whose crafts were empty sang to amuse themselves or to attract customers. They chanted bits of arias and popular music and their voices pranced over the water, young and irresistible. I wandered, following the map, to the Grand Canal, which in the dusk looked black and oily, and with the lighted gondolas skimming along, it could have been the San Francisco Bay burdened with an array of Chinese junks.

I found the Piazza San Marco, and sat at a small table facing the square. I ordered coffee in my tourist-book Italian and sat watching the people in the grand square and the lights playing on the façade of the Basilica of Saint Mark and dreaming of the age of the doges and the city states of Italy which I had read about. The table I had chosen was in a fairly empty area of the restaurant, but the space was filled rapidly. Voices, suddenly closer, burst through my reverie. I looked around and discovered myself hemmed in by strange faces. I was the focus of at least thirty pairs of eyes. They all seemed to be searching my face—my mouth and nose, hairline and ears—for something precious that had been lost. There was a bizarre sense of being caught in a nightmare dreamed by a stranger.

I looked at my book for the necessary phrase. The waiter came over. "I would like more coffee." He chattered something back to me and nodded toward a group of men among the crowd staring at me. I repeated my request and he may have repeated his answer, because he nodded again toward the men. This time I followed his nod and saw three glasses lifted and smiles directed to me. They were toasting me. Surprise did not prevent me from returning their smile with a cool, restrained one of my own. I inclined my head and the crowd burst into laughter.

One woman asked, " 'St. Louis Blues'?"

One man sitting near me stood up and came very near my table. His black eyes were shining.

"*Americano*?" He leaned toward me unnecessarily—his voice carried around the restaurant and out into the plaza.

I answered as quietly as my grandmother would have replied if she was trying to show a loudmouth how to behave "Yes."

His smile widened. "Harlem?"

I nodded again, because I knew what he meant.

He bent his knees and put up his hands in a professional boxer's pose. He jabbed at the air. Everybody laughed. The man withdrew from the position, and looking at me again, asked, "Joe Louis?"

I didn't know how to tell him I knew who Joe Louis was but I didn't know him personally. He repeated, "Joe Louis?"

I put both hands together and raised them over my head in winners gesture, and the crowd laughed and raised their glasses again.

It was amazing that the people were all so handsome. Those at one table motioned that I should join them. I only thought about it a second, then went over and sat down in a chair that had been pulled out for me.

Again there was a general noise of approval. As soon as I sat down, men and women at other tables pulled up their chairs. I put my booklet on the table, pointed to it and smiled. A waiter brought a glass and I had a sweet and bitter Campari, which I'd never tasted before. When I grimaced the people wagged their heads and clucked. I looked through the dictionary for the word "bitter"; it wasn't there. A man took the book and began to look for something, but his search was in vain. A woman held her hand out for the book, and when it was passed to her she riffled through the pages and also failed to find what she was looking for. I was given another Campari. As the book traveled from hand to hand we all smiled at each other and the customers talked among themselves. I was having a lovely time and didn't understand a word that was said except "*Americano*" and "*bellissima*."

It was time to go. I smiled and stood up. About thirty people rose and smiled. I shook hands with the people at my table and said "*Grazie*." The others leaned forward, offering their hands and their beaming faces. I shook hands with each one, and walked out onto the square. When I looked back at the lighted café the people were still waving.

The year was 1954, only a decade since their country had been defeated by my country in a war fought for racial reasons as well as economic ones. And, after all, Joe Louis, whom the man seemed so proud to mention, had beaten an Italian, Primo Carnera. I thought my acceptance in the restaurant had been a telling show of the great heart of the Italian people. I hadn't been in Europe long enough to know that Europeans often made as clear a distinction between Black and white Americans as did the most confirmed Southern bigot. The difference, I was to discover, was that more often than not, Blacks were liked, whereas white Americans were not.

I prepared for bed after examining each object in the small bedroom and bath next door. Touching the washstand, the walls and the fine cotton curtains assured me that I was indeed out of the United States. I slept a fitful sleep, longing for my son and feeling nervous because the next evening I would debut in the role of Ruby.

19

The interior of the Teatro la Fenice was as rococo as the most opulent imagination could have wished. The walls were paneled in rich red velvet interrupted by slabs of white marble and gold mosaic. Heavy crystal chandeliers hung on golden chains. The rounded seats were covered in the same velvet and the wide aisles were carpeted with a deeper red wool.

The dressing rooms had been designed and built by people who possessed a great appreciation for singers and actors. They were large and comfortable to the point of being luxurious. The smaller rooms were furnished with a small sofa, dressing tables and wide lighted mirror and a washstand. And the stars' quarters could have easily passed for superior suites in a first-class hotel.

Irene Williams and Laverne Hutchinson had not been seen all day. In the manner of operatic stars they had been in seclusion. However, singers of the less strenuous roles had walked along the canals and shopped in the small stores. Ned Wright had met a gondolier and arranged a late-night boat ride on the Grand Canal for a few friends. He invited me. I had seen posters of John McCurry and me posted

433

around the city, and as I walked alone in the streets, small boys followed me chanting *"La Prima Ballerina," "La Prima Ballerina."* The children's pale-gold complexions and their joyful spirits reminded me of Clyde.

The stars materialized and dress rehearsal began. I was in costume and in place. There was a marked difference between observing the play—carefully scrutinizing each move, paying the closest attention to every note—and being a part of it and having some responsibility for the drama. The poignancy of Porgy's love for Bess and the tragedy of his fate brought tears to my eyes and clogged my throat, so that I could barely push notes out of my mouth. I was certain that in the course of time the play would become stale to me and I would become partially indifferent to its pathos. Over the next year, however, I found myself more touched by the tale and more and more impressed by the singers and actors who told it. The actual performance put dress rehearsal in the shade. The singers sang with fresh enthusiasm as if they had been called upon to create the music on the spot and were equal to the challenge. When Dolores Swann sang "Summertime," the audience was as hushed as the plastic doll that lay in her arms, and when she crooned the last top note the theater exploded with the sound of applause. Serena's lament and the love duet brought the audience to its feet. In the second half, when I finished my dance, the audience cheered again; as I followed the singers to the wings I received kisses and hugs and pats on the back.

Martha caught my hand and said, "Oh, Pavlova, I knew you were the one."

Lillian gave me a grin and said, "You danced your tail off, girl."

The curtain opened and revealed the theatergoers standing in the brightly lit auditorium. They clapped their hands and shouted up a pandemonium: "Bravo," "Bravo." During rehearsal the theater had been like a large inverted rococo snuffbox, but now, filled with beautifully dressed people screaming their appreciation, it was warm and rich and nearly too gorgeous to behold.

The curtains opened and closed and opened and closed and the audience refused to release the stars. Flowers were brought to the stage. I watched from the wings as Irene received bouquets gracefully in her arms until they piled up, threatening to obscure her face. Laverne bowed and smiled, holding on to her hand, then left her alone to take the kudos. When the curtain closed again, they exchanged places and he stood in the center accepting the applause. When the curtain closed for the last time, we hugged each other and danced with ecstasy.

The opening night of our European tour was a smash hit. The Italians were the most difficult audiences to sing for. They knew and loved music; operas, which were mainly for the elite in other countries, were folk music and children's songs in Italy. They loved us, we loved them. We loved ourselves. It was a certainty: if Italy declared us acceptable we could have the rest of Europe for a song.

We stayed in Venice for one sold-out week. During that time the stars were feted by city officials and the well-to-do, while the chorus was adored by the ordinary folk. We were hailed in the streets like conquering heroes and given free rides on the canals by gondoliers, who sang strains from *Porgy and Bess*. One owner of a glass-blowing factory presented us with delicate figurines, which we stowed in layers of cotton for our imminent trip to Paris.

I bought a French-English dictionary and packed it with the Italian-English phrase book and other belongings and had them taken to the bus which waited in the square. Fans crowded around us, offering cheeks to be kissed, hands to be shaken and flowers. We exchanged hugs and some tears with people who hadn't known of our existence only seven days before.

When the bus drove toward the station where we were to take a train to Paris, I thought of the city as a larger replica of some of its museums. Venice was itself an object of art, and its citizens the artists who had created it and were constantly re-creating it. I waved my hands, wagged my head and made sorry, sad faces to the well-wishers, as if I was being carried off against my will. Loving Venice and Venetians nearly made me Italian.

The Blue Train sped through Italy. I sat in a compartment with Lillian, Martha and Barbara Ann, listening to them talk about recital salons, and concert halls. Lillian mentioned a voice teacher whom someone in New York had recommended. Martha drew herself up and said the greatest voice teacher in the world was her teacher, in New York, and she wouldn't stand for anyone else messing with her voice. (Operatic singers are fiercely loyal to their teachers.) Lillian told her that was stupid: "Your teacher couldn't be the best vocal teacher in the world because I've heard some terrible stories about her." An argument grew and thrashed around the small space between us. I had nothing to add, since Wilkie was the only voice teacher I'd ever met, and I didn't want to mention his name in case I'd be obliged to defend him. I kept quiet. Barbara Ann said conciliatingly, "Well, you know, it's hard to say who is the best voice teacher in the world. That is until you've heard everyone. There are teachers in Texas no one has ever heard of who are very good." That was for Martha. She turned to Lillian and said, "Just because a person is gossiped about doesn't necessarily mean that the person is guilty." She looked at me for confirmation and added, "I mean, look how they talked about Jesus Christ. Am I right or wrong?"

I said I didn't know, and all three singers turned to me, their questions pouncing on my ears.

"What do you mean you don't know about Jesus?"

"They talked about him like a dog."

"Don't you remember about the Philistines and the Pharisees?"

"Your grandmother would have been ashamed of you."

"What about the money lenders in the temple?"

Martha said, "What about 'buked and scorned?" and then she began to sing: "I been 'buked and I been scorned."

Her voice was the most perfect I had ever heard in my life. It was like hot silver being poured from a high place.

Lillian laid her full contralto under the glistening sound:

> "I been 'buked
>   And I been scorned
> I been talked about
>   Sure as you're born."

Barbara Ann wedged her clear soprano between the other voices, embracing first one tone then the other, getting so near the other trills that her sound almost melted into theirs. The music written hundreds of years before soared in the Italian train, erasing the dispute, and placing us all somewhere between the agony of Christ and the ecstasy of Art.

As the train pulled into the Gare du Nord I heard my name shouted above the clamor of luggage carts and the calls of porters: "Maya Angelou," "Où est Mademoiselle Maya Angelou?" I knew I shouldn't have left my son. There was a telegram waiting for me to say he had been hurt somehow. Or had run away from home. Or had caught an awful disease. The train ground to a halt and I forced the conductor aside and opened the door.

Five feet away stood the handsome and rugged Yanko Varda and Annette March, as svelte as a model. They were searching the train and yelling, "Maya Angelou," "Mademoiselle Maya Angelou."

I felt weak with relief. "Yanko, Annette, *je suis ici.*"

We caressed one another like lovers. Annette handed me a basket that held cheese and fruit, a bottle of wine and a loaf of bread. They motioned to me to look back along the track. Victor Di Suvero, Mitch Lifton and Cyril March were handing out similar baskets to some of the singers as they detrained. They said, "Welcome to Paris. This is in honor of Maya Angelou. This is in honor of Maya Angelou. Welcome to Paris."

Yanko called to them, and when they saw me they ran over. Mitch and Victor hugged me and grinned. Cyril, who was always more reserved, gave me the European embrace.

I asked what they were doing in Paris, and they asked me to go with them for a glass of wine. They would explain everything.

I went to Bob Dustin to get the name and address of my hotel and an advance in francs. He agreed to send my baggage along, and my San Francisco friends took me to a sidewalk café.

They had not come to Paris together. Yanko was returning from a trip to Greece.

"Maya, I have found the only beautiful brunette in the world," Victor said. "She is a sculptor, a Greek, a goddess. You will meet her here. She will come to Sausalito. She will light up San Francisco with her black eyes and the men will fall at her feet like Turks. She is Aphrodite."

Victor was en route to Italy on family business. Mitch was on a visit, and the Marches had moved to Paris, where Cyril was practicing medicine. San Francisco papers had run a notice that I had joined *Porgy and Bess*. My friends in Paris had read the company's advance publicity and found when and where we were due to arrive.

I described the fabulous success in Venice, giving myself a little more credit than I deserved. We drank wine, talked about San Francisco and they promised to attend opening night.

20

Paris loved *Porgy and Bess*. We were originally supposed to stay at the Théâtre Wagram for three weeks, but were held over for months. After the first week I discovered that I couldn't afford to stay in the hotel that had been assigned to me. The policy of the company was to pay the singers half their salary in the currency of the country we were in and the other half in dollars. I sent my dollars home to pay for Clyde's keep and to assuage my guilt at being away from him.

I moved into a small pension near the Place des Ternes, which provided a Continental breakfast with my tiny room. There was a cot-sized bed and just space for me and my suitcase. The family who owned the place and my fellow roomers spoke no English, so perforce my French improved.

One evening after the theater a group of Black American entertainers who lived in Paris came backstage. They enchanted me with their airs and accents. Their sentences were mixed with Yeah Man's and Oo la la's. They fluttered their hands and raised their eyebrows in typically Gallic fashion, but walked swinging their shoulders like Saturday-night people at a party in Harlem.

Bernard Hassel, a tall nut-brown dancer, worked at the Folies-Bergères, and Nancy Holloway, whose prettiness brought to mind a young untroubled Billie Holiday, sang at the Colisée. Bernard invited me to see the night life of Paris.

"*Alors*, something groovy, you know?"

We went to the Left Bank, and he showed me where F. Scott Fitzgerald and Hemingway did some flamboyant talking and serious drinking. The bareness of the bar surprised me. I expected a more luxurious room with swatches of velvet, deep and comfortable chairs and at least a doorman. The café's wide windows were bare of curtains and the floor uncarpeted. It could have been the Coffee Shop in San Francisco's North Beach. High up over the façade hung a canvas awning on which was stenciled the romantic name DEUX MAGOTS.

L'Abbaye was a bar owned by Gordon Heath, a Black American who provided his own entertainment. He sang in a weak but compelling voice and projected an air of mystery. After each song the audience showed their appreciation by snapping their fingers. Heath did not allow hand-clapping.

The Rose Rouge on the Left Bank was closer to my idea of a Parisian night club. It had velour drapes and a uniformed doorman; the waiters were haughty and the customers well-dressed. Acrobats and pantomimists, magicians and pretty half-naked girls kept up a continuous diversion. Bernard introduced me to the handsome Algerian owner, who I immediately but privately named Pepe Le Moko. He said if I wanted to do an act in his club, he'd find a place for me. I said I'd keep it in mind.

Around three o'clock in the morning my escort took me to the Mars Club, which he pronounced "Mairs Cloob" near the Champs-Élysées. It was owned by an oversized American man from New York and specialized in Black entertainment. Bernard pointed out the names printed on the door of people who had worked in the smoky and close room. The only one I recognized was Eartha Kitt. Ben, the owner, repeated Pepe Le Moko's invitation. I said I was flattered and I'd think about it. I knew I wouldn't. Where would I find a musician in Paris who could play calypso accompaniment?

Ben asked, "Why don't you give us a song now?"

I looked at the pianist, who was white and thin and had a long sorry face. He sat playing a quiet moody song. When he finished, Ben called him to the bar and introduced us. "Bobby Dorrough, this is Maya Angelou, she's a singer."

He smiled and his face was transformed. His cheeks bunched under sparkling eyes and his teeth were large and white and even. He said, "Happy to know you, Maya," and the drawl made my skin move along my arms. He couldn't have sounded more Southern white if he had exaggerated.

Ben went to the microphone and announced, "Ladies and gentlemen, we have with us tonight one of the stars of *Porgy and Bess*."

I was hardly that, but why correct him? I stood and bowed while the audience applauded fiercely.

The pianist said "Welcome to Paris" in a molasses accent. For months I had been away from the sound that recalled lynchings, insults and hate. It was bizarre to find myself suddenly drenched with the distasteful memories in a Parisian *boîte*.

I made myself speak. "Where are you from?"

"I'm from San Antonio." At least he didn't say "San Antone." "Where are you from?"

"San Francisco." I said it so briskly I almost bit my lip.

"Would you like to sing something? I'd be happy to play for you." The graciousness dripped honeysuckle all over the old plantation.

I said, "No. I don't think you can play my music. It's not very ordinary."

He asked, "What do you sing? The blues?" I knew he would think I sang blues. "I play the blues." I was sure he'd say he played the blues.

"No, I sing calypso. Do you also play calypso?" That ought to hold him.

"Yes. I know some. How about 'Stone Cold Dead in the Market'? Or 'Rum and Coca-Cola'?"

I followed him to the piano in a mild state of shock. I told him my key and he was right. He played 'Stone Cold Dead' better and with more humor than my accompanist did at the Purple Onion. The audience liked the song and Bobby applauded quietly. Everything about the man was serene except his piano playing and his smile.

"Want to sing another? How about 'Run Joe'?"

Although that had been the song which started my career and I always used it to close a show or as a dramatic encore, it was not really well known. I was surprised that the pianist knew it. "Yes. I'll sing one more."

He took only a few bars to fall into the mood I was creating and then raced along with me and the story, never drowning my effects but always holding his own. When we finished I felt obliged to shake his hand over the loud applause.

"Aw, Maya, there was nothing to it. You're very good."

Bernard and Ben met me back at the bar. They were still clapping as I approached.

439

"How about doing one spot a night for me, Maya?" Ben was grinning as he shook my hand. "One show a night. You'll be a sensation in Paris."

Bernard said, "*Cherie*, it'll knock them out."

"But I don't get out of the theater until eleven-thirty." It was nice to be begged to do what I liked to do.

"You could do a show here at twelve-thirty."

I thought about the money. I would be able to move out of the grim little pension that had no luxuries and was minus certain things that I as an American considered necessities. I could afford a room with private bath again and a toilet that wouldn't be at the end of dark stairs. And I could continue sending the same amount of money home. Or, it occurred to me, I could stay where I was—the pension wasn't all that bad—and send more money home. Mom could buy something wonderful for Clyde every other week and tell him I'd sent it. Then perhaps he would forgive my absence.

I asked Ben, "Could you pay me in dollars?"

Ben had been in Paris a long time. His large, round face became wise and hard. "You've got a good connection for exchange?"

I knew some people in the company sold their dollars on the black market and received a higher percentage of francs than banks would give.

I said, "No. I have a son at home. I have to send money for his keep."

His expression softened a little. "Of course, of course, kid, I can give you dollars and you'll be paid every night. That's the way we do it in Paris. You want to talk it over with Bobby? He'll be playing for you."

I waited until the pianist joined us at the bar. "I'm going to start singing here. Ben has offered me a job."

"Well, isn't that nice."

Oh God, I didn't know how I could bear that accent. If he would only play the piano and never speak to me, we'd get along very well.

"When are you going to start?"

Ben asked, "How about day after tomorrow. You could rehearse with Bobby tomorrow and next day and begin that night. How's that, kid?"

That was fine with me and the musician. Bernard bought drinks and we closed the deal by clinking glasses all around.

Bobby Dorrough had a pitch as fine as crystal. I sang snatches of songs to him in the empty bar and as if he were a music machine, the notes went into his ears and immediately his fingers pressed them out of the piano keys. In the first afternoon's rehearsal we ran over my entire repertoire and agreed to spend the next day polishing the numbers. It was nearly dusk when we walked out of the bar.

"Do you want me to get you a taxi, Maya?"

I said, "No, I just live near the Place des Ternes."

"All right then, I'll walk you to your hotel."

"Oh no, thanks. I mean, I feel like walking slowly."

"Well, I wasn't planning to race you down the streets."

"I mean, I'd just as soon walk by myself." I tried to tell him, without hurting his feelings, that I didn't really want to be with him. Suppose some of my friends from the opera met us. I didn't know one person who would be surprised or offended if I was seen with a white man, but neither did I know one who wouldn't be shocked into uncomfortable recall by the Southern accent.

"Would you like to have lunch tomorrow? Before rehearsal?" He was very slow in getting the message.

I said, "No, thank you."

Rejection dawned on him and his pale face flushed with understanding. He said, "All right then, Maya, I'll see you tomorrow."

I walked away, heading toward the Arc de Triomphe.

Martha and Lillian said they'd come down with me to the club. Ned Wright and Joe Attles and Bey promised to drop by for the last show. The news that I had a second job did not displease the company's administration because any publicity I received was good for the opera.

After the midnight show I introduced my friends to the full audience. "Ladies and gentlemen, some members of the *Porgy and Bess* company."

The audience stood up to look at the suddenly modest singers, who refused to rise, but simply nodded grandly from their seats.

I knew what was wrong. I hadn't singled them out and made individual introductions giving their names and the roles they played. "Ladies and gentlemen, I would like you to meet Miss Lillian Hayman, who sings Maria and Serena." She was understudying the two roles. Lillian stood and graciously took the applause. She sat down gratified. "Joseph Attles, Sportin' Life." He stood, waved his long hands and blew kisses. "Ned Wright, Robbins." Ned stood and flashed a smile like a beacon around the room. "And Miss Martha Flowers, Bess." Martha stood up slowly and solemnly. She inclined her head, first to the right, then to the left, then to the audience directly in front. Only after she had bowed did she smile. Her sense of theater was never better—she began the smile slowly, keeping her mouth closed and simply pulling her lips taut. Then she allowed a few teeth to show and gradually a few more, and then more. When her lips were stretched as tight as possible and her teeth glimmering like a row of lights, she snapped her head back and laughed, the high sound tinkling like chimes.

441

The audience was bewitched. They began to shout, "*Chantez*, Bess. *Chantez*, *chantez*, Bess."

Martha suddenly became demure, and shaking her head in refusal, draped her small body in her seat. Her action incited the crowd and their clamor rose in volume. At exactly the correct moment, Martha stood up and shyly went to the piano. She leaned and whispered to Bobby. He struck one note and took his hands from the keys.

> "O they so fresh and fine
> And they right off'n the vine."

She was singing the vendor's song a cappella and her voice floated free in the quiet room:

> "Strawberries, strawberries!"

I looked around—everyone was beguiled, including our fellow singers. Martha ballooned her voice, then narrowed it, dipping down into a rough contralto, and then swung it high beyond the lyric soprano into the rarefied air that was usually the domain of divine coloraturas.

For a second after she finished there was no sound. Then people applauded her and began to crowd around her table. She coyly accepted the attention as if she hadn't worked hard for years to earn it.

One of the lessons I learned from *Porgy and Bess* was that jealousy is conceived only in insecurity and must be nourished in fear. Each individual in our cast had the certainty of excellence.

After the din over Martha's singing diminished, I asked Lillian to please sing.

She stood up without reluctance and sang,

> "Go way from my window
> Go way from my door
> Go way, way, way from my bedside
> And bother me no more
> And bother me no more."

Her voice was as colorful as Martha's was pure, and the customers were again enchanted. Ned Wright sang a medley of popular songs, beginning with "I Can't Give You Anything but Love," which the French people recognized and loved. Joe Attles gave the audience "St. James Infirmary" and they literally stood in the aisles.

Maya Angelou was a crazy success. A smash hit! The audience

thought they had never been better entertained. Ben was certain I would improve business; the bartender and waiters smiled gratefully at me. If I hadn't memorized a story my grandmother told me when I was a knee-high child, I might have become conceited and begun to believe the compliments I did not totally deserve.

The old story came to mind:

Mrs. Scott, a woman well past middle age, fancied young men. She was a great churchgoer and used each religious gathering to search for the objects of her choice. All the young men in her town were aware of her predilections, and she was unsuccessful in snaring them.

One day a new man appeared at the meeting house. He was handsome and although adult, he was still young enough to be gullible.

The woman caught him directly after service and invited him to her home for late Sunday afternoon dinner. He accepted gratefully.

She rushed home, killed a chicken and put it on to fry. While the chicken cooked, Mrs. Scott took a small needle from her sewing kit, and putting on her bifocals, picked her way down the lane from her front door. When she reached a tree a hundred yards away, she stuck the needle in the bark and returned to the kitchen to finish preparing the meal.

When the young man arrived, they sat down to a tasty dinner (for Mrs. Scott was an excellent cook), and after they finish Mrs. Scott invited the man to sit on the porch in the swing, to let his dinner digest. She brought out lemonade and sat with him. Dusk was falling and the shapes of things were blurred.

Mrs. Scott sat bolt upright and turned to the young man "What on earth is that I see sticking in that tree?" She pointed down the lane to the oak, which was barely a shadow in the darkness.

The young man asked, "What tree, Mrs. Scott?"

"Why, that oak tree at the bottom of the lane." She squinted and bent her neck. "I do believe that's a pin."

The young man, squinting, tried to pierce the gloom.

Mrs. Scott, I can't hardly see the tree. And you can see something sticking in it?"

"Yes." Mrs. Scott had relaxed her scrutiny. "At first I thought it was a pin, but when I looked for the head it wasn't there—I saw instead a hole. So it's got to be a needle."

The young man turned and looked at Mrs. Scott with admiration.

"You know, ma'am, when you left church this mroning, some folks told me to be careful. That you were an old woman who loved young men. But I must say, if you can see the hole in a needle a

*hundred yards away after the sun has gone down, you're not nearly
as old as they say you are."*

*Mrs. Scott, proud of her compliments and forgetful of her
subterfuge, said, "Well, thank you for that. I'll just go and get the
needle and show it to you."*

*She flounced up out of the swing and stepped jauntily down the
stairs. When she reached the bottom step she turned to smile at the
appreciative young man, and then continuing, she walked two steps
and tripped over a cow sitting in the lane.*

Yes, I was a success in Paris at the Mars Club. I would have been a
fool to have thought the praise was all mine. Ben liked me because I
was good enough, but appreciated me because the members from
Porgy and Bess were likely to drop in and sing for free. Bobby liked
me because I was good enough, and he had a chance to play music
for which he seldom received requests. The audience liked me
because I was good enough, and I was different—not African, but
nearly; not American, but nearly. And I liked myself because, simply, I
was lucky.

I gave thanks to *Porgy and Bess*, my good fortune and to God. I
wasn't about to trip over a cow.

21

Paris was changing the rhythm of that old gang of mine. Martha took
a two-week leave from the company to give a Town Hall recital in
New York City. Lillian had said to me often, "I'm so glad I wasn't born
here, because I'd never have learned to speak this language," but she
had found new French friends and I seldom saw her after the theater.
Barbara Ann's husband flew from the United States to be with her,
and since they were newly married, they could spare little time for
anyone beyond their tight circle of romance. Ned Wright and Joe
Attles were bent on a ferocious discovery of Paris. After the final bow
they raced from the theater as if an emergency call awaited them.
They unearthed little-known restaurants and bars in obscure corners
of the city.

From my third-floor (which the French perversely called second-floor) room, I assayed my value to Paris and its promise for me. I had accepted the Rose Rouge offer and become a typical Parisian entertainer. I sang a midnight show at the Mars Club, threw a coat over my sparkly dress, hailed a cab and rode across the Seine to do a second show at the Rose Rouge. My songs were well enough received and fans were beginning to remember me. Some sent notes and occasionally flowers to my dressing room. A few expatriates and two Senegalese students I had met advised me to leave *Porgy and Bess* and make my mark in Paris. The Africans said that in France I would never hear of lynchings and riots. And I would not be refused service in any restaurant or hotel in the country. The people were civilized. And, anyway, the French people loved Negroes. Look at Sid Bechet. Lil Armstrong, a former wife of Satchmo played piano at the Le Jazz Hot and had an avid following. Bambi, a tall, deliciously thin model, could hardly walk the streets in Paris without men following her and raving over her Black beauty. Nancy Holloway and Inez, who owned Chez Inez, sang American songs as well as popular French melodies and were welcomed with hyperbolic Gallic admiration. And, of course, Josephine Baker was a national institution.

I considered the advice seriously. I could find an apartment and send for Clyde. He was bright and would learn the language quickly. He would be freed from growing up under the cloud of racial prejudice that occasionally made every Black childhood sunless. He would be obliged to be good for his own sake rather than to prove to a disbelieving society that he was not a brute. The French students wore short pants and blazers and caps, and I knew my son would look beautiful in his uniform. The prospect looked glorious.

A woman asked me to join her table after my show at the Rose Rouge. She welcomed me and introduced me to her friends.

Her voice was tiny but piercing, and a baby-doll smile never left her pink-and-white face, and her eyelids fluttered only a little faster than her hands. She reminded me of Billie Burke and very small door chimes.

"Mademoiselle, do you know who is Pierre Mendès-France?" Smile, blink, rustle.

I said, "Yes, madame. I read the papers."

"I want an affair for him to give." Her English was not broken, it was crippled.

I said in French, "Madame, let us speak French."

She bubbled and gurgled. "*Non. Non.* I love this English for practice to speak."

Alors. She limped along verbally, explaining that she wanted me to sing at a reception which she planned to host. It would be a fund-

445

raising event and they would gladly pay me for my services. I would be expected to sing two songs. Something plaintive that would move the heart, I thought, and loosen the purse strings.

"The blues." Madame said, "Oh, how the blues I love. Will you sing 'St. Louie Blues'?" She started singing the first line: "I hate to see, that evening sun go down."

Her shoulders hunched up to her ear lobes and she made her eyes small and lascivious. Her lips pushed out and I saw the red underlining of her mouth.

"'I hate to see that evening sun go down.'"

She shook herself and her breasts wobbled. She was imitating her idea of a *Négresse*.

I stopped her. "Madame, I know the song. I will sing it at the reception."

She was not fazed by the interruption, but clapped her hands and told her friends to clap theirs. We agreed on a price, and she said, "You are with *Porgy and Bess*. The great opera. If Bess or Porgy or your friends desire to come with you at the reception, they will not be made to pay."

She smiled, laughed, waved her hands and generally jangled like a bunch of keys. I thanked her and left the table.

Since my friends in *Porgy and Bess* were otherwise engaged, I asked the two Senegalese men to escort me to the reception. They were pleased to do so and appeared at the theater's backstage door in tuxedos, starched shirts and highly polished shoes. Their general elegance put me in a party mood. I walked into the salon with a handsome, attentive man on each side, and as we stopped inside the door, I felt that the three of us must have made an arresting tableau.

Madame was informed of my arrival and she floated over in wisps of chiffon, smiling her cheeks into small pink balloons.

"Oh, mademoiselle. How it is kind of you to come." She offered me her hand, but gave her eyes to my escorts. They bowed smartly. "And your friends you brought. Who of you is the Porgy? I do love 'Summertime.'" She had wafted into singing "'And the living is easy.'"

I said, "No, madame." It was hard to wrest her attention from the two men. "No, madame, they are not with *Porgy and Bess*. These are friends from Africa."

When the import of my statement struck her, the smile involuntarily slid off her face and she recovered her hand from my grasp.

"*D'Afrique? d'Afrique?*" Suddenly there were no bubbles in her voice.

M'Ba bowed formally and said in French, "Yes, madame. We are from Senegal."

She looked at me as if I had betrayed her. "But, mademoiselle—" She changed her mind and stood straight. She spoke in French, "Please wait here. I will have someone take you to the musicians. *Bon soir.*" She turned and left.

After I sang, a young woman gave me an envelope with my pay and thanked me warmly. I never saw Madame again.

Paris was not the place for me or my son. The French could entertain the idea of me because they were not immersed in guilt about a mutual history—just as white Americans found it easier to accept Africans, Cubans or South American Blacks than the Blacks who had lived with them foot to neck for two hundred years. I saw no benefit in exchanging one kind of prejudice for another. Also, I was only adequate as an entertainer, and I would never set Paris afire. Honesty made me admit that I was neither a new Josephine Baker or an old Eartha Kitt.

When the *Porgy and Bess* administration informed us that we were moving on to Yugoslavia, I found a woman to give me lessons in Serbo-Croatian and bought myself a dictionary.

Adieu, Paris.

22

In Zagreb the company was called together to be told that the Yugoslav government and the American State Department wished us to be discreet; we were, after all, guests of the country and the first American singers to be invited behind the iron curtain. We would be driven from the hotel to the theater and back again. We could walk only within a radius of four square blocks of the hotel. We were not to accept invitations from any Yugoslavians, nor were we to initiate fraternization.

The hotel corridors smelled of cabbage and the dust of ages. I found the maid on my floor and asked her in Serbo-Croatian if there was anything interesting to see near the hotel. I had little hope that she would understand me, but she readily answered, "Yes, there's the railroad station." I was elated that the money I had spent on language lessons had not been spent in vain.

I said excitedly, "Madame, I can speak Serbo-Croatian."

She looked at me without curiosity and said, "Yes?" She waited for me to go on.

447

I repeated, "I learned to speak Serbo-Croatian two weeks ago."

She nodded and waited heavily. No smile warmed her features. I couldn't think of anything to add. We stood in the hall like characters from different plays by different authors suddenly thrust upon the same stage. I grinned. She didn't.

I said, "Thank you."

She said, "You're welcome."

I went to my room taking my confusion along. Why hadn't the woman been amazed to find an American Negro woman speaking Serbo-Croatian? Why hadn't she congratulated me? I knew we were the first Blacks that had stayed in the hotel and possibly the first that had ever visited the town.

At first I concluded that because the maid had never been out of her country and everyone she knew spoke her language, she thought Yugoslavia was the world and the world Yugoslavia. Then I realized that the staff must have undergone intensive indoctrination before our arrival. In the lobby no one stared at us; obviously, we were being studiously and politely ignored. The desk clerks and porters, waiters and bartenders, acted as if the sixty Black American opera singers roamed the halls and filled their lobby every other week. I was certain that we were the only authentic guests in the establishment. The others, who averted their eyes at our approach and buried their heads in their newspapers, seemed less innocent than Peter Lorre in an Eric Ambler movie.

Outside, however, it was a different story. Ordinary citizens crowded three deep to peer into the hotel windows. When one gawker could catch a glimpse of us, he or she nudged the persons nearby and all craned their necks, eyes bulging, and then laughed uproariously, revealing stainless-steel teeth that looked ominous. They had to be talked to sharply like obstreperous children at a summer fair.

Martha, who had rejoined the company, and Ethel Ayler, the new and glamorous Bess, refused my invitation to go for a walk.

Martha leaned back and looked up at me. "But Miss Thing, they think we're monkeys or something. Just look at them. No, my dear, I'm counting on Tito to keep his people outside and I swear Miss Fine Thing will stay inside."

Ethel laughed and agreed with Martha. "They think we're in a cage. I wouldn't be surprised if they threw peanuts at us."

Ned warned me, "I don't think that's the smartest thing you could do. Look at those silver teeth. Those people might start thinking you're a chocolate doll and eat you up. Stay here in the hotel. I'll play you some tonk and buy you a slivovitz."

I hadn't taken Serbo-Croatian lessons just to try out the language on hotel staff who wouldn't even pass the time of day. I walked out of the hotel.

People crowded around me. Short, stocky peasants from the country wore pointed, knitted hats and had eyes that would have been at home in Oriental faces except for their blue color. I spoke to them. "Good afternoon. Please excuse me. Thank you."

It took a few seconds for those nearest me to realize that they could understand me, and then a hilarity exploded that would have been well received at a Fourth of July Shriners' picnic. They shouted and pushed in closer to me. A small surf of panic started to lap at my inner mind. I held it off. I couldn't afford terror to freeze me to the spot or force me to bolt. Hands began to reach for me. They clutched at my sleeve, at my face. I stretched as tall as possible and shouted, "Excuse me, I am going through." I had followed Wilkie's teachings attentively, and if the quality of my singing did not show a marked improvement, the volume at least, had certainly increased.

I boomed again, "Excuse me. I am going through." The noise abated and the country people's mouths gaped. The crowd parted and I strode through their moment of fluster and down the street. I didn't dare turn to see if any had chosen to follow me. Mobs of any color terrified me, and had I seen the mass behind me, without a doubt I would have taken flight and been lost in a second.

When passersby saw me, they stiffened in their tracks as if I were a fairy queen or an evil witch who had the power to suspend their mobility.

I walked into a small store which sold musical instruments. The salesman took one look at me and rushed back to a draped doorway. He shouted, "Come and see this!" Then, as if I had not heard and seen his action, he dressed his face in the universal sales-pitch smile and asked, "How are you? Good morning. May I help you?" He jerked his face away and toward the door again. "Come. Come now." Then back to me with a courteous manner.

I said, "I'd like to buy a mandolin."

He interested me as much as I interested him. It was fantastic that he thought he ceased to exist for me when he removed his attention."

"A mandolin? Certainly." His eyes fled toward the back room. I grabbed his attention: "Here. How much is this one?"

While he removed a mandolin, beautifully inlaid with mother-of-pearl, children began to tumble through the rear door and into the store. They were followed by a heavy woman with a large, florid face. When they saw me they stopped as if they had rehearsed the scene.

The woman directed a question to the man. He looked at her and answered but I couldn't catch the language. They all began to talk at once, the children's voices stabbing in and out of the deeper sounds. I continued examining the mandolin, strumming on it, turning it over in my hands to appreciate its fine woodwork. I ignored them and said to the man that I would like to buy the instrument.

He interrupted the family dialogue and told me the price; I gave him the money. The family had advanced on me. The mother was holding back as many of the children as she could reach while she inched closer to me.

I spoke to her. "Good morning, madame."

She smiled tentatively, but the incredulous look on her face remained.

"Good morning, madame," I repeated, looking directly in her eyes. If they thought I was a talking bear, then they would have to admit that at least I spoke Serbo-Croatian.

Her husband was wrapping my package, so I contintued, "How are you, madame?"

Finally, her lips relaxed and opened and I saw the bar of metal that substituted for teeth. She placed herself between me and the children, then said, "Paul Robeson."

It was my turn to be stunned. The familiar name did not belong in Byzantium. The woman repeated, "Paul Robeson," and then began one of the strangest scenes I had ever seen.

She began to sing, "Deep River." Her husky voice was suddenly joined by the children's piping "My home is over Jordan." Then the husband teamed with his wife and offspring, "Deep River, Lord." They knew every word.

I stood in the dusty store and considered my people, our history and Mr. Paul Robeson. Somehow, the music fashioned by men and women out of an anguish they could describe only in dirges was to be a passport for me and their other descendants into far and strange lands and long unsure futures.

> "Oh don't you want to go
> To that gospel feast?"

I added my voice to the melody:

> "That promised land
> Where all is peace?"

I made no attempt to wipe away the tears. I could not claim a forefather who came to America on the *Mayflower*. Nor did any ancestor of mine amass riches to leave me free from toil. My great-grandparents were illiterate when their fellow men were signing the

Declaration of Independence, and the first families of my people were bought separately and sold apart, nameless and without traces—yet there was this:

> "Deep River
> My home is over Jordan."

I had a heritage, rich and nearer than the tongue which gives it voice. My mind resounded with the words and my blood raced to the rhythms.

> "Deep River
> I want to cross over into campground."

The storekeeper and his wife embraced me. My Serbo-Croatian was too weak to carry what I wanted to say. I hugged them again and took up my mandolin and left the store.

Porgy and Bess received the expected kudos from sold-out houses in Zagreb, and after a few days we moved on to Belgrade. We had been told that Belgrade was a city that was reasonably cosmopolitan, and we were all eager for the bright lights.

The Moskva Hotel in Red Square was considered a large hotel but it could hardly accommodate our singers, administration and conductors. Bob Dustin, cheery as usual, announced that we would have to triple up, and that if we didn't want to be assigned bed space arbitrarily, we should choose roommates and let him know.

Martha, Ethel Ayler and I agreed to share one of the large high-ceilinged rooms. Ethel had made fast friends with Martha and was an excellent foil for Martha's always sharp, often acid comments. Ethel would smile calmly and say, "Martha Flowers, you are a disgrace. Charming, talented, but a disgrace." Martha would giggle and be coaxed out of her ill-humor.

We had expected three cots in our room, but found one large lumpy bed, a very worn carpet and a single overhead light.

"You mean this is what these people got out of their revolution?" Martha daintily picked her way around the room. "Someone should tell them that they're about due for another." She wrinkled her pretty face in distaste.

Ethel said reprovingly, "Martha, control yourself. Unless you want the NKVD to take you to Siberia. How could you sing with salt in your throat?"

Martha laughed, "Miss Fine Thing can sing anywhere, darling. Even on the steppes of Byelorussia."

451

Our bags were brought to the room by a porter who didn't raise his eyes. We tried to tip him, but he rushed away as if afraid.

Martha said, "*Regardez ça*. Maya, you speak his lingo, why didn't you tell him we wouldn't bite? Of course; only because he's not cute enough." With the mention of men, Martha and Ethel and I fell into an old conversation which had never concluded and was interrupted only by sleep, performances and forced separation on journeys. The value of men. Their beauty. Their power. Their worth, excitement and attractiveness. Were American Negro men better than Africans? Better companions, better lovers? Yes. No. Whoever had a story to substantiate her point of view told it in detail. Were white American men sexier than French or Italian? Yes. No. We told secrets to each other on trains, ships, in hotel rooms and backstage. I was never loath to exaggerate a tale to make my point, and I'm certain that some of the accounts that were told to me were as fictitious as my own. We were all in our mid-twenties, and given that my two friends had spent ten years cloistered in vocal studios and secreted in institutes of music and I had had fewer romantic experiences than most college coeds, our imaginations got more exercise than our libidos.

Ethel slept in the middle and Martha beside the night table. She jumped when the telephone rang.

"Who on earth, what time is it?" The telephone and Martha's outrage awakened Ethel and me. Something must have happened and Bob Dustin or Ella Gerber wanted the company to gather at once.

Martha sweetened her voice. "Good morning." She sang the greeting.

"Mistress who?" We were all sitting upright in bed. "Mistress Maya Angelou?" Her voice revealed her disbelief. "And you are Mr. Julian? Hold on."

She put her hand over the receiver. "Mr. Julian wants to speak to Mistress Maya Angelou. At eight o'clock in the damned morning. Now, ain't that something?" The phone wire wouldn't extend across the bed. I had to get up in the cold and pad around to the other side.

"Hello?"

"Is this Mistress Maya Angelou?" The question was asked by a voice I had never heard.

"Yes. I am Maya Angelou." I answered to a background of disgruntled noises and curious looks from my roommates.

"Mistress Maya, I am being Mr. Julian. It's that last night I am seeing you dance. I am watching you leap across the stage and looking at your legs jumping through the air and, Mistress Maya, I am loving you." The words ran together like dyes, and it was difficult for me to separate them into comprehension.

"I beg your pardon?"

452

Martha groaned. "Oh, my goodness, can't he call you after the sun rises? Or does the sun never rise in Yugoslavia?"

"It's I am loving you, Mistress Maya. It's that if you are hearing a man is throwing his body into the Danube today, and dying in the icy water, Mistress Maya, that man is being me. Drowning for the love of you. You and your lovely legs jumping."

"Just a minute. Uh, what is your name?"

"I am being Mr. Julian, and I am loving you."

"Yes, well, Mr. Julian, why do you want to drown? Why would loving me make you want to die? I don't think that's very nice."

Ethel and Martha were both leaning on their elbows watching me.

Martha said, "Would he promise to die before sundown? Do you think he'll do it in time for us to get a little sleep?"

Ethel said serenely, "Now Maya sees what her saintly lifesaving attitude has brought."

"Look, mister."

"It's being Mr. Julian."

"Yes, well, Mr. Julian, thanks for the telephone call—"

"May I please be seeing you? May I please be taking you to one expensive café and watching your lovely lips drinking down coffee with cream?"

"No, thank you. I am sorry, but I have to hang up now."

Martha grumbled, "Hang up, or down. Just let me go back to sleep."

"Miss Maya, if you're not seeing me, if you're not letting me see your lips drinking down coffee with cream, then today, I am sending you my heart."

Oh, my God. The woman who gave me Serbo-Croatian lessons in Paris was a Yugoslavian émigré. After my last class she told me solemnly, "Don't ever in the warmth of passion tell a Yugoslav that you can't live without him. You will find him, his trunks and his family at your door. Ready to move in and improve your life." I had thought she was making a sarcastic joke, for she had said the best thing about Yugoslavia was that she couldn't return to it. When I chided her on exaggeration, she swore that what she said was absolute truth. That Slavs were passionate and so romantic they would gladly mutilate themselves to demonstrate their sincerity. And here this unknown man was threatening to send me his heart.

"Oh, no, Mr. Julian. Please. I beg you. Don't send me your heart."

Martha said, "Tell him to send you his tongue so he'll shut up."

"Mistress Maya. It is that I am sending it to your theater, by hand, this morning. Good-bye, lovely legs leaping." The line went dead.

Martha flopped back on the bed. "Well, thank God for small favors."

Ethel looked at me, waiting to see if I wanted to talk about the phone call.

I said, "I'm going to take a bath."

She said, "O.K. See you," and wiggled down under the heavy quilts.

I was tickled and frightened. "It's I am being Mr. Julian," indeed. He sounded old and rusty—like aged garden furniture, pushed around on concrete. "It's that I'm loving you. I am sending you my heart." Oh no, please.

I walked down the hall to the communal bathroom, thinking about a gory heart wrapped in newspapers waiting in my dressing room.

I stood in the drafty tub sudsing myself and imagined the blood congealed, clotted around the aorta. I dried with the thin towel and assured myself that no one in the world, even in fiction, had ever cut out his own heart. Then I remembered hara-kiri, or the ritual Japanese samurai suicide where the protagonist arranges for friends to help him perform his self-murder. Were the Yugoslavs as dramatic? I prayed not.

Martha and Ethel woke as I was leaving to go downstairs for breakfast.

"Going to meet Mr. Julian, Maya? Going to bring back his heart?"

"I am going to breakfast, ladies. Just breakfast."

"Don't eat braised heart on toast, girl." I could have wrung Martha's silver throat. My appetite fled on the heels of her remark. Downstairs I forced down tea and continually pushed away the bloody pictures which assailed my mind. I couldn't go to the theater early because we were under the same restriction in Belgrade that had obtained in Zagreb. We could walk only in the prescribed four-block area, and buses took us to and from the theater.

I waited throughout the day. Drinking slivovitz and writing letters, forced happy letters, to my family.

Finally, the cast assembled in the lobby and we trooped onto the buses and were driven to the theater.

"Maya, there's something in the dressing room for you."

He did it. The poor bastard. Actually cut out his heart and had it sent to me. I kept my face serene, but my body trembled and the muscles in my stomach were in revolt.

I opened the room door, half braced to see a bloody organ still thumping like a prop in the *Bride of Frankenstein*. A harmless-looking flat package wrapped in gay paper lay on my dressing table. If it was a heart, it had been sliced sliver-thin. I closed the door for privacy and picked up the box. It might have been a See's box of Valentine candies. The note read: "Mistress Maya, here is my heart. I am loving you. I am wishing to see you. Goodbye, my lovely legs. Mr. Julian."

He had to be alive. Otherwise how could he hope to see me? I unwrapped the paper carefully because I might need it again. I pulled the last layer away.

Mr. Julian's heart was a cake. An inedible concoction of flour dough, water and probably concrete. It was a quarter of an inch thick and a little tanner than uncooked biscuit dough. A wisp of paper warned in Serbo-Croatian and French, "DO NOT EAT!" I inspected the thing and decided the warning was entirely unnecessary. Bits of plate glass and small squares of windows were punched down into the cake and there were shreds of paper doilies and tatters of lace which vied for space with dead leaves and dried flowers. The whole thing was sprinkled over with grains of rice, barley and wheat which were glued to the surface.

I swayed somewhere between relief and indignation. At least I didn't have the onus of trying to explain to the Yugoslavian government and the U.S. State Department how a Communist citizen's heart came to be found in my dressing room. On the other hand, what could I do with the putty heart? My luggage was already overweight. I had bought sweaters in Venice for myself and a few presents for my family in Paris. I wanted a few pieces of pottery in Greece and it had been hinted that we were going to Egypt. Certainly I'd find something there to take home. And here I was, saddled with something I did not want or could not give away. There wasn't a soul in the world I disliked enough to give the ugly thing. There was a small catch in the back of the heart which indicated it was meant to hang on the wall. I placed it under my dressing table behind the shoe rack. There would be time enough to deal with it when I had to pack to leave Yugoslavia.

Mr. Julian telephoned every morning at eight o'clock. When I spoke to him sharply, ordering him to cease and desist, he answered, "It's that I'm loving you. It's that I am dying because of you. It's that I'm falling in front of a train."

I asked the desk clerk to stop putting his calls through to our room. The clerk said, "In Yugoslavia, we answer the telephone." Martha refused to answer the ring any longer, for when she told him on the second morning that I was out, he responded with: "In Belgrade? There is no place for her to go. Maybe she is going to the bathroom. I will telephone later." Ten minutes later he said to her, "This is being Mr. Julian. I am wanting to speaking with Mistress Maya Angelou."

Ordinary courtesy bade me to exchange places with Martha so that I could at least answer the telephone.

"Mistress Maya, it's that I am dying."

"All right, Mr. Julian. I can't help that. Only please, don't send me any other parts of your anatomy."

Harsh words did not deter him, nor did kind words give him solace. I answered the telephone each morning and unemotionally, fuzzily and sleepily told him to get lost.

Other members in the cast reported similar conquests. Women fairly hung on the coattails of the bachelor singers, and one evening when Martha was taken to a ballet by an admirer, I left Ethel in the room manicuring her nails and went down to the bath.

When I returned, she was sitting yoga fashion on the bed and a strange man was spread-eagled, face down, on the floor at the foot of her bed.

I stood in the door in mild shock.

Ethel said, "Maya, I've been waiting for you. Help me to get this fool out of the room."

I threw down my towel and soap.

"Mister, mister. Get up." I turned to Ethel who had risen from her lotus position and was standing at the man's feet. "Is he drunk?"

"No, girl, he's crazy."

"O.K. Mister, we're going to put you out in the hall." His cheek was on the carpet and his eyes wide open. "It is not that I am being drunk. It is that I am loving Mistress Ethel. It is that her love is killing me. It is burning in my heart like a fire."

I said, "O.K. I understand."

Ethel said, "Here, Maya, you take the left foot. I'll take the right. We'll drag him."

The man made no resistance and allowed his body to be scudded across the room. I opened the door and we deposited him, still flat on his stomach, in the hall. Throughout the action, he had continued his litany.

"I am loving Mistress Ethel. I am dying out of love for Mistress Ethel."

We closed the door.

"Ethel, how in the hell did he get in here?"

"There was a knock at the door, and I thought it was you. So I said 'Come in,' and in comes this fool. He takes one look at me and falls flat on the floor. I thought maybe he had died or something so I went around and bent over him. To take his pulse. That's when I saw his eyes were open and he started chanting, 'Mistress Ethel, I am loving you. Dying! Killing myself.' And all that stuff."

"Why didn't you call the desk?"

"I figured you'd be back soon, and he seemed harmless."

We were laughing when we heard Martha's voice at the door and a series of quick raps.

"Hey, open the door. Open up, will you?"

Ethel went to the door and opened it. She called, "Maya, come quick." I raced to Ethel and looked over her shoulder. Martha was trying to disentangle herself from her escort, whose arms were octopus-ing all over her body.

"Get this fool off me, will you?" Ethel and I grabbed the man and untwined his arms.

"Hey, mister. What do you think you're doing?"

He struggled to regain his hold on Martha. "It's that I am loving Mistress Martha. Mistress Martha, I drink your eyes. I drink your nose."

We freed our friend, and as we gained the security of our room and slammed the door we heard the man's muffled voice. "Mistress Martha, I drink your ears, your nose, your fingers. Mistress Martha, it's that I'm loving you. I am dying."

One evening near the end of our Yugoslavian run, I felt I had danced particularly well, and although I might not have sung the music as written by George Gershwin, my fellow singers had greeted my harmonies with raised eyebrows and approved.

A young couple was directed to my dressing room. The man was a photographer and the woman a dancer. They spoke excellent French and complimented me on my dance. The husband asked to photograph me and invited me to their home the next evening for a pre-Christmas party. They said they would pick me up at the theater and would return me to my hotel after the party.

I considered the invitation. We had been told to stay within the allotted areas and I didn't relish the idea of calling down the wrath of two governments on my head. However, I was myself. That is, I was Marguerite Johnson, from Stamps, Arkansas, from the General Merchandise Store and the C.M.E. Church. I was the too tall, unpretty colored girl who had been born to unhappy parents and raised in the dirt roads of Arkansas and I was for the only time in my life in Yugoslavia. I divined that if I ever became rich and famous, Yugoslavia was not a country I would visit again. Was I then to never see anything more than the selected monuments and to speak to no one other than the tour-guide spies who stuck so close to us that we could hardly breathe? No. I accepted the couple's invitation.

Martha and Ethel warned me at the hotel that I had better not contravene the official orders. I tried to explain my reasons, but they either would not or could not understand. Like all company information, the news that I was going to a private party was common knowledge by noon the next day. Friends stopped by my lunch table cautioning me to change my mind. I thanked them for their advice.

Others came by my dressing room that evening to add their counsel to the general consensus. I was amazed when Helen

457

Ferguson said the couple had invited her too, and that she was going to come along. She was one of the youngest singers in the cast, pretty and so petite she looked like a child. I said, "You know, we're not supposed to go away from the group."

She said, "Listen, I'll never come to Yugoslavia again in my life. I want to talk to some of the people here so I can have some real memories."

We waited outside the stage door and were surprised when a strange young man approached us. "Miss Ferguson? Miss Angelou?"

"Yes."

"Please come with me. I am to take you to the Dovic party."

We followed him around the corner to a flatbed truck which held about thirty people crowded together, laughing and talking. With their help, Helen and I climbed up and joined them. The man slammed the flap, ran around and started the engine, and we were off on our adventure.

The men and women were about our ages and they all spoke some French. They passed bottles of slivovitz around and we drank the fiery liquid and tried to talk over the motor's loud roar. Finally, the crowd began to sing. I couldn't follow the words, but the melodies sounded like Hungarian tziganes. They were heavy and touching. I was so busy listening that I was slow to realize that we had left the lights of Belgrade behind and the old truck was struggling along on a bumpy dirt road. The night was clear and cold, and in the bright moonlight the flat countryside looked familiar, as if I had seen it all before. I had to remind myself that I was behind the iron curtain, not taking an innocent ride in central California. The people could be taking us to Siberia. Helen and I caught each other's looks and laughed, for there was nothing else we could do. The engine began to slow down as we went over an even rougher lane when we finally stopped in front of a large gabled Charles Addams-type house. The crowd of people gave a loud shout and began to jump over the sides of the truck. Helen and I and some of the other women waited until the flap was released.

The Dovic couple came out to welcome us and lead us into an already crowded living room. Helen and I were introduced (the rest seemed to already know each other), and while we were welcomed heartily, no one stared at us as though we were apparitions from a nightmare. I soon felt at ease and got into a discussion on the future of art and its relative value to the masses.

In an adjoining dining room we were given festive foods and drink. My hostess told me she had some records I might like to hear and she called for quiet in the room. People sat down on the floor in groups, sharing bottles of wine and slivovitz. The host put the record on a wind-up record player and Lester Young's saxophone yowled out of the silence. My ears and brain were at extreme odds. I was in Yugoslavia and the ordinary people of the country had no freedom to travel. According to my language teacher in Paris, the common citizen found it impossible to obtain an exit visa or a travel document; they were prisoners in their own land. And outsiders seldom visited the iron curtain countries; few wished to come and fewer were allowed. But I was listening to Lester Young. Helen and I exchanged surprised glances. When the record was over, the host replaced it with a Billie Holiday song and then exchanged that for a Sarah Vaughan, then Charlie Parker.

The host saw my startled expression, and said, "We love music. Everyone at this party is an artist. We are painters, sculptors, writers, singers, dancers, composers. Everything. And we find ways to stay aware of innovations in art everywhere in the world. Bebop was the most important movement in music since Johann Sebastian Bach. How did we get the records?" He smiled and said, "Don't ask." I didn't.

The party was slowing down and I had begun to think of the long, bumpy ride back to the hotel when an old woman emerged from a side door. She wore a chenille bathrobe and slippers to match. She shuffled through the thinning crowd, greeting each person informally and receiving embraces in return. She had to be the grandmother of the house. She had made her way to the center of the living room before she saw me. Her face was immediately struck with panic. She squawked and turned, nearly falling, and headed for the room she had just left.

The host, hostess and other guests came quickly and apologetically to me.

"Miss Angelou, please excuse her. She is eighty years old."

"She is very old and ignorant."

"She has never seen a Black person before."

"She does not mean to hurt your feelings."

I said, "I understand her. If I had lived that long and never seen a white person, the sight of one would give me a heart attack. I would be certain I was seeing a ghost."

"Please. You shouldn't be bitter."

It wasn't my intention to be sarcastic. I was sincere.

The hostess went to the door through which the old woman had disappeared and in a moment the two came out together. The hostess, draping her arm across the woman's frail shoulders, gently guided her toward me. When they were about four feet from where I was sitting, I said in Serbo-Croatian, "Good evening, madame."

459

She gave me a very faint "Good evening, madame" in return.

I asked, "Will you please sit with me?" The hostess removed her arm and the old woman inched slowly away from her fear and came to join me on the sofa.

I asked, "How are you?"

She whispered, "I am well," and kept her gaze unwavering on my face. She raised a wrinkled hand and touched my cheek. I didn't move or smile. Her hand brushed my hair slightly, then the other cheek. Without shifting her look from me she called her grand-daughter.

"Go and bring food and drink."

"But Grandmother, she has already eaten."

"Go."

Mrs. Dovic brought a small meat pie and a shot of slivovitz with the accompanying apricot preserve. I took a bite of the savory and one small spoonful of preserves. Without hesitation I gulped down the jigger of brandy and followed it with another spoonful of preserves.

The old woman smiled and patted my check. She began to talk to me so fast I couldn't keep up with her. I laughed and she laughed, showing a full set of the regulation metal teeth. Only after the party relaxed and general conversation resumed did I realize how tense the atmosphere had been. The grandmother patted my cheek again and touched my knee, then she rose laboriously and headed for her room. I called, "Good night, Grandmother," but she didn't respond. The host said, "She has already forgotten you. She is very old. Thank you for being so kind."

We were collecting our coats when the door opened again and the old woman again emerged, but this time followed by an older man. He, too, wore a chenille robe and matching slippers, and sleep had not yet released his face. When I noticed that he did not look around the room for someone or something strange but began greeting the guests closest to him, I knew the old woman was playing a joke on him. He hobbled from one person to another and the old woman stayed close to his side. Suddenly he saw me and almost leaped out of his ninety-year-old antiquity. He screamed and turned as quickly as he could to escape, but the old woman caught his sleeve, and with words I couldn't understand, began to berate him for his ignorance and chide him for being rude.

She guided him to the sofa and made him sit on one side of me while she sat on the other.

"Go bring food and drink."

Again I went through the ritual. When the old man saw I could both eat and drink and I could speak some Serbo-Croatian, he not only decided I was human, he declared me a Yugoslav. Just a very dark one.

460

"What is your name?"

"Maya."

"A good name."

"Who is your father?"

"Bailey Johnson."

"What a strange name for a Croatian. But I am sure I know him. Who is his father?"

"William Johnson."

"Vilyon? Vilyon? What does he do? I know everybody. I am ninety-three years old. Now tell me, was that Vilyon from Split or the one from Dubrovnik? Tell me."

No one could convince the man that I belonged to a different race and country.

As we headed for the door he said, "Tell Vilyon you have met me. Tell him to come after Christmas. We will talk of the old times."

The desk clerk at the hotel had to unlock the door to let us in. He said, "Miss Angelou. Miss Ferguson. Did you enjoy the party at the Dovic home? Did you enjoy the American records and the food? The old man and woman are very amusing, are they not?"

So much for our sense of freedom.

The next morning a clean-cut American asked to see me. I went to a room in the hotel and listened to a strange white man talk to me as if I were a child.

"You have been asked, Maya, not to wander around Belgrade. The Yugoslavs don't want it. They are a different people from us. They don't understand our ways. You are, after all, a guest in their country. Simple courtesy demands that you honor the wishes of your host."

I said, "I am not the one of the two of us who needs lessons in common courtesy. I did not say one thing last night that I didn't mean, nor that I would be reluctant to repeat. Good morning," and I left.

If *Porgy and Bess* didn't like it, they could find another singer who could dance, or a dancer who could sing. I had already seen Venice, Paris and two towns in Yugoslavia. I could go home to my wonderful son and my night club career.

I never heard any more about the incident, nor did I ask Helen if she had been questioned on our return.

"Good morning, Mistress Maya. As you know this is being me, Mr. Julian."

It was also the morning of our closing night in Belgrade.

"Yes, Mr. Julian."

Nothing had deterred him. Neither strong words nor outright insults kept him from telephoning. Martha and Ethel became so used to the ring that it no longer awakened them.

"It's I am loving you yet. It's that when you are leaving tomorrow I am dying."

"Yes, Mr. Julian." The night before, I had joined Joe Jones, Martha, Ethel, Ned and Attles in a slivovitz-and-song fest at a local bar. I felt as if the harsh brandy had baked my brain, and if Mr. Julian could wait until the next morning to die I would best him by twenty-four hours.

"I am not drowning. It is being very difficult for me. Because I am being Yugoslavia's Olympic swimming champion."

Swimming champion? Mr. Julian? Doggone it, I had slipped a bet. His voice had sounded ancient, as if it belonged to a body in the last stages of deterioration. I liked strong and muscular men. Had I known Mr. Julian was an athlete, I'd have seen him the first time he called.

"I am loving you and wanting to see you, oh..."

"Maybe I can see you tonight, Mr. Julian." I couldn't make up for the time wasted, but there was no reason I should lose another night.

"It is true? You will let me take you to one expensive café? And watching you drinking down coffee with cream in your lovely lips?"

"Yes, Mr. Julian." You bet. "After the theater you come to the stage door."

"Mistress Maya, there are always being so many people around your theater. Is it that you can be meeting me one block away?"

"Sure, yes. Of course." It seemed a little late for him to show a shy side.

"One block away near the park. I will be standing. I will be wearing a green suit. I will be smiling. Oh, Mistress Maya, my heart is singing for you. Good-bye, my lovely."

"Good-bye, Mr. Julian."

I hung up the telephone as Martha and Ethel turned over and sat up.

"So, at last. My Lord, we'll get to see this damned Mr. Julian." Martha was grinning and nodding her head.

Ethel said, "Maya, you *are* cold-blooded. You know the man loves you. And you wait until the last night to see him."

Martha added, "It *is* cold—he wants to marry you so you can take him to the States. Now there's no time to get a license. You're just going to use that poor man and toss him away, like a sailor does a woman in a foreign port." She was laughing. "Ohh, you're mean."

I told them both to go to hell and went back to sleep.

Ned met me at lunch. "So you're finally going to see Mr. Julian?"

Annabelle Ross, the coloratura, asked, "Tonight's the night, huh?"

Georgia Burke, the oldest member of the cast and veteran actress, said, "I understand Mr. Julian's finally got lucky. Well, there's nothing like sticking to it, they say."

Barbara Ann sat down at the table. "What made you wait so long, Maya? And what made you change your mind?"

I told her I had thought that he was an ancient lech and I couldn't abide the idea of going out with an elderly stage-door Johnny who would slobber on my cheek and pinch my thighs, but that he had finally told me he was a swimming champion and now I was sorry I waited so long.

She understood and sympathized with me.

An hour later Bey appeared at my door. "O.K., Maya. Got yourself a swimming champion, huh?"

On the way to the theater, a few wags in the back of the bus began to harmonize: "I'd swim the deepest ocean..."

Among the cast no news was private and no affairs sacred.

The audience began applauding in the middle of the finale. They were on their feet, throwing roses and shouting before the curtain fell. We bowed and waved and repeated the bows unremembered times.

Backstage, Marilyn, the wardrobe mistress, was supervising the labeling and packing of costumes. Departures were always her busiest time. She had to tag the clothes that had been torn so they could be sewn or replaced before our next opening night, and to keep separate the pieces due for cleaning and the shoes needing repairs.

As I passed the wardrobe room the door was open on a havoc of disarranged clothes, hats, shoes, baskets and umbrellas. She looked up from her counting. "Going to meet Mr. Julian, huh, Maya?"

My only chance of escaping the curious eyes of my fellow singers was to leave the theater by the front entrance. I gathered my costumes and dropped them in the wardrobe room, as we were required to do. Marilyn's attention was on her work. I slipped past the stage hands who were breaking down the set and stacking scenery. I tiptoed across the stage and jumped from the apron to the theater floor. The lobby was empty and dark as I eased out the door. I had avoided everyone. As I walked to the intersection I looked down the street. I saw a crowd of well-wishers at the stage door; they would keep the company occupied for a least a half-hour. Mr. Julian, I am coming and coming alone. You'll never know what a remarkable feat I have accomplished.

I approached the designated corner, searching for a tall well-built man in a dark-green suit, possibly a tweedy affair. He might be smoking a pipe—pipes and tweeds went so well together.

Mr. Julian wasn't on the corner. I wondered if he had decided, after all, to collect me at the stage door. I crossed the street and stood under the light, planning my next move.

"Mistress Maya?"

I turned, happy to be relieved of the problem. A small, very wiry old man was standing before me. His eyes were large and black and glistening. His bald head looked greased under the streetlight. He was smiling a row of decidedly polished metal teeth. And he wore a Kelly green suit.

"Mistress Maya, it's that I'm being Mr. Julian."

If he was a swimming champion the match took place in 1910.

"Yes, Mr. Julian. How are you?" I offered him my hand and he took it, stroked the back of it, turned it over and kissed the palm.

He mumbled, "I am loving you."

I said, "Yes." And, "How about that coffee?"

If Martha or Ethel or Lillian caught a glimpse of my athletic lover, I'd never be allowed to live it down.

"I can't go far, I must be in the hotel before curfew, you know."

He didn't understand the word "curfew" and I didn't have the time to stand on the corner explaining it.

"Let's go to the café up the street. Is that all right?"

We sat at a small table silently. Each conversational opening I tried was blocked by his statements of undying love. His bright eyes watched me drink coffee. He observed my lips so intently, I had the sensation that his gaze was following each sip slide over my tongue, through the esophagus and into my stomach.

I gulped the last swallow and stood up. "Thank you, Mr. Julian. I must get back to the theater or the bus will leave me."

"I will take you to your hotel." His eyes were begging.

"No, thanks. The buses have to take us. Sorry."

"It's that I will walk you back to the theater. I am loving you."

"Absolutely not! No, thank you. I appreciate the coffee and the thought, but I'd like to remember you right here, having coffee with cream." I didn't offer him my hand again. "Thank you. Please stay. Good-bye, Mr. Julian."

I walked slowly out of the café, but when I closed the door I broke into a run that would have impressed Jesse Owens. The bus was loading as I reached the theater.

As I climbed aboard, Martha said, "Whatever else Mr. Julian is, I can tell he's fast."

Lillian said, "I've got something for you, Maya. You left it in your dressing room and I felt I'd better bring it to you. Your life would not be the same without it."

She handed me a package. It was Mr. Julian's heart.

23

The singers were hardened to the discomfort of travel and the sense of dislocation. Yet the Yugoslavia trip put an unusual amount of pressure on us all. The cold weather, gray and dreary, and the incommodious hotel with its grim corridors and heavy odors pressed weightily on our spirits. The unhappy people in their ugly, thick clothes and the restrictions on our freedom of movement all combined to make us impatient to put the dour place behind us and to bask in the sunshine of North Africa.

Ethel, Martha, Barbara Ann, Lillian and I crowded our personal belongings into the two overhead racks of our compartment. It was seven o'clock on a dark morning. The cast had begun to assemble at the train station at six and we had boarded the fabled Orient Express as soon as Ella Gerber and Bob Dustin completed their head count and were satisfied that no member of the company was still sleeping at the Moskva. Belgradians crowded around the train steps. Some Yugoslavian women sniffled and dried their eyes as male singers embraced them, checked their watches and boarded the train. A few female singers waved good-bye to some native men, who wept openly.

My friends and I nestled down, anxious for the train to move. We were chatting when a noise alerted us. We looked up to see Mr. Julian standing in the doorway of the compartment, holding a small package.

"Mistress Maya?" Tears trickled down his face. "Mistress Maya, I am wishing you joy, happiness and wictory." With that emotional outcry he threw the package in my lap, slammed the door and leaped off the train.

Lillian asked, "*That* was Mr. Julian?"

Ethel said unbelievingly, "No, surely not?"

Barbara Ann asked, "But when was he a swimming champion?"

Martha shifted her small head and said, "He looks like he'd have a hard time floating across a bathtub."

Before I could retort, his face was at the window. He waved his hands in a beckoning motion and the train began to move slowly. Mr. Julian kept up with our window for a while, but as the train gained momentum his face and all the other faces of those left behind began to slide from our view. In a few minutes we were in open country, looking out on lonely farmhouses and sullen fields.

Ned Wright pulled the door open and offered a bottle of slivovitz.

"Here we are, me darlings. Long gone and away. Tito can keep his Yugoslavia. I am meant to sit under sunny skies and sing. What the hell are you crying for, Maya?"

Ethel said it couldn't be for Mr. Julian. "Did you see him?"

Martha laughed, "He looked like a mile of country road in the winter in North Carolina."

I said, "But he persevered. And he was nice. I mean, he never failed to call and he had to get up very early to be at the station before we left. I admire that in anyone."

Ethel asked, "Would you like to go back to Belgrade?"

I didn't have to choose an answer. I said, "No. Pass me the slivovitz!"

The train sped all day through the glowering provinces and we took our meals in an old dining car which smelled like our last hotel. Some of the cast took naps or wrote letters home. We played games of rise and fly bid whist in our compartment with all the passion of addicted gamblers. When the gray afternoon finally surrendered to night, a porter made our beds and we slept.

I awakened to find Martha and Ethel chittering like crickets. The sunlight came boldly through the windows and their faces were lit with a gaiety I hadn't seen for weeks.

"Maya, girl, you're going to sleep all day? Look out the window." Martha edged over and made room for me. The countryside had changed. In one night we had passed from bleak winter to spring. Cows grazed on abundant green foliage and the farmhouses were painted in so many vivid colors the scene resembled a large Matisse painting.

Grownups, smiling broadly, waved at the train, and children bounced, laughing their excitement. The picture touched me so violently that I was startled, and in an instant I realized that I had not seen giddy children since Venice. The Parisian youngsters were so neat in dress and manner they might have been family ornaments created and maintained to adorn. The children I saw in Yugoslavia appeared sensible and level-headed without the buoyancy of childhood. Here were children I could understand. Although their voices didn't carry over the distance and through our windowpane, I was certain they were shouting, yelling and screaming, and I was just as certain that the mothers were saying "Be quiet," "Stop that" and "Hush."

I got up and excused myself. The longing for my own son

threatened to engulf me. As I walked down the corridor, controlling the emotional deluge that swelled in my mind, I passed compartments where other members of the company sat close to their windows, absorbed.

We caught brief glimpses of the white buildings and green hills of Athens, then boarded buses which were to take us to the port city of Piraeus. The road was high and winding, and our moods were high. We sang in full voice every song that was suggested and laughed when someone made the wrong harmonic change or forgot the lyrics.

At the waterfront, Dustin doled out cabin assignments and announced that Lee Gershwin was throwing a champagne party on the ship for the entire cast before lunch.

If only Yanko and Victor and Mitch could see me now. I had dredged up some Greek learned during my marriage and greeted the crew members. They were already excited by the cluster of Black people, and when they heard me speaking their language they nearly saluted. Three men left their posts to help me find my quarters, where my suitcases, books and mandolin were already stacked on a table in the single room.

Martha, Lillian, Ethel and Barbara Ann came down the passageway talking about the ship, the champagne party and the handsome Greek sailors.

I stopped them, and said, "Hey, you guys, aren't you surprised that Lee Gershwin is inviting the humble nobodies to her affair?"

Martha said, "Darling, Miss Fine Thing has never been humble, and for your information, she has always been Somebody. She shall grace the motley crew with her presence." She grinned and flung her head back.

Lillian said, "Dearie, there's going to be champagne?" She nodded, answering her own question. "I'm going to drink Madame Gershwin's champagne."

Barbara Ann said smoothly, "Maya, you've never forgiven her for telling you and Joy what to wear in Venice, have you?" She shook her head and managed a sad smile. "And I thought you were supposed to be a Christian. Shame, Maya, shame."

They continued looking for their rooms and left me thinking about Lee Gershwin. She had approached me and Joy in Venice's Saint Mark's Square on our second day in Italy.

"Don't you girls know you shouldn't wear slacks in Italy? The Italians don't like it." Her narrow face was sour with propriety. "Be nice. Remember, we are all ambassadors."

Joy had told her: "One, it's cold. Two, I'm singing every night on a cold stage and changing in a cold dressing room, and three, I'm

467

working six hours a day with the cast on their roles. Four, I shall continue to wear slacks and, if I need it, a parka!"

I simply looked at Lee. If I had given tongue to my voice, I'd have said too much. I simply continued to wear slacks when I thought it necessary, counting on my own sense of propriety to dictate what I should wear where and when. The incident had slipped from my consciousness, but once reminded of it I had to admit that Lee's maternalistic attitude had so infuriated me that, although she traveled with us, I had erased her from my thoughts.

I unpacked the clothes I would need for the three-night, two-day trip to Alexandria and changed into a dress for lunch.

When I walked up the stairs, stewards grinned and spoke to me in Greek, and as I entered the dining room a large, bushy-haired man in a black suit caught my arm.

"Mrs. Angelos?"

"Yes?"

"I am the purser."

I couldn't dredge up one idea of what to expect.

"You speak Greek?" he asked.

"Yes. A little."

"How did you learn?"

"My husband was Greek."

"Ah." And he grinned a broad approval. "Mrs. Angelos, may I make a suggestion?" He turned his large body sideways and spoke out of the side of his mouth as if he were giving me the secret of building an atomic bomb.

"Yes."

"There is a party. A champagne party." He inclined his head toward the tables where members of the cast were already lifting glasses. "We expect a very rough trip to Alexandria. It would be better if you didn't drink today. Or tonight. Not champagne. Not wine. Not water. Eat lightly. Bread. Biscuits. And no drinking."

I thanked him and asked if he had warned anyone else. He smiled, pulling his lips leftward to reveal a solid gold tooth.

He said, "They are opera singers. I wouldn't try to tell them. But you"—again he grinned—"you are nearly Greek"—he took my hand and kissed it—"and you have my sympathy. Good-bye. Remember."

Sympathy? He thought having married a Greek made me deserving of his compassion? Strange.

My friends had saved a chair for me at their table.

"Miss Thing, hold your glass." Martha held the champagne ready to pour.

"No, I'm not drinking." I told them of the warning. Lillian said, "I've never been seasick in my life."

Martha and Ethel seconded her. They shared the wine and giggled, paying no attention to my admonition. Every table was filled with happy flutters. Even the few nondrinkers were in a party mood. I only half believed the purser, but was glad for an excuse not to participate. I liked to pay for my own drink or at least choose the sponsor who treated me.

"Mother Afrique, your long-lost daughter is returning home..." Lillian was composing another toast and no one was waiting for her to complete it.

"Cheers."

"*Salute.*"

"*À Votre santé.*"

"*Doz vedanya.*"

"*Skoal.*"

An officer at the captain's table stood up, kissed the women's hands, bowed to the men and began to pick his way out of the dining room. He was tall and moved gracefully, hardly shaking the braid that looped across his wide shoulders. He turned his head and looked at our table. He had the most sensuous face I had ever seen. His lips were dark rose and pouted, and his nostrils flared as if he were breathing heavily through them. But his eyes were the most arresting feature. They were the "bedroom eyes" sung about in old blues— heavy-lidded, as if he were en route at that moment to the boudoir of the sexiest woman in the world.

"Mart, Ethel, look at that," I said.

My friends, who usually had a high appreciation of male beauty, were so occupied with their party that they gave the officer only a cursory look.

Ethel said, "Yeah, he's cute."

Martha said, "I'll check him out later. Pour a little more of the bubbly into my slipper, please, for I am Queen of the May."

I watched the man leave the dining salon and knew that when the sexy women in our company got around to noticing him, they would take some of the arrogance out of his swinging shoulders and lessen the bounce in his narrow hips.

After lunch I returned to my cabin, leaving the party in full hilarity. By midafternoon when we were well away from the coast of Greece, the ship began to shudder under the attack of a storm. My luggage shot back and forth across the tiny space between my bunk and the wall, and had I not stood up I would have been thrown out of bed. I shoved my bags tightly into the closet and jammed a chair under the closet's doorknob. I took a book and headed for the main deck.

In the passageway I met my suddenly sober and suddenly sick fellow singers. Those who were able to talk said the party had broken

469

up as drinkers and players became too ill to continue; the waiters had removed all bottles and glasses and were tying the tables down.

The dining room was empty and dark, and I struggled, rolling from wall to wall, up the passageway to a small red sign which invited: BAR. The door opened on a small, empty but lighted room. I sat at a table, trying to glue my mind to the plot and away from the roiling sea. After an hour or so, a young crew member came in, saw me and was surprised. He asked if I was all right: I lied and told him in Greek that I was. He looked at me, astonished for a second, then left hurriedly. A few moments later the purser arrived.

"Mrs. Angelos, are you well?"

"Yes, of course." My composure was paper-thin, but it covered the fear.

"You didn't drink. I noticed." He was proud of himself and of me.

"No. I ate bread and a piece of cold chicken."

"Very good. It is going to be worse tonight, but tomorrow will be calmer. You are not to worry. We have a doctor, but he is very busy. Both the opera company and the movie company are sick and he is kept running between the two."

I didn't know about the movie company. "Who are they? From America?"

"No. They are English. Except the star is French. Brigitte Bardot. They are all in their cabins and I don't expect to see either the singers or actors until we reach Alexandria."

He took my hand. "Mrs. Angelos, if you want me, please ring this bell"—he pointed to a button on the wall—"and tell anyone to come for me. I will be with you immediately." He kissed my hand and departed.

A waiter entered and said tea was being served in the dining room. I thanked him and said I wouldn't have anything.

The ship pitched and rolled and quivered and sometimes leaped, seeming to withdraw entirely from the surface of the water. I was frightened at the violence and my inability to control any part of the experience except myself and there was no certainty that my mental discipline would outlast the physical anxiety. But at least I wasn't ill.

The purser pushed his head in the door. "Dinner is being served. I suggest that you eat. Again the plain bread. And again a small piece of meat. No wine. No water." His head disappeared as the vessel rolled over on its side.

Although I had no appetite I decided to continue following his suggestions. The dining room was not quite empty. The captain and his officers sat quietly in their corner; a few teetotalers from *Porgy and Bess* were at separate tables; and two men whose faces I recognized from British movies occupied a table near the wall. I joined Ruby Green and Barbara Ann and ate sparingly.

470

Barbara asked, "Where have you been? You haven't been sick?"

I told her I'd been reading and I wasn't sick because I didn't drink the champagne.

"You ought to see downstairs. Everybody's sick. I mean, people are moaning like they're dying. The poor doctor no sooner leaves one room than they call him to another. That man's got his work cut out for him. See, here he comes now. Poor thing. Just now getting a chance to eat his dinner."

I looked up, following her gaze, and saw the voluptuous face that had startled me at lunchtime.

"That's the doctor?" I would have more easily believed him to be a gigolo, a professional Casanova.

"Yes. And he's very courteous. He gives the same attention to the men that he gives to the women."

I looked at his retreating back and wondered if Barbara in her naïveté had described the man better than she could have imagined.

After a somber dinner we went below, where the groans of suffering escaped mournfully from each room. I paused before my friends' doors, but I knew I could do nothing for them except sympathize and I could do that without disturbing their agony.

There was a soft rap on my door. When I opened it and saw the purser, I thought he expected me to compensate him for my sound health. I held the door and asked icily, "Yes, what do you want?"

He said meekly, "Mrs. Angelos, I want to show you how to strap yourself in the bed so that you won't fall out and be hurt."

I started to let him in and thought better of it. "No, thanks. I was planning to sleep on the floor. I'll be all right. Thanks, anyway."

He shot his hand in the narrow door opening and grabbed my arm.

"Mrs. Angelos, thank you. You are very sad and very beautiful." He bowed and kissed my hand and released it. I slammed the door. How could he tell I was sad? That was a strange romantic come-on.

I made my actions fit the lie. I stripped mattress and covers ftom the bed and lay down on the floor to sleep in miserable fits and starts.

The morning was dreary and wet, but the sea was more restrained. The purser was waiting for me outside the dining room door.

"Mrs. Angelos, good morning. You may eat a full breakfast. We will have good weather by evening." He looked at me lovingly, concern seeping out of his pores. "How did you sleep?"

"Beautifully, thank you. Just beautifully."

Some members of our company who had survived the storm exchanged stories of the night before.

"Honey, I was so sick I tried to jump overboard!"

"Did you hear Betty? She prayed half the night, then she got mad

471

and screamed, 'Jesus Christ, this ain't no way for you to act so close to your birthday!' "

My visits to Martha's and Lillian's cabins were not welcome, so I made them brief, staying only long enough to see that although their faces were the color of old leather boots, they would survive. I walked around the ship, enjoying the luxury of solitude. For the first time, there was a tender behind the bar and I ordered an apéritif. The very large British movie actor and his companion came in, ordered and sat near me.

"So you're a sailor too, are you?" The man's gruff voice was directed to me.

"I suppose so."

"But the rest of your company have no sea legs?" He laughed and his eyes nearly closed beneath dark, thick eyebrows.

"Some have been a little sick," I said. The man always played friendly characters, so without knowing his real personality, I felt friendly toward him. "But they're better now."

"My name is James Robertson Justice."

Of course I knew the name and had thought it fitted his giant size and huge laughter. He pointed to his smaller, quieter friend. "And this is Geoffrey Keen."

We talked about opera and movie making and I felt decidedly international. I was on a Greek ship, talking to English movie stars, en route to the African continent.

I ate lunch and dinner alone, but joined Ned Wright and Bey in the bar after dinner. James Robertson Justice was there again and the three men exchanged stories. They all laughed together, but it was not clear if they understood each other. Ned tended to talk and snap his fingers in the air like a flamenco dancer, meanwhile wiggling his head. Bey grumbled in a bass-baritone without moving his lips. Justice spoke in all the British accents, gamboling from upper class, middle class to Welsh and Irish like a skittish lamb on the heath.

I left the men laughing and talking loudly and walked down the passageway. The doctor passed me, lips distended and full, his eyes low and dense.

"Good evening," he said.

I said "Good evening," and wished vainly that he would stop. The purser knocked at my door. I opened it a crack.

"Mrs. Angelos, we will dock at eleven. Everyone will be asked to come to passport control. There will be a crowd. I suggest that you meet me after breakfast, at nine o'clock, and I will see that your passport is stamped first."

"Thank you." I held on to the door. "Thank you very much. Good night." I closed the door firmly.

At nine o'clock the next morning he met me outside the dining room. He took my elbow and guided me to the upper deck. An official handed me my stamped passport and medical documents. The purser led me away.

"Now, Mrs. Angelos, I suggest you get your belongings, not your luggage, but handbags and other things you want to carry. Bring them on deck and then you will not have to stand in line with the others." He kissed my hand and gave me a lingering look.

When the two companies lined up on the main deck and on the stairs leading to the officials' temporary office, I stood beside the rail watching the coast of Africa. The ship was being pulled into the harbor by a small, powerful tugboat.

The sea was a beautiful blue, and the tall white buildings on the shore belied the old statement that all Africans lived in trees like monkeys. Alexandria was beautiful.

I had all my hand luggage and was eager to step out on Egyptian soil. A camera swung from my right side, a shoulder bag from the left. I carried my mandolin and Mr. Julian's heart (I was too ashamed of my treatment of him to throw the thing away), and at my feet was a make-up case and a small box of books.

As the ship neared land, streets and the details of buildings became more visible in the bright sunlight, and I fantasized the Africans who designed the houses and laid out the streets. Tall and dark-brown-skinned. Proud and handsome like my father. Bitter-chocolate black like my brother, lightly made and graceful. Or chunky and muscular, resembling my Uncle Tommy. Thick and sturdy, walking with a roll to their hips like boxers or gandy dancers. The fantasy was mesmerizing, and before I knew it men were lashing the ship to the dock.

Except for their long gowns and little skullcaps, the men did look like my father and brother and uncle, and there appeared to be thousands of them, screaming and shouting and running up and down the pier. From my high perch I tried to distinguish the differences between these Africans who had not been bought, sold or stolen and my people who were still enduring a painful diaspora. But I was either too far away or they moved too fast for my purpose. Still, I was determined and kept my gaze fastened on the area below.

"Mrs. Angelos."

I turned and was face-to-face with the doctor.

"Mrs. Angelos, what are your first impressions of your native continent?"

I retrieved my thoughts and longings and made a snappy remark. "It is colorful. And noisy. And the sun shines on Africa."

He fished two cigarettes from a package and lighted them

simultaneously (he had seen *Now Voyager* too, and I wondered how often he had imitated Paul Henreid). He put one between my lips.

"Where are you staying in Alexandria?"

I told him the company was booked at the Savoy.

"Will you honor me with dinner? They have a decent dining room and you won't have to leave your hotel."

I quickly weighed his lips, shoulders, hips and eyes against the chances of finding an interested Egyptian man on the first day. The sea had been smooth for nearly twenty-four hours, which meant that the huntresses were feeling well and would be back in the chase and any available men would be at a premium. "I'd be delighted," I said.

His eyes smoldered wonderful promises; then he tried a smile that was incongruous on the lascivious face. "My name is Geracimos Vlachos. I am called Maki. Expect me at eight o'clock. Until then." He bowed and kissed my hand.

Martha said, "You got him, you fast thing, you. Took advantage of all your sick sisters and snatched that man while everybody was flat on their backs. Dying in the hold."

We were lined up at the rails, ready to disembark.

Lillian nudged us. "Look at the people, will you? Africans. My God. Now I have lived. Real Africans."

Ethel and Barbara were a little more reserved, but just as excited. Our voices nearly equaled in volume the shouts and yells of the dock workers.

I saw that the older singers were as fascinated as we. Katherine Ayres, Georgia Burke, Eloise Uggams, Annabelle Ross and Rhoda Boggs stood facing Bob Dustin, but their eyes continued to steal away to the dock and to the people who were unloading the vessel. When they walked between the gowned stevedores on the way to the buses, their usually reserved smiles broadened into happy grins, and they doled out money, whose value they had not really considered, to the beggars who stretched out their hands.

In the hotel we deposited our hand luggage then raced back to the lobby to look at the Africans. It took less than five minutes to discover that the bellhops, porters, doormen and busboys were black and brown and beige, and that the desk clerk, head waiters, bartenders and hotel manager were white. As far as we knew, they might have all been African, but the distribution of jobs by skin color was not lost on us. The sweetness of our arrival in Africa was diluted, but not totally spoiled.

After all, Gamal Abdel Nasser was the President and every photograph showed him to be brown-skinned. Darker than Lena Horne, Billy Daniels and Dorothy Dandridge. Without a doubt, he was one of us.

We sat in the lounge and ordered drinks. Ned had thrown his cape rakishly across his shoulders and Joe Attles had donned a new and colorful ascot to protect his throat.

Ned asked, "Does anyone want to go with us? We're going to look at The Dark Continent and bring back a sphinx."

We all laughed and clapped our hands. Servants ran out into the lounge and bowed, waiting. We looked at them and each other. If we wore the same clothing no one would be able to say we were not members of the same family, yet we couldn't hold a conversation. (Europeans and white Americans are not surprised to see their look-alikes speaking foreign languages; but except for meeting a few African students in Europe, we had never seen a large group of Black people whose culture, language and life styles were different from our own.)

Martha asked in French if they wanted something. One man answered in French that when he heard us clap our hands, he thought we wanted something. We learned that day, although we slipped up now and then, not to clap our hands at a joke, and that if we wanted to talk across the centuries that separated us from our brothers in Egypt, we had to use French, a language that was beautiful but more attuned to the thin lips of Europeans—it lacked the rhythms of Ned Wright popping his fingers and Martha Flowers swinging her hips. The knowledge made me sullen and I excused myself and went to my room.

The cast assembled for the evening meal. The large dining room was decorated with palm trees and paper ribbons swinging from slow-moving ceiling fans. Alexandria's playboys were present in evening finery, sending champagne to the women and occasionally to a man who caught their fancy. They introduced themselves from table to table, kissed hands, bowed and offered their calling cards. A few women in low-cut satin dresses ogled the male singers; when they netted a man's attention, their red lips split in a smile to welcome a pharaoh. It was sexually stimulating to be the object of such desire, even if the desire was general and the object collective.

I was so busy flirting and watching my friends that I had forgotten about my date with the doctor. He appeared out of nowhere and stood before me.

"Mrs. Angelos, my I present my cousin and cousin-in-law? They live in Alexandria."

I shook hands with a tall, attractive woman and her short, pudgy husband. Maki asked me to join their table. When I excused myself from my friends, they raised their eyes.

We made small talk in a mixture of French and Greek. The tables were cleared, and a small band arranged itself at the back of the room. The men played Greek and Arabic music on instruments I had never seen before. When the belly dancer appeared, tasseled and sequined, our company exploded in approval.

"Yeah, baby. Shake that thing!" And she did. Her hips quivered and trembled and her breasts threatened to jiggle out of the skimpy satin-cup restraints. She bumped so hard she had to be cautioned, "Throw it, but don't throw it away, baby." Her skin was pale brown and her hair straight, and we were all flabbergasted; no white woman we'd ever seen could move that way.

"Shake it, but don't break it."

"It must be jelly 'cause jam don't shake that way."

Later the orchestra played popular songs for dancing and Maki invited me to dance. He held me close and whispered heavily accented words. I gave the appearance of listening, but in fact I was looking around the dance floor for my friends. As busy as they were with their own flirtations they still kept me within sight. I had posed too long as Goody Two-shoes and they weren't going to let me slip without a detailed inspection of my fall. Unity and friendship when needed is reassuring, but sometimes can become an obtrusive and nosy intrusion."

I asked Maki if he knew somewhere else where we might dance. He said he would drop his relatives at their home and we could go to his hotel. "There is an accordion player who specializes in romantic Greek songs. I would like you to hear him."

At once the object of my life was to be in Maki's arms and beyond the scrutiny of my colleagues. I told him I would meet him in front of the hotel. I shook hands with him and his relatives and they rose to go.

Someone at the table said, "Going to let him slide, huh, Maya?"

I said I was going to bed—all the noise had given me a headache. They watched me leave, bemused.

Maki had a taxi waiting, and after we dropped his relatives at their house, near my hotel, we rode in silence for what seemed to be hours. Finally he ushered me into a mean little pension, which would have fitted well on San Francisco's skid row. An unshaven desk clerk handed a key to Maki, who said, "I had forgotten. The accordion player is off tonight. But let us go to my room, I will sing for you."

I considered my options. I didn't know where I was. I didn't speak the language. I was attracted to him. I wasn't married or being unfaithful, for I had no lover. He wouldn't hurt me—after all, he was a doctor, Hippocratic oath and all.

I followed him to the room and his songs were glorious. Early the next morning he said we were only a few blocks from my hotel and he would take a cab and drop me, then return to his ship. I wanted to walk and look at the city. The frivolous night was over; I had enjoyed it. But I needed to think great thoughts about myself and Africa and slavery and Islam; I didn't want a white man at my side—in fact, I didn't want anyone distracting me.

Maki was reluctant to let me go alone. I said, "It's daybreak. And, after all, I am home."

"You do not know this country, Maya."

"I come from this country. I am only returning home."

He said we would meet in two weeks, since his ship was to pick us up again in Alexandria after we finished our run at the Cairo Opera House. He said he loved me and I should think about that; he was married, but would get a divorce and come back to the United States with me; doctors made very good money in the United States and it was difficult to get a visa, but if he was married to an American citizen...

I walked out into a beautiful morning and struggled with a bitter thought. The very country that denied Negroes equality at home provided them with documents that made them attractive abroad. Mr. Julian and Maki, in my case, and hundreds of European men and women who tagged this coattail of Black servicemen and singers and musicians might have found them much less appealing if they claimed West Indian or African citizenship, but since they hailed from "God's country," the "home of democracy" and the richest nation on earth, men were ready to leave their wives and women their husbands for entry into the land of plenty. Avarice cripples virtue and lies in ambush for honesty.

My footsteps disturbed a group of people wrapped in filthy rags and huddled in a doorway. Two small brown children awakened first; they punched and probed in the bundle of clothing until a man's head emerged. When he saw me he began bellowing and a woman sat upright. I was rooted to the pavement, watching the unfolding scene. The two children, joined by two smaller tykes, made their way to me; the mother and father followed, dragging the tatters of cloth that had once covered them. They encircled me, their hands outstretched. The man and woman clutched their fingers together and brought them to their mouths in a jabbing motion, then they stabbed the bunched hands at their stomachs. They were hungry, but I wasn't sure if it was safe to open my purse. Suppose they grabbed it from me, what could I do?

My inaction called for drama from the adults. The mother grabbed the smallest boy and wedged him between her knees facing me. The father took the child's chin roughly and forced it away from the chest. I looked at the baby's face in the soft morning sunlight. It was a biscuit topped with dusty black hair and, like a clean dinner plate, devoid of meaning except for a thick white substance which seeped fron the closed eyes and slowly descended the cheeks. The parents heid the boy's head for my view as if I had caused the condition, as if I had poked out the eyes with a nail and now I must pay for my deed.

I fished out my advance from my purse and peeled off a bill. When I offered it to the child the man snatched it, and the woman flung her blind offspring behind her dirty skirts and grabbed another boy. They showed me his severed arm. The stump looked as blind and final as the diseased eyes. I gave them another bill. When they began to line up the whole family, I said in French, "I have no more money," and turned to walk toward my hotel.

They followed, running beside and behind me. I opened up my stride, and the man ran in front, talking loudly, gesturing and screaming, as if I had just evicted them from their home.

Their noise awakened other beggars who had found sleeping accommodations in doorways, on porches and next to roofless buildings. Their supplications, loud and cacophonous, merged; the adults wept and pushed crippled children in my path, ripping the filthy clothes to show the extent of the horror.

Egypt had stumbled under the imperialist and colonial yokes for two thousand years, and finally in 1953 achieved true independence as a republic. But success in gaining self-rule had not yet affected the lives of the poor. Much remained to be done.

I knew that and journalists in the local newspapers knew it, too. I had read magazine articles analyzing the depth of the problems of the country and I was distressed. But sympathy did not lessen my sense of guilt. I was healthy and, compared to the horde of beggars, rich. I was young, talented, well-dressed, and whether I would take pride in the fact publicly or not, I was an American.

The crowd followed me to the hotel where a large uniformed doorman spied me. He rushed to meet me halfway down the block. Then he began screaming and hitting out at the beggars. Occasionally his heavy fists connected and there was a thud of flesh on bone or bone on bone. I called to the man to stop, but he kept flailing his fists and arms until the beggars took to their heels, their shreds of clothing floating behind them like dirty smoke.

"Never mind, mademoiselle. Never mind." His composure was so complete it seemed as if it had never been ruffled. My father had been a doorman in Long Beach, California, during the great depression. I wondered if he had ever had to chase beggars and hobos from the door. Were they Black? Did he feel no more for them than the Savoy doorman felt for his fellow Egyptians?

Martha was sitting in the lobby when I entered. She still wore the dress from the night before. It was impossible to tell whether she had just come in seconds before me or had sat in the same chair all night.

"Good morning, Miss Thing. First night in Africa take the headache away?"

I told her to take a flying leap and went to bed.

24

We stayed in Alexandria two days before moving on to Cairo, but I would not leave the hotel again and refused to explain my seclusion. My close friends thought I had fallen in love with the doctor and I accepted their teasing without comment.

We were driven to Cairo, and thrown into another world. More black-skinned people held positions of authority. The desk clerk at the Continental Hotel was the color of cinnamon; the manager was beige but had tight crinkly hair. The woman who supervised the running of the house was small and energetic and her complexion would never have allowed her to pass for white.

Beggars still hounded our footsteps and the audiences which shouted Bravos at our performances were largely European, but I felt I was at last in Africa—in a continent at the moment reeling yet rising, released from the weight of colonialism, which had ridden its back for generations.

We toured the city and went en masse to the pyramids. We rode camels and had our photographs taken in front of the Sphinx, but I couldn't satisfy my longing to breathe in the entire country.

I went again to the pyramids, alone. I used the few Arabic words I had picked up to tell the camel drivers and guides that I wanted to be alone. I took off my shoes and dug my feet into the hot sand.

> Go down Moses, way down in Egypt land,
> Tell old Pharaoh, to let my people go.

A Pharaonic tomb rose above my head and I shivered. Israelites and Nubians and slaves from Carthage and Mesopotamia had built it, sweating, bleeding, and finally dying for the mass of stones which would become in the twentieth century no more than the focus for tourists' cameras.

My grandmother had been a member of a secret Black American

female society, and my mother and father were both active participants in the Masons and Eastern Star organizations. Their symbols, which I found hidden in linen closets and night stands, were drawings of the Pyramid at Giza, or Cheops' tomb.

I tried to think of a prayer or at least some dramatic words to say to the spirits of long-dead ancestors. But nothing apt came to mind. When the sun became unbearable, I took a taxi back to town.

North Africa made me more reflective. Other members of the cast reacted similarly to the Egyptian experience.

Ethel and Martha were invited to a private party and they asked Lillian and me to come along. A well-to-do Arab came to the hotel and when he saw that his original invitation had expanded to include four women, he ordered a second horse-drawn carriage. We were driven to a large, lighted villa in Heliopolis, and when we started to climb out of the buggies, he stopped us and shouted at two men who stood by the wide wrought-iron gates. They emerged from the shadows bowing, touching their foreheads and chests like extras in a bad Hollywood film. They were as black as the night which closed in on us.

The host said, "You are not to walk. These servants will carry you." He stepped aside as one of the men walked up to the buggy, his arms outstretched.

Lillian said, "Maya, you let him carry you. I'll walk."

I said, "No. Uh uh. I'll walk with you."

Martha shouted from the other carriage, "Have you ever heard of anything so foul? My dear, Miss Fine's never had to be carried to a party. Come on, Ethel, we'll walk."

We stepped out into mud that oozed up over the tops of our shoes and walked on as if we were doing the most ordinary thing in the world.

We rejected the offer to have house Blacks clean our feet, but accepted towels and wiped away the mud ourselves, chatting vapidly about the pretty villa and the lovely furnishings.

The hosts and other guests were shocked at our refusal to be tended to, not realizing that auction blocks and whipping posts were too recent in our history for us to be comfortable around slavish servants. The party flopped despite flowing champagne and brittle laughter, probably because we couldn't keep our eyes away from the Black men who stood like barefoot sentinels at every door, dressed in old galibiyas, waiting with obsequious smiles on their handsome faces.

When we walked to the door to leave, we found that planks of wood had been laid over the wet walkway that led to the drive. There was only one carriage; we were told that our escort was obliged to stay with the other guests, but that the driver would see us safely back in our hotel.

We were obviously too democratic for the company's comfort and they too feudal for ours.

A sign in the hotel elevator read:

Défrisage
MONSIEUR PIERRE
Reservations Made at Hotel Desk

Martha, Ethel, Gloria and I decided to have our hair straightened by chemicals and be rid for a while, at least, of the heavy iron combs heated over cans of sterno that made our hotel rooms smell.

We sat side by side in a luxurious beauty salon and accepted hot cups of sweet black coffee from a young barefoot boy. Monsieur was visibly French: he pooched out his mouth, rolled his eyes and danced pantomimes with his long, thin fingers. Martha and Ethel were lathered down first; then I was taken into a booth. When the assistant put a green foam on my hair, it trickled down to my scalp and began to sting. I tried to sit still and say nothing—after all, my friends were receiving the same treatment without comment—but when my entire head started burning intensely I screamed, "Take it out! Take this out of my hair!"

"Qu'est-ce que vous dites?" Monsieur rounded the corner, pushing the assistant out of the way.

I shouted, "I said take this crap out of my hair."

Ethel said from the next stall, "Oooh, Maya, don't be such a crybaby."

I turned on the water and pushed my head under the faucet. "It's burning me."

The hairdresser, prompted by my loud shouting, hurriedly rinsed out the chemicals. My hair was still wet when I stalked angrily out into the streets, followed by my friends' snickers.

That evening Gloria's hair was so straight and airy that it flew around her head each time she moved. Ethel, Martha and other singers who had endured the process had only to shake their heads and their hair would bounce up and down and sideways with a sinuous smoothness.

A week passed and the hair that moved so freely began to move completely off the women's heads. Bare patches of scalp the size of small coins appeared at first, then enlarged until they could no longer be covered by an adept combing and plastering and pinning of hair from another side of the head.

A few weeks later my mother wrote me, "I read in Dorothy Kilgallen's column that all the young women in *Porgy and Bess* are

481

wearing wigs. What on earth did you do to your hair?" I did my best not to laugh and sent my mother a photograph taken in a coin-operated booth. I was looking into the lens and had both hands to my head, pulling my healthy kinky hair.

Undeniably, Egypt impressed every member of the group. Irving Barnes, his wife and eight-year-old-daughter, Gail, spent whole days in museums and art galleries. The child who had put on grown-up airs, throwing her tiny hips as she tried to imitate the strut of a provocative Bess, became a little girl again, intrigued with African toys.

Paul Harris forgot his extraordinary good looks for a while and allowed his plump ego to deflate of its own accord. He semi-adopted two young beggars and they hung around the stage door and the hotel entrance until he emerged. He bought the urchins clothes and shoes and took them to restaurants for belly-distending meals.

Earl Jackson, our street-wise Sportin' Life, underwent the most startling personality change. Where he had used colorful profanity to shock the university-schooled and proper singers, he now substituted kind words, softly spoken. His romantic preferences for the local good-time women shifted and focused on the prim soprano of the group. He was to be found in the wings talking low to Miss Helen Thigpen, or finding a chair for Miss Thigpen in the hotel lobby, or rushing to be first on a bus to save a window seat for the quiet and reserved singer. He had begun to act, for all the world to see, like a man in love. And Thigpen, who had only been excited by recitals and her own repertoire, bloomed under the attention.

We left Egypt undeniably changed. The exposure to extreme wealth and shocking poverty forced the frivolous to be level-headed and encouraged the sober to enjoy what they had taken for granted.

Replicas of the Sphinx and the pyramids were packed along with three-inch busts of Nefertiti and small stuffed camels. Ned acquired a carved walking stick, which he kept at hand for the next six months, and Bey bought a red tasseled fez, which, with the giant congo drum that he never let out of his sight, made him look like a Sudanese musician on a pilgrimage to Mecca.

We boarded our Greek ship in Alexandria and the captain welcomed us, Maki smiled when he saw me, but the purser scowled, glum-browed and mean. He arrived at my cabin a moment after I entered.

"Mrs. Angelos." His voice was nearly closed with accusation.
"Yes?"

"Why did you lie to me?"

"I beg your pardon? I don't lie to anyone." I might not tell the truth, but I did draw the line at outright falsehood.

482

"You said you were a widow?"

"What? When did I say that?"

"I asked you how you had learned Greek and you said your dead husband taught you." He was pointing his finger at me as if he had caught me stealing the gold out of his mouth.

"I said to you my husband was Greek."

"Exactly." His smile was malevolent with satisfaction. "So he's dead?"

"No. I mean, he was my husband."

"But he's still alive?" Confusion and disappointment shifted his features.

"Very much so."

"Then why did you say he was Greek? Anyone who is Greek will be Greek until he dies."

I thought about that and thought about my husband who had intended to lock me into the apologetic female role, which he understood was proper for wives.

"Yes. You're right. He is Greek and will be that until he dies. But he is no longer my husband." I wanted to apologize to the purser for the misunderstanding, but I couldn't bring myself to ask for pardon.

"Vlachos loves you now?"

God, men talk about women gossiping. "I don't know. I hardly know him."

The frown was gathering again beneath his overhanging brow. "He said you were going to take him to the United States..."

Lillian knocked at the door. "Hey, Maya, let's have a drink."

I opened the door and the purser gave Lillian a little bow, put his hat on and left the cabin.

"Girl, you don't wait, do you? Well, they say there's no time like the present." She laughed.

I knew there was no use explaining the scene, and I knew that even if I stuck to Lillian's side like white on rice, the incident would be company knowledge before dinner.

"Thanks, I'm going to wait. The doctor ought to be coming soon and I have a few thousand words for him."

She blew air out of her cheeks. "Whew. You're a busy lady." She pulled the door slowly, closing it on her grin.

Maki came to the cabin, his eyes wild. "Maya, I have told my wife everything." He reached for me.

I said, "Hold it a minute." I pushed him away. "Listen, I don't know you. You don't know me."

"But I love you. I want to marry you. I will come with you to the United States."

"No, you won't." I opened the door. "You're nice. I guess. But I'm

483

not marrying anyone. And surely not another Greek."

"But I'm in love with you."

"Really? Could we live in Greece after you married me?"

"You don't understand. Greece is a poor country. In America I could make money and..."

"Mister, my suggestion is that you keep the wife you've got." I walked out into the passageway and held the door open with my foot. "I think you'd better go."

He put his hat on and stepped out of the room. His face was downcast and he was going to say something, but Martha walked by.

"Good morning, Doctor. Good morning, Miss Thing. Still at it, huh?"

I called after her. "Wait, Mart. I'll go up with you."

Except for what I had come to think of as only a reasonable amount of teasing, the rest of the cruise was uneventful.

25

The opera was well received in Athens. We photographed each other at the Acropolis and drank retsina late at night in small bars. I dodged Maki in the hotel lobby and tore up the letters he sent me without opening them.

I could have been wrong. It was just possible that he did like me a little. But I knew I would never marry again, nor would I be the cause of a marriage breaking up. I couldn't introduce another non-Black to my son and family (although my mother might have accepted this one more heartily because at least he was a doctor). But what made marriage impossible was the fact I would have been embarrassed even if I loved the man (which I didn't). No amount of kindness or fidelity on his part would erase the idea that I had bought a mate with a license that gave me little personal gratification: American citizenship.

We flew from Athens to Tel Aviv. The bright sun that pleased us in Egypt shone on Israel too. The palm trees and white sand and tropical flowers were identical, but the streets were washed clean and there was a total absence of beggars. We were met by English-speaking fans who seemed to have drawn our individual names from lots and immediately became our companions and guides.

The very religious among our company visited Jerusalem, the Wailing Wall, the Mount of Olives and the Dead Sea. The rest were satisfied to buy vials of sand from the Holy Land and agate beads from tourist shops.

Lionel Hampton's band had just finished an engagement in Tel Aviv and we met at a party given by the American embassy and the Israeli government. The *Porgy and Bess* company had not seen such a gathering of American Negroes in months. We fell on the musicians as if they were bowls of black-eyed peas.

In the United States—or anywhere else, for that matter—jazz musicians and opera singers would find few topics of mutual interest. Their vocabularies have no unanimity and even their approach to the common musical scales are as different as odds and evens. But at the foreign official welcoming party we were indisputably siblings.

Helen Ferguson talked with a giant baritone sax player. He bent double to listen to her. Lillian and Ethel laughed with the frenetic drummer who pushed his words over and around a wad of chewing gum.

Gloria Davy and Delores Swan listened attentively as Hamp staccatoed his remarks: Yeah. Ha, ha. Yeah. Great. Yeah. Great. Ha, ha."

Joe Jones and Merrit were telling stories to the brass section. I had my eyes on Sonny Parker, the male band singer. We had known each other slightly, but never as well as I wished.

"Sonny, who would have thought we'd meet in Israel?" I batted my eyes and tried to convey that I'd be happy to meet him anywhere.

"Yeah, baby. That's life, though. Yeah. Life's like that. Hey, Maya, who is that sharp chick?"

I said, "Barbara Ann Webb," but was too chagrined to add that she was so in love with her husband that when asked how she liked the weather, she would respond with "Richard says..."

I left Sonny and walked around, rustling myself in the sounds and feasting my eyes on the tasty colors of my people.

I met Arik Lavy, who had the tawny hair and open-mouthed laugh of Victor Di Suvero. He introduced himself and his girl friend to me and told me they were both Sabras, persons born in Israel. Each evening in Tel Aviv after the performance I joined them in an open-air café. The Sabras taught me Hebrew folk songs and I sang spirituals in exchange, always thinking that the real Jordan River was only a few miles away and my audience was composed of the very Israelites mentioned in my lyrics.

I made an arrangement with a dance teacher to give classes in modern ballet and African movement for three weeks in exchange for lessons in Middle Eastern dance.

485

We boarded a plane for Morocco where we would give a concert and continue to Spain. I was downcast at leaving Tel Aviv. I had felt an emotional attachment to Egypt and made an intellectual identification with Israel. The Jews were reclaiming a land which had surrendered its substance to the relentless sun centuries before. They brought to my mind grammar school stories of pioneer families and wagon trains. The dislodged Palestinians in the desert were as remote in my thoughts as the native Americans whose lives had been stifled by the whites' trek across the plains of America.

In Barcelona we were tired. Too many planes, hotel rooms and restaurant meals were exacting a toll on the company's spirits. But the Spaniards had no way of telling the extent of exhaustion the singers experienced. Years of training sustained the quality of performance, and an affection which bordered on kinship reduced the exhibition of ill humor which lay just under everyone's skin.

We went to Lausanne, Switzerland, performed and left, associating the white and icily beautiful town only with one more stop to be checked off our list. Our interests narrowed into petty little concerns and the cities and countries were beginning to melt together.

Genoa was quaint with its narrow streets and sailors—but were sweaters cheaper in Naples? Florence had Michelangelo statues and the Ponte Vecchio, but why didn't the clothes come back from the cleaners really clean?

In Marseilles, Gloria Davy and I tried to lift our spirits. Our birthdays were only two days apart, and we decided to give ourselves a treat. We bought a box lunch and took a small boat to the Château d'If. It turned out to be a dungeon built into the rocks, from which we were told no one had ever escaped, except the fictional Count of Monte Cristo. The guide wanted to show us where prisoners were chained to the walls. We refused and stood aside, gazing wistfully back at the mainland while other tourists ducked their heads and trooped through the small, low opening. I didn't relate the story to my friends because I knew they were too moody to hear another sour tale.

When we reached Turin the company was a drab lot. Merriment had seeped out of our repertoire and we fabricated joy on stage. Sullen and quiet, we went separately to our hotel rooms.

Helen Thigpen announced that she was giving a birthday party for Earl Jackson and everyone was invited. The statement sparked the first light of common interest I had seen in months. We had all noticed that Helen and Earl had become inseparable and had exchanged some character traits. He was more contained and the wise hopping walk had given way to more erect posture, while her reserve had thawed and she smiled more frequently.

Lillian and I made a bet with Martha and Ethel that the lovers were going to announce their engagement at the party. Ned held the bet, declining to join either side.

Helen had taken over the top floor of a restaurant near the hotel. Every table held a bottle of expensive whiskey, and waiters, assigned to our party exclusively, brought food and wine. I sat with Martha and Ethel and her mother, who had just arrived to spend a month with her daughter.

The party began like any party, coolly and dryly at first, but the sounds of a good time increased in direct proportion to the absorption of food and drink. Joy sat down at the piano and Leslie Scott stood to deliver a rich "Blue Moon." We applauded happily. Laverne Hutchinson, without being urged, sang another sentimental song, trying to outdo Leslie. Martha, who was sipping no less steadily than the rest of us, submitted to requests and honored the gathering with a song a cappella. When she finished, another singer took her place. Between songs we talked. People who had found it hard to smile for weeks were suddenly reminding each other of old stories and sharing the hilarious memories. It was a much needed festival.

Rhoda Boggs, at five foot eight inches and nearly two hundred pounds, was called "one of the big women in the company." She wore a mink capelet to all formal affairs, hats that quivered with large silk roses and high-heeled baby-doll shoes, the straps sinking deep into her ankles. She had the lyrical voice and artistic temperament of almost every classical soprano. As the party reached a peak, Rhoda clutched her capelet to her large bosom and started across the small dance floor to share stories with friends at another table. At the same time, Billy Johnson, waspish, impish and balding, decided to traverse the small space en route to another destination. The two collided midway. Rhoda stumbled at the shock while Billy almost fell under the impact. Rhoda was the first to recover. She looked down at the associate conductor as if he were a street urchin laying obstacles in the route of her parade. She rushed to the nearest table."

"Did you see him? Did you see that?" Her indignant voice was sounded like a flute played in anger. "Did you see that he struck Rhoda Boggs?" She went quickly but gracefully to the next table. "Did you see him actually strike Rhoda Boggs? Oh, my dear." She patted her breast and sang a little mean "Where does he live? Oh, where does he stay?" She carried her outrage from table to table, the roses on her hat nodding wildly in agreement at the affront.

Billy Johnson was still wondering in the center of the dance floor when Earl Jackson approached. Rhoda had relayed her news to the hostess and host, and although under Helen's influence Earl had mellowed, it was not safe to think he had ripened.

He caught Billy's lapels and pulled him out of the stupor. "What the hell you trying to do, hittin' that woman? You trying to be funny?" His voice carried over the room to Rhoda who was fanning her face with her hat. "This is my party, you sonna bitch!"

And then he pushed Billy away with his left hand and slapped him with the right. The loud smack pulled us all to our feet, but Billy Johnson spun and dove a full gainer onto the highly polished wood. All movement and sound were suspended for a second and we heard Billy drawl in his plain Oklahoma accent, "That's the first time a man has really ever hit me."

The moment was so brief, there was no time to decide whether the pronouncement was a complaint or a compliment. Some people laughed out of nervousness, others because it was a funny scene, and a few began to down the last of the free drinks and collect their coats.

Behind my chair I heard a waiter say *"Carabinieri,"* I told Ethel to get her mother and I would find Martha, that we should leave at once because the police had been called. I found Martha in a group sympathizing with Rhoda Boggs.

"Mart, we'd better go. The waiters have called the police."

"You're so smart, Miss Thing." Partying and excitement had thickened her tongue.

"Here's your coat." I helped her put it on. "Come on."

I started toward the stairs and she followed me.

"Maya Angelou."

I turned and looked back. Martha was on the landing and I was four steps below her.

"Maya Angelou, you're a smart-ass! Miss Fine Thing doesn't like smart-asses."

Obviously, excitement after such a long period of dullness had intoxicated us all.

I opened my mouth to speak just as she threw the contents of her glass in my face. All the pious self-placating words "Patience," "Tolerance," "Forgive, for that is the right thing to do"—fled from me as if I had never known them.

I could have gone back up the stairs and stomped her face flat into the floor until her features became part of the parquetry design. But she was so small. Five foot tall and absolutely too small to hit. Yet I couldn't just walk out with the whiskey dribbling down my cheeks and into my collar and down my neck.

I grabbed a handful of the hem of her coat and gave it a lusty jerk. Her feet shot out from under her and she came bumping down the stairs. When she settled, a step below me, I saw that her wig had jumped free from the pins and had been turned askew. Long, black, silky hair covered her face and the wig's part began somewhere behind her left ear.

488

When I reached the bottom of the stairs I looked back. Ned Wright was bent over the woman. "Oh, my dearie. Someone pushed Miss Fine Thing down the stairs? Do let Uncle Ned help you up."

The soprano had both hands on her wig. In one move she snatched it around straight on her head and composed her face. She smoothed the hair down to her shoulders, fingering the curls that lay on her collar.

"No one pushed Miss Fine Thing," she said, jaw lifted as she struck a pose on the steps. "I fell."

The next day I sat sulking in my room, feeling betrayed and friendless. I told myself the time had come to go home. I missed my son and he needed me. His letters, printed in large letters, arrived regularly, and each one ended: "When are you coming home, Mother? Or can I come to visit you?"

Breen and Bob Dustin had offered to send for him and give me an allowance for his upkeep. But there were many male homosexuals in the company, and while I wasn't afraid that they might molest him I did know he was at an impressionable age. He would see the soft-as-butter men, moving like women, and receiving the world's applause. I wasn't certain that Clyde wouldn't try to imitate their gestures in a childish attempt to win admiration. Everyone wants acceptance.

No matter what it cost in loneliness, I was doing the good-mother thing to leave my son at home. Thus I had soothed my guilt, never admitting that I was reveling in the freedom from the constant nuisance of a small child's chatter. When the travel had been good, it had been very good. I could send money home, write sad and somehow true letters reporting my loneliness and then stay up all night past daybreak partying with my friends. There were no breakfasts to either prepare or worry about. I could wear my hangovers openly, like emblems of sophistication, without fear of judgment.

The truth was, I had used the aloneness, loving it. Of course, I had to work, but dancing and singing every night with sixty people was more like a party than a chore. And I had my friends.

I thought about Martha and knew I'd never speak to her again. Or to Lillian, or Ned, or any of the others. They had been friends before I came along and I was certain they were closing ranks to push me out, even as I sat in the miserable hotel room. I had lunch sent to my room and made up my mind to hand in my resignation. It was time for me to go. The greatest party of my life was over.

That night I barely grumbled hello to the singers backstage, and when we took our places and the overture began, I was working hard at holding back the tears.

The curtain rose on Bey, Ned, Joe Jones, Joe Attles and John Curry shooting dice. Ned, as Robbins, sang his lyrical tenor line, "Nine to make. Come nine," and won the pot. Crown, angered by the game's outcome, took the baling hook and a fight began. In the struggle, Crown stabbed Robbins with the weapon. Robbins screamed as always and turned upstage to face the company. A small gasp of surprise raced around the stage. He had always played the death scene to the audience, milking the moment for every drop of drama. Now he clutched his chest where the hook was supposed to have struck and said aloud, "He struck me. Oooh! He struck me. Did you see that? He struck Ned Wright."

He stumbled across the stage from right to left. He asked Joy McClain and Delores Swann, "Where does he live? Where is he staying?" He then hurtled over to Freddie Marshall and Ruby Green, "Did you see that? He actually struck me. Oooh weee!"

The company was supposed to be shocked into silence by the murder, and the music rests during the scene, but when Ned began imitating the disaster of the night before, a few soft giggles could be heard onstage.

After thrusting, clutching and stumbling, Ned finally went down to the floor. He then sat up absolutely straight, putting one fist at the back of his head and another to his forehead, gave a vigorous tug, slipping both hands around until they were directly over his ears.

He said prissily, in a loud whisper, "No one struck Ned Wright. I fell." Only then did he lie down and close his eyes.

The giggles might never have increased except that Ned was hunched face down while his body jumped and shook with convulsions, and Bey let out a bass shout of such pure glee that we were all pulled along into uncontrollable laughter.

The conductor looked up from the pit, aghast. He lifted both hands, cueing the singers to begin the dirge; not one voice followed his signal. He lifted his hands higher, imperiously pointing his baton at the stage, but the sopranos had buried their faces in their aprons and the men had covered their mouths with their hats, their shoulders shaking with laughter.

Alexander Smallens' face darkened with fury. He held his baton between his fingers like a pencil and made short stabbing motions at the singers. The orchestra played the entire passage alone. On the cue for the cast to exit stage left in a wild attempt to escape a white policeman who enters stage right, we tripped over each other, falling into the wings.

People leaned on the walls or clung together—some even held on to the curtain—trying to keep laughter under control. Rhoda Boggs wiped the tears from her round face; she managed to steal a breath from her spasms and said, "That Ned Wright. Uh uh. That Ned Wright. He's crazy."

Someone caught me and pulled me around. It was Martha. She looked at me and I wasn't sure if her wide grin was meant to be an attempt to apologize. Suddenly she put her hands on her wig and pulled it askew. When she shoved it back to the correct position.

"Miss Fine Thing didn't fall. Somebody pushed her."

I bent low, laughing, and she put her arms around my neck. Neither begged the other's pardon. We picked up our friendship as if it had not fallen but had only stumbled. A few weeks later she shed the wig. A Black beautician in Rome curled her newly grown hair in a high and luxuriant coiffure, and we never mentioned the incident again.

26

Porgy and Bess was to be the first American opera sung at La Scala. Famous white sopranos, tenors aad baritones from the United States had soloed at Milan's renowned opera house; now an entire cast of Negro singers were nervously rehearsing on the legendary stage.

Photographers and journalists lounged around the stage door and waited in our hotel lobbies.

"Miss Davy, how does it feel to be the star of the first...?"

"I am honored, of course, but then, we all work hard. I am just one of the Besses."

"Mr. Scott, are you nervous about singing at La Scala?"

"Nervous? No. I am excited, yes, but then, I am excited each time I sing."

"Miss Flowers, did you ever think you would have the opportunity to sing in Milan? At the world's most prestigious opera house?"

"Certainly. I do believe in the work ethic. Work hard and be prepared. Naturally, we are all pleased."

Oh, I was so proud of them. Their hands were knotted with tension and their brows moist with perspiration, but they acted cool."

We were told that La Scala audiences reacted to singers in the same way patrons of the Apollo in Harlem responded to the acts. That warning didn't need to be spelled out. The Apollo audiences were famous for shouting mediocre performers out of the theater or joining the entertainers on the stage to show them how a dance should be danced and how a song should be sung.

On opening night the backstage silence was unusual and ominous. Dressing-room doors were not only closed but locked. When the five-minute call was given we all went quietly to our places; not even a whisper floated over the dark stage. The rustling audience was stilled by the gradually darkening lights; they applauded the conductor's entrance and the overture began. The cast remained apart and I felt a little afraid. Suppose Gloria lost her voice, or Annabelle couldn't hit her high coloratura note. Just suppose I tripped over someone's foot on my entrance. I was coiled tight like a spring and realized as the curtain rose that every other member of the cast had also wound themselves up taut for a shattering release.

The moment the curtain opened the singers in concert pulled the elegant first-night audience into the harshness of Black Southern life. When Robbins was killed, the moans were real (didn't we all know people who, unable to talk back to authority, killed a friend over fifty cents?). The entrance of the white policeman was met with actual fear (wasn't the law always on the side of the mighty and weren't the jackals always at our heels?). The love story unfolded with such tenderness that the singers wept visible tears. (Who could deny this story? How many Black men had been crippied by the American oppression and had lost the women they loved and who loved them, because they hadn't the strength to fight? How often had the women submitted to loveless arrangements for the sake of bare survival?)

The first smiles of the evening were shared during our bows. We had sung gloriously. Although we faced the audience—which was on its feet, yelling and applauding—we bowed to compliment each other. We had performed *Porgy and Bess* as never before, and if the La Scala patrons loved us, it was only fitting because we certainly performed as if we were in love with one another.

We arrived in Rome on a late spring afternoon. I arranged my bags in the hotel room and went downstairs to find a telephone directory. In Paris, Bernard Hassel had told me to go to Bricktop's if I ever got to Rome. She was a living legend. He said Bricktop, Josephine Baker and Mabel Mercer had been the high-yellow toasts of Europe in the thirties. They hob-nobbed with the rich and the royal, and although Mabel had gone to the United States and Josephine was semi-retired, Bricktop still owned the most fashionable night club in Rome.

When night fell I walked down the Via Veneto, past the outdoor tables of Doney's Restaurant and into the next block where a small simple sign BRICKTOP'S hung over the door.

I opened the door and found myself standing behind a pudgy broad-shouldered man and a heavily made up woman whose brown

492

hair was frosted blond. A small, very light-skinned, freckled woman with thin red hair stood facing the couple.

"*On dit que vous avez bu trop en Cannes.* (They say you've been drinking too much in Cannes)." She frowned and her French accent was as Southern and sweet as pecan pie.

The man said, "Please, Brickie. I promise not to drink tonight. My word of honor."

Her scowl relaxed when the man's companion added, "I won't let him have a thing, Brickie. We'll just watch the show."

Bricktop called a waiter. "Come here and take King Farouk to a table." My ears almost rejected the name. "But don't give him a drop. Not one *goutte.*"

The couple followed the waiter and Bricktop signaled to me. Her face was closed.

"Are you alone?"

I said, "Yes."

"I'm sorry, miss. But I don't allow ladies in here unescorted." She started to turn away.

I said, "Miss Bricktop, I am sorry too. I have been waiting for six months to come here and meet you." It was flattery, but it was also the truth.

She walked closer to me and stood straight. "What are you doing in Rome?" The question was asked cynically, as if she thought I might be a traveling prostitute, and her eyes said she had heard every version of every lie ever told.

"I'm with *Porgy and Bess.* I am a dancer-singer."

"Uh-huh." I could see her defenses relax. "When did you get in?"

"About two hours ago."

She nodded, appreciating that her place had been my first stop. She turned and lifted her hand. A waiter came scuttling to her.

"Take mademoiselle to a table." She said to me, "Go and sit down. I'll be over to talk to you pretty soon."

The club had thick carpets and heavy chandeliers, and the waiters dressed as handsomely as the customers. Bricktop was a Negro woman away from the United States thirty years, and still her Southern accent was unmistakable. I was even more amazed when she later told me she wasn't Southern at all, but had come from Chicago.

When she finally came to my table, she asked where I was from.

I said, "San Francisco."

"How do you feel, being so far from home?"

I said, "There is no place God is not."

Her face crinkled in a little-girl grin. "Oh, you're going to be my baby. Did you know that I've converted to Catholicism?"

I said I hadn't heard.

She leaned across the table, her eyes sparkling. "I have friends who ask me why. They found out I go to Mass every day and they're shocked. I say, 'Look, for thirty years you saw me running in and out of bars every day and you never tried to stop me and it didn't shock you. Why do you want to stop me now?' " She sat back in the chair and smiled smugly. "Don't you reckon that stopped them?"

She invited me to the club whenever I wanted to come and promised to cook a dinner of black-eyed peas. "I know where to find them in this town. Fact is I know where to find anything and everyone in Rome."

I looked around the room at some famous American and European faces, and at the line of people waiting inside the doorway for tables. I didn't doubt that Brickie had the keys necessary to open the Eternal City.

27

After a few weeks in Rome I received a disturbing letter from Mother. Wilkie had moved out into his own studio. Lottie was looking for a housekeeping job because Mr. Hot Dog was losing money. And mother was planning to become a dealer in a Las Vegas Negro casino—which meant there would be no one to take care of Clyde, who missed me more than ever. He had developed a severe rash that resisted every medical treatment. I wrote immediately, saying I would be home in a month. I was obliged by union rules to give two weeks' notice, but since we were in Europe, it was only fair to allow the company four weeks to find another dancer-singer.

I went to Bob Dustin and explained that I would be leaving in one month and what a pleasure the tour had been. That evening he came to my dressing room, took a seat and looked at me solemnly.

"I am sorry, but I've got bad news for you. Since you're handing in your notice, we do not have to send you home. You'll have to pay your own way. And you'll have to pay your replacement's fare, first class, from wherever we find her."

The fares could come to over a thousand dollars! I had not seen that amount of cash since the war when I had kept the keys to my mother's money closet.

Bob left me alone with my tears. I told Martha and Lillian, who sympathized but had no money to lend me. Desperation began to build. I had to go to my son, but how could I find the money to do it?

Bricktop answered the private phone number she had given me. "Well, now, stop crying and tell me what's the matter."

I told her how I had left my son and that my family was down on its luck and that I needed to have another job to earn my fare home.

"That's nothing to cry about. I've heard of dancers crying because they were worked too hard, but never because they weren't worked enough. Put your faith in God and come down here this afternoon to rehearse with my pianist. You can start tonight."

For the next two months I not only danced in the opera and sang at Bricktop's but also found daytime employment. Some dancers at the Rome Opera House asked me to give them classes in African movement. I charged them as much as they could afford and watched each penny carefully, so that my bankroll grew. Bricktop fed me often, and once when I was so depressed I could hardly speak she asked me to her house. When I entered the large foyer she lifted her skirt and showed me her knees. The light skin was bruised and scratched.

"I went up the holy stairs on my knees for your son. And I've been lighting a candle and praying to the Holy Mother for him every day. Now, will you please have faith and know that he is all right?"

I counted the money unbelievingly; every penny I needed was there. I made reservations on the *Cristoforo Colombo*. Martha and Ethel, Lillian, Barbara, Bey, Ned, the Joes (Attles and James) gave me a lavish farewell party.

Martha said, "Miss Thing, why don't you fly home? The way you're going it'll take you two weeks to reach California."

I was afraid. If the plane crashed my son would say all his life that his mother died on a tour in Europe, never knowing that I had taken the flight because I was nearly crazy to be with him.

Lillian made a face at Martha. "Let her alone, Miss Fine Thing. She gets these hunches and sometimes they work. Let us not forget about the Cairo and the *défrisage*." We all laughed at the good times in the past which were good enough when they happened but were much better upon reflection.

The nine-day trip from Naples to New York threatened to last forever. I seemed to have spent a month going to bed in the tiny cabin where sleep was an infrequent visitor. Uncomfortable thoughts kept me awake. I had left my son to go gallivanting in strange countries and had enjoyed every minute except the times when I thought about him. I had sent a letter saying I was coming two months before and had felt too guilty to write and explain my delay.

A barely adequate band played music in the second-class salon, and after the third restless night I started singing with them.

A very thin and delicate-looking man from first class introduced himself and sat every evening until the last song had been played and the musicians had covered their instruments. Without the band and his company the trip would have been totally unbearable.

My friend was a chronic insomniac, so we played gin rummy and talked until sunrise. He told me he was a friend of Tennessee Williams, and we discussed the future of drama. I recited some of my poetry, which he said was promising.

We exchanged addresses at the dock and I took a taxi to the train station. The three-day trip in a coach deposited me tired, frazzled, but happy at the Third and Townsend Station of the Southern Pacific in San Francisco.

28

Lottie answered the doorbell and gave a shout of welcome. In seconds the family closed around, kissing, stroking and hugging me. They guided me to the sofa, talking and asking questions that they didn't expect to be answered. When I sat down, Clyde jumped into my lap and snuggled his head under my chin. Every minute he would pull away to look at my face, then nestle again against my neck. Mother patted my hair and my cheek and laughed, wiping her eyes.

Lottie said, "She needs a cup of coffee."

"The prodigal daughter," Mother said, "That's who you are. The prodigal daughter returns home."

Lottie, in the kitchen, said, "Oh, baby. We've missed you."

"If we lived on a farm," Mother said, "I'd kill the fatted calf. Oh, yes, baby." She turned to my son. "That's what the mother does when the prodigal daughter returns."

Clyde's arms were wound around my neck.

"Clyde," Mother said.

He murmured into my collar, "Yes, Grandmother?"

"You're too big to sit in your mother's lap. You're a little man. Come on, get up and go find a fat calf. We'll kill it and cook it."

His arms tightened.

I said, "Mother, let him sit here awhile. It's O.K."

The first day was spent dispensing gifts and telling each other snatches of stories. I talked about the company and some of the cities we visited. Mother and Lottie told me about losing the restaurant lease and how Clyde had missed me and how they had taken him to a dermatologist who recommended an expensive allergist, but nothing seemed to help.

Clyde had little to say. The loquacious, beautiful and bubbling child I had left had disappeared. In his place was a rough-skinned, shy boy who hung his head when spoken to and refused to maintain eye contact even when I held his chin and asked, "Look at me."

That evening I went in to hear him say his prayers dully, and when I bent to kiss him good night he clung to me with a fierceness that was frightening. In the very early hours of the morning I heard a faint knock at my door.

I turned on the light and said, "Come in."

My son tiptoed into the room. His face was puffy from crying. I sat upright. "What's the matter?"

He came to my bed and looked at me directly for the first time since my return. He whispered, "When are you going away again?"

I put my arms around him and he fell sobbing on my chest. I held him, but not my own tears.

"I swear to you, I'll never leave you again. If I go, when I go, you'll go with me or I won't go."

He fell asleep in my arms and I picked him up and deposited him in his own bed.

29

Disorientation hung in my mind like a dense fog and I seemed to be unable to touch anyone or anything. Ivonne was happily married at last; she introduced me to her new husband, but my interest was merely casual. At home I played favorite records, but the music sounded thin and uninteresting. Lottie prepared elaborate meals especially for me, and the food lay heavily on my tongue—it had to be forced down a tight, unwilling throat. Mother and I showed each other the letters we had received from Bailey. The sadness I experienced in Europe when I read the mail had obviously been left abroad, and now rereading his poignant and poetic tales of prison life left me unmoved.

I was aware that I was not acting like the old Maya, but it didn't matter much. My responses to Clyde, however, did alarm me. I wanted to hold him every minute. To pick him up and carry his nine-year-old body through the streets, to the store, to the park. I had to clench my fists to keep my hands off his head and face whenever I sat near him or moved past him.

Clyde's skin flaked with scales and his bedclothes had to be changed each day in an attempt to prevent new contagion. I had ruined my beautiful son by neglect, and neither of us would ever forgive me. It was time to commit suicide, to put an end to accusations and guilt. And did I dare die alone? What would happen to my son? If my temporary absence in Europe caused such devastation to his mind and body, what would become of him if I was gone forever? I brought him into this world and I was responsible for his life. So must the thoughts wind around the minds of insane parents who kill their children and then themselves.

On the fifth day home I had a lucid moment, as clear as the clink of good crystal. I was going mad.

Clyde and I were alone in the house. I shouted at him. "Get out. Go outside this moment."

"Where, Mother?" He was stunned at the violence in my voice.

"Outside. And don't come back, even if I call you. Out."

He ran down the stairs as I picked up the telephone. I ordered a taxi and telephoned the Langley Porter Psychiatric Clinic.

"I am sorry. There's no one here to see you."

I said, "Oh, yes. Someone will see me."

"Madame, we have a six-month waiting list."

"This is an emergency. My name is Maya Angelou. Someone will see me."

I grabbed a coat and went to sit on the steps. Clyde came running around from the backyard when he heard the cab stop. He squinted his eyes as if he were about to cry.

"You're going away?"

I said, "I'm just going to see a friend. You go back in the house. I'll be home in an hour or so."

I saw him watching the taxi until we turned the corner. The receptionist was not alarmed at my hysteria. "Yes, Miss Angelou. Doctor will see you now, in there." She showed me to a door.

A large, dark-haired white man sat behind the desk. He indicated a seat. "Now, what seems to be the trouble?" He put his hands on the desk and laced his fingers. His nails were clean and clipped short. His good suit was freshly pressed. He looked muscular. I thought he's probably one of the tennis players who drive expensive sports cars and his wife has Black servants who

498

wash her underclothes and bring her breakfast on a tray.

"Are you troubled?"

I started to cry. Yes, I was troubled; why else would I be here? But what could I tell this man? Would he understand Arkansas, which I left, yet would never, could never, leave? Would he comprehend why my brilliant brother, who was the genius in our family, was doing time in Sing Sing on a charge of fencing stolen goods instead of sitting with clean fingernails in a tailor-made suit, listening to some poor mad person cry her blues out? How would he perceive a mother who, in a desperate thrust for freedom, left her only child, who became sick during her absence? A mother who, upon her return, felt so guilty she could think of nothing more productive than killing herself and possibly even the child?

I looked at the doctor and he looked at me, saying nothing. Waiting.

I used up my Kleenex and took more from my purse. No, I couldn't tell him about living inside a skin that was hated or feared by the majority of one's fellow citizens or about the sensation of getting on a bus on a lovely morning, feeling happy and suddenly seeing the passengers curl their lips in distaste or avert their eyes in revulsion. No, I had nothing to say to the doctor. I stood up.

"Thank you for seeing me."

"If you'd like to make another appointment—"

I closed his door and asked the receptionist to call a taxi.

I gave the driver the address of Wilkie's studio. I arrived in the middle of a lesson. He took one look at me and said, "Go into my bedroom. There's a bottle of scotch. I have another student after this one, then I'll cancel for the rest of the afternoon."

I sat on his bed and drank the whiskey neat and listened to the vocalizing in the next room. I didn't know what I was going to say to Wilkie, but I knew I would feel better talking to him than to that doctor, to whom I would be another case of Negro paranoia. I telephoned home and told Lottie where I was and that I'd be home soon.

The piano was finally silent and Wilkie opened the bedroom door. "O.K., old sweet nappy-head thing. Come on and talk to Uncle Wilkie."

I walked out into the studio and collapsed in his arms.

"Wilkie, I can't see any reason for living. I went to a psychiatrist and it was no good. I couldn't talk. I'm so unhappy. And I have done such harm to Clyde..."

He held me until I finished my babbling.

"Are you finished? Are you finished?" His voice was stern and unsympathetic.

I said, "Well, I guess so."

"Sit down at that desk."

I sat.

"Now, see that yellow tablet?" There was a legal-size yellow pad on the blotter. "See that pencil?"

I saw it.

"Now, write down what you have to be thankful for. "Wilkie, I don't want silly answers."

"Start to write." His voice was cold and unbending. "And I mean now! First, write that you heard me tell you that. So you have the sense of hearing. And that you could tell the taxi driver where to bring you and then tell me what was wrong with you, so you have the sense of speech. You can read and write. You have a son who needs nothing but you. Write, dammit! I mean write."

I picked up the pencil and began.

"I can hear.
I can speak.
I have a son.
I have a mother.
I have a brother.
I can dance.
I can sing.
I can cook.
I can read.
I can write."

When I reached the end of the page I began to feel silly. I was alive and healthy. What on earth did I have to complain about? For two months in Rome I had said all I wanted was to be with my son. And now I could hug and kiss him anytime the need arose. What the hell was I whining about?

Wilkie said, "Now write, 'I am blessed. And I am grateful.'" I wrote the line.

"It's time for you to go to work. I'll call you a cab. Stop at the theatrical agency on your way home and tell them you're ready to go to work. Anywhere, anytime, and for any decent amount of money."

When he walked me to the door he put his arm around my shoulders. "Maya, you're a good mother. If you weren't, Clyde wouldn't have missed you so much. And let Uncle Wilkie tell you one last thing. Don't ask God to forgive you, for that's already done. Forgive yourself. You're the only person you can forgive. You've done nothing wrong. So forgive yourself."

I told the agent I would accept any job and the only stipulation was that I had to have transportation and accommodation for my son. He was surprised at the unusual request, but we signed contracts and I went home.

My lighter mood influenced everyone. I told funny stories about the singers and stopped lying about how miserable I had been.

Mother said, "Well, at least. I knew you had to have some good times."

Lottie was cheered by my new appetite and planned even more elaborate meals for my pleasure. And Clyde began to tell me secrets again. He resurrected Fluke and the two of them held interminable conversations in the house's one bathroom. I took him out of school for a week and we spent days riding bikes in Golden Gate Park and having picnics on the grass.

Before my eyes a physical and mental metamorphosis began as gradually and inexorably as a seasonal change. At first the myriad bumps dried and no fresh ones erupted. His skin slowly regained its smoothness and color. Then I noticed that he no longer rushed panting to my room to assure himself that I was still there. And when I left the house to shop we both took the parting normally, with a casual "See you in a minute." His shoulders began to ride high again and he had opinions about everything from the planning of meals to what he wanted to be called.

"Mother, I've changed my name."

I'm certain that I didn't look up. "Good. What is it today?"

In the space of one month, he had told Fluke and the rest of the family to call him Rock, Robin, Rex and Les.

"My name is Guy."

"That's nice. Guy is a nice name."

"I mean it, Mother."

"Good, dear. It's quite a nice name."

When I called to him later in the day, he refused to answer. I stood in the doorway of his room watching him spraddled on the bed.

"Clyde, I called you. Didn't you hear me?"

He had always been rambunctious, but never outright sassy.

"I heard you calling Clyde, Mother, but my name is Guy. Did you want me?"

He gave me a mischievous grin.

Mother, Lottie and I failed for a time to remember his new name.

"Aunt Lottie, if you want me, call for Guy."

"Grandmother, I have named myself Guy. Please don't forget."

501

One day I asked him quietly why he didn't like Clyde. He said it sounded mushy. I told him about the Clyde River in Scotland, but its strength and soberness didn't impress him.

"It's an O.K. name for a river, but my name is Guy." He looked straight into my eyes. "Please tell your friends that I never want to be called Clyde again. And, Mother, don't you do it either." He remembered "Please."

Whenever anyone in the family called him Clyde, he would sigh like a teacher trying to educate a group of stubborn kindergarten students and would say wearily, "My name is Guy."

It took him only one month to train us. He became Guy and we could hardly remember ever calling him anything else.

30

I received a telegram from Hawaii:

OPENING FOR YOU THE CLOUDS. $350 DOLLAR WEEKLY, FOUR WEEKS. TWO WEEK OPTION. TRANSPORTATION AND ACCOMMODATION YOU AND SON. REPLY AT ONCE.

The three women who owned the hotel and night club met us at the airport dressed in long, colorful Hawaiian dresses. They were white Americans, but years in the islands had tanned their skins and loosened their inhibitions. Ann, a tall blonde and one-time professional swimmer, smiled warmly and draped fresh leis around our necks. Verne, the shortest of the trio, kissed us, while Betty, handsome and rugged, clapped our backs, grabbed our bags and herded the company into a car.

On the drive to Waikiki I imagined Bing Crosby and a saronged Dorothy Lamour standing under palm trees, singing "Lovely Hula Hands." The air was warm and moist and the perfume of our flowers filled the car. Guy asked how deep I thought the ocean was and if there were any sharks. And did they have any life guards?

The Clouds was near the sea, at an angle from the vast and elegant Queen's Surf Hotel, which jutted pink stucco towers near Diamond Head.

We were shown to our separate rooms with a connecting bath and invited to have our first dinner with my employers.

Guy and I took a walk and happiness wound him up so tight he chattered incessantly. We went along the beach and he ran forward and back, laughing to himself, grabbing my hand to pull me along faster, then letting go in impatience and racing off alone.

After dinner and after his prayers, he told me he had left Fluke at home, because Fluke couldn't swim. I reminded him to wake me in the morning and after we had breakfast I'd change a traveler's check so that he'd have some cash. After he went to sleep, I found Ann and Betty. They showed me the club and we drank and talked late into the night.

I awakened and looked at my watch. It was ten-thirty. I thought the long plane trip had exhausted Guy because he usually got up before seven. There was no answer when I knocked on our connecting door. I tried the knob, but the lock had been turned. I went out and tried the hall door leading to his room. It, too, was locked. I called the maid and explained that my young son was sleeping and I was unable to wake him. She unlocked the door. The room was empty. I didn't panic at first. I thought he had decided to let me sleep and one of the owners had taken him downstairs to eat in the hotel restaurant.

I asked the waiter where I could find my son. He said no children had been in the restaurant that morning. Betty was in her office. She said Verne and Ann were still asleep and she hadn't seen him but I shouldn't worry—he'd probably just gone for a walk.

I thanked her and went back to the rooms. Betty didn't know Guy. He might have decided to spare waking me and he might have gone for a stroll, but there was one sure thing he would have eaten. Even when he had been seriously upset and physically ill my son's large appetite never slackened. His normal daily breakfast consisted of oatmeal, bacon, eggs, toast, jam, orange juice and milk. On special days he ate hot biscuits and fried potatoes as well.

The maid let me in his room again. The clothes he had worn on the journey were hanging in the closet and his suitcase was open, but the contents looked undisturbed. His pajamas were at the foot of the bed.

Could he have been kidnapped? Why? I had no money. Could some sex maniac have taken my beautiful son? How could he have gotten him out of the hotel naked? Guy would have fought and screamed. I walked down to the beach, but all the children looked like my little boy. They all had tawny skin and dark eyes. I went back to the hotel and called the police.

Two large Oriental men appeared in the lobby. One of them asked, "What was he wearing, Miss Angelou?"

"Oh, nothing as far as I can deduce. All his clothes are in his room."

"What does he look like?"

I showed them a photograph.

"We'll find him, don't worry."

Don't worry?

I went to the bar and ordered gin and nodded when Verne, Betty and then Ann sympathetically repeated, "Don't worry."

This was the way the whole world ended. One child disappears and the sun slips out of the sky. The moon melts down in blood. The earth ripples like a dark ocean. I had another gin and tried to blank out the headlines that rushed behind my eyes: *Child's Body Found in Alley, Boy Kidnapped under Mysterious Circumstances.*

I had just found a seat in the lobby when Guy walked in flanked by the policemen. He had on swim trunks and was completely covered with sand. Weak with relief, I couldn't have stood up even for a moment. He saw me and rushed away from his escorts to stand in front of me.

"Mom"—his voice was loud and concerned—"what's the matter? Are you all right?"

I said yes, I was all right, because I couldn't think of anything else to say.

"Whew!" He blew out his breath. "Gee, I was worried for a minute."

I pulled enough strength from some hidden resource to stand. I thanked the officers and shook hands. They ran their hands over Guy's head, and sand fell to the carpet like brown snow. "Don't worry your mother like that again, hear?"

They left and I fell back in the chair. "Guy, where have you been?"

"Swimming, Mother."

"Where did you get the swimsuit?"

"Grandmother gave it to me. But why were you worried?"

"You didn't have breakfast. That's why."

"But I did."

"The waiter said you hadn't been in this morning."

"I didn't eat here. I ate at the Queen's Surf."

"But you didn't have any money. Who paid?"

"No one. I signed my name."

I was flabbergasted.

"But they didn't know you. I mean, they just accepted your signature?" That was incredible.

He looked at me as if I wasn't quite as bright as he would have liked.

"Mom, you know your name is up on that thing outside?"

I had noticed when we arrived that a large sign proclaimed MAYA ANGELOU. I said, "Yes. I saw it."

"Well, after I finished breakfast I pointed to it and said I would like to sign the check and that Maya Angelou is a great singer and she is my mother."

I nodded.

He was partially right. Although I was not a great singer I was his mother, and he was my wonderful, dependently independent son.